THE COLONIAL JOURNALS

THE COLONIAL JOURNALS
AND THE EMERGENCE OF AUSTRALIAN LITERARY CULTURE

KEN GELDER & RACHAEL WEAVER

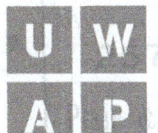

UWA PUBLISHING

First published in 2014
by UWA Publishing
Crawley, Western Australia 6009
www.uwap.uwa.edu.au

UWAP is an imprint of UWA Publishing
a division of The University of Western Australia

This book is copyright. Apart from any fair dealing for the purpose of private study, research, criticism or review, as permitted under the *Copyright Act 1968*, no part may be reproduced by any process without written permission. Enquiries should be made to the publisher.

The moral right of the authors has been asserted.

Copyright © Ken Gelder & Rachael Weaver 2014

National Library of Australia Cataloguing-in-Publication entry:
    The colonial journals: and the emergence of Australian literary culture / edited by Ken Gelder and Rachael Weaver.
    ISBN: 9781742584973 (paperback).
    Includes bibliographical references.
    Australian Literature. Literature and society—Australia. Popular culture and literature—Australia.
    Gelder, Kenneth, editor.
    Weaver, Rachael, editor.
    A820.80994

Printed by Lightning Source

CONTENTS

PART 1
Beginnings and Endings: The Precarious Life of a Colonial Journal
6

PART 2
The Making of Australian Literature
67

PART 3
Colonial Authors, Canons and Taste
110

PART 4
Stories and Poetry from the Colonial Journals
151

PART 5
Colonial Journals and their Artists
196

PART 6
The Journal Covers
221

PART 7
Colonial Types: Emergent and Residual
268

PART 8
Colonial Types: The Australian Girl
312

PART 9
Race and the Frontier
348

PART 10
Colonial Modernity
380

Bibliography
434

Acknowledgments
437

PART 1

Beginnings and Endings: The Precarious Life of a Colonial Journal
KEN GELDER & RACHAEL WEAVER

'Preface', *Australian Magazine; or, Compendium of Religious, Literary, and Miscellaneous Intelligence*, 1 December 1821
19

'Address' and 'Preface', *Hobart Town Magazine*, March 1833 and December 1833
19–20

'Introductory Address', *Tegg's Monthly Magazine*, March 1836
21

'To Our Readers', *Literary News*, 12 August 1837
22

'Editor's Address', *Arden's Sydney Magazine of Politics and General Literature*, September 1843
23

'Introductory Address', *Colonial Literary Journal and Weekly Miscellany of Useful Information*, 27 June 1844
24

'Preface', *Heads of the People*, 9 October 1847
25

Editorial, *Australia Felix Monthly Magazine*, June 1849
26

'Salutation to an Old Friend', *Melbourne Monthly Magazine*, May 1855
27

'Preface', *Illustrated Journal of Australasia*, 1 June 1857
28

'To our Subscribers and the Patrons of Literature in Australia,' *Month*, November 1858
29

'Ourselves', *Australian Magazine*, October 1859
30

'A Few Words at Starting', *Penny Melbourne Journal: A Weekly Family Newspaper of Fiction, General Literature etc.*, 3 October 1862
31

Editorial, *Sydney Punch*, 27 May 1864
31

'The Editor's Address', *Australian Monthly Magazine*, September 1865
32

'To Our Readers', *Australian Journal*, 2 September 1865
33

'To Our Readers and the Public', *Australian Journal*, 22 August 1868
34

'Introduction', *Colonial Monthly*, September 1867
36

'A Prospectus. In One Act', *Colonial Monthly*, March 1868
36

'Introductory', *Colonial Monthly*, January 1870
38

'Preface', *Touchstone*, 2 October 1869
39

'Philosophical Essays, by Q: On the Pleasures of Editorship', *Humbug*, 5 January 1870
40

'Ourselves', *Athenaeum*, 3 July 1875
42

'To Our Readers', *Melbourne Review*, January 1876
43

'Ourselves', *Australian: A Monthly Magazine*, October 1878
43

'A Matter of Public Concern', *Bulletin*, 31 January 1880
44

Editorial, *Australian Woman's Magazine and Domestic Journal*, 1 May 1882
45

'Introduction', *Sydney Quarterly Magazine*, October 1883
46

'Introductory', *Table Talk*, 26 June 1885
47

'Buy the Boomerang', *Boomerang*, December 1888
48

'About Ourselves', *Dawn: The Journal for Australian Women*, 15 May 1888
49

Advertisement, *Australasian Critic*, 1 October 1890
49

'Ourselves', *Scorpion*, 24 April 1895
50

'To Australia', and 'The Month', *Cosmos*, 1 September 1894
51–52

'Introducing Ourselves', *Block*, 15 August 1896
53

'Ourselves', *Ha! Ha: A Merry Magazine for Australians*, 9 April 1898
54

Editorial Notes, *Southern Cross*,
14 November 1898
55

'This Intimation', *Bookfellow*, 31 May 1899
56

'Entre Nous', *Yabba*, 17 January 1900
57

'All About Australians', *A.A.A.: All About Australians*, 3 May 1901
58

'Editorial Notice', *A.A.A: All About Australians*, 29 May 1901
58

'To Our Readers', *Australian Magazine*,
1 January 1908
59

Editorial, *Microbe*, August 1902
60

'To Our Readers', *New Idea: A Women's Home Journal for Australasia*, 1 August 1902
60

'Introduction', *Steele Rudd's Magazine*,
January 1904
61

'As Regards "The Gadfly"', *Gadfly*,
14 February 1906
62

Editorial, *Ye Wayside Goose*, 31 August 1906
62

'The Editor's Uneasy Chair', *Lone Hand*,
1 July 1907
63

'The Native Companion', *Native Companion*,
1 August 1907
64

'The Editor's Earnest Cry and Prayer to his Contributors', *Trident: An Australian Review*,
1 August 1908
65

'Editorial', *Trident: An Australian Review*,
1 April 1909
66

1

Beginnings and Endings: The Precarious Life of a Colonial Journal
KEN GELDER & RACHAEL WEAVER

THIS BOOK MAKES A CASE for the important role played by colonial journals in the establishment and development of Australian literary culture. It takes a broad, inclusive view of the colonial period, regarding it as something that continues right through to Federation and beyond; its influences, values, and ideologies lasting at least until the beginning of World War I, which is where this book draws to a close. We tend to forget just how many journals began, and in so many cases ended, during this time.

The first colonial journal was the Sydney-based *Australian Magazine; or, Compendium of Religious, Literary, and Miscellaneous Intelligence,* which began in May 1821 and closed down in September 1822. In her excellent bibliography, *Australian Periodicals with Literary Content, 1821–1925,* Lurline Stuart notes that 'Over the next hundred or so years, almost six hundred periodicals with varying literary content were published. Most of them were begun in the confident assumption of success…but only about half those produced survived their first year'.[1] Some colonial journals lasted for no more than one or two issues; but others, like the *Australian Journal* (September 1865 – April 1962), had surprising longevity. A significant number of colonial weeklies – especially those associated with the metropolitan daily newspapers – also had very long lives: like the *Sydney Mail* (July 1860 – December 1938), the *Australasian* (October 1864 – April 1946), the *Queenslander* (February 1866 – February 1939), and the *Australian Town and Country Journal* (January 1870 – June 1919). The best-known colonial weekly was of course the Sydney *Bulletin,* the first issue of which was 'cried vigorously in the streets on Saturday morning, 31 January 1880'.[2] For many years an independent journal, it was eventually sold off to newspaper proprietor Frank Packer's Australian Consolidated Press in 1961, finally ceasing publication in January 2008. The Melbourne *Punch* (August 1855 – December 1925) was another long-lasting weekly; so was Maurice Brodzky's controversial *Table Talk* (June 1885 – September 1939). In 1888 *Table Talk* was ranked equal to the *Bulletin* as 'the raciest paper – that is to say the most characteristic of the colonial spirit, and the most daring'.[3] Brodzky claimed to have made a profit of over £4,000 in that year; by 1903, however, he was forced to sell the weekly for a mere £15 and it lived out the rest of its time under the ownership of the Melbourne *Herald*.[4]

Table Talk had modelled itself on 'the leading fashionable journals in England', although its focus was almost entirely on colonial social, political and cultural life. The nineteenth century had of course seen a rapid rise in journal production in both Britain and the United States; journals such as *Blackwood's Edinburgh Magazine*, George Murray Smith's *Cornhill Magazine* (which published Rolf Boldrewood's first short story in 1866), *Harper's New Monthly Magazine* and *Scribner's Magazine* (which had developed an Australasian edition by the 1890s) were influential, and easily available in the colonies. The short-lived *Melbourne Monthly Magazine* (May – November 1855) announced itself as 'a reproduction…of the first-class magazine literature of London, the class of which *Blackwood* may be considered the type'. On the other hand, this journal also serialised colonial fiction about bush life and emigration, and immersed itself in local issues. The *Australian Journal* modelled itself on bestselling British penny weeklies such as G. W. M. Reynolds' *London Journal* and James Elishama Smith's *Family Herald*; but it was also devoted to the publication of local fiction and items of colonial interest (and became a monthly in 1869). Many colonial journals in fact mixed British and colonial material almost indiscriminately. In *Colonial Dickens*, Kylie Mirmohamadi and Susan K. Martin note that local readerships 'carved out a subjectivity that involved being British and Australian, of being both from here and of there'.[5] Charles Dickens's own work in fact provides a good example of English influence and local appropriation. Beginning with a pirated edition of *Pickwick Papers* in Tasmania in 1838, the 'taste for Dickens in the colony' – as Anny Sadrin notes – 'was fed by serialisation in local periodicals'.[6] William Baker's Sydney weekly, *Heads of the People* (April 1847 – March 1848), had serialised Dickens's *Dombey and Son* not long after it appeared in Britain. When Marcus Clarke described himself as the 'Conductor' of the *Australian Journal* in 1871, he was borrowing the term Dickens had used for his editorship of *Household Words* – a high-circulating weekly that ran throughout the 1850s in England and was familiar to Australian readers. But although he was profoundly influenced by Dickens, Clarke also committed the *Australian Journal* to the publication of local content.

The earliest account of the popularity of both British and colonial journals in Australia is given in George Burnett Barton's *Literature in New South Wales* in 1866. Barton – a journalist and lawyer who went on to become a Reader in English at Sydney University in the mid-1860s – had noted that colonial readers were enthusiastic subscribers to imported journals such as *Cornhill Magazine*: 'The demand for English periodicals', he wrote, 'is very great'. All this would seem to suggest that colonial readerships were ready to support local journals, too. But for Barton, local literary networks were not yet established enough to maintain readerships and gain the circulations necessary to survive. 'One or two clever writers alone will not do', he remarked. 'We have rarely or never had among us a sufficient number of professed men of letters to carry on such undertakings'.⁷ On the other hand, the *Australian Journal* – as Barton himself noted (writing just one year after that journal was launched) – was already selling around 5,500 copies per week across the colonies. 'The ablest COLONIAL pens of the day will be engaged on our staff', the editor announced in the first issue of the journal in September 1865 – anticipating the *Bulletin*'s editorial aspirations ('the services of the best men of the realms of pen and pencil in the colony have been secured') by over thirty years.

Significantly, the first issue of the *Australian Journal* opened with the serialisation of Ellen Davitt's *Force and Fraud*, Australia's first murder mystery novel. The serialisation of colonial fiction was crucial to the establishment of a local literary economy, giving it a resource that could enable authors – and journals – to project themselves into the future. Elizabeth Morrison writes that, 'While there were a few isolated and atypical examples earlier, the practice [of serialisation]...[was] introduced in 1863 by the *Sydney Mail* and followed within a few years by the *Australasian* and others'.⁸ Some colonial journals – like the *Melbourne Monthly Magazine* – were in fact already serialising local fiction by the 1850s. By the mid-1860s, the *Australian Journal* was routinely serialising two or three novels in each issue. Some of this material, of course, was either sourced (officially or otherwise) from overseas or set somewhere other than Australia. Toni Johnson-Woods records over 900 serialisations across seven colonial weeklies and journals through the later decades of the nineteenth century, of which just over 20 per cent could properly be described as 'colonial': that is, written by colonial authors, and with colonial settings.⁹ While this sample is relatively small, it gives us an indication of the way in which many of the colonial journals were obliged to balance the temptation to reprint cheap, popular content from overseas with an ideological investment in the development of a distinctively local literary culture.

For Katherine Bode, '[s]erialisation provided the major form of publication for colonial novels from the 1860s to the 1880s'; but she also talks about 'the low cultural value of serial publication...coupled with limited economic reward'.¹⁰ The precariousness of many colonial journals meant that even the commitment that serialisation entailed couldn't always keep them afloat; on the other hand, serialisation enabled journals to build up audiences and gain at least some degree of continuity. Marcus Clarke – as we note in part four of this book – was the editor of several journals, including the *Colonial Monthly* (September 1867 – January 1870) and, for a short period in the early 1870s, the *Australian Journal*. Taking good advantage of his role, he serialised his first novel *Long Odds* in both journals; and *His Natural Life* went on to be serialised in the *Australian Journal* four times over. The author-as-editor was a role that could work both ways, keeping a colonial writer visible (and remunerated, at least to a degree) by providing a regular outlet for his or her work, while supplying the journal with material that was in keeping with its local aspirations. Toni Johnson-Woods notes that 'colonial periodicals were *de facto* publishers and offered many colonial writers their only publishing outlet'.¹¹ Some journals, of course, launched their own occasional publishing ventures: the *Bulletin* did this,¹² and so did *Steele Rudd's Magazine* (January 1904 – October 1907). Donald Cameron was the editor of the *Melbourne Quarterly* (July 1882 – July 1883) and then the *Melbourne Journal* (October 1883 – November 1886). Like Clarke, he regularly serialised his own fiction. (His work was also serialised in the *Australian Journal*.) Cameron, Laing & Co. was Cameron's Melbourne-based publishing house; it printed his journals and published a small but significant number of colonial literary works, including Clarke's *The Mystery of Major Molineux and Human Repetends* (1881) and *The Marcus Clarke Memorial Volume* (1884). Elizabeth Morrison suggests that Cameron, Laing & Co. attempted to maintain 'a financially viable enterprise for publishing Australian literature in a market increasingly dominated by imported products'.[13] But the advertisements for the *Melbourne Journal* – 'Over 150 pages of the best Australian, English, and American Novels' – recognised that mixing local and imported content was still the most economical way to attract broad colonial readerships. The *Melbourne Journal* was almost completely devoted to popular genres like romance and adventure, and it kept itself going by serialising the work of emergent colonial writers in these areas – such as R. P. Whitworth and Grosvenor Bunster – alongside British and American bestselling authors like Bertha M. Clay (Charlotte Mary Brame) and Bret Harte.

In the midst of all this transnational literary circulation, it might be surprising to realise – as we go on to note in part two of this book – that the investment in 'Australian literature' as an identifiable field of writing happens so early on. This investment was built in part on the stimulation of local anxieties that literature from overseas was flowing into the colonies indiscriminately. Even the popular colonial weeklies capitalised on this perception: the *Penny Melbourne Journal* (October 1862 – November 1863) advertised 'the best colonial writers' and 'eminent Australian talent' in order to distinguish itself from 'the European Press daily pouring forth its load of literary trash' (although it relied as much on reproducing the latter as it did on nourishing the former). William Lane and James George Drake's Brisbane-based *Boomerang* (November 1887 – April 1892) claimed something similar thirty-five years later: that their journal 'fosters a national literature that stands in pleasing contrast to the sickly tales imported from the antipodes' (meaning, from this perspective, the northern hemisphere). The colonial journals did indeed see themselves as actively shaping the tastes and sensibilities of colonial readers. Their investment in what constituted 'Australian literature' – which writers counted, who should be remembered, who might become significant in the future, which literary works best evoked the most distinctive aspects of colonial life – was especially important to them, for several reasons. First, it allowed the journals to take on an authoritative role in determining the directions a colonial literary culture might take. Second, it gave the journals something they themselves could invest in, since it was in their interests to see a definitively colonial literature flourish and endure. No matter how much imported material they published, colonial journals had to cultivate their own local (and loyal) readerships. They aspired to offer something unique

in terms of an emergent literary culture; but, more importantly, the business of creating that culture had to be compelling enough to motivate readers to share in, and in some cases even contribute to, that project.

And third, this meant that the colonial journals had to be popular. In order to survive, journals had to rapidly increase their subscriptions and were often candid about doing so. The Sydney-based *Cosmos* (September 1894 – May 1899) put its very existence into the hands of a readership now imagined as fully nationalised: 'Whether it comes to stay or comes to go away again is for Australia to say'. At least thirty journals and magazines between the 1820s and the end of the nineteenth century defined themselves as 'Australian' through their titles in an obvious bid to widen their appeal. When Marcus Clarke took over editorship of W. H. Williams's *Australian Monthly Magazine* (September 1865 – August 1867) he went against the grain and changed the journal's title to the *Colonial Monthly* (September 1867 – January 1870), poking fun at the fashionable aspiration to be national: 'In Victoria alone there are many publications bearing the distinctive term "Australian" or "Australasian"...Indeed, the term has been adopted in the colony above named to such an extent, and for such merely local purposes, that there is some danger that distant readers may come to regard Victoria herself as constituting Australia!' The Sydney-based *Australian: A Monthly Magazine* (October 1878 – January 1881) was one of a number of journals, however, that saw the divisions between the colonies as an unnecessary limitation to circulation: 'We profess in effect to be national in our views, national in our politics, national in our relations to all public and social questions; and our idea of "nationality" is not limited by the artificial obstructions which now split up the Australian people'. When they were successful – and they sometimes were – the colonial journals could indeed travel right across the country. The Sydney *Bulletin*'s national weekly circulation reached around 16,000 by the end of its first year.[14] Popularity was (and still is) something a journal could then capitalise on, a way of promising some sort of future stability. The third issue of J. F. Archibald and Frank Fox's post-Federation monthly *Lone Hand* (May 1907 – February 1921) was able to talk up its future prospects precisely on the basis of having done so well so quickly: 'The Editor acknowledges with gratitude the very generous support given to THE LONE HAND by the public. The first issue of 50,000 was sold out within three days of publication. The second issue (which had to be limited to 50,000) was sold out on the very first day of publication. This will enable the Proprietary to embark with confidence on future plans for improving the magazine; and in future a larger issue will be printed'. For an Australian journal, this was indeed a remarkable level of sales – about half the daily circulation of Melbourne's *Argus* newspaper at this time.[15]

The earliest colonial journals were relatively rigid in their sense of moral and religious purpose: in 1821 the *Australian Magazine; or, Compendium of Religious, Literary, and Miscellaneous Intelligence* was able to announce that 'we have not swerved from the intentions we distinctly proposed'. But editors soon began to recognise that, in order to achieve their ambition of shaping colonial tastes and reaching wider audiences, they had to diversify their content. Colin Campbell's otherwise conservative *Australia Felix Monthly Magazine* (June – October 1849) was innovative in this regard, claiming 'that a magazine cannot, and is not meant to be, the production of any single mind' and calling for the 'free play of intellect' – although it qualified this with the observation that a 'publication without leading principles to stamp its character, is but a body without a soul – a collection of machinery without a moving power'. Even the most distinctive and determining editorial voice could nevertheless accommodate a sometimes radically varied selection of contributions. J. H. Archibald's *Bulletin* certainly earned its reputation as a masculine, nationalist publication (later advertising itself through the slogan 'Australia for the White Man'); but as John Docker notes, it was 'replete with discords as much as harmonies, telling stories in differing rhythms and voices, never in a single tone or single voice'.[16] The early colonial journals typically used the term 'miscellany' to describe the literal mixing-up of content: bits and pieces of literature alongside scientific writing, agricultural information, finance and business, religious tracts, biographies, and so on. But later on – as they spread their range across the colonies – journals begin to reflect the concerns and interests of different constituencies. The *Australian Journal* wrote, in September 1865, 'We do not appeal to a sect, a clique, or a class; for we design to interest, to amuse, and, if possible, to instruct everybody who will read us'.

However, the gesture towards a general readership was countered by the creation of topics and features that were aimed precisely at specific interest groups. The *Australian Town and Country Journal* and the *Sydney Mail*, for example, were well-known 'squattocracy' weeklies. Journals had different political and social investments to make; this might play itself out at the macro level of thinking about the future of the colonies themselves, or at the micro level of an article – for example – on aspects of women's fashion and social etiquette. Women readerships were of particular interest to the colonial journals by the second half of the nineteenth century. The first colonial journal published by women for women was Harriet Clisby and Caroline Dexter's short-lived *Interpreter: An Australian Monthly Magazine of Literature, Science, Art, &c.* (January – February 1861), which included poetry and earnest commentaries on Aboriginal people, medical issues, fashion and beauty, and dreams and spiritualism. By the 1880s, there were several journals devoted specifically to women's issues: notably, the *Australian Woman's Magazine and Domestic Journal* (April 1882 – September 1884) and Louisa Lawson's *Dawn: The Journal for Australian Women* (May 1888 – July 1905). The *Bulletin* launched its own women's page in April 1888, written by 'Sappho Smith' (Alexina Maude Wildman); Louise Mack took over the role ten years later, writing the *Bulletin*'s 'Woman's Letter' under the pen-name 'Gouli Gouli'. By the 1890s, journals such as *Cosmos* or Bertram Stevens and E. J. Brady's *Native Companion* (January – December 1907) cultivated a recognisably 'feminine' aesthetic that saw articles on the 'New

Woman', illustrations and cover designs by female artists such as Ruby Lindsay, and stories by emerging women writers – all published alongside the more generically familiar tales of masculine adventure and bush life.

Establishing a journal is, ideally, a collaborative undertaking: some level of collective input is needed so that production can continue. Colonial journals soon became venues where authors would converge to form a local nucleus of activity. George A. Walstab, the original editor of the *Australian Journal*, was a close friend of Marcus Clarke – who took over as editor a few years later. Through the added involvement of R. P. Whitworth, Henry Kendall and others, a literary network was formed here that led on to other initiatives and also worked as a kind of mutually-supporting cultural (and social) economy. For example, Walstab wrote several chapters for Clarke's serialised novel *Long Odds* when Clarke was ill; Whitworth took over the editorship of the *Australian Journal* after Clarke withdrew; Kendall and Walstab contributed to Clarke's *Colonial Monthly*; and in the midst of all this, Kendall and Clarke started another journal, *Humbug: A Weekly Illustrated Journal of Satire* (September 1869 – January 1870). Of course, these literary networks could also be precarious and journals were expensive to run and maintain. Announcing *Humbug*'s final issue, Clarke brought a typically caustic humour to bear on the sobering fact that 'editing as a business don't pay', with contributors falling by the wayside: 'One went melancholy mad, and another took to the city missionary line of business. He said it paid him better than comic writing. I had to do all the MSS. myself and for some weeks used to write about five pages weekly of brilliant satire'.

Even the most impressive collection of contributors could find success elusive. This was the experience of Robert Francis Irvine's aesthetically progressive but short-lived *Australian Magazine* (March – September 1899), which brought together an extraordinary collection of talented people: the artists and illustrators George W. Lambert, Thea Procter and D. H. Souter, the writers Arthur H. Adams, Roderic Quinn, Ambrose Pratt, Christopher Brennan, and many others. These writers were already familiar as contributors to the *Bulletin*, of course; they were a part of a 'bohemian' literary network drawn to this iconic weekly, which regularly published their work and went on to mythologise many of them as celebrity figures. But the *Bulletin* didn't always successfully accommodate the ambitions of colonial writers. In his 1933 book *The Romantic Nineties*, Arthur Jose remarked that the *Australian Magazine* was the result of a number of writers' belief that the *Bulletin* 'did not welcome…the best of their stuff'.[17] Another fleeting *Bulletin* off-shoot was Norman and Lionel Lindsay's lighthearted *Rambler* (January – March 1899). The Lindsays, of course, were themselves collaborative, illustrating writers' works and contributing to a remarkable number of journals along the way; as we note in part five, Ruby Lindsay is also significant here, illustrating the *Native Companion*, the *Lone Hand*, and C. J. Dennis's acerbic South Australian weekly, the *Gadfly* (February 1906 – February 1909). Contributors to the *Gadfly* included Sydney Partrige and her husband, Hal Stone, who formed a 'tribe' of writers and artists called the Waysiders and produced a series of beautifully-designed, intermittent 'journalettes' that included the *Microbe* (November 1901 – August 1902), *Ye Kangaroo* (September 1902 – 1905), *Ye Wayside Goose* (1904 – October 1906), and the *Red Ant* (a single undated issue in 1912). Although they shared some contributors, *Ye Wayside Goose* ridiculed the *Bulletin* and its choice of fiction, 'especially' – it noted in July 1906 – 'when it runs amok on iguana-swallowing yarns. Surely we Australians have some sense'.

Irvine's *Australian Magazine* was set up as a publishing company and floated on the stock market; it reminds us that journals are indeed commercial enterprises, active participants in the wider colonial economy. Frank S. Greenop's excellent *History of Magazine Publishing in Australia* (1947) begins by noting that the word 'magazine' in fact comes from the French word for store or warehouse, *magasin*: 'it is useful at once', he writes, 'to picture the actual meaning of magazine as a store of varied goods of interest and usefulness'.[18] When writers are published in a journal, they enter a framework to do with both appraisal and commodification: their work is judged and analysed, but it is also advertised and promoted (or demoted) and placed alongside an array of advertisements for other writers, publishers, and a host of other, often unrelated material. Editors knew this very well: alongside all the other skills they brought to the task, they had to fashion themselves as print capitalists in a colonial economy that was often unpredictable and unstable. Leon Cantrell makes exactly this point about the editor of the *Bulletin*'s famous 'Red Page', A. G. Stephens: 'He was certainly obsessed with the idea of literature as a commodity. He delighted in the role of the broker…'.[19] In her discussion of Dickens's *Household Words*, Catherine Waters notes that 'it was of course the nineteenth-century periodical, rather than the novel, which most visibly embodied the commodity form'.[20] This is literally true: by the 1880s, many journals were saturating themselves in advertisements for pharmaceuticals and beauty products, publishing houses, foodstuffs, and so on. Some journals were directly linked to local department stores, like the Sydney weekly the *Block: An Australian Society and Home Journal* (August – September 1896), or Lewis Scott's *Our Quarterly Magazine*, a beautifully designed journal that ran from around 1902 to 1911 and was published by Edward Rich and Co. Advertisements contributed to the aesthetic landscape of progressive journals, too, such as *Cosmos* or the *Southern Cross* (November 1898 – November 1900) or the *Lone Hand* – which published commercial artwork by a number of the same artists who also illustrated their stories and poems. It was part of the business of making the journals as attractive to readers – and to the authors they published – as possible.

This book introduces material from around fifty colonial journals, much of which has never previously been reprinted. We begin with a selection of prefaces and editorials that cover about ninety years of literary development, from the beginning of the *Australian Magazine* in 1821 to the demise of Archibald Strong's Melbourne-based *Trident* (May 1907 – April 1909) – the longest-lasting of four journals (including the *Native Companion*) published by T. C. Lothian around this time.[21] Most of the prefaces are in prose; several are in verse; and one (from Clarke's *Colonial Monthly*) takes the form of a dramatic dialogue in which the editor debates the journal's qualities with its contributors, readers and investors. Each of the journals seeks to intervene in the colonial literary economy, and to advance it in some way. The question of how to foster the development of literature in the colonies and across Australia is always crucial, and every preface or editorial responds to this in its own way, taking a moment to give expression to the journal's particular dispositions and priorities, its aspirations, the things that make it distinctive and unique. It is often noted that journals, magazines, weeklies and so on occupy the disposable end of the literary field, quickly produced and then skimmed over by distracted readers, an emblem of the ephemera of everyday life. But this book addresses the fact that the colonial journals – their precariousness notwithstanding – wanted to participate in something longer lasting. The next three parts of this book look at the various ways in which the colonial journals mapped out the Australian literary field. They debated, analysed and evaluated it, creating genealogies and traditions, recalling pasts and imagining possible futures. Distributing themselves across the colonies and beyond, they played a fundamental and necessary role in the making of Australian literature. At the same time, the colonial journals were also *unmaking* it, dispersing their authors, letting older authors go and finding new ones to take their place, reinventing and re-evaluating them, and identifying trends, canons and schools of writing barely recognisable to us today. In part four, we bring together a series of poems and stories that in some ways probably replicates the 'miscellaneous' quality of the journals themselves: featuring work by writers such as Barron Field, Henry Kendall, Mary Fortune, Louis Becke, Katharine Susannah Prichard and Mabel Forrest. In the selections we have made, privileging some writers over others, placing anonymous authors alongside familiar ones, drawing on some journals and not others, we, too, have generated a canon of local writing that is at once idiosyncratic and (in terms of the way it offers a snapshot of the colonial journals' actual content) representative.

Parts five and six of this book turn to the visual landscape of the journals, their illustrators and artists. As these parts suggest, the appearance of a journal – the cover design, its typography, its illustrations, its layout, its materiality – is also an expression of its disposition. For the *Australian Journal*, even the fact that it uses 'colonial-made paper' is noteworthy. The *Native Companion* goes even further: 'The Literary and Advertising Sections', it tells its readers, 'are printed throughout on a specially-made tinted Australian antique paper of the best quality'. Cover designs can convey the cultural aspirations of a journal and say something about the way it sees – or imagines – colonial potential. The cover of Maxwell Keely's *Southern Cross: An Illustrated Australasian Magazine* (November 1898 – November 1900) was produced by the artist Charles Turner, who later took over as editor (and had also contributed to its sibling journal *Cosmos*). For Keely, Turner's image gave *Southern Cross* 'a pleasing conception of the beauty of the Antipodes': conveying an idealised sense of the nation as feminine, cultivated, and outward-looking. The four remaining parts of this book turn to the ways in which the journals represented the nation as a set of ideals that were nevertheless – like literature itself – constantly in the process of being made, and unmade. Parts six and seven are devoted to what we call colonial 'types': where, even as colonial ideals were being framed and circulated, colonial populations were being fractured and classified in order to identify the kaleidoscope of manners and occupations and dispositions that were appearing (and disappearing) in the wider colonial economy. Colonial types generate narratives, which feed an increasingly diverse field of literary forms: stories, poems, romances, sketches, memoirs, and so on. Part eight takes up the issue of race, as something that both fascinated and troubled the colonial journals – generating a striking set of character types and narratives through which (often brutal) racial encounters were staged. The final part of this book turns to writing from the colonial journals that charted change and development across the colonial landscape: the bush and the forests, the townships and the cities. All of these things turn out to be important to the emergence of colonial literary writing, which continually cross-pollinates with the social and cultural commentaries of the time. Indeed, writers like Mary Fortune, Donald Cameron, Ernest Favenc and many others flowed easily back and forth between fictional and non-fictional representations of colonial life. This is something else the colonial journals made possible: an emergent Australian literature that was fully embedded in the immediacy of its time and place.

1 Stuart, *Australian Periodicals with Literary Content, 1821–1925: An Annotated Bibliography*, p. ix.
2 Lawson, *The Archibald Paradox*, p. 72.
3 cited in Cannon, *The Land Boomers: The Complete Illustrated History*, p. 132.
4 ibid., pp. 132–33.
5 Mirmohamadi and Martin, *Colonial Dickens: What Australians Made of the World's Favourite Writer*, p. 26.
6 Sadrin, 'Foreign English-Language Editions', p. 209.
7 Barton, *Literature in New South Wales*, pp. 6–7.
8 Morrison, 'Serial Fiction in Australian Colonial Newspapers', p. 309.
9 Johnson-Woods, *Index to Serials in Australian Periodicals and Newspapers. Nineteenth Century*, p. 5.
10 Bode, 2012, pp. 113–14.
11 Johnson-Woods, p. 5.
12 see MacKaness and Stone, *The Books of the Bulletin 1880 – 1952: An Annotated Bibliography*.
13 Morrison, p. 318.
14 Lawson, p. 82.
15 Potter, *News and the British World: The Emergence of an Imperial Press System*, p. 59.
16 Docker, *The Nervous Nineties: Australian Cultural Life in the 1890s*, p. 28.
17 Jose, *The Romantic Nineties*, p. 4.
18 Greenop, *History of Magazine Publishing in Australia*, p. 1.
19 Cantrell, 'A. G. Stephens's *Bulletin* Diary', p. 37.
20 Waters, *Commodity Culture in Dickens's Household Words: The Social Life of Goods*, p. 19.
21 Sayers, *The Company of Books: A Short History of the Lothian Book Companies 1888–1988*, pp. 31–33.

'PREFACE'

Australian Magazine; or, Compendium of Religious, Literary, and Miscellaneous Intelligence
1 December 1821

In completing the first Volume of the AUSTRALIAN MAGAZINE, we should depart from established usage, and disappoint the expectations of our Readers, were we to omit offering some prefatory observations.

To expatiate on the merits or defects which it may contain, were a task to which we have neither right nor pretension:—but, as our readers hold over us a kind of judicial authority, by which they are warranted to applaud or to censure, we owe it in deference to them, and in justice to ourselves, to advert to the principles with which we entered upon our labours. Those principles are indeed the only data by which our work can be fairly estimated. It is in literature an unvarying maxim, that the critic should "in every work regard the writer's *end*."

Our design, from the first, has avowedly been, "to disseminate useful knowledge, religious principles, and moral habits." And though some, we are aware, object to our Magazine, that it wears too grave and religious an aspect, candour must compel them to acknowledge, that we have not swerved from the intentions we distinctly proposed.

Political discussion, and party spirit, and personal allusion, we have scrupulously avoided. Literature and science, while we have devoted to them a portion of attention, have been kept subordinate and subservient to our primary design. Of *Colonial* occurrences we have endeavoured to select the most interesting; though this department is in great measure superseded by the weekly Journal. The Meteorological Diary and Agricultural Reports, for which we are indebted to the kindness of two respectable gentlemen, cannot but be esteemed important, as a summary view of the fluctuations in our atmosphere, and the progress of our husbandry. In our Theological articles, we have studiously guarded against "unprofitable disputation;" so that sincere Christians, of whatever denomination, may peruse them with safety and advantage.

In fine, it has been uniformly our object to lead the mind to serious reflection; to explain and enforce the pure doctrines of the Gospel; to restrain vice and irreligion; and to promote social virtue and vital piety.

'ADDRESS'

Hobart Town Monthly Magazine
March 1833

In presenting to the Public of this Colony a Miscellany, exclusively devoted to Literature and Science, the conductors are induced to offer a few remarks in explanation of their views and intentions. The novelty of their plan is, of itself, perhaps sufficient to attract attention in the first instance: but, erroneous indeed will be the opinion of their Readers, if they imagine if this alone will constitute their principal claims to public patronage. Their aim is much higher—their ambition much more lofty and meritorious,—they aspire to establish such a Miscellany, as shall not only prove highly acceptable to their fellow Colonists, but, at the same time, show their friends and well-wishers in "Old England," that Tasmania is not devoid of individuals who have the means, as well as the desire, of cultivating Literature as well as Land, and of devoting their best and liveliest energies to its interests and advancement.

The want of such a work, as that which is now contemplated, has long been experienced in the Colony. The highly intelligent character of the general Settler, and his anxiety to find some means of relaxation and entertainment, beyond the mere gratification of his physical propensities, will induce him to hail the appearance of our Magazine with delight and satisfaction; and it shall be our own fault, if we do not strengthen and foster this gracious and salutary feeling, by our earnest endeavours to please, and, perchance, instruct him. But the general Settler is not the only inhabitant of this territory; neither is he the only individual, whose good opinion we desire, or whose oblectation we shall study to promote. Our exertions will be directed towards all classes, from the very highest personage in the Colony to the lowliest—"who desired instruction, and whose soul thirsteth after knowledge." To those who, happily, enjoy offices of high trust and acceptable emolument, we offer a cheering, harmless, and—we scruple not to say it—an intellectual relaxation from the arduous toils of official duty. We will undertake to promise, that the pages of this Miscellany shall never be stained by political or general personalities—that scurrility shall never find even a dark corner to sculk [sic] in—and that the advancement of intelligence and wisdom, by means rigidly compatible with Morality, Honor, and Truth, shall alone find support and advocacy in the columns of *our* Magazine.

'PREFACE'
Hobart Town Magazine
December 1833

In bringing to a conclusion the first volume of our adventurous Miscellany, we cannot resist the temptation of addressing a few words to our friends—the public—on this happy and important occasion.

For the encouragement we have received, we are, as in duty bound, most grateful. Although we anticipated a very ample share of patronage, our expectations have been more than realized; and we have proved by our exertions, that "Tasmania is *not* devoid of individuals, who have the means as well as the desire, of cultivating Literature as well as Land, and of devoting their best and liveliest energies to its interest and advancement." We cannot be accused of vanity, even by the most fastidious and precise, if we attribute to the combined exertions of *our* literary *coterie*, the diffusion of so extensive a taste for literature, as is now prevailing in the Colony; neither can the same sin be imputed to us, if we affirm, that our little Miscellany has been enriched by communications, which would have done credit to any of the magazines "at home." To particularize individual articles would certainly be invidious; but, we think, we may safely take pride to ourselves for the excellence of the communications, which have been furnished by our poetical friends,—a very convincing proof, by the way, that the higher faculties of the imagination are not excluded from Tasmania.

'INTRODUCTORY ADDRESS'
Tegg's Monthly Magazine
March 1836

The want of a Magazine, whose pages should be devoted to general literature, avoiding the stormy arenas of politics and polemics, and combining amusement with instruction, has long been felt and acknowledged.

A work of this description seems at the present juncture particularly required. There is evidently a growing taste for reading in the minds of our colonial public; and to foster and supply that taste is the object at which we aim.

In following up our plan we shall endeavour, as far as it is practicable, to avoid all invidious distinctions of classes, meting out justice to all. In our dealings with others, we shall invariably make truth our object, and charity our motive; the good of all classes shall find in us a warm supporter, and the bad an unsparing censor.

A portion of our pages shall be devoted to Original Articles on General Literature; and no pains shall be spared to render this division worthy [of] the support we expect from an indulgent public.

A second portion will consist of Extracts selected from the best sources of Periodical Literature, a regular supply of which has been ordered from Britain.

The remaining space will be filled with Reviews of New Books—Colonial and British, Literary Notices, the Drama, and other Varieties.

We trust that in the exercise of our vocation as Critics, we shall ever be found to treat the productions of others with that fairness and candour, which restrains not the freedom of enquiry, nor contracts the limits of just censure.

It now only remains for us to entreat from the public its kind indulgence towards our future labours. We shall spare no exertions to provide for our readers useful and agreeable entertainment. We have endeavoured to secure such literary assistance as lay within the compass of our power. And we call on all who feel anxious to remove from the land, whether of their adoption or their birth, the stigma under which it has hitherto laboured, to unite with us in endeavouring to render Australia

> Great, glorious and free,
> First flower of the earth, and first gem of the sea.

'TO OUR READERS'
Literary News
12 August 1837

The appearance of a literary periodical, of one at least of the present description, is a novelty in our Colony, and a novelty which some, perhaps, may be disposed to think a hopeless experiment. In more than one quarter, we have heard the idea almost ridiculed, of infusing a taste among the Australian public, for literature and the arts, and in one publication, referring to our "Address," we are charged with promising "mighty things," as if the attempt to engage the interests of the colonists in something else besides pecuniary speculations and political squabbles, were really so Utopian an undertaking as to have emanated only from the brains of enthusiasts or egotists. We shall not insult the respectability and intelligence of those whom we are ambitious of counting among our readers, by supposing our design to be so utterly fruitless; for ourselves, we have made no promises, save those which related to our aims and intentions. We are not aware of having been presumptuous enough to announce that we either should or could effect the objects of our paper—we merely stated it was our *desire*, and would be our *endeavour* to do so. We are not arrogant enough to flutter before the public face, "the Literary News," as an oracle or standard, before which they are to bow with implicit faith; but it is humbly and zealously offered as a channel through which they may become acquainted with, and be induced to acquire a taste for, the Belles Lettres in general, and thus be themselves led to explore the original stores from which our own gleanings have been drawn. We are not altogether without hope that we shall receive encouragement from the colonial public, who, it is no dreamy notion to surmise, may probably, whilst maintaining the existence of *five* political journals, give a helping hand to the birth and growth of *one* that professes to be literary. From the conductors of the press, too—devoid as we are of all party feeling or expression—we may reasonably look for support; though, possibly, by joining in the political sympathies of none, we may provoke the editorial antipathies of all. Be this as it may—it must be something startling indeed that shall tempt us to an interchange of hostilities with them. We would rather have

their praise than their censure; but if we cannot obtain the first, we shall not suffer ourselves to be betrayed into acrimony or uncourteousness by the last.

'EDITOR'S ADDRESS'
Arden's Sydney Magazine of Politics and General Literature
September 1843

It is with great satisfaction that we conclude our first month's laborious application, and it is with difficulty we find a corner to speak of our personal feelings on the subject.

The Editor is fully aware that a reading public, in reviewing this publication, will judge of it, as they have a right to, by its results. He may be allowed, however, in closing the last sheet, to offer some extenuating remarks for the frequent faults which its pages display.

The various pieces of which our Magazine is composed must bear evident marks of hasty construction; but, while we frankly acknowledge that the compilation deserves much critical censure, we may be permitted to advance, as an excuse, the severe tax which its production has been upon our abilities. Nearly the whole of the present number has been composed by the Editor himself, and the exertion to produce variety in the original articles has demanded no little versatility of mood and imagination. We must rely, indeed, upon gaining the generosity of the reader by informing him that little more than a fortnight has been afforded for the composing, illustrating, arranging, compiling, and printing the First Number of ARDEN'S SYDNEY MAGAZINE; and all we shall lay claim to at present is the spirit and industry with which we have completed the task, under all the difficulties, of a novel attempt in literature, in a place where the Editor has not the personal advantage of being publicly known.

The supporters of the Magazine will, at least, appreciate the talent we have secured in the illustration of the work, and we are inclined to hope that Mr. Prout's connection with our literary labours will not be disadvantageous to his fame as an Artist.

Our intended arrangements for contributions are necessarily incomplete, and the size of the Magazine falls short of the quantity of matter which it was announced to contain. No pains, however, shall be spared to render its successor equal to the expectations of our friends, and the ambition of the Proprietor.

Limited as the means of private parties are, from the depression of monetary affairs, it is not too much, we venture to say, to request that the substantial reward which each individual has in his power to offer, may be early accorded.

No. 2, of Arden's Magazine, will be punctually issued on the 5th of October.

BEGINNINGS AND ENDINGS

'INTRODUCTORY ADDRESS'
Colonial Literary Journal and Weekly Miscellany of Useful Information
27 June 1844

Unprecedented as is, in this colony, the appearance of a *Weekly* Literary Miscellany, we commence our present undertaking in the hope, that thereby may be supplied that deficiency, which, it seems to us, has hitherto prevented success from attending similar efforts of this nature. We have been led to believe that a weekly publication is more in accordance with the public taste, than one issued at a longer interval; and we now present our subscribers with our commencing number, in the humble hope that it may receive their approbation. We must request their most favourable consideration for a few unavoidable omissions and deficiencies in our first number, which, we trust, will not occur again.

To, by far the greater portion of, the inhabitants of this colony, *periodical* literature must ever be the most welcome, and, if rightly selected by them, the most instructive. The pressing calls of business, or of duty, will ever deprive many of the means of pursuing literature or science in any better way than desultory reading. It is therefore a pleasing reflection, that, with the general increase of occupation, has also decreased the difficulty of obtaining useful entertainment and instruction. Information, once to be found only in expensive books—the ponderous quarto and the laborious folio—is now dispersed in a thousand minor channels, and diffused in so cheap a form as to be accessible to every one. We propose, therefore, by means of the *Colonial Literary Journal*, in some measure, to supply to this colony her share of an advantage so desirable, and so conducive to general satisfaction; being assured, that every advance in the pursuit of knowledge, which the mind makes toward attaining perfection, must necessarily increase the rational enjoyments of life.

If it be inquired, what are the particular principles we maintain; we reply, that we intend to uphold the Christian faith, being equally opposed to bigoted intolerance, and averse to reckless sectarianism or misjudged liberalism. No acerbity of party-feeling, either religious or political, will be designedly admitted in the columns of the *Colonial Literary Journal*; but its pages are open to fair and temperate argument; for, without enquiry, there can be no feeling of security; and without controversy, the truth cannot well be elicited.

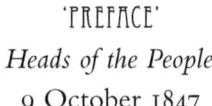

'PREFACE'
Heads of the People
9 October 1847

In presenting our readers with the first volume of the HEADS OF THE PEOPLE, we beg to express our most sincere acknowledgements for the support we have hitherto received; and to assure them that no exertions will be spared on our part to deserve a continuance of public favor. Our undertaking was, indeed, a "matter of grave consideration." To publish a periodical, from the pages of which all personalities were to be excluded;—which was to interfere as little as possible with party feelings or politics, whilst it contained matter at once instructive, amusing, and adapted to the perusal of any class in the community—required far more exertion—far more determination of purpose than will, perhaps, be generally credited.

Some periodicals exist by being almost entirely devoted to business; others are upheld by particular parties on account of the politics they advocate;—others, again, by controverting, in rather strong language, the party prejudices of a particular class;—and some are supported more on account of the peculiar style of the writings they contain, than, perhaps, of any intrinsic merit they may possess. We have endeavoured to avoid wounding the feelings of anyone; but we have also determined to "shoot folly as it flies."

Vice of every kind has always received, and will always receive, our severest censure. We fear not to expose the folly or vice of any public individual; but his private or domestic affairs have ever been held sacred by us. In our pages no spurious moral has been inculcated; no reverend institutions have been insulted; no peace of families violated; and no pranks played which deserve a severer sentence than a peal of laughter.

It has often been mentioned as a reproach to the inhabitants of Sydney, that although several literary journals have been published here, they have all failed in consequence of not having received that support which such undertakings are almost certain to receive elsewhere. They have been spoken of by a publication of the present day as a people "devoid of all intellectual attainments"; and accused of "intellectual barrenness". These censures may once have been just, but can be so no longer; for we flatter ourselves, from the support which we have already received, that there is now growing up in Sydney a taste for other writings than mere local and matter-of-fact news—violent political articles, or those gross vituperative writings which once seemed to be so much relished. In fine, we feel sure that a more liberal spirit is springing up amongst us, and that Literature is in the ascendant.

It has been objected that we have selected our HEADS rather indiscriminately. To this we reply, as we have already done, that we cannot undertake to please every one. We invariably make our selections, not only with a view to please our readers generally, but to bring into notice rising talent, and drag from obscurity real merit wherever we find it. Besides, our Head is only given as the type or representative of a class; we cannot, therefore, expect to please any number of persons, and at the same time exactly coincide with the opinions of some fastidious individual, who looks upon himself as a sort of index to the feelings and opinions of the great body of the people, which he estimates by his own.

In thanking those gentlemen who have, from time to time, favored us with their contributions, we beg to state, that our columns will always be open for the reception of any production which may be considered deserving of publication, hoping that we shall thereby contribute to excite a spirit of emulation in useful literature.

EDITORIAL
Australia Felix Monthly Magazine
June 1849

The AUSTRALIA FELIX MAGAZINE, in introducing itself to the public, (and the Editor in this case must do the honours,) is not called upon to explain its principles and its plans, which will be found embodied in its pages, but may be fairly indulged in a few prefatory remarks, calculated to prevent mistakes. In the first place it must be kept in view, that a magazine cannot, and is not meant to be, the production of any single mind, so that absolute unity in thought and feeling is neither to be expected nor desired. Variety, however, while it has its charms, may also beget a feeling of discrepancy, but this is essential to that free play of intellect, without which thought itself is not worth having. And yet we know well, that a publication without leading principles to stamp its character, is but a body without a soul—a collection of machinery without a moving power. The *Australia Felix Magazine*, as long as we are responsible for its contents, will, then, avow itself to be Protestant in its religious views, British in its politics, progressive in its practice, and all contributions written in a christian [sic], or in a constitutional spirit, or on points contributing to the advancement of the comfort and happiness of the colony, will find a welcome and a corner. Those who are prepared to devote time and study to further the best interests of their adopted country, have good hopes of forming a band, in which, indeed, every instrument will have its distinct sound, but which nevertheless in its unified effect may produce, after some practice, an harmonious symphony. The public may look upon this attempt as hopeless, but the hopelessness lies in themselves, and, half represented as we are in Sydney, and half represented as we are at home, a publication which will be the local organ of those who care enough about the country to give an hour's thought to its welfare, is the best hope we have, and affords us what we have long wanted, a means of speaking out for ourselves, and proving that we are fit for an independent existence.

'SALUTATION TO AN OLD FRIEND'
Melbourne Monthly Magazine
May 1855

In ushering into being the first number of a new publication of a character different from anything yet produced in this colony, it will be a sufficient explanation of our design to say, that we purpose a reproduction—as far as the circumstances of the colony and the resources at our command render possible—of the first-class magazine literature of London, the class of which *Blackwood* may be considered the type.

This has hitherto, as far as we are aware, been unattempted in Victoria. Two or three serials have appeared at distant intervals, and from the operation of various influences have failed. These, however, have approximated much more closely in character to the weekly illustrated miscellanies of the London press than the publications we intend to imitate. Even by these the field has long been left unoccupied, and when the *Melbourne Monthly Magazine* was projected, the colony presented the singular spectacle of a civilised country without a literature—a condition which the subsequent appearance of the *Rural Magazine*, a mere manual of gardening operations, cannot be thought materially to have changed.

Victoria is not destitute of newspapers: Melbourne itself boasting as many as three *dailies*, all conducted with a certain amount of ability and spirit. It is to be regretted, however, that partly from the homage paid to a false theory, and partly from the unworthy spirit to which it has suffered itself to become subject, colonial journalism can scarcely claim a standing in the literary world. We say this with sorrow, remembering the great services the newspaper press of England has rendered to the cause of intellectual, moral, and political progress. But no man accustomed to the conditions under which the British press works, and the spirit in which political and social discussions are conducted, can feel otherwise than humbled at seeing the functions of a great institution perverted to the gratification of sentiments that are mildly described as those of petty jealousy and personal animosity.

The *Melbourne Monthly Magazine* will partake more of the character of a purely literary than of a political journal. Political discussions will not indeed be excluded, but they will be sparingly introduced, and will invariably be conducted in the calm and impartial spirit of the historian, rather than with the passion and partisanship of the controvertist.

The Editor has some hesitation in presenting this number as a specimen of what his journal is designed to be. It has been very hurriedly got up, with little more than three weeks having elapsed since the project was finally determined on. Ignorant at first of the literary resources that would be at his disposal, the Editor has to some extent perhaps made use of materials that might have been rejected had he been as cognizant as he is now of the literary wealth that really exists in the colony. He must plead also that many distracting causes have interrupted his attention to very responsible functions. But in spite of all he trusts that his first number will be a "child of promise," and, without further professions and apologies, throws himself upon the sympathies, and appeals to the support of a public who cannot have forgotten, he would fain hope, the reading habits of home.

'PREFACE'
Illustrated Journal of Australasia
1 June 1857

It is with extreme regret, shared by many contributors and friends, that the proprietor of the JOURNAL OF AUSTRALASIA announces the completion of the fourth volume as the finish of that work. The amount of encouragement and support accorded to it by subscribers and casual purchasers has not been equal to one-third of that necessary to have made the same an ordinary, fairly profitable printing order. He thought that, by uniting proprietor, publisher, and printer, in one person, a remunerative magazine, then (as, equally, now) a fiction, might be realized a fact. Six hundred pounds, it is thought, will hardly cover the loss sustained by this attempt—an attempt which, considering the character and choice of the literature contained therein—the printing, which safely can be averred to be unequalled in the Australias (and in but few instances in the mother country), either as to typography or careful reading—or the introduction of a class of fine engravings and popular music, he still thinks has hardly met with that support it was entitled to.

True, it is not all people who care for or appreciate "fine" printing. Some would be as well satisfied with the style of the "*Scientific*" or the "*Month*" (Sydney), and feel just as and, perhaps, more comfortable when reading its pages than if they held in their hands one of Robson, Levey, and Franklyn's presentation books, printed with ink specially made for the purpose, on extra superfine thick glazed tinted paper, also made for the book, with beautiful new type, and enriched with the most exquisite engravings.

Some have thought the magazine too "light," and others, again, have declaimed against it as being too "heavy." The first didn't care for "romance"—they could get it in large quantities at the booksellers, for about eighteenpence a pound in "Long Primer," or two shillings in "Bourgeois," never caring—not they; they did n't believe in it—to encourage those who would and could hold up the colony to "nature's mirror." The second thought too many of its pages were occupied by scientific articles. They did not care to know anything about the exploration of the interior; or the appearance of the earth of the colony, either under or upon its surface; or the curious creatures that lived thereon; not they.

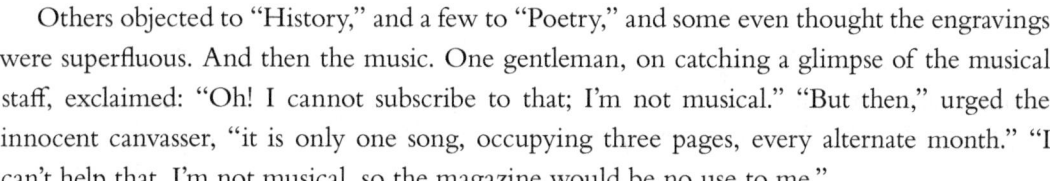

Others objected to "History," and a few to "Poetry," and some even thought the engravings were superfluous. And then the music. One gentleman, on catching a glimpse of the musical staff, exclaimed: "Oh! I cannot subscribe to that; I'm not musical." "But then," urged the innocent canvasser, "it is only one song, occupying three pages, every alternate month." "I can't help that. I'm not musical, so the magazine would be no use to me."

The proprietor might go on, and, perhaps, by detailing the troubles consequent upon magazine publishing in Victoria, manufacture a guide book for the future producer of the like article. Experience is a bitter pill, and, as he hopes some day to have his revenge for the one he is swallowing, he prefers keeping the remainder of his ills to himself. But, whilst parting (he trusts for a time only) from the few who have, by their contributions and subscriptions, so liberally supported the Journal (not forgetting his advertising friends), he cannot do so without returning them his most sincere thanks; and it affords him some consolation to know that Literature and Art have been helped on to some extent by the existence of the *Journal of Australasia*.

'TO OUR SUBSCRIBERS AND THE PATRONS OF LITERATURE IN AUSTRALIA'
Month
November 1858

The present number completes the third volume of this Magazine.

A vigorous effort will be made early in the month of December to increase the number of Subscribers. For this purpose not only our own friends and patrons will be called upon for co-operation, but all those who are popularly known to have the encouragement of Polite Letters at heart.

A New Subscription List will be opened. Several ladies and gentlemen have volunteered to canvass for Subscribers.

In the conduct of the new series of the MONTH the following canons will be rigidly observed:—

1.— There will only be one continued Story in each number.
2.— A "London Letter," being a rapid historical essay on the events or facts of the month, will appear in each number.
3.—One Australian Sketch of scenes or scenery in town or country—or a paper on the wild sports of the Australians will appear in each number.
4.—The acknowledged Literary and Critical character of the serial will be maintained.

BEGINNINGS AND ENDINGS

It may be well to remark that Mr. Frank Fowler and Peter "Possum" are permanently engaged to write for the Magazine; Messrs. Wilkie Collins, author of "Basil," &c., and James Hannay, author of "Singleton Fontenoy," &c., have promised to contribute occasionally.

Mr. Frank Fowler's Essay on "Disraeli's Books," written during his voyage to London, will appear in the January number.

The January number will be published on or abour the 24th of December. It will contain a Christmas Story of Sydney in the Old Times.

The success—if not the very existence of the Magazine—depends on Subscribers *paying in advance*; or, at least; at the end of each quarter, *without waiting for a Collector to call*.

J. SHERIDAN MOORE, EDITOR.
"Month" Office, 29th November, 1858.

'OURSELVES'
Australian Magazine
October 1859

This first number of the AUSTRALIAN MAGAZINE is given to the public under circumstances of great encouragement, not unmixed, however, with some grounds of anxiety and apprehension, owing to failure after failure having been the result of similar speculations of considerable promise, which have struggled through a brief existence to an early demise—or put forth prospectuses, that have met with but little or no support. Such, at least, will not be the fate of the present undertaking,—whether from more energetic efforts, or from personal remembrances, we have been so readily met with promised aid and countenance, that we now feel the success of the current undertaking certain. The execution of our designs, on the comprehensive scale we have laid down, and the completion of that arrangement in the liberal spirit which we flatter ourselves that we have given proof of at the outset of our labours,—will require an extent of circulation which can only be secured by the kind and active co-operation of all who take an interest in our present undertaking. It will be our part to excite and foster that interest; and while we point to the unquestionable usefulness of such publications as the present, as periodical organs of communication between the sister Colonies of Australia on all subjects connected with their mutual advantage, as its great claim to support, independent of the amusing and instructive contents of its lighter pages, we promise our unremitting endeavour to make all its departments complete.

'A FEW WORDS AT STARTING'
Penny Melbourne Journal: A Weekly Family Newspaper of Fiction, General Literature etc.
3 October 1862

THE MELBOURNE JOURNAL, of which this is the initiatory Number, will be published every Saturday. Each Number will contain a great variety of original matter, comprising Essays, Fiction, Poetry, History, General Literature, Mechanical Inventions, Scientific Discoveries, Fine Arts, Amusements, &c., contributed by some of the best colonial writers and arranged by eminent Australian talent.

The design of the Promoters of the JOURNAL is to supply a CHEAP and GOOD weekly publication—a deficiency which has long been felt by the colony. They are fully aware of the amount of moral responsibility entailed by such an undertaking. The cry—"Give us something to read!"—uttered by our vast reading population—especially the youthful portion of it—is promptly answered by the European Press daily pouring forth its load of literary trash, which is so calculated to lower instead of elevating the moral tone of the youthful mind—ever prone to choose the evil rather than the good. This we would supersede—and to the demand for intellectual food which the present acme of civilisation makes so urgent, and which is imbibed regardless as to whether it be poisonous or nutritious, we would subscribe our mite; but in such a manner as to place before the public a work blending instruction with entertainment, admonition with amusement, and general knowledge in a pleasing form—a work containing matter to please those able to make a healthy choice of literature for themselves, and one which shall not be pronounced "dull," "dry," and "insipid" by those accustomed to be amused by the perusal of the poisonous mass of literature at present in circulation.

'EDITORIAL'
Sydney Punch
27 May 1864

On the morning of the twenty-fourth day of May, in this joyously saltatory leap year, one thousand eight hundred and sixty-four, Mr. PUNCH completed his pilgrimage from Fleet Street to the shores of this Southern Italy—Italy without the ruins, and poverty and brigands in steeple-crowned hats. Mr. PUNCH's ship cast anchor in front of the strong sponge-cake-looking fortification which appears to be armed with a gun, or a big telescope, or a bit of stovepipe, and presents such an imposing appearance to strangers. Mr. PUNCH felt rather dizzy at first from the sunny blaze of scenic magnificence supervening on prolonged sea-sickness. Still, strong in the Christian panoply of good conscience, and lofty purpose, he went ashore, landed, in the first instance quite alone, and addressed some feeling and suitable remarks to himself. Subsequently, he repaired to a convenient hostelrie, and drank his own health in a goblet of the generous juice of the sun-fed vines of this blue-heavened Colony. He then returned himself thanks, in a neat and appropriate soliloquy; and proceeded on his way, solemnly impressed with the exalted and hopeful nature of his mission. Having happily arrived on the birth-day of our Most Gracious and Benign Sovereign, Mr. PUNCH promptly prepared the path for a fittingly ceremonious introduction to her Britannic Majesty's gubernatorial vicar. With a tone and manner singularly felicitous, His Excellency expressed his gratification at meeting a fully accredited representative of the important Fleet Street item of governing consequence. Mr. PUNCH, in his reply, embodied in a voice husky with emotion, begged to truthfully repose this assurance, that he had arrived here with the simple intention of aiding, loyally, nationally, colonially and humanly, the truest aims of editorial action.

Mr. PUNCH, having but just arrived, yet feeling strongly and warmly respecting the purpose of his mission, begs to say that he confidently trusts that his oracular and facetious utterances will be of a character and tone that will not offend any justly sensitive colonially human feeling.

Laughter is the distinctive blessing and exclusive privilege of the human race; and Mr. PUNCH purposes to stimulate this healthy agency week by week, for an indefinite series of hebdomadal periods.

Mr. PUNCH defers a more extended exposition of his aim and sentiment till he recovers from the consequence of the sudden blaze of this brilliant atmosphere.

'THE EDITOR'S ADDRESS'
Australian Monthly Magazine
September 1865

To adopt the humble, but not very original or elegant, metaphor with which some periodicals have announced the beginning of their existence, we ought to say that our "frail bark" is now fairly launched upon the ocean of public opinion, and that we hope for it a prosperous and successful voyage.

But, in truth, we are not inclined to be content to introduce ourselves to our readers with such modesty. We are determined to have the birth of *The Australian Monthly Magazine* ushered in with some flourish of trumpets, though we ourselves are the trumpeters.

In our prospectus we stated there was a favourable field open in Australia for the establishment of a good monthly magazine, and we intimated that we should endeavour to fill that opening. Our first number is an earnest of what our future efforts will be; and we trust that we give a good guarantee that all reasonable anticipations that may be formed of our enterprise will be realised.

The contents of the following pages, and the style in which the magazine has been got up, are sufficient proofs that we have set before us a high standard for our aim. There are difficulties inseparable from the inauguration of a new project of this character, especially in a country like Australia; and, making due allowances for those difficulties, our first number, we venture to affirm, both as to its literary and typographical merits, is not only a creditable, but a highly successful, production.

It is a remarkable fact that at the present time there is not a single representative published in the Australian colonies, except *The Australian Monthly Magazine*, of this description of periodical literature. Many of the obstacles which have long existed to the successful establishment in this part of her Majesty's dominions of a magazine, worthy to be compared with any of the English monthlies, have been gradually removed during the last few years; and the projectors of this magazine may fairly claim the credit of being the first to take advantage of the altered state of circumstances to supply the blank which has long been felt in our periodical literature. While confidently relying on our first number in support of our claim for public approbation, we are not unconscious of our defects and shortcomings. These it will be our endeavour to remedy in future issues.

The establishment of a magazine of this character is an enterprise of considerable magnitude, and the expense and labour attendant upon the production of the first number have been by no means light. We trust that the public will look with favour upon our undertaking, and give *The Australian Monthly Magazine* a cordial welcome.

It is the fashion of some people to say, more than doubtingly, "Can any good thing come out of Australia?" They sneer at everything colonial, and affect to despise native enterprise in whatever direction it may be developed. This class of grumblers is, however, a small one, and is gradually becoming less and less as the colonies give some fresh proof—which they do almost every day—that their own resources can supply the people, to a very great extent, with all the luxuries as well as the necessaries of life which they require.

If the *Australian Monthly Magazine* receive that measure of encouragement which is due not less to its intrinsic merits than to the fact of its being a new colonial enterprise, we shall accept that encouragement as a stimulus to renewed exertions to make the magazine worthy of Australia.

'TO OUR READERS'
Australian Journal
2 September 1865

Inexorable fashion exacts from us an exordium to our new periodical; and we gladly avail ourselves of the custom to come face to face with those whom we trust to hold in social intercourse for many a month of happy companionship. Let us bespeak, if we can, their sympathy, their goodwill, their kindly judgement, for we cannot flatter ourselves that we shall never deserve their censure, though we would fain hope we shall never receive it.

We do not appeal to a sect, a clique, or a class; for we design to interest, to amuse, and, if possible, to instruct everybody who will read us.

Yet we do hope to embrace a wide and genial audience: to record the phases of Colonial literature; to direct attention to the triumphs of art; and to explain the most recent efforts of mechanical genius; until these pages reflect the Literature, Art, and Science of Australia. Neither shall we neglect to satisfy our readers with abundance of matter for mirth and entertainment, mingled with food for thought. We shall lead them into the realms of romance; into the fairy-land of poetry.

The ablest COLONIAL pens of the day will be engaged on our staff. Historical Romances and Legendary Narratives of the old country, will be mingled with Tales of Venture and Daring in the new; Nouvellettes, whose scenes will be laid in every nation, varied occasionally with Fairy Stories for the Young; and Parlour Pastimes for boys and girls. Then there will be the Fashions; and last, though not least, Answers to Correspondents.

In a word, we seek to please everybody, and shall succeed if we can but carry out the work which with a full sense of its high responsibility, we have commenced; and with the confident hope of success, we know launch into the world the first number of

"THE AUSTRALIAN JOURNAL."

Welcome it, O readers!

'TO OUR READERS AND THE PUBLIC'
Australian Journal
22 August 1868

The present number (156) of the AUSTRALIAN JOURNAL completes our Third Yearly Volume. In the face of fierce competition, which has for some months past been carried on among the importers of European periodicals, it is worthy of mutual gratulation, on the part both of proprietors and readers, that the JOURNAL has not only been able to "build its own," but that, keeping the even tenour [sic] of its way, it has every prospect of attaining a still higher measure of success than has hitherto marked its steady progress in popular favour throughout these colonies.

Commenced, in 1865, with an explicit announcement that it would "not appeal to a sect, a clique, or a class," the AUSTRALIAN JOURNAL has uniformly acted up to its avowed purpose—namely, that of 'reflecting the Literature, Art, and Science of Australia; affording mirth and entertainment, mingled with food for thought; and leading its readers into the realms of romance, and the fairy land of poetry."

As considerable stress has of late been laid upon the 'duty of fostering colonial industries', it may be permitted us, on this occasion, to offer a few remarks upon the applicability of this principle to colonial literature, as one—and by no means the least important—of the "native industries," to foster and promote which is pronounced to be the duty of all who have made Australia their home.

The proposition naturally suggests the fostering of colonial literary and artistic talent by the conductors of periodical publications; who, in return, have a right to expect that the public will award corresponding patronage to their colonial productions, without which support it is obvious that all efforts on the part of a publisher to encourage native authors or printers must prove utterly futile.

There are at this day many persons, in each of these southern colonies, who can remember the time when the best British fabrics—woollen cloth and carpets, for example— were very far inferior, as regards texture at least, to the imported continental articles. But it became fashionable to encourage the home manufacture, and what is the fact now? The men of Yorkshire, and of the West England, daily produce broad-cloths that, for texture, beauty and durability, cannot be surpassed by Saxony or any other part of the world; whilst the men of Wilton and Kidderminster now successfully compete with their Brussels rivals, their former haughty superiors. It is by similar means alone that literature, like the more substantial productions of a country, can hope to be successful, or even self-sustaining.

So far as *their* portion of the "duty" of fostering native industry is concerned, the proprietors of the AUSTRALIAN JOURNAL appeal, with pride and satisfaction, to the experience of their fellow colonists, during the three years their periodical has been before the public. Whilst articles, of European or American origin, possessing extraordinary interest for their scenes and incidents, have been judiciously selected on occasions, it has been the uniform practice of the Editor to give preference to matters appertaining to Australia, and articles from the pens of colonial writers. A cursory glance at the contents of the three yearly volumes will suffice to show that this aim has been faithfully carried out in all departments, by authors and artists, contributors and printers, and, as far as possible, by colonial-made paper. The proprietors feel, therefore, that they are justified in looking with confidence to the reading public of these colonies for that measure of patronage without which all efforts on their part must prove ineffectual.

BEGINNINGS AND ENDINGS

INTRODUCTION
Colonial Monthly
September 1867

It is due to the readers of the COLONIAL MONTHLY that some words should be spoken as to the views of the proprietors in taking up the *Australian Magazine*, and the adoption of the present title, in place of the former one, for a periodical essentially Australian in aim. These words shall be brief; and they shall be final.

The title, COLONIAL MONTHLY, has been chosen as much for convenience as for its comprehensive character. In Victoria alone there are many publications bearing the distinctive term "Australian" or "Australasian," and this is found not unfrequently to confuse correspondents and to lead to other inconvenience. Indeed, the term has been adopted in the colony above named to such an extent, and for such merely local purposes, that there is some danger that distant readers may come to regard Victoria herself as constituting Australia!—a conclusion fairly to be resented by her sister colonies.

'A PROSPECTUS. IN ONE ACT'
Colonial Monthly
March 1868

EDITOR, ARTIST, PROPRIETORS, CONTRIBUTORS, *and* FRIENDS *discovered seated at a table in the Fig Tree Tavern. Dinner has just been removed. Thermometer at 70 in the shade and mosquitoes troublesome.*

    EDITOR *(rising)*. Gentlemen,—We have met this evening—(hum, ha)—to confer about a plan of operations for the new COLONIAL MONTHLY. ("Hear, hear, hear!") The success which has attended the small publication which has hitherto borne that name—(CONTRIBUTOR—"N. or M.?")—has induced the—hum—the ha—the m, m—proprietors to enlarge the magazine, and present it to the—the—(A CONTRIBUTOR—"Public Library!")—to the public in a more attractive form. It has hitherto been a matter of regret that no articles by English writers have been contributed. I have made arrangements, gentlemen—(*suppressed groans*)—for a serial story by a well-known English author, which will appear in due course. I intend to make the MONTHLY a feature in colonial literature. There is no reason why a well-printed, well-written, amusing and instructive—("bravo, bravo!")—periodical should not succeed in Australia. I believe that such a periodical will succeed, and I think we can produce such a periodical. ("Hurray!—quite antithetical! like Burke, begad!" etc.) It only remains, gentlemen, for us to discuss calmly, quietly, and dispassionately—("hear, hear")—the course we intend to pursue. (*Sits down amid immense cheering.*)

TOMMY TURNOVER (*a contributor, from behind a huge cigar*). The question is—

EDITOR. The question is—Will it pay?

CHORUS OF FRIENDS. Pay? of course!

JOHN PENNYLEX (*an ingenious contributor, lighting his pipe.*) It must be made to pay.

EDITOR. Ha! (*Spits into fire-place.*)

MELBŒUS (*a squatter*). What are your plans? Are you going to support the wool trade?

A CIVIL SERVANT. Oh! we'll have no politics!

TREGARTHEN (*a barrister with a knack for lampooning his friends*). You want smart social sketches.

EDITOR. Yes; and a good serial story.

JOHN BROWN (*a practical man, with money*). Not too long, though. The public don't like long stories.

TREGARTHEN (*helping himself to brandy and water*). You are right, Brown, my hearty. We want stories with "go" in them.

JEROME PATUROT (*a talented journalist*). Exactly! Plenty of *verve* and dash!

PENNYLEX. You must get one from Europe!

MELBŒUS. No! Stick to "Colonial Industries."

EDITOR. By all means! Give [me] one really good novel by a colonial author, and I will publish it. But we must have no trash, you know.

A TALENTED CONTRIBUTOR (*suggestively*). The Bleeding Bedoween, or the Bounding Boatman of the Bosphorus.

EDITOR (*severely*). This is not a comic journal, young man!

CONTRIBUTOR (*derisively, after the manner of the late Mr. O. Smith*). Ha! ha! ha!

(EDITOR *frowns, and helps himself to brandy by mistake.*)

SAURIAN PODICEPS (*a scientific man, with spectacles*). We must have one heavy article a month!

TREGARTHEN. Only one.

JOHN BROWN. On some current topic of the day.

ALL. Hear! hear!

BEGINNINGS AND ENDINGS

'INTRODUCTORY'
Colonial Monthly
January 1870

PROCLUS has happily remarked that the best deeds are generally those which are prefaced by few words. I intend to act upon the apothegm of the old philosopher, leaving the readers of the New Year's number of the COLONIAL MONTHLY to appraise for themselves the contents which follow this brief "introduction."

In divesting myself of the "singing robes," in which I usually appear before the public, I may be allowed to say, that I have accepted the invitation of the proprietor of the COLONIAL MONTHLY to write the present preface, with some misgivings as to myself but with great confidence as to the future success of the magazine. That is to say, I thought, and still think, he might have secured a better man to put the number before the public, seeing that it appears to be to be a really good one. It is an excellent indicator of what we might expect from Australian authors, if Australian literature were fairly encouraged. That it has received some material help of late may be assumed, from the facts that the COLONIAL MONTHLY is now completing its fifth volume, and that its proprietor has been tempted to add to it an important feature, in the shape of an enlarged number, to be issued once a year—on New Year's Day. The present issue is the first of the series; the readers will gather from its contents the proprietor's intention to make its successors special and appropriate in character.

The COLONIAL MONTHLY has, from its start, been accredited as the only high class magazine in the colonies; the principal Australian writers have, from the beginning, been constant contributors to it; one of the most brilliant novels written this side of the equator, was introduced to the public through its pages; another of equal calibre, is being issued at the present moment through the same medium; articles of a scientific and social nature, from University professors and other leading scholars, have, from time to time, graced its columns; so that if the proprietary had not achieved success, they would have deserved it. It now remains for the reading public to recognise the proprietor's further efforts to please them. I have no intention to word this preface like an advertisement for that gentleman, but I cannot help remarking, that when a man shows pluck, for the attainment of a useful end, he is entitled to encouragement which takes that best of all forms, namely, the form of practical assistance.

We are in a new country; in the midst of a virgin society; in the dawn of a literature which, even if its beginnings are poor and pale, may, at no very remote period, form one of the healthiest branches of the good old British stock; and, with respect to the proper cultivation of that literature, it is time that a start was made. We have men amongst us who can and have

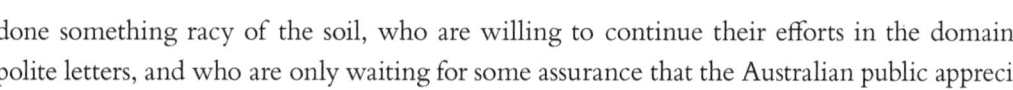

done something racy of the soil, who are willing to continue their efforts in the domain of polite letters, and who are only waiting for some assurance that the Australian public appreciate those efforts.

Such appreciation is best shown by the adequate support of magazines like the COLONIAL MONTHLY. It is not only the hope of Scholarship in Australia, it is *emphatically* the desire of Scholarship in England, to see some gold from the vast unworked quarries of thought in this new El Dorado.

HENRY KENDALL.

'PREFACE'
Touchstone
2 October 1869

"Why did he leave the forest of Ardennes?"

The question has been asked a thousand times, by all manner of people, in all kinds of places, at all sorts of seasons.

"Could TOUCHSTONE," I reply, "have brought his wisdom to a country in which it was more needed, or his folly to a community in which it is held in higher honour?" In truth the hours began to hang heavily on my hands. Audrey is not an entertaining companion on a long winter evening, and the melancholy moralist having relapsed into cynicism, has grown more controversial, cautious and quarrelsome. Therefore I resolved to quit my old woodland haunts, and my co-mates and brothers in exile; and, gathering up my scrip and scrippage, I journeyed hither, and hung up my cap and bells under the very shelter of your civic palace. Shall I do violence to the modesty of my nature by relating how the Governor of Victoria, and all the members of his family, the Ministers of the Crown, the Judges, the two Houses of Parliament, the Mayor, Aldermen, common Councillors of Melbourne, the puntman in Studley Park, the Inspector of Nuisances of Flemington, and other distinguished personages waited upon me in a body—in several bodies, indeed—entreating me to brighten the dulness of their daily lives, by occasional discourse, moralizing after the manner in which I was want to do in the purlieus of the forest, with Corin for my butt, and the lady Rosalind for the sharp correction of my wit!

I am but human and I smiled assent. My suitors departed in a rapturous frame of mind, and the joy-bells of the two cathedrals proclaimed to a hundred thousand people that TOUCHSTONE has consented to become their guide, philosopher, and friend:—

BEGINNINGS AND ENDINGS

> A guardian angel o'er their lives presiding,
> Doubling their pleasures and their cares dividing.

Ought I to maintain a diffident reserve respecting the good I have effected, and the evil I have abated or destroyed? Are not these things written in the history of the colony? Or rather is not that history comprised within the limits of the present volume? Picture to yourself what the community would be without TOUCHSTONE. But no! the imagination refuses to conjure up anything half so horrible and distressing. Victoria might part with its representative institutions—at an alarming sacrifice. It might exist without its Ministers and its nuisances. But what could replace its TOUCHSTONE? The Public and the Parliament Libraries might perish, like their Alexandrian prototype, but there is one work which, if rescued from the flames, would be found to embody the choicest intellect of the nineteenth century, to mark its highest stage of civilisation, and to perpetuate the names and actions of every man of note who figured in the political, civic and social life of the colony, and that work is

THE FIRST VOLUME

OF

TOUCHSTONE.

'PHILOSOPHICAL ESSAYS, BY Q: ON THE PLEASURES OF EDITORSHIP'
Humbug
5 January 1870

It is a very fine thing, but it is rather expensive. For the last fifteen weeks I have been editing this respectable journal, and my experience is that editing as a business don't pay.

As I informed the no doubt intensely interested public some time ago, my habitual melancholy and an incurable tendency to spiritous liquors caused me to be selected from a host of claimants as the Editor of the miserable rag you see before you.

The pay was to be unexceptional, and the work nominal, and I thought I had dropped into a good thing. "You must look over the MSS. old fellow, arrange about the Cartoon, and draw your 'screw.' It's as easy as lying."

It wasn't by any means.

No, sir, I was HAD! HAD emphatically in the biggest possible print.

It began all right. The screw was drawn with refreshing regularity, and the MSS. were plentiful. I suppose I had used up about 3 cwt. of the best paste in the first month. But by and

by the contributors fell off. One went melancholy mad, and another took to the city missionary line of business. He said it paid him better than comic writing. I had to do all the MSS. myself and for some weeks used to write about five pages weekly of brilliant satire.

The Proud Proprietor I believe thought that I had several thousand yards of that article coiled away inside me, and had only to pull thirty feet or so out, and cut it off.

Then my friends used to make suggestions. One wanted a page of social chat spiced with Greek quotations; another said that unless I parodied a Spurgeon's sermon every week, he wouldn't subscribe; another wanted "more conundrums" (insatiable beast!); and a fourth quarrelled with me because I wouldn't go about in a buggy drawn by a pair of piebald jackasses, and distribute *gratis* copies in a blue tunic and a Roman helmet.

I was told that I must have nineteen page engravings, two chromolithographs, and a satirical copperplate sketch if I wanted to make the public buy.

Jones drew out an elaborate calculation to show that if I would have cut the pictures, publish in a broad sheet, and sell for twopence half-penny (I was to be very particular about the half-penny), I should make any fortune.

Brown was a very hopeful fellow. He said that if *he* had the paper he would put in advertisements for nothing, and give away 30,000 copies weekly.

When I refused to adopt these suggestions, my friends went away, and said that I was a most impracticable fellow, and confoundedly conceited into the bargain.

I suppose that, taking them all round, fair give and take, I have made at least nine deadly enemies, and sown the seeds of dissension in ninety hitherto happy families.

I have been called a murderer, a villain, a thief, and an infamous and degraded hound, by numbers of worthy people whom I never met. And scarcely a week passed but I received a note from some respectable bachelor, or baker, or candlestick maker, starting "the paragraph commencing so and so" is an "atrocious and cowardly libel," and informing me that the curse of generations yet unborn will be poured out on my devoted head.

I have discovered that, not only am I myself a venomous and malignant scoundrel, endowed with every vice save that of literary ability, but that my family, from the twentieth generation, have been habitual criminals, and that all my relatives, whatsoever and wheresoever, are branded indelibly with the brand of Cain.

I was told that no man ever conducted a comic journal successfully unless he was either a Capitalist or a habitual Drunkard. Nobody would lend me the money to become the former, so I made an attempt to become the latter, and brought on five useless fits of *delirium tremens* in consequence.

I am at present writing in a hot bath, with a blister behind each ear, ice on my head, a bailiff outside the door, and a man from the Yarra Bend smoking his pipe on the steps—ready for me when I come out.

BEGINNINGS AND ENDINGS

'OURSELVES'
Athenaeum
3 July 1875

It is usual, in introducing a new paper to the public, to state its pretensions and intentions. Whether the practice has anything to recommend it, is doubtful, for promise and performance are by no means synonymous terms in the newspaper dictionary. The custom exists, however, and we bow to it, merely premising that our readers will do well to remember that many circumstances may arise which may cause us to somewhat alter our programme, or fail in attaining the standard at which we aim.

The ATHENAEUM is intended to serve as a means for fostering and encouraging Australian Literature, Science, and Art. It will contain a serial tale, and poetry, &c., by Australian writers, together with reviews of works published in Australia or having connection with Australian affairs. We rely on being able, through the kindness of certain scientific gentlemen, to furnish our readers with occasional articles in this branch of our programme, and we are promised similar assistance with reference to Art. It will easily be seen that, for the satisfactory carrying out of our designs, we are dependent in a great measure upon non-professional writers, and we trust the desired aid will be accorded us.

Some space will be devoted to the consideration of the social and political topics of the day, and we also propose to furnish copious extracts from the leading articles of provincial newspapers, which we assume will serve somewhat as a guide to the opinion of the country Press on matters affecting the welfare of the colony at large.

Arrangements have been made to secure honest and capable criticism of musical and theatrical performances; and we shall also publish general items of intelligence with reference to Literature, Art, Science, and Drama in Australia.

We hope that the foregoing programme embraces a sufficient variety of subjects to make it probable that we shall secure readers in all classes of the community, and no means will be left untried by us to carry it out to the best advantage. At the same time, we must again repeat that we cannot furnish matter for the production of which special knowledge is required, without the aid of gentlemen possessing that knowledge—which, however, we trust, and have reason to believe, will be accorded us.

It must be conceded that the ATHENAEUM, if properly conducted; will supply a want in the community and, in making our first appearance, we do so with large promises of support, and a confident hope that, ere the close of the year, this paper will have obtained a secure hold upon the favour of the public.

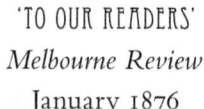

'TO OUR READERS'
Melbourne Review
January 1876

It is an old and reasonable custom in commencing an undertaking like the present to say a few words in explanation of its plan and purpose. In this instance it is the more necessary as the present venture is in many respects a novelty in these Colonies. It is true that several previous attempts have been made to acclimatise periodical literature in the form of Monthly Magazines, but these have been chiefly devoted to Fiction and light literature, and have consequently been brought into direct and unequal competition with our abundant supply of English periodicals, and with our own excellent weekly papers. This, together with the practice of dealing too exclusively with local topics of no intrinsic interest, has probably contributed in no small measure to their uniform want of success.

The conductors of the *Melbourne Review* will, as far as possible, avoid these presumed causes of failure. Though a certain amount of space will be reserved for Poetry and Belles-lettres, the main portion of its pages will be devoted to subjects of a more solid character and of more permanent interest: thus, articles on Philosophy, Theology, Science, Art, and Politics will form the leading feature of the *Review*. It is moreover intended, and this will form one of its distinctive characteristics, to admit contributions of ability on any of these questions, no matter from what school of thought they may emanate;—the soundness of this eclectic principle having been demonstrated by the marked success of the only two English periodicals that have adopted it, the *Contemporary* and the *Fortnightly Review*.

The social and intellectual development of Victoria is now sufficiently advanced to render such a periodical as has been indicated a desideratum to the daily increasing class of thoughtful men and women, who it may be presumed are hardly satisfied with the necessarily brief and partisan treatment of important questions by the daily or even the weekly press.

'OURSELVES'
Australian: A Monthly Magazine
October 1878

In assuming the title of "THE AUSTRALIAN," we hope to make good our right to the name, our wish being to establish a Magazine written for Australians by Australians—Australians in the truest sense—those who have made this land their own equally with their kinsmen born on the soil.

BEGINNINGS AND ENDINGS

We profess in effect to be national in our views, national in our politics, national in our relations to all public and social questions; and our idea of "nationality" is not limited by the artificial obstructions which now split up the Australian people.

Our ambition is to place before the reading public such literary diet as they will approve, and we think that we understand the palates of those for whom we purpose to cater.

We intend that our monthly bill of fare shall offer something for everybody—good substantial staples, economic and political—served up with plain speaking and sound logic; science dealt with in a lucid fashion, best loved by the student; and side by side with these we hope there will be found a lighter diet—seasoned with art and fancy—prose and poem, as much as may be written from a local point of view, and smacking racy of the soil.

We hope and fondly trust that we may thus escape the fate of many of our deserving predecessors in the same line of adventure, namely, the verdict of being "damned with faint praise."

We make one solemn promise, and that is, we shall do whatever we can to avert the fate of being pronounced insipid—or, a doom we dread even more—condemned as unsaleable.

Our readers will after all judge us by our performance and not by our professions; so in committing our venture to the winds and waves of opinion, we ask merely a good word and good will from our friends, and fair play from all.

'A MATTER OF PUBLIC CONCERN'
Bulletin
31 January 1880

To-day we send broadcast throughout the colonies the first number of THE BULLETIN. That it goes to an appreciative public we have no doubt. Excellence is the passport to success in colonial life, and THE BULLETIN bids to win. The aim of the proprietors is to establish a journal which cannot be beaten—excellent in the illustrations which embellish its pages and unsurpassed in the vigor, freshness, and geniality of its literary contributions. To this end the services of the best men of the realms of pen and pencil in the colony have been secured and, fair support conceded, THE BULLETIN will assuredly become the very best and most interesting newspaper published in Australia. With our first issue begins a new departure in journalism. We give to the public what is dictated by the result of twenty years' experience on the colonial Press. The substance of the ordinary daily and weekly newspaper is gathered by the average reader in a few moments. The public eye rejects as uninteresting more than half of what is printed in the publications of the day. It is only the other half which will be found in THE BULLETIN.

EDITORIAL
Australian Woman's Magazine and Domestic Journal
1 May 1882

In presenting the second issue of *The Australian Woman's Magazine and Domestic Journal* to our countrywomen, we can but repeat the sentiments expressed in our prospectus—that we desire to fill a void long felt in colonial literature, by issuing a periodical calculated to elevate and sustain the tone of our home readings, and to develop the resources of native talent and genius.

We have in our Australian-born population many men and women noted for their learning, benevolence, and true worth; while not a few possess rare and special gifts.

We expect much from the younger generation. A great deal is being done publicly, as well as privately, for their advancement in everything that will tend to make them true women and true men; and it will always be a pleasing part of our work to supply the young people's columns with matter interesting and beneficial to them.

Fifty or sixty years ago we had little, if anything, in the form of juvenile literature, and we often wonder how our grandmothers and grandaunts got along when they were little girls; and it must have been dreadfully hard on the boys, as they must have got into mischief much oftener than they do now, notwithstanding we frequently hear the remark that "boys and girls were *so* good when *I* was young."

The supply of intellectual food for our children is a grand feature of the literature of the present day. We must admit there is much that is indigestible—a good deal of dross, but the gold deposit is very rich.

Our Australian youths and maidens are highly privileged. They have ample scope for literary and artistic talent, and the sons and daughters of honest toil can earn enough and to spare.

Much has yet to be said and sung of Australasia's past, and the future of the seven sisters is grand to contemplate. Yes, we have already a past, a history full of incident, adventure and romance—a past rich in themes for the Poet's pen, and subjects for the Painter's brush. And even we, blind as we are, can look forward through the years that increase, and what do we see? A great nation—great because enlightened, good and happy: a free people, not free to break established laws, to be ignorant, to retrograde; but free to be educated, free to toil upwards.

In again alluding to our enterprise, we take this the earliest opportunity of gratefully acknowledging the large amount of encouragement, favour and support we have received from our countrywomen, and would also express, although we can only do so in feeble words, our heartfelt thanks for the kindness and sympathy bestowed upon us, and the helpful aid given by our helpful literary gentlemen friends and well-wishers, including the representatives of the press, whose very favourable opinions will be an incentive for us to do still better in the future. Out motto is "Onward and upward." No doubt we shall make mistakes in wandering sometimes a little to the left, or a little to the right; but we are resolved not to go backwards. Having fixed our minds upon the goal of excellence to be attained, we shall endeavour, notwithstanding sundry divergences, still to make progress, and by following this course we feel certain that we shall receive a continuance of that kind appreciation which accorded such a cordial welcome to the first appearance of *The Australian Woman's Magazine*.

'INTRODUCTION'
Sydney Quarterly Magazine
October 1883

There is much ground for the frequent complaint that, in Australia, the progress of literature—in fact, of all branches of mental culture—is, when compared with the advance in population, wealth, commerce, and other respects, disproportionately small. The reply of apologists to this complaint is familiar and ancient. It is contended that a new country must always develop its physical resources first; and that, in the struggle with primeval nature, the more ornamental concerns of life are pardonably disregarded. This, it is argued, creates an indifference towards intellectual progress which can only be gradually overcome. The rapid accumulation of wealth is made the chief business of existence; sport and amusement its pastimes. Thus, the positions of patrons to the arts and sciences in older countries are, in these newer lands, filled by those who, as a rule, have sedulously devoted their energies to pursuits which have placed them out all of sympathy with such lofty objects. And, continues the apologist, these circumstances—this unmarketableness of intellect it is which renders it possible for a "King-of-the-Ring" in his four-in-hand to drive past a poor forlorn Marcus Clarke in all the anguish of impecuniosity; for a Kendall to depend almost upon private charity for his daily subsistence; or for the proprietor of a successful ballet troupe to look with purseproud pity upon the author of the "Crown of Thorns." Of course there is an obvious moral to be drawn from each of the instances we have cited. But, as Bulwer Lytton very truly observes, "the world satisfies itself too easily when it dismisses the memoir of one of its benefactors with some trite maxim drawn from the errors of genius."

Our contention is that new scenes and new countries ought but to create fresh fields for literature; that struggling with and overcoming primeval nature should but impart vigor of style and resoluteness of tone. And in proof we can point to the writings of such men as Bret Harte and others of that school, who have by their genius invested the roughest possible types of humanity, viz., the heterogeneous horde that composed the pioneer camps in the Sierra Nevada and California mines—their sayings and doings, their journeyings, their very vices and profanity,—with a pathos and humour that have gained for their authors world-wide renown.

Why then is it that Australia is so barren of literature distinctively and characteristically her own? We entertain various theories on the subject, which need not be promulgated here. One thing, however, we will state—and emphatically. It is our intention to leave upon record another attempt to arouse young Australians from their lethargic indifference, and to afford an opportunity for the display of any literary prowess which may be lying dormant or unrecognised in our midst. And who so bold as to predict the result, or scoff at the possibilities of such an endeavour? A glance at the contents of this number will show that we have secured the co-operation of those whose names should dismiss the idea of failure. And we believe that there are many others who will come forward to help us, when they are thoroughly satisfied as to our singleness of purpose and integrity of aim. But should our effort fail for lack of support (as many a worthier has done ere this) as we gather round the tomb of our strangled enthusiasm, no touch of shame—save for the spiritless ones who let it die—will embitter our regret.

'INTRODUCTORY'
Table Talk
26 June 1885

In entering into the journalistic arena with TABLE TALK, we are acting upon a well-founded belief that Colonial Society has attained such a definite stage of development, has become crystallised into such a concrete and enduring form, that it merits more systematic and comprehensive treatment than it has hitherto received at the hands of journalists. The daily newspapers of Melbourne and their weekly offshoots have done much in this direction, but our effort will be to do incomparably more. The journalists referred to have to fulfil certain duties to the public; they have to constitute themselves as a mirror of the hard, practical details of daily life, wherein are reflected political campaigns, diplomatic designs and motives, "battles and murders and sudden death," and all the other factors, great and small, which go to make the total sum of public life in our community. It is impossible, under these conditions, that they should find time or space to deal exhaustively with the other side of life's picture, and supply correct and minute information respecting that Society, which to a large and honoured class in the Old World, is the "be-all and end-all" here, and which has begun to assert its influence in these colonies in no uncertain or ambiguous manner. To remedy this state of things, attempts have previously been made to publish journals devoted exclusively to the interests of Society, but in most instances failure has resulted through the originators taking a low and utterly false view of their subject. The life-blood of Society is, we submit, not supplied by "the sins of emptiness, gossip and spite and slander," and we venture to assert that elevation in the social

BEGINNINGS AND ENDINGS

scale does *not*, of necessity imply a fiendish delight in the soiled or lost reputation of another. We believe that Victoria possesses ladies and gentlemen of the highest rank, as well as of the highest character, whose chief delight does not consist in the reputation of a Society friend shattered by a worthless scribbler in a more worthless journal. In short, "if we have writ our annals true," we affirm that Society does not live upon the garbage which is so often dished for its delectation by journals which started on a misconception, and which must inevitably find speedy death as the fitting end of such misconception.

It is our intention to conduct TABLE TALK upon the lines of the leading fashionable journals in England, so far as the widely different conditions of Colonial Society will permit; and we trust that we shall be able to make it no unworthy representative of its great English prototypes. Arrangements have been made for a constant supply of the latest fashionable intelligence from all the principal towns in the Australian colonies, as well as New Zealand, and we assure our readers, that expressions of "envy, hatred, and malice" will find no place in our columns.

With these few prefatory observations we submit our journal to the criticism of an indulgent public, with the conviction that our efforts will meet with cordial recognition. To adapt the words of the poet:

Go little work, from this our solitude;
We cast thee on the waters; go thy ways;
And if, as we believe, thy vein is good,
The world will find thee after many days.

'BUY THE BOOMERANG'
Boomerang
December 1888

All readers of the Christmas BOOMERANG should subscribe for the weekly issue, published every Friday morning, price 3d. It contains 20 pages, is profusely illustrated by first-class artists and full of entertaining and original reading matter. It is essentially Australian in spirit, advocating progressive nationality and political reform. It gives at once and together the latest news from the world of fashion and from the world of labour. Its business column is a special feature. Its original story page fosters a national literature that stands in pleasing contrast to the sickly tales imported from the antipodes. It is the cheapest and the best threepenny publication in Australia; 12s. per annum in advance, or from all newsagents.

'ABOUT OURSELVES'
Dawn: The Journal for Australian Women
15 May 1888

"Woman is not uncompleted man, but diverse," says Tennyson, and being diverse why should she not have her journal in which her divergent hopes, aims and opinions may have representation. Every eccentricity of belief, and every variety of bias in mankind allies itself with a printing-machine, and gets its singularities bruited about in type, but where is the printing ink champion of man's better half? There has hitherto been no trumpet through which the concentrated voices of womankind could publish their grievances and opinions. Men legislate on divorce, on hours of labor, and many other questions intimately affecting women, but neither ask nor know the wishes of those whose lives and happiness are most concerned. Many a tale might be told by women, and many a useful hint given, even to the omniscient male, which would materially strengthen and guide the hands of law-makers and benefactors aspiring to be just and generous to weak and unrepresented womankind. Here then is DAWN, the Australian Woman's journal and mouthpiece—a phonograph to wind out audibly the whispers, pleadings and demands of the sisterhood. Here we will give publicity to women's wrongs, will fight their battles, assist to repair what evils we can, and give advice to the best of our ability. Half of Australian women's lives are unhappy, but there are paths out of most labyrinths, and we will set up fingerposts. For those who are happy—God bless them! Have we not laid on the Storyteller, the Poet, the Humorist and the Fashionmonger? We wear no ready-made suit of opinions, nor stand we on any ready-made platform of women's rights which we have as yet seen erected. Dress we shall not neglect, for no slattern ever yet won the respect of any man worth loving. If you want "rings on your fingers and bells on your toes" we will tell you where that can best be bought, as well as sundry other articles of women's garniture. We shall welcome contributions and correspondence from women, for nothing concerning women's life and interest lies outside our scope. It is not a new thing to say there is no power in the world like that of women, for in their hands lie the plastic unformed characters of the coming generation to be moulded beyond alteration into what form they will. This most potent constituency we seek to represent, and for their suffrages we Sue.

ADVERTISEMENT
Australasian Critic
1 October 1890

For some years past the lack of an Australasian critical review has been making itself felt among the reading public. Of newspapers we have many; of magazines we have a few; of reviews we have none. The promoters of **The Australasian Critic** believe that the time is ripe for the establishment of such a review.

The Australasian Critic will not resemble any publication which has hitherto originated in Australasia. Its purpose will be to give reviews and criticisms of works of literature, science and art and of dramatic and musical productions, a record of what is being done in the world of pure and applied science, and news, notes, and articles concerning matters of literary, scientific, and artistic interest.

In its judgements **The Australasian Critic** will endeavour to be clear and sober, eschewing violence, exaggeration, and personality.

In the conduct of **The Australasian Critic** it will be carefully borne in mind that it is addressed to Australian readers; hence especial attention will be paid to such matter as concerns the Australasian colonies.

The Australasian Critic will be published on the 1st of every month, and each number will contain twenty-four quarto pages (double columns), each page containing about twelve hundred words. The price will be Sixpence monthly.

'OURSELVES'

Scorpion

24 April 1895

Every journal has an object in its existence. The majority which are to be found in Sydney to-day have one common cause, and that is, the aggrandisement of wealth, and support of the upper classes. We have no such ambitions. We are satisfied to live for the day, and hold the mirror to the public. Our prayer is that of the seer in the Bible—"Give me neither poverty nor riches, feed me with food convenient for me." We are not allied with any pronounced class, but are devoted to the people. The so-called Labor Party is not in our confidence, and the leather-lunged orators who prate in the name of Democracy have no part with us. We have a humble mission in life—and yet a very responsible and perilous one—the exposure of the wrongs of Society, be the sin that of the rich and powerful, or the chicanery and duplicity of the insects who live on the Labor Party. Allied with no party, hampered by no prejudice, working for ourselves, we make the effort of shewing in this journal life as it is in Sydney. As the name "SCORPION" indicates no desire to fight with lavender, we boldly throw down the gauntlet in the cause of true Democracy, and promise to ruthlessly expose the shams and frauds which are so plentiful in Australia. We trust therefore that a generous public recognising the mission on which we have embarked will do us the justice of supporting THE SCORPION.

'TO AUSTRALIA'
Cosmos
1 September 1894

From small beginnings everything has sprung;
The ladder's top is but the highest rung,
The Austral nation now a pride and strength
Where freedom reigns and sways its breadth and length,
Was a place decried as desert waste
When men essayed to judge it in their haste;
A place for outcast wrong to be redrest,
And man's emotions curbed or else supprest.

So ancient Rome, that ruled the world, was but
A lifeless valley from existence shut,
Till fleeing outcasts took it for their home
And made it, by their patience, Mighty Rome.

From small beginnings has the "cosmos" sprung,
And with its life and influence scarce begun
Its future reign cannot as yet be seen,
And yet—why should not what before has been
Be once again? And from a seedling tome
Be patient energy upreared, as Rome
Was built, why should not there arise a pow'r
For something more than whiling past an hour!
Or rather why, within this Austral land
Should not success attend the willing hand?

You Austral people hold the riddle's sign;
Yours is the power to answer or decline.
Be loyal to yourselves and help your own;
To help a nation heed what seed is sown
The "cosmos" starts—nor strives for aught that's less
Than merit won, Australian, success.

BEGINNINGS AND ENDINGS

'THE MONTH'
Cosmos
1 September 1894

September—"yellow haired September"—the month when Australia awakens from its brief winter, and the harbingers of Spring gild the landscape and prepare the way for countless buds and blossoms that lighten the country side; the month when the Austral year should commence for human as well as vegetable things. It is the time for buds and efforts to be put forth, and with it comes the *Cosmos*.

"Another attempt at an Australian magazine," as an alliterative journalist informed his readers, prior to foretelling them of the failure that was bound, from precedent, to follow it.

"Tis better to have loved and lost,
Than never to have loved at all."

If failure in others were to deter fresh efforts from being made it would be a sorry circumstance for the world, and how much more so for Australia, where effort is the mainspring of existence?

In the face of opposition as cold and persistent as it well could be, the individual effort has been made, and with the wattle bloom, Australia's golden emblem, comes the *Cosmos*.

Whether it comes to stay or comes to go away again is for Australia to say. It is a venture to reach the public mind, to amuse the public brain and satisfy a public want. The public by their acceptance and support give back the answer whether it shall or shall not stay. The anticipated answer is "stay."

Does Australia realise the fact that with nearly 5,000,000 inhabitants, a national feeling growing up in spite of provincial demarcations, a distinctive mode of life and an ever-increasing love for a starry banner yet to be unfurled, that it has no living production of its own in the realms of magazine literature, beyond that of which this is the first number? Does it realize the fact that it, one of the great sections of the English-speaking people, is dependent, but for the *Cosmos*, upon publishers in other parts of the world for its home circle reading matter? Does it realize that of the vast field of fictional opportunity, the bush, the settlement and the township offer, scarcely an acre has been taken up? And does it realize that of the writers it has bred scarcely one but has been forced from its shores in search of a market for their creations? Even of those who remain true to their country and cling to the soil that is to them their mother-land, how many of them but are compelled to send all their choicest productions

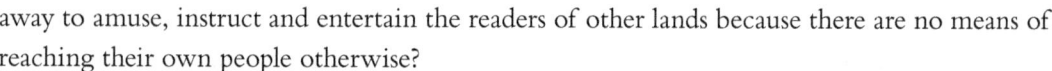

away to amuse, instruct and entertain the readers of other lands because there are no means of reaching their own people otherwise?

That the want exists for a literary magazine here, is more than amply demonstrated by the consumption of foreign importations, periodicals which as often as not contain articles from the pens of authors who are Australians and in Australia. The *Cosmos* aims at filling this void, and supplying this want in Australian literary life. To do this it will be conducted on broad lines, having no policy save the entertainment of its readers, and endorsing no creed save that of an ever-increasing circulation. But its columns will be open to well written articles on all or any subjects, no preference being shown, nor predilection allowed beyond the ever-present search for matter of interest and entertainment. It will not undertake to instruct its readers nor to educate the public upon any "fad" or "ism" of the hour, although if an article of the necessary quality is to be obtained from them, it will be utilized for the interest that it contains. In fiction as in other branches, the *Cosmos* aims at being Australian, and writers, especially of short stories, are desired, who will reach beyond the bushranger and the blackfellow yarn, and enter the real sphere of Australian life. The stories published from month to month will have as their guiding principles, that they are Australian in colour, healthy in tone, and above all, *human* in characterization. Poetry, as the higher grade of literature, has not received all the attention from Australians that it should have done; often it is to be feared through the want of other mediums of publication than the daily newspaper, and if the *Cosmos* can develop a clearer tone, and more distinct enunciation in the flights of poetic fancy amongst the Austral singers, it will have done well. In all branches of literature the *Cosmos* is open to receive contributions, giving remuneration for those that are accepted, returning those that are accompanied by stamped addressed wrappers and ignoring all that are written on both sides of the paper or in illegible characters.

'INTRODUCING OURSELVES'
Block
15 August 1896

For the first time in Sydney a Journal, destined to be the mirror of its social life, is presented to the public by the Proprietors of THE BLOCK. It has hitherto been taken for granted that any publication dealing with social topics must necessarily be exclusively devoted to fashions and frivolity, and, with a few household hints and recipes thrown in to suit the more domestic section, cater solely for women. This being the case, home journals and social columns are, as a rule, passed over or given the most cursory survey by average citizens—the men because their interests lie elsewhere, and intelligent women because such matters have become subordinate through the higher mental training they have secured, and the liberalising tendencies of modern thought. Men and women are more on a par than they were a quarter of a century ago. In the Universities the women are winning the most coveted prizes and positions in the honours lists, and women doctors and nurses are becoming most useful allies to the medical profession in combating disease and suffering. In tennis, and even cricket, women are gradually winning their way in competition with the stronger and sterner sex, while as cyclists, many a long spin and country excursion is made the pleasanter by the companionship of husband and wife, and in the chief cities of Australia gay parties of cyclists of both sexes proclaim that a new era for men and women is at hand.

In Literature and Art, Australia is rapidly coming to the front. At the present time there is a bright galaxy of young writers of both sexes attracting the attention of critics in the old world, quick to detect the signs of budding genius in the volumes which are being rapidly issued by colonial printers and publishers; while works by our native-born artists and sculptors find a place in the Art Exhibitions of Europe.

Australia has, perhaps, furnished the strongest proof of the interest taken in music in the Southern Hemisphere by the immense sale of pianos among all classes. Over a hundred thousand have been imported into New South Wales alone, and the schools of Music and Examination lists show how earnestly the young Australians are striving to reach the highest musical standards.

Returned colonists affirm that in Australia the leading shops in the large cities can furnish costumes as elegant and fashionable as those to be found in West End shops, the weekly communications by mail steamers bringing the latest novelties for the adornment of our society leaders. Mayfair, therefore, presents a gay and brilliant appearance, whether at Government House functions, theatres, races, weddings, or social gatherings of all kinds. Descriptions of these will form a prominent feature of the BLOCK.

It will be seen, therefore, that the field is large for a paper of the kind designed by the Proprietors of the BLOCK, and in the hands of capable managers and writers it is destined to become a favourite in every household.

'OURSELVES'
Ha! Ha: A Merry Magazine for Australians
9 April 1898

Ha! Ha!! We really cannot help it! Has anyone seen the "terrible monotony of colonial life?"—we can't find enough of it to fit a microscope.

One would think that after wading through the usual Australian literature that "the awful gloominess of the Australian bush" is a reality, and that this continent must be the most woe-be-gone spot between the poles.

We have diagnosed the whole case and have come to the conclusion that the aforesaid awful monotony is simply 'neath the hat of the bush penman.

Let a man feel happy and his surroundings are congenial.

It is just as natural to expect a cockie, whose pet corn has just been scrunched beneath the hoof of his heaviest, plough mare, to burst forth into joyful praise, as to expect a joyful poet to see joy in anything (bushy or otherwise).

Our plan is to look at life as something to make the best of. Smile on the petty troubles fornist us, and as we step out with a clear conscience the so-called monotony will become a field of beauty. We will see new and undreamt of colours in the old blue gum—we will trace new wonders in the shadows on the track, and our swags will feel as light as the kiss of dawn!

We don't apologise for coming into the field of newspaper life; we are sure we will be kindly welcomed by our many contemporaries as a younger brother, and so we reciprocate merry greetings.

It's the fashion now-a-days to look at the world through big blue spectacles—ours are white, and so we see things as they really are. You'd be surprised to see the amount of genuine colonial humour going to waste, so we're going to garner it in, and dish it up, and serve hot and cold.

Our first big wrestle therefore will be to burst up the depressing pessimism in Australian literature.

We have the healthiest climate under the sun, and if your liver is not in good working order, for goodness sake don't blame the scenery!

Having said so much about ourselves, we will now retire—and blush!

EDITORIAL NOTES
Southern Cross
14 November 1898

The Editor feels justified in calling attention to both the literary and decorative features of this issue of the *Southern Cross*. The cover is by Charles Turner, who is gifted with a true inspiration of art, and has given us a pleasing conception of the beauty of the Antipodes. In harmony with this is the artistic scene of interior illustrations by Spence, Mahony, Morris, and Lyall, thus making the *Southern Cross* the most attractive penny periodical ever issued south of the line; and the reading matter is no less pleasing. This issue has been hurriedly brought out, and it is only a slight degree indicative of what the publishers promise for the

BEGINNINGS AND ENDINGS

future. It is intended to make the *Southern Cross* the best family magazine in the colony, Fact, Fiction, and Illustration of a high order being our guiding star for the future, in the constellation of Australian realism, idealism and art. Before the issuance of the next number, a half-dozen or more brilliant writers will join the editorial staff and thenceforth conduct interesting departments over their respective signatures. In regard to the advertising columns the management desire to state that absolutely no bogus or irresponsible firms will be allowed to present announcements to the public through the columns of this magazine at any price or under any circumstances. All firms using our columns as an advertising medium will be sound and reliable and entitled to the trust of the public.

'THIS INTIMATION'
Bookfellow
31 May 1899

With this number *The Bookfellow* dies to the soft music of the tears of many well-wishers, in the sure and certain hope of a ruddy resurrection on the Red Page of *The Bulletin*. Subscribers' surplus stamps will be returned to them; and friends will please accept this intimation as final.

In spite of hundreds of kindly notices, and subscriptions weekly increasing, *The Bookfellow* does not pay; and it is not likely to pay unless advertisements are obtained; and, except the class of advertisements which would be a desecration of the shrine, these things which no *Bookfellow* can stand without appear to be unobtainable.

To merely print *The Bookfellow* costs for 2500 copies about £25; and to fill it as per sample is worth at least another £30–total £55. Take 2500 *Bookfellows* at 3d.—and many are sold at 2d. to booksellers; multiply and subtract according to Colenso; and the result is Loss. It would take a sale of at least 5000—allowing for sundry deductions, and calculating on the lesser proportionate cost of the greater quantity—to repay cash expenditure; and there is still much worry and anxiety unpaid for. A sale of 5000 at 6d. would be encouraging enough; but that is judged not possible at present.

So here is another cairn of Experience piled for the guidance of travellers along the local literary road.

BOTTOM BOOKFELLOW.
(Translated.)

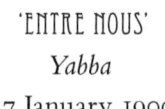

'ENTRE NOUS'
Yabba

17 January 1900

Yabba, in the language—if such it can be called—of the Australian aborigine, means to talk, while *budgeree yabba*, when translated into English, represents good talk; the *yabba* of YABBA will always be *budgeree yabba*. It really makes us blush to open with such a personal compliment, for right from birth we have resolved to avoid all self-laudation and—so far as our own virtues were concerned—remain as shy as the proverbial oyster. However, good goods, like a murder, will always find prominence. The main reason for a reticence in the proclamation of our merit is not in consideration of the general public—far from it—simply the belief that noise proves nothing. Often a hen who has merely laid an egg cackles as if she had laid an asteroid, and numberless newspapers have been born with high-sounding names, issued with a flourish of trumpets, and, for a time, have existed on the promises of the fine heroic deeds they were going to perform. The Registrar General's Office shows more newspaper registrations than you could count in a week. Each new medium, in its own day, was going to revolutionise journalism, and break things generally. Now, YABBA does not attempt to do anything of the kind. It does not aspire to fill a "long-felt want." The public at a pinch could get along fairly well without us, but, we cannot help adding, it will get along a trifle easier with us. Don't imagine for one moment, gentle reader, that our object is to lift you into a higher sphere of education, for such is not our mission. Woman's suffrage will not form one of our planks, neither will we devote any special space to the particular parallel of latitude or meridian of longitude you must follow in order to reach the Golden Gates. But for one shilling a year—payable in advance—we will post once a month to any address in the colony, YABBA, the brightest, snappiest, cleanest and most useful sixteen-page paper you could wish for. It will contain amongst other things stories, original and cribbed, versus ditto, notes on home conduct and home comfort, wrinkles to fathers, mothers, sisters and brothers, chatty news for the cool of the verandah, or the warm chair by the fireside, well balanced paragraphs on political and social matters, tit-bits of society life, hints on culinary matters, and information on household management, talks on frocks and fashions, frolicsome columns for little ones; in fact, items of interest, laughs and sighs, and information for everybody. To sum up YABBA, it will be a welcome visitor in every home, a magazine which people will read, praise, and pay for.

BEGINNINGS AND ENDINGS

'ALL ABOUT AUSTRALIANS'
A.A.A.: All About Australians
3 May 1901

All about Australians! Well I never!
    It will take a lot of precious time and toil
To tell the plucky deeds and great endeavour
    Of the sturdy children of Australian soil.

There's the Member, the Alderman, the J.P.,
    There's the Actor and the Singer and the Crank,
There's the Cricketer, the Sculler and the Jockey
    There's the gentleman who manages the bank.

There are wealthy men of commerce, clever writers,
    There are men who play at golf, and sail a yacht,
There are boys who wear the khaki, gallant fighters,
    And that's not half the kind of men we've got.

They are not so very many; but they're mighty,
    And they're moving on with progress every day,
So tell about their deeds, and point out to them their needs
    The very chief of which is A.A.A.

'EDITORIAL NOTICE'
A.A.A.: All About Australians
29 May 1901

We have received many compliments upon our first issue, but the compliments have been tinged with doubt as to whether "you can keep that standard up." All we ask of our friendly doubters is that they should watch and see. Be assured, dear reader, that the A.A.A. will not seek to achieve any financial success by debauching the literary taste of our countrymen, by sneering at the honour of men or the virtue of women, or by undermining the loyalty, now the brightest star in the British firmament.

We do not believe that despair is the dominant note of Australian life. The ne'er do well at home sent out to the bush to watch by the camp fire or to ride the boundary, is a type of a small class, and he is immortalised in Banjo Paterson's "Jim Carew." But he, *et hoc genus omne*, does not represent Australian life or Australia's aspirations.

We believe that the dominant note of our country is something far nobler. It is a note of faith in our fellow man, of confidence in the future of our country, and trust in the great All Father whose everlasting arms are beneath us all.

We have been told that high-class literature does not pay. We look at the *Sydney Morning Herald* with its high-class reports and its thoughtful articles. It is the greatest success of Australian journalism. Next to the *Herald* comes the *Melbourne Argus*, lofty in tone and pure in matter. Verb sap:

We enter into competition with no publication that is clean and clever. For ourselves, we are assured that there is a place and a name in our native land. We are here to stay and whatever success we may attain will be gained by elevating our readers in taste and in thought.

We shall be glad to receive the co-operation of our subscribers. Tell us the features you like and those you don't like. There is no false pride about us, and if we make a mistake as soon as we find it out we will remedy it.

If you know anything done by an Australian that is worthy of being chronicled let us know. If you have an idea for a bright sketch or story send it along.

This continent is just beginning in earnest. It feels its strength, it rejoices in its youth. We are all hopeful. We can hold our own, and so can A.A.A. We sneer at nothing that is good. The editor of this paper does not sit in the seat of the scornful; the doings and the writing of our fellow Australians will be treated in a spirit of sympathy and appreciation.

'TO OUR READERS'
Australian Magazine
1 January 1908

It will be observed that the "A.A.A." has developed into "The Australian Magazine." The change was necessary, as the old name had outlived its period of usefulness. The magazine needed some wider and more all-embracing title. Very shortly it will enter the eighth year of its existence. This we believe establishes a record for Australia. That the public has been appreciative of our efforts to produce something that does not suffer too much by comparison with the best of the world is gratefully acknowledged. It has been solely through the generous support received that we have been enabled to gradually extend, and to improve. The limit of improvement has, however, not yet been reached. Possibly it never will. The Art of

BEGINNINGS AND ENDINGS

printing and of illustrating are making rapid strides forward, and it will be the business of the proprietors of "The Australian Magazine" to keep pace with the times.

EDITORIAL
Microbe
August 1902

To our generous correspondents, the public and the world: This organ of culture and advanced ideas herewith takes up its hat and passes out into the deep, dark night. If our aesthetic audience will allow the term, we go absolutely and irretrievably BUNG. We wanted assistance and it came not, we went out on the highroad and called for literature and the housewives ran out with penny novelettes.

It is not a pleasant sensation this "going under," and we owe an apology to those interested in our going. We owe debts of gratitude all round, and because we pay nothing more solid than gratitude we expire. Also there is not a single reader who knows what work is required to produce this paper, and this is our apology.

'TO OUR READERS'
New Idea: A Women's Home Journal for Australasia
1 August 1902

"The New Idea" is a new departure in Australian journalism. No publication worthy of mention has hitherto been published devoted exclusively to the needs and problems of the Australian home and its mistress. Its name reveals its aim—to present the newest ideas continually arising in every branch of woman's life and interest. It will contain, each month, the best that is thought or written, the world over, on every topic which appeals to women. While it will adequately reflect the life and doing of women beyond these colonies, special care will be taken to make "The New Idea" a perfect reflex of local affairs and interests by the introduction of such regular features as, "Marriages of the Month," "Social Chit-Chat," "Pretty Fashions for Women," "Doings of Noted Women," etc.

A WIDE OPEN MAGAZINE

We want the readers of "The New Idea" to feel that this is a wide-open magazine: wide-open to them, their wives, their perplexities, their questions, their criticism, their praise, their manuscripts. It bars its doors to none. If you have a message to this magazine or its public send it along, it matters not what department of this business you wish to reach; all the branches of this publishing house are open to you. We wish to perfect all departments of our business in every way we can. But a business cannot be more successful than its system. We want that system to be as good as it can be made, and the man or woman who helps us to perfect that system by pointing out some defect is the one whose interest we value. Our business is a large one, as you can readily understand. Naturally, mistakes and oversights are bound to occur. It cannot be otherwise. But the only way we can find out where our system is not what it should be, is for someone who has found a weak spot to tell us about it. Don't nurse a wrong. Don't keep it to yourself. Don't suffer in silence. Let us know about it and we will quickly see if the facts are as they seem to you to be.

So with frankness let us meet one another: reader and editor. We are anxious to make "The New Idea" the best and most helpful magazine that Australian women read. We shall strive for that result. But help us with the encouragement of your suggestion and criticism. Feel that you can reach the editor who speaks to you now. If we can be of help to you, our resources are open to you in any way in which we can serve you. We know that you can be of help to us. Help us to make the magazine what you want it to be.

'INTRODUCTION'
Steele Rudd's Magazine
January 1904

This Magazine is issued in the interests of Australian Literature and Art. It is believed, in order to effect large sales, both advertisers and readers should receive full value for their money, and, with that object in view, it is proposed to fill its pages with nothing but first-class work both as regards writing and drawing. *Steele Rudd's Magazine* will be edited by, and as regards its literary part, be under the absolute control of the well-known writer, whose pen-name it bears, "Steele Rudd" (Mr. Arthur Hoey Davis). He will also write the greater part of it, while most of the drawings will be the work of one of the best black and white artists in the commonwealth, Mr. E. Ashton Murphy. It is the first Australian venture of its kind embarked upon in Queensland, and it is hoped that it will receive such encouragement as will justify its expansion into a more substantial monthly volume.

For all contributed matter printed in the Magazine liberal payment will be made.

STEELE RUDD & CO., LTD.
39 Adelaide Street,
Brisbane, Queensland.

BEGINNINGS AND ENDINGS

'AS REGARDS "THE GADFLY"'
Gadfly
14 February 1906

The old-time journalist, timidly proffering a new publication for public approval, almost invariably remarked, "For this, our first appearance, we make no apology," thereby immediately suggesting an apology was necessary, or at least expected. For an honest endeavour to interest and amuse the public we cannot see that any apology is needed. We shall possibly do all our apologising later on. Our chief object in coming out is to make money, which money we desire, with much fervency, to earn honestly, by giving our subscribers fair value. It is not the intention of the *Gadfly* to assault the public with vast areas of type, as it credits the public with sufficient intelligence to be discriminating, and the idea that said public is a fat-headed crowd that delights in the possession of many yards of stodgy and uninteresting reading matter is an idea that will not be shared by this paper until the public proves its own title to fat-headedness. It is just possible that the opinion we hold of our fellow-man is too exalted, but until he forces us, in tears, to other convictions we shall go on regarding him, in the average, as an animal of some intelligence, almost, if not quite, as intelligent as our noble and high-minded selves. But in coming out we have other besides mercenary motives. the *Gadfly* is run by Australians in the interests of things Australian. Our opinions, such as they are, belong to us, and the paper is not published, influenced, or subsidised by any clique, league, political party, or organisation. We are independent and intend to remain independent. Our party is "The Public," our policy our own. It is our intention to encourage, so far as it is in our power, Australian literature and art, and here, again, we credit the public with no unreasonable and unpatriotic prejudice against the literary matter or illustration that is "Made in Australia." Finally, we desire to apologise for not appearing long ago, as we feel in our inmost heart that we are supplying a "long-felt public want."

EDITORIAL
Ye Wayside Goose
31 August 1906

We do not send this Journal out into a cold, cruel world for the mere joy of issuing it, but rather that we may induce you to disgorge the sum of One Shilling for a year's subscription. If this note, glaringly displayed, fails to unloosen your tightened purse-strings, then we

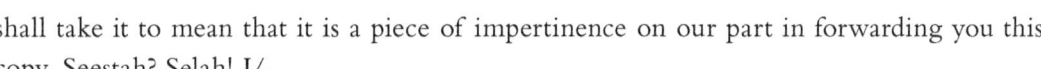

shall take it to mean that it is a piece of impertinence on our part in forwarding you this copy. Seestah? Selah! I/-

STONE'S PRINT SHOP,
355 Post Office Place West, Melbourne. Vic.

'THE EDITOR'S UNEASY CHAIR'
Lone Hand
1 July 1907

Spring in other lands is welcomed with a feeling of relief from a long and weary sadness. In Australia it is not a wakening from the dead, as in the colder North. Winter here is but as a little break in the eternal sunshine. For a few brief weeks the pulse of life beats slower, the bloods seems less warm, there is a pause in the quick beat of Nature's music.

So, in Australia, Spring steals in unnoticed. The days lengthen, the sun reddens more the cheek, the vivid scarlets of the winter flowers disappear for the colder colors of narcissi and daffodils. There is a change rather than a recrudescence of color.

THE LONE HAND will strive to put a little extra color into this Australian Spring. With September it will begin to include color-prints, and artists are invited to submit paintings, in water and oils, suitable for reproduction. As our arrangements are perfected, we hope to give the public several pages of Australian sunlight each month.

The memoirs of J.F. Archibald—which have now reached nearly to the point at which he came to Sydney to found, with John Haynes, THE BULLETIN—will possibly be interrupted next month to allow of the printing of the late W.H. Traill's record of the early days of THE BULLETIN. This short history has been purchased from Mrs. Traill by THE LONE HAND, and it is necessary to a full knowledge of the early days of THE BULLETIN, of which paper Traill was, in the words of J.F. Archibald, "the first real Editor." J.F. Arhcibald's memoirs, it will be noticed, do not attempt to keep chronological order, and have already dealt with some part of his BULLETIN experiences.

The Editor acknowledges with gratitude the very generous support given to THE LONE HAND by the public. The first issue of 50,000 was sold out within three days of publication. The second issue (which had to be limited to 50,000) was sold out on the very first day of publication. This will enable the Proprietary to embark with confidence on future plans for improving the magazine; and in future a larger issue will be printed.

Criticisms and suggestions from various sources have led THE LONE HAND to somewhat modify its style and make-up. The smaller-faced type will be very little used. The stories

BEGINNINGS AND ENDINGS

will be allowed more length in some cases. The receipt of many hundreds of letters of personal congratulation, added to the great weight of press approbation from all parts of Australia, have been of splendid encouragement. No less so has been the perusal of two or three savage attacks. THE LONE HAND hopes to make an enemy of every public pest. When it ceases to be abused in some quarters it will know that, whilst it may still be entertaining, it has ceased to safeguard "the public good."

'THE NATIVE COMPANION'
Native Companion
1 August 1907

The July issue of *The Native Companion*, dated August 1st, inaugurates a new Australian sixpenny magazine. The publisher is T.C. Lothian, of Melbourne, whose enterprise and success in the Australian publishing field have already attracted attention.

Mr. Lothian, Jr., is in years the youngest publisher in this country, probably in the Empire; but books and writing have been his familiars since boyhood. His father was for 25 years co-manager for the firm Walter Scott & Company, England.

The editorial chair of *The Native Companion* is occupied by a well-known Australian writer, E.J. Brady, author of "The Ways of Many Waters," and other books. His celebrity as a writer of sea songs, ballads and chanteys is world wide. In the current issue of *The Native Companion* Mr Brady begins the interesting illustrated story of a wagg on a trip from Sydney to Townsville, which he undertook and completed, despite all difficulties, some years ago.

The Native Companion marks a period in Australian Magazine Publications.

The Literary and Advertising Sections are printed throughout on a specially-made tinted Australian antique paper of the best quality. The illustrations, even among the Advertisements, are all Line Drawings, executed by artists. The cover is beautifully printed on art paper in three colours, with a tasteful picture by Ruby Lindsay, showing a group of Native Companions, performing their peculiar dance before a full moon, on the front.

'THE EDITOR'S EARNEST CRY AND PRAYER TO HIS CONTRIBUTORS'
Trident: An Australian Review
1 August 1908

List to the words of a weary thrall
Who bends to the oars with an aching spine:
Listen awhile, ye minstrels all,
As ye sit at meat with the Maidens Nine!
Singing, singing in shade and shine,—
Dancing nimbly on metric toes,—
Ye souls ablaze with the Fire Divine,
Give us, O give us, a little prose!

Like autumn leaves on our desk they fall,
Many a sonnet of rare design;
Many a sparkling madrigal;
Songs that gladden the heart like wine.
Genius gloweth from every line
Of your blithe ballads and your sad rondeaus;
Still we cry, with a piteous whine,
Give us, ah give us, a little prose!

Verse is loved in hamlet and hall,
But the loveliest things (as the sage opine)
After a season are apt to pall.
Sweet is the breath of the eglantine,
But the cabbage, too, hath a fragrance fine
That strongly appeals to the world's sad nose;
On fire and dew can an editor dine?
Give us, yea give us, a little prose!

Bard, if a pitiful heart be thine,
Turn not away from the tale of our woes;
Lest an editor's reason snap like twine,
Give us, *do* give us, a little prose!

BEGINNINGS AND ENDINGS

'EDITORIAL'
Trident: An Australian Review
1 April 1909

After this month the *Trident* will cease to appear. It is sorry for its subscribers, against whom its only complaint is that they are so few in number. It is sorrier still for the great majority who might have been expected to buy and read it, but have never done so. To the one class it extends its thanks, to the other its compassionate forgiveness. It bears practically no malice, and dies well pleased on the whole with everybody, including itself. It has always taken considerable interest in its own existence and has endeavoured to inspire something of the same feeling in its readers. If it has succeeded in doing this, it has not lived in vain. It may adapt the prayer of Alcestis and express a hope that it will be some day succeeded by a review possessing, not indeed greater merit, but better fortune.

PART 2

The Making of Australian Literature
KEN GELDER & RACHAEL WEAVER

'Colonial Literature', *Colonial Literary Journal and Weekly Miscellany of Useful Information*, 27 February 1845
73

'A Prospective Glance at the Advantages to be derived from the Creation of an Australasian Literature', *Tasmanian Monthly Magazine*, September 1853
77

Frederick Sinnett, 'The Fiction Fields of Australia' (extract), *Illustrated Journal of Australasia*, November 1856
79

'Australian Literature', *Athenaeum*, 24 July 1875
80

James Smith, 'Colonial Literature and the Colonial Press. A Note', *Melbourne Review*, July 1878
83

G.B. Barton, 'The Status of Literature in New South Wales. II. How the Publishers Look at it', *Centennial Magazine*, September 1889
88

'The Characteristics of Australian Literature', *Australasian Critic*, 1 November 1890
93

'Eric', 'Australians in Fiction', *Cosmos*, 20 October 1894
97

Arthur A.D. Bayldon, 'A Review of Australian Fiction', *Lone Hand*, 1 August 1907
100

John H. Garth, 'Should Australian Literature be Cheerful?' *Australian Magazine*, 1 July 1908
106

'Editorial Note', *Lone Hand*, 1 March 1909
108

2

The Making of Australian Literature
KEN GELDER & RACHAEL WEAVER

THE COLONIAL JOURNALS BEGAN TO think about 'Australian literature' as a category – a definable body of writing – long before Federation. They invested in it as a shared cultural value, something that the colonies already seemed to recognise as larger than themselves. It is as if Australian literature had to transcend its colonial borders, in order to convey a set of overarching ideals about what a national literature should become. In fact, the journals express a much larger aspiration: that Australian literature, even in its earliest stages, should be recognised at a global level, becoming sufficiently distinctive (and competitive) to attract the attention of readerships overseas. A strident interest in a national literature making its way in the world means the journals also invest in what they think Australian literature should do and say. They continually identify points of origin, writers who were there at the beginning; but they also capture the vitality of emerging writers who seem to speak for future possibilities and new directions. Australia itself seemed to offer an abundance of imaginative resources for writers. The problem for the journals, however, was to do with how all this was depicted, and what forms a national literature might take. Australian literature had the capacity to be *too* Australian; paradoxically, it had to loosen its grip on its native material in order to realise its aspirations and become nationally representative.

James Reading and Francis Sandoe's Sydney-based *Colonial Literary Journal and Weekly Miscellany of Useful Information* (June 1844 – March 1845), spoke up for 'a cheap Periodical Literature' that could be accessible to a wide range of colonial readerships. Among other things, it published stories and serialisations about bush life, as well as the work of colonial poets like Charles Harpur and Daniel Deniehy. The anonymously authored article 'Colonial Literature' celebrates Harpur alongside an earlier poet, Charles Tompson, whose *Wild Notes: From the Lyre of a Native Minstrel* was published in Sydney in 1826. Foundations are important here: the article also praises James Martin's *The Australian Sketch Book* (1838), 'the first literary production that has ever emanated from the pen of an individual educated in Australia' – written when

Martin was just eighteen years old, and influenced by the American writer Washington Irving. For this article, North America (rather than Europe) provides a model for an emergent national literature, and it cites writers such as Irving, Nathaniel Parker Willis and William Ellery Channing. The term 'colonial' prevents that model from flourishing; what is needed instead is a more ambitious project that aims, ultimately, 'to stamp Australian literature as among the national literature of the world!' In the more remote colonies, this aspiration was no less apparent. The *Tasmanian Monthly Magazine* (September 1853) lasted for just one issue. But the article, 'A Prospective Glance at the Advantages to be Derived from the Creation of an Australasian Literature', is very much about imagining the possibility of a literature that binds the colonies together. North American models are again important: interestingly, the article invokes Harriet Beecher Stowe's *Uncle Tom's Cabin,* published in the previous year. But the imperative, once again, is to develop a literature that is globally recognisable: 'we shall be as nothing in the scale of nations', the article writes, 'until the effort succeeds'.

The writer and scientist William Sydney Gibbons and journalist Frederick Sinnett, who both helped to establish Melbourne's *Punch* (August 1855 – December 1925), were also the editors of the *Illustrated Journal of Australasia* (July 1856 – June 1858), a socially progressive journal with a wide range of interests. Sinnett's 1856 article 'The Fiction Fields of Australia' is the first extended piece of Australian literary criticism. For Sinnett, the role of a national literature is to develop character and 'render local vernaculars in dialogue'; on the other hand, too much emphasis on local colour ('manners and customs') would limit the fiction aesthetically. In the extract we publish from his article, he praises the South Australian writer Catherine Helen Spence's 1854 novel, *Clara Morison*, precisely because its characters are so convincing: distinctively Australian but not ostentatiously so, and free of the vulgarising effects of what Sinnett calls 'Australian peculiarities'. Elsewhere, other articles on an emergent Australian literature give a more buoyant and accommodating account of the field. The anonymously authored 'Australian Literature' was published twenty years later in the *Athenaeum* (July 1875 – February 1876), a short-lived Sydney journal edited by H. W. H. Stephen and P. J. Holdsworth. Colonial poetry was important to this journal, but so was theatre and other urban entertainments. The article is enthusiastic about the role played by colonial journals – like Melbourne's *Australian Journal* – in promoting more popular kinds of local writing. It even speaks up for genres like burlesque that might otherwise seem peripheral to the aspirations of a national literature, citing the example of Marcus Clarke's *King Billy's Breeches*, first published in 1871. This article knows that literary maturity is something to look forward to, but in the meantime it enjoys the 'genuineness' and 'vitality' – as well as the peculiarities – of what seems by now to be a highly productive and varied literary scene.

Not everyone was so positive about the early predicaments of Australian literature. James Smith was a prominent journalist and critic who had also been involved, with Sinnett, in establishing Melbourne's *Punch*, becoming editor in 1857 and proprietor a couple of years later. Smith was in fact an active contributor to a large number of colonial journals: for example, with Henry Kendall he founded *Touchstone: A Saturday Journal of Criticism, Commentary and Satire* (October 1869 – December 1870), and he contributed to H. Mortimer Franklyn's *Victorian Review* (November 1879 – February 1886) and, so it seems, the *Melbourne Review* (January 1876 – October 1885). The *Melbourne Review* was edited by a group of well-known literary figures: Henry Gyles Turner, Arthur Maning Topp, A. Patchett Martin and, later on, Alexander Sutherland. Some of its contributors were academics from the University of Melbourne, like E. E. Morris who became a professor of modern languages and literatures there in 1884. Elizabeth Webby notes that the *Melbourne Review* and the *Victorian Review* were in competition with each other;[1] even so, they shared a number of regular contributors, including Marcus Clarke, Francis Adams, Catherine Helen Spence – and James Smith. There is some dispute, however, as to whether Smith was actually the author of the 1878 *Melbourne Review* article we reproduce here, 'Colonial Literature and the Colonial Press'. In her fascinating biography, *James Smith: The Making of a Colonial Culture*, Lurline Stuart writes that, although his name was attached to it, Smith – who was also working for the Melbourne *Argus* – 'denied authorship'.[2] On the other hand, one of the *Melbourne Review*'s editors, A. Patchett Martin, wrote to the *Argus* (on 8 July 1878) to protest that the article's author was indeed 'James Smith'. Because 'Colonial Literature and the Colonial Press' is critical of newspaper journalists, it may well have been embarrassing for Smith and for the *Argus*; and we can perhaps see the article as an example of the tensions and differences in perspective that often existed between the newspapers and the colonial journals.

Smith's article – if we can assume he is the author – argues that local literary writing is still relatively undeveloped: 'Colonial literature', he says, 'has not yet emerged from the Grub-street condition'. The problem, however, lies not so much with the writers themselves, as with the lack of local support and infrastructure: small readerships, inadequate remuneration, and in particular, scant attention devoted to colonial literature by journalists ('critics') in the newspapers – which is no doubt why the *Argus* saw this article as damaging to Smith's reputation. But Smith's pessimism about the state of colonial literature was not untypical. As we noted in the first part of this book, G. B. Barton wrote an important early literary history of New South Wales in 1866. Much later, he wrote a series of articles for Ernest Blackwell's *Centennial Magazine* (August 1888 – September 1890) that were especially despondent about the current state of Australian literary production. Like Smith, Barton calls for a more supportive local industry, to make it worthwhile for Australian authors to be published and read in Australia. At the moment, he writes, 'all that an author can expect, when he publishes his book in Sydney, is that it will pay its expenses'. For Barton, the suicide of the debt-ridden poet Adam Lindsay Gordon in 1870 was emblematic of the plight of Australian writers generally; in this,

he anticipates the famous complaint at the end of Henry Lawson's '"Pursuing Literature" in Australia' – an article that we reproduce in the following part.

Gordon's suicide does indeed become a defining moment in the history of Australian literature; among other things, it generated a sensibility or state of mind that colonial writing found difficult to move beyond. Marcus Clarke's 1880 preface to a posthumous collection of Gordon's poems characterised this state of mind as a 'weird melancholy' and famously infused it into the Australian landscape, as if it was now nationally representative. The short-lived *Australasian Critic* (October 1890 – September 1891) was closely tied to the University of Melbourne, edited by the classical scholar Thomas G. Tucker and the eminent biologist and anthropologist Walter Baldwin Spencer; the literary contributions were edited by E. E. Morris. Morris might well be the author of the unsigned 'The Characteristics of Australian Literature', a lively article that thinks about Clarke's preface but tries to extricate itself from the influence of what by now seems like an entrenched tradition of Australian literary melancholia. Like Sinnett, the article also doesn't want its writers to reproduce colonial clichés: 'We have had almost enough of bushfires in blank verse', it caustically remarks, 'and of tales of convict murders in pentameters'. Optimistically, the article then places its faith in an entirely new generation of local writers, most of whom, however, are now completely forgotten: Alfred Domett, P. J. Holdsworth (one of the editors of the *Athenaeum*), John Farrell, Thomas Heney and Alfred Chandler. By the time we get to the journalist and writer Arthur A. D. Bayldon's 1907 article 'A Review of Australian Fiction', published in J. F. Archibald and Frank Fox's *Lone Hand*, Marcus Clarke's writings are old enough to be identified as 'Australian classics': influential, but no longer dominant. Australian literature has indeed moved on, a busy, diverse field of activity. Bayldon is now able to identify various quite different schools or genres of Australian literature, like the Emotionally Creative School (Henry Lawson) or the more exacting Literary Critical School (Albert Dorrington). His lists give us an eclectic mix, gathering together a few authors who are still remembered today (Rosa Praed, Louis Becke, Rolf Boldrewood) and a host of authors who have since faded into obscurity (E. Baldwin Hodge, A. E. Kearney, C. A. Jeffries, Ethel Mills, John Nicholson, Helen Jerome, and so on). The work of some of these writers – like Mabel Forrest and Roderic Quinn – appears elsewhere in this book.

Caroline L. Montefiore is another forgotten local writer; but among other things, she contributed some interesting essays to Annie Bright's *Cosmos* under the pseudonym 'Eric'. In 'Australians in Fiction', Montefiore returns us to the question of representation in Australian literature. Now, it seems, readerships outside Australia are increasingly fascinated by Australian life: 'The interest taken in England concerning Australian affairs has of late years increased so much that the English public has been ready to read almost anything that might be put before them about the colonies'. The problem here is that Australia had now become a resource that anyone could tap, including English novelists who may have had little local knowledge. Montefiore is scathingly critical of Helen Mathers' *Sam's Sweetheart* (1883) and E. W. Hornung's *The Bride from the Bush* (1890) for exactly these reasons; but she also attacks local writers such as Catherine Martin for their inauthentic Australian characters, creating 'false impressions'. In its seventh year of operations, the *A.A.A.: All About Australians* (May 1901 – January 1908) changed its name to the *Australian Magazine*, needing (as it wrote) 'some wider and all-embracing title'. The question of how Australian literature might look to the rest of the world was something this journal carefully considered. John H. Garth's July 1908 article, 'Should Australian Literature be Cheerful?' is another attempt to break away from examples of Australian literary melancholy that were still in currency. Morbidity is one problem for Garth; mediocrity is another, and his view of the role played by journals like the *Bulletin* here is ambivalent. The *Lone Hand* was much more enthusiastic about the *Bulletin*, of course, but it, too, wanted a local literature that was (as its editorial puts it) more 'conspicuously gay'. The question of what constitutes an authentic or 'real' Australian literature is increasingly a matter of competing ideologies and investments; but it also returns us to those early accounts that imagine Australian literature taking its place on a world stage. Whether it is melancholy or cheerful, critical or celebratory, Australian literature gains its significance not only through the images it projects back to itself, but also through the way these are absorbed and evaluated by readerships elsewhere.

1   Webby, 'Before the *Bulletin*: Nineteenth Century Literary Journalism', pp. 29–30.
2   Stuart, *James Smith: The Making of a Colonial Culture*, p. 98.

'COLONIAL LITERATURE'
Colonial Literary Journal and Weekly Miscellany of Useful Information
27 February 1845

"But we have no colonial literature, nor do I see any materials from which a literature purely colonial could be raised."

"I wish you would abolish the word 'Colonial' at any rate with regard to literature, and call it either 'Australian' or 'National.' Depend upon it that Australia will never be more than a cipher among nations, until her sons assume to themselves national characteristics, and proudly stamp them by the pen to be acknowledged and admired by the world!"

"All very good,—but no answer to my position, that both literature and the materials for forming it are wanting to Australia."

Such was the commencement of a conversation unintentionally heard, while sauntering on the Circular Wharf, at a time when no incentive beyond that offered by cool breezes, rippling waves, fleecy clouds, merry seamen, richly laden barques, lightly freighted yachts, dashing oars, distant woods, rocks, trees, and flowers had led me forth for the refreshment of both body and spirit.

What accident had begun, curiosity, aided by a desire to avail myself of any information regarding so interesting a subject, prompted me to continue, and without appearing to do so, I held the same course with the disputants, who, mounting the steps at the end of the quay, led me into the Domain, where, seated in a rocky nook, they continued their conversation.

I could not but regret the unsparing use that had been made of the tomahawk and pruning knife, for where it had been easy a year or two back to have sat down within a few feet of any person quite unsuspected, I was obliged to have recourse to *ruse* in order to seat myself within earshot, unobserved by my friends: after trying from several points to gain a favourable view of the *Adrastus*, at anchor in the stream, a seat slightly removed and in part hidden by a ledge of rock, offered me the possibility of working very busily on pages that serve me as a waste book for views, notes, incidents, and events, while I could catch some portions of what was said.

"You contend well for your country, and I applaud you for it, but until supported by better evidence than even *your* assertion, I still hold out."

"Little has yet appeared, I grant you, to warrant the high ground I have chosen to take in this argument; yet of what has been published, so great a proportion is really good, that I cannot help repeating that, with the same amount of talent, to say nothing of any addition, a literature might be formed, distinctively and strikingly Australian! and as for material! whence the material of American literature? In the woods, and prairies, on the rivers, and lakes. Among the red Indians and snowy mountains, ay, and in the city too, in the drawing room, in the counting house, in the cottage and in the hall! If anything be wanted here, it is the man and not the matter, nor do I believe that even they are absent, but that if the Australians as a nation would cherish and be proud of literature as of national and not of European character and interest—a Fenimore Cooper, a Washington Irving, a Channing, a Franklin, and a Willis, would soon spring up in our midst to spread a halo over Australia, by seizing each in his own manner on the materials presented in the town, in the bush, among sheep stations, homesteads, squatters, blackfellows, kangaroos or parrots; among seamen or landsmen, native-born or emigrant, military, naval, or civilian!"

"Well, if I listen much longer, you will fairly run me down."

"If I am earnest, I am warranted in being so, and if you have patience, I will illustrate by passages from writers that have been, what I have ventured to assert concerning those that may be, I had almost said those that will be: Thompson [sic] and Harper [sic], the first of Australian poets, are the first I will refer to,—Hear Thompson's [sic] description of the village where he was educated:—

"'Fair Castlereagh! I trace thy landscape round,
Each well-known spot to me is sacred ground;
In every mead—in every bower or tree,
Some dear companion—some old friend I see;
The myrtle grove that skirts thy sloping sides,
And the tall summit from the plain divides,
The rich acacias waving o'er the rill
That pours its scanty streams beneath the hill,
Thy spreading vale—but here let mem'ry tax
The rude invasions of the spoiling axe,
That chas'd the Dryads from th'affrighted glade,
And lopp'd each shrub that once composed the shade.
Thus art extends her civilising reign,
Bows the tall wood and casts it on the plain—
Drives nature's beauties from their seats away,
And plants a train less lovely far than they;
The landscape shines beneath a borrowed hue,
But graceless more, and different from the true.'

"His eulogy on Macquarie, if I can remember it, I will repeat:—

"'Macquarie; candid, generous, noble, free,
all 'neath perfection, blended, shine in thee!
Thou, when the hapless widow pin'd for bread,
Shed bounty o'er, and raised her drooping head;
When affluence spurned the beggar from his door,
Cheer'd by thy smiles he felt no longer poor;
The orphan child, whose supplicating tongue
Crav'd scanty pittance of th' unbending throng,
His artless tale despised, or disbelieved,
Asked but of thee, was pitied and relieved.
Did mis'ry to thy door a victim send?
Thy willing influence proved a saving friend;
Large were thy means, yet far beneath thy will,
Here praise must cease, for language here stands still!'

"Twenty years ago the anniversary was welcomed with an ode not unworthy [of] the spring times of poetry—opening thus:—

"'Strike, strike the bold convivial lyre!
 Let lofty Pœans wake the soul!
Let ivied bands each heart entwine
 In one harmonious whole!
 Fill, fill the goblet high!
 The full libation pour!
Why should decrepid care intrude,
 When Bacchus rules the hour?
E'en age resigns his cynic rod,
And smiling, owns the potent god,
 With dropping clusters crown'd;
The jovial hours their pinions hide,
And unregarded swiftly glide
 When bumpers flow around!'

"Harper [sic] in his closing stanzas of the song addressed to the Lyre of Australia, is almost prophetic—

THE MAKING OF AUSTRALIAN LITERATURE

"'With her green forests around me, above—her blue sky,
    I see in thy measures some national dream;
And I find that the notes, though unstudied are high,
    When the glory of future Australia's the theme!

And ever this lay, to her sons and her daughters,
    Should breathe of the land where the evergreen grows—
To men's souls like a strong wind which swelleth the waters,
    To the heart, like a spring-breeze that opens the rose.'

"Who can read his song for the spring without feeling joyous?

"'The mimosas are blooming,
    For summer is coming,
I felt her warm breath in the forest to-day,
    Where the river is streaming,
    And nature lies dreaming
Of new love and beauty—come dearest away!

    Like passion's first feeling,
    It's joy half concealing,
In each green nook some rare flower is blooming for thee;
    Where, as infancy clinging,
    The woodbine is ringing
All wildly the boughs of the kerrigong tree.'

"In prose I will only quote 'Martin' as the first who ventured upon a volume at all approaching to nationality—and will repeat as nearly as I may, a descriptive passage in his sketch of Botany Bay.

"'The broad bosom of the deep, placid as a sleeping infant, without a ruffle on its surface, without a breath of wind to agitate it, reflecting the morning sun with scrupulous exactness, unbroken and undistorted; the balmy freshness of the atmosphere; the dewy fragrance of the shrubs around; the solemn stillness of the place; and the harmony of every surrounding object—were circumstances sufficient to captivate the attention of the least sensitive individual, and cause the most vitiated and artificial taste to acknowledge the genuine majesty of nature!'

"His apostrophe regarding the listlessness of Australian youth to objects of national interest, will just suit us now:—

"'Is it ever to be the case,' he writes, 'that the sordid desire of accumulating wealth, should occupy the whole attention of our youth, and blunt those finer feelings which set off and give an air of elegance and dignity to the most rigid particles of our nature? Perish the thought! a more refined and a more intelligent race of individuals are now rapidly rising up amongst us, and will shortly emerge from the vale of youth, and take their destined places, in full and vigorous maturity, among the ranks of their fellow citizens and their countrymen.'

"I could multiply quotations from these same writers, or from others not less noble as the pioneers to literature in Australia, but I think that I have recited quite enough to prove that talent *has been* in Australia.—Talent is here yet, and it needs but the spur to rouse Australians to exertion, and my position will be fully upheld, that neither materials nor men are wanting to stamp Australian literature as among the national literature of the world!"

Having finished my sketch, I rose and departed, resolving to repeat my visit to the same spot, in the hope of learning something further concerning Australian national literature.

'A PROSPECTIVE GLANCE AT THE ADVANTAGES TO BE DERIVED FROM THE CREATION OF AN AUSTRALASIAN LITERATURE'
Tasmanian Monthly Magazine
September 1853

In plain terms—Is there a Colonial Literature,—such, at least, as is worthy of the name,—in any of the Austral settlements? If not; have we arrived at that state of civilization, and is our onward progress so rapid and so portentous of future nationality, that we ought not to be without one? Being ripe for those intellectual efforts, which a national Literature would require, are we bound to make them, and prepared to maintain them? And lastly, how are they to be maintained? Each of these divisions of the subject, pregnant with considerations of vital importance to the advancement of our adopted country, might well merit a discussion of much greater length than our limits will allow; and accordingly, with a promise not to lose sight of a question so deeply interesting in all its bearings, we must dismiss them for the present with greater conciseness than we could have wished.

With respect to the existence of an Australasian Literature, under any form which deserves the name, we are driven at once to the confession,—somewhat humiliating indeed, though scarcely surprising,—that it is still *in nubibus*. In the result of literary effort, properly so called, Tasmania has unquestionably the advantage of her sister colonies: but, with the exception of a Scientific Journal, of which the value is inestimable, she has merely a Newspaper Press, tolerably organized, but made up principally of English and inter-colonial extracts, and supported *by* and *for* its advertisements. All circumstances considered, however, our Colonial Journalism is indeed a wonderful creation: and the talent employed upon it, and the energy displayed in the conduct of it, afford ample proof that we are fully ripe for the establishment of a Literature in all its branches, and, by consequence, that we ought not be without one. In support of this position, it must suffice, in this paper, to advert to the requirements of Science and Education. By the time that any new English discovery has found its way into these Southern latitudes, it may not improbably have been superseded by some added improvement, or set aside by some detected fallacy: not to mention that the very irregular, uncertain, interrupted, and disjointed communications which are received on scientific matters, the scanty importation of scientific treatises, and the straggling sources of information calculated to arrest attention, can only be compensated by an extensive and well-appointed division among ourselves. In the event too,—by no means an unlikely one,—of some important Australian contribution to the advancement of Learning, or Science, or the Arts, it would be a melancholy reflection that we had no efficient means of making it known, or testing its value, of discussing its relative merits, or establishing its reality. Then as to works of Education, there is scarcely one of those which are in use in our Schools and Colleges, and none of any real educational worth, which are adapted to our peculiar position, to our altered habits and local propensities, to our social wants and domestic necessities. The cost of procuring them is, moreover, so great, that the time, we are persuaded, must shortly come, when she shall be driven by the mere dictates of a prudential economy, to prepare a series of volumes embodying a Course of Study for the Youth of Australasia.

From the combined assurance, then, that we have at this moment no genuine Australasian Literature, that we are equal to the enterprise necessary for its creation, that the advantages to be derived from it are sufficient to give encouragement to the effort, and that we shall be as nothing in the scale of nations until the effort succeeds, it is an easy, indeed the only inference, that the effort should be made. When made, it must be supported with energy; the same energy will ensure its maintenance; and the result is certain. Look at America. Her Literature was based upon that of English; but one of her own daughters was the authoress of "Uncle Tom's Cabin," and the effect has been such that no English author could have produced. A like achievement may at no distant day be wrought in Tasmania. Reading will beget writing; but both the reading and the writing must be of a kind and character adapted to awaken the sympathies of the people of Tasmania in particular, and of Australasians generally. As already hinted, we have yet much more to say on a subject so congenial to our feelings, and, as we trust, to the feelings of our readers: nor are we weak in hope that we shall one day look back with pride upon the birthday of an Australasian Literature as coincident, or nearly so, with that of the TASMANIAN MONTHLY MAGAZINE.

FREDERICK SINNETT, 'THE FICTION FIELDS OF AUSTRALIA' (EXTRACT)
Illustrated Journal of Australasia
November 1856

Decidedly the best Australian novel that we have met with is "Clara Morison," the work (as we learn from the preface, written by some friend in England, where the book was published) of a young lady who, for many years, has resided in South Australia, in which colony the story is laid. Considered entirely apart from its Australian scenery and coloring, "Clara Morison" would be a book deserving careful criticism and much praise. It stands, we think, quite alone among all Australian stories yet published, in that it is free from the defect of being a book of travels in disguise. It is not written exclusively for distant readers, and as a means of giving lazy people an idea of what they call "life in Australia." It is not a work of mere description, but a work of art. The novel is no more Australian than results from the fact that the author, having been long resident in Australia, having a gift for novel writing, and writing about what she knew best, unavoidably wrote an Australian novel. But the wish to illustrate local peculiarities has had very small sway over the mind of the author of "Clara Morison". She has merely illustrated Australian life insensibly in the process of illustrating human life. Paul de Kock describes Parisian life because he writes novels and is a Parisian. Dickens describes London life because he writes novels and is a Londoner. The local coloring in each case is the accident—the pourtrayal [sic] of human life and interest being the essential. In the same way the Australianism of "Clara Morison" is not obtruded. The story is thoroughly Australian, but at the same time is not a deliberate attempt to describe the peculiar "manners and customs" of the Australians. The points of resemblance are more numerous than the points of difference between the inhabitants of various countries, and it is therefore destructive to the completeness of any picture of human life to give great and obvious prominence to mere local peculiarities. If any of us, who have lived in this country for some years, pass in review our memories of what we have done, undergone, and witnessed, we shall find that, only occasionally—not every day and all day long—have we been encountering either persons or circumstances strikingly and distinctively Australian. Such persons and circumstances are, indeed, sufficiently numerous to give a description of life in Australia a special character, but the specialities should no more be obtruded than in a picture of Australian scenery, where the artist has to paint the outlines of cloud, and hill, and plain, and wood, and water, and to obey the laws of perspective, which hold good equally all over the world. It is by a judicious regard to tints—by a few artistic touches about the foliage and so forth, that the distinctive Australianism of the landscape is conveyed. If Australian characteristics are too abundant—if blackfellows, kangaroos, emus, stringy barks, gums, and wattles, and any quantity of other things illustrative of the ethnology, zoology, and botany, of the country are crowded together, a greater amount of detailed information may be conveyed upon a given number of square inches of canvass than would otherwise be possible, but the picture loses character proportionately as a work of art.

We remember to have seen, many years ago, a print of "organic remains restored," in which earth, air, and water were crowded with all kinds of flying dragons, and slimy monsters, and antediluvian nondescripts, with necks as long as their names. "The world must have been very full of life in those days," was the reflection of our ingenuous youth; for we mistook the artist's design, which was not to shew how the earth looked before the flood, but what kind of creatures then lived. He treated the subject with an eye to science, not art. Had he wanted to make a good picture of the antediluvian world, he would have foregone to crowd it with creatures, and perhaps one long neck upreared from the waters of some vast and desolate swamp, and a few enormous tree ferns, would have sufficed to convey to the mind a vivid conception of what sort of a place this globe would have been to live upon in those times. Some stories written deliberately to illustrate national habits remind us, by the unnatural crowding together of local peculiarities, of that engraving of organic remains restored.

We have dwelt at such length upon this matter, because the fault we point out is one into which the writers of Australian fictions, for many years to come, are peculiarly likely to fall, and because it would be fatal to the claims of any story to rank in that higher class of literature, for the possible cultivation of which upon Australian soil we have been contending. From the fault in question "Clara Morison" is almost entirely exempt. The writer took too vital an interest in the fictitious personages she had created, in the development of their characters, in the furtherance of their fate, and in their mutual relations, to let the grand aims of fiction be subordinated to the desire of working up Australian peculiarities for the information of distant readers.

"Clara Morison", indeed, deals with a time and place so peculiar that it was only necessary for the author to put her people down then and there, and to let them play their parts easily and naturally among the circumstances by which they were surrounded, to ensure the result being a thoroughly and unmistakeably (but not obtrusively) Australian novel.

'AUSTRALIAN LITERATURE'
Athenaeum
24 July 1875

It is probable that before long the fossil remains of the eocene period of the earth's history will possess more interest than others for the geologist. He would like much to know what the modern world was like when it lay in its cradle, ages before the articulate voice of primeval man was first heard; when the fauna and flora of the past began to die out, and above all when the first of the new forms of life in tree and flower, in reptile, bird, and beast, began to appear on the surface of the planet. We fancy, and perhaps not unwisely, that "the boy is father to the man," and that the life of the last is united to that of the first by a chain with uniform links, so that the qualities of the most vigorous manhood may be discovered in their germs in earliest infancy.

And as it is with life, so also is it with thought. Those periods of the world's history in which a new literature is born, possess a singular attraction for students of poetry, romance, art, philosophy and science. When the magnificent old Roman Empire crumbled away before the attacks of barbarians from the four winds of heaven: of Goth, Vandal, Hun, Frank and Lombard, for centuries there was a sort of midnight blackness overspreading the literary world. But the dawn came. The first spontaneous products of modern thought were works of imagination. The Trouveres or romance composers in the north of France, the Troubadours or minstrels in the south of what is now the same kingdom, and the music-singers of Germany were the little twittering song-birds of an early spring, but they presaged the arrival of the skylarks and nightingales of summer, the strong-winged Dante, Shakspeare [sic], Milton, Göthe of a later time. And there is a marvellously glad vitality in these earliest of modern poets. As we listen to their lays we seem to be wandering a little after dawn in bright spring, or through some green primeval forest, surrounded by

> "The balm, the bliss, the beauty and the bloom
> The gracious prodigality of nature,"

And to use grand old Milton's words on a kindred subject, the revival of modern thought, "the fresh odours of the coming morn embathe the soul in the fragrancy of heaven." Take as one instance among a thousand that might be given, that little poem by the Troubadour, Anaud de Merveil, recited by Sismondi in his "Literature of Europe." There is not a particle of speculative thought in it, but a world of poetical feeling. Here are the lines —

> "Oh! how sweet the breath of April,
> Breathing soft as May draws near,
> While, through nights of tranquil beauty
> Songs of gladness meet his ear;
> Every bird his well known language
> Uttering in the morning's pride,
> Revelling in joy and gladness
> By his happy partner's side.

THE MAKING OF AUSTRALIAN LITERATURE

While around me all is smiling,
While to life the young birds spring,
Thoughts of love I cannot hinder
Come, my heart inspiring.
Nature, habit, both incline me
In such joys to bear a part;
With such sounds of bliss around me
Who can wear a saddened heart?

Fairer than the far-famed Helen
Lovelier than the flowrets gay
Ruby lips, and eyes truth-telling,
Heart as open as the day,
Golden hair, with fresh bright roses,—
Heaven who formed a thing so fair
Knows that never yet another
Lived who can with her compare."

Childish in many respects? Yes, that is its excellence. It was written when the modern world was very young, and the butterfly was very much like the flower on which it settled.

And somewhat of this character is most of our original Australian literature. I say "original Australian literature," for I would not call the polemical literature of Australian newspapers original. It is very good of its kind, but it is an exotic. All that is best—and in the Australian journals of the day there is very much of vigorous thought clearly expressed—is of British origin. Adam Smith and John Stuart Mill have written the old and new scriptures to which the best of our newspaper writers, directly or indirectly, owe the inspiration of their choicest productions. But our imaginative literature is to a large extent the spontaneous product of the thought and feeling of our younger men and women. Take the most popular by far of the literary journals of Victoria (the colony in which I now write), *The Australian Journal.* It is almost entirely composed of stories and poetry, contributed apparently by young people. There is any amount of juvenility about it, but at the same time, also, a genuineness, a cheerfulness, even a vitality, which I always like. In the sister colonies, the tendencies of colonial literature seem to be in much the same direction as they are in Victoria. You have your Henry Kendall, with his strange mixture of strong poetic feeling and vague unnerving mysticism; we have our graceful George McCrae, and our high-souled, spirited, unfortunate Gordon—all alike the troubadours or minne-singers of the Australia of to-day. Nor are we wanting in our trouveres, or story-tellers. Far and away the best, in my opinion, of all our Australian romances is Marcus Clarke's "His Natural Life." Besides the sustained interest of the story, and the dramatic power with which some of the characters are pourtrayed [sic] (notably the insolent, obtuse Maurice Frere, his good-natured and too susceptible wife, and, best of all, the wrecked, dissipated, but still high-souled clergyman, North). This novel is so true, on the whole, to Australian life, that it is by no means unlikely that, at a future time, it may be cited as evidence of the manners and customs of our early Australian life, just as we refer to the pages of Fielding for a life-like portraiture of what London life was in the last century, and to Thackeray for what it was in the early part of this.

There is also a kind of literature in which young Australia has not been unsuccessful. I refer to burlesque. In this, also, I should concede the prize to Marcus Clarke for his "King Billy's Breeches," which appeared in *The Australasian* about two or three years ago. The keenness of the satire and richness of the humour displayed on the red-tapeism of the Government offices, both in Australia and in London, are, as it seems to me, superior even to the display of the same powers by Dickens in his well-known description of the "Circumlocution Office."

On the whole, I believe our original Australian literature, with all its juvenility, to be full of promise. At present, we have only our troubadours and trouveres. A generation or two may pass away, and these may have paved the way for an Australian Chaucer or Spencer, a Petrarch or a Boccaccio.

JAMES SMITH, 'COLONIAL LITERATURE AND THE COLONIAL PRESS. A NOTE'
Melbourne Review
July 1878

Colonial literature has not yet emerged from the Grub-street condition, and the "poor author," unless on the staff of a newspaper or in the safe anchorage of a Government appointment, occupies much the same social position as he did in England in the time of Goldsmith and Richard Savage. The reasons commonly assigned for this, especially by local *litterateurs* themselves, are usually very wide of the mark. We are confidently assured that our literature would flourish if publishers would only display less rapacity or more enterprise; but it must be quite evident to any unbiased person that they would only be too glad to publish colonial books if there were any likelihood of profit accruing from the speculation. There are people who gravely attribute the alleged decline of the drama to the popularity of music halls, or the modern practice of dining in the evening, quite overlooking the fact that these are but effects which show, if anything, that legitimate dramatic performances no longer attract. And so it is with the question we are now considering. The real underlying cause is the absence of public demand for stall tickets or colonial books. Leaving the theatre for the present to take care of itself, let us in these few pages consider the question of Australian literature, its position, and its prospects, and what may hinder, and what foster its development.

"That," said a theatrical acquaintance to me on one occasion, pointing to a very shabby and melancholy-looking individual, "is a colonial author. You may tell by his *make-up*." I have never found time to peruse the writings of the gentleman of whom I caught this passing glance. Judging merely from the titles of his stories, I should infer that he devoted his talents to the production of those garish sketches of aristocratic immoralities which make such publications as the *London Journal* so widely popular. It must be confessed that colonial authors, as a rule, do not attempt any very lofty flights, and that the public neglect of which they complain may, in most cases, be accounted for by the worthlessness of their wares. Still we have in our midst gentleman—and at least one lady—who can write in a far different style to that of the "Penny Dreadfuls," but who find it almost impossible to gain the public ear, except perhaps through the medium of a weekly newspaper. Why is this?

I think it is undeniable that there is a tendency, even among ourselves, to underrate colonial productions—especially artistic productions. When Mr. B. L. Farjeon, the well-known author of "Grif," was here, we thought very little of him, and would not even give him a hearing. We asked, "Is not this Benjamin, the tobacconist, and the penny-a-liner of the *Bendigo Advertiser*?" and exclaimed, like they of old, "What good can come out of Bendigo?" But now that he has established himself in London, we freely purchase, peruse, and praise his stories; and if he came to Victoria to give public readings from them, as he has lately been doing in America, we should crowd to hear him, and the leading journals would be lavish in their laudations. Yet I venture to assert that we have here an abler novelist than Mr. Farjeon; and I think most critical persons, if unbiassed [sic], will agree with me that "His Natural Life," however repulsive the story itself may be, is, from an artistic point of view, worth all that Mr. Farjeon has written or is likely to write. But Mr. Clarke is only a colonial author, whereas Mr. Farjeon is now an English one, and, consequently, enjoys a far greater amount of fame and remuneration. This one illustration may serve to show the difference, apart altogether from merit, in the position of a London and of a Melbourne *litterateur*.

[...] There can be no doubt, then, that the position of the colonial author is a very unequal one, and that he is heavily handicapped in the race for wealth and fame. Now let us consider the one agency that can either retard or foster the growth of our young literature—I allude to the Press.

There can be no doubt that the influence of journalism, especially in a young modern community, is overwhelmingly great. It is the only kind of literature possible to such a community, and people come to regard the utterances of their newspaper as oracular. What, then, has been the attitude of the colonial press towards colonial literature?

It would seem that, in addition to the almost universal bias against colonial productions (except perhaps boots and shoes), the professional journalist often displays what may be somewhat paradoxically termed the Bias of Age and Experience. If he has attained to any position he is generally a man past middle life, and worn in the daily service of letters, but from the fact that his voluminous writings are anonymous, and upon ephemeral topics, he receives but scant personal recognition for his labours. Whatever his intellectual ability and acquirements may be, so long as he takes refuge under the anonymity of the press, he is *vox, et præterea nihil*. Naturally, it annoys him beyond measure to notice on the title pages of books the names of obtrusive young men—unless they happen to reside on the other side of the equator. He, himself, has not published a sonnet to his mistress' eye-brow these many years, and has not thought of bringing out even a sketchy book of travels for the last quarter of a century. There was a time when he may have attempted odes to Liberty, or love verses to Melinda, but now he devotes his talents to the more practical questions of Underground Sewage and Roll-stuffing. He has outlived the period when literature appears as a brilliant mistress, and has learned to regard her as a useful but prosaic wife. What can be more aggravating to him than those pert attempts of his juniors to bring themselves (too often, alas! at the expense of the printer) into public notice; for there is no sin in others, so hideous in our own eyes, as that for which we have a natural though restrained propensity. This will serve to show what I mean by the bias of age and experience; and it is only by presupposing the existence of this bias, that we can account for the utterances of local journalists—who are often undoubtedly men of ability—upon colonial books and authors. As an illustration take the case of the late A.L. Gordon, whose writings, now that he is dead, we all agree to praise. Upon the appearance of his first volume, "Sea-Spray and Smoke-Drift," which it is difficult to read without perceiving the fresh originality and the power of vivid narration it displays, albeit commingled with inartistic crudenesses of expression, he was subjected to this criticism—"We have received a copy of a volume of poems by a Mr. Gordon. We can only say that it reflects great credit upon the printer, the binder, and the paper-maker."

Only this, and nothing more; and it may be that poor Gordon thought it rather too much. Could such a criticism as this have been penned except the writer allowed his judgment to be warped by the bias to which I have shown he is, by his profession, peculiarly susceptible?

In Victoria, as in all young dependent communities, we are too prone to regard journalism and literature as synonymous. Our newspaper press bears favourable comparison with any in the world, and is a very prominent feature of our social and political life, whereas our independent literature is small in quantity, and often contemptible in quality. Newspapers must be produced on the spot, but books can be, in the case of a colonial dependency, most advantageously imported. And so, from the mere fact that we have hardly any literature but that of the daily and weekly press, we naturally come to regard a journalist as the typical man of letters. Yet it should never be overlooked that newspapers, however useful they may be, are certainly the most ephemeral of literary productions, and have merely an incidental connection with art. Without in any way agreeing with the leisured and fastidious Walpole, in his contempt for those "who daily scribble for their daily bread," one cannot but see that the exigencies of the newspaper press are entirely opposed to the conditions of all high-class literary workmanship. By turning to account those bright portions of life which are not engrossed in mere bread-winning, Charles Lamb produced a slender volume of essays, but they will be read by the cultivated for generations to come, and are indeed "a thing of beauty and joy for ever." In a very short space of time, a press writer will produce three or four times as many essays in the form of leading articles, but they will have no value the day after publication. This is the difference between literature as art and as mere merchandise. In saying thus much, I do not wish to underrate the important social functions of those trained experts who gather together the news and scandal of the hour, and so diligently furnish the public with dissertations on the topics of the day. The journalist is, in many respects, the priest and the schoolmaster of the adult world. All that is contended for is that, in larger or less dependent communities, literature is understood to mean something quite apart from mere journalism. When we speak of the English literary men of the day, we do not refer to the leader writers on the *Times* or *Daily News*, but to such men as Tennyson, Ruskin, Browning, Froude, Newman, and Matthew Arnold, who are in no sense of the word journalists. And even, as in the case of Black the novelist, and others, where an author is likewise a journalist, it is not by his labours on the press, but by his independent writings that the public recognize him as a man of letters.

We thus very clearly see that as yet we have hardly any literature at all. We have produced a few writers whose names are more or less known throughout the colonies, and who may have, from time to time, received some measure of recognition in England. Colonial literature is a very young and very feeble offspring (albeit of a vigorous parentage), and, in its awkward attempts to run alone, has many ignominious falls. But so surely as we are developing a national life and national types of character, resembling, no doubt, but yet distinct from, that of the mother country, so surely shall we develop, whatever may be the difficulties and obstacles in the way, a genuine literature of our own. For all literature is merely the artistic expression of national life and character. Shall we, in our own small measure, attempt to foster or to thwart this social development? It is because I feel that most thoughtful men and women will agree with me in desiring to cultivate and advance our literature that I have ventured to be so outspoken in my remarks on the colonial press. It seems to me that any individual who can circulate his opinions anonymously and authoritatively in a newspaper, has an important and almost judicial function to discharge. He should certainly try, as far as poor human nature will

permit, to disabuse his mind of any bias for or against an author or a publication. Of course, such a critic could flourish only in Utopia, but it is the ideal towards which we should strive, if we wish to have either a school of criticism or a literature of our own. Byron, smarting under the lash, wrote—

> "A man must serve his time to every trade
> Save censure—critics all are ready made."

And the history of literature would perhaps, more than anything else, show the fallibility of human judgment. It would be highly suggestive to republish certain of the criticisms passed by their contemporaries upon men and women whose names we now venerate, and whose writings have become classic. Such obsolete judgments would reveal to us the startling fact that our great writers are in many cases imbeciles and imposters, and that immortal renown has often been confidently predicted for books and authors now utterly forgotten. The critical faculty is indeed very rare, and few of us are competent to express an independent opinion in matters of literature and art.

[...] Probably the vast majority of would-be authors deserve the treatment they receive, while many are grossly overpraised (especially in England, where literature seems to be becoming a question of cliques), but when we remember that in the realm of letters, as in that of politics, we have so largely to repeal the decisions of our predecessors, it behoves us to be circumspect in awarding praise and blame.

Whether or not it would be advantageous to the public for critics and newspaper writers generally to append their names to their contributions, it is difficult to say. Much may be said on both sides of the question. This, however, is clear, that, in the case of signed articles, the public would come to regard what they read in print as merely individual opinions; and although journalists would lose some of that power which is so well expressed in the proverb, *omne ignotum pro magnifico*, yet, on the other hand, they would acquire personal notoriety,—which is so dear to all public performers.

These remarks are offered in no ungenerous spirit, and with only the barest allusions to particular cases. It would have been easy had it been thought desirable, to show that almost every colonial author has been harshly treated by the colonial press at first, and that only after great persistence, supplemented by the good opinion of English critics, have any, as a rule, obtained press recognition here. When one considers the small number of halfpence, and the large number of kicks to be obtained by colonial authorship, the wonder is, not that our literature is so scanty, but that we have any at all.

THE MAKING OF AUSTRALIAN LITERATURE

G.B. BARTON, 'THE STATUS OF LITERATURE IN NEW SOUTH WALES. II. HOW THE PUBLISHERS LOOK AT IT'
Centennial Magazine
September 1889

Some years ago, when passing down a street in Melbourne, I noticed a parcel of small books in a bookseller's shop-window, conspicuously labelled, "'Leaves from Australian Forests,' by Henry Kendall; price of one shilling." Not having previously seen, or even heard of, the book, although it had been published some years previously, I went in to buy a copy, and in reply to my inquiry how it was that a volume of Kendall's poetry could be sold at such a price as a shilling? the shopkeeper told me that there was no sale for the book, that he was glad to get rid of it at any price. It was the second of the author's publications, the first—"Poems and Songs"—having appeared in Sydney in 1862, seven years previously. A third volume, entitled "Songs from the Mountains," was published by him in 1880—two years before his death. A collected edition—"Poems of Henry Kendall"—was published four years after that event by his friend, Mr. R. P. Holdsworth. Three of these books were published in Sydney, where the poet was best known during his lifetime; and although the friendly editor of the last says nothing about their reception in his biographical sketch of the author, we may safely hazard the assertion that the sale of these books, which represent the life's work of a man of genius, did not realise a decent year's income for their unfortunate author.

The surprising thing in this case, and in others of the same kind, is not so much the commercial failure of the publications as the fact that books should be published in Sydney, where there is no market, while it would be so much less expensive, and therefore less risky, to publish in London—the best market in the world. If the painful experiences of the past were not enough to deter authors from launching their frail barks on so perilous a sea, covered as it is with the *disjecta membra poetæ*, a very little investigation of the facts should be enough to show them the folly of their venture. Of all the books that have been published here, I do not know one that can be said to have repaid the author for the time and labor devoted to the task of producing it. Poetry has no show, under any circumstances; but some may think that a good novel would pay as well in Sydney as anywhere else, in proportion to the population. That idea may be put to the test by an example as conclusive in its way as the fate of Kendall's poems.

Robbery under Arms is the title of a novel written by a well-known writer, known to his readers as Rolf Boldrewood. It was originally published some years ago in Sydney, in a weekly newspaper, and it was republished last year by McMillan, the London publisher, as one of the cheap reprints entitled The Colonial Library. I knew nothing of the book until a few months ago, when I saw it mentioned in a critical article in the London *Spectator* as one of the three good novels that had been written in Australia. Feeling a little ashamed that I should obtain my knowledge of an Australian masterpiece through a London journal, I bought a copy of McMillan's edition at once, and in a few minutes read enough to justify the *Spectator*'s opinion. The merits of the work could not fail to be recognised immediately by anyone who had lived long enough in this country to learn something about the bush and the wild characters that figured so conspicuously in it before and after the discovery of the gold-fields. The work deserves to take rank with Marcus Clarke's celebrated novel, as a perfectly faithful picture of certain phrases of life in the old days, now happily fading out of memory. But what sort of success attended the publication of this remarkable romance? In a note to the London edition, the author tells us that, "but for the prompt and liberal recognition of the proprietors of the *Sydney Mail*, it might never have seen the light." In other words, if it had been refused by that journal, it would not have been published at all. From which it may be inferred that the columns of a weekly newspaper form the only available means of publication open to a novelist; and, as everyone knows that the scale of remuneration allowed by newspaper proprietors for fiction is a very low one, it follows that the production of a novel in that form cannot possibly give the author any adequate return for his work. Facts of this kind are enough to show that, as there is no market here for literature even in its most popular forms, authorship as a profession, under existing circumstances, is practically closed to literary men. It may seem strange that it should be so, considering that there is now a total population in the colonies of over three millions to work upon. Some people, perhaps, may be unkind enough to say that the fault lies with the authors, whose books are not worth buying. The authors, on the other hand, are inclined to think that the responsibility should be divided between the public and the publishers, since neither will offer them the slightest encouragement in their work.

They think that the case might have been very different if the public had not always shown so much apathy as they have done in matters of this kind; and they point with some emphasis to the unmistakeable enthusiasm shown in the encouragement of *le sport* in all its varieties—the large sums of money so readily obtainable when required for that purpose—and the frantic exultations indulged in whenever a local champion carries off the stakes in a contest on the racecourse or the river. There is some force in this argument; the contrast between the two pictures is too deep and too marked to be soon forgotten. One of our poets has left us a silhouette sketch of himself, writing in a shabby lodging by the side of his dead child, "to earn the undertaker's fee." The other side of the question might be represented by an etching, in Hogarth's style, of a brawny embodiment of muscular training in his professional costume, loaded with prize money and silver cups, and carried on the shoulders of the mob to the doors of a public house—where he lives happily and dies respected.

But what have our authors to say against publishers? They have not made any formal complaint on the subject. Whatever they may have to say, they are too few and too scattered to think of forming combinations in self-defence; and consequently they have said nothing in public about their unfortunate experience. Let us see what an author has to encounter when he proposes to publish. In the first place, all the risk of the publication falls on him; the publisher will take none of it under any circumstances. Secondly, owing to the higher rates prevailing here for printing, binding and paper, an author who determines to publish in Sydney has to pay some fifty percent more on those items that he would have to pay if he published in London. Thirdly, publishers here insist on charging forty percent of the receipts from sales—a charge which they justify on the ground that they have to allow twenty-five percent discount to the trade, (that is, the other booksellers, who may take a certain number of copies on sale or return), leaving themselves, as they say, only fifteen percent for their trouble in bringing the work out and putting it on the market. The author's share of the profits—supposing there are any—will therefore amount to sixty percent of the total receipts, probably just enough to pay his printers' bill and other expenses, leaving him nothing to show for his hard work and the time devoted to it. But this is taking a very rosy view of the speculation, because it assumes that a sufficient number of copies will be sold to pay all the expenses of the publication. It is more than probable that in ordinary cases the sale would not be sufficient for that purpose. There are only two or three publishing firms in Sydney who are in a position to publish successfully, from the fact that they employ travellers who are always moving about from one town to another in the colonies, taking orders for books published by their firms. The publishers who do not employ travellers are not in a position to operate outside their own localities, except by means of agents—that is, other booksellers. Any publisher may employ canvassers, no doubt; but that method could not be adopted in the case of ordinary books, because the expense of canvassing would be too much for them.

As a general rule, then, all that an author can expect, when he publishes his book in Sydney, is that it will pay its expenses. If he is sanguine enough to calculate on making a substantial profit, sufficient at any rate to pay for his time and labor, the chances are that he will be disappointed. Nor will he find compensation in any other shape. "The honor and glory of the thing," to which he should look for his real recompense, will probably prove equally delusive. He cannot wake up one morning and find himself famous; the work that would make him famous in London would leave him very much where it found him in Sydney. With all its charms, the old place is not a literary centre yet; it is just like a quiet old seaport town in the mother-country, many miles away from the great metropolis, to which it looks for its literary supplies as regularly as it does for its news, its fashions, its political sensations, and everything else that makes up the excitement of city life. What English author would think of publishing a book in Bristol or Dover? If anyone should be eccentric enough to do so, and then send it to

a London publisher to be sold on commission, the great man in Paternoster Row would take no interest in it; he would do nothing to push it; and it would drop quietly into the waters of oblivion like a kitten thrown into a well.

Now an author might resign himself to the loss of his money, but it is hard that he should have to go without his reward in the shape of fame and reputation, especially if he took to his work from ambition—*lo gran desio dell' eccellenza*, as Dante calls it. Yet, in spite of all this bitter experience, we still find books occasionally issuing from the local press, and no doubt it will continue to be so until our authors learn to look a little more closely after their own interests. Supposing that their eyes were fully opened on that interesting subject, it would not be difficult to point out a course by which they might obtain some of the profit, as well as recognition, they deserve. If a society were formed on the plan of the English and French institutions, known as the Incorporated Society of Authors, and the *Société des Gens de Lettres*, the obstacles which now stand in the way of successful publication might be removed. Why should there not be an Australian Authors' Society, or a Society of Australian Men of Letters, composed, not exclusively of literary men, but of all who take an interest in the development of Australian Literature, and who would be willing to assist in promoting it in a practical way? If one hundred—or even fifty—such persons would signify their readiness to meet and form a society of the kind, it might be established with every prospect of success; and it would not be difficult to show that, in the course of a few years, such an organization would produce a very great change for the better in the present condition of things. Its chief object would be to enable authors to have their books printed and published in London, and published in all the Australian colonies immediately afterwards. That could be done by means of a yearly subscription of say, five guineas, entitling the subscriber to send in the manuscript of any book he might desire to publish to the council of the society for approval. The council would be composed of six or more members, elected annually at a general meeting, whose duty it would be to receive and examine manuscripts sent into them, and to arrange for the publication of such as they might think fit. Under this system, the publication of a book would not cost the author anything in the event of its not proving a success, because the loss would fall on the subscribed funds of the society; but if it did prove a success, then he might be reasonably required by the rules to reimburse the society in a certain proportion from the profits. But as no work would be recommended for publication unless the council were satisfied as to its prospects, the risk of failure would not be great, supposing, as we may fairly do, that the members of the council did their work conscientiously.

There would be some little difficulty, no doubt, in establishing a society of this kind. In the first place, there is the everlasting *vis inertice*, that apathetic indifference which has to be encountered whenever men are asked to combine for the purpose of accomplishing results not directly profitable to themselves; and in the second place, the unselfish devotion to their work which would be required on the part of the council, might possibly operate to deter members from undertaking the duties of such a position. Objections of that kind, however, would soon disappear if the society were well established, and some energy and determination shewn in its management. The examples of the French and English societies prove that literary men can combine when they like in order to protect their own interests, and that such institutions can be as effectually worked as any organization connected with trade. The scope of such a society would not be confined to the encouragement of authors; it could be made to embrace the whole range of literary activity—that of journalism in particular—with a view to improving the position of its members. The number of literary men now engaged in journalism must be considerable in each of the colonies; taken altogether, they constitute a formidable body, especially in connection with the agency they have at their command. Supposing the movement to succeed, a branch of the proposed society might be established in each colony, and whenever occasion might require, the various braches could act together so as to bring their united weight to bear on any particular question.

It is not necessary to say much as to the advantages of such an institution. Surely the simple fact that it would be the means of opening the door to the noblest of all professions—that of authorship—is enough to justify the proposal. That door is practically closed, as things stand; and there does not seem to be any prospect of its being opened by any other means. There is no need to be pathetic on the subject of struggling genius; we may be told that there is no genius amongst us; but at least it may be assumed that there are many men in the colonies, to say nothing of women, who would willingly make their appearance as authors if they had the same facilities for the purpose that writers have in England. Look, for instance, at the degree of ability shown in Australian journalism. The newspaper press in these colonies does not suffer by comparison with that of the mother-country. There is nothing more remarkable than the fact that, although literature itself is still in such an undeveloped condition among us, that particular section of it which we call journalism displays so much conspicuous excellence. It is hardly possible to pick up a newspaper without meeting with unmistakable evidence of talent in its columns. So much is this the case, that one can hardly help wondering why men of proved capacity should be content to confine their energies to newspaper work, which, at the best, lives but for a day. The reason why they do so is not far to seek. Journalism is at present the only field in which literary talent can find profitable occupation, and it will continue to be so until means are found for the purpose of opening up a better career for it in the shape of authorship.

It is difficult to close this subject without a passing reference to the experience of those who have long since made a name in literature. Harpur, Kendall, and Gordon, for instance, succeeded in accomplishing the great object of their ambition—that of establishing their fame as Australian poets. But with what result to themselves? The story of their sufferings is much too familiar to invite any repetition here. Harpur's unfortunate career is told in touching language by his widow, in the preface to an edition of his poems published in Sydney a few years ago. Kendall has left sketches of his domestic life which remind the reader of the most dismal period in English Literature—when the attics in Grub Street were tenanted by starving men of letters, and Johnson used to eat his corned beef and carrots behind a screen in his publisher's shop. Gordon, by far the most popular of our poets, blew his brains out the day after his volume of Bush Ballads was published in Melbourne. A great deal of pitiful wonder has been expressed on that subject; it seems so strange to the uninitiated that a popular writer should take so desperate a remedy for his troubles on the very day, of all days, when Fortune might be supposed to smile upon him. But considering the usual result of a publisher's balance sheet there was nothing very surprising in the tragedy after all. The really surprising thing—a cynic might say—is, not that Gordon should have done as he did, but that every other Australian author should not have done the same thing; for there was no more reason for the act in one case than in any other. The question for us now is, why should not our authors in the years to come have something better to look forward to than a tragic *finis*!

'THE CHARACTERISTICS OF AUSTRALIAN LITERATURE'
Australasian Critic
1 November 1890

In the preface to Gordon's poems, Marcus Clarke devotes one of the most eloquent passages penned in Australia to the theory that the characteristic note of Australian poetry is melancholy. This, however, is no responsible opinion uttered by a careful thinker after wide consideration. It was the impression left on the impulsive mind of a man of genius after the mournful perusal of the works of a friend but recently departed.

It is undoubtedly true that Gordon's poetry has a deep undercurrent of melancholy throughout. But this was the result, not of the country in which the poet lived, nor yet of any of his surroundings in it, but solely and strictly of this own temperament and of his own personal experiences in life. A wayward boyhood, unruly and defiant towards parents whose only failing had been a too tender indulgency to himself; a youth full of evident power and with rare opportunities, but wasted in recklessness and extravagance, were certain to leave in a soul so honourable and sincere a long tale of years, like those concluding ones in the lives of Burns and of Byron, marred by self-dissatisfaction and remorse. The cheerlessness of dust and ashes occupied the cold hearth where once the fire had burned brightest and merriest, and a gloom was spread where mirth had been loudest.

Marcus Clarke has himself no little flavour of melancholy due to this cause. A year or two of fast life, while he was yet a boy, followed by a manhood which never showed the slightest trace of that "prudent, cautious self-control" which, as Burns declares, "is wisdom's root," left him the victim of restless longings and regrets. Now, if it had happened that these shores of ours had received any very large number of young men, gifted with genius, but of reckless habits; youths who brought to the colonies not only the sad reminiscences of their follies, but also the power to give voice to their woes, then we might have had something which would have looked like a national characteristic, though really unconnected with the country itself.

But of these exiled geniuses Gordon and Clarke were the only notable examples. There is, unfortunately, a third to be added who, though not an exile, had yet very much the same reason for self-dissatisfaction. Kendall had experienced a hapless boyhood and a youth full of high ideals, thwarted by cheerless circumstances. His subsequent life was one long series of strong endeavour, sudden temptation, and miserable degradation, followed by an anguish so keen that, as he tells us,

> The hell the Christian fears to name
> Was heaven to his fierce remorse.

Thus three out of our six most famous writers presented an undertone of melancholy, not because of anything in the country, but merely because they had the seeds of melancholy in themselves. But with these exceptions the great body of our nascent literature is cheerful and vigorous, as becomes the pioneer writers of a young and hopeful country. Brunton Stephens, though he can handle a solemn theme in grave and stately fashion, is, as a rule, either gay or boisterously merry. Gordon M'Crae, amid all his refinement, exhibits no tendency to melancholy. Charles Harpur, though his life was marked by heavy sorrows, is by no means a gloomy writer; he may be mystical; he may often recall Coleridge by his vague aspirations grandly formed but imperfectly accomplished; but he is assuredly not pervaded by any sentiment of sadness.

Dommett [sic] tells his Maori tale without the least indication that his views are pessimistic or his disposition sombre. Where will anyone find any trace of sadness in old Dr. Lang? Does Macarthur show any signs of unusual melancholy, or Wentworth, or Woods, or Bonwick, or indeed any of our elder writers, save Gordon, Kendall, and Clarke?

This theory of the melancholy which necessarily underlines Australian literature is explained by Marcus Clarke as an effect of the sombre effects of the Australian forests. But in the first place, it is to be noticed that those of our writers, such as Harpur, who lived all their youth and early manhood in the bush, exhibit no unusual strain of sadness. And in the second place, can it be truly said that the Australian forests are peculiarly melancholy? Are not all primeval wildernesses more or less oppressive? Even such woods as those of Brazil, more richly stored with life than any other on the face of the earth, are declared by Bates, after eleven years of residence among them, to have an awful and oppressive effect upon his spirits, by reason of their deadly stillness during the day and the weird noises of the night. The Australian bush is, at mid-day and at midnight, like almost all forests—silent, heavy, and full of a vague suspense. But like most forests, it is cheerful in the early morning and when the evening falls. Who that has dwelt in the bush has not recognised the merry voice of the ubiquitous magpie as the herald of a cheerful dawn? What with flocks of cockatoos and parrakeets, what with crows and kingfishers and smaller birds, the bush is lively and often enough noisy after the heat of the day has begun to decline.

Australian forests are not peculiarly sombre. As a rule they are open park-like lands, upon which the sun shines richly, and through which the breaths of heaven pass freely. They are as fully peopled as other forests with those feathered tribes which alone make up the vivacity of the primeval woods. Why then should they be peculiarly melancholy? And it is equally untrue, if we will but examine it widely enough, to say that there is apparent any marked infusion of sadness in our infant literature.

But it is much easier to show that this is not its prevailing characteristic than to indicate what is or is likely to be its most notable feature. There is, indeed, among those who have made their mark no common feature discoverable. Stephens and Gordon and Kendall and M'Crae and Dommet [sic] and Harpur are pervaded by no one sentiment or manner which could be treated as a bond of union, welding them into something like a single school. But it might be a little more profitable to look for such pervading feature in the younger men—those who have made as yet no great name for themselves, but who are likely enough, some of them at least, to have their names enrolled among our pioneers in literature;—writers like Farrell, and Holdsworth, and Heney, and Sherard, and Chandler, and Sadler, and quite a long train of young aspirants, who are even now pressing forward to enter the shrine of fame and sing for their mother Australia songs that shall perhaps build up for her a reputation in the years to come.

Even here, however, we find but little that is truly characteristic. In manner they have nothing in common that could be chosen as indicating a coming national school of poesy. The stately lines of Heney, ringing out a classic tone in spite of a sort of purposed carelessness, remind one of Shakespeare's sonnets, or the work of Keats, or the more placid poems of Shelley; for they disdain to descend to the levels of human interests. They belong to the artist's world; they please the student who gives a little care to them; they will never please the passing reader. How different in all these respects from the work of John Farrell, forceful even to coarseness, little worth any prolonged study, but full of that action and vigour and heartiness which give an immediate zest to the reader's appetite. How different again from the verse of Philip

Holdsworth, sweet, but a trifle tame; clear, natural, and sincere; simple thoughts welling up from a mind of much elegance, and expressed in verse that is moulded on the highest models. Widely different, again, is the style of Alfred Chandler, with its varying moods, now recalling Gordon in its simple, straightforward way of telling a bush story or hitting off a description of colonial scenery, now dropping down into ballads of almost Della Cruscan vapidity. Allan Sherard, again, with his finely musical lines, recalls the swing and the glamour of Swinburne.

There is, in truth, so wide and so healthful an eclecticism of style among our rising writers that it seems useless to search for any common feature which may be taken as the promise of a future national school. But in regard to subject matter, however wide their range may be, and however various their methods of treatment, they all are marked by a restless, and sometimes unnecessary, patriotism. There is no very perceptible, and certainly no offensive tinge of what the Americans call the spread-eagle tendency. There is no depreciation of what their fathers have done who have hailed from older lands, and whose toils have made this country what it now is. But there is a resolute determination that as Australia has not yet been sung about and praised and glorified as other lands have been, it must be their duty to rectify that omission at once. This is very laudable, and in many cases the work has been fairly well done; but it is work that will necessarily fail of a high artistic effect. It is one thing to give voice to a strong national feeling when danger or oppression or the glow of victory has furnished a fitting occasion, but it is a wholly different thing when no such occasion has arisen and no such sentiment has been awakened to try to simulate it. Because England has a national anthem, is it really necessary that Australia should have one also? More than a hundred have been composed, but they all deal in vague abstractions. Half the literary skill that has been displayed in the artificial concoction of many a single one of these might not have been necessary for the composition of comparatively rude verses, which should give utterance to some national outburst so strong that the lines would live as a national inheritance long after the feeling itself had become purely historical.

The same want of opportuneness is displayed in much of the description of Australian scenery. It is often described not as incidental to a tale, or as tinged by or tinging the emotions of the describer. The wattle has never been celebrated in song. It is as good a tree, they think, as the oak or the elm or the holly; these have often been sung. Therefore, the wattle must be also enshrined in song. But it makes all the difference whether the oak is to be only the background of the picture or is to be the picture itself.

This slightly obtrusive endeavour to be above all things Australian is the only national feature that can at present be detected in our literature. It is not, perhaps wholly undesirable, but it partakes too much of self-consciousness to be wholly pleasant. It is what our young poets are urged to by many of their guides and advisers. They are warned not to describe at second-hand the sights and scenery of other lands, but to describe what lies all around them, and in so far as it is necessary to describe at all this advice is sound and reasonable. Yet there is an inevitable baldness in poetry which contains too many sonnets to the wattle tree and to the magpie, to the varnished native and the lost explorers. We have had almost enough of bushfires in blank verse, and of tales of convict murders in pentameters. Hymns to Australia and odes to Australasia are plentiful beyond reckoning.

This, and this alone, is the common feature which prevails in our young Australian poets; this too conscious effort to be Australian. With high ideals and no mean powers of execution, they very often fail of all the effect they might easily attain because they are not content to let the country and the nation be the setting in which their subject is framed, but wish to make the country and the nation themselves the subjects. It is one of the great merits of Gordon that while he is almost everywhere unmistakably Australian, he never goes out of his way to be Australian. It is the chief weakness of our rising poets that they too often write for no other purpose than to be Australian; and it is just possible that their laudable desire to rouse a thrilling patriotism for their native land may defeat itself by over-shooting the mark.

It is Heney who writes—

> He is secure who trusts himself and sings,
> And is content if he do satisfy
> That sense most inly set which only brings
> Assurance that his verse shall never die.

It is just the want of this security which is most characteristic of our rising school of poets, and in an almost equal degree of our writers of fiction. They have a restless self-consciousness of being Australian, which in the future will probably disappear as their strength increases, but which in the meantime interferes a great deal with the artistic fulness and greatness of their work.

'ERIC', 'AUSTRALIANS IN FICTION'
Cosmos
20 October 1894

Fiction is (or is at any rate supposed to be) imaginative writing, and a novelist is considered at liberty to invent the *dramatis personæ* of his tale at his own will and pleasure. If he chooses also to place the scene in a purely imaginary country he will not be found fault with by the public, provided he carries out his ideas with a fair amount of skill. But if he takes it upon himself to describe the manners and customs of a country of which he knows little or nothing, relying on his fertile brain to supply his deficient knowledge, then the inhabitants of that country have a distinct right to complain of any injustice that he may do them.

The interest taken in England concerning Australian affairs has of late years increased so much that the English public has been ready to read almost anything that might be put before them about the colonies. At the same time their knowledge of the actual condition of things in Australia, and even of Australian geography, was, and is still very limited. They are thus unable to judge of the accuracy of impressions given by various writers, and novelists are tempted to pitch the scene of their romances on Australian ground without taking much trouble to ascertain in what points life in the new country differs from life in the old. For instance, Miss Helen Mathers, some years ago, published a novel entitled "Sam's Sweetheart," which as a picture of Australian life and Australian people is simply a tissue of absurdities from beginning to end. Miss Mathers did not even avail herself of a map of Australia which would have saved her from the error of making some of her characters embark for England from the town of Bathurst, which is not exactly a sea-port. That Miss Mathers should have made her hero a Maori and her heroine a half-caste Maori, if it slightly lessens the improbability of the plot in one way, heightens it in another, since her endeavours to account for the presence of Maoris in the midst of the Australian bush are vague and inconclusive. Yuntha, the young Maori woman who gives the book its title, having been brought up nearly all her life in New South Wales, may be considered to all intents and purposes as an Australian girl, but we can hardly suppose that the authoress ever either met or heard of an aboriginal Australian bearing even a remote resemblance to this beautiful and fascinating creature, or to her noble and unfortunate lover. Still, there is no more to be urged against Miss Mathers' heroine than that she is untrue to nature; she is neither ill-mannered nor disagreeable, and if her innocence appears abnormal, at any rate it is not an unfavorable trait.

A later writer, in attempting to pourtray [sic] an Australian girl (not a half-caste this time), has fallen into very different and less excusable errors. After all, even an ignorant reader would be in doubt if he should take "Sam's Sweetheart" seriously, but he would read the whole of "A Bride from the Bush" without recognizing that it was a libel on Australian girls in general, and would accept the very singular and aggravating "Bride" as a very fair type of her country-women. That any Australian girl, even one brought up in the Never Never country, should be so utterly without any sense of *savoir vivre* or knowledge of the usages of polite society as to give vent to a prolonged coo-ee while driving through Hyde Park in the height of the season is absolutely incredible; indeed, the whole account of Gladys' conversation and conduct when in the great metropolis, her gross ignorance and utter want of refinement, constitute a picture which is certainly not a fair representation of Australian women.

Scarcely less misleading, though in a totally opposite direction, is Mrs. Macleod's novel "An Australian Girl." The young women of our country ought perhaps to be flattered by the portrait. The girl who can quote Kant's "Kritik of Pure Reason" in the original (and does so at every opportunity) must, we should imagine, be rather a *rara avis* in most countries; but the authoress does not lead one to suppose that her attainments excited any surprize in South Australian society, or that her friends were at all over-awed by her knowledge of German Philosophy. They may, perhaps, have been bored by it, but they discreetly kept their feelings in the back-ground.

After reading "A Bride from the Bush" the uninitiated Englishman might naturally conclude that it is the usual thing in Australia for girls to crack stockwhips, introduce all kinds of slang into their conversation, and give frequent evidence of a complete lack of education. On the other hand, after reading "An Australian Girl" he would probably imagine that the feminine portion at least of the rising generation at the Antipodes comprised some of the most erudite people on the face of the globe, and he would no doubt be surprized that these learned ladies had not done more to leave a mark on the literary history of the 19th century.

Unfortunately, even those whose knowledge of Australian life ought to prevent them from representing it in false colours do not always keep within the bounds of probability. Mrs. Campbell Praed's heroines too often conduct themselves in a manner which would be denounced as impossible for an English girl, but which is looked upon as perfectly natural for a young Australian. There are, no doubt, girls in our country whose manners leave a good deal to be desired; there are some here, as elsewhere, whose conduct is not irreproachable, but these are the exceptions, not the rule, and the injustice lies in representing the contrary.

There is a class of Australian novels from which one would draw the inference that all the men in the colonies are either squatters, stock-riders or bushrangers, with a few miners thrown in out of deference to our mineral resources. These are mostly written by authors who have never visited Australia and who have a vague impression that it is a vast half-cultivated region, with widely scattered townships about the dimensions of an English country village. This is partly to be attributed to the novelist's natural desire to seize on the most salient points of difference between the old country and the new, and to shut his eyes to points of resemblance. Australian bush life has no resemblance to English country life, whereas, in all essential respects, life in one city is very much the same as in another.

Such writers as "Tasma" and Ada Cambridge are, however, doing a good deal to remove false impressions as to the manner of life in Australia, and in process of time, our fellow subjects on the other side of the globe will doubtless realize that there are Australian men who are neither hirsute nor rough-mannered, and Australian women who can compare favourably with their sex in the old country.

THE MAKING OF AUSTRALIAN LITERATURE

ARTHUR A.D. BAYLDON, 'A REVIEW OF AUSTRALIAN FICTION'
Lone Hand
1 August 1907

Since nearly every Australian weekly contains one or more short stories, often the first printed copy of would-be authors, it is out of the question to expect a brief review of Australian fiction to be exhaustive. The most I can attempt is to dwell on the characteristics of the most prominent authors, in my opinion.

Perhaps it is as well to first pay tribute to the two authors who seem to stand aloof from the others, partly by virtue of their literary significance, partly that their work was done before most of our moderns had begun. It is too late in the day to criticise Marcus Clarke's "Term of His Natural Life" and Henry Kingsley's "Geoffrey Hamlyn." These novels are not only popular, but are looked on as Australian classics. Even when it is admitted that the strength of the first was fed by Hugo on the one hand and by Read on the other, and that some of its material was too brutally handled, and that the second frequently degenerated into melodrama, ludicrously out of place in a novel, written in the gossipy literary style of Thackeray—even with these admissions, the two novels have deservingly won, and retain Australia's profound admiration.

To catalogue the most important of local writers and their kinsmen in alphabetical order, we get:—

BAYNTON, BARBARA	KEARNEY, MRS.
BECKE, LOUIS	KENNA, FRANCIS
BEDFORD, RANDOLPH	KINGSLEY, HENRY
BOLDREWOOD, ROLF	LANCASTER, G. B.
BOOTHBY, GUY	LAWSON, HENRY
BRERETON, J. LE GAY	MACK, LOUISE
CAMBRIDGE, ADA	MILLS, ETHEL
CLARKE, MARCUS	MONTGOMERY, ALEC.
COLLINS, TOM	MUTCH, T.
DORRINGTON, ALBERT	NICKOLSON [sic], JOHN
DYSON, EDWARD	PATERSON, A. B.
FLETCHER, H.	POYNTON, MISS
FORREST, M.	PRAED, MRS. CAMPBELL
FRANKLIN, MILES	QUINN, RODERIC

GOULD, NAT. RUDD, STEELE
HODGE, MRS. SORENSON, –
HUME, FERGUS TURNER, ETHEL
JEFFRIES, C. A. WATSON, J. R.
JEROME, HELEN

To simplify and to abbreviate my review, I shall arbitrarily classify the writers of marked affinity in schools of my own designation. There are two authors in the above list who can readily stand as extreme exponents of two antithetical schools: the Emotionally Creative and the Literary Critical. And I will deal with these before inventing labels for the other schools.

Henry Lawson completely exemplifies the characteristics of the Emotionally Creative School. A highly emotional temperament, with quick objective perceptions and an excellent memory, are his literary make-up, supplemented by grim humor at times and a laudable desire to stick to facts—scouting everything invented, the trickery of plots, the artificiality of preconceived literary effects, as little less than a crime. To give birth to the pulsing characters obsessing him, without sacrificing any of their human attributes, seems to have been his one object in fiction. A man of little education he has been severely handicapped. So long as the stories contained his conceptions—the emotions, the feelings that possessed him—he troubles little how these have been presented. The result is that his best work seems torn out of life itself. Though his range is short, almost confined to illiterate bush and city types, yet within its circle are individualised living, thinking, acting beings. He has been likened to Bret Harte by superficial critics. The American, however, had a literary facility and a theatrical dexterity beyond Lawson, who probably does not desire them. But he lacked that dreadful earnestness, that tragic intensity of hopeless misery and cheerless mirth; his stories have never Lawson's dire undertones of pain with a shudder at the drop scenes. Lawson is so deadly realistic that one can imagine Zola embracing him had he met him. But much of his work has been written without the emotional mood. His characters then do not impress. We perceive they are drawn from life, but they are self-acting automatons, not living beings. At these unemotional times Lawson is tediously prolix, losing his motif and his readers' interest amid a *debris* of insignificant details. Notwithstanding, there is one fact always patent: you are getting a faithful transcript of the bush, or whatever it is he is describing, just as it is to the average man. The beauties of Nature have no charm for him. Hence, his popularity with swagmen who (as I know from experience) can walk past the finest of the Blue Mountain scenery without a second glance toward it, unless there were a chance of its ministering to their physical needs.

In Albert Dorrington we have Lawson's antithesis—the exponent of the Literary Critical School. There is not a breath of emotion in all Dorrington's characters. In lieu of it he has, when at his best, a hard intensity. Lawson's best work pours out of his heart without brain check. On the other hand, Dorrington is all brain. His inventive and constructive faculties are remarkable. Though his vocabulary is not copious, his discrimination is keen. An idea striking him he immediately plans out the story, with the passionless exactitude of an engineer. Then he writes it, selecting only those precise words that vividly respond to the effect he desires to get. Should there be a savage heat in the concept—a man fighting with sharks, for instance—his intensity drives out without an effort the precise vocabulary that presents the picture to the mind. His characters seem to be embodied moods, rather than human beings—sometimes only pegs on which to hang the fine drapery of his verbiage. When the mood is morbid, or cruel, or pitiless, or monstrous, the character, frugally yet brilliantly presented, strikes with an electric stroke the chord of appeal. His best work wins your admiration, never your sympathy. It hits on the polished surface of the mind with resonant ring. Your intellect marvels at the stroke, and getting critical, yields homage to the consummate Art that propelled it—but your heart is unmoved. With the simple human feelings Dorrington is out of touch. Though his inventive faculty (I repeat) is remarkable, yet he has no imagination. His pictures are vivid reproductions of the impressions of the senses. Thus, an English writer's imaginative touch of dawn on the Alpine glaciers—"each in itself a new morning"—is distinct from, and beyond, his word-flashes of sense impressions. Nevertheless, I know of no writer superior to him on his own special plane. He rivals Crane at his best, with the kicking force of his cutting, sounding epithets; his characters, however, fall in value when compared with the American's as actual human portraits. Inventive and constructive ingenuity, a grasp of simple and yet effective expression, with much mental energy, and a sense of dramatic fitness and reserve, and climax—these are Dorrington's prominent characteristics.

With this clear definition of the two leaders of the above opposing Schools, we can quickly dispose of their kindred workers. Barbara Baynton's bush studies bear the creative impress of an emotion more modified than Lawson's. Though she lacks his sardonic humor and versatility, her work is more artistically presented. Her stories have the solemn gloom and silent depth of subterranean pools. Another conspicuous member of this school is Steele Rudd. Though as yet no tragic chord has been struck, no pathetic element introduced into his literary household, yet "Dad" and the others are such vital humans, the incidents so matter of fact, that the autobiographical illusion of his books is complete. Several critics have insisted that Rudd's studies are caricatures. This erroneous impression has arisen from the critics forgetting that each particular sketch is a glance into the household on such occasions as a series of humorous episodes were in progress. There were, of course, days of normal monotony when Rudd had nothing of interest to record. These critics, reading his books, and making no allowance for the gaps of time between story and story, reviewed them from a wrong standpoint. Much as I desire to do adequate justice to Rudd's work I must pass on, otherwise my space will not suffice to more than touch on the authors demanding attention.

Miles Franklin's "My Brilliant Career," though raw and crude, contains scenes—that squalid bush hovel, for instance—instinct with life. Miss Poynton has deservedly gained a place in this school. One of her Chinese studies would have more than pleased Bret Harte.

Ethel Turner, a student of child-life, has not only the keen perceptions, but much of the creative emotion of Lawson. The death of Judith is in itself a passport to membership.

Several writers, lacking, or having not yet expressed, enough creative instinct to entitle them to full membership, may be mentioned as sympathisers with this emotional school. The value of Sorenson's stories is in the astonishing knowledge he possesses of animal and bird life, and of the out-of-door subjects connected with that particular part of the bush he has studied. His work is a storehouse of useful information. G.B. Lancaster, under the influence of Kipling, is a writer of tragic stories of movement. Mutch, a young recruit to our literature, with a quick eye and a readiness to depict with crude fidelity what he sees, has yet to prove his claim as a possessor of creative emotion. Brereton, with quaint humor and a sympathetic insight into "sundowners," prefers to draw off in verse the oozings of sentiment to cultivating his innate talent, peculiarly attractive. There is so much evidence of scholastic lore, allied with considerable power of etching home bush scenes, in Tom Collins' work, that I'm almost afraid I'm at fault in not mentioning him earlier.

Other writers less concerned with the primitive bush types may now be dismissed with a phrase or two interpreting their characteristics. Ethel Mills has busied herself with studies of the feminine mind and the orthodox male with clean simplicity. Mesdames Hodge and Kearney now and again print stories betraying their interest in the attractions and repulsions at work around the hearth and in the social circle. Ada Cambridge, with more weight but less grip, essays the wordy novel, and should be transferred to the conventional school of novelists. Among English writers, Ouida in the past, and Marie Corelli of to-day, are examples of the popularity that is achieved by meeting mediocrity half-way with efflorescent sentiment and an hysterical verbiage. M. Forrest furnishes us with Australian example. Though loth [sic] to find fault, I am compelled, out of justice to her fellow-workers, to put a finger on her ephemeral sentimentality, that is preferred by the great mass of undeveloped readers to more sterling qualities. I may fitly close this paragraph with Helen Jerome, who is rapidly developing a sleightness of movement in her handling of the short story.

I will now select such writers as bear the most characteristics of the Literary Critical School. Not one of them can approach Dorrington as a literary craftsman, but all of them surpass him in sinking nearer the mark of illusion with their characters. Alec. Montgomery is an author potentially capable of work calculated to make him a popular writer of romance of the Rider Haggard description. With a personal knowledge of the Malay Peninsula, a memory filled with unexploited material, fine inventive and constructive faculties breathed over by an ideal atmosphere, with an analytical bent and a cleanly-cut literary style, he has, through either an indifference to fame or a constitutional dislike to exertion, only presented the world with a few stories, of which the best are admirable. With less literary equipment, but with perhaps more actual contact with an adventurous life than Montgomery, and with almost a ferocious desire to make the most of his wares, Louis Becke stands to-day the most widely-read writer of South Sea Island stories. Allied with these writers through his literary style, that approaches the nearest to Montgomery's; through his lack of emotions; through his perceiving, turning critically over and deliberately presenting his characters without heat; through his self-obliteration—is Edward Dyson, a worthy member of this school. Dorrington and Montgomery attract each other by an affinity of several faculties, and are a little apart from Becke and Dyson, who lean more on close observation regarding their characters, getting into their work a more human note in place of the remote scenic effect of the inventive faculties of the other two writers. It will be perceived that the first School is very human, has warmth of feeling; that its expression is natural and often commonplace; that the second is cold, critical, inventive; its expression artificial, having at its best a hard polished surface. The emotional writers are mainly occupied with their material; the literary writers with their medium of presentation.

Kenna and Watson represent the Psychological school—the first, after displaying brilliant promise in a batch of sex studies of sombre strength and an avowal of relentless pessimism, passed into the political world. Watson, however, introducing himself with "Fate's Puppets," a short story of remarkable insight into motives, set to work on a bigger canvass. His novel, "In a Man's Mind," whilst displaying his subtle intuitions, exposed his defects and weaknesses. Lacking imagination, and without the power of disconnecting his characters from his own individuality, and projecting them into the world of space and time, he had been snared by the mannerism of Henry James. His style, too, has become stilted, and suggests the influence of Meredith.

The leaders of the Ideal or Poetic School are Roderic Quinn and John H. Nickolson [sic], and their work is shot through by visionary lights. In face of awakened reminiscenses of Hugo's Gilliott in "Toilers of the Sea," I am disposed to think "Margaret" is Quinn's highest achievement in literature. His prose is so finely tempered that this oceanic dream quivers through it as a jewel through sunny waters. Indeed, so rich is he in ripe epithets and phrases, and moves with such meandering melody, that I rank Quinn, at his best, among the foremost of our stylists. Unlike the characters of several writers of the Literary School that are dry detachments of the inventive faculty, and seem driven by mechanical forces, Quinn's are creations of the imagination. Nickolson's [sic] "Halek," an allegory, written in the style of the school of Queen Anne, is an etherealised "Pilgrim's Progress" studded with aphorisms and out-breaking into passages like subdued music. These writers, however prosaic their material, cannot help flavoring it with an occult idealism.

Before I pass to other Schools, I will dismiss Louise Mack, whose brilliant style is of the Critical school, whose material is of the outer world around her, sometimes catching in its passage through her mind a gleam of poetry; Bedford, with his explosive vocabulary, his matter-of-fact outlook and fine animal spirits, boisterously loving freedom and fresh air; Jeffries, with exaggerated epithets and a passion for farcical scenes and adventurous episodes connected with railway life, to which he largely confines himself; H. Fletcher, with his criticisms of current topics uttered by humorous Dads out-back in their vernacular; Daley, with a Bohemian sketch or two, interesting as biographical reminiscences of an Australian poet; Paterson, familiar with the bush, with an observing eye, a shrewd mind, and a fund of humor.

Guy Boothby and Fergus Hume (who worked mainly in England) belong to the Sensational School. Their object is to carry their readers rapidly from the first page to the last. Plots and counter-plots, and every device conceivable to create astonishment and stimulate curiosity, are dexterously dove-tailed and fitted on to their characters, like machinery to propel them to fulfil their respective roles in the melodramas.

In Mrs. Campbell Praed and Rolf Boldrewood we again come nearer to actual beings. Both, however, rely more or less on the interest excited by incidents apart from the evolution of character. Mrs. Praed's studies of station life carry favor through their truthfulness. A knowledge of the rough and stirring life of the gold-diggings in the early days, a faculty for exciting incidents, and a happy knack of sketching in characters of primitive instincts, are the most serviceable of Boldrewood's equipment.

Nat Gould, a disciple of Hawley Smart's, with none of his master's refinement, breadth of range, and perception of character, is the chronicler of the Australian racecourse. His novels, therefore, are popular with the gambling fraternity, and cleverly illustrate the plots and stable secrets, the tricks of touts and welshers, the movement of horses and rustle of silks, the spectacular views and vociferous enthusiasm—the whole machinery, in short, of our racing world.

In my desire to keep this review within a desired compass, I may have been too curt with some writers. I have, however, endeavored to be precise in my remarks and not include any haphazard opinions. I have tried to review the authors from an impersonal standpoint, from that of a critic who countenances not at all his own special attitude towards the works of the authors referred to. Naturally, as a reader, I have my own favorite author among the number reviewed. I flatter myself this review does not betray that predilection.

THE MAKING OF AUSTRALIAN LITERATURE

JOHN H. GARTH, 'SHOULD AUSTRALIAN LITERATURE BE CHEERFUL?'
Australian Magazine
1 July 1908

It has been widely accepted that morbidness must of necessity be the distinctive note in Australian literature, that Nature herself has decreed the great bulk of our literary output shall always be "sicklied o'er with the pale cast of thought." But if we look into the matter we will find that this idea is as wrong as it is mischievous.

The casual observer, glancing back upon Australian prose and verse, found that a very large percentage of it had morbidness as its motif; took it that it was natural this should be so, and, in casting about for the cause, decided at once that the big empty spaces of the back country and the mysterious "bush" were responsible. They were strengthened in this conclusion by the dictum of a certain weekly journal which they had come to regard as an authority, although, on this occasion at least, it was merely seeking to saddle Nature with its own questionable taste.

In any enquiry into the tendencies of Australian writing we are compelled to take this particular paper into consideration because of the influence it has had in building up a certain school of authorship and because of the misconceptions here and abroad as to the representative character of that journal. While the "Bulletin" was the first paper in Australia to make it worth while for budding writers to put pen to paper, and in so doing undoubtedly laid the foundations of our literature, such as it is, it will always be a debateable point as to whether Australia would not have been better off had the "Bulletin" done nothing of the kind. The paper wanted a certain class of matter, and, speaking broadly, it paid for none other. This meant that with this as practically the only profitable means of publication open to them, our story writers turned themselves entirely to the type of stuff that stood a reasonable chance of acceptance. Thus the school of "smart," morbid Bulletinesque writers came into being. Looked at from any point of view, it is not an admirable school, and judged by it alone the "Bulletin's" influence on our literature would be wholly deplorable. But the fact remains that, whatever mode of expression it demanded for itself, that paper turned our young thought pen-and-inkwards, and blazed the trail, however crookedly, for men and papers outside its own sphere. It is because of this we speak of the effect of the "Bulletin" on our writing as debateable.

Some there are we know who hold that the paper from the outset merely offered itself as a medium for Australian expression—that had our writers not in the first place wanted to so express themselves, and had not the public from the beginning wanted such an expression, there would never have been a "Bulletin" School. This is the old story about the readers making a paper instead of the paper making the readers—an absolutely absurd proposition.

On such an assumption the journal with the biggest circulation would necessarily reflect the views and aspirations of a community. Yet thousands of people who buy say the "Sydney Morning Herald" all the week read the "Bulletin" on Thursday, and even "Truth" on Sunday! As a matter of fact it often happens in the newspaper world, just as in the big human chorus, that the man who "sings out of tune" gets the greatest amount of attention. It may not be very flattering attention but in the case of the newspaper at least, it can conceivably be very profitable.

To return to the writers, our authors have always written to the newspaper market. Mediocrity always does write to its market. Only genius breaks away—and we have developed no genius yet. If at the outset there had been one paper only and it had bought and paid liberally for only humorous matter, we would have long ago developed a strong school of humor. Similarly, had cheerful stories been demanded, so would they have been supplied, and ere this we would have been well on a sane, national literary road. The thing is forcibly illustrated by the astonishing advance that has been made in the matter of story writing during the past few years since a wider journalistic market has been opened to the writers of healthy fiction; for to-day we have a big detachment of writers in the weekly and monthly press who are doing really excellent work on rational lines. They are rapidly recruiting, and as rapidly improving, and it is clear that they have firmly laid the foundation of a big school of writing destined to leave a permanent mark on our literature. On the other hand, the school of "smart" writers neither expands nor advances, and it has become a common-place among Australian readers that you can safely wager months ahead who the contributors to certain publications will be on any given date.

What, then, apart from newspaper considerations, makes for morbidness in our fiction, and should it in the sum logically outweigh the tendencies to cheerfulness? In the first place there is always a tremendous appeal in intense emotionalism for youth, and so it is with the young writer, whatever his years. And from highly-strung emotionalism to morbidity is but the smallest step. Then the morbid story seldom fails of some effect by sheer strength of its idea. Further, its motif can easily cloak a multitude of literary sins, just as a few splashes of violent color may bring effect to a poster though its draftmanship be distinctly faulty. Similarly the effect in such a story can be achieved in shorter space than in any other—a fact of extreme importance in these days of high pressured readers. But these things are not peculiar to Australia. The same applies all over the world—yet they have been lived down elsewhere, and a cheerful and healthy literature has sprung up in, let us say, two or three countries.

What has been said of the melancholy effect of the "bush" is certainly to a great degree true. But the bush isn't all Australia, and, further, our writers do not come from the bush. If they did we would have a wild and woolly literature indeed. Those of our penmen who write best about the black country have lived there—or we hope they have—but they have been either merely sojourners there, or, having spent their boyhood in the wilderness, have drifted to the towns. In neither case can we rationally blame the poor bush for any unhealthiness they might give expression to.

Turning to the other side there are overwhelming reasons why cheerfulness should be the dominant note in our literature. The Australian himself is a cheerful animal. Look at a crowd of him at work or play in the cities, observe his habit in the country towns, live with him for a week or two on farm or station and there is no room for doubt. Certainly you find many men isolated from their fellows by the exigencies of their calling out back, who naturally evidence a gloomy mentality born of loneliness and overmuch introspection. But these latter do not write—printable stuff. No; the Australian, taking him generally, is cheerful. Indeed it would be a ghastly commentary on his mental makeup if he were not so. His environment is so utterly opposed to it. He lives in a country of sunshine and elbow room—two of the prime essentials to man's well-being; he has to exert himself less to acquire the necessaries of life than in any other civilised country; in a month's march he is not confronted with the nerve-depressing sight of that abject, pitiless poverty that he would continually meet anywhere in the old world. His country has gone through no heart-searing experiences of war or pestilence, and up till the present at any rate, he has been free from big national worries of any kind. Add to this the fact that the scenery of most of that part of this country in which he lives is inspiring, and of a bigness that begets nobility, and you have the last excuse for morbidness exploded.

Weigh the whole thing critically and you will find in the first place that the worst that can be said of the natural conditions in Australia is that they tend to a happy slothfulness rather than to a diseased activity, and in the second place that the morbid blight which early fastened itself upon our literature, was a thing of accidental growth which has already begun to atrophy.

'EDITORIAL NOTE'
Lone Hand
1 March 1909

There is a curious disparity in Australian life as it is lived and as it is limned in Australian letters. The Australian is hereditarily, climatically, destined to be a gay, sport-loving, somewhat *insouciant* national type. He is heir in possession of the finest sunshine, the bluest seas, the creamiest beaches in all Nature. His dreams are not haunted by the shadows of old tragedies; his mind is singularly free of superstitions. Many faults he has, arising from a "don't-care," "can't-bother" spirit carried to excess. It is certainly not among his faults that he is gloomy. More of a devil than an angel, perhaps, good orthodoxists, but anyhow, a cheerful devil! Yet what national literature Australia has so far produced in book form is not conspicuously

gay. Marcus Clarke, Gordon, Kendall, Daley, Lawson—these names occur at once as those of the best known Australian writers. They are all, in the main, rather gloomy. In Australian literature which has not, as yet, become so "classic"—such as that which flowed week by week for many a year through the pages of THE BULLETIN—the national humor, gaiety and cheerful cynicism have found better expression. But the foreigner does not always see that, and Australian literature is usually judged by the authors above mentioned.

PART 3

Colonial Authors, Canons and Taste
KEN GELDER & RACHAEL WEAVER

Henry Kendall, 'About Some Men of Letters in Australia', *Australian Journal,* October 1869
116

A.M.T. (Arthur Maning Topp), 'The Australian Ladies' Annual', *Melbourne Review,* January 1879
118

H.G. Turner, 'Marcus Clarke, Australian Author and Journalist', *Once a Month,* 15 October 1885
120

'Homemade Haggardism', *Australasian Critic,* 1 January 1891
126

Mary Gaunt, 'The Three Miss Kings', *Australasian Critic,* 1 September 1891
127

Rolf Boldrewood, 'How I Began to Write', *Australian Town and Country Journal,* 1 October 1898
129

Mrs Charles Bright, 'Miss Louise Mack', *Cosmos,* 31 October 1895
133

Review of Henry Lawson's *While the Billy Boils,* 'The Bookshelf', *Block,* 29 August 1896
136

Henry Lawson, '"Pursuing Literature" in Australia', *Bulletin,* 21 January 1899
137

'A note from "Steele Rudd"', *Bulletin,* 27 May 1899
144

'An Australian Authoress', *Bookfellow,* 25 March 1899
144

A.H.A. (Arthur Henry Adams), 'Roderic Quinn. An Appreciation', *Australian Magazine,* 29 April 1899
146

'A Man Akin to Nature', *A.A.A.: All About Australians,* 31 October 1901
147

Review of Barbara Baynton's *Human Toll, Native Companion,* 30 April 1907
149

'Books Reviewed' (*Human Toll*), *Steele Rudd's Magazine,* May 1907
150

3

Colonial Authors, Canons and Taste
KEN GELDER & RACHAEL WEAVER

THE COLONIAL AUSTRALIAN JOURNALS PROVIDED venues for the establishment of often tightly-knit literary networks, featuring groups of writers who worked (and often socialised) together and who would write about each other, reviewing and promoting each other's books. Some of the longer-lasting journals would also try to sustain the literary careers of writers in their 'circle', offering regular payment for contributions; the serialisation of a novel, for example, or a series of articles on a particular topic. The writers associated with a journal helped to make it both distinctive and recognisable in terms of style, content and values. And they also determined what counted (and what didn't) in the ongoing project of establishing an appropriate literary canon. At one level, journals are all about literary ephemera, the kind of writing that lasts only a moment and then disappears. But at another level, they work hard to establish longer-term views of literary production, memorialising certain writers and speculating about their legacies. The colonial journals enabled writers to talk candidly about their influences, their aspirations, their fortunes and their misfortunes. As we look back on them now, we can say that the journals played a vital and constitutive role in structuring an Australian literary field: investing in it, evaluating it, gathering it together and then distributing it across the colonies and beyond.

The poet Henry Kendall was a remarkably active contributor to the colonial journals, including Marcus Clarke's *Colonial Monthly* and *Humbug* (September 1869 – January 1870); he was also one of the editors of *Touchstone*. We begin this section with Kendall's 1869 article 'About Some Men of Letters in Australia', published in the long-lasting *Australian Journal*. Here, Kendall wants to establish a 'foundational' poetic canon in New South Wales, turning back to Charles Harpur and Daniel Deniehy, both of whom had died just a few years before his essay was published. Past appreciations of these poets' work become important here, and he cites early commentaries by G. B. Barton – whose *The Poets and Prose Writers of New South Wales*, which discusses Harpur and Deniehy (as well as Kendall himself), was published in 1866 – and William Bede Dalley, a successful barrister and writer. But Kendall also wonders about posterity.

COLONIAL AUTHORS, CANONS AND TASTE

His comment about 'future Halliwells or Colliers' looking back at his own essay and using it as a historical resource refers to the well-known Shakespearean scholars and collectors, James Orchard Halliwell and John Payne Collier – the latter of whom, interestingly, was exposed as a literary forger. At the same time, Kendall simply wants to celebrate literary personalities, with his own recollections of Dalley (who would later defend Kendall on a charge of forgery in 1870) and the 'bohemian' circle of Sydney's *Punch* testifying to the vivacious cultural life of a colonial journal.

Marcus Clarke was also part of Kendall's literary circle, working with him during his time in Melbourne. H. G. Turner's 1885 article on Clarke for *Once a Month* (July 1884 – June 1886) is worth comparing to Kendall's article on Harpur and Deniehy. Published four years after Clarke's death and coming in the wake of an 1884 memorial collection of his writings, it enables Turner – and *Once a Month* – to commemorate Clarke as an 'Eminent Australasian'. Turner gives us a broad-based appreciation of Clarke's oeuvre, including his many contributions to the colonial journals. He perceptively describes Clarke as a *flaneur*; but this also troubles him, because it means that Clarke's work is spread too thinly for him to be truly canonical. The question of how substantial an author's work might be is one that comes to preoccupy the journals as they go about evaluating the worth of colonial writers. They think carefully about who is important and who isn't, as they attempt to develop and promote an appropriately distinctive canon of local literary writing. The different values, priorities, affiliations and prejudices that each journal brings to the task of defining an Australian literary canon, however, mean that this ambition was just as contested and variable then as it is today.

The work of colonial women writers was especially scrutinised in terms of whether or not it measured up to prevailing literary values. This section includes a review by Arthur Maning Topp – from the *Melbourne Review* – of the playwright and pastoralist Francis Hopkins's *Australian Ladies' Annual*, a collection of stories by colonial women writers. Topp likes the idea that colonial women are getting their work published, but he complains that the stories are 'wild and absurd'; what he wants instead is a serious literary realism that invests in local scenes and local characters, along the lines of European writers like Balzac and George Eliot. We also reproduce two reviews from the *Australasian Critic*. The colonial writer Mary Gaunt's review of Mrs. Cross's (Ada Cambridge's) *The Three Miss Kings* (1891) celebrates the realistic qualities of this romance novel and distinguishes it from 'the flood of rubbish purporting to be "New Australian Novels"'. In an important article about colonial writing, Susan Sheridan has argued that women's romance was eclipsed by a parochial investment in literature about rural Australian life – where '"The Bush" comes to signify nationalism, literary originality and, by implication, masculinity'.[1] This is certainly true at a general level, but there were all sorts of local variations and exceptions to this binary – which the journals could often tease out. The problem of 'literary originality', for example, could apply to some exclusively male genres as much as it could to women's romance. A lively review of James Francis Hogan's *The Lost Explorer* (1890) – titled 'Home-Made Haggardism' – complains that adventure writers such as Hogan, George Gilbert Aimé Murray (author of *Gobi or Shamo*) and the Canadian popular novelist James De Mille (the anonymous author of *A Strange Manuscript Found in a Copper Cylinder*) had more or less completely imitated the formula of bestselling British author H. Rider Haggard. The adventure novel in this instance couldn't be any more masculine, or any less original.

Two of the most important male writers in the colonial bush nationalist tradition are Rolf Boldrewood and Henry Lawson. Boldrewood's 'How I Began to Write', from the weekly *Australian Town and Country Journal*, looks back at his career, which saw him turn to writing after financial ruin as a squatter. Not long after the *Australian Town and Country Journal* was established, Boldrewood met its owner, Samuel Bennett, and began regularly to contribute bush sketches. Interestingly, the journal later refused to serialise Boldrewood's novel *Robbery Under Arms* (1889), rejecting it 'without comment';[2] it was serialised instead in another weekly, the *Sydney Mail* (July 1860 – December 1938). Boldrewood's article reminds us of the way a colonial writer's career was so closely tied both to the journals and to material circumstances, which were often difficult and unpredictable. Even so, his reputation by this time is secure enough for him to offer his blessing to local writers whose careers were just beginning, 'my Australian brothers and sisters of a newer generation'. Henry Lawson is quite a different case. A review of Lawson's *While the Billy Boils* (1896) in the weekly *Block* (August – September 1896) values the quality of the publication (by Angus and Robertson) and enjoys Frank Mahony's illustrations. Its account of Lawson's 'pathetic and squalid' realism might seem to suggest a criticism; but in fact, it is in sympathy with the cultural logics of bush nationalism, even though the journal itself is metropolitan. Lawson's account of his own career, however, is much less forgiving. His famous essay, '"Pursuing literature" in Australia', was published in the *Bulletin* in January 1899. Much more so than for Boldrewood, financial hardship bedevils Lawson and saturates his output, producing a kind of desperate, revolutionary and embittered sense of purpose. The *Bulletin* seems to be only too familiar with Lawson's discontentment: it introduces the article with the wry comment, 'Henry Lawson unburdens his soul'. Interestingly, Lawson's article reveals just how closely tied he was to the colonial weeklies, the *Bulletin* in particular, which gave him much-needed (although often meagre) financial support. His remarks to local writers whose careers were just beginning is utterly different to Boldrewood's: 'My advice to any young Australian writer whose talents have been recognised would be to go steerage, stow away, swim, and seek London, Yankeeland, or Timbuktoo – rather than stay in Australia'. But Lawson's jaundiced view wasn't always shared – or even taken seriously – by others. We also reproduce a brief reply to Lawson in the *Bulletin* from Steele Rudd, who would later go on establish his own literary journal: 'Poor Lawson, and that Hard-up Confession of his', he jokes, 'nearly made me sad'.

COLONIAL AUTHORS, CANONS AND TASTE

The careers of colonial women writers can be framed in quite different ways. Annie Bright's appreciation of Louise Mack in *Cosmos* begins with an account of Mack's early association with the *Bulletin* and notes her contributions to a number of other colonial journals and newspapers. Mack is claimed as a 'native-born genius', but the article is also tentative about how she will be remembered in the future: 'In these early days it is not possible to predict the place that Miss Mack is destined to fill in Australian literature'. Louise Mack and Ethel Turner were contemporaries at Sydney Girls' High School, where they edited rival school magazines. The article on Turner from A. G. Stephens's *Bookfellow* (January – May 1899) casts her as an industrious bestseller, a 'good woman-of-business'. As a much-loved writer of children's fiction, her reputation is secure; but as she notes herself at the end of the article, it isn't canonical. Even so, her financial success is enough for her to provide the article with a cheerful antidote to Lawson's pessimism: 'A total of 115,000 copies of the books conceived in one brain, written by one pen, sold in five years: this is the *real* pursuit of literature in Australia – and the attainment'.

The question of the early Australian literary canon was complicated not only by women writers, but also by a number of male writers who did not seem to bear out the values attributed to bush nationalism. Arthur Henry Adams was an influential journalist and critic who would later replace A. G. Stephens as editor of the *Bulletin*'s 'Red Page' and go on to edit the *Lone Hand*. He also contributed to Arthur Jose's *Australian Magazine*, a short-lived journal that – although it published Lawson and other bush nationalist writers – embraced a progressive, European aesthetic. Adams' article on Roderic Quinn defends the poet's ethereal, lyrical style which, he suggests, will be remembered 'when the more robust and riotous chorus of Australian singers is lost in the rattle of galloping hoofs'. In fact, Quinn is almost completely forgotten today. But he regularly contributed to the *Bulletin*, which published his collection *The Hidden Tide* in a limited edition in 1899. John le Gay Brereton also published his poetry in both the *Bulletin* and Jose's *Australian Magazine*. The Sydney-based journal *A.A.A.: All About Australians* began just after Federation and was deeply interested in both local writing and the fortunes of Australian writers overseas. The anonymously authored article on Brereton, 'A Man Akin to Nature', wonders what it means to be an erudite, university-educated Australian poet who, like Quinn, is published in limited editions. In one sense, Brereton is a quintessential poetic type, a 'Bohemian of the Bohemians'. To make him more canonical, the article puts him back into the bush nationalist tradition, 'with a swag on back and billy in hand'; but this was now a much healthier, more positive view of bush experience, distinguished from Lawson's despair and pessimism.

Perhaps surprisingly, the post-Federation backlash against despairing portraits of bush life played itself out most intensely in relation to a woman writer. We end this part with two short reviews of Barbara Baynton's 1907 novel, *Human Toll*. Bertram Stevens and E. J. Brady's *Native Companion* developed a feminine, metropolitan aesthetic built around a number of emerging women writers. For this journal, Baynton's novel is an admirable attempt to produce bush realism; but it exaggerates its wild descriptions to the point of 'pathology'. The review of *Human Toll* in *Steele Rudd's Magazine* is another backlash against Australian literary pessimism, giving a lively caricature of what the darker side of late colonial writing has become. The problem now is not so much about the need to establish canonical reputations. It is much more pragmatic: to do instead with how 'useful' literature should be, and how to respond to the kind of writing that seems to radically contradict the aspirations of an emergent nation.

1   Sheridan, 'Temper, Romantic; Bias, Offensively Feminine: Australian Women Writers and Literary Nationalism', p. 54.
2   de Serville, *Rolf Boldrewood: A Life*, p. 201.

COLONIAL AUTHORS, CANONS AND TASTE

HENRY KENDALL, 'ABOUT SOME MEN OF LETTERS IN AUSTRALIA'
Australian Journal
October 1869

The names I am about to mention are—allowing an exception or two—not likely to outlast the present generation; but as they belong to men who have attempted to lay the foundation-stone of Australian literature, this paper may be of some service to future Halliwells or Colliers in their search for particulars relating to our contemporary writers and contemporary writings.

New South Wales may fairly lay claim to be the birthplace of the most distinctive literature Australia has produced. She has no novelist equal to the brilliant author of "Long Odds;" no historian to be named beside the Rev. J.T. Woods; no journalists comparable to the leader-writers of the *Argus*; but she has given us two men at least—Charles Harpur and Daniel Henry Deniehy—whose writings, however ill-balanced they may be, have an indigenous flavour that we cannot discover in any other local literary result. Into the first-named author the spirit of the forest had passed; and the most of his verses contain syllables having no other origin than the fresh solitudes of his native country. It is a matter of surprise to me that this poet, whose recent melancholy death was made known to us by the *Argus* and *Colonial Monthly*, did not take with his countrymen to the degree that might have been reasonably expected. There is something, however, in the fact that his poetry is hardly of the popular kind. There is an austere tone in even the best of it—a want of softness and fluency that repels the ordinary reader. The cold neutral tints of the "Creek of the Four Graves," for instance, are apt to frighten those away who have not the stamina to dig for gold in ice.

Harpur is no meet minister for the young and full-blooded; for Passion, with him, is like a vestal virgin with her veil down. Nevertheless, the man was an authentic Levite—one whose face was well-known in the gates of the Temple named Beautiful. In other journals I have pointed out more fully the freshness of his songs, the distinct and dignified character of his blank verse, and the Australianism which runs through the whole body of his writings. These are filled with that sense of vastitude and spectral silence which the mind cannot help associating with our forest solitudes, and which Harpur, of all local writers, has been the most successful in describing.

I met Harpur for the first time about six months before his death. He was then suffering from the earlier effects of the disease which terminated so fatally; and he appeared to be the almost empty shell of his former self. He had the frame, and must have had in younger years, the strength of a giant. The man was a noble ruin—one that had been scorched and wasted, as it were, by fire. His face looked as if it had been through the hottest furnaces of sorrow; indeed, it reminded me of Coleridge's description of a countenance whose strange, almost terrible, weariness told of agonies that had been, and were, and were still to continue to be. Biography has nothing to offer darker than the story of this poet's life. It is so sad, so full of hopeless trouble from beginning to end, that I do not care to dwell upon it.

Harpur was anything but a brilliant table-talker; still he had a conversational power that always secured him willing listeners. One could not be ten minutes in his society without having cognisance of his genius. He had fitful flashes of enthusiasm, during which he never failed to give utterance to memorable things. There were times, however, when he was as dull as poor Goldsmith—times when, perhaps, the devil of despondency had got him by the throat.

Charles Harpur's earliest and most loyal admirer was the late Daniel Henry Deniehy. A review of the poet's lyrics was almost the last thing that came from poor Dan's brilliant pen. Of Deniehy, I can state but little from personal knowledge, and that little is not worth the recording. I fell in with him a year or so before his death, at a stage when his physical and mental powers were all but gone. Nevertheless there were some flashes of the old light in him even then. When the spirit came upon him, as it did on rare and fortunate occasions, his wasted face was want to become like the face of one glorified. I have been in his company in moments when his countenance, plain in repose, has caught a fire and a beauty that looked like phases of actual transfiguration. In this respect, he resembled the author of "Atlanta in Calydon," whose face—according to Lord Houghton—while under the influence of enthusiasm, seems to have an inspired light about it.

After the complete papers of Messrs. Barton and Dalley on Deniehy, I need not dwell upon his life or genius. That the latter is accredited throughout the colonies, and wherever he was known, there can be no doubt. He has been likened, by several of his reviewers, to De Quincey; and, to my thinking, his friends cannot very well find fault with the coupling together of the two names in criticism. Deniehy's high and holy love for the divine revelations of nature and art—a love which lasted through all the vicissitudes of a really hard life—was not surpassed by that of the great English opium-eater. A physical resemblance, a parallel experience with its tales of unappeased and pursuing grief; and a divine thirst for the authentic and remote sources of things—the fountain heads of truth and loveliness—must ensure for once and for ever the association of these men in our local records. They were both high priests at a sanctuary where love becomes religion, and the favoured few see nature face to face in her naked and immortal beauty.

Charles Harpur was buried on the windy banks of the Tuross River. It is a fit sepulchre for one whose songs were set to forest tunes. Deniehy lies under the barren red clay of the Bathurst cemetery; a spot antithetical in its character to Keats's resting place, the beauty of which, Shelley said, made him "feel almost in love with death." The site of a grave cannot be of much moment to a dead genius; but it seems to me that men like Deniehy, who worship nature all the days of their life, are entitled, in right of their love, to sleep their last sleep where the first, the most exalted, and the most harmonious manifestations of The Beautiful are made.

Probably the most brilliant of living Australians, is William Bede Dalley. Nature and fortune are combined in favour of this pet son of theirs. No native of these colonies has achieved more unequivocal success; and certainly none has better deserved it. The subject of this part of my paper is still a young man, but he is already a leading member of the Bar of New South Wales; and within the last ten years he has been a member of the local Parliament, as well as a Minister of the Crown. The latter office he vacated in a very short time; indeed his literary and social tastes hindered him from following up the promising political career that was opened to him. Mr. Dalley was editor and part proprietor of the Sydney *Freeman's Journal* in the palmiest days, when, notwithstanding its sectarian character, it had a great influence over the politics of the colony. No doubt this was owing to the vigour and brilliance of its editor's leading articles, some of which were worthy of Sydney Smith in his best vein. Since his retirement from the journal referred to, Mr. Dalley has almost, if not entirely, deserted the walks of political literature; but, from the day of its start up to the present date, he has been a constant and leading contributor to *Sydney Punch*. His papers—founded chiefly upon social subjects—are, perhaps, the most popular, and certainly the most genial and scholarly that have appeared there. Mr. Dalley writes with the grace and precision of Landor. His satire is in the delicate and keen manner of Peter Plymley. As to his touches of pathos—and there are many of these scattered through his unpretending pictures of social destitution—they are characterised by a realism that cannot be surpassed. The description, for instance, of a dinner given to the reclaimed arabs on board the nautical training ship "Vernon," is worthy of Thackeray.

Dalley is an embodiment of good nature and good humour. His face ripples, as it were, with animal spirits. Eminent for his social qualities, he is a lion wherever he goes. I do not know a man in his position who has more friends and fewer enemies. Whether at the Bar, or at the literary or social gathering, he is the same brilliant foremost feature. When I was a member of the *Sydney Punch* staff, the contributors used to meet once a week, over cognac and cigars, to think out a cartoon for the next issue, and to decide upon the character of the corresponding letterpress. On these occasions Dalley used to sit oozing with wit and humour. Some of the happiest hits made by *Punch* were originally suggested by him; and his knack of concocting subjects for happy topical cartoons in the dullest of times was something remarkable.

A.M.T. (ARTHUR MANING TOPP), 'THE AUSTRALIAN LADIES' ANNUAL'
Melbourne Review
January 1879

Mr Hopkins' idea of publishing an Annual composed entirely of contributions by ladies is not a bad one, as, if carried out yearly, it may enable us to see what kind and degree of literary talent there is in these colonies among the fairer half of our rising generation. The present volume is in many respects interesting, as showing some of the tendencies we may expect to find in the poetry and fiction contributed to our scanty colonial literature by the women of Australia. As may be supposed, both their merits and their defects are much the same as characterize the literary productions of their sex all the world over. Chief among their faults is one which is mainly attributable to their want of experience and knowledge of human nature—namely, the unreality and extravagance which pervade most of the tales in this volume. Instead of describing faithfully the incidents and characters of real life, the writers invent wild and absurd stories, and make men and women talk and act as they never do outside the walls of a lunatic asylum. We have been tempted to notice this fault, as a writer of a critical article, the last in the book, entitled "Heroines of Fiction," remarks that women, though less practical, are more imaginative than men. This is a great mistake. Women have far less imagination than men, and nothing shows it more strongly than their tendency to depart from truth and nature in their delineation of life and character. True imagination is based upon experience, and is shown far more in a faithful and life-like description than in the wildest and most fantastic departure from reality. Without this basis of knowledge and experience the imagination can produce little better than the visions of a dreamer, or the crude outpourings of children and savages.

"Tasma's" contribution, "The Rubria Ghost" is, as usual, clever and well written, though the story is not very pleasing. On the whole, we prefer this lady outside the field of fiction. She has not the story-telling faculty in a high degree, but undoubtedly possesses many of the qualities of a first-rate essayist. The thoughtfulness and frequent originality of her remarks and the elaboration of her style are peculiarly suited to the essay. Most of the tales in this volume, notably "The Three Troopers" and "The Empty House," are wild and improbable. They might suit the pages of the *London Journal* or *Family Herald*, but are scarcely adapted for the more cultivated tastes to whom the "Australian Ladies' Annual" may be presumed to appeal. The slight sketch—it can scarcely be called a story—"A Romance of Coma," is better and more promising, as the writer keeps on the plain pathway of everyday life, instead of wandering into the hopeless mazes of sensational incident and melodramatic character. We are sorry we cannot speak favourably of the verse contributed to this volume. It is mostly fairly and fluently written, but lacks the individuality and concentration which distinguishes poetry from mere verse. It suggests that the author has sat down with the intention of writing a poem, rather than that she had been impelled to write by being filled and inspired by a particular subject. If these remarks are severer than may seem called for by the slight and unpretending character of the contributions to this volume, they are made because it seems desirable to convey to the writers how their efforts impress an impartial reader. Criticism is always an ungrateful task, and on the present occasion it would be more pleasing to apply the language of indiscriminate praise. To do so, however, would be to pay but a poor compliment to the ladies who have so creditably stepped forward to assist in the production of Mr. Hopkins' Annual. In conclusion we would like to express a hope that in future issues the fair authors will draw a little more upon their actual experiences, and a little less upon their pure invention. Let them bear in mind that each one ought to have something to tell of her own life, and the people she had met, that would interest others; and if she had not, then it is hopeless to attempt high flights of imagination. The writers who have most successfully dealt with the extraordinary and improbable are those who have had the strongest grasp of the actual. Shakespeare was able to create Caliban and Titania because he could delineate Falstaff, and Bottom, and Polonius. The tendency of the age is to realism in fiction as well as in art generally, which simply means that people prefer what is natural to what is false and artificial. If, then, we Australians are to make any worthy contributions to the world's fictitious literature, it can only be by following in the track of the great modern realists—Balzac, Thackeray, George Eliot, Tourgenieff, and the most recent addition to their ranks, the excellent American writer, Henry James. These authors should be read and studied. But, after all, the source of the truest inspiration to the novelist is the great world of men and women. And surely, in a city like Melbourne, in a country like Australia, there are incidents occurring, and characters to be met with every day, that afford material ample and interesting enough, if artistically treated, to satisfy the craving of the most eager seeker after novelty in the wide field of fictitious literature.

H. G. TURNER, 'MARCUS CLARKE, AUSTRALIAN AUTHOR AND JOURNALIST'
Once a Month
15 October 1885

The untimely death of the gifted young litterateur, Marcus Clarke, in August 1881, evoked a wide-spread expression of sympathetic interest throughout Victoria. It found utterance in numerous articles in the daily and weekly press, eulogistic of his originality and talent, and it took the still more earnest form of a voluntary subscription towards providing for the immediate wants of his bereaved widow and young orphaned children. When it is borne in mind that a considerable portion of his literary work was veiled by journalistic anonymity, and that he was chiefly known to the reading public by one powerful romance, dealing with so terrible a subject as the horrors of convict life, the wide area from which these subscriptions flowed in was an unmistakable indication of the vigour of style and realism of treatment which has fascinated so many readers.

His literary career, and the circumstances which influenced it, were very fully dealt with in the *Melbourne Review* shortly after his death, and last year there was issued by subscription a memorial volume, containing a more detailed biography, and a judicious selection of extracts from his writings, giving an admirable idea of his surprising versatility, and ranging from the exquisite pathos of the story of "Pretty Dick" to the hilarious abandonment of the "Wail of the Waiter."

Though born in a London suburb, in 1846, Marcus Clarke may be claimed as essentially an Australian writer. He was but eighteen years of age when he arrived in Melbourne, and by the influence of his uncle, Sir Andrew Clarke, formerly Surveyor-General of Victoria, was placed on the staff of the Bank of Australasia. The dull routine of office life was too suggestive of Pegasus in harness, and though he secured the admiring regard of all his brother clerks, he utterly failed to acquire those methodical habits of patient application which might have made him equally esteemed by the management. Within a year he was relegated to the Ledcourt station in the Wimmera district, to gain what is euphoniously described as "Colonial Experience." Here, in the uninterrupted loneliness of bush life—for the selector's farms which now cover the whole district had not then been called into existence—he was thrown back upon his own resources, and passed much of his time in writing weird stories and quaint sketches of the hangers-on of pastoral life, the photographic accuracy of which is unsurpassed in Australian literature. His keen perception took in alike all the quiet beauties of the sombre forest primeval, with its ghostly suggestions; the dappled shade of the ferny gullies; the glaring stretch of hot dusty plains; the wealth of colour with which the rising and setting sun painted the rocky face of the rugged Grampians; the eccentric blasphemy of the half-drunken bullock driver; the authoritative swagger of the representative of King Cobb; the pretentious gentility of the bar loafer, who had "known better days;" and the score of half-developed fragments of humanity that made up the life of such a centre as "Bullock Town," by which name he has immortalized the post town of his district, known to the official mind as Glenorchy.

In the exquisite story of "Pretty Dick," and in the admirable introduction which he wrote for a volume of Gordon's poems, he has described the prevailing characteristics of the Australian bush and its effect upon the imagination, in a manner that leaves nothing for his successors. In the more humorous sketches, where he deals so realistically with the eccentric humankind that animated the deadly dullness of "Bullock Town," his style bears a strong resemblance to that of Bret Harte. In no sense, however, can he be said to have copied that entertaining writer, for the humour is essentially and radically Australian, and the characteristics delineated are as racy of our own soil, as the creations of his American prototype are distinctively Californian. "How the Circus came to Bullock Town," "Grumbler's Gully," "Poor Jo," and "An Idyll of Bullock Town," are all of them so redolent of a phase of life that has now quite passed away in Victoria, and are so clearly and sharply outlined, that they may be said to serve a similar purpose to that of a photograph of some whilom important building that the march of progress has ordained to destruction. The "Colonial Experience" which he gained on Mr. Holt's station did not appear to have been of sufficient value to warrant him in devoting his life to the then lucrative business of rearing sheep. He is very severe on the ordeal he went through, and in one of his sketches, entitled "In a Bush Hut," gives an amusingly exaggerated account of the lenten fare and general discomfort of his surroundings. When at length an opportunity offered of his returning to the more congenial atmosphere of metropolitan life he gladly availed himself of it, and, with a determination to embrace literature as a profession, commenced his chosen career in the office of the *Argus*. It is not necessary here to enter upon the particulars of his relations with the press. They were not altogether happy. Marcus Clarke was so essentially a Bohemian in his ideas, and a free lance by inclination, that he could not conform to editorial discipline any more than to banking restraints, and he seems to have wilfully ignored the recognized code of journalistic ethics. His pen was fluent, his style vivacious, his ideas quaintly original, and his productive power voluminous; but he could not work within defined limits, or restrict himself to one supervision. Thus it came about that his cynical and sometimes caustic comments on social matters flowed in turn from various and somewhat antagonistic sources. For a long time he gratified the readers of the *Australasian* by the lucubrations of "The Peripatetic Philosopher;" he wrote the "Buncle Correspondence" for the *Argus*; he became the weekly exponent of morals in the *Leader* over the signature of "Atticus;" and he contributed to the *Daily Telegraph* the series of papers entitled "The Wicked World." Of course, spread over so long a period, it may be assumed that these contributions are very unequal. The weekly column of this kind of pabulum that has to be furnished, whether the writer is in the humour or not, must, of necessity, be produced at times under adverse circumstances. It may be safely said, however, that they are quite equal to anything of the kind that the Victorian press has been able to command before or since, and they contain more humorous philosophy and epigrammatic point than the long drawn out series with which "G.A.S." had regaled the readers of the *Illustrated London News*. A selection from the "Peripatetic Philosopher's" sayings was published some years since by George Robertson, and has doubtless assisted to while away many an hour on a tedious journey or in a sick room. The humour may occasionally be a little forced, but there is not a line in the book to shock the most fastidious.

It has frequently been alleged that Marcus Clarke lacked the necessary industry to make the best use of his undoubted talents. The long list of his published writings, his extensive anonymous work as a journalist, and his official duties at the Public Library for nearly ten years, out of so brief a career, give an emphatic denial to this allegation. He wanted method in his industry, and he lacked close application to work out more enduring results, but he was foolishly prodigal of himself, and frittered away energies, that, carefully husbanded, would have made him a greater posthumous reputation. The whole of his literary work was accomplished within about fourteen years, and in that time he gave to the world two complete novels, upwards of thirty shorter tales and sketches, a most interesting volume of "Old Tales of a Young Country," and a "School History of Australia," about a dozen dramatic works, including original comedies, burlesques, and adaptations from the French, some pamphlets on topics of the day, and he once plunged recklessly into controversy with the Bishop of Melbourne, on the well-worn topic of the Christian Evidences. Concurrently with these indications of mental activity, it must be remembered that he had for some portion of the time daily journalistic work, and for the remainder the responsible duties of assistant librarian in Sir Redmond Barry's great foundation. He wrote many capable review articles on such divergent subjects as "The Comptist Philosophy," "Balzac's Place in Literature," and "Gustave Doré and Modern Art;" while his summing up of Lord Beaconsfield's contributions to the world of fiction is about the most outspoken and scathing criticism that had been written on that gilded genius. Finally, it must not be overlooked that for a long time he edited a colonial monthly magazine, which was a financial disaster, and, for a shorter period, a weekly comic paper called *Humbug*, to which he was a considerable contributor himself.

Had Marcus Clarke been better endowed with worldly wisdom, he would doubtless have concentrated his power on the production of a few books that would have shown him at his best, and ensured some more tangible return than can be secured by the lighter labours of the *flaneur*.

That he was capable of such work no one who has read "His Natural Life" can doubt. Terribly depressing, nay, almost revolting as is the burden of this most powerful romance, it masters the reader by its enthralling interest, and the care with which all its incidents are worked out, so that we seem to be spectators of the action. Moncure Conway mentioned that he first met with it on board an Atlantic steamer, and it so fascinated him that he could think of little else during the voyage. He declared that he could not think of leaving Australia until he had visited Port Arthur and the surrounding districts so graphically described. The story has been translated into several European languages, and has had an enormous circulation in America. It was originally published in instalments in the *Australian Journal* in Melbourne, but great changes were afterwards made, both in the opening chapters and in the *denouement*; and in its improved form it was published in the ordinary three volume style by Bentley, of London, with a dedication to Sir Charles Gavin Duffy, who had warmly expressed to the author his opinion of its great power. This edition, and the Australian one published by George

Robertson, are both long since out of print, and a new issue in a cheap form has just come into circulation with the prospect of a very large renewed demand.

The sustained effort, the tedious gathering of facts connected with the old convict *regime* of Port Arthur, and the labour attendant upon writing, and practically re-writing this book, superimposed upon his other work, did not altogether accord with Marcus Clarke's temperament. The humorous column of the *flaneur*, the fanciful story for the weekly journal, the quaintly philosophical social essay, or the graceful *vers de société*, flowed readily enough from his pen. He was permeated with Bohemianism, and liked, when "consuming the midnight oil," also to sacrifice at the Nicotian shrine. In a little Christmas volume called "'Twixt Shadow and Shine," we get an unreserved picture of the comrades with whom he solemnized the "High Jinks" of that rollicking fraternity.

[…] There was a curious twinkle in his eye when in the humorous vein, and a certain hesitancy of speech, almost amounting to a stammer, often gave unexpected point to a ludicrous story. To those with whom he had tastes in common he was a most genial companion and attractive talker, but he had strong dislikes, often upon most inadequate grounds. Unhappily, too, he possessed a fund of such caustic repartee, not always under discreet control, that he managed, over trivial differences, to alienate many who would gladly have remained his friends. To some extent this feeling was probably due to the sensitiveness engendered by a chronic condition of financial trouble. Having somewhat heedlessly entangled himself in the toils of the usurers, probably without any conception of what sixty per cent. really implied, he worked for years to pay the interest to his bond-masters, until it seemed that, after all his labour, there was only bread and cheese for himself, and no reduction in the weight of the oppressive incubus. In one of his humorous papers, entitled "On Business Men," he assumes to be rather proud of the rollicking Bohemianism that cannot vex itself about "the cursed lack of pence," and he enjoyed the luxury of borrowing without allowing his pleasure to be overclouded by anticipating the carking cares of repayment. In one sense he certainly did not value money, and nothing but the absolute inability to raise it could restrain him from a free expenditure, in which he was always ready to share his windfall with any less fortunate brother of the craft.

This Skimpolian proclivity was apparently incurable, and while during his bachelor days it brought only the semblance of trouble on himself, it became a very real and harassing anxiety when his responsibilities were increased by a wife and family. In extenuation of the happy-go-lucky system that led him into these financial entanglements it must be borne in mind that he was physically somewhat weak, with an apparently inherited tendency to self-indulgence, which was stimulated by his injudicious treatment in boyhood. In the early days of his literary career in Melbourne he met with a severe accident in the hunting field, being thrown and kicked in the head by his horse, sustaining a slight fracture of the skull and some injury to the brain. Though making a remarkable recovery he was liable to an occasional recurrence of the symptoms whenever overworked or mentally excited.

This inability to estimate at their proper value such qualities as frugality or prudential forethought was not removed by experience, and at last, like many before him, he came to look upon people who practised self-denial and acquired property with a certain feeling of dislike and contempt. Hence, though always humorously cynical, he became in later years bitterly caustic in his fanciful comments on the smug world, which makes up the majority of our fellow creatures, and his radicalism was very red.

He was married in 1869 to Marian, the second daughter of the late John Dunn, the well-known comedian. His widow is left with five orphans to make their way in the world, with little more than the reputation of their father, and the histrionic abilities of their mother, to help them on. Kindly offers have been made to Mrs. Clarke of the gratuitous education of some of her bright boys, and, as already mentioned, the general public contributed a subscription towards defraying urgent necessities. It is to be feared that no substantial returns will accrue to the family from any of the literary works of the lost parent, although from the interest recently exhibited there appears every prospect of a considerable sale of the new edition of his great romance.

"The Marcus Clarke Memorial Volume" will give the casual reader a good idea of the wide field covered by the writer's inventive faculty, and, lest the published price of half a guinea should restrict its circulation, it is well to point out that it was produced with a view to assist the fund being raised for the benefit of his family, hence the purchaser will have the satisfaction of assisting to that praiseworthy end, in addition to the entertainment derived from its perusal. To those who are unwilling to incur this outlay there is a small volume available, published by George Robertson, for one shilling, entitled "Holiday Peak and other Tales," which contains about a dozen sketches full of character, and redolent of Clarke's peculiar humour. It contains, *inter alia*, the beautiful story of "Pretty Dick," which few persons can read aloud without a break in the voice.

As a versifier Marcus Clarke was clever, and apt in facile rhyme, but the majority of his contributions must be described as capital imitations. In his young days he had been an omnivorous reader, and, with the aid of a fine memory, a good classical education, a correct ear, and keen perceptive faculties, he could fall back on his mental storehouse for the materials of a story or a lyric, and dress it in appropriate language with little effort. He was fond of pondering over psychological problems, and in the extraordinary papers called "Cannabis Indica," "Human Repetends," and, still more noticeably, in the uncanny narrative of "The Mystery of Major Molineux," published after his death, he ensures the breathless attention of his reader in a manner quite equal to the most powerful efforts of Edgar Allen Poe. It is not perhaps desirable to lengthen this notice by extracts from his published writings, because its object is to induce in the reader sufficient interest to ensure his reading some of the books, and judging for himself how far this estimate of what Australian literature owes to Marcus Clarke is justified.

COLONIAL AUTHORS, CANONS AND TASTE

'HOMEMADE HAGGARDISM'
Australasian Critic
1 January 1891

The Lost Explorer: An Australian Story. By J.F. Hogan. Edwards, Dunlop and Co., Sydney and Brisbane.

Before further remark, we may state that, in our opinion, this is a very creditable story of its kind. It is spiritedly written, full of life, and rather over-full than under-full of incident. To him who is not yet sated with the blend, recently so fashionable, of adventure-*cum*-weirdness, it can be confidently recommended. As there are, no doubt, many such persons, the book is likely to be popular, and, seeing that taste in novels is as various as taste in anything else, we have no intention of denying that any popularity it may gain will be merited. Quite certainly *The Lost Explorer* better deserves to amuse a novel-devouring public than four-fifths of contemporary works of fiction.

For ourselves, however, we frankly confess to being just a little weary of the framework on which Mr. Hogan has built. It was first constructed, we believe, for *King Solomon's Mines*, was utilised again in *She* and *Allan Quatermain*, was borrowed by Mr. Murray for the erection of *Gobi or Shamo*, and was, we have a right to suspect, begged, borrowed or stolen by someone unknown for his *M.S. Found in a Copper Cylinder*. There are those who deny to Mr. Rider Haggard himself the divine honours of originality. When examined, the charges seem somewhat captious. At most, they concern mere details, and though Mr. Haggard may have *trouvé son bien* in various places, *King Solomon's Mines* is in every sensible sense a distinctly original production. The architecture is that of a genius, no matter whence he procured sundry bricks. Upon a bored and critical public *King Solomon's Mines* came with the lively shock of a new sensation, and Mr. Haggard forthwith bounded into fame and success. Success means imitators, and Mr. Haggard's imitators are upon us, with Australians, Mr. Murray and Mr. Hogan, prominent among them. It would not have been amiss if under their titles they had printed "after Rider Haggard."

Imitating a new style of fiction might be likened to imitating novel cookery. The imitator may discover and compound the several ingredients of a dish, but the result may strangely lack the savour of the preparation by the original *chef*. Mr. Hogan, like Mr. Murray, has noted the ingredients of the romance a la Haggard, and has compounded them. The result will differently please different tastes. For ourselves, we confess to feeling a little cloyed with *toujours perdrix*.

The recipe for an essay in Haggardism is, we take it, something like this. Take one unexplored or barely explored country, one English gentleman of an adventurous turn of mind, one MS. or its equivalent relating to something in the unexplored country which makes him badly want to go there; add one or two English, Irish or Scottish gentlemen by way of seasoning, also one prodigiously powerful and impossibly-sagacious native; mix therewith one hair-erecting journey through dire and horrible regions; pour in one most particularly weird people, one malicious high-priest or his equivalent, one friendly faction, one most opportune civil war, half-a-dozen incredible Homeric feats; let the mixture simmer for half an hour, then add one comparatively easy return home. These, with slight experimental variations, are the ingredients in *She* and *Allan Quartermain*; they are mostly to be found in *Gobi or Shamo*; and Mr. Hogan has got them all in, as becomes an observant pupil in literary cookery. Nay, his conscientiousness goes further. In *King Solomon's Mines* a rough guiding-map (of which we get a facsimile) comes conveniently to hand; in *The Lost Explorer* there comes conveniently to hand a rough guiding-map (of which we get a facsimile). In *Allan Quatermain* the party is attacked by swarms of land-crabs; in *The Lost Explorer* the party is attacked by swarms of snakes. We need not take the *dramatis personae* and point out the equations, Uralla the blackfellow, Umslopagas the Zulu, and so forth. He who runs may read the several analogues.

We do not propose to tell Mr. Hogan's story here. It is concerned with a mysterious volcanic region and a no less mysterious volcanic people in Central Australia, where a lost explorer, Louvain (=Leichardt) [sic], who has been a prisoner for a score of years, is ultimately discovered and rescued by his son. There is an abundance of persons on the boards, and plenty of stage-effects. The descriptions are good, and often eloquent, though the style is for the most part not one of distinction, and the author displays a tendency to lapse into that kind of journalese, of which "he returned to the combat with such renewed strength, vigour, agility and determination that his redoubtable antagonist was quite taken aback," may be taken as a mild specimen. In working out the narrative, Mr. Hogan seems to have made a curious slip. Though Arthur Louvain is obliged to use Uralla and Wonga as interpreters in communicating with the natives, he is none the less able on occasion to understand anything he overhears said in Maluan.

We have spoken candidly, but, we hope, not unkindly of this Australian production. If we ask Mr. Hogan for more originality, it is because we think it probable that he has more originality to give.

MARY GAUNT, 'THE THREE MISS KINGS'
Australasian Critic
1 September 1891

The Three Miss Kings. By Mrs. Cross (Ada Cambridge). London: Heinemann. Melbourne: Melville, Mullan & Slade.

COLONIAL AUTHORS, CANONS AND TASTE

The three Miss Kings are three charming young ladies, in whom we take the deepest interest from the moment we open the book, which has for its title their name. Elizabeth, tall and stately, whom it has never occurred to anyone to call by any pet diminutive; Patty, outspoken, warm-hearted and incautious; and Eleanor, the most shadowy of the three, lovable and winning, but shallow—are all well drawn. They are nice, good girls—natural girls—whom it can only do girls in real life, and men, too, for that matter, good to read about.

The story is of three unknown, lonely girls, who have not a relation in the world, and for friends in the beginning only an old lawyer and his son. Brought up in a quiet Australian seaport, they are as ignorant of the world and the world's ways as it is possible for well-read, well-educated young women to be. On the death of their father, they, on finding themselves possessed of three hundred a year of their own, come to Melbourne as a first step towards that world which they have read about and are determined to see. And here begins their story, or perhaps we should write stories, for each of the Miss Kings has a lover of her own, and her anxieties and troubles thereon interest us greatly.

Elizabeth meets her fate in a crowd on the day of the opening of the first exhibition, and we are grateful to Mrs. Cross for making no mystery of it, and telling us there and then that Kingscote Yelverton is her fate, and relieving our minds of any anxiety on that score, for this eldest Miss King is a conscientious young woman, and having been brought up in the straightest sect of the Pharisees, is horrified at discovering that her lover has strayed from the fold, and she is more than half-minded, though she realises his goodness, to give him up for conscience sake. Possibly it would be hardly fair to tell here the way in which her scruples are suddenly overcome; but her meeting with her lover in the German picture gallery of the Exhibition—"as pleasant and convenient a rendezvous," says Mrs. Cross, "as lovers could desire"—is very prettily told; and if these two made up their minds on the subject of matrimony rather promptly, it only seems the natural outcome of the rest of the story.

Patty is far and away the most lovable of the three heroines. She falls in love "right off" with the old lawyer's son, Paul Brion, how, is not exactly explained, for since they lived in lodgings alone, Paul Brion, with a prudishness, which with all due deference to the author, we think overdrawn, refused to visit them; still she did fall in love. Being only a cold-blooded reviewer we don't understand the process ourselves, but we have read somewhere that it doesn't take long. Very heartily and naturally Miss Patty falls in love too, and the heartburnings and misunderstandings that arise therefrom are thoroughly well told. Patty herself is so delightful from the moment she cut Paul at the Cup, because she had been told he admired and—oh, worst of sins!—dangled after a woman of whom she entirely disapproved, till she apologised and made it up with him in the most unconventional of fashions in his own rooms. It is good, we feel, that Patty should have her heart's desire. She desired it so honestly and truly, and yet is so reserved and maidenly withal. There is a most excellent description of the three girls' feelings after their first ball from which their kind patroness—do lonely girls in real life ever come across a Mrs. Duff Scott we wonder—has gone home thoroughly well pleased with her girls and the attention they have received. Yet each of the girls, though she has put a fair face on it to the world, retires to bed and cries her heart out because her own particular affairs have gone so utterly wrong. Elizabeth has discovered that the faith of the man that she loves is not as her faith; Patty remembers that though she is a social success, Paul Brion is not in her charmed circle, is out of her life and is likely to remain out of it, and what is the worth of any success when the one thing needful is beyond her reach? and Eleanor cries herself to sleep from wounded vanity, simply because the man she had thought in love with her and whom she has made up her mind to accept, not because she cares for him, but because he is rich and can give her the position and wealth her shallow little soul hankers after, has thrown her over for a richer girl. There are a good many Eleanors in this world, we fancy, and we feel that the little snub in her successful career is good for her, but we are much more in sympathy with Patty who can stand her trouble no longer and comes in and sobs out her sorrows in her sister's arms because "when I have had just one good cry perhaps I shall get on better."

Later on it is Elizabeth who turns to Patty for advice and sympathy in her perplexity, and she receives it in characteristic fashion from that young lady, "Now if it were my own case, I should take the man I loved, no matter what he was, if he would take me."

Now-a-days when such a flood of rubbish purporting to be "new Australian Novels" is being launched on a long-suffering people, it is refreshing to come across so thoroughly a good book as this. We might have given a few extracts, but the difficulty would have been to know where to stop. We can only recommend our readers, those of them who read novels, to read it, and indeed those of them who do not might make an exception in favour of *The Three Miss Kings*.

ROLF BOLDREWOOD, 'HOW I BEGAN TO WRITE'
Australian Town and Country Journal
1 October 1898

For publication I mean. Having the pen of a ready writer, by inheritance, I dashed off occasional onslaughts in the journals of the day, chiefly in defence of the divine right of kings (pastoral ones); I had assailed incoherent democrats, who perversely denied that Australia was created chiefly for the sustenance of sheep and cattle, and the aggrandisement of those heroic individuals who first explored and then exploited the waste lands of the Crown. The school of political belief of [sic] which I belonged derided agriculture, and was subsequently committed to a scheme for the formation of the Riverina into a purely pastoral kingdom of the colony. A petition embodying a statement to the effect that it was wholly unfitted for the sustenance of a population dependent upon agriculture was forwarded to the Secretary for the Colonies, who very properly disregarded it. The petitioners could not then foresee the stacking of 20,000 bags of wheat, holding four bushels each, awaiting railway transit at one of the farming centres of this barren region in the year 1895. Allied facts caused me to reconsider my very pronounced opinions, and, perhaps, led others to question the accuracy of theirs. My deliverances in the journals of the period occurred in the forties and fifties of the century, and gradually subsided.

I was battling with the season of 1865 on a station lately purchased, at no great distance from the flourishing town of Narrandera, then consisting of two hotels, a small store, and a large graveyard, when an uncertain-tempered young horse kicked me on the ankle with such force and accuracy that I thought the bone was broken. I had ridden at daylight to count a flock of sheep, and could scarcely crawl back to the huts without assistance, such was the agony. I sat down on the frosted ground, and pulled off my boot, knowing how the leg would swell. Curiously the thirst of the wounded soldier immediately attacked me. My room in the slab hut, preceding the brick cottage then in course of erection, was, to use Mr. Swiveller's description, "an airy and well-ventilated apartment." It contained, in addition to joint stools, a solid table, upon which my simple meals of chops, damper, and tea were displayed three times a day by a shepherd's wife, an elderly person of varied and sensational experiences.

I may mention that the great Riverina region was as yet in its unfenced, more or less Arcadian stage, the flocks being "shepherded" (expressive Australian verb, since enlarged as to meaning), and duly folded or camped at night. Something of Mrs. Reagan's independence and advanced tone of thought may be gathered from the following dialogue, which I overheard:

Shady township individual—"Your man shot my dorg t'other night. What d'yer do that fer?"

Mrs. Reagan—"Cause we caught him among the sheep, and we'd a shot you if you'd bin in the same place."

Township individual—"You seem rather hot coffee, missus! I've 'arf a mind to pull your boss next court day for the valley of the dorg."

Mrs. Reagan—"You'd better clear out and do it then. The P.M.'s a comin' from Wagga on Friday, and he'll give you three months, like as not. Ask the pleece for yer character."

Township individual—"D—n you and the pleece, too! A pore man gets no show between the traps and squatters in this bloomin' country. Wish I'd never seen it."

This was by way of interlude, serving to relieve the monotony of the situation. I could eat, drink, smoke, and sleep. But my injured leg—worse than broken—I could not put to the ground. Neither had I company of any kind nor description, save that of old Jack and Mrs. Reagan, for a whole month. So, casting about for occupation, I bethought myself that I might write something for an English magazine. The subject I pitched upon was a description of a kangaroo drive or battue, such as were then common in Western Victoria, which I had lately quitted. The kangaroo had become so numerous that some were eating the squatters out of house and home. Something had to be done; so they were driven into yards in great numbers and killed. This severe mode of dealing with the too prolific marsupial in whole battalions, I judged correctly, would be among the "things not generally known" to the British public.

I sat down and wrote a twelve-page article describing a grand muster for the purpose at a station about twenty miles from Port Fairy, and seven miles from my own place, Squattlesea Mere.

The first time I went to Melbourne I posted it, with the aid of my good friend, the late Mr. Mullen, to the editor of the "Cornhill Magazine," and thought no more about the matter. A few days afterwards my neighbour, Adam McNeill, of North Yanko, hearing of my invalid state, rode over, and carried me off to his hospitable home. I had to be lifted on my horse, but after a month's rest and recreation was well enough to return to my pastoral duties. I was lame, however, for quite a year afterwards, and narrowly escaped injuring the other ankle, which began to show signs of over-work.

Just about the time of my full recovery, I received a new "Cornhill Magazine" and a business-like note from Messrs. Smith and Elder, forwarding a draft, which added to the honor and glory of seeing my article flourishing in a first class English magazine, afforded me much joy and satisfaction. The English review notices were also cheering. I thereupon dashed off a second sketch, entitled "Shearing in Riverina," which I dispatched to the same address. The striking presentment of seventy shearers, in a big Riverina shed, all going their hardest, was a novelty also to the British Public.

> The constant clash that the shear-blades make
> When the fastest shearers are making play,

As Mr. Barton Paterson ("Banjo") has it, in "The Two Devines," more than twenty years later, challenge attention. This was accepted. I received a cheque in due course. This came at a time when such remittances commenced to have more interest for me than had been the case for many years past.

The station was sold in the adverse pastoral period of '68–'69, through drought, debt, financial "dismalness of sorts," but that is another story. Christmas time found me in Sydney, where it straightaway began to rain with unreasonable violence and persistency, (as I thought), now it would do me no good; never left off, in fact, for five years. The which, in plenteousness of pasture, and high prices for wool and stock, were the most fortunate seasons for squatters since the "fifties," with their accompanying goldfields prosperity.

COLONIAL AUTHORS, CANONS AND TASTE

The last station having been sold, there was no chance of repairing hard fortune by pastoral investment. "Finis poloniae." During my temporary sojourn in Sydney, I fell across a friend, to whom, in my palmy days, I had rendered a service. He suggested that I might turn to profitable use a facile pen, and some gift of observation. My friend, who had filled various parts in the drama of life, some of them not undistinguished, was now a professional journalist. He offered to introduce me to his chief (the late Mr. Samuel Bennett), proprietor of the "Town and Country Journal," and did so. That gentleman, whom I shall always remember gratefully for his kind and sensible advice, gave me a commission for certain sketches of bush life, a series of which appeared from time to time. Shortly afterwards, I wrote my first tale, "The Fencing of Wandaroona," succeeding which, the "Squatter's Dream" and others, since published in England, appeared in the weekly paper referred to. Thus launched upon the "wide, the fresh, the ever free" ocean of fiction, I continued to make voyages and excursions thereon, mostly profitable, as it turned out. Varied colonial experience, the area of which became enlarged when I was appointed a police magistrate and goldfields commissioner in 1871, supplied types and incidents. This position I filled for nearly twenty-five years.

Although I had, particularly in the early days of my goldfields duties, a sufficiency of hard and anxious work, entailing serious responsibility, I never relinquished the habit of daily writing and story weaving. Nor did I, on that account, neglect my duties, I can fearlessly aver. The constant journeying, riding, and riding over a wide district, agreed with my open air habitudes. The method of composition which I employed, though regular, was not fatiguing, and suited a somewhat desultory turn of mind. I arranged for a tale, by sending the first two or three chapters to the editor, and mentioning that it would last a twelvemonth, more or less. Then the matter was settled. I had but to post the weekly packet, and my mind was at ease. I was rarely more than one or two chapters ahead of the printer; yet, in twenty years, I was only once late with my instalment, which had to go by sea, from another colony. Every author has his own way of writing, and this was mine. I never but once completed a story before it was published. And on that occasion it was—sad to say—declined by the editor. Not in New South Wales, however, and as it has since appeared in England, it did not greatly signify.

In this fashion, "Robbery Under Arms" was written for the "Sydney Mail," having been refused by other editors. It has been successful; and, though I say it, there are few countries where the English language is spoken, in which it has not been read. I was always satisfied by the honorarium which my stories yielded. It made a distinct addition to my income, all of which, as a pater-familias, was needed. I looked forward, however, to making a hit some day, and with the publication of "Robbery Under Arms" in England, that day arrived. Other books followed, which have had a gratifying measure of acceptance by the English-speaking public at home and abroad.

As a prophet, I have not been "without honor in my own country." My Australian countrymen have supported me nobly, which I take as an especial compliment, and expression of confidence, to the effect that, as to Australian matters, I knew what I was writing about.

In all my relations with editors, I am free to confess that I have always been treated honourably. I have had few discouragements to complain of, or disappointments, though not without occasional rubs and remonstrances from reviewers for carelessness, to which, to a certain extent, I plead guilty. In extenuation, I may state that I have "hardly ever" had the opportunity of correcting my proofs. As to the attainment of literary success, as to which I often receive inquiries, as also how to secure a publisher, I have always given one answer. Try the Australian weekly papers, if you have any gift of expression, until one of them takes you up. After that the path is more easy. Then perseverance and practice will ordinarily discover the path which leads to success.

A natural turn for writing is necessary, perhaps indispensable. Practice does much, but the novelist, like the poet, is chiefly "born not made." Even in the case of hunters and steeplechasers, the expression "a natural jumper" is common among travellers. A habit of noting, almost unconsciously, manner, bearing, dialect, tricks of expression, among all sorts and conditions of men, provides "situations." Experience, too, of varied scenes and societies is a great aid. Imagination does much to enlarge and embellish the lay figure, to deepen the shades, and heighten the colours of the picture; but it will not do everything. There should be experience of that most ancient conflict between the powers of Good and Evil, before the battle of life can be pictorially described. I am proud to note among my Australian brothers and sisters, of a newer generation, many promising, even brilliant performances in prose and verse. They have my sincerest sympathy, and I feel no doubt as to their gaining in the future, a large measure of acknowledged success.

MRS CHARLES BRIGHT, 'MISS LOUISE MACK'
Cosmos
31 October 1895

So many letters have reached me from literary people in Sydney and the other colonies, asking for information concerning the writer of the sketches and poems that have appeared in *Cosmos* from the pen of Miss Louise Mack, that a portrait and sketch of this promising young writer's career seems the most satisfactory way of answering the diverse questions addressed to me. It is all the more appropriate, as in this issue of *Cosmos* appears the first instalment of a serial from her pen, written expressly for the magazine, entitled "In an Australian City." The short sketches, "Compensation," "To-morrow and To-morrow and To-morrow," "A Study in Invitations," and "A Lyric Evening," are mere fragments, but the widespread interest they have aroused have led to the more speedy development of the young writer's artistic literary gifts; and several finished works are now in the publishers' hands. Experienced writers have remarked on the artistic touches and "insight" displayed in Miss Mack's verse and prose alike, and it is to the encouragement of one of the soundest, if most austere, critics in the colonies, the editor of *The Bulletin*, that Miss Mack delights to attribute her first success. Nothing of the Brummagem order passes that lynx-eyed censor, but anything good is sure of quick and hearty recognition, as many a prominent writer in Australia can testify.

It was not until about three years ago that Miss Mack had any serious intentions of devoting herself exclusively to literature. She had written verses almost from the time she could remember, and when a pupil at the Sydney Girl's High School had edited a paper, "The Girl's High School Gazette." Miss Ethel Turner was a pupil at the High School at the same time, and became editor of a rival paper, "The Iris," the schoolgirls dividing their favours between the two. This was clear evidence of the bent of mind of the two budding writers. Australia, however, has an exclusive claim to Miss Mack, as she, unlike the author of "Seven Little Australians," who is of English birth, was born at Hobart over twenty years ago, where her father, the late Rev. Hans Mack, was then stationed as Wesleyan minister. Miss Mack is, therefore, a native-born genius, and *Cosmos*, being exclusively Australian, is glad to welcome this young literary aspirant.

"I have always loved the feel of a pen in my hand," says Miss Mack, when telling me her brief experience, "but it had not occurred to me that I might write, except to gratify or relieve a passing mood, until a critical friend advised me, about three years ago, to send two sets of verses I had just written to the *Bulletin*. Everyone has red-letter days in his or her experience, and one of mine is a memorable morning when the postman brought a letter addressed to Mr. L. Mack, asking that gentleman to call on the editor of the *Bulletin*."

Miss Mack had signed her verses, "Soul Flight," "M.L. Mack," and as the first line runs:

"I am a man long smil'd upon by Fate,"

and the poem has a certain virile strength about it, Mr. Archibald may be excused for thinking a man was the author. The lines are given in full in another part of this issue, so that readers may judge for themselves of their literary merit. Business is not Miss Mack's forte, and six times the young author went in search of the *Bulletin* office, and missed it, but the lucky seventh time, she says, "I found myself walking up the stairs with a most violently beating heart, that nearly suffocated me. At last I was in the presence of the editor and announced myself to him." He seemed slightly surprised to see a blue-eyed girl before him, and told the trembling poetess that "he thought it was a man who had written 'Soul Flight'." "In the kindest manner imaginable,"

Miss Mack continues, "he discussed the verses with me, and advised me about my writing, and, shortly afterwards, 'Soul Flight,' my first paid-for poem, appeared in the columns of the *Bulletin*, under the signature of M.L.M. Stimulated by this success, I wrote a short story, 'The Curse of Smith, Senior,' and sent this after 'Soul Flight,' and it was the encouraging manner in which this story was editorially accepted that determined me finally to adopt literature as a profession. Short stories and verses seemed to be the form of literature in which my pen was most at home, and I wrote these for *Cassell's Magazine* and nearly all the Sydney papers, including the *Bulletin, Mail, Town and Country Journal, Illustrated Sydney News, Daily Telegraph, Sunday Times* and others. One day, as I was in the train, there came into my head, in a most irrelevant way, the title of a story, 'The World is Round,' and at the same time the outlines of a plot seemed to come ready made from my brain. I did not begin to write it for some months, and then worked very slowly; it was, in fact, a year from the time it was commenced until I had finished it. About four months ago I sent it to Fisher Unwin and Co. the London publishers, who had already received a volume of collected stories and verse, and one longer story, and by return of post, received news of its prompt acceptance, and proposals for all my future work. The letter dropped right from my hands with incredulous delight. Here, at last, was the fulfilment of my waking dreams, and for days I walked as on enchanted ground." This London critic wrote: "your story is a brilliant little study of two men and two women, sparkling and witty, and told in a graphic style." The other story, "God's Girl," is in the same publisher's hands. Besides these completed works, Miss Mack is collaborating, with Miss Ethel Turner, [on] an "Australian Fairy Book"—the first of its kind—in which aboriginal myths and stories, founded on Australian natural objects, will form an attractive volume. But the last written, "The World is Round," may be described as Miss Mack's "first book."

It is always a wonder to outsiders how writers, some of world-wide fame, manage to produce their *chef d'oeuvres* in the midst of unpromising surroundings. Charlotte Bronte is a perpetual illustration of the fact. A prominent American wrote of the author of "Jane Eyre," some years ago: "The world bends with infinite tenderness over the story of that woman, who had no beauty and no blessing, out on the Yorkshire moors. We pity her for the dismal, scranny school of her childhood, where food for the outer and the inner life was alike hardy and crusty, and mouldy ... We watch her a woman, while yet a child—a woman because other little children, still more helpless, are motherless, and can find no other nature large enough to take them in and understand them and adopt them ... and then, at last, a woman grown, walking over great stretches of wild country to go back and bear her burden of a bare, rugged life."

Although Miss Mack's life and genius may bear no comparison with that of the gifted Charlotte Bronte, it is wonderful how—the central figure of a family of thirteen—she has found time and opportunity to develop her literary bent. She is the seventh child, the first daughter to gladden the eyes of her parents after six little boys had come to share the frugal life of a Wesleyan parsonage. Now there are eight brothers and five sisters, and a family tradition tells of the delight of the six little brothers who stood beside the mother's bed waiting to be shown the little sister who had at last put in an appearance. Family life is an ever-present teacher to receptive minds, and Miss Mack owes much of her development to her mother's literary tastes, and the varied training that an intellectual father can bestow on his children.

In these early days it is not possible to predict the place that Miss Mack is destined to fill in Australian literature. At present she shines chiefly in dialogue, and a quaint, satirical style, peculiarly noticeable in sketches like "A Study in Invitations." In time she may develop a faculty for descriptive writing, which will supply the only element now lacking to ensure her high rank among the popular novelists of the day.

REVIEW OF HENRY LAWSON'S *WHILE THE BILLY BOILS*, 'THE BOOKSHELF'
Block
29 August 1896

"But he didn't see the dirty blind wall, nor the dingy window; nor the skimpy little bed, nor the greasy washstand; he saw the dark-blue ridges in the sunlight, the grassy flats and sidings, the creek with clumps of sheoak here and there, the course of the willow-fringed river below, the distant peaks and ranges fading away into a lighter azure, the granite ridge in the middle distance, and the rocky rises, the stringy bark and the apple-tree flats, the scrubs, and the sunlit plains—and all I could see it, too, plainer than I ever did."

"'You thundering jumped-up crawlers! If you don't (something) well part up, I'll take your swags and (something) well kick your gory pants so's you won't be able to sit down for a month—or stand up either!'"

Both these extracts are from Lawson in his last book *While the Billy Boils*, published and forwarded to us by Messrs. Angus & Robertson, Sydney. And both are characteristic examples of the matter, pathetic and squalid, more often the latter, that mark the fifty-two pen-and-ink photographs that make up the volume. Personally I prefer the former style, and think Lawson at his best in such pieces as *Going Blind* and *Drifted Back*. But, for all that, the force and vigour and absence of all restraint, and above all, their absolute and realistic truth to nature, human and otherwise, will, I have no doubt, appeal eloquently to a large circle of readers on behalf of the rest. Drovers, rousabouts, shearers, swagmen, selectors, and diggers, their language, and their manners, and their want of them, and their customs and their slang, are all hit off with that rare microscopic power of observation that Lawson shows himself possessed of in a very

eminent degree. Nor could any man have written these brief, and in many cases fragmentary and abrupt sketches, without having been through the mill himself. And in this, of course, from a literary point of view, lies their value. Above all, Lawson is a descriptive writer with an eye for details that nothing escapes; and that these details are mostly squalid and unconventional ones is not his fault. Other writers, whose lot was not cast amongst such material, and whose fame is wide, have gone in search of and revelled in it. And through all his prose, as well as his poems, runs that half-hearted sort of pessimism; and that half-declared revolt against the pain of the world, so characteristic of the man himself. The language of his vigorous and live people is certainly, at times, frequent and free. But if a man is to be photographed, you must put up with all his features. A mutilated picture is useless. And when you write of the bush—as of any other place—and its inhabitants, you *must* reproduce them in their entirety, or you lose your effect and the value of your work. Prunes and prisms have no room in such stuff as Lawson gives us—strong, raucous, biting stuff, reminiscent of the shearers' and the rousabouts' huts; the bush shanty; the coasting steamer's steerage. His men are men, not bloodless shadows; and their language is redolent of blasphemy, their breath of rum. Men—and women too—he puts them on his pages as he found them, lived with them, worked with them. Whether they were worth the trouble of limning, their more fortunate brethren will presently let us know. To some, human nature is always worth reproducing, in whatever guise it comes to the artist; and the clearer you make your picture, slurring nothing, extenuating nothing, so much the better. Other people think quite otherwise. These may perhaps as well leave *While the Billy Boils* alone. Lawson does not write for the unco guid. The letterpress is varied by eight of Mahony's drawings; and the style of the book, inside and out, is a credit to the publishers.

HENRY LAWSON, ' "PURSUING LITERATURE" IN AUSTRALIA'
Bulletin
21 January 1899

Henry Lawson unburdens his soul—

In the first fifteen years of my life I saw the last of the Roaring Days on the Gulgong goldfield, N.S.W. I remember the rush as a boy might his first and only pantomime. "On our selection" I tailed cows amongst the deserted shafts in the gullies of a dreary old field that was abandoned ere Gulgong "broke out." I grubbed, ring-barked, and ploughed in the scratchy sort of way common to many "native-born" selectors round there; helped fight pleuro and drought; and worked on building contracts with "Dad," who was a carpenter. Saw selectors slaving their lives away in dusty holes amongst the barren ridges: saw one or two carried home, in the end, on a sheet of bark; the old men worked till they died. Saw how the gaunt selectors' wives lived and toiled. Saw elder sons stoop-shouldered old men at 30. Noted, in dusty patches in the scrubs, the pile of chimney-stones, a blue-gum slab or two, and the remains of the fence—the ultimate result of 10 years', 15 years', and 20 years' hard, hopeless graft by strong men who died like broken-down bullocks, further out. And all the years miles and miles of rich black soil flats and chocolate slopes lay idle, because of old-time grants, or because the country carried sheep—for the sake of an extra bale of wool and an unknown absentee. I watched old fossickers and farmers reading "Progress and Poverty" earnestly and arguing over it on Sunday afternoons. And I wished that I could write.

The droughts of the early Eighties, coming with the pleuro, the rabbits, crop and vine diseases and other troubles, burst a lot of us round there. Some old selectors did pick-and-shovel work in the city, or drove drays, while their wives took in washing. I worked for sub-contractors in coach factories, painting; tramped the cities in search of work; saw the haggard little group in front of the board outside the HERALD office at 4 o'clock in the morning, striking matches to run down the "Wanted" columns; saw the slums and the poor—and wished that I could write, or paint.

I heard Tommy Walker, and Collins, and the rest of 'em, and, of course, a host of Yankee free-thought and socialistic lectures. I wore the green in fancy, gathered at the rising of the moon, charged for the fair land of Poland, and dreamed of dying on the barricades to the roar of the "Marseillaise"—for the young Australian republic. Then came the unexpected and inexplicable outburst of popular feeling (or madness)—called then the Republican riots—in '87, when the Sydney crowd carried a disloyal amendment on the Queen's Jubilee, and cheered at the Town Hall for an "Australian Republic." And I had to write then—or burst. THE BULLETIN saved me from bursting.

"Youth: the first four lines are the best. Try again." Answers to Correspondents, BULLETIN, June 18, 1887.

The first four lines were printed. I haven't felt so excited over a thing since. The fire blazed too fiercely to last; but it lasted for ten years.

"H.L.; will publish your "Song of the Republic."

I was up at daylight every publishing morning and down to the earliest news-agent's, but "The Song of the Republic" was held over for a special occasion—Eight Hours' Day (Oct., 1887). Democracy and Unionism were alive those times, and Eight Hours' Day was called "The Carnival of Labour."

I was a coach-painter's improver at 5s. per day, with regular work, and only needed to practice "lining," or tracing, to be master of the trade. I helped write, machine, and publish a flyblister called *The Republican*. I wrote some versus [sic] called "The Song of the Outcasts," or, "The Army of the Rear;" also "Golden Gully," "The Wreck of the Derry Castle," and one or two others (rejected.) I took the parcel to the old BULLETIN office, in Pitt-street, after dusk, intending to slip it surreptitiously into the letter-box; but the charwoman, broom in hand, opened the door suddenly, and gave me a start. I thrust the screed into her hands and made off.

In Dec., '87, I was coach-painting at Windsor, Melb., for 6s. a day, when I got *my* first Xmas BULLETIN. I tore it open, tremblingly; glanced through it, to make sure I was there, and hid it in a hearse I was "rubbing down"—for the boss was a fierce Wesleyan. I rubbed hard with the pumice-stone till my heart didn't thump so much, and I felt calmer. I stole glances, behind the hearse, at "Golden Gully" and "The Wreck of the Derry Castle," and the kindly editorial note to the effect that I was a mere lad (aged 19), earning a living, under difficulties, at house-painting, and that my education was as yet unfinished (N.B.—I couldn't spell), and that my talent spoke for itself in the following poem. I was in print, and in the Xmas number of a journal I had worshipped, and devoured every inch of, for years. I felt strong and proud enough to clean pigstyes [sic], if need be, for a living, for the rest of my natural life—provided THE BULLETIN went on publishing the poetry. Varnish an old hearse hard as flint; but I made a good job of that one, and a quick job—for I "rubbed down" on air if I didn't walk on it. It was the shortest eight hours' graft I ever did.

When house-painting on Mt. Victoria early in '88 (8s. a day—trade was good then) I got my first cheque, £1 7s., from THE BULLETIN. It was totally unexpected, for, being in constant work and getting what I thought such a grand outlet for my thoughts and feelings, I hadn't dreamt of receiving payment for literary work—which might be a hard fact for the present cashier of THE BULLETIN to swallow. But before that I had written and worked, and I have written and worked since, for Australian unionism and Democracy—for nothing. I had a strong, deep-down feeling against taking money for anything I wrote in the interest of "the Cause" I believed in; and I felt red-hot about—

> I hate the wrongs I read about! I hate the wrongs I see!
> The marching of that army is as music unto me!
> —*"Army of the Rear,"* '87.

And I went a bit mad over—

> We'll make the tyrants feel the strength
> Of those that they would throttle!
> They need not say the fault is ours
> If blood should stain the wattle!
> —*"Freedom on the Wallaby,"* '88.

But I believed what I wrote was true.

When out of graft a while in Sydney, I helped turn the old *Republican* machine, and wrote "Faces in the Street," for which I received a guinea. Along in these times I wrote bush ballads for the *T. and C. Journal,* but only got an occasional half-sovereign. I tried "Tom" Butler of the *Freeman's Journal*, of whom I have kindly recollections. He told me when I first saw him that they didn't pay for poetry; but I might bring something round to him; and if it was fairly good and suitable for his readers, he would see what he could do. I wrote a few bush rhymes for him; whenever I brought one round he reminded me that they didn't pay for verse—except, perhaps, at Xmas, and by special arrangement or for special stuff; and whenever he wrote me a cheque he never failed to draw my attention to the fact that the *Freeman's Journal* didn't pay for poetry. The *T. and C.* proprietary treated me a little better later on—but only took Xmas matter; and, when I got "finally" hard-up in Sydney, contributed £1 towards my fare to Maoriland.

But it was before that—in '89—that I went to Albany W.A. I painted; and wrote articles at a penny a line for a local paper. Came back, and hung out for the best part of '90 in a third-rate hash-house in Sydney, where I got some good "copy." Up-country again, and started house-painting at 8s. or 9s. a day, with every prospect of a good run of work; but one day, as I was painting a ceiling, I got a telegram to say that Brisb. *Boomerang* offered £2 per week and a position on the staff. I was doubtful of my abilities, and wired to an old friend in Sydney for advice. He advised accept; so I accepted.

It was the first, the last, and only chance I got in journalism. I wrote pars., sketches, and verse for six months for the £2; and barracked, spare times, for Democracy, in the *Brisbane Worker*, for nothing. I got very fond of the work, and was with difficulty kept out of the office on Sundays, publishing days, Saturday afternoons, and other holidays. I might have been an experienced journalist to-day, with a good "screw" and no ambition, but the *Boomerang* "ghost" was fading fast. We hashed up a couple of columns of pars. from the country papers every week, with the names of the papers attached—to curry favour with the country press; and I conceived the idea of *rhyming* this "Country Crumbs" column, and having it set as prose, and kept two columns a week going for a couple of months. You can rhyme anything if you stare at it long enough between whiles of walking up and down and scratching your head.

Perhaps the "Country Crumbs" in prosy rhyme had the same effect on the readers as at first on the comps.; anyway the spectre grew less and less discernable, and deputations of comps. went up oftener to the sanctum to discuss the inadvisability of their taking shares in the paper in part-payment of wages. A piece I wrote, called the "Cambaroora Star," was the *Boomerang's* own epitaph.

I came south, steerage, with £2. It wasn't the first time I went saloon and came back steerage, so to speak. I got as far as Bathurst once, during an unemployed period, and came back in charge of the guard.

I hung out (with difficulty) in a restaurant in Sydney, getting an occasional guinea from THE BULLETIN, and painting for nigger-driving bosses at 5s. a day. Hard times had come to Sydney, and it took a good, all-round tradesman to be sure of seven or even six "bob" and fairly constant graft. When the trade failed me I used to write a column of red-hot socialistic and libellous political rhyme for *Truth*. I still believed in revolutions, and the spirit of righteousness upheld me. *Truth*'s "ghost" was eccentric, and the usual rates for outside contributions were from 5s. upwards; but John Norton gave me 15s. to £1, for special stuff. He cursed considerably; and there were times when it wasn't advisable to curse back; but he saw that I, and one or two other poor devils of scribblers on their uppers, were paid—even before the comps. I haven't forgotten it.

Towards the end of '92 I got £5 and a railway ticket from THE BULLETIN and went to Bourke. Painted, picked up in a shearing shed, and swagged it for six months; then came back to Sydney "in charge of five trucks of cattle." Bourke people will understand that dodge. (Most of my hard-up experiences are in my published books, disguised but not exaggerated.)

Most of the matter in "While the Billy Boils" (and some of what my reviewers considered the best) was written for Syd. *Worker* for 12s. 6d. a column. During one of the frequent interregnums I edited the *Worker* a while gratis, on the understanding that I should get the permanent editorship—for "the Cause" didn't loom so big in my eyes as it used to, and I was only then beginning to find out that others had not been quite so enthusiastic as I was. But that mysterious inner circle, the trustees and their friends, brought an editor from another province.

Towards the end of '93 I landed in Wellington with a pound in my pocket—just in time to see the women vote for the first time. Got a little painting to do now and then, and a guinea (5s. "out of the editor's pocket," I understood) from the *N.Z. Mail* for a 1½ col. rhyme called "For'ard." And I wrote some steerage sketches at the rate of 5s. a col. Did a three-months' unemployed "perish," and then went with a mate to a sawmill in the Hutt Valley, for a boss who had contracted to supply the mill with logs. We two bullocked in a rough, wet gully for a fortnight—felling trees, making a track for the bullocks, and "jacking" logs to it over stumps and boulders. But we were soft and inexperienced, and at the end of the fortnight the boss said we weren't bushmen—which, strange to say, hurt me more than any adverse criticism on my literary work could have done at the time. The boss had no cash; and my mate was only restrained from violence by the fact that he was a big man and the boss a little one. He gave us each an order for our wages on the owner of the sawmill in Wellington, and as we had no money for railway fares, we "tramped in"—twenty miles, without tucker or tobacco. Those orders have not been cashed yet.

I house-painted a bit; then got on with a ganging lineman on a telegraph line in South Island. It was hard graft at first, through rough country, in the depth of winter, and camping-out all the time—humping poles some times where the trace-horses couldn't go. The boss was a bit of a driver, with a fondness for "hazing" the gang when his liver went wrong; but it's better to be driven to the benefit of your muscles, general health, and consequent happiness, than to be brain-sweated in the city to the danger of your reason through brooding over it. In four or five months I was too healthy to read or write, or bother about it, or anything, or to hate anybody except the cook when "duff" didn't eventuate at reasonable intervals. But there came a letter from the *Worker* people to say that a *Daily Worker* had been successfully floated, and there was a place for me on it. I said, "Get behind me, Literature!" but she didn't go; so I threw up the billet, and caught a steamer that touched the coast to deliver poles. I arrived in Sydney three days after the *Daily Worker* went bung.

After a deal of shuffling-humbug, I was put on the *Weekly Worker* as "provincial editor," but in a month I received a notice alleged to come from the trustees to the effect that, on account of the financial position of the Workers' Union, they were regretfully obliged to dispense with my services—"for the present at least." No one was responsible for the *Daily Worker*, nor for the thousand pounds sunk into it, nor the crowded staff, exorbitant "screws" and gross mismanagement of the *Weekly Worker*, nor for me—except, perhaps, the "last committee."

House-painting was dead; clerical work was always out of the question—I couldn't add a column of figures without hanging on like grim death till I got to the top, and two trips with poor results utterly demoralised me. Deafness stood in the way of a possible Government billet.

My two books published by Angus and Robertson, "In the Days when the World was Wide," and "While the Billy Boils," are advertised as in their seventh thousand and eight thousand respectively. The former is sold to the public at 5s.; the latter has been sold in various editions at from 5s. to 2s. 6d. My total receipts from these books have been something over £200; and I have sold the entire rights. The books represent the cream of twelve years' literary work. I estimate my whole literary earnings during that period at £700.

Up to a couple of years ago THE BULLETIN paid me at the fixed rate of a guinea a column; but advances written off and special prices for special matter brought it nearer 30s. per col. all through. The only thing I have to complain about with regard to THE BULLETIN is that the paper is unable to publish the sketches and stories within reasonable time. Some of mine published lately were written and paid for as far back as '91. While the publication of "W.B.B." was being arranged for THE BULLETIN held some stories and sketches which were to complete the "Steelman" and "Mitchell" series; and, as THE B. would not rush them through, an idea of having the matter arranged with an idea to sequence had to be abandoned. Which explains the apparently hap-hazard appearance of the order of the stories and sketches in that volume, and will be responsible for the same thing in my next prose volume—which will contain some *introductory* sketches to others in W.B.B.

There are, perhaps, a score of Australian writers known to THE BULLETIN, and most of them little more than lads, who could write better stuff than had been appearing in the shoal of popular English magazines lately (no offence intended); but they have no scope, and, as far as I can see, no hope of future material encouragement from the "great" and wealthy Australasian weeklies and dailies, only one or two of which (excepting the *Sunday Times*) that I know of have, up to date, offered even the most niggardly assistance to purely Australian writers, and this is only after THE BULLETIN had introduced them and established their Australian reputations. Many papers, notably in Maoriland, clip their racy Australian sketches from THE BULLETIN; and in at least one of these offices that I know, and have hearty contempt for, it would be thought as an act of charity to offer a hard-up BULLETIN writer 5s. per col.; while in another it would be a mark of special favour to offer him a chair. I have stood (and walked up and down and boiled over) for two hours in the passage outside the office of a paper which has been "clipping" my work for years and this because they knew I was hard-up and wanting them to pay for a contribution by way of a change.

Meanwhile, our best Australian artists and writers are being driven to England and America—where the leaders are making the mark, and a decent living; and the rest would follow in a lump if *they* got the show.

The work of some of those who have gone brightened Australia for years, yet no one asked how they lived, and no one, in all the wide Australias, stood up and asked whether a native-born artist or writer went aboard the boat with a decent suit to his back, or a five-pound note in his pocket. And they talk about our "cheap," "unhealthy" or "affected pessimism"! The fools!

A last word for myself. I don't know about the merit or value of my work; all I know is that I started a shy, ignorant lad from the Bush, under every disadvantage arising from poverty and lack of education, and with the extra disadvantage of partial deafness thrown in. I started with implicit faith in human nature, and a heart full of love for Australia, and hatred for wrong and injustice. I taught myself a trade—the first years in Sydney I rose at five o'clock in the morning to go to work with a rough crowd in the factory of a hard taskmaster; and learnt the little I did at a night-school; and I worked even then, before I could write, for a cause I believed in. I sought out my characters and studied them; I wrote of nothing that I had not myself seen or experienced and wrote and re-wrote painfully, and believed that every line was true and for the right. I kept steady and worked hard for seven years, and that work met with appreciation in Australia and a warm welcome in London. When desperately hard-up and with a wife to provide for, I at last was forced to apply to the Govt. for temporary work. I was kept hanging about the office for weeks; and when, as a last resource, I applied for a railway-pass for a month, to enable me to find work in the country and gather new material for literary work, I did not receive a reply. I was obliged to seek the means of earning bread and butter from the Govt. of a province (M.L.) in whose people's interest I had never written a line.

My advice to any young Australian writer whose talents have been recognised, would be to go steerage, stow away, swim, and seek London, Yankeeland, or Timbuctoo—rather than stay in Australia till his genius turned to gall, or beer. Or, failing this—and still in the interests of human nature and literature—to study elementary anatomy, especially as applies to the cranium, and then shoot himself carefully with the aid of a looking-glass.

'A NOTE FROM "STEELE RUDD"'
Bulletin
27 May 1899

Dear BULLETIN,—You won't hear much from me this year; have been "off," and ordered to exercise vigorously—am doing so, going strong on polo, developing a dangerous passion for the sport. And when there is a horse to belt and bullock about, Dad and Dave and the selection and the 'roo and the Red Page can all slide—and it won't matter whether the 'roo swims or whether he don't, or whether the woman murdered in her bed would have been nicer butchered in the bath or under the house. Lord, give us plenty sport, and keep us full and merry, and never mind the money! Poor Lawson, and that Hard-Up Confession of his, nearly made me sad. Would like to have him in a spring-cart with the winkers off the horse, just to shake those funeral services out of his bright head.

P.S.— "Dad's" in town—first time for *41 years*. Forty years in the wilderness!—good old Dad!

'AN AUSTRALIAN AUTHORESS'
Bookfellow
25 March 1899

One finds Ethel Turner at home in a cottage at Mosman, on the shores of Sydney harbour, looking towards the sea. Though now merged in the stream of Australian life and literature, it was near Doncaster, in Yorkshire, England, that our children's storyteller was born, and from England she came at eight years of age, to be educated at that famous square brick building in Elizabeth-street, Sydney—the High School for Girls—which has nourished so many bright young hopes and efforts. Even at school Ethel Turner wrote stories: with her sister Lilian, author of "The Lights of Sydney," she edited the timid *Iris*, a schoolgirls' magazine; and later there was another magazine, *The Parthenon*, over which much anxious ink was spilled.

It was when she wrote her "Children's Page" in the *Illustrated Sydney News* that Ethel Turner's real literary life commenced; and when the *News* died the fanciful, conversational commentary on little people's ways was transferred to Sydney *Town and Country Journal*, where it is still continued over the signature of "Dame Durden." In 1894 "Seven Little Australians" was published by Ward, Lock, and Bowden, Ltd., and since then the busy pen has never rested. We have recently heard much of the troubles which spring from "pursuing literature in Australia"; but the quiet persistence of the small figure at the desk in the Red Road County, writing and destroying, destroying and writing again, perfecting style and art, and winning at last a well-deserved success, holds a lesson for many an ambitious author who refuses to learn that the second-best of genius, the best of talent, is the capacity for taking pains.

And Ethel Turner has kept on as well as she began. An approximate list of her books and their sales reads—

Seven Little Australians, 1894, seven editions	30,000
The Family at Misrule, 1895, four editions	15,000
The Story of a Baby, 1896, two editions	10,000
The Little Duchess, 1896, three editions	6,000
The Little Larrikin, 1896, three editions	16,000
Miss Bobbie, 1897, two editions	16,000
The Camp at Wandinong, 1898, one edition	12,000

A total of 115,000 copies of the books conceived in one brain, written by one pen, sold in five years: this is the real pursuit of literature in Australia—and the attainment. Nor is there a quality-cavil to insinuate; for the books which have sold best, though not pretending to be the high plane of intellectual or imaginative achievement, are among the few charming stories written for and about children: in their class can one name better?

Ethel Turner was fortunate in her choice of publishers; she is a good woman-of-business; and she does not rest on her laurels or her income. This year's book, "Three Little Maids," is being printed for Christmas publication; next year's book is being written;—"I find it no trouble to write a book a year—one of *my* books, that is," the author confesses apologetically. "*Some* days indeed, the pen will not write: you sit down and make sketches on the blotting-paper. But as a rule I go to my room about ten o'clock, and by noon or so I have done my day's work. So many days work to a chapter; so many chapters to a book—a regular literary arithmetic." […]

"Charming stories written for and about children"—there is hardly necessity to define Ethel Turner's work farther. Even her books more especially designed for older readers might be included in the same definition. For though her charm never leaves her, it is only her childish characters who are fully realised—made lifelike, genuine, convincing. Ethel Turner's "grown-ups" are still childish characters—have some quaint air of delightful boys and girls masquerading in their elders' clothes. She has the key of the children's paradise only. That is enough; but there is one person in the world who demands more, and her name is Ethel Turner. "I am so tired of writing children's books," she says; "I do wish to write a big book." So she is trying.

COLONIAL AUTHORS, CANONS AND TASTE

A.H.A. (ARTHUR HENRY ADAMS), 'RODERIC QUINN. AN APPRECIATION'
Australian Magazine
29 April 1899

Emphatically the poet of the poets is Roderic Quinn. Simple, naïve, wistful, delicate, fanciful; his range is not wide, yet within that range how perfect! Above all, Quinn is intensely personal. With the great tides that "noise" along the outer world—this harsh world of confused and conflicting humanity, with its million different outlooks, all of which may be right,—Quinn has little to do; the flow and ebb of the hidden tide of his own soul absorb him. His melody is simple, and winged with a theme of wistful sadness; yet the music is haunting, and lingers tenderly in the heart, when the more robust and riotous chorus of Australian singers is lost in the rattle of galloping hoofs. One looks in vain for local colour in this poet's work; he has to do with souls, and they have no local colour.

Yet all Quinn's verse seems veiled in a grey mist. It comes from the great distance, and the haze of its travel is upon it yet. His sight is "inward set and blurred"; he has much sweetness and grace to give; and the dreams in which his sentences are wrapped make his fancies only the more beautiful. He is an impressionist, conveying rather a moral than a message—rather an emotion than a truth. He has no clear-cut, vivid thought for the world; only delicate, tremulous dream-fancies that seem too fragile for publication, except in the dainty booklet-form chosen by the *Bulletin*. Quinn sees the world by moonlight; the vagueness and subdued beauty of his work remind me of the first dawn. He is the poet of the dawn, of mists, of clouds, of neutral tints; he never shocks his reader with the blinding glare of broad noon. His songs are all in the minor; his pictures harmonies in grey. His verse is for twilight reading, when the day and the mood are dying.

And in this aspect Quinn's work is novel and perfect. His book of poems, by its zealous selection, is, in my opinion, the best of the poetical work which the younger writers of Australia have put forth. It is so, not for the heights he reaches, but for the depths he avoids. Out of Ogilvie's bulky book there are only six small poems that I like—that is a mere personal and, perhaps, unfair preference; but out of Quinn's seventeen poems there are only seven that I could do without. This I consider high praise. Like the subjects he chooses—the sea, the soul, the wind, and love—his style is simple, grave, and quiet. Here and there are jewels of phrase and thought; and though there are jangling alliterations that make some of his lines gasp, generally he has chosen the fit and only word. How the heart stirs at the picture of the tides that *noise* along the soul, of the troop whose souls were "visited by strange, dark angels of regret!"

'A MAN AKIN TO NATURE'
A.A.A.: All About Australians
31 October 1901

Clothes do not always "proclaim the man," but they are generally an index of character; occasionally the attire indicates the bank balance, or empty purse; at other times—though more rarely—it is very misleading. A draper's clerk will be most fashionably dressed while a millionaire stock-owner will be content in a slouch hat, easy boots, and any clothes that will sit lightly on his shoulders. The one man studies appearance and abases himself before an outfitter's wooden image while the other conforms to the usages of civilised society without sacrificing his individuality. If you have no individuality you cannot sacrifice it, and if you have no exceptional ability you can easily fall into the ruts worn deep in the city thoroughfares by the votaries of conventionality.

Australia is such a free country and there is so much scope for stretching your arms and legs that it would be pitiful in the highest degree if all Australians fell into city ways. We have great respect for men who can go into the country and leave the city behind, or who can live in the city and not sleep in a long sleeve silk hat, and frock coat. One such man is Mr. J. Le Gay Brereton; he has seen the country and he loves the country, because he views it healthily. Australia is a "sad country" to Max O'Rell because he hoteled it and trained and trammed through it, and therefore never saw it. Some of our own men, like Henry Lawson, are apt to decry it through not being able to hotel it, train and tram it. Those that can see the country and its infinite moods without confounding it with the writers' misfortune are the men who need to speak to their fellowmen in either prose or verse. One such is Mr. Brereton. He has one good failing, and that is his excessive modesty; he has just issued a book of verse dedicated to his wife that would make any writer's name, yet he has but published six copies, written in his own clear hand and bound by himself.

The other day a friend began to lament the general exodus of New South Wales poets to the "Big Smoke." "Paterson, Lawson, Ogilvie, Miss Mack are all gone," he said, "we'll have no one left soon."

Things aren't quite so bad as all that, however. We have still Daley, Quinn, Brennan, and the subject of our sketch, Le Gay Brereton, and in the last named people predict the finest and in many respects the most characteristically Australian of them all.

Mr. Brereton was an early apprentice of the great trade. At the Sydney Grammar School, where he spent much of a discontented boyhood, he was a frequent contributor to, and for some time editor of the *School Magazine*, and under his regime it prospered as it never did before, and never has since. On three occasions he won the Cape Verse Prize. In 1891 he went up to the University, and there carried all before him in the study of English literature, winning prizes both for English verse and essays. As an editor of *Hermes*, the 'Varsity paper, he incurred financial loss, and narrowly escaped academic penalties and legal proceedings. *Hermes* has never been so lively since.

During his later schooldays, and while he was at the University, Mr. Brereton wrote much for *The Sydney Quarterly Magazine*. At a later period he was one of the little band of writers and artists who started the ill-fated *Australian Magazine*.

In 1896 appeared his first book, *The Song of Brotherhood*, published in London by George Allen, a volume of poems, most of which had previously been printed in magazines, and which, though necessarily showing traces of immaturity here and there, suggested notably in the poem entitled "Hill and Dale," that big things might be expected from this young Australian bard now brought prominently before the reading public for the first time.

This impression was further strengthened by a booklet of sonnets, *Perdita* (issued in a limited edition by George Robertson & Co.), which, though published in the same year as his *Song of Brotherhood*, contains later and therefore maturer work. Meanwhile Mr. Brereton, who is one of the finest scholars of English literature in the State, had been devoting his energies to critical work, and in collaboration with J. P. Pickburn, his quondam fellow-editor of *Hermes*, produced an edition of Ford's "Perkin Warbeck," which has been since adopted for examination purposes by the University.

In 1897 Angus & Robertson produced a second booklet, entitled *Sweetheart Mine*, which was received with a chorus of applause from the Sydney reviewers.

In '99 appeared his most considerable work, "Landlopers," published by Wm. Brooks and illustrated by D.H. Souter. This is an account, in prose, of a long trip through the Blue Mountains and down to the coast "on the wallaby," told with the greatest animation and charm, and interspersed with delightful little lines. This is one of the most distinctively Australian books yet published, and unlike most native writings, indebted to no one. In fact, all through Mr. Brereton's work we are struck by his originality. A Bohemian of the Bohemians, a poet in the truest sense—a lover of man with nature—of wide sympathies and humanity. Mr. Brereton has seen that among "the men that blaze the track," the selectors, the hard toiling pioneers on the land, true generosity and high instincts are to be found no less than among the gilded race of the saloon bar. Accordingly, he has gone among the people as one of the people, with swag on back and billy in hand, and much of his most charming work is the result of experiences gained in his wandering far and wide.

In Mr. Brereton's poetry, we notice an intense virility, a great *joi de vivre* and depth of passion, along with the most delicate play of fancy and nicety of phrase and metre, qualities seldom found side by side.

It has been said that he "lacks strength," "lacks blood," etc. This is absurd—unless by "strength" is meant sheer brutality, too common in Australian writers. A refined and cultured mind can be deep and strong no less than an uneducated one. All through Mr. Brereton's writing we are struck by the intensity of passion.

There is no room to dwell on Mr. Brereton's love for and knowledge of English literature, his wide reading and erudition, his stringent self criticism, but for which we would see much work, which tho' of a high quality, seems to its author not to have reached his standard or his personal modesty in spite of his achievements and position among Australian men of letters.

Unfortunately, much of Mr. Brereton's work has been published in such limited editions as to be inaccessible to the general public. Indeed, his best book of verse, "Sea or Sky," has had an exclusively private circulation. But if Mr. Brereton has not appealed to so large an audience as could be desired, it is not because of his inferiority, for judges predict him a high, a very high, place in Australian literature.

REVIEW OF BARBARA BAYNTON'S *HUMAN TOLL*
Native Companion
30 April 1907

Human Toll. By Barbara Baynton. London, Duckworth and Co., 1907.

Readers of *Bush Studies*, a little volume published by the same firm in 1902, know what to expect from Mrs. Baynton. There was abundant evidence of a vision that was attracted by the ugly, the gruesome, and the inhuman aspects of bush life, and a power of embodying them and forcing them relentlessly upon the consciousness of the reader. *Human Toll* is really a "Bush Study" on a large scale; but more powerfully painted, and more objectionable. There is, of course, much that is sordid, ugly and cruel in the Australian bush, as in any similar country, but these are not its characteristic features. To concentrate attention upon the exceptional beastliness of any kind of life is to malign that life, and is bad art. This book is altogether out of proportion. It begins with a death, several deaths occur through the story, besides various other more unpleasant incidents; the characters are knaves, bigots or fools—save the eccentric Boshy, who supplies the sole relief to the general depravity of the piece. The Bush is no factor in the story until the end, when, with pitiless detail, the experiences of the heroine are recounted, on her running away into the bush with the child of a drunken woman, who had wished to murder it. She loses her way, and is without water; the child dies in her arms, and she becomes insane. Fiction is not the province of such work as Mrs. Baynton's; it is rather in the dry field of pathology. *Human Toll* is a remarkable and powerful piece of writing; an extraordinary production from a woman; but it has no more right to appear in the guise of a novel than an anatomical chart has to be regarded as art.

COLONIAL AUTHORS, CANONS AND TASTE

'BOOKS REVIEWED' (*HUMAN TOLL*)
Steele Rudd's Magazine
May 1907

The Australian writer, with a few honourable exceptions, is a pessimist of the darkest colour. He writes of droughts, derelicts, dust, degradation, and delirium tremens. His heroines are never nice, cuddlesome, eight-stone girls, but gaunt women, women worn to haggardness by the five D's aforesaid. Yet, one remembers girls in the country—Ah, well!

When a writer is not a he, but a she, the result is usually a wild caricature of the decent, cleanly bush, a nightmare of erotic hysteria, religious mania, and plain blathers. And this he, which is a she, has recently broken out in a book which is surely the most unpleasant book that ever came out on a sunny land and to drive away its much-needed immigrants. This remarkable thing was praised as a work of genius by the *Bookman*; and the authority of our own, own Australian Red Page, while agreeing with the present writer that the book is unnecessary, picks out two of the worst examples of female vapours as fine writing. The Lady's ugly ferocity passes for strength, her maunderings for intensity. Is such harrowing stuff as "Human Toll" Art? It is not, for Art's essence is beauty. It is Truth? It may have a trifle of that commodity. Is it useful? It is not. Then, what is it?

PART 4

Stories and Poetry from the Colonial Journals
KEN GELDER & RACHAEL WEAVER

Barron Field, 'On Seeing the Bible Society's Map of the World,' *Australian Magazine; or, Compendium of Religious, Literary, and Miscellaneous Intelligence*, September 1821
157

Henry Kendall, 'The Wild Kangaroo', *Australian Home Companion and Band of Hope Journal*, 15 June 1861
157

'Waif Wander' (Mary Fortune), 'The Stolen Specimens', *Australian Journal*, 14 October 1865
159

Marcus Clarke, 'The Acclimatised Sparrow. A Story for Children', *Colonial Monthly*, January 1870
166

'M', 'To a Native Bear', *Sydney Quarterly Magazine*, January 1884
174

Louis Becke, 'On an Austral Beach', *Australian Town and Country Journal*, 21 August 1897
176

John le Gay Brereton, 'The Bush and… Smith', *Australian Magazine*, 29 April 1899
179

K. S. Prichard, 'The Coach-drive to Willara', *New Idea for Australasian Women*, 6 May 1906
184

Sydney Partrige, 'The Woodheap', *Native Companion*, 1 August 1907
190

Roderic Quinn, 'In Town', *Lone Hand*, 1 October 1907
192

Katherine Mansfield, 'Silhouettes', *Native Companion*, 1 November 1907
193

Mabel Forrest, 'Emily's Present', *Lone Hand*, 1 October 1914
193

4

Stories and Poetry from the Colonial Journals
KEN GELDER & RACHAEL WEAVER

THE COLONIAL JOURNALS COMMITTED THEMSELVES to publishing Australian poetry and fiction right from the beginning. Even journals with only an incidental interest in literature would publish at least the occasional Australian verse – partly because poetry could be so overtly declarative, able to give strident expression to the ideological imperatives that a journal stood for. H. M. Green described the first colonial Australian journal – Ralph Mansfield's *Australian Magazine; or, Compendium of Religious, Literary, and Miscellaneous Intelligence* – as follows: 'most of its subjects have no connection with the colony, but there is an article on the platypus, and Australian subjects are sprinkled through the Religious and Miscellaneous sections. There are the usual negligible local verses…'[1] This last remark is interesting, because it suggests that colonial poetry – 'negligible' as it may sometimes be – is about the only thing that properly connects this early journal to its colonial context. We want to go against the grain of Green's off-hand account by beginning this section with Barron Field's 'On Seeing the Bible Society's Map of the World', published in the *Australian Magazine* in September 1821. Arriving in New South Wales in 1817, Field went on to become a colonial magistrate, a founder of the Society for Promoting Christian Knowledge among the Aborigines, a supporter of public schooling, and the first president of the New South Wales Savings Bank. His *First Fruits of Australian Poetry* was published in 1819 by George Howe and reprinted (in expanded form) in 1823 by Robert Howe – the two proprietors of the *Australian Magazine*. Neither 'negligible' nor 'local', Field's poem is in fact foundational, which is why we reproduce it here. It pays tribute to the global responsibilities of the British empire as it spreads its influence across its 'dominions', including Australia. But the emphasis is no longer on military conquest; rather, it is on the roles played by education and the Christian missions – which literature ('Bookmen and penmen') is now called upon to serve.

As they developed, the colonial journals were increasingly accommodating to poets, but this sometimes meant publishing poetry that was not always quite so in tune with their editorial agendas and aspirations. We have already noted Henry Kendall's extensive involvement with a number of journals throughout the 1860s and 1870s. His poem 'The Wild Kangaroo' was published in June 1861 in the fortnightly *Australian Home Companion and Band of Hope Journal* (January 1859 – August 1861). This journal soberly devoted itself to 'labouring in the cause of Temperance, Morality, and Religion'; but Kendall's poem is a flight of fancy that takes us somewhere else altogether, linking the colonial poetic sensibility to an almost pagan celebration of blood sport in the Australian bush. Forty years after Barron Field, it is probably no surprise to see that colonial poetry is no longer doing the work of empire. Kendall's poem takes us back to H. M. Green's throwaway comment about the 'usual negligible local verses' to be found in the early journals. But the 'local' is now invested with energy and made vernacular, or even pseudo-indigenous; and the colonial journals increasingly invest in this kind of space, sometimes almost in spite of themselves.

As we have noted, many editors of colonial journals were also literary writers who contributed heavily to that journal's content: none more so, perhaps, than Marcus Clarke. By 1867 Clarke had become editor and co-proprietor of the *Colonial Monthly*, serialising his novel *Long Odds* there the following year. When Clarke took over editorship of the *Australian Journal* at the beginning of 1870, he began to serialise the novel that secured his reputation, *His Natural Life*; he also re-serialised *Long Odds* in that journal in 1873. The multiple serialisation of literary works across the journals was sometimes a striking feature of colonial publishing practice, as we have already suggested. Clarke's *His Natural Life* was serialised all over again in the *Australian Journal* between 1881 and 1883, in 1886 and 1888, and interestingly, once more, beginning in June 1913, where the editorial noted that the novel was a 'production of no ordinary kind'. It had also been serialised by several other colonial journals and newspapers, including the *Queenslander* and the *Sydney Mail*. The extensive and repeated circulation of Clarke's novel across the colonies – especially in the 1870s and 1880s – certainly refutes the conventional view that colonial journals were simply venues for literary ephemera. The story by Clarke we reproduce here, 'The Acclimatised Sparrow. A Story for Children', was first published in the *Colonial Monthly* in January 1870, and printed again in the *Australian Journal* one year later when Clarke was unable to produce an episode of *His Natural Life* to deadline. Later on, 'The Acclimatised Sparrow' was incorporated into a collection of Clarke's short fiction, *Four Stories High* (1877), where it was added (without a separate title) to the end of 'King Billy's Breeches' – a satirical account of the colonial administration of Aboriginal welfare – and framed as a tale that a father tells to his young son. The original version in the *Colonial Monthly* has no narrative framework; instead, it launches straight into its evocative and whimsical account of a family of sparrows who emigrate to Australia to seek their fortune. Most of the family adapts to its new environment, but the eldest son – a little cock-sparrow – is unable to let go of his attachment to London life. We can note in passing here that sparrows were introduced to Melbourne in 1863, the same year Clarke himself arrived from England. Native species and introduced species are already encountering each other by this time, as the story suggests. We also include in this section a delightful, anonymously authored poem from the *Sydney Quarterly Magazine* (October

1883 – December 1892), 'To a Native Bear', which carefully reflects on the colonial future of a native species. It is worth comparing with Kendall's 'A Wild Kangaroo' and also perhaps with Norman Lindsay's koala Billie Bluegum, which we shall see in part 5 of this book.

The *Australian Journal* was from the outset committed to publishing, and popularising, local material; and with the serialisation of Ellen Davitt's crime novel, *Force and Fraud*, its first issue set the tone for the journal's distinctive and long-lasting investment in popular genres and women's writing. When Marcus Clarke took over editorship from George A. Walstab, the *Australian Journal* renewed its policy of supporting local writing about colonial life. 'The Conductor', Clarke wrote in the July 1871 issue, 'is willing to protect native industry in the matter of tale-writing, but the tales must be "Colonial", and suited for "Colonial wear", not bad imitations of the French and English imported article'. By this time, the journal had already begun to publish short crime fiction stories under the title 'The Detective's Album'. The key contributor here was Mary Fortune, who wrote under the pen-name 'Waif Wander' or 'W.W.' and, remarkably, continued to contribute stories to the *Australian Journal* for around forty years. Lucy Sussex notes that '"The Detective's Album" was to become one of the longest-running series in the early history of crime fiction…written by Fortune from 1868 to 1908…a total of over five hundred detectives stories in all'.[2] We reproduce here a story that Sussex identifies as Mary Fortune's first contribution to the *Australian Journal*, 'The Stolen Specimens', published in October 1865. This story introduces a young, unnamed detective who is a precursor to Fortune's later protagonist, Mark Sinclair. It is a goldfields narrative that recognises the ways in which the line that divides lawlessness and the law is difficult to determine, tracing the tensions that emerge in the detective's relationship to the communities he is employed to police. It is worth noting that 'The Stolen Specimens' is published only four years after Kendall's poem in the *Australian Home Companion and Band of Hope Journal*, with its emphasis on 'temperance' and 'morality': something Fortune's story preserves as it charts the dissolution of a once-respectable young woman who has fallen in with shady types.

We include three stories in this section that take their characters on a journey into the Australian landscape – creating, as they do so, a vivid sense of the 'local' in late colonial Australia. Louis Becke, a popular and much-respected Australian storyteller, was a regular contributor to the *Bulletin* and best known for his tales of Pacific island adventure. His biographer A. Grove Day notes that Becke is indeed 'remembered more for his South Seas stories than for his accounts of Australia'.[3] However, we have included Becke's short, evocative piece, 'On an Austral Beach', published in W. J. Jeffrey's *Australian Town and Country Journal* in August 1897 – Becke was at this time, incidentally, this journal's London correspondent. Here, the narrator travels along the New South Wales coast, celebrating the beauty and plenitude of nature and native species. This story is also worth comparing to Kendall's kangaroo hunting poem; but the 'fishing and shooting' that Becke's story recommends at the end is tempered by a respect for, and fascination with, natural ecologies. We have already seen John le Gay Brereton in part 3; he was an important contributor to colonial journals such as the *Bulletin*, the *Sydney Quarterly Magazine*, Norman Lilley's *Lilley's Magazine* (June – October 1911) and the *Lone Hand*. His story 'The Bush and…Smith', published in the *Australian Magazine* in April 1899, sees two characters setting out for Cooloongolook in northern New South Wales, and then losing their way. The narrator expresses his reverence for the wild, natural world; but his companion is 'grotesquely at variance' with his surroundings, and the story animates the bush as a vengeful, sinister force that can retaliate against those who ignore its rhythms and plunder its resources.

The third story to take its protagonist on a journey into the Australian landscape is Katharine Susannah Prichard's 'The Coach-drive to Willara', published in Thomas Shaw Fitchett's *New Idea for Australasian Women* in May 1906. This is Prichard's second published story; a few years earlier, in December 1903, her first published story 'Bush Fires' – a melodramatic account of a squatter's daughter who sacrifices herself to be with her lover – was the winning entry in *New Idea*'s 'Love-story Competition'. Based in Melbourne, this journal was aimed at women readers, with articles on housekeeping, girlhood and motherhood, fashion, work, and so on. It published popular literary genres such as detective fiction and ghost stories; but it also supported the work of important writers like Miles Franklin and Mary Gilmore, and encouraged high-quality women's investigative journalism. Prichard's literary career could be fairly said to have started in *New Idea*. 'The Coach-drive to Willara' is the first of a series of six pieces about a young woman's life as a governess at an outlying station – based on Prichard's own experiences in western New South Wales. This is an adventure that sees a 'wilful' young woman threatened by locals as she travels inland under the protection of a sturdy bushman, Bill Northwest. Popular romance was also important to *New Idea* and to the literary careers of so many early Australian women writers. Kit is attracted to the bushman, apprehensive about what her new life will bring her but exhilarated by the way outback experience gives shape to romantic predicament: 'I loved the wild life that had left the man with his rough chivalry'.

In the early aftermath of Federation, Australian journals became increasingly invested in new kinds of writing that were more in tune with developments in literary modernism in Europe and elsewhere. The 'local' remains important here, but newer metropolitan – and cosmopolitan – influences help to shape the fiction and poetry. The *Native Companion* was especially instrumental in drawing together a group of young women writers who were beginning to experiment with modernist aesthetics. 'The Magazine', E. J. Brady wrote in an unpublished letter written in October 1937, 'drew writers and artists from all over Australia and New Zealand as a honey jar draws flies. My most notable find was Katherine Mansfield. Her copy intrigued me immediately. Her covering letter, signed Kate Beauchamp, informed me that she was a girl of 17'. In fact, the *Native Companion* published Mansfield's first four stories (one under the pseudonym of Julian Mark), written when she returned to New Zealand after a period of living in London and travelling in Europe. As with Prichard and the *New Idea*, Mansfield's professional literary career thus begins in an Australian journal. In her brief story 'Silhouettes', a young New Zealand woman looks out of her window, full of illicit yearning for something far beyond the domestic setting. Sydney Partrige (Kate Partridge) was also born in New Zealand, later moving to Adelaide where she married Hal Stone, collaborating with him on the Wayside Press and other publishing ventures, and editing and contributing to Stone's small magazines, including *Ye Wayside Goose* and *Ye Kangaroo*. Partrige's novel *Rocky Section: An Australian Romance* was serialised in *Steele Rudd's Magazine* in 1903 and published by Steele Rudd & Co. Ltd. in 1907, reminding us again of the supportive role journals could play in the development of literary careers. 'The Woodheap' is a fine example of an emergent Australian modernism, an elderly man's meditation on a local suburban space that triggers a sequence of sensory recollections of a past life in the bush that is still keenly remembered. What we have with these two vignettes from Mansfield and Partrige is a new kind of aesthetic, consciously nurtured by the *Native Companion*: feminine and literary, local in focus and yet cosmopolitan in reach.

We have already seen Roderic Quinn in part 3. Here, we reproduce his poem 'In Town', published in the *Lone Hand* in October 1907: the same year as the stories by Mansfield and Partrige. 'In Town' is a vibrant celebration of a moment of arrival, where rural Australians are drawn into the city ('A syren-song invites') with all its physical and commercial attractions. Like the *Native Companion*, the *Lone Hand* was interested in an emergent local modernism; it also shared a number of regular contributors, including Quinn, Sydney Partrige, John le Gay Brereton – and the prolific Mabel Forrest, whose story 'Emily's Present', published in October 1914 (several months into World War I), concludes this section. This is a story about a progressive young woman in Sydney who breaks away from her family to become modern and independent. Unconventionality looks as if it might be punished here, with the bedridden uncle Elias as 'the only wild one' in his family, intemperate and profane. But the story wittily situates its protagonist in this rebellious tradition, using it as a way of launching her into a free-thinking future. The poem that opens the transcripts of this part – Barron Field's 'On Seeing the Bible Society's Map of the World' – might now seem to be a very long way away from all this. But the evangelical zeal of that poem and its investment in empire as an ever-expanding Christian institution is something Forrest still registers, through the dour, brittle perspectives of Aunt Sarah and the narrator. 'Emily's Present' is a whimsical story that nevertheless works hard to separate its protagonist from this moral legacy. What we see in this story is another kind of emergent Australian modernism that is still in the process of defining itself against the earliest of colonial literary moments.

1 Green, *A History of Australian Literature*, p. 127.
2 Sussex and Gibson, *Mary Helena Fortune*, p. 9.
3 Grove Day, *Louis Becke*, p. 127.

BARRON FIELD, 'ON SEEING THE BIBLE SOCIETY'S MAP OF THE WORLD'
Australian Magazine; or, Compendium of Religious, Literary, and Miscellaneous Intelligence
September 1821

A moral change is stirring up the world,
And England! the great lever rests on thee.
'Tis as it should be: let all nations know,
Now that all paths are free—all swords are sheath'd—
What nobler conquests Peace can gain than war,
What holier alliances are hers—
Leagues not in blood cemented, how to plant
The cross where first the sword has delv'd; but war
That truly may be counted holy—war
Of reason and pure faith with idols foul—
The Bible for its ensign, and for soldiers
Bookmen and penmen—teachers—missionaries!
ENGLAND! the map of thy dominions paints
Shores in thy liv'ry, eastward both and west;
But pride thyself the rather on that chart
Which thou hast colour'd with the Bible's march,
The lands which thou hast won unto its league,
Or planted with thy Missions and thy Schools.

HENRY KENDALL, 'THE WILD KANGAROO'
Australian Home Companion and Band of Hope Journal
15 June 1861

The rainclouds have gone to the Deep—
The east like a furnace doth glow;
And the day-spring is flooding the steep,
And sheening the landscape below.
Oh! ye who are gifted with souls
That delight in the music of birds,
Come forth where the scatter'd mist rolls,
And listen to eloquent words!—
Oh! ye who are fond of the sport,

And would travel yon wilderness through,
Gather—each to his place—for a life-stirring chase
In the wake of the wild Kangaroo!
    Gather—each to his place—
    For a life-stirring chase
In the wake of the wild Kangaroo!

Beyond the wide rents of the fog,
The trees are illumin'd with gold;
And the bark of the Shepherd's brave dog
Shoots away from the sheltering fold!
Down the depths of yon rock-border'd glade
A torrent goes foaming along;
While the blind owls retire into shade,
And the "echu"★ beginneth its song.
By the side of that yawning abyss,
Where the vapours are hurrying to,
We will merrily pass, looking down to the grass
For the tracks of the wild Kanagroo!

Ho! brothers away to the woods—
Euroka★★ hath clamber'd the hill;
But the morning there seldom intrudes,
Where the night shadows slumber on still
We will roam o'er these forest lands wild,
And thread the dark masses of vines,
Where the winds, like the voice of a child
Are singing aloft in the pines.
We must keep down the glee of our hounds—
We must *steal* through the glittering dew;
And the breezes shall sleep, as we cautiously creep
To the haunts of the wild Kangaroo!
    And the breezes shall sleep,
    As we cautiously creep,
To the haunts of the wild Kangaroo!

When we pass through a stillness like Death,
The swamp-fowl and timorous quail,
Like the leaves in a hurricane's breath,
Will start from their nests in the vale;
And the forester,*** snuffing the air,
Will bound from his covert so dark,
While we follow along in the rear,
As arrows speed on to their mark!
Then the swift hand shall bring him to bay,
And we'll send forth a hearty halloo;
As we gather them all, to be in at the fall
At the death of the wild Kangaroo!
    As we gather them all,
      To be in at the fall—
At the death of the wild Kangaroo!

* THE ECHU is a bird called by bushmen, "The Coachman's Whip." I am indebted to Mr. Harpur for the more poetical appellation.
** EUROKA – An Aboriginal name for the Sun.
*** FORESTER – a title commonly given to the Kangaroo.

'WAIF WANDER' (MARY FORTUNE), 'THE STOLEN SPECIMENS'
Australian Journal
14 October 1865

We, members of the police force of Victoria, are, I think, a little—a very little—less despised in this year of grace, eighteen hundred and sixty-five, than we were when I first donned the uniform twelve years ago.

I was a "Cadet" then, and now I'm a—; but I dare say you don't care much what I am, so I may go on with my adventures.

Well then, although we may be, on the whole, a little more thought of than we were, I don't know that we are any better off as a body.

No one can deny that we get less pay at any rate, and just as little thanks for our trouble; witness the names they called us about those bushranging affairs, but I suspect they will let us alone about *that* now.

Strange scenes during the license hunting, eh? but it was nasty work that; work that I don't like to speak of, nor is it necessary that I should.

There are many incidents connected with the force, quite amusing and interesting enough to relate without going back to the despicable days of the "traps."

Poor devils, the name has stuck to them yet, and a sore point it is, I can assure you.

There was another arrangement by which we were treated very badly. I allude to the making us act the parts of common spies and informers in "sticking up and causing to be stuck up," and so bringing beneath the lash of the law, persons who sold or permitted to be sold on their premises spiritous liquors without Her Majesty's license thereto.

Dirty work that was too: work which reflected little credit upon all concerned in it, and which placed us sometimes in positions the most uninviting and derogatory to the dignity of a preserver of Her Majesty's peace; that is if he is supposed to have any of that—at times, rather expensive article.

In connection with this branch of our service, I recollect some incidents that may while away the time, and will, I have no doubt, be remembered by some of my mates, as they had many a laugh at my expense at the time of their occurrence.

Eight years ago then I was stationed within two miles of diggings, where many large nuggets had been turned up, but where the fine gold was so scarce that a poor man had no chance. The consequence was, that it never was a large rush, the diggers being limited to those who could afford to wait for weeks or months on the chance of finding a "big one." The camp had been originally in what appeared to be the most convenient locality, but the richness of distant gullies had led the population away from its neighbourhood, and, at the time I write of, it stood, as I have said, at the inconvenient distance of two miles from the nearest tent.

The camp consisted of a single wooden sided, iron roofed erection, so familiar to the many; and its only occupants were myself and a foot constable, who spent most of his time lying upon the grass under a tree smoking.

I often wondered how Jerry managed to exist at all; read he did not and *think* I am sure he could not, for his brains, poor fellow, were not overladen with intellectual power. He and I got on very well together, however. I was in charge of the station, and allowed him to do just as he liked, while I did as I liked myself, and neither of us reported the other.

My first act on coming to these diggings was one not at all likely to impress the general public favourably. I received orders to "stick up" all stores and shanties that sold grog without a license, and though I much disliked the work of a "dirty informer," and foresaw the consequences of my becoming one, I could not avoid it; my instructions were strict, and so my first step was to find a man willing, for a bonus of ten pounds, five on engagement, and five on conviction, to do what nothing but "duty" would have obliged me to do myself.

For two or three days I lounged about with my eyes open and my mouth too, for in my anxiety to make myself agreeable, I am afraid I over did it; and, indeed, it is useless to deny that I felt mean enough even in the prospect of such a job, to feel grateful to any honest man who met me with a friendly greeting. At length, with great perspicuity, I settled on my man—a low sneaking looking wretch—and after engaging him to do some fencing at the camp, I sounded him on the point, and he agreed to be my fellow-informer—two witnesses in these affairs being required by law.

The next day he commenced fencing, and during the week which followed there were many opportunities, without arousing suspicions, of doing the business; and we succeeded in drinking nobblers and not paying for them at seven or eight different stores and shanties. Of course I summoned them all, and plenty of black looks I got in consequence.

However the day came, and we were all at the court house, some twenty or thirty miles from the diggings at which I was stationed, and which I will call the Gully Diggings. There we were I say, the summonees looking as black as midnight; and I, with my note-book in hand, feeling anything but comfortable, and peering anxiously at the door for my expected witness. I might have looked till now, I expect, with the same success, for he never came, having levanted with the five pounds and left me to do the dirty work myself. Of course all the cases fell to the ground, and I was covered with ridicule. Some of the rowdy characters "Joed" me the next day when I returned to the Gully; but two or three of the more respectable storekeepers only laughed at the whole affair—"shouted" for me to my heart's content, taking out the worth of the trouble to which I had put them in the most unbounded "chaff." Many were the inquiries made as to whether I had heard from my mate yet, and how the fence was getting on, but fortunately I am an easy tempered chap, and it does not pay to indulge in sensitive feelings in the force, so I lived it down.

To one of these parties, however, it will be necessary to refer more particularly. His name was "Larry:" Larry *what*, I don't know; it was the only name he had, his place being invariably denominated "Larry's."

This Larry kept a grog shanty of the lowest description, which was frequented by all the old hands in the neighbourhood. He himself was ostensibly a digger, while a woman who lived with him, took in washing, as a simple blind, no doubt, for in those days their grog trade must have been a paying one.

It was certainly my interest to keep on friendly terms with Larry's household, as there was one or two of its frequenters over whose movements I was anxious to keep an observant eye, for reasons best known to myself and to the *Government Gazette*.

To Larry's young woman then, I weekly carried my washbag, calling regularly for the same, while I used every means of ingratiating myself with the occupants of the shanty; succeeding at length in making myself rather a favourite with some, I have reason to believe, but entirely failing with the master of the establishment.

STORIES AND POETRY FROM THE COLONIAL JOURNALS

Larry evidently viewed me with suspicion and ill-concealed dislike, and I many a time caught his black looks fixed upon me with such an expression as led me to suppose that if I calculated upon a friend in him I reckoned sadly without my host. With Ellen, however, I was successful, and I have no doubt that the little extra attention which she bestowed upon me in the way of getting up my linen with great care, giving an extra polish to the tumbler ere she mixed carefully my favourite drink, went a good way in confirming the dislike of her amiable partner towards my humble self, although he did not recognise the prudence of expressing it more openly.

Ellen was a young and goodlooking woman, the mother of a baby that she carried almost constantly in her arms, serving customers and even preparing meals with the other, as is often the custom of women with fretting infants. I have often thought it a pity that the poor girl's lot should have been cast amongst such rascals, to whom she was much superior in many respects, having been, I should judge from her appearance and manner, a servant in some honest household; while Larry and his mates were the very offscourings of humanity. Poor Ellen, simple minded, and I always think a little weak headed, was daily becoming reduced more and more to the level of those around her. She was getting more and more addicted to the cursed liquor amongst which she lived; and it at length became no uncommon thing to see her staggering up the street, still carrying the unfortunate child, with its clothes, as well as her own, a picture of neglect and untidiness.

At the distance of perhaps a mile from Larry's, at the very further end of the diggings, was another shanty to which I shall be obliged to introduce my readers; with what hesitancy and dislike they may be able to judge when they read further.

A man does not like to blow much about circumstances and places in connection with which he has made an *ass* of himself, but occasionally it is beneficial to sacrifice one's touchiness, so here goes.

This *other* shanty then, was kept with an air of respectability that did not belong to the calling, by a brother and sister; the brother digging during the day, the sister minding the house. The sister was—; bah! I needn't describe her. I thought her perfection in every way; and to make a long story short fell over head and ears in love with her, making myself the veriest spooney that ever disgraced the silver striped arm of Her Majesty's blue police jacket. I saw the foolery of the course I was pursuing, but at last we settled it all comfortably thus. After a little time I was to resign, marry my inamorata, and keep a shanty myself for all I knew; nothing of that sort troubled me; only let me become the happy possessor of my angel, and everything else might go to old Nick, Her Majesty's police into the bargain!

With such feelings as these it is no wonder that I set public opinion at defiance, and day after day was I to be seen in all the paraphernalia of my mighty office, riding down to "Mack's Shanty," at the door of which my charger remained tied up, while I basked in the smiles of beauty within, to the detriment I do believe of my beauty's trade in grog.

Didn't I think something of myself—idiot that I was—when, after bestowing extreme attention upon my accoutrements, I macassared my soft curls, mounted my well-groomed animal and cantered along with my cap cover as white as the driven snow; my boots shining like mirrors, every buckle about me "polished up to the nines," the palm of my left hand laid so gracefully, and with an air so *dégagé*, upon my left thigh as it rested on the saddle. Well, I was young you know, and I don't think even now that I'm at all a bad looking chap, quite the contrary indeed.

One evening—it was Saturday by the bye—I started as usual for the accustomed spot. On my way I had to pass a crushing machine, the company connected with which I happened to be on very friendly terms. In galloping past I was called upon to stop, in order to admire some splendid pieces of quartz that had just been raised from the shaft. They were richly impregnated with gold, and, it was calculated, would go a hundred ounces to the ton. The shareholders were, of course, in high spirits at such a "rise," although it appeared as if the rich stone was only a patch—no indication of its continuance being visible. However, it was a great lift to pushing men, there being about half a ton of it, in seven or eight solid pieces, thrown out at one blast; so congratulating them on their luck I went on my way.

Having fastened my horse as usual to one of the poles of the "fly," I spent some time with Miss Mac, and at last, the hour being a late one, I was obliged to tear myself away.

'Twas a pity I had not done so a little earlier, for when I went into the dark I found that my charger had gone, loosened on purpose I had no doubt, and I felt in about as pretty a mess as my worst enemy could have wished me.

It was a dark night, and no tent near, and it was entirely useless my doing anything else but walking home, which I did in a humour which my readers can, I dare say, imagine. My reveries on the way were not very agreeable either, you may depend upon it. That the horse would turn up somewhere I had no doubt, but that it would be in some way to secure me as much disgrace as possible I also felt convinced, as it must have been taken from anything but a friendly feeling towards myself.

It is fortunate that I have since repented of all the evil thoughts in which I indulged during my three miles tramp in the dark; for I swore enough of oaths internally to have swamped the most buoyant vessel that ever floated. Not much sleep did I get that night you may guess; and at the first dawn I was up, to try and find out something of the affair.

I walked out to the stable with some faint hope of finding the missing animal there, and there he was, sure enough, standing as quiet and unconcernedly as if he had not been the occasion of the slightest trouble in the world. I was glad to perceive that nothing was broken; the saddle, I could see when I removed it, had been ridden upon, for there were marks of dirty trousers or something of the sort upon it, and two or three scratches upon the leather—the branches of some bush thinks I; and "Ah, my lads," said I to myself, "let me find you out, that's all!"

Well, I went back to my room, and busied myself in removing from my boots some mud with which my pedestrianism in the dark had plentifully bespattered them, while my mate prepared breakfast; shortly after which we heard the gallop of a horse approaching the camp, and Driscol—one of the shareholders I mentioned—came in.

He had come to give information of a robbery the night before; after the men had knocked off work at the machine, the tool chest (to which had been consigned the quartz I had been admiring) was broken open, and every one of the specimens abstracted.

"Too bad, wasn't it," Driscol asked, "two hundred pounds worth."

I promised to attend to the matter immediately on getting my breakfast and Driscol left.

Not a word had I said about the temporary loss of my steed, not likely, but now the conviction that had before taken possession of my mind, namely that Larry had something to do with its abduction, strengthened considerably, and I said to myself, "whoever took my horse took the specimens;" and I went out to examine, under a new light, my saddle and accoutrements.

Oh, it was quite evident—dusty bags had been on my saddle, and sharp corners of quartz had scratched it; and in case there might be anything dubious about the matter, on unbuckling the holster pipes, I found a piece of identical stone, containing gold, which had undoubtedly been placed there on purpose to make a perfect laughing-stock of me. They had actually used my horse for the purpose of conveying to a place of safety the stolen property!

I felt furious; but knowing there would be no good done without a great amount of dissimulation, I removed every trace from the leather, and held my tongue.

Every search was made about the machine premises, but unsuccessfully as to the finding of any traces sufficient to throw the shadow of a suspicion upon any person. The tool chest had been forced open with an old pick belonging to the works, and on the dry hard floor no traces of footsteps remained to give the slightest clue; and so, with the offer of a reward posted up in every direction, the thing to all appearance ended;—the shareholders leaving in my hands the attempt to solve the mystery, pretending at the same time that they had given up all hope of a capture, so as to lull the watchfulness of any neighbouring participators in the robbery.

The next day I called at Larry's with my washing, and found that worthy busy in some little carpentry about the bar. He appeared on particularly good terms with himself, and indeed with me, for he "shouted"—an unusual thing with him—and I, of course, returned the compliment. We discussed the robbery, and I hinted to him my suspicions that the chap who played me the trick about the informing business was very likely to know something about it, as he knew the premises, &c.

Larry said it might be so, and promised to keep his eyes open.

So will I, Larry, thinks I, and so I did. It takes very little to hang a man; and before I left the place I had gained a clue, which, though slight in itself, was of the very greatest service to me in the affair. It was a raw sort of a day, and Larry had on an old, worn monkey jacket.

On his turning his back to replace upon the shelf a bottle, I noticed a rent under the arm and slightly behind it, a small piece of green stuff, that had every appearance of having inserted itself during the pressure of the wearer upon some bush. I managed before he turned to gain possession of it, and shortly after left the shanty.

I was not long in examining my acquisition, and found it was a scrap of tea-tree scrub; but this was in itself no trifle, for there was only one patch of that scrub within a distance of miles, it being at least two miles away from the nearest part of the gully. It was a place upon which I had dropped in some of my kangaroo hunting excursions, and one in which Larry, who was no sportsman, and owned no cattle of any description, could have no reasonable business.

I went straight to the camp and then across the bush to the tea-tree scrub patch; and riding around it, cautiously though, and where by tracks would not be likely to be noticed, I came upon a sort of opening through the thick bushes. My horse seemed to know it, and of course he did, so I gave him the reins, until he brought me to the bed of a creek, where, under the heavy branches of an old gumtree that hung over the steep bank, I found a carefully concealed "drive," and at the end of the drive, among many other articles, were the identical specimens, still remaining in the bags in which they had been removed.

This was a grand affair for me, and I was soon after galloping home, so that I might think quietly upon what would be the best course to pursue. Of course, I had no doubt that Larry was the man now, but to bring it home to him was my business, as well as to recover the stolen property.

For two or three nights then was my animal tied as usual to the shanty of my lady love, while my mate spent his nights in watching near the "plant" in the scrub. At length he was rewarded. Larry began to be off his guard and anxious to break up the stone, so as to render the gold available.

One night we let him hammer away in peace; the next we went together, and after an hour's watch, during which period Larry hammered away regularly and contentedly, we discharged a revolver in front of the drive, and seized the gentleman as he rushed from his place of concealment.

He was an active powerful fellow, but two to one, he had no chance, and we clapped the handcuffs on him in a trice.

"Now my clever fellow," said I, "you shall go to the lockup on the horse that you found so convenient the other night, and believe me, I am prouder to see you there than if you were ten bags of specimens;" and so I was, for I had a personal down on the rascal himself.

To make a long story short, Larry was convicted, and sentenced to seven years on the roads, and I was at liberty to prosecute again my *affaire de coeur*.

Well, the said affaire does not end at all to my credit; but never mind, 'tis like taking a dose of physic—down with it.

One evening, after having been away for several days finishing off the Larry concern, careless of the condition of Her Majesty's charger, off I started to my charmer's residence, full of delight at my recovered liberty.

Hallo! the tent was gone—not a vestige of the spot to me so sacred was left, save indeed the remnants of a pipeclay chimney, and a number of bottles scattered about.

Whatever was up? I had parted with her only a few days before, giving her the last of my last month's pay to settle some pressing account or other as I had often been happy to do before, and now she was gone!

I turned my horse's head campwards, and dreading the quizzing I was sure to get if I asked any questions up the street, I galloped home across the bush.

Jerry was lying as usual under a tree, and the broad grin with which he greeted my unusual return struck me as significant.

"What has become of the Macs, Jerry?"

The loud guffaw which served as Jerry's reply, I fancy I hear yet, and don't want to hear again, at my expense at any rate; but the amount of the matter was, that Miss Mac was not Miss Mac at all, but the mistress of her *soi-disant* brother, and they had not gone off without making a complete laughing-stock of me all over the gully. Nay, Miss Mac had not hesitated to tell all my friends of our intended marriage-arrangements, and laughed until the tears ran down her cheeks at the bare idea of marrying a "green downy-faced trap!"

That cured me; for, as I caressed my delicate moustache, with the twirl of which macassar had so much to do, I felt that a woman who could ridicule *that* was not worth—. Well, I got over it at any rate, after chaff enough to make me more cautious in the future.

As a wind-up to this episode, I may mention the fate of poor Ellen. One day I went to look after her a bit—the neighbours having raised suspicions of her sanity—and found her dancing idiotically before her child, which she had hung up to the tie-beam of the tent, and whose black and distorted features seemed to afford her the most satisfactory amusement. The child was quite dead, and some months after Ellen died herself, the inmate of the hospital of an asylum, another victim to the curse of intemperance so prevalent in our colony.

MARCUS CLARKE, 'THE ACCLIMATISED SPARROW. A STORY FOR CHILDREN'
Colonial Monthly
January 1870

Once upon a time, when pigs were swine, and turkeys built their nests in old men's beards, there lived a family of Sparrows.

The Papa Sparrow was a gentleman of parts, and had the reputation of being a bit of a rake; but Mrs. Sparrow—poor soul!—was only a good motherly little bird, who looked after the house and was wrapped up in her children. Mr. Sparrow was well connected, and had a cousin in the Household at Buckingham Palace; while the wife was a mere nobody, and had been hatched in a citizen's garden at Peckham Rye. His aristocratic friends at the Clubs could not make out how it was that Mr. Sparrow threw himself away on such a silly creature; but Mr. Sparrow winked his bright little eye and dropped hints as to a tree root full of worms to which his wife was sole heiress, and then his friends were satisfied of course, for sparrows are quite as wise, in their own way, as human beings are, you know.

So they were married, and Mr. Sparrow disappeared from his favourite corner of the roof of the Rag and Famish, and went away to enjoy his worms. But after some little time he came back again, looking rather ruffled in mind and feathers, and it was reported that the worm speculation had not turned out as well as was expected. However, Mr. Sparrow never said so—bless your heart, he was much too proud for that—and held his head as high as ever. A fat old Cockatoo, however, who had bachelor chambers in the Albany, said that the cousin in Buckingham Palace had told *him* that Mr. Sparrow was living over a livery stable in great poverty, and that he was only able to appear abroad because Mrs. Sparrow—"a good little body, 'pon honour," the cousin said—was such an excellent manager.

Of course they had a large family—poor folks always have—and when Mr. Sparrow would come home from his afternoon's stroll in Pall Mall, and see all their little beaks gaping for food, his heart sank into his varnished boots, I can tell you. He got quite moody did this poor little fellow, and used to think about suicide in the horse's trough, and other dreadful things.

"The country is overcrowded, my love," he used to say; and Mrs. Sparrow, who thought her husband the cleverest man on earth, would sigh, and say,

"She supposed it was so if he said so."

Now in a milliner's window hard by lived a Parrot—a great green fellow with a red top-knot—who was a retired Port Admiral, and who had the reputation of being a shrewd man of the world, chiefly, I think, because he used to swear terribly. He was not a communicative bird, but everybody knew that though he did not say much, he thought a great deal and that is of more importance.

To this Parrot Mr. Sparrow applied for advice, and that Ancient Mariner after turning himself upside down and drawing several corks, in order to show his loyalty, put his beak between the brass wires and said, "Emigrate!"

"By Jove," said Mr. Sparrow, "Just the thing!" and went home by a short cut, to tell his wife.

Says she, "What of the children?"

Says he, "Take them with us, my dear, of course!"

But when he looked around and saw ten gaping beaks, his heart went into his boots again.

This conversation was overheard by the eldest of the family, a pretty little Cock-sparrow who was the image of his father.

"I hope not," said he, for he was quite a man, and had already vowed eternal love for the pet Canary of the livery stable keeper's daughter.

But the notion had taken firm hold of Mr. Sparrow's mind and he liked it more and more.

But how about the children!

He asked the Parrot, but the Parrot was suffering from indigestion owing to sugar, and putting on his Quarter Deck manner, swore so dreadfully when he was spoken to that Mr. Sparrow flew away in a fright.

He flew right into the back yard, where the Little Boy kept his rabbits.

"How am I to take the children?" said he to the Buck rabbit, and told him the whole story.

"Children!" cried Mr. Buck. "Why, look at Mrs. Doe! Children indeed! That is just what they want!"

And then he laid his ears back, and nipping a piece out of a cabbage leaf, said, "Assisted emigration of course. Try the Acclimatisation Society!"

So after a little trouble the passage was taken, and the Sparrows went on board. Mrs. Sparrow cried a good deal, and Mr. Sparrow sulked, for I am sorry to say that his genteel friends gave him a parting supper under the Haymarket Colonnade, and he was brought home at six the next morning by the milkman, very rumpled and with several feathers out of his tail. But they all got safely away, and on the whole were not sorry to go—all except the naughty little Cock-sparrow before mentioned, who said that he was sure it was a "horrible colony, and that London was the only place for a gentleman to live in."

Now when they got to Melbourne, it was blowing a hot wind, and the dust was whirling down the streets in big red clouds. The Horses didn't mind it so much, but the prize Leicester Rams put their tongues out and panted; the little Cock-sparrow pecked at his wires, and said he was confident that he shouldn't live a month in such a climate.

But his reflections were put to an end by a sailor, who took the cage containing the Sparrow family and whipped it over the side, before they even had time to say good-bye to the one fowl that had escaped the curry-pot.

They went to the Society's gardens, and were soon comfortable enough,—all except the little Cock-sparrow, who said that he hated the place, and wished he was at home again.

There were many strange creatures in the Gardens. There was a Kangaroo, with melancholy eyes and long legs, who leapt twenty feet at a spring. There was a Black Swan, with a yellow bill and a red rim to his eye, who gave himself airs because one of his ancestors had been mentioned in the Classics. There was a queer animal with a duck's bill and a rat's body, whose life was a burden to him, because he couldn't determine whether he was a beast or a bird. There were white Cockatoos with yellow crests, who spoke a foreign language, and said that they knew nothing about the green Parrot at home, unless he came from the Sydney Side. There were Hares and Rabbits, and even Axis Deer. There was a Llama—with long hair, like a walking she-oak tree, and there were several Laughing Jackasses, who called themselves Philosophers, and laughed at everything. Some people said it was because they were so clever, and others, because they could do nothing else. I don't pretend to say why it was myself,—I only know that they laughed.

But our little Cock-sparrow turned up his beak at all his companions, and said that they were people of no family, and had never been to London.

The Kangaroo hopped up with that sudden obtrusiveness which belongs naturally to timid people, and said, "How do you do, my little brown bird?"

"Brown yourself!" said the Cock-sparrow. "I am a Londoner and have lived in good society, I can tell you. Put that in your pouch, my long-legged friend!" Whereat the kangaroo hopped off again, and talked to the Black Swan.

The Axis Deer passed the time of day, and said that it was warm. "Warm!" said the little Cock-sparrow—"Warm do you call it? It was much hotter in London." Nevertheless he was gasping for breath all the time.

"And what do you think of the colony?" said the Lyre-bird, spreading his tail out best side foremost.

"Oh, so-so," said the little Cock-sparrow. "It is not half as big as London though!" at which the Laughing Jackass burst into such a roar, that the Keeper, who was smoking his pipe at the door, began to laugh too, though he could not tell what he was laughing at for the life of him.

All this time poor Mrs. Sparrow was silently weeping in a corner of the cage, for two of her children had died on the way out, and being only a poor woman and a good manager, she felt the loss of them. But the little Cock-sparrow never went to comfort her. He was too much wrapped up in his own thoughts. "Never mind," he said to himself, "wait till I get out into the world!"

The next day the Keeper came and put the Sparrow family into a cage, and sent them up to Ballarat by rail, for the farmers round about wanted sparrows to kill the grubs, which were destroying their crops. So, when they got to Ballarat, they were taken outside the town and set free. Oh, how nice it was! A lovely summer's evening, with the sun going down behind the big purple hills, and the air cool and balmy.

"Here is a big worm!" cried Mr. Sparrow. "And another, and another!"

So they all had supper, and when they had done, Mrs Sparrow put up her head and said, "Tweet, tweet!" which is the Sparrow for grace, you know.

Then Mr. Sparrow found out a triangular hole in a stable roof, and flew in among the sweet clean straw. A lovely nest! And his family all followed him; and, as he put his head under his little weary wing, he said,

"How—glad—I—am—that—we—have—em-mi-gra—."

And then he went fast asleep.

But the discontented little Cock-sparrow remained behind, and cried,

"What is the use of a vulgar stable? I have been used to live in a town. This is a horrible colony." And then he flew away.

"I will go into the world and seek my fortune," said he.

The first place he came to was an Engine Shed—a thrashing engine, I mean—and he went in and slept upon some oil-rags. But before daylight a boy came to light a fire, and tried to catch him with his cap; but the Sparrow was too quick for him and got away.

"Now, isn't this a horrible colony!" said the Cock-sparrow.

The next night he came to a Bush Tavern, where two men were drinking, and as he sat on the iron ring of the verandah post, he heard one say to the other,

"I say, Jem, I'll bet you drinks that I knock that bird over."

"Done!" says the other.

And before our poor little Sparrow could fly away, a big quartz pebble came whizzing past his head, and the men burst into a roar of laughter.

"*That* wouldn't have happened in London!" said the Cock-sparrow.

By and bye he came to a Corn Field—for instead of going back to Ballarat he was flying further up the country—and he got down among the stalks for a night's rest, but just as he was dropping off, a big black snake glided by, and startled him.

"I *hate* snakes," said the Cock-sparrow; "they have none in London."

And he flew off again in disgust.

The next night he came to a Fruit Garden, and made a luxurious supper.

"Come," he said, "the fruit is not bad any way!"

But in the morning out came the owner with a big blunderbuss, and says he, "Small birds again!" Bang! bang!

But he had been sitting up late the night before, and his hand shook, so he missed; and the Cock-sparrow flew away, only singed.

"What a terrible colony this is!" says the Cock-sparrow. So he got quite discontented and wished himself home again.

"I could do some good at home," said he to himself. "London is a place where they appreciate talent. There is no opening for a bird of my abilities here. I do not so much mind the hot winds, or the rough living, but it is the gross ignorance of the inhabitants I object to! Fire at me indeed! I wonder what they would say to that in London!"

He told this to a Toad, who lived under a stone in a Squatter's garden, and the Toad said,

"Ah, you are young. You will know better one of these days. I thought so myself when I was a child."

"Why, were you born in London?" asked the Sparrow.

"No," said the Toad. "I was born in a British copper mine, about two thousand years before London was thought of."

"Oh, what a story!" cried the Cock-sparrow; "why, London is as old as the World!"

And the Toad said nothing because he was ugly and poor and accustomed to be contradicted.

There was a Hen in the Squatter's family, and when the Sparrow told her his grievance, she began to cluck in the most angry manner.

"Tut-tut-tut," said she. "You miserable little Cock-sparrow, go and do some good in the world. Don't twitter to me, don't. Can you lay eggs?"

"No," said the Sparrow.

"Tut-tut. Then what's the good of you, I should like to know! Master Chickabiddy, if you don't come out of that kitchen directly this minute, I'll peck your pole for you!" And she went off in high dudgeon.

"Oh dear, dear," said the Sparrow, "what shall I do to be useful?"

So he went on, and on, and on, until he met a Mole.

"Please, Mr. Mole," said he, with his little heart sinking nearly as low as his father's did when the beaks used to gape, "tell me what I must do to be useful."

"Dig," said the Mole. "Everybody who is worth anything digs!"

"But I can't dig," said the Cock-sparrow. "I wasn't made for it!"

But the Mole didn't hear him, for he was already six inches below the surface.

Then he went on, and on, and on, until he met a Sheep-dog.

"Please, good Mr. Sheep-dog," said he, "tell me what I must do to be useful."

"Drive sheep," said the Sheep-dog. "Everybody who is worth anything drives sheep!"

"But I can't bark," said the Cock-sparrow.

"Hoot mon," said the sheep-dog—he was of Scottish extraction—"that's no affair of mine," and went away.

Then he went on, and on, and on, until he met a Magpie.

"Please, Mr. Magpie," said he, "tell me what I must do to be useful."

"Can't you steal?" asked the Magpie, with his knowing head on one side.

"I don't know," said the Cock-sparrow. "I never tried."

"Oh, you're a fool!" said the Magpie, and flew away in a hurry, for he was a Member of Parliament, and he had some "proper representations" to make.

So the poor little Cock-sparrow sat down on a stone by the road-side and began to cry.

"I am a fool, I suppose," said he, "and that is it. I can do nothing but eat and drink, and cry 'Tweet-tweet.' Oh dear, why was I ever hatched?"

Now close to the roadside was a little cabin, made of wood, with a brick chimney, and in this little cabin lived an Old Woman and her son. The son used to be away all day sinking a shaft—for the cabin was on the outskirts of a gold-field, and in some of the great red mounds that rose up among the dusty gum saplings, much gold had been found in days gone by.

But the diggings were half deserted now, for the Quartz Reefs which had broken out some five miles off had attracted all the people, and only those who were very poor, like the old woman and her son, lived on the spot. They had built the hut in the good times, and had fenced in a little piece of ground with a wattle fence, thinking that the rush was going to last, but the tide of fortune had rolled back again, and left them stranded on the shore. The Old Woman said that she would stay in the old hut until she died; and her son, who was a good stupid fellow and loved his mother, said that he would stop with her. So all day the son went away, in his short-sleeved flannel shirt, and his moleskin trousers all stained red with earth, to the big mound, with the windlass standing up clear against the fierce blue sky, and every night he came back with as many gold grains as would pay the bill at the store.

The floor was of earth, the door was half off its bullock-hide hinge, there was a hole in the roof, and the Old Woman lay upon a stretcher, in the inner of the two rooms, dying.

The day was very hot, and the air seemed to simmer. The goats had all crept under the dusty gum saplings, and a hobbled horse hard by kept clanking his fetters, as he stamped to get rid of the flies. From a break in the purple line of hills seen from the hut window, a thin column of white smoke rose up,—a bush fire, and no sound broke the stillness save the buzzing of the blow-flies and the occasional crack of a whip over the shoulders of the whim-horse down in the hollow.

All of a sudden the little Cock-sparrow hopped up on one of the broken palings that surrounded the desolate place, and said

"Tweet, tweet! Tweet, tweet!"

The Old Woman had been lying in a sort of stupor, looking at the sordid Australian landscape, and waving from time to time her withered hand before her face to keep the flies off. At the faint sound, she raised her head.

"Tweet—tweet!"

What was it? Did she dream?

"Tweet—tweet!"

She had not heard that sound for years; not since she was a merry young girl at service in the house of the merchant at Peckham Rye, where John wooed and won her.

"Tweet-tweet!"

She began to think of her childhood, in the old Kentish Farm, when the harvest moon rose, full orbed, over the apple blossoms, and the sparrows twittered in the orchard.

"Tweet-tweet!"

How pleasant it used to be in those times, when she was young, and rosy, and light-hearted! How well she remembered parting at the garden gate, with the coach waiting down the road, and her mother's white apron! She herself wore a print dress with lilac spots, and a straw hat with cherry-coloured ribbons.

"Tweet-tweet!"

Ah, but her courting days! The snug back kitchen in the prim merchant's house, with the cuckoo clock tick-tick-ticking from the snowy wall, and John, the carpenter, sitting on the edge of his shiny wooden chair, and looking sheepishly at her as she worked. Then the wedding dress, and the ring, and the clasped bible that her good mistress gave her. She remembered that the clergyman had an iron-mould spot on his surplice, and that it would catch her eye, do what she might.

"Tweet—tweet!"

The little house in the big city, with herself sitting, working and rocking the home-made cradle, and John coming home to supper from the warehouse, long, long before they thought of emigrating. Ah! happy days of youth, gone never to return! She could see it all; the little by-street, the narrow lattice, with the box of mignonette, and the—

"Tweet—tweet!"

She raised herself, and turned her fast glazing eyes to the window.

There it was!

A little brown bird, perched, half timidly, half boldly, on the wooden ledge, with his head on one side, and chirruping, "Tweet—tweet!"

A miserable, dusty, acclimatised, discontented—London Sparrow!

A smile of strange sweetness passed over her withered lips, and then the eyes closed, and the weary head fell back on the pillow.

"A London Sparrow!"

When the son came home, his old mother was dead; and as he came near the body, a bird flew away from the window sill, crying, "Tweet—tweet!"

It went up, and up, and up, until one could see it no longer; for it had done its appointed task, and had gone to join the soul of the Old Woman.

But this is only a story.

STORIES AND POETRY FROM THE COLONIAL JOURNALS

'M,' 'TO A NATIVE BEAR'
Sydney Quarterly Magazine
January 1884

The Grecian age of art has fled;
But Grecian noses lived instead,
Close welded to the modern head.

In men we trace their outlines fair;
And thou—our classic native bear—
Dost this admired appendage wear.

It suits that placid face of thine,
And other charms with it combine
Thy whole appearance to refine.

Devoid of wonder or surprise,
Most supernaturally wise,
In the expression of thine eyes.

When perched in thine exalted chair
Thou seem'st in dignity to wear
An almost professorial air.

Dost thou in solemn state preside
While woodland fairies round thee glide,
Or on the silver moonbeams ride?

Art thou that oracle whose cry
Fills with the note of destiny
The pathless woods and open sky?

Or does thy apathetic life
Protest against the ceaseless strife
With which the busy world is rife?

We know not; for thou dost not deign
Of aught to grumble or complain,
Unless impelled by fear or pain.

And then thy cry is purposeless—
A wail of infinite distress,
Or grunt of grim unhappiness.

Thy simple life few storms disturb;
No passion needs the constant curb—
Thy self-possession is superb.

Men call thee slothful; but we know
That all thy quiet movements flow
As parts in acrobatic show.

We sorrow for thy tailless state,
As, storm-tossed ship with living freight,
Thou art left rudderless to fate.

Thy ways are innocent and mild
As those of Nature's gentlest child,
By arts persuasive unbeguiled.

A vegetarian in thy food—
A lover of deep solitude,
With calm ascetic tastes imbued.

Unlike thy cousin near the pole,
Who loves upon the ice to roll,
Thou hast no malice in thy soul.

Thou would'st not love, 'tis manifest,
That strong-armed prowler of the west
Who strains the hunter to his breast.

And yet these twain are of thy race,
And bear thy name, though we can trace
But scant resemblance in thy face.

Their policy is blow for blow
Or squeeze for squeeze; and this they know
Is answer fit to any foe.

"Bear and forbear" thy creed must be;
And, high exalted in thy tree,
Thou holdest war but vanity.

Thus, sometimes fettered and subdued,
Thy kin are led from solitude
To fill the blanks in hearts unwooed.

Hast thou ne'er worn the captive's chain,
Or caused some maiden lady pain,
By fleeing to thy woods again?

Methinks thy home of flower and leaf
Would charm me more than all the grief
That damps the fair one's handkerchief.

LOUIS BECKE, 'ON AN AUSTRAL BEACH'
Australian Town and Country Journal
21 August 1897

As we sat, half asleep, on the shady verandah of the local "pub" (otherwise the Royal Hotel) listening to the ceaseless, pounding hum of the surf on the ever-restless bar, a dusty, slouch-hatted horseman rode along the baking street, pulled up when he saw us, and, in a voice indicative of a mighty thirst, besought us to have a drink with him. We consented, and then Sandy Macpherson—that was his name—gladdened our hearts by telling us that he and his mate wanted us to come out to their camp on Cattai Beach for a couple of days' fishing and shooting. The two men were beach-mining, that is, working the deposits of auriferous sand that are to be found all along the beaches of the coast of New South Wales, and their camp

was situated on the margins of a tidal lagoon at Cattai Beach, fifteen miles away from the little township where my friend and myself were awaiting the arrival of a steamer to take us to Sydney.

By daylight next morning we had breakfasted and saddled up, and long before the inhabitants of the sleepy old country town were awake, we cantered through the silent streets and out along the winding forest road leading towards the coast. Five miles or so from the town we emerged from the gloomy shadows of the grey-boled gums out upon the summit of a hill whose seaward side, clothed with a soft green nap of low shrub as smooth as an English privet hedge, was shining bright in the first rays of the morning sun; while at its base of black trap-rock the lazy ocean swell had not yet heart to break, for only the lightest air ruffled the surface of the sea beyond. To the north, cape and cape and headland and headland of pale misty blue were fast purpling in the glorious sun, and southward there trended in a great sweeping curve a noble beach full fifteen miles in one unbroken stretch. Beneath us, where it began, its hard surface at the water-margin was dotted with countless groups of snow-white seagulls and jetty-plumaged "redbills," all standing or sitting in motionless array with heads facing to the sea; further on the line of the beach was yet but half revealed, for the smoky haze of a semi-tropic sea still hovered o'er it, and floated in gossamer-like clouds up towards the green fringe of scrub-clad hills. Oh, the beauties of a summer's morn upon that wild and lonely coast! The strange, sweet earthy smell of the rich red soil beneath our horses' feet, the sweeter calls and cries of awakening bird life around us, the glint of the blue Pacific before and the dome of cloudless turquoise above, and the soft coolness of the land breeze as it stole gently seaward from the mountains, and stirred and swayed the leafy banners of the lofty gums and tapering bangalows! And then, as we turned and followed the bearded Mac adown the narrow fern-lined track that led us to the shore, the blue sky above us vanished and showed but here and there through the thickly overarching branches and clustering vines and serpent-like lianas; a big black wallaby leapt across the path just in front of our leader's horse, then another and another, and all three crashed into the thick undergrowth of the seaward hill-slope; a flock of green and golden parrots shrieked angrily at us from the boughs of a blossoming honeysuckle—and then we came out again into the light and warmth of the sunshine and the noise of the tumbling surf and seaward clamour of the open beach.

"Now we can go as hard as we like," said Sandy, and away he shot before us over the hard, firm sand, riding close to the water's edge, and hurrooing wildly at the whirling clouds of seagulls and divers as they rose with hoarse, protesting croaks at the galloping feet of our shoeless steeds. Two miles onward, and then a tiny, shining stream of water that cut its way through the sand to the sea brought us up sharply—for our horses knew the danger of a quicksand—and we walked cautiously up to beyond high water-mark and there crossed. Then, for the next hour or so we walked or trotted soberly along, smoking our pipes and watching through the transparent green of the rollers as they curled to break fifty yards away, the darting forms of countless thousands of great sea-mullet swarming beachward with the rising tide. Sometimes as we approached too near to the water there would be an agitated swish and swirl and bubble and a compact body of keen-eyed "blue fish" or whiting that were cruising in water scarce deep enough to swim in, fled seaward with lighting-like rapidity. That we should see plenty of fish along this beach we knew, but we were not prepared for the extraordinary sight that we witnessed a mile or two further on: for here, at the mouths of two little creeks, which ran down to the sea in parallel lines not a hundred yards apart, the water was literally teaming with countless thousands of silvery bream, trevally, whiting and garfish, and every wave seemed to add to their number. Swimming so close to the shore that every now and then some hundreds would be left stranded on the sand by the backwash, were swarms of dark-green backed garfish about fifteen inches long. It did not take us long to discover the cause of this gathering of the clans—the banks of each rivulet were covered with layers and ridges of fine big prawns, and by the turmoil at the creeks' mouths it was evident that numbers were being swept down into the hungry jaws that awaited them. On the previous evening, so Sandy told us, there had been a violent thunderstorm, the creeks had risen suddenly, and rushing down to the sea had met the incoming spring tide, and every wave that broke upon the shore left some hundredweights of stranded prawns behind it, where they remained to be devoured by the gulls and divers and the vast bodies of fish which, when the tide again rose, were enabled to ascend to the highest parts of the beach. The greater number of these delicious crustaceans were still alive—only those which had been washed apart from the thicker masses and ridges of the others having succumbed to the rays of the sun. Sandy had come prepared; for now he dismounted and began to fill a sugarbag with them. Prawn soup, he told us, was "verra good." Also he observed that if he could only get but one-half of those masses of prawns up to the Sydney market they would be worth £25 to him—and that was more than he could make by three months' hard work at beach mining. Before we mounted again we watched our chance and picked up nearly a dozen stranded garfish; these Sandy popped into the bag on top of the prawns.

For another mile or two we rode slowly along the hard, unyielding sand till we came in sight of a high sand head—the northern side of the entrance to Cattai Lagoon, and then turned away up from the beach to where a thin, wavering line of smoke ascended from the scrub. This was the digger's camp. In a few minutes Sandy's mate came to meet us, carrying a couple of fat, black ducks he had just shot. Their tent was situated on a little grassy bluff that overlooked the lagoon, and while Sandy and his mate set about to cook our breakfast of grilled garfish and grilled duck, my companion and I took our guns and set out along the lagoon bank, taking care to walk with discretion, for black snakes were very plentiful.

A ten minutes' walk brought us to an open space, from where we had a splendid view of a lovely scene. The broad, shallow lagoon, with its shores lined with she-oaks and clumps of flowering, golden wattle, growing literally on the sandy beaches, stretched inland for many miles, while towards the camp we could see the blue Pacific showing against the high white wall of glistening sand that separated Cattai from the sea. The heavy storm from the previous evening had brought down a vast volume of water, and the lagoon was quite a foot or two higher than the sea-level. In the evening we saw the sea and lagoon on a level, and only divided by a narrow strip of sand. Another thunderstorm or a heavy sea or two would have washed this away, and a wide entrance have been formed, only to be closed up again in a few weeks. All over the placid lake (whose waters are very brackish) were parties of black swans swimming lazily to and fro, or resting asleep, and not deigning to notice the noisy ducks and water-hens around them. On the other bank, long rows of pelicans stood in solemn silence. The waters were alive with fish, and, indeed, that afternoon the four of us caught whiting and bream till we were tired. One only needed to stand on the sand and fling his line into about two feet of water, when it would be literally rushed—for the lagoon entrance having been closed to the sea for over a month, the fish had all gathered at the sea-end, their instinct telling them that it might force a passage through at any moment. After spending half an hour in attempting to get a shot at a flock of black ducks, we returned to the camp and devoured our fish and game. We spent two delightful days at Cattai, and if any readers want to revel in fishing and shooting let them go there. It is not on Cook's itinerary, but they can find it easily enough.

JOHN LE GAY BRERETON, 'THE BUSH AND...SMITH'
Australian Magazine
29 April 1899

Dear Broome,—

There was a demonstration when we left Bullah Delah this morning. A crowd of men clumped on the verandah of the pub and cheered, and women stood in every doorway. I kissed innumerable children, and took off my hat right and left. Smith says he can't stand tommyrot; but then nobody offered him a drink.

We were making for Cooloongolook, but we missed one turning through there being no sign-post. Later on I wished they had consistently omitted their posts right along. We left a path which we should certainly have followed if a sign-board, ambiguously placed, hadn't misled us. Gradually our bush road became a faintly-marked dray-track, and at last petered out in a gully. It was merely the spoor of a timber-cutter.

STORIES AND POETRY FROM THE COLONIAL JOURNALS

LATER.

What were we to do? Go back miles, for the second time? Smith said there was no other possible course, and abused me for leading him astray. That decided my plans. We rested by the creek for a while. The gully was deep with fern, and here and there a lovely white orchid spread its delicate blossoms—so delicate that a finger-touch leaves livid bruises. We sat on the rocks and smoked, till Smith said:

"We'd better hurry or we'll never get to Cooloongolook to-night."

I said: "Hurry, then. I'm not going to Cooloongolook."

"Where are you going?"

I pointed with my pipe.

"Up there! Rot! What for?"

"Top of the range, and northward, to the Maclean."

"But there's no track; it's as wild as they make it!"

I filled the billies and started, Smith expostulating till he was breathless. We climbed laboriously up the steepy spur, through ferns and rotting foliage, round or over great logs. Our hearts thudded and our bodies steamed, and the salt sweat stung our eyes. We gasped in the still heat. The summit appeared to recede before us. Whenever we rested Smith swore at me faintly. He was so incongruous—so grotesquely at variance with the grand silence of the expectant bush—that I could not help laughing; yet, somehow, the humour of the situation seemed as grim to me as the Dance of Death. The bush mutely protested, and rounded in my ear some inarticulate threat. The ferns that brushed my hands gave mysterious warning. But a lyre-bird sang in the myrtle-shade, and my soul danced in the shower of his notes. Still, there is a mood in these waiting trees that I have never felt before.

I thought that there would be fairly smooth walking on top of the range (as there is in the Blue Mountains), but I was badly mistaken. The tangled jungle on the ridge is worse than the canopied ferneries of the lower land. Vines—many of them armed with strong, hooked claws—clutch at our arms, trip us, lasso our swags, and drag us this way and that in their serpent coils. Often I walked ahead, slashing a way with my sheath-knife, while Smith stumbled behind, spilling the water, and wailing in gasps. I try to shut out his voice—to forget and ignore him—but he is as persistent as fate. I thought the bush was fiercely glad to see him falling, and tearing himself through the brakes, and panting up the slopes. We pass many snakes—copperheads mostly—and I almost wonder that they do not feel this irresistible spirit of the solitude urging them to turn and strike at him with deadly fangs. Once he said he was too tired out to go a step further. He dropped his swag, and bundled himself down beside it, and there he lay, with arms thrown wide. I sat at a little distance from him—out of range of conversations. Then he squealed, and I saw him jump up, grabbing at his legs, slapping himself, squirming, and jerking. He had thrown his swag upon a nest of hopping ants, and the ground about him was a flickering swarm of venom. He tore off his clothes, and I got a stick and scraped away such of the creatures as he couldn't easily reach. I found it necessary to scrape energetically. He has been in a sort of high fever ever since—thirsty and flushed, and regretting that he hasn't brought his bottle of somebody's patent pain-killer.

We are very travel-worn this evening. My clothes are torn; my hands and arms are covered with bleeding scratches, and I feel as though I had been wading to the knees in sand. Smith is a haggard wreck. We have made a fair course northerly, and have found no great difficulty in striking the saddles, although they dip low and are thickly veiled. Of course our rate of progress has not been great. We see a good many lyre-birds. Once I found the playground of the bower-birds, and left them a few coloured blanket-threads for decoration. We have had to go a good way down into the gullies each time we wanted water, and consequently use it sparingly. Whereat Smith—but bust him, anyway! He lost his blessed old sketching-block to-day!

We've pitched our camp between the roots of an enormous tree, on one of the saddles. The water is not too far away, in a gully full of palms, myrtles, orchids, ferns, and creepers. The bush is beginning to wake in the dusk, and a multitudinous whisper rises from the sinister shadows. Nature is murmuring against intrusion.

Smith has found a big leech on his leg, and is gibbering because he has heard that the Northern River leeches get under a man's eyelids. We searched, and caught six, looping towards us, or standing on their tails and wavering. I shouldn't be surprised to find Smith sucked nearly dry in the morning; but it is too dark to shift camp in this network of wilderness. The arms of the bush are about us. But Smith is her enemy—an alien, as distasteful to her as a leprous Cabbage-Chinaman would be to a gathering in high society. The aromatic scent of wild foliage floats from the dusky jungle, and pleasant sounds are filling the night with sympathetic thoughts, and the life of the bush flows over and through me; and yet I am sick at heart.

NEXT DAY.

I wish to God I had come on this journey by myself, or with anyone but Smith! But I'll keep to my word with you, and give you a letter-diary, telling you everything of note in due order.

This bush is very noisy in the night, when all the wild creatures are abroad—mopokes and curlews, and birds whose notes are strange to me; wombats tearing up earth and rotten logs in search of roots; wallabies thudding in the scrub; bears grunting to each other in the trees; bandicoots squealing and tumbling; on every side a woof of uncouth sound—squeaking, drumming, shouting, flapping, and rending; and the leaf-mattressed earth full of a tiny, creeping rustle; and high up in the tree-tops a brush of the night-wind's trailing skirts. Once an old bush-giant fell, somewhere to the south-west, with a groaning rush and crackle, followed by one grand crash. Spare me the task of recording Smith's comments.

Early in the morning the birds began their concert, and the bush was washed from end to end with their fresh, unfaltering notes. A lyre-bird settled on the ground a few feet from me, and hopped cautiously towards me, uttering short, enquiring whistles. I lay still and watched him; but when Smith snorted and heaved in his blanket, the frightened creature rose, screaming. I got up and looked about. Within a stone's throw I saw a pair of beautiful round-breasted wonga pigeons, parading on a log. I went a little closer and watched them. They showed no fear; probably they had never before seen anybody in that part of the mountains. I left them murmuring, breast to breast, and took the billies for water (I am always the one to get water, light the fire, and cook our food). I waded slowly down through the thick ferns and decaying foliage. At each bird-note, blossoms of pure emotion sprang to sudden fulness, and drenched me with inspiring fragrance. I sat for a few moments by the creek and let the mood have play. Then a cold breath whispered up the glen, and I thought of Smith. I hastily filled my billies to the brim, and scrambled back to our camp.

"How's that for luck, Jack?" said Smith. It was the first time he had spoken with enthusiasm since the day we left Newcastle.

"What?" I asked, without looking.

"That bird—bust you!"

I glanced hastily where he pointed. There, with ruffled plumage, lay the body of a pigeon—a male wonga. Its head was crushed and bolted with blood, and its feet were curved in helpless immobility. A steam of rage rose in my brain, and dimmed my eyes, and filled my soul with dangerous apathy. As I set down my load, I asked:

"How did you get him?"

"I chucked a stick at him. He was pretty tame, you know, but it was a good shot all the same."

"Why did you kill him?"

"Because I wanted fresh meat, of course."

He sat down, and began tearing the feathers from the bird.

"Here, you don't want all that water. I want a bit to clean this brute."

I poured out some water on the ground, and left just enough for our cooking. He protested:

"Don't be a fool, Jack! Hang you, don't look at me like that! I'm not going to be looked at as though I were a murderer, even if you do eat nothing but nuts and grass!"

He used some of his tea to wash the blood and entrails from the poor creature's body. But he had not finished roasting the meat when I shouldered my swag and started.

"Wait a bit!" he shouted. "I haven't half cooked this pigeon."

I took no notice.

"Aren't you going to wait for a smoke? Oh ★ ★ ★!!"

He thrust the carcass into his pocket, and hurriedly rolled his blankets. He was afraid of being lost.

※

We plunged through the thickets until midday, and then halted on a saddle. I threw the billies to Smith, and told him I thought the water would be nearer on the western slope.

"Take care," I added, "that you come back the right way."

"You'd better go," he replied, sulkily; "I know nothing about this mountaineering rot."

But he went.

I can't tell you intelligibly what followed. You have not endured Smith and his eternal befouling of clear waters. You have not sat and listened to the almost articulate prompting of the trees. You don't know what it is to have the bush about you filling you with primeval passion till you are pure savage. I cannot even attempt explanation. I don't want to dwell on it, either; so you must pick your way as best you can.

As soon as he was out of sight a rush of determination swelled up and engulfed me like a tide. "Determination" I call it, for lack of a better word; but I seemed to have surrendered my will to the vast powers that reign in that solitude. I was their all-but-passive instrument. With the stealthy watchfulness of a prowling beast I hid our swags among the ferns in the edge of the eastern gully, and lay beside them, listening. The day was hot, and fairly still. He came up and looked about carefully; but I had concealed all traces of our halting-place. Then he shouted, carelessly:

"Hey, Jack!"

In the silence a dead branch snapped and fell almost at his feet. The bush had flung her gage. He sang out louder, and walked about the saddle, searching. As he passed me I could see the sweat on his face, and I could hear his muttering. He cried out as loud as his lungs would let him, and was answered by the ironical whispers of the wind. He started north along the range, but missed his way. I followed him quietly. When he went, shouting wildly, into a gully, I skirted the dip, and waited among the ferns on the opposite spur. I heard him labouring through the mazes of that hostile wilderness. When I caught sight of him I noticed that his eyes were starting and his jaws twitching. He stopped and cooey'd in a strange voice. Then, as though he had lost time, he ran along the edge of the hill, without noticing that he was going back to his starting-point. I tracked him with the relentless patience of a panther. I can't tell you all about it now—it's too fresh. When he threw away the billies I picked them up, and hung them on a tree where I could easily find them.

He shrieked and tore at random about the range. His clothes were tattered by the thorny growths; his face and arms were astream with blood. Three times he blundered across the gullies. And I moved in his trail and lurked in the coverts of the snakes. At last he sat down and buried his face in his arms. I watched him from behind a log. His whole body, retaining its attitude of rest, was writhing in each separate muscle. He sprang to his feet, facing me, and stretching his hands towards the sky, burst into uncontrollable laughter. Good heavens, Broome, do you know the sound of a madman's laugh? I could have stood his shrieks; but I knew that if I left him in the ranges now, my life would be a hollow dome filled with echoing peals of mirthless laughter. That hideous sound would ring in my ears for ever. With such unnatural yells did the furies pursue Orestes! In mere self-defence, I rose to my feet behind the log, and stood glaring. I could feel my face set stiff against the fore-bones of my skull, and my teeth impressed upon their protecting flesh. He saw me and gaped in dead silence. He shrank and cowered, and by degrees there came into his eyes a knowledge of what had happened. He knew what I had intended. So we stared at each other, till I said coldly:

"You'd better come for the swags."

But the stark trees droop their leaves in bitter reproach. I have broken faith with the bush.

K. S. PRICHARD, 'THE COACH-DRIVE TO WILLARA'
New Idea for Australasian Women
6 May 1906

> Willara Station,
> Back o' Beyond,
> New South Wales,
> May 24.

Dear Mother,—This whim of mine to go governessing in the wilds of N.S.W. is a bitter pill to you, I know. I'm going to write a sugar-coating—such long letters—and tell you all about everything! I'm wilful, dear! but do love wild things, and can't help it. I wish I could stay at home quietly, and be the eldest daughter, as you want. I'd be tabby, and purr to please you, dearest; but the restless spirit, Ma-Mie, will always be seeking "beyond the sunset and the baths of all the western stars." It grieves you, I know, that I can't make puddings and pies and patches. Father is breaking his heart over it.

To begin with, I'm happier alone, and spreading my wings. They're young and strong, dear, and I'm not going to be eaten by blacks or married by a squatter. All my thoughts are running over each other in the bewildering novelty of the new surroundings. The journey was wonderful. The route from Adelaide to Melbourne is "pays de connaissance" and uninteresting. We'll skip that part. Of course, I was too excited to sleep in the mid-night express. It was almost terrifying to think of the monster rushing away with me through the darkness; the yellow, goggle eyes of him restlessly flashing, his stertorous, fiery breath, and the clouds of ghostly vapour he exhaled. I imagined myself some beautiful maiden of romance being carried off by a dragon.

Dawn came on the edge of the ninety-mile desert—a red, splashing break in the ashen sky, over the grey level of the dead plain.

We did not reach Broken Hill until next day. I saw the dawn again—a pale, chill dawn—felt lonely watching it, dear, out there in the way-back sandhills.

THE COACH AND ITS DRIVER

I had to coach for three days, you remember, dear, from Broken Hill to Willara. Such a rickety, Gretna-Green affair rattled up to the station. A gaudy red and yellow it was, patched up with rusty tin, and dragged by a weedy, wild team of four horses. A miscellaneous crowd of miners, dust-stained stock-drivers and bullockies, tattered Afghans, and dirty Chinese were collected round it.

The driver came to see me. He told me Mrs. Lyne had told him to expect me. His name was Bill Northwest, and he was at my service. The man was youngish—a weather-brown, bearded fellow. He had a Virginian cow-boy look. I liked him, though his clothes did whiff of vile tobacco and stale whiskey. They were rough and uncleanly too. The primitive nerve, sad to relate, Ma-Mie, approved both the odour and the garments, congratulating itself on having found something genuine.

The wind was in my wings. They absolutely flapped with independence; so I thanked him with a dignified little air. I got inside the coach, feeling rare—the only thing in petticoats within sight, and an object of interest to the miscellany. Had my governess face on—was so demure in the grey coat and the little red hat with the long grey veil you gave me.

The only passengers beside myself were two wretched-looking men on the box; and, inside, a disreputable tramp, who was tipsy, and sprawling, half-asleep, on one seat. I sat back quietly in a far corner, hoping not to disturb his slumber. The interior of the coach was small and stuffy. It had no windows, and only a doorway.

Beyond the flourishing and altogether prosperous and commercial aspect of Broken Hill, the country began of which, vaguely, I'd been dreaming. On the outskirts of the great western silver-town began the rough life of which I love to catch glimpses. Round a big mine were settlements of miners' huts—hovels built of mud and stones, shelters of sacks sown together, and beaten-out kerosene-tins rusted and dusty.

Everything in and near Broken Hill is red with dust. A few filthy and begrimed women watched the coach pass, standing in their doorways. Children grey with smoke and dirt were playing in the dust near the road-side. The air was fine, clear, and dry; the sky infinitely blue. The lower hills of the Barrier Ranges seemed almost purple in the distance. There were patches of vivid green in their valleys. It was the only fresh colour in the landscape of red-dust plains and bare brown hills. At last we left the long, low lines of broken, rocky hills, and swept out on to the stretch of plains. Blue-grey, it is covered with salt-bush, cotton-bush, and blue-bush. Treeless and infinitely wide, for about fifty miles before you lies the unbroken, blue-grey upon the red sand of the desert.

BILL NORTHWEST INTERVENES

My fellow-traveller began to awaken at this stage. He was filthy and evil-smelling as an animal. The red face of the beast leered at me. I cowered inwardly. The wings were folded very tightly, and I gazed fixedly from the doorway. When his ugly eyes had taken me in he began to talk. I got so frightened at last, and called out to the driver. He hollered to the brute;

"Let the female passenger alone!"

The team was a fresh one, I suppose he couldn't stop. I sat down again, feeling very much the "female passenger"—and all the airs and graces of Mdlle. Gouvernante very limp. The man was clumsy and big, one of those low Irish types. He was an ugly brute, with the most vicious face unhanged. He tried to sit next to me, and put his hands on me. Nearly crying with rage and fear I called out to Mr. Bill Northwest. I'm sure my voice was pitiful enough to melt the heart of a stone.

"Sorry, lady!" Bill said, shortly, but gently. "It's about forty miles from anywhere. No water, neither; so I can't put yer out."

I heard him ask one of the men on the box to let me have his seat for a little while, but the surly brutes wouldn't move.

"Tell y' what, y' brute!" said Billy, harshly, to the tramp, "if y' don't behave yerself 'n let the female passenger alone, I'll dump y' out, 'n leave y' here in the middle of the desert, by—!"

"The horses is pretty fizzly, Miss! I can't leave 'em or I'd try me hand on him," he said, again, to me!

So I had to squeeze back into the corner again.

The drunken Irishman was uproarious at the threat. He was about twice the size of Billy.

"Ye'd put me out!" he roared, shaking his great fists out the doorway, "Ye—ye skinflint! I'd break every bone in yer body, ye-ye-rat! I'd smash you up wid a blow."

Thereat the driver threw his reins to one of the men on the box. He got down and grabbed the Irishman by his dirty red beard, and dragged him out of the coach. The road was stony, the beast too drunk to stand. Billy kicked him a bit, and gave him a bang on the head when he tried to get up. His horrid face was bleeding, his mouth full of sand. He spluttered and roared like a bull. Billy bundled him into the coach again, and got on the box.

"You get down!" he said, shortly, to the man nearest him. "You've got to get inside, or I'll treat you the same way. The female passenger's to come up here." The man cursed me, but climbed down. Can't you fancy the odious wretches!

WITH BILL ON THE BOX

Oh! I did love Bill Northwest for his fierceness! Though his anger was brutal, there was a gruff gentleness in his manner to me. Sitting next him on the box, still quivering as I pressed against his rough coat, I loved him. The old coat had the smell of old tobacco and old beer about it. Such a climb-down from my "dignified air" of the early morning, wasn't it, Ma-Mie? Billy seemed to remember that, too, because his eyes had a comical little smile; but he didn't say anything.

Before we started he put down his head, and yelled to the pair in the coach, who were quarrelling furiously already, "I'm going to prosecute yer when we get to 'Cannia, for being disorderly; 'n if yer don't leave off 'f damagin' this coach, I'll get yer six months!"

The Irishman began bawling again, "Skin a man, would ye? Bate out his brains, then prosecute him, would ye? Oh! The ill-natured baste ye are!"

We heard him yelling incoherently till it was dark. I tried to laugh, but it sounded so tearful that Billy only looked at me. We weren't quite sure how to begin to talk at first. Billy cracked his stock-whip, and called to the horses! I watched him. His arms were tough and sinewy, all hairy like Samson's. After a bit he told me yarns, all about his road-adventures, hair-breadth escapes, accidents with horses, queer passengers, and storms, and how once the coach was stuck up, coming from the opal fields. Often he is driving all night and all day; but it's the best life in the world, Bill says; and no coach-driver is ever much good at anything else.

Just as the moon was sailing up the sky in the east, and the flames of the sunset fading into the west, we pulled up at a little tin shanty, a way-side bush-in—for eating and sleeping that night!

Billy Northwest advised me to go straight to bed, after getting something to eat. He said there would be, most likely, a rowdy night in the bar-room, but he'd see I wasn't interfered with.

There were only two rooms in the place—the drink store and a big bare room with an earthen floor. Only a big wooden table was in it, and some benches. At one end, behind a screen of bags, I went to sleep, leaving Bill Northwest smoking before the fire. I woke with a racket of tipsy swearing and horseplay. Looking through the bagging, I could see Bill, standing before the fireplace, with a savage, sullen look in his eyes. The men were wild with drink, and trying to make him go back with them to the bar-room. Blind horror came over me till I heard him telling them, hoarsely and angrily, to "go to—!" When they had left him, my hero threw himself on that earthen floor. I could see all the muscles of his body fighting, the blood knotting the veins in his head and hands. He made a murmuring groan that seemed agony to me. I could not sleep again till he seemed quiet. Then my head dropped like a child's, so wearily, and I dreamt of a cavalier in moleskins, with a dark, emotionless face, keeping silent watch over the shed where I slept! Wasn't it splendid of the man, Mother dear!

Stories and Poetry from the Colonial Journals

SUNRISE ON THE PLAINS

We left Little Nolo at dawn. Billy kept the box-seat for me. Our only traveller was an old selector, who had been on the spree, and was just suffering the recovery. The undesirables of the day before were too drunk to come on. Have you ever seen a raw, four-in-hand start, Ma-Mie? There's a little kicking play, a bewildering clash and jiggle of chains, a jerk, and a struggle, and off you swing. Billy, flourishing and cracking his whip, called to the animals, making them race along. Oh! the wind in the morning was glorious—fine, clear, and chill. Sunrise on the blue-grey plains was lovely. You could see, first, the faint crimson glimmer creep out of the shadows, and a tint of pale light. The red, fading, spread in pink cloudlets over the morning sky. From a rent in the pale horizon the light splashed forth, and the sovereign gold of the sun burst on this wide, primitive world. Flocks of galahs screeched and scattered in their morning preamble across the plains, tossing their rose-pink breasts against the sky. A mob of bullocks passed on their way to the Hill—great, big Queenslanders, about five hundred of them. The morning light made golden haze of the dust that rose at their heels. In it the drovers, whose rough and raggedness delighted my heart; the big-boned, lean horses and the mob moved across the plain. I loved to hear the stock-whips cracking, like rifle-shots in the clear air, and clashing horns and bellows of the beasts.

On the salt-bush plains Bill pointed out mirages to me, and told me how often even experienced bushmen were deceived by these apparent tree-fringed, shallow lagoons.

We stopped about mid-day, at a rough shelter-shed made of bagging and boughs. Bill brought me a bit of sodden bread, with currents in, called "brownie," and a pannikin of tea, which he had unearthed from somewhere. We got a change of horses and went on. Turpentine and thorn-bushes were scattered along the roadside. In the stony rises beyond Millungara, the mulga country begins. Some way-side trees were out in a downy yellow blossom. We got a bad team at the next change. A sketchy young black horse in the rear kicked. Such a vicious little brute she was, mere skin tied over a skeleton, too.

It was splendid to watch Bill when the leaders played up at a paddock gate. His face was as hard as wood, cool, and strong. The little black kicked like fury. She kicked her heels into the mid-leader's trace. Billy ordered the man recovering from the spree to go out and undo her. The fellow was scared of putting himself near the black's heels. He fixed up, however, and then Billy thrashed the little black mare's hide to a lather.

A COUNTRY OF CROWS

Oh! the wide, weary country, the dull blue-grey of the trees, the bare, barren blue of the skies; I can't tell you how weird and wild it is! So different from the lovely green of my own sweet Southland. At first the bass of the crows, melancholy and ceaseless in the wilderness, the immensity, the vagueness, the desolation of the wide, grey plains clutches your heart and fills you with unconscious fear. The crows are in thousands all along the mulga country, and their huge rough nests are built in the fork of every tree. Only the long, dead road, with its stony declivities, the bare, grassless waste in the dense mulga scrub, meets the eye. I could not help philosophising on the wild, lonely life, the cruel, hard life of these birds of ill-omen. About here we crossed the track of Burke and Wills.

It was late moonlight when we rattled into 'Cannia. All I saw of the township was quaint and old-fashioned, tree-planted streets; the broad river beside the main road; and rose-gardens. It was a very oasis in the wilderness. Wearily I slept that night, mother dear, in a queer little square-box hotel.

Early next morning we were off again. It was blazingly hot, though supposed to be winter in this region. The roads were heavy with sand. We passed a camel-tram and a bit further on a bullock wagon that had got bogged. Billy Northwest was a bit afraid of our chance, with the heavy coach and the poor team. Heavy rains had made the roads soft in some places. Our cargo consisted, beside baggage, of an old woman, and a beggarly-looking Chinaman. In the heavy stillness at noon nothing could be heard save the plough of the wheels in the heavy sand. Not a sound of wind or bird stirred the deadly, oppressive stillness. When night came the sun sank down in the dull, flaming red behind the wave of the mulga scrub. Before the moon rose, the darkness was heavy and thick. Everything silent, even Bill's whip. He did not call to the horses, tired and toiling through the sand-hills. The old woman inside the coach was getting excited. We could hear her voice in loud exclamation. At last a fat head was thrust through the doorway.

"Ye're lost! Ye're lost! Yer fule driver!" she yelled. "This ain't Dead Man's Corner way! Don't I know the road with me eyes shut! The fule's lost the way!" She turned to the unresponsive Celestial.

I took a startled glance at Billy Northwest. I could only see his sombre shape in the blackness. Even the best drivers lost their way, sometimes, among the shifting plains, he had told me. Sand-hammocks drifted away, covered landmarks, and silted up in different places.

"The moon'll be up in a jiffy!" he said, indifferently.

"We'll be out in the desert all night!" shouted the old woman. "Oh the fule—the fule—why don't 'e git out 'n' look for the way with matches!"

The moon swam up slowly, serenely. A big yellow moon it was, that waned silvery as it climbed the sky. The old woman spluttered at intervals: "Fule! Fule! Get a match! Strike a light!" But I had boundless confidence in Bill.

By the clear silver moonlight we could see the dry courses of water—the stream that the silting sand had filled. A few grey-leafed gums, still standing, marked its course. We drove through a shallow lakelet. The splashing sound of water was delightful after those two hundreds of miles of dreary, dry desert.

STORIES AND POETRY FROM THE COLONIAL JOURNALS

Do you know, in all those days' travelling I saw no habitation or human being except at the horse-exchanges stationed on the wayside.

From the top of a hill, Billy Northwest pointed out Willara to me. It looked like a whole white township in the moonlight. At last my journeying was ended. I tried to tell my coachman and cavalier, simply, the grateful thanks of my heart. He was Australian, real and racy, a bush-man, and quoted me Gordon in the wilderness, swearing in a God-forsaken way that would make your hair jump. I enjoyed the novelty, though, of having hot words whizzing round my ears. Billy didn't say them wickedly; just carelessly, as he cracked his whip. I loved the wild life that had left the man with his rough chivalry. He wouldn't hear my prim little phrases of gratitude. We shook hands and said "good-bye" with the frankest of eyes.

I must tell you about Willara another time. But now, "Good-night, Ma-Mie."—Lovingly your own daughter,   KIT.

SYDNEY PARTRIGE, 'THE WOODHEAP'
Native Companion
1 August 1907

There are pepper-trees in my backyard, a rosebush, some vines and a woodheap. Next door, on the right, there are grass plots and fruit trees, and a shed with piles of neatly sawn lengths of wood, all exactly two feet long. Next door, on the left, is a pomegranate, oriental and gorgeous, and a quince tree, which once a year hides its spring garment of pure pale green under a veil of pinky-white. Next door to this—but come back to my yard.

No one in this long suburban street has a woodheap like mine. It comes straight from the bush in huge logs of all lengths and sizes; a great stump of peppermint, grubbed out of the ground, with earth still clinging to its roots; a six-foot length of pink gum, a foot and a-half through; a ten foot pole of white gum, to burn with it; one or two short, dark, rough bits of sheoak, very precious; a high criss-cross pile of wattles, and slabs of thick, soft bark, or slivers of thin, brittle candle-bark.

Colonies of ants come down with a load, so many that my backyard boasts an ant-hill. No one dares to touch it, for it is potent to bring before me, like a well-trained jinnee, scenes of far-off times and places. Black beetles and brown come, too, and one marched out like a grenadier a very fine fellow, whose coat gave off bright violescent gleams, mixed with a green and coppery sheen, as beautiful as anything in the Household Cavalry. All sorts of spiders lurk in the hollow logs, and if there is a bit of rotting wood, centipedes and scorpions.

Under that piece of bark by the fence no doubt you will find Ned Kelly the lizard, who came down eight loads ago. He has become domesticated and friendly. His fondness for milk carries me back in memory to the old cow-yard at home, where the lizards came every milking-time for the milk we children would squirt over their heads and into their mouths.

Some of the wood is green still, and gives out its own strong smell when cut. Odours are like connecting wires to the brain cells where old memories lie stored. The smell of that green wood brings back instantly days of ring-barking in New England with Long Ned, who afterwards shot a mate in mistake for a kangaroo, and went west and carried Matilda, to die at last of thirst out beyond the Last Fence somewhere; days of timber-cutting in the ranges, and post-splitting on the plains—when I was young, and mates and girls followed each other like figures in a kinematographe.

What does that mottled pole of white gum, with the branchlet of withering leaves still fastened to it, do for me? Where are now the great boles of its brothers that dotted the slopes of the Suntrap Hills? My God! I'd give my eyes to be galloping again under the spreading branches, with 16ft of stockwhip at my saddle-bow, and a horse under me that could turn on a dinner-plate, with a young, young heart in my breast!

The rooty peppermint, clodded with dirt and crawling with ants, flashes home to me a wide sunny flat and a crowd of people, buggies and carts and horses, a very rough-and-ready track and in-and-out racing through the trees—laughter and yells and excitement—a young chap in pink heading the race past the judge's box (a stump of peppermint), and later a flush like a sweetbriar bud on a girl's face, and a few words spoken low.

Gone—gone are the days on Suntrap, Long Ned, and the girl with the wild-rose cheeks, the horses that carried me, the youth and the strength.

An old man dreams in the sun, beside a city woodheap.

OCTOBER 1, 1907 — THE LONE HAND

IN TOWN

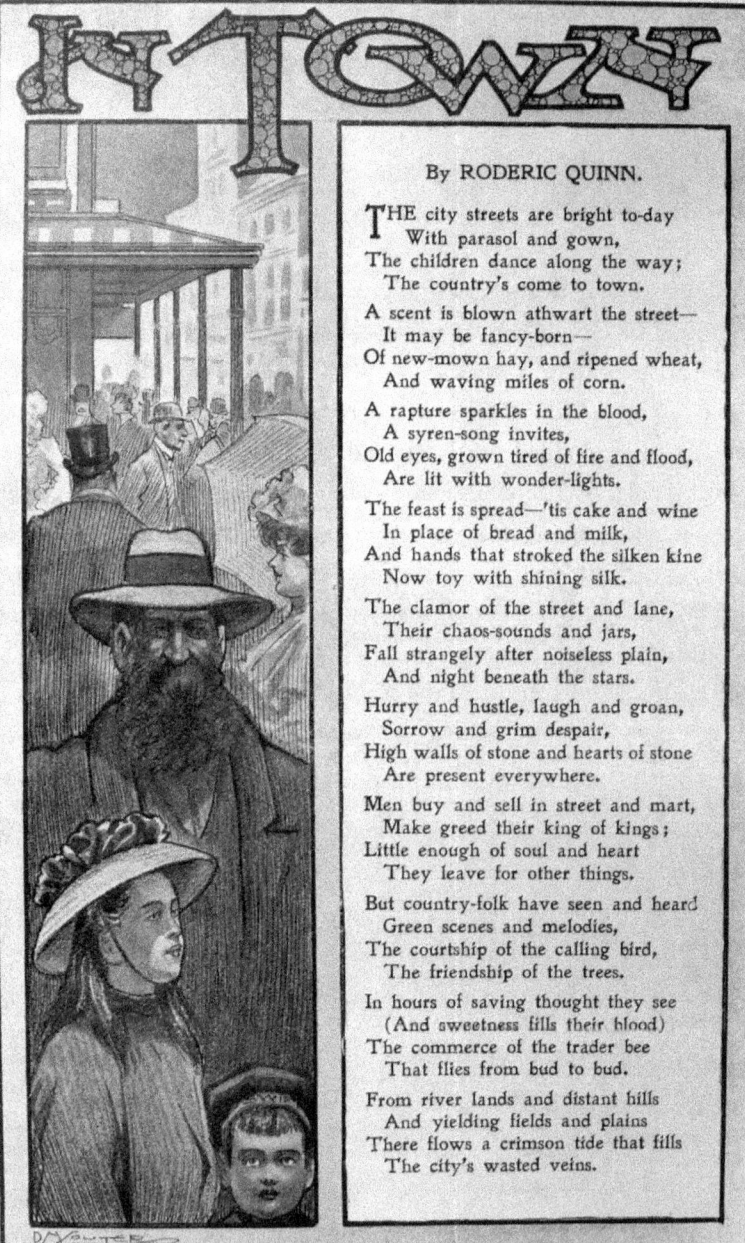

By RODERIC QUINN.

THE city streets are bright to-day
  With parasol and gown,
The children dance along the way;
  The country's come to town.

A scent is blown athwart the street—
  It may be fancy-born—
Of new-mown hay, and ripened wheat,
  And waving miles of corn.

A rapture sparkles in the blood,
  A syren-song invites,
Old eyes, grown tired of fire and flood,
  Are lit with wonder-lights.

The feast is spread—'tis cake and wine
  In place of bread and milk,
And hands that stroked the silken kine
  Now toy with shining silk.

The clamor of the street and lane,
  Their chaos-sounds and jars,
Fall strangely after noiseless plain,
  And night beneath the stars.

Hurry and hustle, laugh and groan,
  Sorrow and grim despair,
High walls of stone and hearts of stone
  Are present everywhere.

Men buy and sell in street and mart,
  Make greed their king of kings;
Little enough of soul and heart
  They leave for other things.

But country-folk have seen and heard
  Green scenes and melodies,
The courtship of the calling bird,
  The friendship of the trees.

In hours of saving thought they see
  (And sweetness fills their blood)
The commerce of the trader bee
  That flies from bud to bud.

From river lands and distant hills
  And yielding fields and plains
There flows a crimson tide that fills
  The city's wasted veins.

KATHERINE MANSFIELD, 'SILHOUETTES'
Native Companion
1 November 1907

It is evening, and very cold. From my window the laurestinus bush, in this half light, looks weighted with snow. It moves languidly, gently, backwards and forwards, and each time I look at it a delicate flower melody fills my brain.

Against the pearl sky the great hills tower, gorse-covered, leonine, magnificently savage. The air is quiet with the thin rain, yet, from the karaka tree comes a tremendous sound of bird song.

In the avenue three little boys are crouched under a tree smoking cigarettes. They are quite silent, and though terrified of discovery, their attitudes are full of luxurious abandon .... And the grey smoke floats into the air—their incense, strong and perfumed, to the Great God of the Forbidden.

Two men pass down the avenue, talking eagerly .... In the house opposite are four beautiful squares of golden light .... My room is almost in darkness. The bed frightens me—it is so long and white. And the tassel of the window blinds moves languidly to and fro. I cannot believe that it is not some living thing ....

It is growing dark. The little boys, laughing shrilly, have left the avenue.

And I, leaning out of my window, alone, peering into the gloom, am seized by a passionate desire for everything that is hidden and forbidden. I want the night to come, and kiss me with her hot mouth, and lead me through an amethyst twilight to the place of the white gardenia ....

The laurestinus bush moves languidly, gently, backwards and forwards. There is a dull, heavy sound of clocks striking far away, and, in my room, darkness, emptiness, save for the ghost-like bed. I feel to lie there quiet, silent, passively cold would be too fearful—yet—quite a little fascinating.

MABEL FORREST, 'EMILY'S PRESENT'
Lone Hand
1 October 1914

"If Emily would only take a little advice," sighed Aunt Sarah as she finished off the woollen skirt that was for Aunt Betsy's mid-summer baby.

Aunt Sarah is always so sensible. We go to her to help us to choose our Christmas presents and birthday gifts for the family. The family is a sacred thing with us. Only Emily, who is studying medicine, being up-to-date and not believing as we do, that the home is the first consideration in a woman's life—only Emily refuses to consult Aunt Sarah about anything. Consequently she makes grave mistakes. "If ever Emily gets a young man he will be someone out of a freak show, or a person of no breeding," Aunt Sarah says, because aunty has a most penetrating eye, and she always passes her opinion—sentence, Emily calls it—upon our admirers. True, Rose's husband, whom aunty chose herself from amongst some pattern Sabbath-school teaching youths who believed in Adam and Eve, and thought the world was created in a week, walked out one day with all his best shirts, and never came back. He left a note which stated, rather rudely, that he was "sick of the whole dam' family." It was inconsiderate, but inadvertent things will sometimes happen; though I do not agree with Emily, who said it was "bound to occur. If you marry a man who has never sown wild oats, the mildewed grain will rise in his gorge and choke him." I suppose Emily thinks, because she has been plucked for one medical exam, that she knows all about anatomy.

Personally, I always go to aunty for advice. I gave up Roger McCann because she said Scotchmen were often intemperate, and when that sandy-eyed Bodge girl caught him—she was always a bold creature—I only pitied her and him. He is the President of the Temperance society now, but that is possibly only a blind; one can never tell. Aunty declares that if we watch long enough he will break out. Then Emily snapped, "Pish! his wife is a good cook," as though that made any difference.

The matter under discussion was the giving of a Christmas present to Uncle Elias. In spite of his name, he was the only wild one in Father's family; and we think—though, of course, one mustn't be uncharitable—that his illness came as a judgement upon him. For he was not an old man when he was smitten. When Aunt Sarah heard of it she said it would give him time to repent. Aunty is always pious. Emily! Well, Emily was very nearly blasphemous. She doesn't choose her language. I expect she mixes too much with medical students. They are usually profane; and the girls at the women's college go out without chaperons into Paddy's market and places that smell and have an evil reputation.

Emily's skirts are transparent, too, and she shows her throat and bosom and part of her ankle. I go boned to the ears and wear two petticoats in the summer. I think with Aunt Sarah that it is so dreadful to reveal the contour of the limb. Emily says that it is because my ankles are thick. But then, Emily—I never can understand how she came to be my sister. Tom Clinker said that, too, and yet I never can quite believe he is sincere, for after that he bought her chocolates.

We made a list of our presents for Uncle Elias—useful things like air cushions and bed rests and a reading stand for his Bible. Aunt Sarah herself was giving him the Bible—an illustrated one, with a realistic picture of the Evil One in blue and yellow.

But Emily refused to tell us what she was getting for him. Uncle has been bed ridden for years. Because of his spine he has to lie flat, which he does from morning to night in a room looking on to the esplanade, Manly. He says he likes to see the girls surf-bathing. Aunt Sarah says it is truly terrible to think how much chastening it takes to humble some hearts. She shakes her head over uncle. He will not give up his brandy and tobacco either, though the doctors have told him to; and he talks in the most irreligious way about the next world, and believes we were once monkeys. But because of his affliction, Aunty encourages us to visit him.

Besides, he has money to leave.

On Christmas day we took an early boat from Circular Quay. The others, Aunt Sarah and myself meant to go to morning service at Manly after we had presented our offerings; but Emily said she would stay with uncle and watch the surfers. It was an oppressive day, and the waves came tumbling in with a lazy sound. Uncle was staring sideways through the window.

"Distrust the Greeks and those that bring gifts," he said cheerfully, with his queer, twisted smile, when he saw our parcels; especially when Aunt Sarah's Bible was unwrapped.

I cannot say he showed any pleasure in our presents, though he thanked us, because he belongs to a generation when people had manners. But when Emily's cardboard box was put into his hands he laughed, "What's she giving me? A jack in the box I'll be bound, for the old man to pull the string."

There never was anybody so ridiculous as Emily. The idea of buying a new hat for a man who never goes out of doors, who can't rise from his reclining position, who will never move till the undertaker carries him off. The notion was fairly indecent.

Aunt Sarah, who believes in being honest, said as much. But uncle's sunken eyes flashed. "The very thing I wanted; the very thing!"

It seems he had been pining for a new hat for months and was ashamed to ask his valet to get one; for uncle has the vain man's dread of ridicule, and Emily had somehow guessed his desire. Now he wears it all day in bed, and looks at himself in the hand-mirror placed near him, and the doctors say he is ever so much brighter.

After that we went to church. Aunt Sarah had a good deal to say about human pride, and the ruling passion strong in death as we went down the Corso to the dissenting chapel. She told us to turn our eyes from the half-naked women promenading with members of the other sex on the beach. She was obliged to look herself, to be able to tell us what to avoid; so she arrived at the chapel hot with indignation. She said she did not know what Sydney people were coming to, with undraped statues in the gardens, and tango teas and mixed bathing. That she went to sleep during the Christmas sermon was solely due to her exhaustion after all she had gone through in the morning.

Uncle Elias gave away every present we had so thoughtfully prepared for him. The Bible went to the Salvation Army. He was a most ungrateful and unrepentant old man.

When he died quite suddenly six months afterwards it was Emily who inherited all his fortune.

She lives in a flat now, estranged from her family. We cannot but feel she took a mean advantage. If only *I* had thought of that hat.

PART 5

Colonial Journals and their Artists
KEN GELDER & RACHAEL WEAVER

Julian R. Ashton, 'An Aim for Australian Art', *Centennial Magazine*, 1 August 1888
200

Mrs Charles Bright, 'Mr Livingstone Hopkins: "Hop", of the *Bulletin*', *Cosmos*, 30 March 1895
203

'Titian Redde' (A.G. Stephens), 'Artists in Australia: Frank Mahony', *Bookfellow*, 25 March 1899
206

'George Taylor and his Art', *A.A.A.: All About Australians*, 1 December 1902
208

George Taylor, 'Caricature and its History', *Steele Rudd's Magazine*, April 1905
212

'Phil May…By One Who Knew Him', *Our Swag*, 22 December 1905
215

Phil May, 'Phil May in Sydney', *Bulletin*, 22 December 1905
217

Edward Dyson, 'Billy Bluegum', *Lone Hand*, 1 August 1912
218

Norman Lindsay, 'Billy Bluegum', *Lone Hand*, 1 August 1912
220

5

Colonial Journals and their Artists
KEN GELDER & RACHAEL WEAVER

THE VERY EARLY COLONIAL AUSTRALIAN journals were visually plain, with the covers showing little adornment beyond the typography of the journal's title or perhaps a patterned border or a few generic flourishes in the corners. By the late 1830s, however, editors were drawing on the skills of local artists and designers. According to Frank S. Greenop, James Tegg's *Literary News* (12 August 1837 – 3 February 1838) was the first colonial journal to include an illustration, an image from Australian natural history: 'Apart from being a creditable weekly publication, the *Literary News* left behind it one innovation: it had broken the even type measure of its column to include in one issue an illustration which was engraved on wood, a picture of a platypus illustrating an article describing the creature. Only once before had a magazine included an illustration, and that was the lithographic frontispiece which appeared in some issues of the *Hobart Town Monthly*'.[1] Not long afterwards, however, colonial journals began to employ local illustrators to develop their visual content, livening up the printed page. The short-lived *Arden's Sydney Magazine* (September – October 1843) highlighted its association with the immigrant lithographer and painter J. S. Prout: 'we're inclined to hope', George Arden wrote, 'that Mr. Prout's connection with our literary labours will not be disadvantageous to his fame as an Artist'. Prout's sketch for the first issue, 'The Tank Stream, Sydney, 1843', is generically typical of the kinds of illustrations found in the journals around this time. They give realistic black-and-white snapshots of aspects of colonial urban development (the Tank Stream had provided fresh water to Sydney in the early days of the colony), bush landscapes, local natural history and portraiture. In fact, they work precisely as precursors to documentary photography – which made its way into the colonial journals much later on, towards the end of the century.

Sketches of colonial types soon began to populate the pages of those journals that aimed for popular readerships. This was the focus of the lively Sydney journal *Heads of the People* (April 1847 – March 1848), which featured character sketches on its cover each week of recognisable colonial types like government officials, public figures, and peripheral urban characters like the 'night auctioneer' or the 'poet'. Edited by the lithographer and printer William Baker, it took its title from a series of illustrated character studies published in England in 1840–41 by a group of writers and artists that included William Thackeray, Leigh Hunt and Douglas Jerrold. Jerrold had been a key contributor to the satirical illustrated London magazine *Punch*, which began in 1841 with Henry Mayhew as one of its editors and quickly developed distinctive styles of caricature. *Punch* soon came to Australia, published in Melbourne in 1855 and then in Sydney in 1864, later spreading across the colonies with local versions published in Adelaide, Ballarat and a number of other provincial centres. The journalist Frederick Sinnett – an extract from his serialised essay 'The Fiction Fields of Australia' (1856) appears in part two of this book – was a founding editor of the Melbourne *Punch*. Satirical sketches soon became important to other colonial journals too, like Henry Kendall and James Smith's *Touchstone* – which featured a jester as the figurehead on its front cover – and Marcus Clarke's *Humbug*. Caricature went on to become a defining feature of journal publishing in Australia. The 1880s gave a new prominence to the role of the satirical sketch artist. The *Bulletin* hired the American illustrator Livingstone Hopkins ('Hop') in 1883 and he remained a key contributor for over thirty years, designing many of the journal's striking covers. The *Bulletin* also brought the British cartoonist Phil May over in 1886, with May's illustrations going on to become celebrated worldwide. A prominent figure in Sydney, he cultivated a 'grotesque' cartoon style that he brought to bear even on himself in his various self-portraits. We have included an affectionate recollection of Phil May from *Our Swag* (April 1903 – August 1906), written a couple of years after his death.

George Augustine Taylor was another prominent *Bulletin* cartoonist in the 1890s, who also sketched for Melbourne's *Punch* and numerous other local journals and newspapers. In his article for *Steele Rudd's Magazine*, he pays tribute to a number of local artists and illustrators, asserting that in Australia 'our spirit of caricature rises beyond that of any other nationality in its fearlessness'. Taylor even established his own short-lived monthly, *Ha! Ha: A Merry Newspaper Magazine for Australians* (9 April – 18 June 1898), bearing out this satirical ethos. But the article about his work in *A.A.A.: All About Australians* sees Taylor – a member of the bohemian Dawn and Dusk Club and the Art Society of New South Wales – defending higher artistic tastes in Australia as well.

Julian Ashton was an art teacher, painter and advocate for Australian art, establishing the Sydney Art School in the 1890s. His article in the *Centennial Magazine* argues for an Australian art that is contemporary rather than conspicuously colonial ('from the back blocks'). By this time, the local journals were indeed fostering higher aspirations for the colonial art scene; on the other hand, their artists frequently worked across a range of genres, from the decorative arts right through to cartoon sketches and commercial advertising. Images of contemporary life jostled for space alongside more traditionally colonial kinds of subject matter that by this time would have been all too familiar to readers. Norman Lindsay, a prolific illustrator of stories and poems, drew extensively for the *Bulletin*, the *Lone Hand* and *Steele Rudd's Magazine*; he went on to become one of Australia's most successful popular artists. His comic sketches of the waist-coated koala Billie Bluegum – a city-educated character energetically devoted to improving bush conditions – accompanied Edward Dyson's stories in the *Lone Hand* in 1912 and were the precursors to Lindsay's Bunyip Bluegum character in *The Magic Pudding* (1918). Despite Ashton's aspirations for a properly contemporary Australian art, by the end of the nineteenth century Australian journals continued to invest in the visual stereotypes of earlier bush experiences. Frank Mahony sketched for the *Bulletin* and the *Australian Town and Country Journal*, among others; as we noted in part three, he also illustrated Lawson's *While the Billy Boils*. The article we've included here from the *Bookfellow* (January – May 1899) by 'Titian Redde' – aka A. G. Stephens, the journal's editor – celebrates Mahony's fascination with horses and horsemen and identifies his name as 'a bush-word over broad Australia', although it is critical of his capacities as an artist. Stephens' article reminds us of the ongoing significance of bush themes in the visual repertoire of the colonial journals.

At the same time, some colonial journals were developing their interests in the decorative arts, influenced by modern, fin-de-siècle aesthetics imported from Europe. George W. Lambert had studied under Julian Ashton in Sydney and sketched for the *Bulletin*. But alongside his iconic bush paintings, he developed a more figurative approach that saw him contribute a striking cover design to the first issue of the short-lived *Australian Magazine*, in March 1899. His image of a naked man on a demonic horse leaping through a bed of waratahs could not be further removed from the bush horsemen sketched by Mahony and his contemporaries. The *Australian Magazine* brought together a dynamic group of writers and artists, including Roderic Quinn, John le Gay Brereton, D. H. Souter, Thea Proctor and Lambert himself. Its florid, decorative artwork reflected decadent and symbolist influences, although these were in fact shared across a number of colonial journals including the *Bulletin*, the *Bookfellow* (which reproduced some of Aubrey Beardsley's artwork), the *Lone Hand* (with its columns on 'French Literature') and the *Centennial Magazine,* which had published Oscar Wilde's poem 'Symphony in Yellow' ten years earlier in February 1889. Souter was a remarkably prolific late colonial artist, regularly contributing cartoons to the *Bulletin*. Influenced by Art Nouveau, Souter's slender black and white cat – 'Kateroo' – soon became iconic, decorating Doulton chinaware but also featuring on the covers of journals like the *Lone Hand*. Souter also provided cover designs for the *Native Companion*; so did the painter and feminist Dora L. Sommers, and also Norman Lindsay's sister Ruby, who signed her drawings 'Ruby Lind'. We can think about the journals around the turn of the century as fostering two distinct styles and sensibilities: a characteristically masculine form of nationalism that sees bush images reproduced with increasing sentimentality, and what might be considered a more feminine cosmopolitanism (in work by both male and female artists) that continued to draw its influences from contemporary Europe.

---

1   Greenop, *History of Magazine Publishing in Australia*, p. 74.

COLONIAL JOURNALS AND THEIR ARTISTS

JULIAN R. ASHTON, 'AN AIM FOR AUSTRALIAN ART'
Centennial Magazine
1 August 1888

To anyone interested in Australian Art, the diversity of opinion as to what should be its aim and motive is bewildering in the extreme. One critic insists that historical subjects should be the theme to inspire our artists. The landing of Cook; the Burke and Wills expedition; or some episode in the life of Bligh—these are favourite examples of the subjects which artists are invited to take up. Then there is the gentleman who sees no beauty in any subject unless it is from the back blocks. Treeless plains covered with parched grass, the blackfellow, kangaroo, and emu, men dying of thirst or being speared, men in any form of agony or danger, and landscapes void of every feature which charms the eye, are to him subjects peculiarly Australian in character.

Australian in character! That is the keynote of Australian criticism. We are expected to have an Art which no one can mistake for that of any other country than Australia, totally forgetting the fact that Art belongs to no country, but to all time. Men and women are formed here as they are all over the world. The same language and ideas, and to a large extent the same customs and dress are adopted here, that are in use over a great portion of the civilised globe, but our Art must be something apart from all this. Because the artists of other countries are endeavouring to paint the beautiful, we as Australians should take as subjects those which are repelling and ugly. Because modern artists are beginning to see that true historical painting consists in reproducing the scenes which lie around them, Australian artists should go back two generations and give us imaginary pictures of a gentleman in the cleanest of knee-breeches landing on a rock and declaring a country of which he knew nothing one of the possessions of His Most Gracious Majesty King George the Fourth.

What a common idea it is that Art is more dignified when it deals with bygone times! No artist is supposed to be so well employed as when he is painting things he has never seen. The things he does see round him are too commonplace and unpoetical to merit attention. This is the usually received opinion, and a most difficult opinion it is to eradicate from the common mind. There is nothing poetical in the steam engine, yet Turner reproduced the railway train in one of his most noted pictures. Can such a thing as an Orient steamship be beautiful? The answer is, that Wylie can make it so. In truth, the only pictures of past times which will live, will be those which reproduce the life and scenes of the times in which they were painted. Velasquez and Rembrandt will inspire artists as long as Art exists, because they saw beauty in their everyday life and surroundings, and frankly expressed it in their work. The old Greek statues, of which we fortunately possess many examples, will live forever, for the reason that their sculptors reproduced the figures they saw constantly around them. Their gods and goddesses were the faultless forms of the Greek men and women they found in the streets or market place. To us they are ever true, and fresh, and wonderful, because they show us the beauty of the human form. Those artists saw nothing undignified in making use of the materials round them. It may be that one of the chief things Art has to teach, is the lesson that all great Art of past times was represented by men who frankly accepted their own time and did not escape from it. If men could but see it, there is as much beauty and poetry now, not only in the human figure but in the commonest forms of life around us as ever there was,—and there is no doubt that beauty of some sort should be insisted upon.

It does not need the artist to bring bare material fact before us, stripped of that poetic grace and charm, which he knows how to impart to it. The photographer can do that. Indeed one of the highest attributes of the artist seems to me to be the power of selection, or that power which enables him first to discern the beautiful, and then to set it free from all lets and hindrances which prevent the world from seeing it with him. I forget who it was who said "Art is the power of selection"; if this is not quite true, it is very nearly so. Naturally the finer the perceptions of the artist, so much the truer will be his rendering of the accepted fact. It seems a bold thing to say, but to an artist the subject of a picture matters but little. So that the composition and color satisfy the eye, or rather, so long as beauty of line, and truth and delicacy of tone is attained, the educated lover of pictures is satisfied with the simplest theme.

To the general public a picture full of incident, no matter how it is painted, so that it be ludicrous, possesses greater interest than, for example, any portrait can ever do. But this is not the case with the lover of painting. He has noted with wonder the lovely color on the cheek of a child, the delicate graduations of hue from chin to brow, the exquisitely soft blending of the hair into the face, and the silky tresses full of most subtle differences of tone. The reproduction of these in a masterly manner, without faltering or hesitation, fills him with honest satisfaction.

He has watched the opalescent tints of the morning; the glow of sunset has touched him with its glory and sadness. He feels the introduction of a false note of color as a musician would a discord; it hurts him. The lovely blue of the distant hills strikes some chord in his nature which does not demand a clearly defined subject carefully worked out by line and rule, but is fully satisfied with this beautiful and mysterious tint. He sees and feels and is satisfied. The common man sees nothing of all this. A child's face! there's nothing in that, there are too many of them. The sunrise he does his best never to see, and in his opinion sunset is a daily recurring institution, designed by Providence to let him know that it is time for him to take boat or tram to his dinner. The blue of hills affects him not one jot, unless they contain good feed for cattle or sheep, in which case they are very fine hills indeed.

COLONIAL JOURNALS AND THEIR ARTISTS

Some of the most estimable people in Australia do not know a beautiful thing when they see it. Everything that the heart can wish for seems to be theirs, but go to their homes, and it is easy enough to note that there is one virtue they do not possess. Heaven has not granted them the artistic eye and sense, the power to perceive the beautiful in nature, in dress, in manner, or in conversation. They are hopelessly and irredeemably commonplace.

The aim of Art should be to educate and refine such minds, not by themes chosen from the past, but alone—rich and fruitful as the past is in inspiration for the present—by interpreting with grace and beauty, the simple themes that every day life will furnish. Many beautiful subjects for pictures have I seen, and still see constantly around me, which would touch into sensibility such natures as these, not perhaps at first from any love of art, but because of the fact that they were things or scenes well-known to them; and their interest and attention would be excited by the recognition of landmarks familiar from childhood. Places where they had made love, the scenes of their early good fortunes, spots hallowed in their minds by the fact that there they had silently fought through some such dark and bitter trial as comes at some time or other into the life of every man born of women. Very gradually the sense of seeing would be awakened, and a keen and fresh delight would be experienced in making use of those powers granted to every human being, but so often allowed to lie dormant. This is the true meaning of the educational power of Art, and a very noble meaning it appears to me.

The artist should preach the beautiful in our commonplace and everyday existence, not only to those who will listen, but to those who will not. That the seed may fall upon barren places is none of the artist's business. He paints because he must. It is the only thing worth doing or living for; else is he no true artist. But before all he must learn that in spite of the suggestions of the critics and his friends' advice, he has little or nothing to do with the Past. The Future he may look forward to, but it can never be his. The Present alone belongs to him, with all its varied forms of life, its color, and its romance.

I have seen finer subjects in Australia, England, and France than any ever painted by the old masters. Not finer than they saw, perhaps, for in painting as in all other Art the execution falls far short of the conception. But, indeed, no country is so God-forsaken that poetry and romance may not find some abiding place therein. It but needs the artist's hand and eye to place it before the world, and sooner or later this fact must surely be recognised.

If the artists of Australia, whose hands are daily strengthening, will band themselves to paint the Australia of to-day, they will leave behind them historical pictures of the greatest value to coming generations. Pictures which, in spite of all criticism, must perforce be eventually Australian: and which will serve as a high educational power to those poor folk of whom unfortunately it might sometimes be written, "Eyes have they but they see not; ears have they but they hear not."

MRS CHARLES BRIGHT, 'MR LIVINGSTONE HOPKINS: "HOP", OF THE *BULLETIN*
Cosmos
30 March 1895

There are few people throughout the length and breadth of Australasia who are not familiar with the name of "Hop," of the Sydney *Bulletin*. From Coolgardie to the capitals of the Australian colonies, in every hamlet, woolshed, or mining township, the *Bulletin* finds each week a circle of eager readers. Travellers say that by the camp fires of stock-drivers and swagsmen, nothing is hailed with so much satisfaction as a stray copy of the racy Sydney paper, while, when the incoming mail steamers touch at Albany, it is seized by the weary voyagers, as a welcome relief from the monotonous platitudes indulged in by the average saloon passenger. But all turn first to the cartoons as a sure index of the trend of public affairs in Australia. However much people may declaim against the rough radicalism of the reading matter, "Hop's" illustrations are studied and admired for the wonderful skill that sometimes with a few pencil strokes presents the irresistibly comic side of social or political life. It is thirteen years since a representative of the *Bulletin* called on Mr. Hopkins in his Nassan-street studio, New York, and offered him a three years' engagement on that paper. For more than a dozen years Mr. Hopkins had occupied a distinguished position in the States as illustrator of magazines like *St. Nicholas* and the *Century*, contributing sketches of his own composition, or illustrations for comic stories and verses. There was hardly an illustrated American paper or periodical of repute in which his work did not appear, and he occasionally wrote short articles, bursting out into prose or verse when least expected. Work of this kind leaves little time for relaxation, and when the invitation to Sydney was tendered he was considering the advisability of following in the wake of many brother artists, and migrating to Paris for a season, as a means of escaping from a fixed groove. The sudden appearance of the emissary from the Antipodes was as dramatic and startling as that of Mephistopheles in *Faust*, and after assuring himself that his visitor was not an escaped lunatic, but a gentleman very much in earnest for the reputation of his paper, he decided to pitch his tent under the Southern Cross with his wife and three children. The three years have extended to thirteen, and Mr. Hopkins is working with as great success as ever, throwing off from his pencil, each week, sketches that occasionally convulse the whole Continent with laughter.

Although the magic word "Hop" draws our eyes with lively expectation to the picture bearing his signature, we do not know much of our favourite caricaturist. Like many other hard workers, society, in its usually accepted sense, has no charms for him. A club man, *par excellence*, he is one of the most welcome *confrères* at many a gathering at the Atheneum Club, or valedictory banquet, or supper when some artist is given a "send off." It is a first duty to secure "Hop" as chairman for such a gathering, for he is a matchless after-dinner speaker, and spreads a halo of good humour around that seems contagious. The same effect has been noticeable at the few lectures he has given in Sydney. When talking of so serious a matter to himself as "Picture Writing," in which he held forth at the Art Society's Rooms and elsewhere, he will suddenly, after going deeply and learnedly into the technical side of his subject, give a comic turn to the whole that keeps his audience in a simmer of good-humour and expectation. As ladies are not yet privileged to enter a club, my first introduction to Mr. Hopkins was at his studio. Like a wise man, he does not allow his work to subjugate him; but, instead, subjugates his work, by what Schopenhauer would call the righteous Will. Everything is ordered by rule—the days at the studio, and the days for recreation—and to this may possibly be attributed the freshness of his style. When his week's work is over, he has several hobbies to occupy his attention—etching, carpentering, and, when he is not making a dog's house or other accessory to his home, playing quoits, at which he is an expert, or fishing. When the time arrives for his subjects to be evolved, he sits down, and, almost to the minute, may be depended on to have reproduced the ideas threshed out at the editorial conclave where the work of the artist is allocated. This characteristic reminds one of Anthony Trollope, who waxes eloquent in his "Autobiography" on the efficacy of a piece of cobbler's wax on the seat of the would-be author. According to this prolific novelist, if a person endowed with any literary gift will but sit at his desk, and doggedly do his utmost, he must eventually succeed. It is not often, however, that this characteristic is allied to striking originality. In "Hop's" case, however, you might search illustrated papers throughout the world in vain to find even a "cue" to any of his productions. He is essentially an originator.

Chatting with Mr. Hopkins about his art it is interesting to a lay person who only knows how to admire effective drawing to hear him dilate on the various kinds of illustrative work. The distinction between the comic and the serious artist has been gradually lost, he says, and in most of the so-called humorous pictures it is the letterpress that tells the joke, not the artist. Cover the printed matter, for instance, under one of Du Maurier's pictures in *Punch*, and the sketch will be generally found to be that of high-bred society as seen in London drawing-rooms. The lovely women, and their cavaliers and environment do not explain the joke. You must read below the sketch to see what you are intended to laugh at. So it is with rare exceptions in every other publication of the kind. Specimens of the caricaturist's work are very rare, the most notable English examples being those in *Vanity Fair*, where the artist takes a public man and exaggerates any personal characteristic or defect. Hogarth, who is generally accepted as a typical caricaturist, was nothing of the kind, such pictures as "The Rake's Progress" and "The Industrious and Idle Apprentice" being a sort of illustrated moral lesson. Even Cruickshank was not exactly a caricaturist, and Mr. Hopkins considers that the early illustrations of Dickens' works were inadequate. "For some reason" he says "the artists considered him a humorous writer," whereas he was essentially a caricaturist, with a purpose. Of all the artists who have essayed their hand on Dickens' novels, Mr. Hopkins suggests that the most successful was Luke Fildes, whose work on the unfinished novel "Edwin Drood" is beyond all praise.

When speaking of Charles Dickens, it was an easy transition to revert to the genesis of the "Pickwick Papers" and recall how that volume owed its existence to what was apparently mere chance. It is well-known to many that a number of illustrations, notably of a sporting character, were prepared by the artist, Robert Seymour, who wished to have a story written up to them. Several gentlemen were invited to attempt the work, among them being Mr. Charles Whitehead, afterwards on the Melbourne press, author of a successful novel, "Richard Savage," published by Bentley and Sons. Eventually Charles Dickens undertook the task, and under the *nom-de-plume* of "Boz," fairly electrified the public by his opening chapters. But the pictures were nowhere. The genius of the young writer had evidently refused to be trammelled by the illustrations, and the only character that preserved any of the artist's ideas was that of Winkle. The success of the story was so great that Dickens was allowed a free hand, and the artist's suicide a few weeks later was a tragic ending to his share in the business. Illustrations have something to do with the success of a work, Mr. Hopkins considers, and Du Maurier's "Trilby" was instanced as a case in point. There seems to be a recollection of Thackeray all through this extraordinarily popular novel, but with this enormous difference. When Thackeray illustrated his own works, the drawings were imperfect and the writing was superb. In Du Maurier's book the exact opposite is the case. The illustrations make the book, which, though pleasant enough reading, is not, by any means, a work of genius. Of the character in "Trilby," supposed to be meant for Whistler, Mr. Hopkins thinks that artist has himself to blame for the attention drawn to it—a case of hypersensitiveness, he conceives, as it is difficult for the ordinary reader to detect the resemblance so much resented.

In answer to an interrogatory concerning his own authorship, Mr. Hopkins has a curious story to tell of the only volume he has as yet published. It was at the time of the Philadelphian Exhibition, in 1876, when a great wave of national pride surged over the United States, that Mr. George W. Carleton, the publisher of Artemus Ward's, Josh Billings', and Bret Harte's earlier works, suggested to Mr. Hopkins the idea of a "Comic History of the United States" as an apt subject for the prevailing spread-eagleism. Mr. Hopkins had illustrated some of Josh Billings' books for this publisher, and at once prepared 75 pictures for the contemplated volume, besides writing the text. As after events proved, it was a creditable publication, but on its first appearance met with a howl of derision from the newspapers. It was hustled almost out of existence by the sapient critics, who, over-impressed with the solemnity, if not sanctity, of the Fathers of their glorious Constitution, whose Centenary was being celebrated, stigmatised the man who dared to joke on the subject as one who "would dance a jig on his grandmother's grave." The position was philosophically accepted by the object of their wrathful indignation. The book only ran through its one edition of 1000 copies, and for the time was dropped. A year or two later when this fever of patriotism had evaporated, and the Philadelphia Exhibition and its commemoration faded from recollection, Mr. Hopkins made the acquaintance of Cassell & Co., the great publishers. Their manager mentioned "The Comic History of the United States," on one occasion, and expressed surprise that so good a book should have been unsuccessful. He proposed to re-publish it, if the plates, the joint property of Mr. Hopkins and Mr. Carleton, the publisher, could be obtained. A generous response was made by the latter gentleman, who at once gave Mr. Hopkins *carte blanche* in the matter, and an order on the printers for the blocks, The book was immediately brought out in a cheaper edition at 3s., and has had a continuous sale ever since, Mr. Hopkins receiving royalty to the present time on every copy sold. It was strange, he said, as showing the inception of similar ideas, that it was not until his book was published that he became acquainted with Gilbert a'Beckett's *Comic History of England*, which was then brought under his notice. One grows out of this sort of thing, Mr. Hopkins remarks, and my maturer judgment would not lead me to publish a volume of the kind now, although it has met with so much appreciation.

Many of Mr. Hopkins' sketches have become immortal, as it were. Who among us can ever forget "The Roll Call of the Soudan Contingent," "The Landing of the Forefathers," or still later ones, such as that when the Cricket mania was in full possession of the place, a few weeks ago, called "The Relative Value of things in Australia just now," where a huge cricket ball overshadows politics, religion, spooks, and everything else. He is essentially a caricaturist. "Laughter holding both his sides" is his familiar spirit, and the sketches inscribed with the pseudonym "Hop" have undoubtedly added to the sum of human enjoyment throughout the colonies. Mention has been made of Mr. Hopkins' ability as a lecturer, and since writing the above, it has been intimated that a long-contemplated plan of his is about to be put into execution. In order to obtain a wider acquaintance with the colonies, and to secure temporary relaxation from his artistic work, Mr. Hopkins has arranged to give a series of lectures throughout Australia, extending over three months. In this way, the public will be able to gain the personal knowledge of the genial caricaturist it has been the writer's desire to convey.

'TITIAN REDDE' (A.G. STEPHENS), 'ARTISTS IN AUSTRALIA: FRANK MAHONY'
Bookfellow
25 March 1899

Francis Mahony—affectionately and conveniently Frank: the not-very-recent portrait is moderately like him—is not only an artist in Australia, he is an Australian artist. And though theoretically the world is a good man's country, and his humanity should bond all men in brotherhood, the rooted instincts of family, friends, fatherland, will not yet be denied supremacy. To be Australian need better no man's work; but it betters his Australian claim. He and you start acquaintance from the vantage of many common sympathies, aims, ideals. He is kin, and closer: to be alien is necessarily to be alienated.

Born in what is now Flinders-lane, Melbourne, Mahony remains in his middle thirties a young man of promise. Will he ever perform, in a large sense? He hopes so; he thinks so. "I feel to have more strength now than ever I had: I can see better, and do better. If I get a chance—" Ah, the good chance! denied to so many of us, and to none more than to our artists. For an artist-painter—such as Mahony is—has at the beginning to acquire by long, laborious study a difficult and complicated technique. No matter how ardently he may imagine, he must learn to draw, to colour, to compose. He needs schooling—have we schools? That is, though we have classes and teachers, have we the inspired instructor, born to the task, living not for himself, but wholly and solely in his pupils? Then the young artist wants patrons—he must live; and we have few purchasers, no patron as Ruskin was a patron. More than all he wants atmosphere—the environment which talks, thinks, dreams Art, eats and drinks Art, wakes and sleeps Art; and alas! we have no atmosphere (none of artistic accomplishment, though there be ample for natural inspiration). Sum it up in this: that Art is old and Australia new, and the ragged flowers on our hillsides, though they have a fresh grace of their own, cannot emulate the rich blooms cultured in European compost. As Mrs. Gamp observed in another relation, we are born into a wale, and we live in a wale, and we must take the consequences of such a situation. Genius, of course, can fly beyond the hemming peaks; but there is thus far only question of a good pedestrian talent. So on the whole Mahony remains a young man of promise.

Frank Mahony's father was Irish, his mother Cornish—the blend which brought the Brontë sisters. From the same Mahony stock sprang he of Watergrasshill, Francis Sylvester Mahony, the brilliant "Father Prout." (The "P." of Mahony's familiar signature "F.P.M." fancifully suggests this relationship, but has no baptismal warrant). Mahony is tenth of a family of eleven, of whom four survive: his elder brother is M.P. for Annandale in N.S.W. Legislature.

Mahony came to Sydney when he was ten years old, and has stayed there ever since. His taste for picturing was early shown, and grew in spite of obstacles. His father, having little faith in the artist's vocation, wished him to adopt some "substantial" profession; and when his school days were over Mahony was for a short time draughting in a Sydney architect's office, by way of vague compromise. He drew horses instead of plans; attended Signor Anivitti's at the Art Gallery school; and gradually acquired confidence and skill enough to go painting for a livelihood.

For the last ten years Mahony's work has been prized in Sydney studios, and his drawings in the *Bulletin* have made his name a bush-word over broad Australia. Always his art has hovered round horses: he has instinctive fellowship with horses, has studied horses more than men; and it is as a painter of horses that he has been hitherto best known and most valued. Certainly no one in Australia paints horses with equal truth, and sympathy, and power. Mahony carries these qualities throughout his work: though still purely objective, it shows a sense of and a striving for the ideal. He is perhaps less apt with the pen; but with the brush—and time—there are few "effects" in the line of his likings which he cannot accurately and adequately realise.

The drawing here produced from *The Bulletin*, though on too small a scale to do the artist justice, may hint the admirable "feeling" which Mahony puts into his animal-pictures. He is really a master of a horse's moods, and his pictures really utter them. The "hack" that young Sliprails begins with is a very different animal from the one which moves dispiritedly away after the contest. Mahony has undertaken book-illustration, with success when the themes suited him; and the volume of Barcroft Boake's poems, in particular, contains some fine examples of his skill. There is force and motion in the glimpse of a woman controlling a runaway coach, here given by the courtesy of Boake's publishers, Messrs. Angus and Robertson.

Mahony's pictures of importance number a dozen or so, nearly all in oils. None of them is memorable; all are interesting; some are remarkably successful in reaching the result sought-for. Of the three hung in N.S.W. National Gallery, "As in the Days of Old," here reproduced from a photograph by Messrs. Kerry and Co., is perhaps most attractive to general tastes. It is an episode of bush-ranging days, thoroughly felt, strongly presented. "The Cry of the Mothers" is a picture of horses and cattle on the margin of a flooded river; "The Straggler," another animal piece, is very effective in its way. In "The Centaurs," shown at Sydney Art Society's Exhibition last year, Mahony attempted on a larger canvas a more ambitious design—two centaurs struggling for mastery on the edge of a cliff, with a bevy of nymphs waiting for the conqueror. The idea and treatment were rightly praised; but the subject demanded a technique still beyond Mahony's capacity. Yet there was a brave attempt.

Here, for the present, one may hopefully leave our young man of promise. Will he go far? At least he will go farther.

'GEORGE TAYLOR AND HIS ART'
A.A.A.: All About Australians
1 December 1902

The venerable chestnut that "a prophet is without honor in his own country," is disproved in the case of Mr. George Taylor, for there is hardly a journal of any consequence in Australia that has not been decorated with the work of this versatile artist. Considering his art advent only dates back to 1896, his rapid rise to a foremost position in the ranks of art-humorists is remarkable.

Born in Sydney, Mr. Taylor has not worked out of his native place, though his work has been published as far off as London and New York. His humor has effervesced in no less than twenty-four Australian journals, among which may be mentioned *The Sunday Times, Sydney Mail, Town and Country Journal, Bulletin, Star, Arrow, Referee, Melbourne Punch, The Field, Adelaide Critic*; and if the scope of his work is any evidence of his popularity Mr. Taylor easily holds a front place. Being always a free lance he can command a wider field than if tied to any particular journal.

He is a stickler for originality, as his work testifies. One of his styles of drawing first produced in the *Bulletin*, having [sic] the honor of being plagiarised in England and America. He has created many novel methods of reproduction, and there are few better experts in color printing in the Commonwealth.

Mr. Taylor is thorough in all his work. For local color he has "humped bluey" in the west. He has as well "fossicked" on Turon (also probably for "local color"), and he spent two awful nights in the Sydney opium dens in order to gather material for a painting entitled "The Ebb Tide," which was exhibited in Sydney in 1897, afterwards in New Zealand, as well as in the Brisbane Exhibition, where it held the post of honor.

Like many others, he was originally fired with the hope of making his mark as a printer, and his ambition still lies somewhere in that vicinity. His acceptance of a post as Art Critic, however, rendered his resignation from the Council of the Art Society a matter of fairness. The same spirit has retained his paintings from the Art Exhibitions for the past four years.

On the matter of art-criticism Mr. Taylor holds decided views, and that such opinions are of value is testified from the fact that he wrote critiques of the late Art Exhibition for five metropolitan papers, as well as for the London *Studio* which he has represented for the past four years. It may be also mentioned that he has been offered the post of Australian Art Commissioner for the St. Louis Exhibition, the English representative by the way being the President of the Royal Academy.

"I am a native of Sydney," said Mr. Taylor, born just thirty years ago—"so I'm sorry to say I cannot furnish you with the usual interesting reminiscences of the Tank Stream or other pre-historic items. School life? well nothing of interest. I had a fairly easy time, for the simple reason I somehow edited a school magazine, and my home lesson invariably consisted of putting one of Æsop's Fables into verse! A task? Not much, you see I usually adopted blank verse, it was so much more like Shakespeare, (and a bit easier)."

"I may mention that that poets Rod Quinn and E. J. Brady went to the same school, so you see it had a lot to answer for."

Leaving school with a naturally artistic bent, Mr. Taylor served two or three years in an architect's office, where he incidentally mentions "he learnt a few good points."

COLONIAL JOURNALS AND THEIR ARTISTS

"I learnt for instance," said Mr. Taylor, "that architect millionaires weren't very common just about that time. The other points came in useful later on."

Mr. Taylor then joined the Professional Staff of the Mines Department, where passing the Public Draftman's examination he yearned for the salary usually attached to that position, but as his yearning didn't bear fruit he resigned, and devoted himself entirely to art.

Of Mr. Taylor's art career much could be written. He commenced on the *Elector* in 1896, continued thereon till '97, when he turned his attention to the *Bulletin*, where his work was reproduced till 1898, when he gave birth to that curiously original publication *Ha! Ha*, for which he not only produced the pictures and most of the letterpress, but engraved some of the blocks himself, "which," he interrupts, "evidently settled it."

Since the sad demise of that affair, Mr. Taylor has been cartoonist to the *Sunday Times* Propriety. He was also cartoonist for *Melbourne Punch*, and a regular contributor to many other sources of reproduction, when an event happened which materially altered his plans. It was this way—whilst doing poster work for "John Sands" he sought a material by which posters instead of being printed could be cast in high relief. His experiments were highly successful, and his colored caricatures in relief of well-known characters issued by that firm earned a great deal of notoriety.

Mr. Taylor's previous architectural experience came in here, and he saw the great possibilities of the new material for building purposes. It was placed on the market, and has proved one of the greatest successes in building circles. It was awarded a gold medal at the last Interstate Exhibition, and has since been planted all over the world.

We had occasion to review in our August number the great factor it is in developing a national school of decoration, and it is now being manufactured by the Bagasse Company, Limited, of which Mr. Taylor is one of the principal shareholders.

Mr. Taylor's individuality breaks out in multifarious places, not only in humorous art, but as an art craftsman he takes a lead, and he is a "lightning sketcher" of considerable popularity. Just at present he is devoting his late hours to a novel Christmas publication, *The Swag*, which will be printed throughout in colours.

Questioned as to what he considers his best work, Mr. Taylor is hardly quite satisfied with any of his work to date; in fact, he thinks that any artist worth his salt cannot but pull his own work to pieces if he likes. His next picture is going to be his best. As regards his most popular cartoon, well, if repeated reproduction is any evidence, "The Lion and the Kangaroo," originally published in the *Sunday Times*, comes easily first, being reproduced, as far as could be ascertained, by *London Black & White,* the *Outlook, London, Daily Mail,* and a New York journal. "Outside of hard plodding," said Mr. Taylor, "I can't say I've had any exciting episodes worth chronicling. However, I may mention one little adventure I didn't *participate* in. It was thus:

"Sculptor Simonetti," said Mr. Taylor, "was dying. I went over to see him. Leaving him early in the afternoon I stepped into the Balmain colliery close by, as I desired to make some studies below to fill in a picture I had in mind at the time. The next shift was about to descend, but on a sudden fit of laziness (if you like) I excused myself, and the shift went without me. Before I reached bottom, every man in it was smashed up!"

"How do our politicians like being caricatured?" Well, they seem to welcome it. There is Mr. Reid, he is perpetually throwing himself under the notice of the humorous artist. For instance, his intimation that he had been taking up heavy-weight lifting looked like a deliberate play to the comic art gallery. Then there is Mr. O'Sullivan—with his public bout with 'yours truly' is too recent to be re-told. Another politician, who shall be nameless, often suggests to me some would-be humorous episode, in which he may have figured as a hero. I hope he'll take this hint and—*don't*."

Questioned as to sources of inspiration, Mr. Taylor opines that a humorous artist possessing the least unobtrusive bump of originality ought to depend upon himself, for the originality of suggestions made by kind friends, cannot always be guaranteed, and for a humorous artist to put his mark upon a "chestnut" is as commercially wicked as the grocer who thins out his sugar with pulverised sandstone.

Mr. Taylor has in hand a History of Caricature from the earliest times, which is to be published at Easter, and his theories upon the spirit of caricature in the Commonwealth, fill a number of interesting pages in the *Commonwealth Annual*.

Of the future of caricature, Mr. Taylor speaks hopefully.

"From its present widespread demand it should develop to great brilliancy. The cartoon sends its moral right home and tells its story in a flash, and that's an important item in these days of hurry. Can you not imagine the Premier of the future delivering his policy. 'This,' says he, standing in front of a huge board, and making a lightning sketch, 'is my policy.' 'And that,' explains the leader of the opposition, making another sketch, 'is my idea of it.' Amid breathless silence the leader of the female party—the balance of power—will step up, select a few highly-coloured chalks, and so decide the fate of the country. Reporters will take snapshots, and the House will retire early and respectably. Hansard reporters will bless the innovation, and perhaps have a marble bust of the inventor placed in the Legislative Council chamber."

Regarding the oft-quoted assertions of the lack of Australian art taste, Mr. Taylor cannot see anything in it. "If," says he, "a party purchases an artist's picture, the lucky artist naturally opines the art taste of the purchases is good enough and *vice versa*. I may be exceptionally fortunate—well perhaps I am lucky having a good demand for my work, so I may be biased in cracking up the art appreciation of my native land, but Australians are not fools, and I have noticed that some who discredited Australian art appreciation, and considered our artistic taste not much above the aboriginal, and so in disgust left to try the maelstrom of London, have been glad enough to come back again."

COLONIAL JOURNALS AND THEIR ARTISTS

GEORGE TAYLOR, 'CARICATURE AND ITS HISTORY'
Steele Rudd's Magazine
April 1905

[…] In Australia the spirit of caricature long lay quiescent, and a glance at its development will not be out of place.

Like many of our institutions…. the spirit of caricature early shaped itself upon the English style, as embodied in the London *Punch* of the forties, the illustrations being almost imitations of the styles of its artists.

One can, therefore, understand how eager our spirit was to materialise itself when it was glad enough to adopt as a medium a barefaced parody of an old-world affair. However, having found its feet it gradually eliminated the heavy English idea of humor, and adopted more national characteristics, till the eighties saw the advent of Livingstone Hopkins and Phil May, who lifted the art to a very high level. These brilliant caricaturists were greatly assisted by the great field of originality presented by the developing colonies. Australia, as an "open sesame" to fortune, attracted a multitude of human types—small wonder the spirit of caricature grew under the hands of these two brilliant exemplars to such maturity as to give it to-day a particularly strong position in the world's art.

It was in 1886 that Phil May commenced his Australian career, and his remarkable economy of line which presented a maximum of effect with an apparent minimum of effort, soon won wide appreciation. It has been stated that Phil May's famous economy of line was the result of open drawing to suit inferior printing machines in Australia. This is absolutely incorrect. His vigorous handling was simply the perfection of the broad and open technique so well seen in the work of Linley Sambourne, for whose work May, as a fellow-craftsman, expressed unbounded admiration.

The spirit of Hopkins's caricature, essentially American, found in our independent conditions a welcome field. The many humbugs intruding on the establishment of a new nation were caught by this knight of the pencil, and ridiculously routed before they swelled to any dangerous size. For instance, mention may be made of the humorous castigation that annihilated the idea of a State Dead House, and the trenchant satire that burlesqued Senator John Cash Neild's attempts at poetry and successfully turned him from the broad poetic path. "Hop's" technique is varied, and, being remarkably fertile in his ideas, his work is ever fresh. His creations—"The Little Boy of Manly," "Reid's Dry Dog," and his "Hop's Understudy"—are well known. A considerable amount of controversy has arisen as to who this understudy can be, but I am fortunate to be able to throw a little light upon the subject.

In the photograph reproduced the party playing the cello is very like Hopkins, and I may also mention the fact that the fellow with the blunderbuss likewise bears a remarkable likeness to the same individual. I can, however, safely say that one of them is the understudy, but which one is it, and why one wishes to annihilate the other, is as great a mystery as the Sphinx or George Reid's idea of political economy.

Hopkins is Yankee born. The year of his birth is a mystery, upon which he will not throw any light, but a casual glance at his portrait reveals the fact that he is more than seven. He commenced making pictures at a very early age, but at the outbreak of the American War in the sixties, evidently thinking the sword was mightier than the pen, he enlisted and went through the campaign without doing any particular damage, and to-day is proud to state he is about the only survivor that does not happen to be a colonel.

He was landed in Sydney in good order and condition nearly twenty years ago, and—is still there.

I am fortunate to be able to present a reproduction of his happiest hit, the "Roll Call" (the return of the Soudan contingent). It will be seen that the famous "Little Boy of Manly" occupies a prominent position in the foreground.

The origin of this myth is mysterious to many, but it may be explained that during the excitement of despatching that pioneer band of soldiers, the Right Hon. W.B. Dalley originated a patriotic fund, and among the subscribers thereto was "A little boy at Manly—one penny;" and as Dalley was of small stature and resided in that suburb, the *Bulletin* tacked the title on to him with hilarious success.

"Hop's" present caricaturing partner, Alf. Vincent, has won a high position in Australian caricature by his clever draftsmanship. The spirit with Vincent is light and on the face, taking every advantage of his remarkable facility of execution and economy of line.

Vincent is a young man who first came into prominence through brilliant work on Melbourne *Punch*. Joining the *Bulletin* staff some years ago with a rapidly improving pen, he stands to-day one of our most brilliant pen draftsmen. Originally influenced by Phil May's simplicity of technique, he has developed therefrom a vigorous style. Just here it may be pointed out that styles in caricature are rarely created. They generally develop upon the technique of another, and in the process of evolution the style is generally improved and added to. As in life the work develops by the acquisition of knowledge by the correlation of new truths with old, so in the art, the development through the progression of "the men who come behind." For instance, I may mention Raven Hill's style developing from that of Charles Keene, and Phil May's early work resembling the vigorous handling of Linley Sambourne, but whereas Sambourne had reached his highest level, May carried the style to still higher paths, and gave it an individuality of his own.

In the work of Alek Sass and Ambrose Dyson the spirit materialises in clever burlesque.

COLONIAL JOURNALS AND THEIR ARTISTS

Sass delights in foreshortenings, and this gives his work a quaintness that always holds attention. Born in Wiltshire, England, in 1876, he reached these parts at a tender age. Some years ago he hesitated whether he should go through life as a poet or a humorous artist, but lacking the necessary cash to purchase a rhyming dictionary he got his hair cut, and took to the pencil. He still hopes to buy that dictionary some day; meanwhile he keeps on drawing things.

The work of Ambrose Dyson betokens a bright young caricaturist with a fine sense of the incongruity of things in general.

Originally influenced by Hopkins and Zimmerman, he has developed a strong technique thoroughly permeated with humor.

With his brother, William Dyson, the spirit shines brilliantly through a technique quaint and effective, and possessing the true ring of genius, and it hardly requires a seer to predict a very high level in the art of these two clever brothers.

Norman Lindsay is a decorative artist of promise. His work is well thought out, and when applied to caricature brings to the fullest possible effect any suggested humor and holds attention not only by its excellent technique, but from the decorative composition inseparable from this young man's work. Born at Creswick, Victoria, Lindsay—at an age when the ordinary lad is struggling with the intricacies of the multiplication table—was going to revolutionise modern comic journalism, and though for this publication he did a good deal of work, from pasting up his posters to hacking the cartoon of the week from a piece of Kauri, advertisers wouldn't bite, and so another dream was wrecked. As his portrait shows he is still quite a lad, and his present work betokens a future of exceptional brilliance.

In G.H. Dancey, D.H. Souter, Leist, and E.M. Grosse, we meet a coterie of artists whose chief characteristic is brilliant draftsmanship. Dancey's cartoons are usually in wash, and are finished with delightful taste, so that each of his efforts is a veritable work of art.

Dancey, originally intended for ecclesiastical decorative art, was the chief cartoonist for Melbourne *Punch*. He has a remarkable facility of catching the expression of his victim, and models his figures excellently. His work is solid, and stamps him as the finest brush cartoonist in the Commonwealth.

If imitation is really the sincerest form of flattery, then D.H. Souter should blush furiously. His drawings are reproduced in numberless American and English journals. Perhaps no greater compliment could be paid to the artist. His work is decorative to a degree, and always in keeping with its smart gag—which he usually furnishes himself. Of Scotch birth, Souter, after an attempt to pick a fortune out of South Africa with his pencil, landed in Sydney some twenty back, and has ever since been turning out delightful copy. He shows great facility for daintily picturing the humors of Australian society, and his technique is very vigorous and clear.

Grosse on rare occasions wanders into the realms of caricature with notable success. Few of our artists possess such exquisite feeling for gradations and contrasts in black and white. His absolute command of the pen or brush can be imagined when it is mentioned that not only is he a black and white artist of exceptional excellence, but he has no equal in the world as a scientific draftsman—one, for instance, who can depict with microscopic exactness the gradations in tone of the antennæ of the *Rolyat Australiensis*.

A. J. Fischer is a specialist. His speciality is the humorous fossicker of the Australian mining fields. No one realises him better. His work on the Brisbane *Boomerang* will be remembered.

Of other Queensland caricaturists mention must be made of Cecil Gasking's clever work on the *Courier* journals, and A.J. Hingston, who is rapidly advancing in his art, and whose work is receiving wider and more welcome appreciation every day.

In the work of Hugh McCrae, H. MacLean, and J. McDonald (Pasquin), the spirit of caricature finds congenial quarters.

Thus we stand at the beginning of the new century enjoying a freedom which permits the drastic annihilation of social humbugs, by whom naturally enough the art is constantly derided. After all, 'tis a poor theory that cannot stand the light of criticism, for the honest man fears not the light of truth.

'PHIL MAY...BY ONE WHO KNEW HIM'
Our Swag
22 December 1905

A good deal has been written concerning Phil May and his early struggles, but little light has been cast upon his Australian career—that period when he found his feet and began to climb.

A more grotesque figure than Phil in Sydney could hardly be imagined. A cadaverous lantern-jawed face, almost colorless, gums toothless from ruined digestion, his thick brown hair plastered to his forehead and cut straight an inch above his eyebrows, a nose most pronounced and one that Phil often took liberties with in his lightning sketching, and an ever-present cigar in his mouth.

Many mistakenly fancied Phil aped the eccentric, but it was simply his don't-careness.

Many a sketch he did of himself, with his teeth out in order to render his pictures more grotesque, as will be seen from the sketch here shown.

His Australian engagement was more a matter of luck than judgement. W.H. Traill was introduced to May by Haddon Chambers, whose drama "Captain Swift" was then doing well in London. May was offered £750, but Mrs. May, who chaperoned Phil's business dealings, rather considerably considered his services were worth a thousand. The deal was therefore off, and Baxter, who then was doing wonderful caricatures on "Ally Sloper," was offered the post. Baxter couldn't go, so Phil's demand was accepted.

A good deal of nonsense has been written about his method of working. Some experts state he always drew his pictures over and over again to obtain the right effect, but anyone who knew Phil couldn't imagine him taking such trouble as that. His method was simplicity itself, and I don't think it has been mentioned before. Phil first drew his sketches roughly on soft paper, placed a sheet of blue transfer paper beneath, and traced through the most important lines onto a sheet of cardboard, and ran over the tracing with his pen. By that simple and ingenious method he was able to rapidly build up his pages of cartoonlets without wasting any space. […]

Many tales are told of Phil in Sydney. One related to a trip taken to the mountains. His weekly page of cartoon was not forthcoming. He was evidently having a good time. Repeated wires from the office brought back a lovely page of mountain caricatures, with a capital sketch of Phil in the corner sitting on a mountain peak, with his thumb up his nose: "Where's the cartoon? Come up and get it."

Phil was most erratic regarding his cartoon work, and a *Bulletin* man had to keep Phil in tow till the weekly page was finished. It was Saturday, and the page had not arrived. Sunday morning found the *Bulletin* man seeking Phil. Phil was eventually discovered among a number of pals and successfully detached. Reaching his chambers, for he lived in town, he regretfully pointed out that Mrs. May was out of town all day, and had the only key to the door. "You see, old chap," he remarked, "I could get in by smashing the fanlight and climbing through, but the damage would eat up any cash I got for the sketch, and it would make such a draught the wife would never forgive me for it. Let's look round the back." And they inspected the back premises, and by means of a friendly waterpipe, entry was effected through an open window some way up. Phil disappeared through the window, tripped upstairs to his room, and in a few minutes reappeared with the completed picture, the ink still wet. The *Bulletin* man wept for joy, and Phil rejoined his mates with a lighter heart. The origin of "The Parson and the Painter" has received many versions, but to Phil's credit it must be mentioned that he never purposely gave undeserved offence to any of his caricatured. In the case referred to, it appears that Phil was conversing with a group of friends at Katoomba, and the reverend gentleman purposely insulted May, who, however, walked away apparently unconcerned. May could easily have retaliated in the *Bulletin,* as the person referred to was very well known locally, but Phil was generous, and four years later in England, where the clergyman could not have been known, he, perhaps unconsciously, resurrected the impression as the type he desired, and in the pages of that wonderful book, "The Parson and the Painter," the Sydney clergyman cavorts joyously. Phil was once taken to task about his apparent malice, but disclaimed any such intention. "At any rate," said he,

PHIL MAY IN SYDNEY

(Sketched by himself).   From *Bulletin*.

"I am told he has had crowded congregations of curious individuals who come to see if he is like the sketches, so he hasn't got much to complain about. I, therefore, have the worse deal of the two."

Many think that the old clergyman, Phil's most famous Sydney model, is the original of the parson. The old party referred to was an old penniless priest, and Phil's ever-open pocket kept the poor old chap alive. Many a drawing has this fine old face decorated. He is the original figure for "The Temptation of St. Anthony," "A Sydney Type," and numberless sketches. The two pencil drawings shown herewith, and now published for the first time, are most interesting as showing the marvellous detail he could place in his work when he cared. See the world-lost sadness in the eyes, how the very flesh hangs tightly round the skull; and in the other the free facility of placing his lines and the little highlight that just touches the tip of the nose. Referring to May's pencil work, of which there has not been much shown, Longstaff said he believed no artist has ever drawn anything better than them. No reproduction has yet given the slightest hint of their quality.

There have been many tales of Phil May's Australian earnings. I have seen it mentioned that his remuneration here was very small, but in justice to the *Bulletin*, ever liberal in its dealings with its artists, the fact should be mentioned. Coming here at a salary of £1000, Phil, in addition thereto, was paid for extra pages. This, during his stay in Melbourne during Exhibition time, ran into over 50 and 75 pounds per week. And before he left they offered to double his salary if he would stay another three years!

Phil at times, like Silas Wegg, "dropped into poetry." The wondrous jingle he perpetrated had for its text Bishop Barry's famous remark that the recklessness of Australians was caused by their eating too much meat, and Phil's "poem" contained almost every word in the Dictionary that rhymed with "meat". It was a very lengthy affair, and as a rhyme it was a huge success, but no doubt the Bishop looked upon it as an awful example proving his remarks.

EDWARD DYSON, 'BILLY BLUEGUM'
Lone Hand
1 August 1912

Billy's bright ideas came to him at the oddest moments. For instance, it was when Dr. Dandylion, Archbishop of Bruin, was delivering his celebrated sermon on the Electrification of Hades that Billy remembered the urgent need of a fire brigade.

Billy Bluegum simply ran out of church, and the males of the congregation followed him, leaving the Archbishop of Bruin preaching to a pitiful array of wenches.

In five minutes a fire brigade was formed, and dressed in bright red uniforms and large helmets. As it happened, there was a hose-reel in the bag.

The brigade looked quite smart. At least it would have looked quite smart if it had not been for the helmets, which were rather large, so large in one or two cases that they had to be propped up in front to enable the firemen to get out.

"For what is a fire brigade used?" asked Blackbutt, K.C.

"For torchlight processions chiefly, but also for competitions and to put out fires."

"We have no fires."

"They can be made without difficulty now we have an influential daily press. I shall make some."

"But they burn, I understand."

"They do. They burn very severely, but the brigade will extinguish them almost immediately."

PART 6

The Journal Covers

Australian Magazine; or, Compendium of
Religious, Literary, and Miscellaneous Intelligence
1821
223

Hobart Town Magazine 1833
224

Australia Felix Monthly Magazine 1849
225

Tasmanian Monthly Magazine 1853
226

Illustrated Journal of Australasia 1858
227

Australian Magazine 1859
228

Magpie 1865
229

Colonial Monthly 1867
230

Colonial Monthly 1870
231

Australian Journal 1870
232

Australian 1878
233

Australian Woman's Magazine and Domestic
Journal 1882
234

Sydney Quarterly Magazine 1884
235

Melbourne Journal 1884
236

Once a Month 1885
237

Victorian Review 1886
238

Centennial Magazine 1888
239

Boomerang 1888
240

Pacific Quarterly 1890
241

Australasian Critic 1890
242

A.H.R.: Australasian Home Reader 1894
243

Block 1896
244

Clarion 1897
245

Cosmos 1897
246

Cosmos 1897
247

Cosmos 1898
248

Southern Cross 1898
249

Rambler 1899
250

Bookfellow 1899
251

Australian Magazine 1899
252

Bulletin 1900
253

A.A.A.: All About Australians 1901
254

Microbe 1902
255

Ye Wayside Goose: A Journal of Intelligence 1905
256

Ye Kangaroo: A Quaint Magazine 1905
257

Australian Bookman 1906
258

New Idea for Australasian Women 1906
259

Native Companion 1907
260

Steele Rudd's Magazine 1907
261

Our Quarterly Magazine 1908
262

Lone Hand 1908
263

Trident: An Australian Review 1909
264

Lilley's Magazine 1911
265

Red Ant: An Australian Magazine 1912
266

Australian Journal 1913
267

THE AUSTRALIAN MAGAZINE;

OR,

COMPENDIUM OF

RELIGIOUS, LITERARY,

AND

MISCELLANEOUS INTELLIGENCE.

VOLUME I.

FOR

1821.

"THE SOUL, UNEASY AND CONFIN'D FROM HOME,
"RESTS AND EXPATIATES IN A LIFE TO COME."   POPE.

SYDNEY:

PRINTED BY ROBERT HOWE, GOVERNMENT PRINTER.

THE HOBART TOWN MAGAZINE.

No. 8.

OCTOBER, 1833

EMBELLISHED

WITH A

LITHOGRAPHIC VIEW

AND A CHART OF THE SOUTHERN HEMISPHERE

VAN DIEMEN'S LAND

H. MELVILLE

ELIZABETH STREET, HOBART TOWN

Price Two Shillings and Sixpence, cash; credit, Three Shillings.

THE AUSTRALIA FELIX MONTHLY MAGAZINE.

JUNE, 1849.

GEELONG:—JAMES HARRISON, MALOP STREET.
MELBOURNE:—G. COOPER, ELIZABETH STREET.
1849.

THE
TASMANIAN MONTHLY
MAGAZINE,
AND
Journal of Australasian Progress
IN
CIVILIZATION, LITERATURE, SCIENCE, EDUCATION, AND RELIGION.

SEPTEMBER, 1853.

Scire tuum nihil est, nisi te scire hoc sciat alter.—Pers. Sat. I. 27.
Hac studia adolescentiam alunt, senectutem oblectant, secundas res ornant, adversis perfugium ac solatium præbent; delectant domi, non impediunt foris; pernoctant nobiscum, peregrinantur, rusticantur.—Cic. Orat. pro Arch. Poet. VII. 16.

HOBART TOWN:

PUBLISHED BY PRATT AND SON, HOBART TOWN, AND A. DUTHIE,
LAUNCESTON:
AND SOLD BY MESSRS. WALCH AND SONS, HUXTABLE, ROLWEGAN, AND FLETCHER,
STATIONERS, HOBART TOWN.

PRATT AND SON, PRINTERS.

Vol. 4.—No. 20.   FEBRUARY, 1858.   Eighteenpence.

THE ILLUSTRATED JOURNAL of AUSTRALASIA

A

MONTHLY MAGAZINE.

CONTENTS:

	PAGE		PAGE
London Literary Gossip	49	Companion to the Kitchen Garden	86
Poetry: My Home, Farewell	53	The Journal of Current Events:	
Mrs. Tribble's Tea Party, and what came of it	54	Journal of Politics	86
History of Victoria. Chapter VII.	62	Journal of Social Progress	88
Music: O! think not that I can forget thee	72	Journal of Science and Industry	92
The New Custom House (with an Engraving)	75	Journal of Literature and Art	95
Tent Life. Chapter XV.	77	Notes and Queries	96
The Agave Americana (with an Engraving)	85	Chess	96
Meteorology of the Month	86	Notices to Correspondents	96

PRINTED AND PUBLISHED BY

W. H. WILLIAMS,

94 BOURKE STREET EAST, MELBOURNE;

And SOLD BY ALL BOOKSELLERS.

No. 2.] [Vol. I.

THE
AUSTRALIAN MAGAZINE.

NOVEMBER, 1859.

CONTENTS:

ARTICLES---
  Science of Legislation
  Mining Revolution
  Chinese Question
  Library and Museum
  Summary of News
  Summary of English News
  Notices

REVIEWS---
  Life of a Criminal
  Philosophical Transactions for 1858

POETRY---
  Tales of the Pig-Tails

  The Emeu and Native Companion
  To a Deserted Cottage
  A Good Natured Man
  King Time's Carol
  The Maiden to Her Dying Lover
  Swiss Chamois Hunters
  Memory of the Departed

REPORTS---
  Philosophical Institute
  Horticultural Society

MISCELLANEOUS---
  Gold Discoveries in S. America
  Doings in Gibraltar
  Napoleon Irritated

MELBOURNE:
PUBLISHED BY THE PROPRIETOR, W. H. COMPTON,
20 FLINDERS LANE EAST.
SOLD BY ALL BOOKSELLERS.

PRICE TWO SHILLINGS.

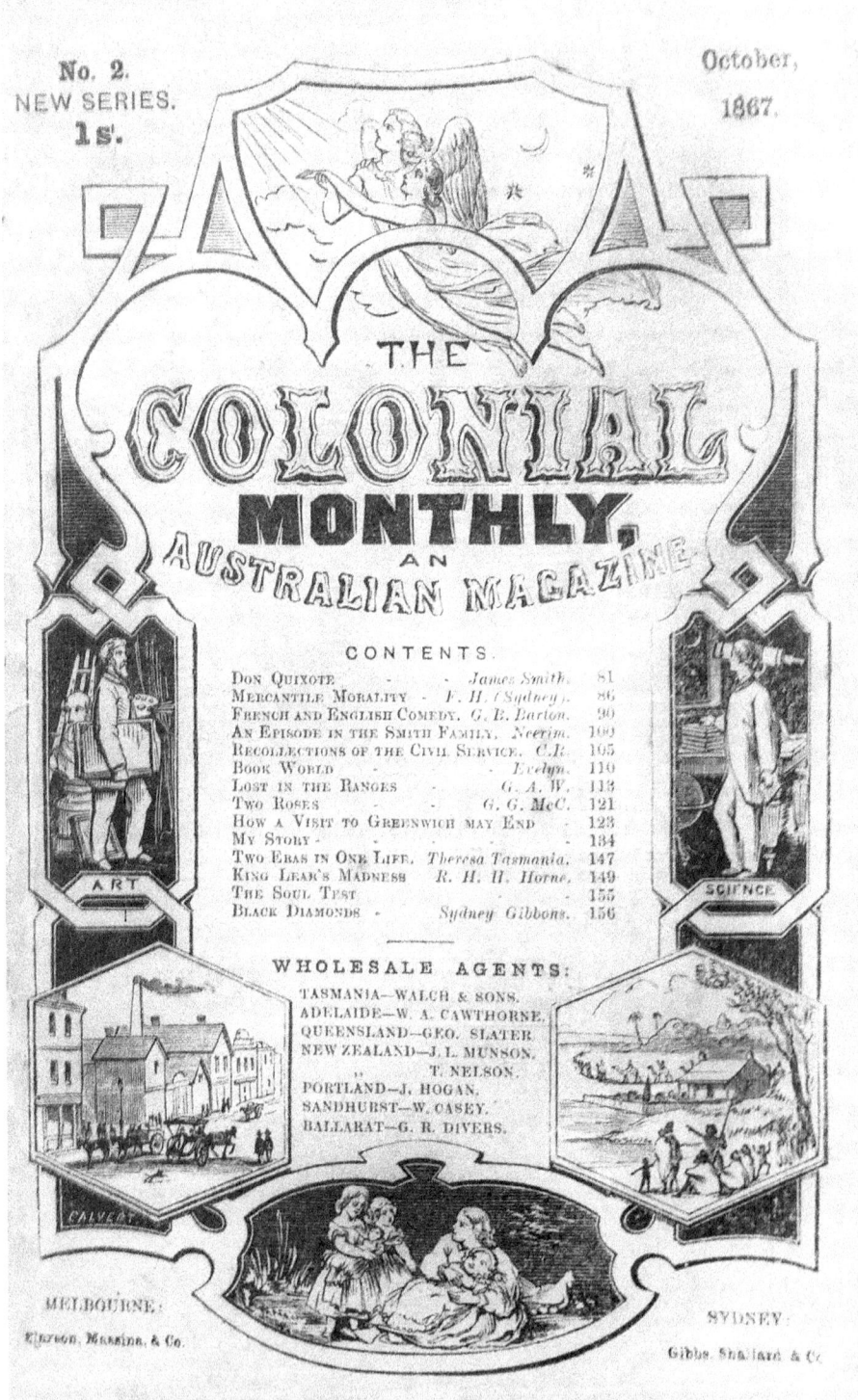

Posted to England and her Colonies for One Penny.

1/– THE COLONIAL MONTHLY

NEW YEAR'S NUMBER

January, 1870.   No. 29.

CONTENTS:

PREFACE. By Henry Kendall 321
DOUBLE HARNESS; OR, PIERCE CHARLTON'S WIVES.
    By G. A. Walstab 323
    Volume II.—Chapter I. Under the Southern Cross.
AT HER WINDOW. By Henry Kendall. *Illustrated by T. Carrington*. 331
A BIT OF CLAY 333
THE SICK STOCKRIDER. By the Author of "Ashtaroth" . 342
THE ACCCLIMATISED SPARROW. By Marcus Clarke . . 345
    Illustrated by T. S. Cousins.
THE PRISONER. By G. Gordon McCrae 354
THE GRAVES ON THE ISLAND. By R. H. Haverfield . . 357
A SWEATER WITH THE CHAMPION PEDESTRIANS. By "Olympus" 379
"LOT 33." A New Year's Story. By G. A. Walstab . .
DIES IRÆ. Translation by F. H.
THE MONTH IN MELBOURNE, SYDNEY, AND ADELAIDE.

MELBOURNE: CLARSON, MASSINA, & CO.
SYDNEY: GIBBS, SHALLARD, & CO.
TASMANIA—WALCH & SONS.   ADELAIDE—W. C. RIGBY.   QUEENSLAND—
GEO. SLATER.   NEW ZEALAND—J. L. MUNSON.   G. H. MOSS.
SANDHURST—W. CASEY.   BALLARAT—G. R. DIVERS.
OFFICE: 87 LITTLE COLLINS STREET EAST, MELBOURNE

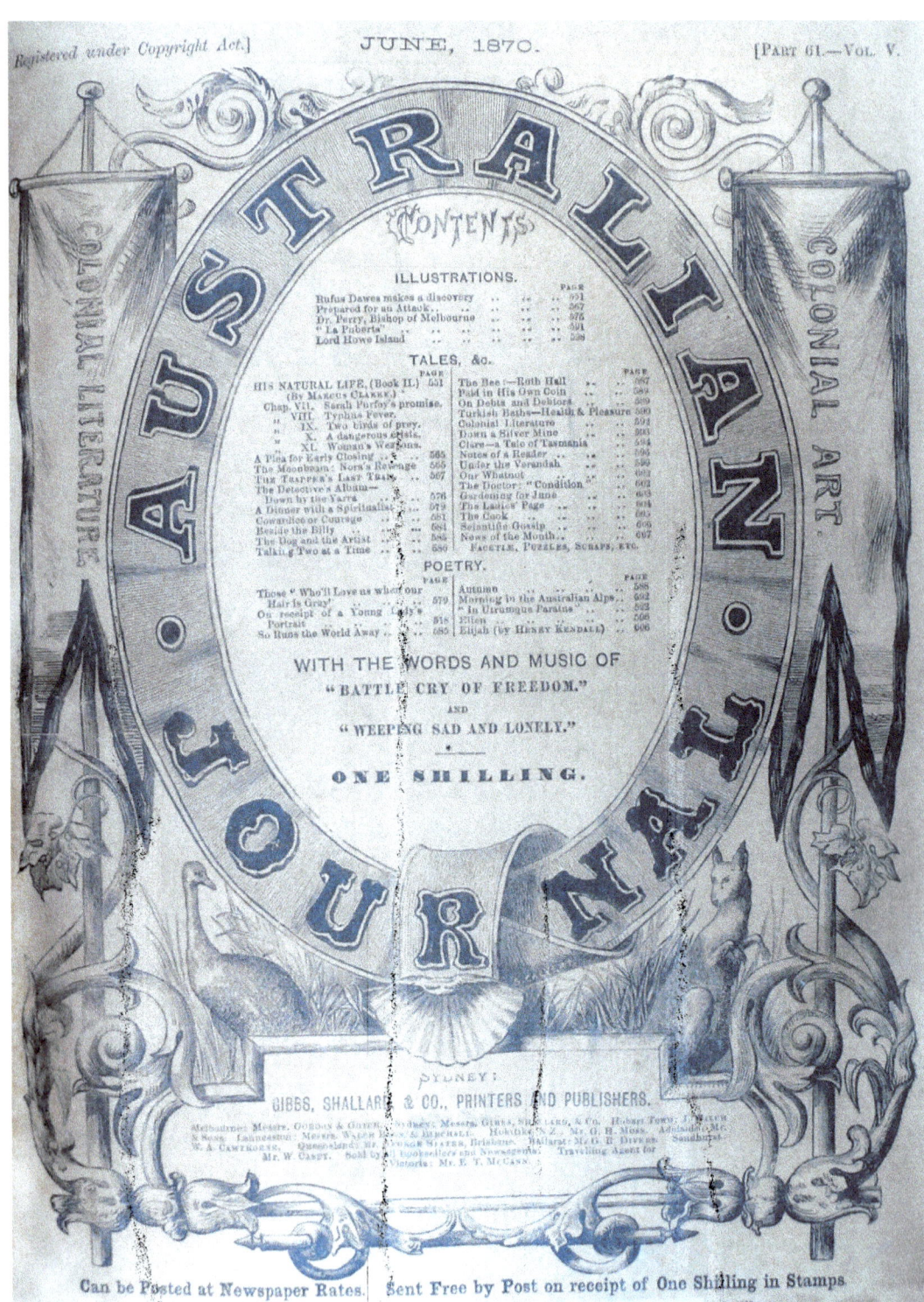

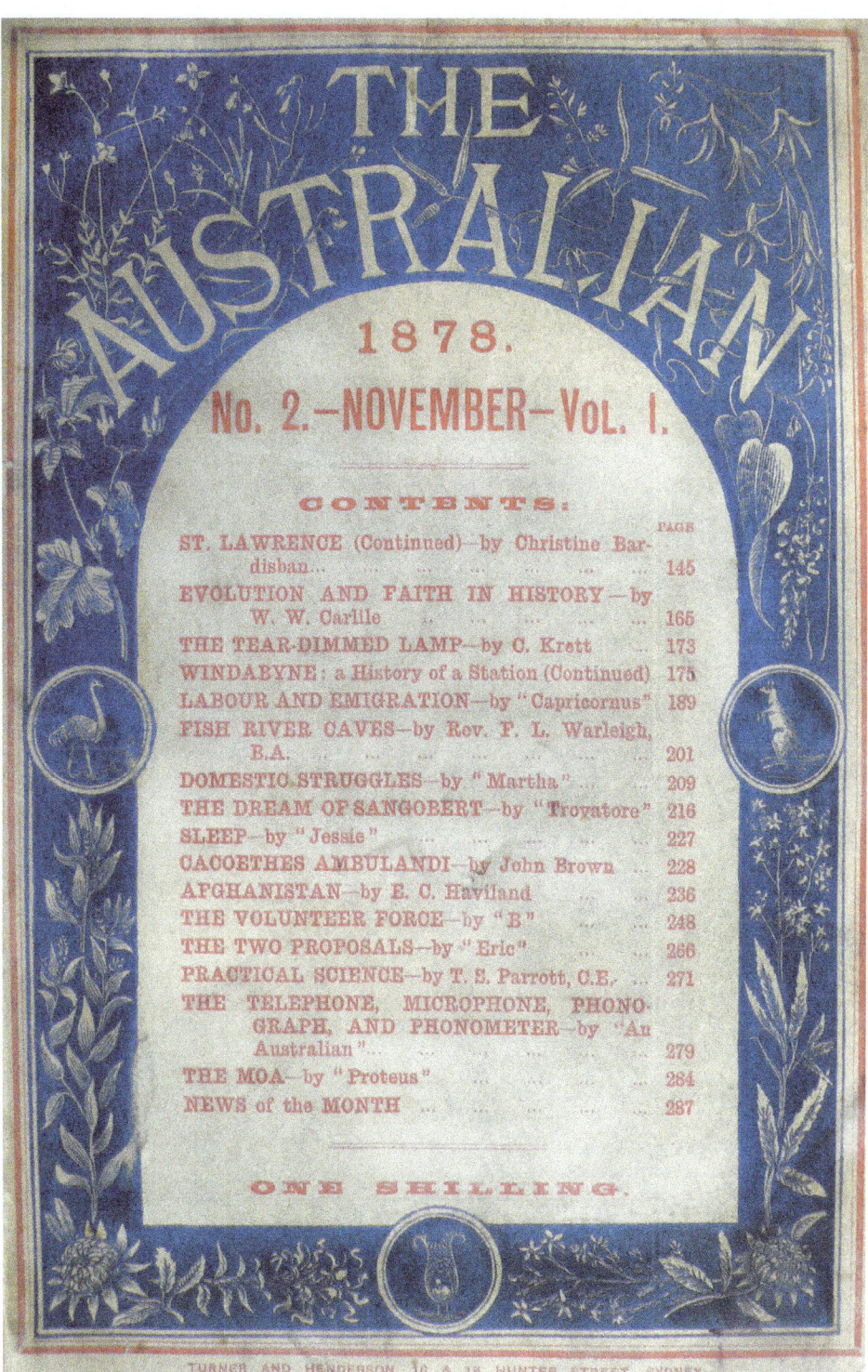

THE AUSTRALIAN Woman's Magazine AND DOMESTIC JOURNAL.

No. 3. (Registered for Transmission as a Newspaper.) JUNE, 1882. Price 6d.

CONTENTS.

Stories:
The Widow Blane. Chapters IV. and V. By N. Page
Walter Swan 65
Temptation. By Australie .. 69
Robinson Crusoing with a Baby Chapters IV. and V. By Robin Goodfellow .. 71
Rupert Godwin's Revenge. By Louise .. 77
Magna: An Australian Girl. By Janet Carroll .. 83

Poetry:
El Sabor del Vino (from the Spanish of Cadalso). By F. W. Scrivenor .. 65
Love, or the Story of Clytia. By F. W. Scrivenor .. 77
Lines on a Passage in Lord Lytton's "Eugene Aram." By Francesca .. 79

Essays and Sketches:
Long Hours and Legislation. By David Blair .. 80
Woman, No. III.—Her Influence. By the Editress .. 81
Society. By "Somebody." .. 82
Katrina. By Evelyn .. 82
H.I.J.M.S. "Rinjio." By G. G. McCrae .. 75

The Fashions:
Fashion Notes .. 90
Fashion Plate .. 91
Description of Fashion Plate .. 93

Fancy-Work Notes .. 91

Music:
Evening Bells. By Sidney Johnson .. 94

Pastimes .. 95

The Cuisine:
Hints on Practical Cooking. (Continued.) By E. Harrie .. 95
Morning Visits. By H.E.P.H. .. 89

Library and Studio:
Review of New Books .. 92
Review of New Music. By E.A.C. .. 93

Pearls from the Poets .. 93
Golden Gleams .. 96
Scientific Notes .. 95

Children's Hour:
The Genii of the Trees. By Indi .. 87

Answers to Correspondents .. 96
Freaks and Fancies .. 96

W. H. ROCKE & CO.
The Largest Stock in Melbourne of
FURNITURE. | CARPETS
LINOLEUMS. | CRETONNES.
GENERAL FURNISHINGS.
BEDSTEADS. | BEDROOM
BEDDING. | FURNITURE.
Every Requisite for Furnishing Throughout.
SOLE AGENTS FOR DOULTON & CO.

36, 38, 40, 42, COLLINS ST. EAST, MELBOURNE.

FACTS WHICH OUGHT TO BE KNOWN.

TOOTHACHE and **NEURALGIA** may be cured by taking "**Hooper's Neuralgic Powders**," which are a perfectly safe medicine for delicate constitutions. Price **1s. 6d.** and **2s. 6d.** a Box.

ASTHMA is instantly relieved by inhaling the smoke from "**Hooper's Herbal Compound**," sold in Tins, **1s. 6d.** and **2s. 6d.** each.

DANDRIFF is cured by "**Hooper's Desideratum Hair Wash Powder**;" and the hair is strengthened by its use. Price **6d.** a Packet.

CORNS are cured by "**Ogston's Painless Corn and Wart Paint**," price **1s.** a Bottle.

MARKING INK for Marking Linen, &c.—Hooper's is the best—it never fails to give satisfaction. Price **1s.** and **1s. 6d.** a Bottle.

The above preparations may be obtained through any Chemists, or per post from the Proprietor on the receipt of Victorian Postage Stamps for the value of the article required.

E. G. HOOPER, PHARMACEUTICAL CHEMIST.
69 BOURKE ST. WEST, MELBOURNE.

PUBLISHED AT THE HEAD OFFICE:—83 QUEEN STREET, MELBOURNE.
AGENTS: Sydney and Brisbane, Gordon and Gotch; Adelaide, A. H. Cargeeg; Hobart, Walch Brothers; Launceston, Walch Brothers and Birchall.

THE elbourne ournal.

ILLUSTRATED CHRISTMAS NUMBER

→*CONTAINING A SERIES OF EXCELLENT ORIGINAL STORIES, POEMS, ETC.*←

No. 7.　　　　MELBOURNE, JANUARY, 1884.　　　　ONE SHILLING.

ALSO, FIVE COMPLETE NOVELS, ENTITLED

"ON THE BLACKMAN'S LEAD,"
BY HENRY WINSTANLY.

"I BEG PARDON, SIR; BUT I EXPECTED TO SEE MY FATHER."

"HARRIETTE HURST'S CHRISTMAS," AND "COLOR-TAINTED,"
BY JANET CARROL.

"WAIREWA'S LOVE," BY SILAS WEGG.

"URBAIN AND ISETTE," By G. R. SIMS.

No. 76.   February 1, 1886.   Price 2s. 6d.

THE VICTORIAN REVIEW.

Edited by H. Mortimer Franklyn.

CONTENTS.

	PAGE
I. The Secret of Happiness. By James Smith	341
II. Over the Water. By Douglas B. W. Sladen, B.A., LL.B.	359
III. Communism. By H. W. Boyd Mackay, LL.B.	362
IV. Translations from Horace. By James Laughton (Hobart)	378
V. Byways of Literature. XV.—Maginn's Miscellanies. By David Blair	380
VI. Trades Unions. By Chas. O. Montrose	398
VII. Transactions of the Shakspeare Society	419
VIII. The Political Situation in New South Wales. By H. Mortimer Franklyn	428
IX. The Contemporary Thought of Great Britain, Europe, and the United States	443

MELBOURNE:
14 FLINDERS LANE WEST.

London: Gordon & Gotch.
Paris: Librairie Galignani.
Berlin: Asher & Co.
Vienna: Gerold & Co.
Sydney (N.S.W.) Turner & Henderson.
Adelaide: E. S. Wigg & Son.
Brisbane: Gordon & Gotch.
Dunedin: H. Wise & Co.
Boston: W. B. Clarke.

New York: The International News Company.
Philadelphia: Porter & Coates.
San Francisco: San Francisco News Company.
Chicago: W. M. Smith.
Calcutta: Brown & Co.
Bombay: Thacker & Co.
Madras: Higinbotham & Co.

[All Rights Reserved.]

Advertisements to be sent direct to Manager "Victorian Review" Flinders Lane W.

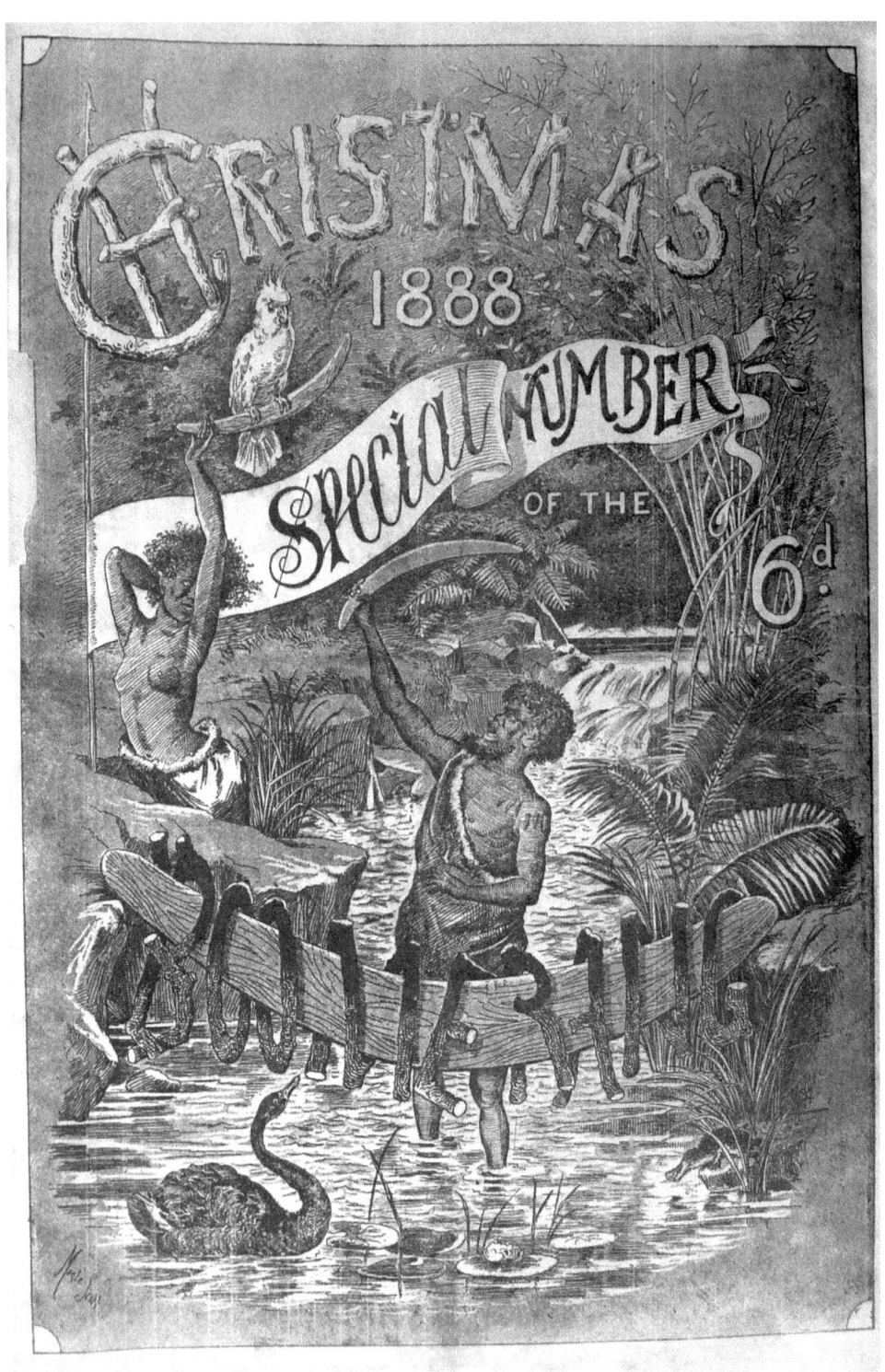

The Pacific Quarterly.

Vol. I. AUGUST, 1890. No. 1.

✢ CONTENTS. ✢

	Page
PROTESTANT UNION. J. BARCLAY JACKSON	1
VIEWS BY DR. THORNTON, Bishop of Ballarat	
DR. MACDONALD, Moderator of the Presbyterian Assembly	
REV. E. WASON NYE, President Wesleyan Conference	
PROFESSOR GOSMAN, Chairman Congregational College.	
THE BUSH FIRE. W. N. PRATT	6
BLOOD AND IRON. R. ARMSTRONG	7
THE CRIMSON THREAD OF BROTHERHOOD. WM. L. LUMLEY	13
A HYMN OF LIFE. T. S. ROBERTSON	16
THE YOUTH OF THE COLONIES. ALEXANDER SUTHERLAND, M.A.	17
THE AUSTRALIAN NATIVES' ASSOCIATION—	
THE CHARGE—GEO. K. KERR	21
THE DEFENCE—G. FITZSIMMONS (Member of the Board of Directors)	25
THE SOURCE OF LIFE. E. WILSON DOBBS	29
LOOKING BACKWARD—A REVIEW	30
LEGISLATIVE COUNCIL REFORM. JOHN J. CARRUTHERS	35
RECENT AUSTRALIAN POETRY	42
THE STUDY OF INDIVIDUALITY. MISS MITCHELL	45

MELBOURNE:
E. W. COLE, BOOK ARCADE, BOURKE STREET.
1890.

SIXPENCE.

Crabb & Yelland, Printers, Prahran and St. Kilda.

The Australasian Critic.

A MONTHLY REVIEW OF LITERATURE, SCIENCE & ART.

VOL. I., No. 1.   1st OCTOBER, 1890.   PRICE SIXPENCE.

GENERAL EDITORS—PROFESSOR T. G. TUCKER, M.A., AND PROFESSOR W. BALDWIN SPENCER, M.A.

EDITORS OF DEPARTMENTS: LITERATURE—PROFESSOR E. E. MORRIS, M.A. PHYSICAL SCIENCE AND CHEMISTRY—MR. E. F. J. LOVE, M.A. BIOLOGY—MR. A. DENDY, M.Sc., F.L.S. GEOLOGY—MR. G. S. GRIFFITHS, F.G.S. APPLIED SCIENCE—MR. J. B. LEWIS, M.C.E. MEDICINE—MR. T. CHERRY, M.B., CH.B. MUSIC—ART—PROFESSOR SIDNEY DICKINSON, M.A. DRAMA—MR. W. LEWERS, LL.B.

MANAGER—J. STEELE ROBERTSON, B.A.   ASSISTANT MANAGER—J. STEPHEN HART, M.A., B.Sc.

All books noticed in The Australasian Critic may be obtained from Melville, Mullen and Slade, Booksellers, Melbourne.

CONTENTS:

LITERATURE.

The Early Life of the Speaker	1
A Literary Causerie	2
Constitutional Experiments of the Commonwealth	2
The Village Community	3
The Passion Play at Ober-Ammergau	4
English Lands, Letters and Kings	4
Illustrated Journalism	5
The Squatter's Dream	5
Themes and Variations	6
The Journal of Marie Bashkirtseff	7
The Heriots	8
Ballads from "Punch" and other Poems	8
Charity Organisation	8
Views and Reviews	9
Literary Notes	9

SCIENCE.

The Relation between Boiling Points and Molecular Volumes	12
The Food of Coral Polypes	12
The Training of an Engineer	13
Consumption as a Contagious Disease	14
Traité d'Optique	15
Introduction to Fresh-water Algæ	15
Characteristics of Volcanoes	16
William Kitchen Parker	17
Science Notes	18

MUSIC, ART, AND DRAMA.

Are We a Musical People?	20
Professor Marshall Hall	21
What Should Australian Artists Paint?	21
The Art Society of New South Wales	22
"School" in Melbourne	23
"Macbeth" in Sydney	24
The Gondoliers	25
Musical Notes	25
Art Notes	26
Dramatic Notes	27
New Books	26
Meetings of Societies	28

PUBLISHERS:

Melbourne: Melville, Mullen & Slade, 262 & 264 Collins St.   Sydney: E. A. Petherick & Co., 333 George St.

Vol. 3, No. 6. September, 1894.

THE
A. H. R.
(Australasian Home Reader)

Published by the Australasian Home Reading Union.

CONTENTS:

About Reading ... ... ROLF BOLDREWOOD

Browning's Victory ... ...Rev. J. S. HART, M.A.

Carlyle and Social Problems ... EDW. TREGEAR, F.R.H.S.

Australian Explorers II. ... ... K. I. H.

The Book of Common Prayer as Literature ... C. O. BURGE

Notes and News.

Sydney University Extension Lectures.

Sydney:
WM. ANDREWS & CO., PRINTERS, BOOKBINDERS, &C.,
315 Pitt Street.

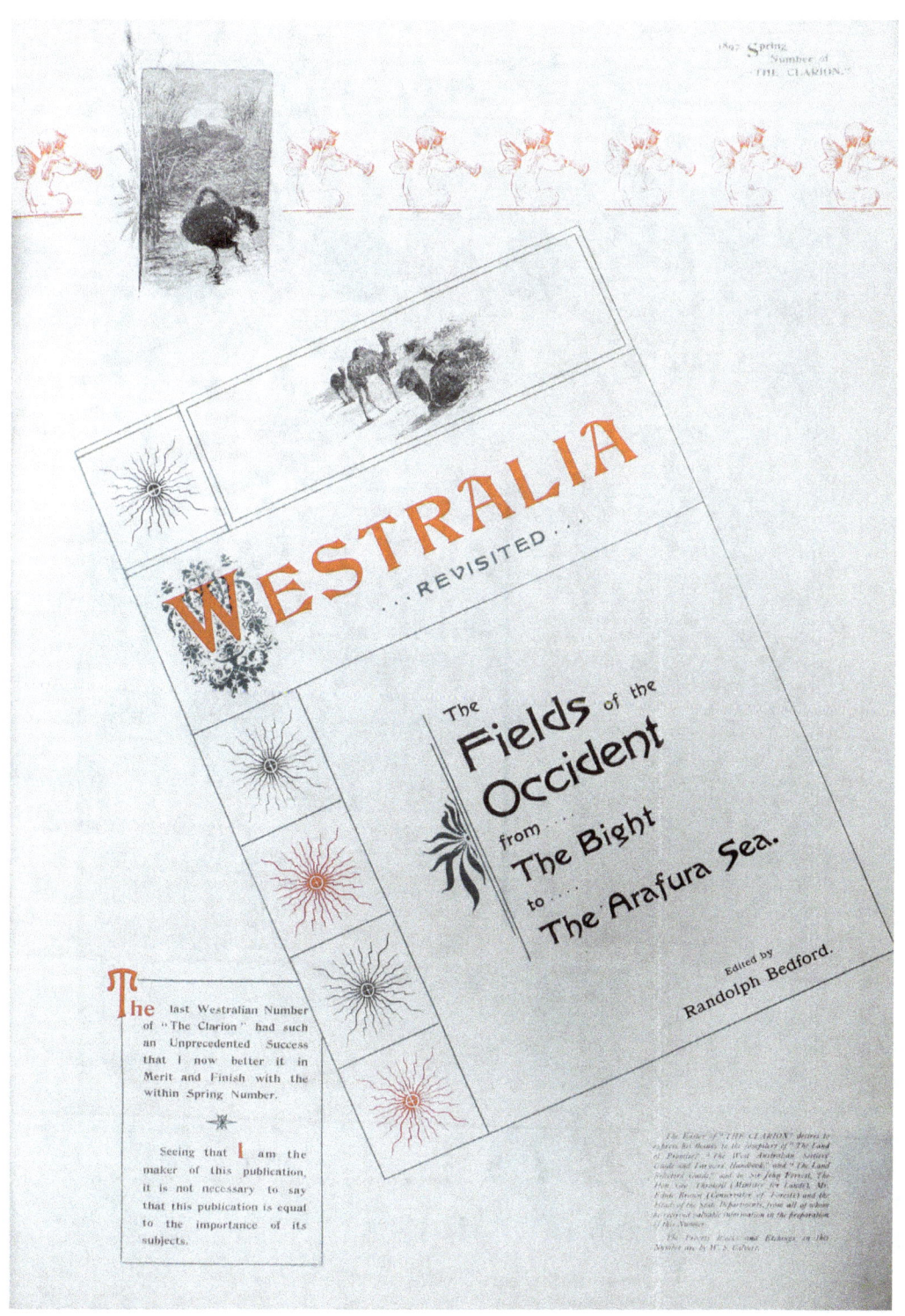

Vol. I.—No. 1.   Melbourne, Monday, 2nd January, 1899.   PRICE, ONE PENNY.
If Posted, 1½d.

Unkind.

HE: "I am a most unfortunate kind of a beggar; people either take me for a rogue or a fool."
SHE: "Oh, I am sure that nobody would think you a rogue!"

The Bulletin

SATURDAY, MAY 19, 1900.

RAT-TAT-TAT!
"I really must look in here just to prevent inter-provincial jealousy."

ALL ABOUT AUSTRALIANS

WITH A LEAVENING OF OTHER INTERESTING SUBJECTS.

Registered at the G.P.O., Sydney, for transmission by Post as a Newspaper.

No. 1. Vol. I. [An Illustrated Monthly Journal] Sydney, May 3, 1901. With Supplement. PRICE 3d.

S.L. Prima Donna Corsets
(REGISTERED)

THESE MOST PERFECT FITTING
LONG-WAISTED CORSETS
ARE NOW MADE IN THE
NEW STRAIGHT FRONT HIP SPRING
CORSET.

Specially designed to give a straight front, and produce most perfect Hips, as required by

Each pair is stamped on band inside **THE LATEST FASHION.**

S.L. PRIMA DONNA,

To be obtained of the Principal Drapers.

Wholesale Agent: **G. PHILLIPS, 18 Barrack Street.**

Purveyors to His Excellency the Governor General

T. S. Prescott & Co.,
IMPORTERS OF HIGH-CLASS
HAVANA CIGARS AND EGYPTIAN CIGARETTES,
**17 HUNTER STREET,
SYDNEY, N.S.W.**

Telephone 3667.

"STRONGEST AND BEST." —Health.
FRY'S COCOA
Highest Honours, Chicago, 1893. | Over 100 Prize Medals and Diplomas.

N.S.W. BOOKSTALL COMPANY,
Sole Proprietor:— A. C. ROWLANDSON

NEW BOOKS BY EVERY MAIL.
Cheapest Firm in Australia. All Books at Published Prices.

Branches at all the Principal Railway Stations in New South Wales and on the North Shore, Mosman and Neutral Bay, and Manly Wharves, Circular Quay. Also Elizabeth Street, Park Street, Liverpool Street, Redfern, New L. Ferry Wharf, Erskine Street, and **861 George Street, Sydney.**

All communications to be addressed: 861 George Street, Sydney.

BLACKWELL, BARTER AND SCOTT,
Manufacturers Agents & Commission Merchants

Indents executed on the best possible terms for all classes of European and Continental Goods direct from the Manufacturer.

We have on view at our extensive Show Rooms

257 GEORGE STREET, SYDNEY,
THE MOST UP-TO-DATE SAMPLES in
Plain & Fancy Earthenware, China, Glass, Enamelware, &c.

We are SOLE AGENTS for Australasia for the following Manufacturers:
Alfred Mekin, Limited, Charles Allerton & Sons, Wood & Barker, Limited, Matthew Turnbull, Wortmann & Elbers, Merkelbach & Wick.

A visit to our Showrooms will at all times be appreciated.

PURE   **PURE**

ROBINSON'S COCOA

PURE   **PURE**

Drink Teacher's HIGHLAND CREAM Whiskey
SOLE AGENTS: PLUMMER, LOVE & Co. 240 George St., Syd.

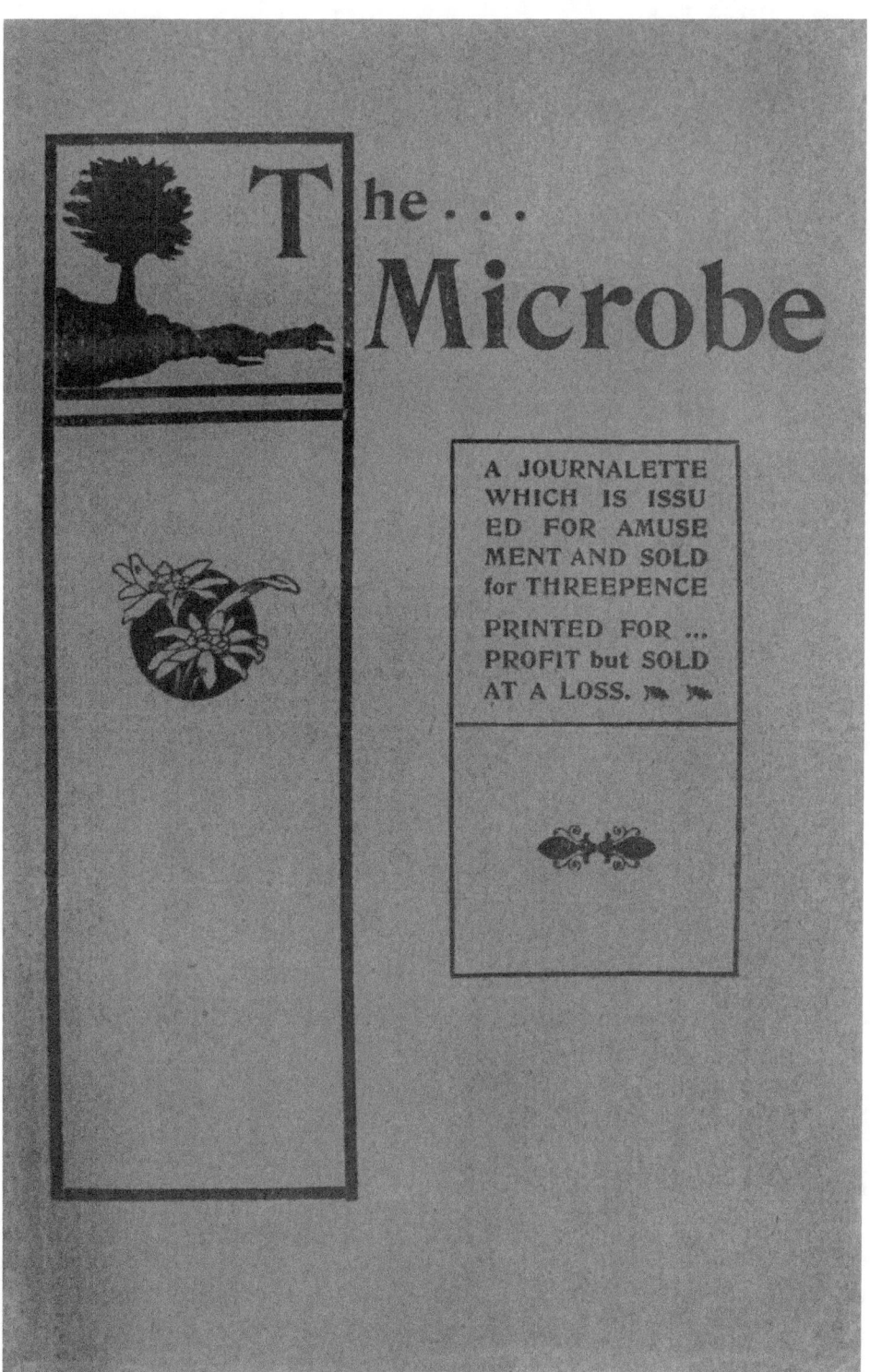

Designed, Engraved on Metal, and Printed by Phil Stone, Melbourne.

Ye Wayside Goose

A Journal of Intelligence

*Registered at the General Post Office, Melbourne,
for Transmission by Post as a Newspaper*

WEDNESDAY, SEPT. 27, 1905

Drawn on zinc by Frank Wilmot

...Price Twopence...

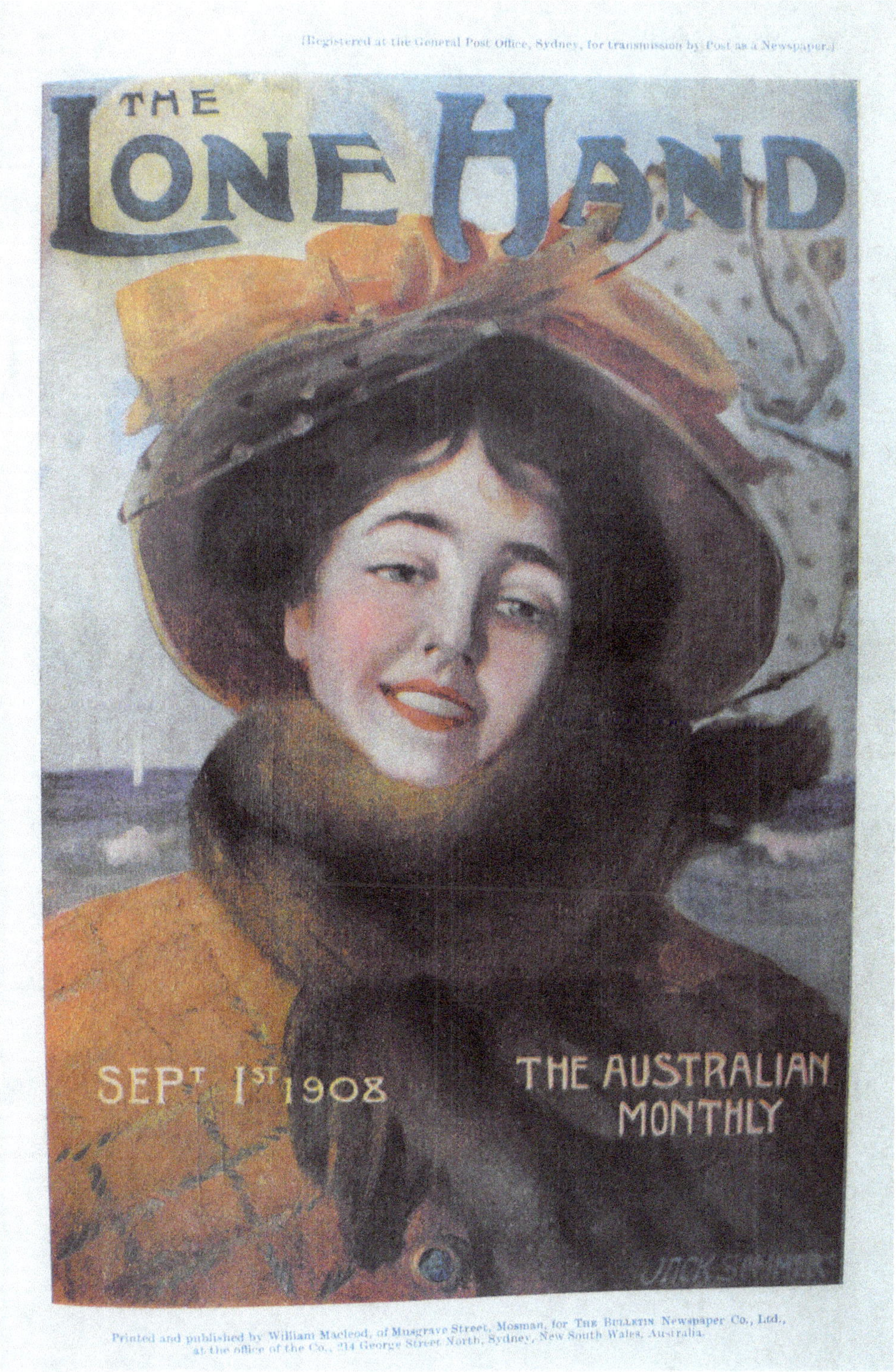
[Registered at the General Post Office, Sydney, for transmission by Post as a Newspaper.]
THE LONE HAND
SEPT. 1ST 1908
THE AUSTRALIAN MONTHLY
Printed and published by William Macleod, of Musgrave Street, Mosman, for THE BULLETIN Newspaper Co., Ltd., at the office of the Co., 214 George Street North, Sydney, New South Wales, Australia.

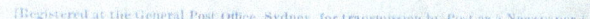

THE RED ANT

AN AUSTRALIAN MAGAZINE

3ᴰ

PART 7

Colonial Types: Emergent and Residual
KEN GELDER & RACHAEL WEAVER

'The Pieman', *Heads of the People*,
7 August 1847
273

'The Melbourne Auction Dealer', *Illustrated Journal of Australasia*, March 1857
275

Donald Cameron, 'The Melbourne Dandy', *Australian Journal*, 26 May 1866
277

E.C. Spicer, 'A Holiday Ramble in Victoria', *Sydney Quarterly Magazine*, October 1883
282

'The Australian Young Man', *Australian Magazine of Contemporary Colonial Opinion*, September 1886
284

Ethel Castilla, 'Nouveaux Riches', *Centennial Magazine*, February 1889
291

'The Oscar Wilde's [sic] of Sydney', *Scorpion*,
24 April 1895
296

K Somerton, 'Jackeroos', *Cosmos*,
19 October 1896
297

'I'm a Hawker and I Hawk…',
Bulletin, 22 October 1898
301

Judex, 'Larrikinism and Hooliganism',
Southern Cross, 1 February 1899
304

Ernest Low, 'Why is the Australian Disliked?'
Lone Hand, 1 October 1910
306

1

Colonial Types: Emergent and Residual
KEN GELDER & RACHAEL WEAVER

THE PRIMARY TASK OF THE colonial journals was to reflect colonial society, to analyse and dissect it, to chronicle its fashions and foibles and to comment on its prospects for the future. The colonial scene was never homogeneous; in fact, it was remarkably diverse, composed of numerous different interest groups interacting with each other, competing with each other, and so on. Given all these different constituencies, who then could be properly identified as a colonial? The journals all wanted to invest in the idea of a representative type who could carry the aspirations of a developing nation. At the same time, the colonies were busily distinguishing themselves from one another; and besides, there was little agreement among commentators as to the qualities that best typified colonial ideals. The journals soon turned their attention to the dynamics of colonial populations, chronicling an extraordinarily wide variety of practices, dispositions, social classes and occupations. The proliferation of character 'sketches' across the journals during this time reveals an increasingly fractured social economy. It also brings a great deal of colonial literary writing – think of some of Henry Lawson's short stories and poems, for example – into close proximity with the interests of social journalism. Alongside the quest for a representative national character we see the emergence of a multiplicity of minor colonial types, some inherited from Europe and America and some locally developed. Each type inhabits its own set of narratives and is given a life-cycle – a destination – that is always assessed in terms of its ability to contribute to the nation's wellbeing.

In the late 1840s, William Baker's Sydney journal *Heads of the People* built itself around precisely the question of who best represented the interests of colonial society. The 'Preface' to this journal, included in the first part of this book, is alert to the objection that its selection of representative types has been made 'indiscriminately'. But the journal deliberately mixes up its types, dismantling conventional hierarchies by placing senior government officials alongside the most marginal of colonial figures. 'The Pieman' might seem to describe one of the latter. But the journal charts his arrival in the colonies and gives him a kind of mock-heroic status, finally linking him into the successful operation of colonial life. 'The Melbourne Auction Dealer' – from Frederick Sinnett's *Illustrated Journal of Australasia* – introduces another marginal type, even though his profession brings him into contact with almost everyone in the colonies. In this first-hand account, the auction dealer casts himself as an active participant in the colonial scene, parasitical in some ways but useful in others, plying a trade that muddles the distinction between what is fake and what is authentic – and helping the colonial economy to flow more freely. The colonial writer and publisher Donald Cameron wrote extensively for the *Australian Journal*, contributing among other things a series of fascinating articles on Australian social types. Cameron's 'The Melbourne Dandy' appears three years after Charles Baudelaire's famous account in 1863 of the imminent demise of this figure in Europe. 'Dandyism is a setting sun', Baudelaire wrote in *The Painter of Modern Life*; 'like the declining star, it is magnificent, without heat and full of melancholy. But alas! The rising tide of democracy, which spreads everywhere and reduces everything to the same level, is daily carrying away these last champions of human pride…'[1] But for Cameron, colonial Melbourne is a place in which the dandy can prosper. This roguish, seductive figure is able to carve out an existence in the city, fleecing new arrivals but also helping them to circulate their money.

The question of who is useful to the colonial economy – and who isn't – can sometimes be difficult to answer. Colonial commentators were preoccupied with the future prospects of young Australians, routinely worrying about what they would become and what their impact on colonial life might be. The Anglican minister Edward Clarke Spicer's 'A Holiday Ramble in Victoria' – from the *Sydney Quarterly Magazine* – compares young men from the different colonies, describing their characters as shaped by the environment of each city and the pleasures it offers. While this is a benign account of robust colonial youth, it does measure one type against another, finding admirable qualities (like hospitality) in some that others don't have. Other accounts of young men in the colonies can be much more critical. The anonymous article 'The Australian Young Man', from James McDougall's *Australian Magazine of Contemporary Colonial Opinion* (July – September 1886), is a marvellous rant against the destructive qualities of an emergent type who seems to reject all the civic virtues that colonialism puts into place, vandalising public spaces, refusing to work, and so on. K. Somerton's 'Jackeroos', from *Cosmos*, is especially disappointed in the capacity of a particular kind of colonial young man to make something of himself. The jackeroo might seem to be an iconic Australian type, tough, masculine and resourceful. Here, however, he is lazy, self-centred, racist and useless; he stands in contrast to the squatter, who is much more essential to the project of nation-building.

In the city, it only seems to get worse. The Sydney *Scorpion* (24 April 1895) was an outspokenly critical journal that lambasted both the wealthy classes and the 'so-called Labor Party', although it lasted for just one issue. Published just a few weeks after Oscar Wilde initiated his ill-fated libel action against the Marquis of Queensberry at the Old Bailey in London, 'The Oscar Wilde's [sic] of Sydney' is anxious about the prevalence of male homosexuality in this colonial city, placing the blame squarely on decadent British influences. On the other hand, in 'Larrikinism and Hooliganism' from *Southern Cross* (November 1898 – November 1900), the locals have preceded and far outstripped their British counterparts. Larrikins as a type generated widespread social anxieties about colonial youth, especially in the wake of violent crimes like the 1886 'Mount Rennie outrage' involving the gang-rape of a teenage girl or the 1889 'Bondi riot' when 'larrikins' fought with police. They soon provided a local version of what Stanley Cohen would later call 'folk devils'; that is, 'visible reminders of what we should not be'.[2] Melissa Bellanta has suggested that larrikins in fact heavily invested in their own wicked image: 'Though they were people rather than types', she writes, 'they still took pleasure from the stylised villains and vamps in the popular culture of the day'.[3] In the article from *Southern Cross*, the solution seems clear enough: more parental discipline, and a harsher state regime. In other accounts, however, neither of these things seems to count for much. We've included a contribution to the *Bulletin*'s 'Red Page' in 1898, a first-person narrative of an itinerant hawker. Each social type provides a vision of the world that is unique to their predicament. For the hawker, the question of where he comes from is irrelevant; and, like the editor of *Heads of the People*, he doesn't seem to care much for conventional social hierarchies. He brings two other types into his framework, the 'sundowner' and the 'larrikiness', the 'two most typical figures in Australian life' – although his account of them might seem to us today to be remarkably eccentric. His country racism is casually evoked, but he also speaks against the kind of despair about bush life attributed to Henry Lawson. For this hawker, Australia's heroes lie hidden among ordinary rural workers such as 'Sydney Bob the Rider'; but his problem is that young Australian men never seem to encounter these obscured sources of inspiration.

Social types in the colonies were rigorously debated in the journals. Commentators asked which types were to be admired, which would carry the nation forward, and which were best left behind. Particular social types might inhabit (and generate) a variety of narrative forms; their life-cycles lead them in different directions, too, and for better or worse this impacts on the ambitions of a nation still preoccupied with its own development. The Victorian writer and art critic Ethel Castilla's 'Nouveaux Riches', from the *Centennial Magazine*, comes to the defence of an emergent class of prosperous colonials, typically represented in fiction as socially awkward, vulgar and low born. Interestingly, she reserves her only criticism for the *nouveau riche* woman, whose wealth is ostentatious: 'The very rustling of her gown', Castilla writes, 'is suggestive of crisp bank notes'. The men, however, gain her approval because they seem to spend their money unselfishly, for the good of the nation. The wealthy colonial's task, for Castilla, is to become philanthropic: 'to encourage all that beautifies and elevates colonial life'. 'Nouveaux Riches' is worth comparing to an article we include in the final part of this book,

COLONIAL TYPES: EMERGENT AND RESIDUAL

'The Duties of a Leisure Class in Colonial Society', since they both think about who might take responsibility for an emergent nation's cultural and aesthetic development. By the time Australia becomes a nation, of course, the type that is of greatest interest is the 'Australian'. In 1910, the journalist Ernest Low published a controversial piece in the *Lone Hand*, titled 'Why is the Australian Disliked?' The *Lone Hand*'s editorial was indeed anxious about the article's reception – 'It will come as news to many an Australian', it wrote, 'that outsiders could have any ground for considering our national type an objectionable one' – and it published a spirited rejoinder from the novelist J. H. M. Abbott in the same issue. Low's article clearly touched a nerve, but in fact it continued themes that were already apparent in earlier accounts of colonial types: vulgarity, boastfulness, self-interestedness, and so on. Localness – the local character of a colonial city, for example – is necessary in order to bring a social type into being. But for Low, the local inhibits the development of the Australian as a social type. The provincial here has now become a disadvantage; it makes the Australian 'conspicuous' away from home, and it also prevents him from becoming cosmopolitan.

1   Baudelaire, *The Painter of Modern Life*, p. 39.
2   Cohen, *Folk Devils and Moral Panics*, p. 2.
3   Bellanta, *Larrikins: A History*, p. 100.

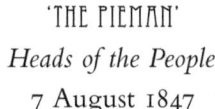

'THE PIEMAN'
Heads of the People
7 August 1847

"What!" we fancy we hear some of our readers exclaiming, "Is the Pieman a head of the people?" We reply, that he undoubtedly does come within that category. "Kidney, pork, apple, or mutton pies: hot pies!" are now among the most prominent of the Sydney "cries". The vendors of these savoury articles here, are much more respectable, too, than the same class at home, and are more extensively patronised. In London, no one of delicate stomach would think of eating what is termed a mutton pie; fearing that the crust would envelop not "the flesh of muttons, beefs, or goats", but that of some carnivorous animal that neither parted the hoof nor chewed the cud. Here, however, no such fear need prevent the epicure in these delicacies from indulging therein; the cheapness of the genuine article not rendering it necessary for the purveyors to run the risk of encountering the claws of the feline, or the fangs of the canine species. The abundance of our flocks and herds will always prove a sure guarantee that recourse will not be had to such nauseous substitutes, as we fear the high price of animal food at home too often leads to the adoption of.

The piemen are, in this colony, a useful class. How often have we noticed the relish with which jurors, witnesses, and spectators at the Darlinghurst Court House, have eaten their little pie, handed to them, smoking hot, from a highly polished tin machine, in a diminutive blue or white plate, and swimming in delicious gravy! How often have we ourselves, in the same situation, enjoyed the same little luxury, rendered doubly piquant by the sharpness of appetite—"Fames optimus coquus". How frequently, too, has the lonely bachelor, on leaving the theatre between 11 and 12 o'clock, paused at the corner of the street, and partaken of these pasties of sweet smelling savour, who might otherwise have gone supperless to his solitary pallet; his landlady having retired to her slumbers some hours previously?

But a truce with further dissertation on this part of the subject: come we now to speak of the eccentric individual whose portrait is herewith submitted to our readers, most of whom we feel assured will immediately, on looking at it, identify it with the living original.

William Francis King, as we have been informed, was born in London, in March, 1807, and is the eldest son of Francis King, Esq, late paymaster of petty accounts in the Treasury at Whitehall. His father intended him for the church; but it soon appeared that his innate love of field sports, and boisterous recreations, was not befitting the sacred character, and he entered into partnership with Smith and Simpson, stock and share brokers, in London. He did not remain long attached to this firm, but fancying it was getting into difficulties, he sold his share in the concern and obtained a situation as clerk in the Treasury Office, in the Tower, which his restless disposition did not allow him to hold long; and he left England for this colony in

COLONIAL TYPES: EMERGENT AND RESIDUAL

1829, with the expectation, from the high recommendations he brought with him, to obtain a government appointment. In this expectation he was, however, disappointed; and he took the situation of schoolmaster and clerk at Sutton Forest, near Bong Bong, presented to him by the then Archdeacon Broughton, the present bishop of the diocese. From this he went as tutor to the children of Mr. William Kern, and remained with him several years. Here again his unsettled temper prevailed over every other feeling, and he left Mr. Kern, with the determination of returning to England. Many unforeseen difficulties, however, presented themselves, and he was induced to hire as barman with Mr. H. Doran who then kept the Hope and Anchor, at the corner of King and Pitt streets, the present Rainbow Tavern. This kind of life did not suit King, and he commenced performing a series of feats of pedestrianism, in which he seems to have taken great delight; and so far from considering he was executing a task on such occasions, he always enjoyed it as a past-time. We will enumerate a few of the exploits of this extraordinary individual, as it is unquestionably owing to his notoriety in these matters that he has acquired the cognomen by which he is now so generally known,—"The Flying Pieman." One of his earliest feats was walking one thousand six hundred and thirty-four miles in five weeks and four days, out of which period he had only nine days fair weather. It was at the time of the flood on the Hawkesbury. Some heavy bets were made on this feat; but it did not appear that the poor pieman reaped any advantage beyond his self-gratification at having acquitted himself so well. He then walked from Mr. Kern's estate, near Campbelltown, and back, a distance of sixty-two miles, in twelve hours and a half. From the Obelisk in Macquarie Place, Sydney, to the sixteen mile stone at Parramatta, and back again in six hours. He beat the coach from Windsor to Sydney, arriving seven minutes before it. He walked from Sydney to Parramatta and back, twice a day, for six consecutive days. He undertook, on one occasion, to carry a dog, weighing upwards of seventy lbs., from Campbelltown to Sydney, between the hours of half-past twelve at night and twenty minutes to nine the next morning; which he accomplished twenty minutes within the given time. He was backed to carry a live goat, weighing ninety-two lbs., with twelve lbs. dead weight besides, from the old Talbot Inn, on Brickfield Hill, to Mr. Nash's, at Parramatta, in seven hours; which he performed, having twelve minutes to spare. He walked from the Parramatta Church to the church at Windsor, a distance of forty-three miles and a half, for three successive days; the first day he occupied eight hours in going to and fro; the second, seven hours and a half; and the third, seven hours and twenty-five minutes. But we fear we are getting tedious, or we could enumerate a variety of other feats performed by this remarkable man. No doubt his natural bent for such undertaking, and his readiness upon all occasions to be backed therein, have made him the dupe of many; whilst his peculiar and vivacious manner rendered him the butt of almost all; and for which he possesses the qualifications described by Sterne.

"A man is not qualified for a butt," says he, "who has not a good deal of wit and vivacity, even in the ridiculous side of his character. A stupid butt is only fit for the conversation of

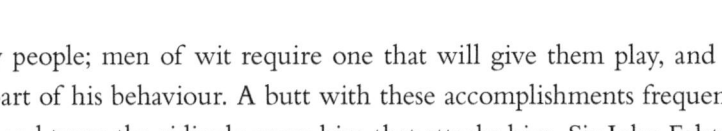

ordinary people; men of wit require one that will give them play, and bestir himself in the absurd part of his behaviour. A butt with these accomplishments frequently gets the laugh on his side, and turns the ridicule upon him that attacks him. Sir John Falstaff was a hero of this species, and gives a good description of himself in his capacity of a butt, after the following manner:—'Men of all sorts,' says that merry knight, 'take a pride to gird at me. The brain of man is not able to invent anything that tends to laughter more than I invent, or is invented on me. I am not only witty in myself, but the cause that wit is in other men.'"

'THE MELBOURNE AUCTION DEALER'
Illustrated Journal of Australasia
March 1857

I am a Melbourne dealer—a regular buyer and seller at all auction rooms, and a hawker, sometimes, of any odd article which sells best at people's houses in the suburbs. I try to make a living, as everybody does in the colony, and, if I am not the most conscientious of men, all I can say is, there are heaps of folks in the city who hold their heads a great deal higher and perform worse actions than I do. Auction rooms are strange places, and a good bit of life can be seen there. Once bob behind the scenes, and a man picks up a great deal of the affairs of his neighbours. The *made-up* genuine sales; the sales *without reserve*; the *ex recent* arrivals! La! bless us! I was once gammoned by those advertisements myself; but it is a long time ago now, and before I was quite up to the trade I practise. Of course folks of my class (and I should astonish you if I attempted to number them) don't attend at the real genuine sales which do sometimes take place. Perhaps, when there's a cargo of spoiled goods, or a sale for the benefit of the underwriters, or something like that, we attend, and now and again get a decent *pull*, but, in general, we turn our attention to the smaller tribe of auctioneers, and glide amongst those gentry who are knocking down every hour in the day six days in a week; and who will, for the proper commission, sell the same article three or four times over the course of the day. Before there were so many traders in Melbourne, when business was brisker, and there were fewer folks to share it, we dealers often made a good penny by buying up a lot of goods and selling them ourselves to a regular city shopkeeper. But those days have gone by: commission agents and three months' bills have knocked that trade on the head. Nobody gives the dealer "paper tic," although the gentry that cut up his ready-money business are, after all, not a bit safer. As it is, our work is confined to buying and selling by auction; snatching up a purchase made at twelve o'clock at one end of Elizabeth street, and selling it by half-past two in an auction room at the other end. That's constantly done. As for the wares, we keep on buying in till we get a real buyer: that's a matter 'tween the auctioneer and ourselves, and it won't do to spoil

COLONIAL TYPES: EMERGENT AND RESIDUAL

business. There's a great number of secrets open to us, however. A B, who buys "on paper" of D E F G H and Co., sends in his goods to the auction room, *without reserve*; when they MUST go, and at a very small profit; and when he hopes "things will be better next week," we know all that. Some of us are always on the look-out, and, when a strange dray is called to A B's door, loaded, and the carman gets his instructions two doors off, we don't want to know any more, but just pass the word to one another, and A B's goods, butter, shirts, or brandies, pass through our hands, that is, we dealers get them uncommonly cheap, share them amongst us, and hawk the goods round at a first-rate profit. I'll just tell you one of those jokes. There was once an article very scarce in town, and only a few held it; one of these few wanted to sell it, for cash, mind, and, thinking the time was favourable, in went a lot of it to auction. We saw it. One of our trade noticed all this, and gave us all word. The room was packed. The goods were ours just thirty per cent. under wholesale price, and Collingwood cleared us all out in the course of the day. I think that was one of the best specs. I ever made, but it did up the seller.

Then look at the genuine buyers that attend the sale—country parsons, who will persist in believing them to be bona fide; old women, 'specially if its China or furniture; storekeepers from the interior, who will buy cheap and won't buy good: why, these folks can be (and are) crammed with all the rubbish in the place. If there's any old stock of mine knocking about the room when these folks enter it, I tip the wink, and up it goes. Just bid once or twice against a woman, and her "dander" rises so awfully that, if I hadn't some grains of conscience in me, I'd ha' cleared out many a one's purse with a cracked dinner service, or a plated bread basket. Time was when a decent hit could be made by getting a lot of eggs, oranges, or such like, and whisking them off to Geelong by steamer, but that game's all over: the "pivot" had such a lot of storekeepers, compared to their customers, that they all ran up to Melbourne themselves, and did us out of our "quarterings." It isn't worth a man's while to take goods down there now. Us dealers, too, are sometimes of use to the detectives. There was a case the other day.—Some jewellery had vanished. It would n't do to pawn it; it would n't do to sell it openly anywhere; but, a watch at this room, and a chain at that, would soon get off the swag ('specially with such a lot of auction rooms), and none be the wiser. Well, some of us were put up to this, and, keeping our eyes open, the stuff was soon spied out, and the parties concerned taken. I know many folk do n't think we're a bit better than the chaps that took the jewellery, but, after all, it is n't our faults. The Government will license people to call things Cold and silDer, therefore we poor men employ them to do it. There are a set of people who will believe gold and silver goods can be bought at a less price than the value of old brass. Therefore we poor men supply them. It's all a matter of sharpness, real or assumed; that's where it is.

Take up a morning paper—*Argus,* or *Auction Mart*—there's a sale of somebody's furniture, at such a place. La! bless us, it's the sweepings of all our goods for the last six months. I give in, perhaps, a bedstead, my friend M. sends in three chairs and a flat-iron, and so on; that's the

way a genuine household furniture sale is often made up; hire a cottage for a pound note, send the things in on Monday night, and clear off on Tuesday. Why, there's "genuine cargoes" of potatoes, onions, and coast produce that's hawked all round the suburbs long before it arrives in the Bay. Can't anybody see that? There's always the captain of the vessel in the room to vouch for its genuineness,—a chap with a lot of jewellery and black hair, who don't know the saddle of the bowsprit from the bridle of the bowline; but it goes down with some people. Ay, and what's more, whoever reads this will say they believe there are such places and such trickery as I mention, but they are too old colonists to be caught by them, and then rush into the first sale room they meet and fall in the trap neatly. It's human nature, and nothing can kick against that. I can't see for the life of me, not that it's any business of mine, and not that I care, but I can't see how the grocers and tailors can pay rent or taxes—any one can go into a small auction room and get "Two pound o' tea with the option of taking a chest," or "a pair of trowsers, with the option of half a dozen." Then if I get the half dozen cheap, off I go to Prahran, or St. Kilda, or some of these places, and quickly sell 'em. It is'nt as at home, where decent folks do'nt like buying of hawkers; anybody buys of anybody else, which, of course, is so much the better for the dealers and so much the worse for tradespeople. It is n't a bad business, after all. It is n't such hard work as the diggings, although we can't plead being licensed vagabonds; a chap with twenty pounds, with some talk, and a judge of articles, generally can knock out a first-rate living for himself and family. Of course, sobriety is necessary, so is punctuality, likewise quietness. Temper wont [sic] do in an auction room; and a loss one day can be made up the next. Of course, as nobody trusts me, I trusts nobody, auctioneers nor none of 'em, and so I rub on. It's not the worst, if it is n't the best, of callings; perhaps it's got a worse name than it deserves, but what of that. Everybody knows lawyers have a better, and so edge one side against the other and we'll all come right some day. That's my maxim, and it's kept me out of many a scrape, and made me take many a rough jest smoothly; and if there's a thousand people in Melbourne better off than I am, who ought n't to be, at least there's another thousand not so well off who ought; so, as I said before, all things come equal, and it's no use endeavouring to overturn human nature.

DONALD CAMERON, 'THE MELBOURNE DANDY'
Australian Journal
26 May 1866

Perhaps my readers may fancy that this character is not an Australian one; but when they have read this article, they will agree with me that it is essentially so. The Melbourne dandy is a peculiar character.

COLONIAL TYPES: EMERGENT AND RESIDUAL

Willie Gordon was as fine a specimen of this genus as could be selected. As for his age, no one had noticed any change in him for years, and he seemed to be about nineteen ever since Bourke-street loungers had known him. His dress was always unexceptional; he wore the most aristocratic pegtops, the finest sac, and his small feet were covered by the best of boots. A beautiful gold chain, with pendant seals and coins, were always on his breast, never performing, even on the most urgent occasions, a journey to the obliging "uncles" who grace the eastern side of Elizabeth-street so conspicuously. He eschewed "four-and-nines," and wore the smart black hat now in fashion, round which a white silk "bandage" was always worn. This hat showed the turn of his head just to his liking. A gold headed cane, the handle of which was an unfortunate dog who was always about to spring, but for some reason or other didn't, might convey to the spectator an idea that Willie was fond of sport, in which he distinguished himself so greatly afterwards.

Our readers have, no doubt, been deceived by the heading of this article. Ten to one but they thought we intended to give them a sketch of the aristocratic Collins-street Dundreary; but he bears too great a resemblance to well-known originals. We choose to give a real Australian creation.

How Willie managed to live and keep himself so primly dressed, few could tell. It was well known he had no property, and his parents were but indifferently well off. Willie used to talk about the "office," but he could never give any satisfactory geographical information on the subject. His "office" evidently lay in Bourke-street, and it was here he used to spend the most of his time. He lived in a great hotel, and made himself "necessary" to all new comers from the country. Willie knew a new arrival "flush" with the ready, as easily as a dog smells game. He could keep off a penniless man with admirable instinct. Few rich young men came to town bent on having a "spree" but Willie would become their *chaperon*; and ere they left Melbourne, Willie was pretty sure to have made "his own" out of them. He would make them pay for his amusement as well as their own, and very few days passed but his bewitching "Hang it, Bob, lend us a shiner or two," would prove successful. In fact, to confess the truth, Willie had such wheedling, coaxing ways about him, that no man or woman could resist him. As regards the weaker sex, Willie was a perfect "lady killer." There was not a barmaid in town, from the famous coterie at the Princess's to Scott's, who did not believe that Willie was their adorer. It was fortunate they were ignorant of Willie's universal and convenient love. If they were there might have been a little hair pulling.

It was Willie's glory to walk around Bourke-street with a new acquaintance with a well-filled pocket on any stirring night. There he might be seen arm-in-arm with his "gull," smoking the most fragrant cigars brought by the aforesaid "gull," and twirling his gold-headed cane. But the summit of his felicity was to sit in the Temple of Pomona, drinking something extra delicious, with a plate of luscious fruit, and confections innumerable before him, all of which, of course, was paid for by the new acquaintance; in return for which Willie told him innumerable stories, and introduced him to the mysteries of Melbourne life.

Once on a time, however, Willie was taken-in dreadfully by one of these gentlemen and severely punished, for leading him astray and spending his money; and it is our purpose now to relate how this happened. We must premise, however, before we go farther, that Willie had never been "out of town in his life," to use an expression so common; but we really don't understand how he could have been out of town before.

This young gentleman was an Echuca squatter, a young man who had just come into possession. He had fallen in love with Willie at first sight, and Willie had fleeced him disgracefully. In fact, we are afraid that Willie outshot the mark in his eagerness this time. He paid for it, however.

When Mordant's money was exhausted, of course he returned home, but insisted that Willie should accompany him. Now, Willie had never been out of Melbourne, and this was rather a perilous adventure. True he had gone up to Sunbury in the train, and stood on a hill to see the volunteers manœuvring. He had been to Brighton and Ballarat. But to go into the bush about forty or fifty miles from a decent town! Why, it was a hazardous experiment. He instantly called to mind Chevalier's pictures, and fancied himself going over these awful ranges on a buck-jumper.

"Very nice, very romantic," said Willie to himself, tapping the pictures with his cane, "but I'd much sooner sit here looking at them, than ride over them. However, when I come back—that is, if I come back alive—I can crow over all the rest, and say I've been up-country."

And up-country Willie went, after giving many a sigh as he lost sight of beloved Melbourne. But matters went very smoothly with him until they reached Echuca. Next morning two fiery-looking horses stood before the inn-door, and our unfortunate town boy had to mount the most vicious-looking—the little black imp who held it telling him, by way of consolation, with every tooth in his roguish head revealed, that the horse was "berry good, massa, him only jump about—baal him buck only when massa spur him!"

Willie saw and did more that day than had been dreamed of in his philosophy. Forty miles a-day is no easy task for a man who never rode above an hour; and when Willie arrived at the home station, after riding over mountains which would put Chevalier's pictures in the shade, he found that a certain portion of his skin had taken leave of him, and that every bone in his body was stiff and sore. He was laid up for three days, and never ventured out of his room, which looked out on a mountain, instead of overlooking the brilliant Bourke-street pavement. Ah! if he would only get back to Bourke-street alive, he would never tempt fate any more by venturing out into the bush.

But his enemies seemed to be determined to torment him. No sooner did he venture out of his room than Mordant told him to get ready for a real kangaroo hunt, which was to take place next day.

COLONIAL TYPES: EMERGENT AND RESIDUAL

"You must be up at dawn of day, mind," was Mordant's parting admonition, "and recollect you must wear a riding-dress, or they'll all laugh at you. I've sent a riding-dress to your room."

Willie heard all this like a culprit about to be executed. His appearance at Wondilly had been an utter failure. He had tried to assume the town-bred gentlemen; but, owing to his antecedents, the attempt was a total failure. Every one knew what he was. What use to him was his natty and genteel appearance, his town manners and his clever ways. He was the admiration of the kitchen, but the butt of the drawing-room.

Precisely at daylight—when Willie, according to his usual course of life would be turning into bed—he was woke up, and being chary about rising so early, he was tumbled out of bed without ceremony, and, by way of aiding him to rouse up, he received a shower-bath gratis. He soon dressed himself in his new dress—what a different one from the loose fitting pegtops!—and walked into the breakfast-room with the same feeling as a newly-breeched boy feels. Here a lot of fellows similarly dressed were partaking of a repast so rough that Willie could hardly refrain from crying when he thought of the beautiful breakfasts he had had at the Albion or the Criterion at others' expense.

"I wonder which of us will be killed to-day," said Mordant.

"Heaven only knows," said a young fellow who sat close to Willie. "Of course you are a good rider?" he said to Willie.

"I think I can ride a little," said Willie.

"You had better be sure," said the other. "It is not long since a young fellow, who came up for colonial experience from Melbourne, was killed at a kangaroo hunt."

Very consolatory to Willie was this; and still more encouraging were the stories he heard his companions relate as they moved on—of hair-breadth escapes up hill and down dale. At last the game was started, and with a tremendous shout, which rose up cheerfully in the morning air, the company applied the spur to their steeds, and away they flew after a huge old man, who bounded away with lightning speed. Willie gladly would have kept back from the break-neck race, but the horse he rode was an old "kangarooer," and would follow the sport, whether Willie liked it or not. The game took to the hills, but he was driven into the plain, and an exciting chase ensued. The plain was dotted with clumps of brushwood. They were very picturesque to the eye, but Willie found them extremely difficult to get through, especially when his horse would follow the chase whichever way it went. At last the horse brought him under a leaning tree, and it happened to him, as it happened to Absalom in the days of old—with this difference, however, that poor Willie was completely stunned, and fell to the ground.

When Willie woke from his trance he knew nothing of what had occurred. His first cry was, "Waiter—sardines and sodawater!" Finding this unheeded, he rose, and seeing some trees around him, he thought he had slept in the Carlton or Fitzroy garden, and he rose up and vociferated, "Cabby, cab, cab," and was about to curse Melbourne cabbies after his usual manner, when he gave a more discriminating glance around, and he instantly understood how matters were. Oh! how can we depict Willie's utter discomfiture. Talk of a countryman being bewildered in the wilderness of London; it is nothing compared to Willie Gordon's bewilderment in the wilderness of Australia. Wherever he turned he saw nothing but the wild, hopeless bush. Oh! that he was back in Bourke-street again. Verily, Mordant was revenged.

Presently, to Willie's unbounded delight, a voice was heard singing close at hand the following appropriate lines:—

They may say what they like of the mountains and trees,
Of the rocks and the waters, and cool healthy breeze,
The snow-covered mountains, and far-stretching plain—
Oh! I wish I was back in old Melbourne again.

They may talk of their sports and the wild kangaroo,
And the feats in the saddle that bushmen can do;
For my part all these ideas can bring me but pain—
Oh! I wish I was back in old Bourke-street again.

When I think on the Temple Pomona so grand,
Where fine dinners and suppers my gulls used to stand,
And the fruit, and the hock, and the sparkling champagne—
Oh! I wish I was back in my old haunts again.

Oh! should fate in her kindness me once more restore
To the scenes where I've triumphed so often before;
Admired by the fair sex, and envied by men,
I shall never lose sight of dear Melbourne again.

And no sooner had the singer finished than the whole company came from behind one of the clumps laughing immoderately, their voices sounding merrily on the fresh morning air. They had all stopped the chase when the "spill" had occurred. Mordant laughed heartily at Willie's mishaps, and told him he forgave him for all, in consideration of all he had suffered; and Willie was sent home in charge of the same grinning aboriginal who had assured him his horse would only jump about, while the rest of the party resumed their amusement.

Willie walks Bourke-street as often as ever, and he can talk about his tour in the country as well as the best, and say he has been in at the death. But we are happy to say he has given up his tricks, and has taken to an honest occupation. But he cannot forget Bourke-street, and one may see him promenading in that street any Saturday night they like to look for him. They will know him by his spruce dress, gold-headed stick, and impudent swagger.

E.C. SPICER, 'A HOLIDAY RAMBLE IN VICTORIA'
Sydney Quarterly Magazine
October 1883

There can be little doubt that these colonies are already drifting into racial peculiarities. No one who is ordinarily observant can fail to mark the difference between the manner, behaviour, and physical peculiarities of the residents in, say, Adelaide, Melbourne, Sydney, and Hobart. The quiet, self-reliant, hospitable man of business, surrounded by an atmosphere of English refinement, proud of the hills that surround his city, glorying in his Botanic Garden, and conscious of no stain of debt or dishonour on his colony's escutcheon, is perhaps a type of Adelaidean. Very different indeed is the finely formed, erect young squatter from the Western District of Victoria, whom you meet in Collins-street on any day, with firm mouth and slightly bronzed cheek; or at his club, discussing the probable winners in the coming race at Flemington; or howling himself hoarse in the midst of a crowd of thousands at a Melbourne *verses* [sic] Carlton football match. He remembers the days at Geelong, when, swift of foot, and keen of eye, and sound in wind and limb, he pursued the *pila velox* himself "with many a merry shout, 'mid riot, revelry and rout," glorying in the pride of power and the acknowledged supremacy of his school, *quorum pars magna fuit*.

He again differs from the taller, and perhaps paler, Sydney youth; who, lithe and active at cricket and all manly sports, and generosity and kindness itself in his nature, still lacks the boundless enthusiasm, the dash and vigour of his Melbourne brother. But your Melbourne friend is somewhat selfish and prefers to enjoy himself in a crowd; while your Sydney friend will take you to his charming home, and, pointing out to you the special loveliness of his particular view of the harbour, will say to you in effect, what the Spaniard says in fact, "This house, sir, is your own."

In thinking of Hobart who thinks of men? I suppose the type of "fortis Hobartia" is an active figure muffled and draped in furs, with cheeks blushing almost crimson under the clear sky and sparkling air that rushes down from the mountain glittering with snow. Such a figure suggests Spring excursions among busy hop-pickers, backed by the long softened rows of poles twined over with the ripening hops; or dreamy boating days, when gliding up or down the Derwent, with its charming spots where cultivation and a kindly air has persuaded a luxuriant soil to clothe itself with flowers of many a varied hue, and, later in the year, with such gooseberries, strawberries, and kindred English fruits as make the chubby school-boy, home from hard study in grinding hexameters for his A.A. degree, shout with joyful anticipation.

Even the architecture of the streets and buildings is characteristic. Melbourne has its grand stone fronts with brick backs and sides; Adelaide, thorough as usual, has its buildings of cut stone even in the back lanes. Sydney has florid decorations upon its splendid edifices, and a singular penchant for "carvings," which sometimes develops itself in weird gargoyles and smiling heads where you expect, if not severity, at least sobriety.

And while Melbourne has splendid streets in the suburbs planted with rows of graceful trees, Sydney, alas! has its beehive terraces, staring, comfortless and atticked. How different, too, from the stone cottages, with broad cool verandahs and gardens all round, so characteristic of the suburbs of the City of Wheat!

And perhaps in nothing is the characteristic peculiarity of the different colonies so marked as the manner in which their inhabitants amuse themselves. Not only in crowds; though the thousands of vehicles at Brighton Beach on a holiday, and their separate groups of happy picnickers, and sufficiently different from the holiday-makers indiscriminately disgorged from a steamer at Clontarf; but in the smaller groups that arrange themselves in parties at any time of the year for a day's picnic or excursion. Sydney possesses so many lovely resorts close at hand, that the most natural course is to step on board a steamer and glide past sheltered bay and woody headland until some favourite spot is reached, where a scramble over rocky hills, or a hunt for rare ferns and flowers, and a well-stocked basket opened under some shady tree, furnish pleasant pastime for a sunny day.

But Melbourne has little natural beauty surrounding it. The Bay is open and flat, and its sandy shores are uninviting. A day's excursion down to the Heads 60 miles away is pleasant enough in summer; but to young, energetic, active youth Melbourne presents few attractions. There are the hills some 20 miles off, on summer evenings half hidden by a purple glow of sunset, where are tall gums, clustering sassafras, dropping ferns, and water splashing over rocky beds of steep valleys. The hills, separated from Melbourne by a long stretch of undulating country covered with small tress, and here and there fertile spots with gardens profusely filled with flowers, and teeming with fruitfulness of every kind;—the hills, with their fresh, invigorating air, and their pleasant memories, inspire the enthusiast to rush forth from the city—after donning his oldest suit, his amplest boots and softest hat,—to climb their steep sides, rest pleasantly wearied under the shade of some spreading fern, and breathe the cool air, scented with a thousand odours.

COLONIAL TYPES: EMERGENT AND RESIDUAL

'THE AUSTRALIAN YOUNG MAN'
Australian Magazine of Contemporary Colonial Opinion
September 1886

He is distinguished prominently by his confidence in himself. He has no doubt of his own merits, his own powers, his own superiority. Consistently, as might be expected, he has a low opinion of the merits of others. Consequently, he disdains advice. He does not seek it, and if offered to him he declines to accept it. But he gives it freely. He gives it on every conceivable subject, for he has a fixed conviction that he is endowed with universal knowledge.

It will be observed that herein the average young man is referred to. Necessarily, among the whole class, there are exceptions to the rule of self-confidence. Perhaps the exceptions are numerous, and some of them are brilliant. They are brilliant enough to encourage the belief, that in the future the average will be the other way, and that modesty will be his leading characteristic. Up to this time, modesty has had only a subordinate share in making up the sum of the Australian young man. The absence of modesty has been justified on the ground that, in all new countries, modesty is a bar to individual development. What is wanted is progress, and progress is difficult if hampered with diffidence or self-distrust. Pioneer work, we are reminded, is rough work, and rough work is not to be done if the worker be sensitive or fastidious about forms, or too considerate for others. He must leap over obstacles, push through crowds, elbow his fellows if they get in his way, tread on their corns if they have any. In any case, he must never yield. He must never confess that others are better informed, more experienced, more accomplished than he is. Before all things, he must never show the weakness of acknowledging that there is such a quality as sensitiveness in others. He may be sensitive himself—that is to say, he may be sore-boned, or, as we have it, thin-skinned—but he must decline to recognise the right of other people to be sensitive.

[…] A walk, at any time, in any large town of Australia, would enable even a superficial observer to discover plenty of evidences of a consuming desire to spoil or to destroy. The excuse is sometimes urged that it is the work of children, and no doubt in some instances it is so; for the almost total neglect of home-discipline, in this part of the world, permits the congenitally destructive instincts of infants to have the fullest scope for their development; and in this way, no doubt, we may explain the over-mastery of the habit at a later period of youth-life, when, in by no means solitary instances, it reaches an altitude of absolute savagery. The evidences of destructiveness to be noted in such a walk, however, are not suggestive only, but conclusive, that the perpetrators are not limited to young children. Let us take the Fitzroy Gardens in Melbourne, for example. We shall there find almost every one of the statues and

vases mutilated or destroyed. These figures are for the most part of plaster or cement, and no doubt they break easily, but some of them are marble, and a few are of bronze. The bronze figures are not broken, for the good reason that the material is hard enough to resist the impact of stones and sticks, but they are scarred by the persistent throwing of missiles at them, while the marble figures are all mutilated. The fountains are filled with all the rubbish that happened to be conveniently handy enough to pick up and throw into them; the ornamental fences are broken or bent, wherever it is possible to break or bend them; branches of young trees are torn away, and flowering plants are wantonly plucked up by the roots. Some time ago the ponds of this garden were stocked with gold-fish, where they bred abundantly, but they no longer glitter in the pools, they have all been stolen. The songbirds, which once made such delightful music of a morning, are stoned to death. It is clear that the labour of laying-out and beautifying this pleasure-ground has been thrown away. For any pleasure it affords the young people whom it was intended to benefit, it might have remained the wilderness it was thirty years ago. The conclusion to be drawn is, that the minds of these persons are unsusceptible of any pleasure which is not gross, coarse, and merely animal. They cannot perceive the reason why all this trouble and expense should have been incurred. To them, green grass is a surface only to be made bare by hard trampling upon; the fringe of flower-beds is clearly contrived to be stamped out of shape; and the footways are receptacles only for the litter of torn paper, which the visitors always bring with them on their visits to this pleasure-ground. These indications of a disregard for the better influences are so common that they appear to occasion little remark. Statues are, apparently, made to be broken; fountains are rubbish-bins; ornamental trees are cultivated to supply switches; flowers are a preposterous weakness; gold-fish are only to be captured for sale; and winding walks are receptacles for waste-paper. And herein is the mischief and the misery of this practice of animalism. The effect is to familiarise people with it, and, haply, to cause them to regard it as inevitable, or such indications may be considered of little import. Perhaps they are only the exuberance of youth. They represent the working-off of latent energy. This cant excuse is sometimes brought forth when complaints of the kind now being made are preferred. We are told that youth is impetuous, and that we cannot engraft the gravity of age upon the energy of adolescence. We are told to regard these evidences of savagery as hopeful signs of vitality. They are manifestations of exuberant growth, not disease. If they were only exceptionally manifested, perhaps they might be so regarded; but it is of interest to note that they show themselves continually, and in many different ways, some of them, it may be, apparently trivial, because the consequences of the mischief are of little moment; but they are not of less moment on this account. Thus we may refer to the persistency with which picture-placards are torn down from bill-posting hoardings. Some of these pictures are, in their way, genuine works of art; not high art it is true, but certainly good art of its kind. They are well-designed, cleverly drawn, and tastefully coloured, and, to an undebased mind, are capable of affording a good deal of pleasure. But they are uniformly torn where they are placed low enough to be reached; and where they cannot be reached, they are bespattered with mud. The persistency with which they are spoiled demonstrates the correctness of what is now asserted, that a positive pleasure is derived from the practice of mutilation. Now, the youths who destroy these pictures would, if they had the opportunity, similarly scratch, tear, and blot out with mud, Titians, Correggios, Raphaels, and Millaises, if they were let loose in a gallery containing such works. They cannot have their will on the Public Art Gallery, and they do not always find "show" pictures upon the hoardings, so they will chalk, scratch, or daub a newly painted or freshly white-washed wall, and get their pleasure in that fashion. So consuming is the desire for mutilation that, if they have neither stick, nail, nor chalk with which to deface a surface, they will use their feet for the purpose; or if they be carrying a burden, they will, with some inconvenience to themselves, rub it on the walls as they pass along.

The habit of match-striking may also help to illustrate this practice of disfigurement. It is true that the habit of smoking is not confined to young men, and that perhaps the scraping of matches on walls is not limited to that class, but as young men almost uniformly smoke everywhere, always, and with total disregard of the preferences of others, they strike their matches with a corresponding indifference to consequences. In doors and out of doors, it is always the same; where there is an approximately rough surface, there they will strike a match. You may go into even well-appointed houses and find doors, walls, and furniture disfigured in this way. The doorways of the law-courts, the town-hall, the theatres, and, indeed, every public building, not excepting the churches and chapels, are disfigured in this fashion. In hotels you will find the wall, for some distance round every gas-jet, trellised with lucifer-scrapings.

And while still referring to trifles as illustrative of this habit of defacement, and of deducing from this habit a condition of mind the very opposite of refined, we may speak of doors. Doors are usually opened by taking hold of the handle, but the impetuous young Australian will not bend himself to such condescension. The door may be exquisitively [sic] painted, curiously gilded, polished with consummate care. What of that? It is his right to protest against such Sybaritism, and so he lays violent hands upon it—dirty hands, hands greasy with the handling of rankly sweating objects, themselves being rankly sweating also—and he will leave his mark upon that door. So also of pictures. He does not care much for pictures, as we have seen in the case of the "show" placards, but he will condescend to look at a picture if you desire him to do so, and then he will paw it as if it were a bullock he was examining. If there be in it any part to which he wishes to direct your attention, he will put his dirty finger upon it, and thereon leave his mark. Some photographic albums are veritably rubbed to pieces in this way. He recognises his friends in an album, and he must die or rub his index finger upon every one of their faces by way of making clear the recognition. If he were not compelled to give up his stick or umbrella on going into an art gallery, he would drill holes in the pictures in pointing out what interested him in them.

So also of books. He is not a great reader of books, but those he does read he maltreats cruelly. He thumbs them, bends them back so as to rip the binding, turns over the leaves by taking hold of them at their inner instead of their outer margin, whereby they become torn. If the book be quarto or folio it is sure to be much ripped, but this tearing does not concern him. Probably books were made to be torn. Occasionally it will occur to him to make marginal notes in books. These are always of the most fatuous kind, but that does not distress him. He speaks fatuously, and, therefore, if his written words are fatuous it is only consistent with the rest of what he says and does fatuously.

Passing from books again to houses, it may be pointed out, as what cannot but be regarded as an inherent disposition in young men to destroy for the mere pleasure of destroying, that an empty tenement, if it remain empty for any length of time, is sure to be a mark for assault. More especially is this the case if it be a detached house, and the landlord be away, and no one has been appointed to look after it. The garden is first operated on; if there be fruit trees, the fruit is gathered by the summary process of breaking off the branches, and the flowering plants are gouged out of the earth. Next, the windows are broken, at first singly, then in a fusillade, until, in say about a week, there is not a whole pane of glass left. Then the marauders get into the house by one of the back rooms, and presently it is known that the house may be sacked at pleasure. And it is sacked accordingly. The doors are converted into fuel, and so are the stair banisters and the stairs, and, at a later period the flooring boards. At last there is nothing left but the walls and the roof, and sometimes even these are operated on. It is by no means unusual for the owner of a house to return from a visit to the Old Country and find his property a melancholy ruin in a desert. The peculiar interest of such a situation, however, is less in the melancholy picture the scene presents than in the illustration it affords of the passion for destroying, and the total absence of reverence, or of any perception of the beautiful. The garden may have been a pleasance, and the house a fair abode, but neither one nor the other has had any effect upon the devastating barbarians. They have worked their will, and compassed a certain kind of enjoyment, in laying them waste, and they are ready to repeat the process as soon as ever the opportunity again shall serve. It may be that the looting included in the process accentuated his satisfaction, but the looting is only an auxiliary pleasure. It is the spoiling, the breaking, the tearing, the effacing, which constitute the real joy. The barbarian spirit which animated the fierce hordes which poured down from the north, and laid waste the cities of Europe, where a thousand years of poetic art had established the worship of the beautiful, seems to live again in these days that we sometimes think are so much better than the days of old. It may not, perhaps, declare itself in an inundation such as flooded Europe in the sixth century, but it runs in many muddy streams, and trickles in a thousand unfertilising rills. We

COLONIAL TYPES: EMERGENT AND RESIDUAL

see it only as commonplace destructiveness, it is manifested in the smallness of its opportunity, but it is the same evil spirit as that which plunged the Western World into a thousand years of darkness, and which, at a later epoch, ravaged the fanes and castles of the Old Country.

But it is not so much the simple fact of this destruction and defacement as the condition of mind it infers which concerns us. It is nothing in itself that a coarse-minded youth should tear down a brightly-coloured placard, but it is a lamentable thing as evidencing the current disposition of the young persons who are to build up our future manhood. It is easy to say that the violence, the turbulence, the boisterousness, the truculent insolence, of a just-let-loose school or factory, disclose only a healthy effervescence of pent-up forces. They show themselves in continual acts of destructiveness. To these young persons the fascination of a good picture, or the engrossing influence of a noble piece of sculpture, is unknown. They would fling road-metal at "The Transfiguration," and set up the Venus of Milo for an "Aunt Sally."

It is to be confessed that nothing in the homes of our young men reminds them that there are beautiful things in this world, the contemplation of which may haply lift them into a better life. To them, flowers are vegetables bunched together to make a cauliflower-shaped "bouquet," and trees are only collections of poles and sticks to be cut down or broken off as may be required. They are not taught that the morning sun is glorious, that the clear blue sky of noonday is gladdening, nor that the clouds that glow in the western heavens of an evening are coloured with the radiant glory of heaven. They have no conception of what is elevating in nature, and therefore they cannot perceive its reflex in art. So they throw stones at the statues; tear the pictures from the walls; knock off architectural projections with an iron bar they may have picked up; kill song-birds out of sheer wantonness; assemble in gangs to wreck an inoffensive house; make innumerable scratches upon newly-painted walls or doors; borrow a diamond, and with it scrawl their ill-sounding names on the windows of railway carriages; wear away the plinth of a Corinthian shaft by sharpening upon it their sixpenny jack-knives; cut ill-formed letters upon the bark of the trees or garden seats that never did them any harm; or rip out of a tree-fern a graceful frond, and fling it on the roadway, to wither or be trodden into mud by feet all careless of its tender grace and transparent colour.

The entire unconsciousness of this true poetry of flowers is a very salient feature in the character of the Australian youth. They will gather them, beg them, even buy them, and they will perhaps put them in jugs or tumblers on tables or mantelpieces, or, maybe, they will insert them in their button-holes. But they have no knowledge of their meaning or their influence. They have no genuine respect for them. They never arrange or display them lovingly, as if they were sentient creatures. We hear sometimes of floral decorations on certain public occasions, and there are persons who make this kind of decorative art their business; but a true art-worshipper can always perceive with how little sympathy this kind of ornamentation is effected. Pot-plants are jostled into corners without any reference to the principles of effect.

Flowers have to be used, and they are used, much as a load of earth would be shot down. The young men who might direct and assist in this work of floral decoration have no feeling in it. They will save their money for the hire of the flowers, and that is enough. It may be only a piece of sentiment to regret the death of a flower, and yet a flower that has memories and associations may be so loved; but an Australian youth has no such weaknesses. He will toss his flowers into a dust-bin with as little regret as if they were potato-parings. It is easy to say that a dead flower is only fit to be buried, and, therefore, why should we weep over it? And yet what fancies into fancies are often linked by a dead and dried nosegay, found pressed, it may be, between the leaves of some book, years after it was given to us by someone who, like itself, is lifeless. Your practical, unsympathetic young Australian is likely to sneer at a dead flower, a faded ribbon, an old glove, or such other trifle as may be found mixed with the odds and ends contained in a long-unopened drawer or box. But it is such waifs as these which often take us back to happier times, when hope had not been crushed out of us by many disappointments. Some of us plant flowers upon the graves of those we have loved in life, and when we visit those little gardens it is to us a true joy to see them marking with their tender presence the place where we have buried our dead out of our sight. And what a violence of distress it causes us to find, as we often do, that these same enclosures have been despoiled and trampled upon. And a Sunday afternoon's visit to the cemetery quite explains how this despoiling is wrought. The crowds of young persons who assemble there, with no motive apparently other than to engage in mere conversation, are seen to be entirely regardless of the feelings of those who own those grave-gardens, for they scamper over them as violently as if they were engaged at football. They are as devoid of pity as unpossessed of taste; they are gross, insensate, ruthless.

But it is in the streets, perhaps, that the Australian young man is seen at his extremist point of offensiveness. Here he is quite master of the situation, and he makes the most of it. His leisure being abundant, he has much of it to spend, and he spends it with great liberality. In places of public amusement he also commands attention. He issues directions to the management, he addresses the performers in terms of familiarity, he demands repetitions of musical performances with an imperativeness there is no resisting. He indulges in conversations in loud tones and unchoice terms. He is not abashed by remonstrance; indeed, remonstrance encourages him to persist. He pays attention to the proceedings on the stage or platform as he thinks fit; and if his interruptions disturb the attention of those who wish to listen, it is nothing to him. He is Young Australia, and he has the only right to be heard. The country is his, and all that is in it. Those who are not Young Australians are aliens, without civic rights.

It may probably be observed that the young man herein referred to belongs to the class which, if not uneducated, is at least uncultured; that he is not of the better order of society, does not move in circles that, for the sake of distinction, are called "upper." But it is only the truth to say that, while the uncultured youth of the Australian Colonies represent, perhaps, an

COLONIAL TYPES: EMERGENT AND RESIDUAL

extreme degree of ungentleness, the same kind of ungentleness, only modified by the accident of circumstances, prevails through all the grades of Australian society. This imputation of want of refinement in manner and feeling will, no doubt, occasion a resentful denial from those who are so charged; but the truth is, the unrefined bearing is so common that it is scarcely observed, and it is quite certain that those who are thus lacking in the quality are not conscious of the defect. They can no more recognize their infirmity than can a man suffering from colour-blindness perceive that he is colour-blind. It is a part of his sensory nature, and it is generally congenital, and therefore incurable. It is a serious question, therefore, whether the Australian youth, being from his early years in the habit of comporting himself with a disregard for the tendernesses of existence, can return to a normal apprehension of the offensiveness of his condition. It is not that he lacks intelligence, or neglects to acquire information, or is deficient in reflective capabilities, or is unobservant, or is really corrupt-hearted. He can upon occasion show considerable generousness, and although his vanity often causes him to be selfish, he can at times be disinterested. But he is so wrapped up in an envelopment of self-esteem, he is so continually contemplating his importance—an attribute, no doubt, born of independence and freedom from the control of his elders—that he comes to think that whatever he does or says is justifiable. He has become a law unto himself. He has formulated a code both of manners and morals, which fits well into his prepossessions, and consorts with his self-esteem. What pleases him should be agreeable to others. If it is not agreeable to them it is their misfortune, it cannot, to his thinking, be his fault. It may be even that he is wishful to please and to conciliate, and it astonishes him to discover that he does neither. It is no wonder, therefore, that he is indignant at remonstrance, that he resists law. It is no wonder that when he enters public life, in whatever capacity, he is an infliction; for either his vanity makes him quarrelsome because he is impatient of question, or his volubility renders him tedious, or his official authority causes him to be tyrannical, or his limited information results in his being dogmatic, or his commercial eagerness develops into greed. In any case he lacks the quality of benevolence. He has no community of feeling with his fellows. He cannot get away from the belief that he alone is the most important element in every aggregation of atoms in which he may be concerned. He cannot rise to the occasion of large-mindedness, because his mental vision is limited, and is invariably bounded by his own interests and desires.

The prospect is not encouraging in a country whose youth has so little of sympathy, of reverence, of consideration for others, or perception of excellence, of generosity, of sentiment. And the real question arising out of this confession of defects is this: Are we to regard the condition as one of immutable fixedness, and consequent upon changes which are common to the rest of the world, or is it a transition-stage, a point of incompleteness in development? Is it reasonable to hope that, in the necessary attrition of Australian communities—themselves becoming steadily larger and more highly organized—this crudity of soul will ripen into a sweetness of tenderness, nobleness, and benevolence? Will the Australian Young Man, with all his hardness, his roughness, his insensibility, his selfishness, his consummate vanity, become manly and gentle? Will he turn him from his evil ways, and regard the rest of the world with the feeling of brotherhood instead of distrust? Before all things, will he be tender and sympathetic to those who are weaker than himself? Will he cease to rejoice in a strength that he abuses, and exult no more in the opportunity of inflicting suffering when he could so easily communicate pleasure? No doubt this is an age of new moral developments, and it is equally certain that this is a country of exceptional social manifestations. The reversal of many of the conditions which ages of conservative habit have sanctioned, and even made venerable, in the Old Country is an admitted characteristic of Australia. It may be, indeed, that the Australian Young Man is an advanced institution upon that of the older land. It is possible that we may be compelled to admit that the qualities which used to be insisted upon as part of the moral organisation of youth are effete and obsolete, but up to this point we have regarded them as otherwise, and we can, therefore, but express a hope that they will one day be the distinguishing attributes, as now they are only exceptions, in our national character.

ETHEL CASTILLA, 'NOUVEAUX RICHES'
Centennial Magazine
February 1889

There is no class of the community oftener held up to ridicule and even opprobrium than *nouveaux riches*. In theory we agree to honour the individual who is a "self-made" man or a *nouveau riche*; but in practice we much prefer the son or daughter of "a hundred earls," who has inherited wealth, position, manners and sometimes a lack of brains. Like princes, *nouveaux riches* find few real friends. It is difficult for the man who has begun life as a blacksmith and ends it as a millionaire, to know whether the men that haunt his house are attached to his society or his champagne, or whether the women who visit his wife are not solely attracted by her sumptuous entertainments. Stinginess in a *nouveau riche* is counted a vice of deeper dye than the same failing in the heir of a noble house, and even the generosity of a *nouveau riche* meets with scant recognition. His very efforts to improve himself and raise himself to the level of a society for which he was not born, have been a favourite subject for the pen of the satirist. The immortal struggles of Mr. Boffin with Gibbon's "Decline and Fall-off the Rooshan Empire," and those of the hero of "The Golden Butterfly" with Robert Browning's "Red Cotton Nightcap Country" are by no means the only examples of this species of sarcasm that are familiar to novel readers. Even in Australian literature one seldom finds *nouveaux riches* represented as either amiable or estimable. Too often the charming but weak-minded heroine

COLONIAL TYPES: EMERGENT AND RESIDUAL

of an Australian novel marries a wealthy and illiterate man because she is tired of dependence on her relatives, and then meets her affinity represented as the scion of an old British family who has come to the colonies to make a noble manhood more complete by travel. The object of the novelist is henceforth to destroy the reader's sympathy for the *nouveau riche* by showing him to be truly odious, and to kill him as soon as possible in order to leave the heroine free to marry the British nobleman, to endow him with the wealth left her by her late husband, and to breathe at once in "an ampler ether, a diviner air." All the *faux pas* of society are attributed to the *nouveau riche*. He is popularly supposed to eat peas with his knife in private, and to address the ladies of his acquaintance as "m'am," while his female counterpart is supposed to fill her rooms with what she calls "objects of bigotry and virtue", and to speak of going to Rome to have her portrait painted by the "old masters." The *nouveau riche* who once interrupted the languid conversation at a *recherché* dinner-party given by his wife, by remarking to that lady, "Kathleen, do you remember when I used to drive my pigs to market?" has been accepted as a type of the whole race.

Australia is a country that owes so much to her self-made men, that the British idea of despising them ought not to prevail here—like other men, they are neither saints nor demons, but mere mortals. It would, indeed, be difficult to distinguish a *nouveau riche* from any one else, were it not from the fact that he is seldom sure of his ground, and is, therefore, either assertive or timid, according to his nature. The timid *nouveaux riches* are usually those who have occupied a humble position in life for many years, and then are suddenly lifted into "society" by an unexpected legacy. Bret Harte—who sees humour and pathos in everything—has thrown a halo of pathetic interest round such beings. He represents a low-born heroine, whose father has suddenly "struck ile," indicting an epistle to an old lover, in which she shows plainly enough, that the path of the *nouveau riche* is not always strewn with roses. "Her Letter" is familiar enough to many Australians:—

" And how do I like my position?
" And what do I think of New York?
" And now, in my higher ambition,
" With whom do I waltz, flirt, or talk?
" And is'nt [sic] it nice to have riches,
" And diamonds, and silks, and all that
" And aren't it a change to the ditches
" And tunnels of Poverty Flat?

" Well, yes—if you saw us out driving
" Each day, in the park—four-in-hand!—
" If you saw poor, dear mamma contriving
" To look supernaturally grand!
" If you saw papa's picture, as taken
" By Brady—and tinted at that—
" You'd never suspect he sold bacon
" And flour, at Poverty Flat!"

" And yet, just this moment, when sitting
" In the glare of the grand chandelier,
" In the bustle and glitter befitting
" The finest *soiree* of the year;
" In the mists of a *gaze de Chambéry,*
" And the hum of the smallest talk,
" Somehow, Joe, I thought of the 'Ferry,'
" And the dance that we had on 'The Fork!'"

* * * * *

" Of the moon, that was quietly sleeping
" On the hill, when the time came to go,
" Of the few valley-peaks, that were peeping
" From under their bedclothes of snow,
" Of that ride—that to me was the rarest
" Of—the something you said at the gate;
" Ah, Joe! Then I wasn't an heiress
" To the 'best paying lead in the State.'"

* * * * *

" And I'm to be finished by travel,
" Whatever's the meaning of that,
" Oh! why did papa strike pay gravel
" In drifting on Poverty Flat?"

COLONIAL TYPES: EMERGENT AND RESIDUAL

It has often occurred to me that such a wish is not seldom echoed by the daughters of a man, who wakes one morning to find himself wealthy. Timidity in society is, however, by no means confined to such *nouveaux riches* as these, who, perhaps, are more to be pitied than any other members of the class. We have all met men of vast possessions, which they have accumulated, year by year, and which should give them, one would think, *aplomb*, who are yet nervous, timid, and decidedly not at their ease, amongst the butterflies of society; the butterflies have, often, neither the wealth, nor the sterling qualities of the *nouveaux riches*, but the former understand the difficult art of conversation, whilst the latter have nothing to say; the butterflies know how to move about a room, whilst the men of many acres remain seated awkwardly on the edges of their chairs; and the butterflies, moreover, can steer their way through the intricacies of a modern dinner-table, while the *nouveaux riches* are in a maze, as regards doilies and glasses. These are all trifles, but life is made up of trifles, and they are enough to often render a *nouveau riche* miserable in society. When one meets a man of this kind, one begins to understand the sketch drawn by the pencil of a modern satirist, representing a *nouveau riche* escaping from the intolerable luxury of his wife's apartments to his own little snuggery, where he solaces himself after the strain of entertaining titled grandees, by performing various humble domestic avocations in his shirt-sleeves—such as that of brushing his own boots.

I fear I must admit that a sketch of *nouveaux riches* would be incomplete without mention of the disagreeable ones. They do exist, even in Australia. The unpleasant *nouveaux riches* are oftenest women, who are apt to take credit to themselves of the faculty of their husbands or fathers for money-making. If Chrysos in Gilbert's "Pygmalion and Galatea" is a study from life, so is the wife of Chrysos, and she is more often to be met with in real life than her husband. The life of the unpleasant *nouveau riche* is one long assertion. She may be well informed or she may be ignorant, but her society is equally depressing in either case. The reason of this may be crisply summed up in a remark this present writer once heard passed by an indignant street *gamin* on a woman of fashion, who had brushed past him so carelessly as to knock the match-boxes he was offering for sale from his hand: "She may call herself a lady, but she ain't got no manners." The unpleasant *nouveau riche* may describe herself as a lady amongst ladies, but the fact nevertheless remains that she is without the graces of life. When Mrs. Crœsus is naturally clever she is often a very trying individual. She is ashamed of her antecedents, and this makes her the more desirous to assert her importance in society. Her only idea of conversation is setting her friends right in their erroneous opinions in art, literature, and science. For it is needless to say that Mrs. Crœsus herself never errs. She has a political, a social, and an artistic creed, and she shows plainly enough that she scorns anyone who dares to object to any of her tenets. As she is accustomed to be made much of on account of her wealth, she judges her neighbours entirely by their position in society, by the size of their houses, and by the fit and texture of their coats and gowns, and takes small pains to conceal her contempt for those who are not rich in this world's goods. It was a *nouveau riche* of this kind who avowed that she never called on the inhabitants of cottages; she drew the line at two-story [sic] houses. I cannot say that the unpleasant *nouveau riche* is less disagreeable when she is ignorant. She is as assertive as her cleverer sister, without having the same excuse for so being. She is obtrusively rich. The very rustling of her gown is suggestive of crisp bank notes, and rich as her dress is it cannot conceal her native vulgarity. For vulgarity is strictly the attempting to appear what one is not. And the ignorant *nouveau riche* not infrequently poses as an authority on dress, china, and etiquette, not to speak of higher things. When she has "done Europe," as the fashion now is, she will discourse on her travels, murdering the Queen's English the while, and occasionally, like Mrs. Malaprop, "bursting into a fine confusion of epitaphs, like an allegory, on the banks of the Nile," till her interlocutors wonder why there is not a law preventing such individuals from entering the eternal city, or from gazing on the heights and glaciers of the Alps. The *nouveau riche*, who may, however, be accepted as a type of the class in the land of the Sunny South, is a man of whom any community might be proud. The Australian *nouveau riche* is most commonly a thoroughly good fellow, and his female relations are thoroughly likeable women. He constantly proves that it is more blessed to give than to receive, by his donations to educational and charitable institutions. He accepts his money as a trust to be used both for his own good and that of the community at large. His home is filled with the works of Australian artists and sculptors, and his life is a record of good deeds done by his right hand, unknown to his left. Australian society is inferior, doubtless, to the best English society in many things, yet in this new country we have certain advantages, peculiarly our own. Australians are freer from the failing known as "humbug," than the members of old-established communities. The love of order and reverence for precedent, peculiar to a Briton, sometimes leads him to commit follies because they have been ordained to be correct by the unwritten law of society. It is thought to be correct, for example, that a British family of the upper or middle classes, should leave London for a certain season during the summer. Thackeray has often described in his novels the struggles of the De Veres to appear "out of town," when the state of their finances forbid their migration, by retiring to the back rooms of their house, drawing down the front blinds, and being "not at home" to such of their acquaintances as might happen to call. This is a species of humbug from which Australians are happily free. We consider ourselves perfectly justified in taking a summer trip, or in not taking one, just as our inclinations lead us, and no one would dream of thinking any the worse of us for so doing.

In the same way the notion of despising *nouveaux riches* prevails in Britain to some extent, because from time immemorial it has been considered the right thing for a member of good society to be of an old family and to have inherited wealth. In Australia we should be brave enough to judge a man by what he is in himself, and not to enquire who his father was. When we do this we shall find that our *nouveaux riches* are amongst the most valuable of our citizens. They alone amongst us have the means and the leisure to give a strong impulse to the improvement of Australian art, literature, and science. According to Carlyle, one of the chief trials of life is the difficulty of finding an aim in it. Australian *nouveaux riches* should then be amongst the happiest of created beings, for their mission in life is clearly marked out for them. It is to encourage all that beautifies and elevates colonial life. I use the word "encourage" with regard to art and literature advisedly. The word "patronise" is too suggestive of the relations of a Chrysos and a Pygmalion. I believe that our *nouveaux riches* are already recognising their responsibilities in this respect, and I confidently look forward to a time when the phrase *nouveaux riches* in Australia, far from being a term of reproach, shall stand for the name of a class that we all delight to honour.

'THE OSCAR WILDE'S [SIC] OF SYDNEY'
Scorpion
24 April 1895

London Society has been shocked by the recent disclosures in the Oscar Wilde – Marquis of Queensbury case. Social Purity men, men of position, clergymen, and high-minded people generally have been holding their noses to avoid the dreadful stench coming from the social sore which the Marquis of Queensbury opened. The Cleveland-street Scandal was as nothing to this awful exposé. People who hitherto held reputed blameless lives, and who were respected, have been fleeing the country to save themselves from prosecution. The state of things in London as regards this horrible vice is also the condition of affairs in Sydney. It is idle for people to shut their eyes to this fact. It has found root and been planted here by the English exiles. The men who escaped the Cleveland-street prosecution found shelter in Australia, and there are many of them at present in Sydney. One is in gaol for an exactly similar crime. The judge, in sentencing him, believed his statement that he was drunk when he attempted the offence. Even in this affair of Oscar Wilde two boys have actually been sent within the last few days from here to England, as witnesses in the charge against the apostle of "culchaw" and aestheticism. One is said to have accompanied Lord Alfred Douglas to Australia. Of course the hotel authorities were not aware of the relations between the sprig of aristocracy and the sycophant who accompanied him. The fact however remains that many of the leading hotels and billiard saloons are haunted by these characters, whose presence is advertised by an effeminate style of speech, and the adoption of the names of celebrated actresses. America has sent over many of this class, in the person of so-called variety artists. A haunt is said to exist in Bourke-street, Surry Hills, and that part of College-street from Boomerang-street to Park-street is a parade for them. Plain clothes men and ordinary policemen are put on duty to hunt unfortunate fallen women off the streets, but these wretches go unmolested. It is idle for the police to say that they cannot secure convictions. They can gaol the cunning burglar, the forger, and the outlaw, and yet are powerless to stamp out this fast increasing acquisition to our criminal class from England. As Australians, let us show the world that the crime of which Oscar Wilde stands charged is detested and abhorred in Australia.

K. SOMERTON, 'JACKEROOS'
Cosmos
19 October 1896

The word jackeroo originally meant a gabbler, being, according to Mr. Meston, the name given by the old Brisbane blacks to the pied crow shrike, a gabbling, garrulous bird. These blacks applied the same name, "Tchaceroo," to the German Missionaries of 1838, because they were always talking. Afterwards they applied it to all white men. But gradually its meaning became narrowed to its present every day use, and means, as now understood: genus, man; species, new chum; habitat, Australian Back Blocks.

The Bush of Australia is, what the Church was once supposed to be—a refuge for the fool of the family. Boys, who are not smart enough to pass the stiff exams., which now obtain for the services, are sent into the Bush—there to go through a process called jackerooing, which is supposed to initiate them into the mysteries of squatterdom.

In other trades than that of squatting, a would be craftsman buys his knowledge, or at least pays his own mess account. But, with jackeroos, it is mostly otherwise—they are quartered on a station like the troops in an enemy's country. Housed, fed, laundried, the run of books, papers, and anything going, gratis.

In return, should the youth be English, he generally gives his hostess muffled growlings of the British Lion stamp; his host evidences of his sulky incompetence to do anything, worth doing, on a station.

He may begin by being graciously patronising, but when he finds that the Australian bushman suffers patronage from no one, he subsides into the sulky attitude.

To take a typical case. A jackeroo arrives on the station. The Boss does his best for him at first. Knowing he is necessarily green to the work, he takes him under his own wing for awhile, that he may spare him the strong language and chaff his incompetence would meet with from others.

In time this teaching of the young idea how to squat, falls up the Boss.

He requests Mac—the sheep overseer, overseers are always Mac something in locally coloured Australian literature. The Boss requests Mac to take Jackeroo in hand. Tells him to

COLONIAL TYPES: EMERGENT AND RESIDUAL

make him work, dam-making or something of that sort to begin with, to tan his hands and make a man of him.

"I'm full up of him. He can neither work nor play. Said he shot in Lord knows what coverts in England, but he can't hit a haystack in Australia, let alone a plain turkey. He shall waste no more of my cartridges; he took out a dozen the other day—his bag was an unfledged hawk and a galah. Get him to work. Don't let him shoot a beast—he'd wound a yard full and kill none."

"How shall I mount him?" asked Mac. "I want to save the regular stock-horses. The grass is none too good, frost taken the substance out of it; horses barely holding their own, won't stand knocking about. Jackeroos are the very devil on horses; knock spots out of them—ride the tails off them."

"You are right, Mac. This fellow blows to my wife of daring deeds he has done on an English hunting field, but I'm hanged if I don't think, from the shape of him outside a horse, that his hunting field was his nursery-floor, and his gee a rocking-horse. Give him any old screw. A broken down brumby, old Pig, or some of that sort for a start. Then if you see he can stick on, promote him to some of the rough youngsters. Take him gently, don't kill the beggar. Only I can't risk my good horses—not for the use of jackeroos. I've been had too often; if I let it go on the station brand would be a sore back."

Thus was Jackeroo made over to the mercies of the overseer.

Mac put him through his squatting paces, paradoxical as such an operation seems, only to find in the end that his schooling had been wasted.

One day Mac was frightfully exasperated with Jackeroo's utter stupidity in the sheep yards; he used some strong bush language absolutely reeking of gore.

Jackeroo let go the swing gate and said, "Do you know who you are talking to? I have blue blood in my veins!" He levelled a look of scorn at Mac, who rushing to the gate to prevent the sheep from boxing, called back:

"Damn your blue blood. It's deuced sluggish. An old black gin would be more use in a sheep yard. I give you best. Clear out of this."

A thoroughbred Jackeroo declines to learn anything—refuses to allow that there is anything for him to learn, his creed being that an Englishman is born knowing all.

He has a fixed belief in the Divine Right of Englishmen. That Australians have different ways from Englishmen is their misfortune, but no reason that he should learn them. All proverbs and philosophies evolved therefrom are vulgar—in particular the one advising those who go to Rome to do as the Romans do.

It were meter in his eyes that, provided the travellers to Rome were Englishmen, the Romans should do as they did.

The laws of Englishmen, as those of the Medes and Persians, altereth not.

Fully imbued with this idea, Jackeroo has a profound contempt for things and persons Australian. His air is distinctly that of the Eton boys when their school was challenged by Cheltenham—was it not? And who replied:

"Harrow, we ken, and Winchester, but who are ye?" The Jackeroo transhapes his reply and seems to say—

"Scotch, I know, and Irish, but Australians who are ye?"

From his lofty attitude he looks down upon his surroundings, which are dwarfed into insignificance as he gazes from the self-made pedestal on which he has placed himself.

The squatter's wife he looks upon as a housekeeper, with whom according to the savage custom of the country he has to feed. She is distinctly an evil socially, but necessary as adding to his comfort domestically. He scruples not to increase her burdens as a housekeeper's, in a country where trained servants are at a premium. He crumples up his ties and shirts not laundried to his liking, flings them out to be washed again, not realising how lucky, comparatively, with new chums of the old regime, he is to have his clothes washed at all. The old rule obtaining on stations having been, "Every man does his own washing and buys his own soap."

Jackeroo's Boss had lively recollections of having, in his colonial experience days, scrubbed down his moles with a brush and flattened his collars with a stirrup-iron.

But the advent of the as yet, petticoated sex had changed all that. The roll of the mangle is heard in the bush laundries and those of Mrs. Pott's have superseded the stirrup-irons.

As to the blacks, the original proprietors of Australia, or if not original proprietors, at least the people in possession, when the cocksure Britishers exploited, for them Jackeroo has nothing but contempt. He wonders audibly that the Boss's wife allows the black gins to scrub, and more especially to scrub the bedroom hallowed by his august presence. He thinks if she did her duty she would rather scrub it herself. Yet he does not disclaim, by means of these same despised gins, to add to the census.

They have a fine pride, these Jackeroos! A time inevitably comes when the Boss, full up of his specimen, says he is reducing the staff. Jackeroo goes. He probably gets a temporary billet elsewhere in the neighbourhood on the strength of having been with Jones, say for two years.

His new Boss does not stand him long. Smith cannot understand how Jones stood him and his conceited incompetency for two years; he cannot suffer him for two months. He does not know that Jones was obliging a friend, or obeying a banker. Neither of whom thinks anything of sending to a poor squatter, out West, his son or friend's son to be a member of squatter's household gratis for a couple of years. Jackeroo to be taught the squatting profession, for which teaching he and his friends expect him to be remunerated at the local rate of wages given to a trained workman. Although perchance Jackeroo, when set to manual labour, will say, as one did when set to work: "I came to learn how the work was done, not to do it."

COLONIAL TYPES: EMERGENT AND RESIDUAL

In return for his good-natured acquiescence in this impost the squatter is rarely even thanked. Probably more often abused for his meanness in not giving the lad a higher screw, and keeping him longer.

It may chance the Jackeroo is someone socially in the metropolis.

The banker, or friend, who sends him out West, thinks, if he stops to think at all, that he is doing the squatter a good turn by sending him a social prodigy. One who can perhaps play the banjo, shoot his linen and claim distant cousinship with a sprig of nobility. On the station they grow to loathe the twanging of the banjo, to abhor the shooting of linen, and don't care a curse for the nobility. Thus his attributes, far from being affording, are rather against him.

When Smith sacks Jackeroo, that youth packs up his old portmanteau, labelled with his name aristocratic, and returns to Jones.

There he is received with the instinctive hospitality of the true Australian squatter. There he loafs. Presumably perhaps waiting for a remittance, which rarely, if ever, comes, English relatives considering Australia a Tom Tiddler's ground. While waiting, he consoles himself with Jones' tobacco and whisky. That is his occupation. For recreation, he amuses himself with Mrs. Jones' maids, black and white indiscriminately. There are, of course, Jackeroos and Jackeroos; but striking an average, the species is useless and bumptious. The exceptions almost compensate for the rule: they are the typical English boys, of whom we more often read than hear or see.

Jackeroos being as they mostly are, it is not to be wondered at that station managers now distinctly object to receive them.

There is an old story of a globe-trotting sportsman who went inland to sample the sport. He complained to his host, after having dealt death and destruction to unlimited kangaroo, wallaby, turkey, duck and the rest, that he was disappointed, for he had never been given a chance of a shot at a jackeroo. He had heard that they were quite the best Australian sport.

"And, by Jove! so they would be," said his host; "but I'm afraid they are preserved; always close season on, eh? what? Mac," turning to his overseer, "don't you think we could rig the Stock Protection Board to declare them vermin and put a price on their heads, eh? what? Anyway, we can well spare Double-Shuffle. Trot him round; let the Captain have a parting shot at him."

The Captain, however, elected to forego the entry of a Jackeroo amongst the list of slain in his sporting diary. Having escaped his duns in England he had no notion of being brought up for manslaughter in Australia. For though squatters may rightly reckon Jackeroos a menace to the lives of their horses and stock generally, the Stock Protection Boards have not yet included them as vermin. They will probably never have to be so treated. Being so eminently unfit their survival is only a question of time; they are dying out.

Practical squatters are giving them best. They know that though Jackeroo eats a good man's tucker, he rarely does a good man's work. Hence his abolition has been one of the first economies to be practised in these days of curtailment. This abolition is the silver lining to the cloud of retrenchment which hangs over squatterdom.

The edict from the long-suffering squatters had at length gone forth: "We take what the Gods and our bankers send us these troublous times—bar Jackeroos."

'I'M A HAWKER AND I HAWK...'
Bulletin
22 October 1898

I am a hawker, and I hawk. I peddle laces, boots, buttons, anything, from Port Darwin to Port Davey, and back again by way of Albany and Bundaberg. Order from me a ton of ice-cream at Georgetown, or a crocodile at Kalgoorlie, and you shall have it. Terms, cash in advance; delivery any time from Monday week to the Day of Judgement; but I guarantee delivery. As a rule I have no time for literature; it is merely literature. Hawking is Life. I tell you that lying near my horses in a dried-up Diainantina waterhole, from which I had just dug out the last quart of mud to make tea that Scotch Tart never equalled, and watching the stars glimmer over the baked plain, I have had emotions higher than Shakespeare's. To be sure, Marinoopna's head was on my knee; and she is the best gin I ever had. Inspector Willshire, who saw her when we were on the Finke River, was mightily taken with her; and Willshire is a judge. My dog's head was on the other knee; and his eyes are as soft as Marinoopna's. And I felt .... if I could only tell you!

Who am I? It is no business of yours. Maybe I was born of poor but unferinented parents: maybe I am the descendent of a highly-flavoured race who habitually ran because the arm of the law was gesticulating after them. I have danced at your Government Houses; I have dined at your threepenny restaurants; and—I have reflected that your Governors are far less important that the kitchenmen at your threepenny restaurants. The governor is a male, fascinating but useless; the kitchenman is a male, useful but unfascinating. Take away the Governor, and the metropolitan earthquake of traffic recurs daily as usual; take away the kitchenman, and the metropolis becomes chaos crying for its dinner. [...]

COLONIAL TYPES: EMERGENT AND RESIDUAL

Yes, I know your Australia—no man better; and I love this sea-girt virgin sprawling under the southern stars. I know your cities—your warm, genial Australian cities—what crowds and life-tales pass through them! Some, happy as sunlight on a toy-shop window; some, godly as the gilt edges of a good girl's prayer-book; others, wicked enough to make a town-hall clock wring its hands in despair. Melbourne, like a stuccoed sultan in a seraglio of town halls; Adelaide, that precocious young paradise of amateur angels; Brisbane, city of lovely lightnings; Rockhampton and Townsville, like parched mermaids beneath an ocean of sunlight; Perth, a handmaiden pointing to the great golden spare-room; best of all, Sydney the shepherdess of human cities, on a shore where the sea has wandered inland and lost itself in loveliness. All health and sunshine to Australia, and may her evil critics be sterilised! She is still the new-life land, the oasis-country, the welcomer of all wanderers.

The two most typical figures in Australian life are the sundowner and the larrikiness. The sundowner works hard at being out of employment, and walks through the country in order to run short of provisions. The larrikiness arrays herself like a cracked kaleidoscope in a fit, and her language is calculated to make the stoutest hearted peach blush itself off the tree. Yet she can love, and battle for her love like a prize-fighting duck. She may be as wicked as a capsized angel. She sympathises deeply with her female comrades when they return from a forced visit to Cockatoo Island prison. She meets the boat that brings them from their brief incarceration at 6 o'clock in the morning; away go all the girls to the back parlor of an adjacent hotel; they rejoice over rum or beer; then they go home, swap clothes or hats, and quarrel over their bargains in the back-yard when the afternoon comes.

The larrikiness eats fried fish in bed, and when her larrikin wakes up in the morning he finds he has been sleeping on the bones and the stopper of a vinegar-bottle. Then he curses all the curl out of her fringe, till she says, "Nark it; you are ratty," and plays a fantasia of finger-nails on his cheek. Sometimes at night, after a brawn supper bought in a Rocks eating-house, she arises in a frightful nightmare and performs weird incantations with her larrikin's straw hat, shocking the moon, when there is any moon. Then she blunders back to bed, and lies down like a horizontal horror beside her paramour, who snores as if he had been born in an organ-pipe out of tune.

When her youthful charms fade, the larrikiness is often so hard-up that she has to sleep out all night. Perhaps one early morn she espies an elderly man who looks as if he had money and was at the fag-end of a nocturnal spree. For fun, he takes her into a hotel. She is so poor that she is determined to captivate him, so, while he is drinking and talking to the landlord, she sneaks into the back-yard to black her boots. The landlord comes and yanks her out. She has another drink, and sneaks back again. This time the landlord finds her taking a rouged rag from her stocking and daubing it over her features till her face looks red enough to take a first-class prize in a tomato-show. She is "making up" in her simple, humble, determined way.

Much of the bush of Australia may be compared to a panorama of poles. The wind blows through the gaunt eucalypti, and, like harps, they moan back, crying for rivers and waters unknown; the axe beats time to the slow, hot anthem of air; and men and women drink tea as if in a previous existence they had lived through millions of years of drought on a waterless planet. As a rule, the people are kindly and cheerful; but some of them keep themselves alive by working their animals to death; the men cultivate the soil, and the horses cultivate a fasting capacity superior to Succi's. Then there is the laughing-jackass; he alights on a branch, scratches his ear with his left wing, shakes his tail, and cachinnates enough to widen a cracked joke into a miniature earthquake. Who knows what the bird laughs at? The native bear is an oddity; he climbs up a tree at dusk, and, like a little fool in fur, lifts up his voice to let people know where he is. He sings a vesper song wherein seems mingled the purring of a cat, the braying of a phantom donkey, and the grunting of a spasmodic pig, ending with a forlorn suspiration like a crazy cookmaid sighing through a nutmeg-grater.

Don't tell me the Bush is the abode of misery and desolation. I know better. These things are there; but they are not all the Bush, are not even most of the Bush. I know your Henry Lawson and admire his talent; but when he talks continually of the accursed country out-back—Bah! A town-man who made one trip into the back-blocks five years ago, and has stuck to the cities ever since! I tell you the Bush is beautiful and terrible; but she is more beautiful than terrible. She has days and nights of Glory. If your painters could only paint the spirit of Australia with her frowning eyes and smiling lips—Australia, the mother of heroes. For there are heroes among your drovers and horse-breakers—men who in obscurity display courage and dash that the most daring cavalry leader known to history never surpassed. Did you ever meet Sydney Bob the Rider? What, never met the most famous and capable bush-horseman in Australian history! Young man, your life has been as much wasted as a consignment of patent stoves to Gehenna. [...]

JUDEX, 'LARRIKINISM AND HOOLIGANISM'
Southern Cross
1 February 1899

So London at last, in common with the great cities of America and our own larger communities, is suffering from an acute attack of the social-hyæna plague in its more pronounced and organized form!

Many and strident have been the contentions amongst literary and philosophical geniuses over the origin of this species of vice, and numerous and divergent the suggestions for its cure, but with the exception of Sydney the measures taken for the eradication of this curse to society have met with but small success, and even in our own city the strong hand of repression, assisted by so long and bitter an experience of the evil, has not been entirely triumphant. Until comparatively recent years the gang, or as it is locally termed, the "push" system, was unknown in the mother country; that is to say, in connection with the species of wolfishness for which our larrikin element is so notorious. Of course, the criminal gang was a recognized entity with regard to swindlers, burglars, and robbers generally, but the malicious, unprovoked, senseless brutality, in which robbery only enters as an apparent afterthought, was rarely the outcome of any attempt at organization. In American communities the gangs assimilated closely to our "pushes," though even there the evil existed in a minor degree, and, as in London at the present time, these pestilent associations assumed the patronymic of their leaders to distinguish them from the members of similar gangs. In this was constituted a point on which they differed from the Australian larrikin, whose title to fame rested upon the fact that he belonged to the "Rocks," "Liver," "Surry Hills," "Woolloomooloo," or other "push," while his confrere across the water boasts that he is a "Hooligan," a "Brownie," a "Murphy," or a "Scaddsie."

But it is in his personal aspect that the Australian scum presents the most marked contrast with his foreign competitors. In other countries the "tough" is a half-fed, ill-clad, often ragged object, whose very appearance is in itself a warning to the uninitiated; whereas, in our own country, the larrikin is invariably well-fed, well-clothed (often "well-connected"), and as far as can be gathered from externals, a different being altogether. No exploitation of dirt-boxes provides *his* meals—his food is that of any respectable citizen. No gathering of kennel rags keeps him skirmishing for his very existence; his employment, when not engaged with a large party of his kind in maltreating some inoffensive individual, consists in leaning against a corner post, smoking cheap cigarettes, spitting upon people's clothing, and insulting in obscene remarks any defenceless female who passes.

In character he is veritable wolf. With his "push" he is ready to insult, maltreat, in his insensate brutality, even to murder, anyone where helplessness renders him an easy victim. Singly he is the rankest, wretchedest cur on the face of the earth. His means of subsistence, when not derived from his parents, is wrung in the form of blackmail from the "unfortunates" with whom he is always on terms of intimacy, or obtained in some equally despicable manner. In fact, there is only one trait in his character which can be viewed with tolerance, viz.: his always absorbing desire to smash up (always with the assistance of his confederates) and maim the members of rival "pushes." Dog may not eat dog, but wolf eats wolf, whether *ferae naturae* or *genus homo*, and the larrikin differs nowise in that respect from his fourfooted congener.

The Hooligan being of more recent origin has not the traditional prestige which attaches to the larrikin, whose predecessors date back to the early forties, when the Cabbage-tree Mob, which existed as late as the early seventies, earned undying fame as the champion terror of Sydney residents.

In the majority of instances the *raison d'être* of the Hooligan's existence is the condition of abject poverty which forms his early surroundings. He is born in the circumscribed area of a tenement house or a "Rents"; his parents are either dissolute or compelled by the exigencies of their caste to leave their children to their own devices while they themselves are earning their bread—hence the education of their offspring is the education of the street. It is this education of the street which creates our own type; and though, as we have said, in Australia the larrikin as a rule only robs his victim as an afterthought, the English hoodlum makes plunder, in greater or less degree, his primary object, for the simple reason that want is the chief cause of his existence. The larrikin's education of the street arises either from the laxity of parental discipline or parental indifference. Particularly among what are known as the "Straw-hat Push"—perhaps the most difficult of all to deal with—is this the case. Nearly all of at least respectable parentage, instead of being compelled to find some rational amusement or occupation in the home, or having some such found for them, they are permitted, as soon as the evening meal is concluded, to wander into the street, where with other congenial spirits they seek the nearest lounging place, generally the street-corner, and in default of something better to do, and strong in the power of numbers, fall to making personal remarks upon the passers-by. As a moral certainty, some individual will sooner or later, probably sooner, resent this, and there is a quarrel, in which all take action against the insulted party. From the first misdemeanour to graver offences is but an easy step, and the nucleus of a flourishing gang of larrikins is formed—*voila tout!*

We will probably be called anything but humane for saying so, but never was a more effective instrument for the suppression of larrikinism invented than *the lash*. We are perfectly cognizant of the inane howl which at once arises from the *soi-disant* philanthropist with

COLONIAL TYPES: EMERGENT AND RESIDUAL

reference to the degradation of humanity incurred by the application of such a barbarous instrument. We are told that we are only brutalizing the subject, that we are treating men (*men?*) like wild beasts. In the name of heaven, what are these creatures but wild beasts? Time and again have milder measures been resorted to, and with what result? Absolutely nil. On the other hand, the exercise of severer coercion has been productive of absolute good, and the ethics thereof are not difficult to understand. The larrikin is essentially a coward of the most malicious description. Other wild beasts may become cruel in their methods, but what wild beast inflicts *malicious* injury? It is safe to say—not one. Wild beasts slay, each in its own fashion, for self-preservation only; that is to say, their victims, however cruelly despatched, are secured for food, and with that object only. But, from the earliest outbreak, along through the Bondi, the Pearl, and numberless similar horrors, down to the recent Newtown outrages, the larrikin has delighted in the infliction of physical injury merely for the pleasure of witnessing the sufferings of his unfortunate victims; yet he is the very one who howls longest and loudest when called upon to undergo a dose of his own medicine. And the remedy is lasting, for the feat which is his predominating characteristic gives him solemn and protracted pause before the committal of another offence which might render him amenable to another dose.

Since Sir George Dibbs wisely overrode morbid sentimental opposition (which to a superficial observer looks remarkably like sympathy with crime), and armed the police, the change in the criminal element has been simply wonderful. The kicking to death of policemen has ceased entirely, and the guardian of lawful security can now with comparative safety extend to the aforesaid morbid sentimentalist that protection which the latter is the readiest to fly to him for, from the fact that he has been rightly placed in a position of physical equality with those with whom it is the nature of his occupation to deal.

Let parents exercise proper discipline and proper supervision of the *amusements* of their sons; let corporal punishment quickly follow the wanton infliction of physical injury, and the curse—be it known as Larrikinism, Hooliganism, or any other "ism"—is doomed.

ERNEST LOW, 'WHY IS THE AUSTRALIAN DISLIKED?'
Lone Hand
1 October 1910

Yes, "disliked" is most emphatically the word. Not "hatred," as I was momentarily of a mind to say. All over the world the homebred Britisher may perhaps be hated for his non-adaptability, his clinging to the old ways of life, whatsoever the clime and the environment, and for his easy assumption of an unquestioned claim to superiority. The American for his irresistible "push," his tendency to go right to the top and stay there, whether as a mining engineer, a financier, or in any walk of commercial or professional life. The German—well, the German, commercially successful (which he usually is!) or not, is always a German; in North America or in Equatorial Africa—he mixes with his kind, continues to drink his lager beer, rarely becomes naturalised in the spirit, though for business reasons he may do so according to the strict letter of the law.

But, go where you will, the Australian is not hated in this honest, outright Johnsonian fashion. He enjoys the minor, but, if anything, more odiously significant distinction of being cordially disliked. In Africa, in the Old Country, in India—practically everywhere outside Australia itself—he is unpopular, looked at askance, tolerated, may be, but usually debarred by the community from that degree of close intimacy which might lead him to feel he was "one of themselves." In a word—and a very expressive word, too—he is the "outsider."

It will be my endeavour, by pointing out dispassionately some of the traits and characteristics of the over-seas Australian, to furnish an answer to the question as to why he is so disliked.

First impressions go far, and the average Australian met with in far lands rarely prepossesses one in his favor. His main cause of offensiveness is his irrepressible tendency—apparently inherent—to "blow." And, in case the word is meaningless to the superior reader, I will explain it by saying that it denotes empty, vainglorious brag of the most grandiloquent and bombastic character—what the Americans call "skite"—and it takes the most aggressive and offensive form. The Australian with the characteristic audacity of the provincial—of the man who has never had it borne in upon him that there are other and wider outlooks upon life than he has hitherto dreamed of, immediately seeks to judge all things and people by the standard of comparison of his own country, his own people—and himself.

Before he is five minutes in a public place, it is a hundred to one that every person present knows he is an Australian. He makes himself conspicuous everywhere; he will not be denied. If there is a public function he will probably be more in evidence than the honored guest; more than likely that he will insist upon forcing himself upon the latter (who may be a man whom the world delights to honor) and expounding his—the Australian's—view of the universe to his bewildered auditor. He cannot remain unnoticed; he has a yearning to advertise his blatant personality—better to cause rows, to get into trouble, to be laughed at than not to be noticed at all. He certainly in the main does achieve part of his object; every place you go to "the Australians" are well known. But their continual and inescapable "blow" goes past the point where it can be passed over with a good humored smile of tolerance. It is too insistent, too persistent, too actively violent not to evoke annoyance, irritation, and the desire to escape.

No matter what the subject or the person mentioned, it is all the same to our "blowing" friend. He may not—probably does not—know anything about the subject in hand; still it is incomprehensible that Australia and Australians cannot know as much and do as much as these effete products of the Old Country whom "Bull," in his dull old way, thinks such marvels.

COLONIAL TYPES: EMERGENT AND RESIDUAL

Taxed on any point, he will not attempt anything in the shape of a logical, temperate argument, of which, indeed, he is generally incapable. No, his idea is to shout down all opposition, to drown dissent, by "blowing" harder and louder and continuing to repeat his shibboleth that what Australians do not know and do is neither worth doing nor knowing. The Australians won the Boer War (by the way, I heard a fairly intelligent man in Sydney give vent to this astounding hallucination a few weeks back); they have given the world a lead in legislation; they are the only people who can ride, who understand sheep, who can conduct horse-racing properly; they not only live in "God's country," but the assumption is, if you are to believe the men whose motto is "While I live I blow" that they are also "God's People," and that nobody and nothing else counts.

It becomes a trifle boring and wearing, this perpetual blare of that trumpet. One is apt to strive to give it a wide berth. There is a limit to the forbearance of everyone; and when, for instance, two men of cultivation and scholarship are constantly interrupted in a chat about Homer and Dante and Shakespeare by such queries as "What about 'How We Beat the Favourite?'" and "What d'ye think of Harry Lawson?" they may be pardoned if the indulgence extended to sheer ignorance gives way to a contemptuous irritation. This is no suppositious case. I have literally come across it. And it is not isolated; on the contrary, only too typical of the awful exhibition this type of Australian will make of himself in his overweening desire to "blow" at all costs.

It will be urged that in this respect he is "not the only pebble on the beach"—that assuredly the American, for one, gives him points and a beating at the game. Well, I have not found it so; and I fancy this opinion will be shared by most people who have travelled. Apart from the typical American tourist ("typical" mainly of the humorous writer and farce), the American man (not the American woman, who is frequently *vox, et præterea nihil*) abroad is a hard-working, self-contained, energetic citizen, chiefly remarkable for a rather dignified reserve. His "skiting" is simply a tactical move in a business campaign; has a definite objective; is part and parcel of a well thought out scheme of advertisement. That, surely, is a very different matter from the mere objectless attempt at "showing the other fellow what I am."

The whole thing was put very neatly to me by the American head of a very large business house in Johannesburg. "Yes, my firm is one of those which holds to the legend 'No Australian need apply.' We've tried them—and, frankly, they're a nuisance. They're a disturbing element; bring discord into the place; other men won't work with them. They're such awful skiters; won't learn our ways, think their way is the best and only way, and want everyone to follow their lead. Some of them, of course, are able, clever fellows; but they never forget to let you know it—and the inferiority of everybody else."

Here I interjected a remark which might have, but did not, offend my friend; and he took up the point with avidity.

"Yes, our people do a bit in that way, and so do the Britishers. But, hang it all, we have some reason to brag, haven't we? We have done something in this world, and every sensible American admits what we owe to the parent stock. But what has Australia done, I should like to know? They may have 'God's country,' and they have shown their appreciation of the fact by getting into the most hopeless tangle of political and commercial mismanagement conceivable. A young country? Why, take our case with California; why ——"

Here he broke off with a smile at himself, as of one who had just successfully resisted a tendency which he was deploring. But it would be hard to gainsay his words. Boasting, always objectionable, may be condoned if it has a record of solid achievement behind it. Whereas—"No Australian need apply."

The word "provincial" has been used in connection with the Australian; and really it is the one word which thoroughly describes him. He seems to lack that cosmopolitanism which all the other folks—even the most conservative and tradition-bound Englishman—seem to acquire to a greater or less degree in their wanderings.

After twenty years' sojourn abroad the Australian is still as Australian as on the day he set sail from Circular Quay—that is, he still retains unblemished all the attributes which least redound to his credit. His clannishness, his pitiful belief that in his "crowd" alone are to be found all the courage, energy, brains and push of the world, are only to be compared with those of the most aggressively patriotic sons of Scotland.

Bluntly, the Australian has not earned the best of reputations for reliability, trustworthiness, "straightness." He is suspected of shiftiness, of a desire to get the better of his neighbor, and of not being over particular in the means he adopts to achieve this aim. Has this reputation been justly earned? Is it merited? Assuredly there must be some foundation for such a very widespread impression. Perhaps it may be due to the fact that while the Australians abroad may not all precisely have "left their country for their country's good," it is undeniable that many of them belong to the least desirable section of the population of any country. This is the section which does not take kindly to regular occupation, which hangs upon the outskirts of racing and "sport" of all kinds, whose means of livelihood is wrapped in mystery to all but the initiated. Of course, no one asserts that all the Australians abroad come within this category; but it is an ugly fact that those who can fairly be so placed do indeed furnish an unduly large proportion of the total community.

Has the question been fairly—if not exhaustively—answered? I anticipate the crowning objection to all that has been set forth, the reply which is calculated to shatter into dust the whole fabric which has been raised. It will be urged that my facts and deductions, even if admitted, only apply to a section of the Australian population; and that, as regards the last count of the indictment, I myself freely allow that the section under ban may consist of individuals of whom Australia is very glad to be rid. The answer to that is obvious. I am not laying down what should be, what ought to be; I am simply concerned with the facts as they are.

COLONIAL TYPES: EMERGENT AND RESIDUAL

After all, the people amongst whom these Australians dwell can only judge from what they see—if their judgment casts an unfair reflection upon all Australians because of the shortcomings or misdeeds of an unrepresentative few, that, alas, is only the way of an unrighteous world. But again, I say amid the mists and shadows of the why and the wherefore, the verdict looms out large and black, and not to be argued away by any sophistries whatsoever. Perhaps the Australians are less fairly typical than the representatives of all the other nations of the earth who have taken up their habitat in the great cosmopolitan centres of wealth and commerce; perhaps they were born under an Evil Star; perhaps the general failure to yield them appreciation is the measure of their greatness; perhaps Heaven and Earth and the multitude are in dark conspiracy to do them injustice. Perhaps!

"Yes!" I can hear it exclaimed; "in your cheap satire you have unconsciously hit the mark. They are not appreciated because they are not understood. The judgment is unfair because it is superficial; to find their good qualities you must go deeper."

"Go deeper?" said a sage old mining man to me, years ago, when I was expostulating with him on his coldness to an individual regarding whom I had just used precisely the same argument. "Life's too short, my boy," said he, quietly, "to bother about going down deep when the surface indications are no good. A man would be mad to waste his time sinking a shaft in the hopes of finding good stuff when the outcrop holds out no promise." That's it in a nutshell—people have not time to sink shafts in order to discover valuable stuff, which may or may not be there. They pass by on the other side, and look for something more promising.

But I shall not leave these objections altogether directly unanswered. I believe that the away-from-home Australian, of whom I have been writing, is not only not exceptional, but is essentially representative and typical of a very large class which dwells in our midst, and from which he springs. Until I came to Australia, after much travel I, too, believed that it would be unfair to judge any large section of the Australians by specimens I had met. I, therefore, came to Australia with an "open mind." It has not taken me long to become convinced of my former error. A large—very large—proportion of the Australian public—almost what in England might be said to correspond with "the masses"—displays just those unamiable traits, those ignorantly provincial traits, which everywhere earn derision and contempt. The cheap sneers at everything which is not Australian, the assumption of superiority to "poor old played out Bull," the pitying attitude towards "the effete Old Country," the refusal to learn anything from the experience and knowledge of the older countries—all these are just as noticeable.

Great commercial and industrial enterprises in the United States will offer fabulous sums to a foreigner who has made his mark in a special direction—in order to secure his services; Canada will cull its experts from any region of the world; Germany willingly imports men to teach it what it does not at present know. And Australia—a howl goes up to the skies at the idea that any "alien" (that, by the way, is the charming epithet applied by one of our "popular" writers to the home-born Britisher who dares to descend upon these shores!) could possibly know half as much about electrical engineering, or teaching or railways as the man from Bungawatta or Fleecemooloo.

Possibly when a generation of travelling—if not emigrating—Australians arises which has been bred in a different school, which has gained a sense of proportion, which has learned enough to grasp what vast potentialities for learning the world holds—then perhaps there may be a prospect of living down the prevalent feeling. With more real self-respect, in place of a blatant self-sufficiency, the respect of others may be commanded. But to bring this about the Australian papers and people must cease to "blow," must look inwards a trifle more, even have the courage to admit the astounding fact that other peoples may excel them in some respects. Much will be achieved when they come to realise that their little minnow pond is not the mighty ocean.

PART 8

Colonial Types: The Australian Girl
KEN GELDER & RACHAEL WEAVER

'Vaga', 'Woman's Work', *Australian Woman's Magazine and Domestic Journal*, 1 July 1882
317

William Gillies, 'The New Governess', *Centennial Magazine*, June 1890
317

Ethel Turner, 'Women's Department', *Cosmos*, 20 October 1894
322

'The J Nib', 'An Australian Girl', *Cosmos*, 19 November 1896
322

J. Steele Millan, 'The Women of the Future', *Cosmos*, 19 February 1897
327

George Taylor, 'The Australian Girl', *Ha! Ha: A Merry Magazine for Australians*, 9 April 1898
330

'Sydney's Leading Political Lady', *New Idea*, 1 January 1903
330

George Taylor, 'The Quest of the Australian Girl', *A.A.A.: All About Australians*, 1 February 1907
333

Fred Leist, 'The Leist Girl', *A.A.A.: All About Australians*, 1 February 1907
338

Beatrix Tracy, 'The Girl in Waiting', *Lone Hand*, 1 June 1908
339

Florence Young, 'The Australian Chorus-Girl', *Lone Hand*, 1 June 1908
343

D.H. Souter, 'The Australian Girl', *Lone Hand*, February 1912
345

Colonial Types: The Australian Girl
KEN GELDER & RACHAEL WEAVER

THE AUSTRALIAN GIRL BECAME VISIBLE as a type early on in colonial print culture, occasionally invoked in ladies' columns and popular romances in the 1860s and 1870s. By the mid-1870s, the *Australian Town and Country Journal* began to invest in the type as a way of valorising the distinctive traits of colonial Australian women. In 1874 it serialised T. A. Browne's novel *Incidents and Adventures of My Run Home*, in which a protagonist named 'Rolf Boldrewood' sings the praises of Australian girls to his English companions. Paul de Serville notes that through this character, Browne created 'an energetic, patriotic squatter of educated literary tastes...[who] could carry the good name of Australia in the motherland with credit';[1] Browne, of course, went on to adopt 'Rolf Boldrewood' as his pen name. Celebrating the virtues of the Australian girl abroad soon became part of the colonial project of nation building; and as Angela Woollacott suggests, the Australian girl was often promoted 'at the expense of her discursive foil "the English girl"'.[2] In September 1888, the *Australian Town and Country Journal* celebrated the centenary of the colonies by publishing Ethel Castilla's now-famous short poem, 'The Australian Girl', an early attempt to define this type's essential qualities and measure them against her English counterpart. This part begins with an extract from the *Australian Woman's Magazine and Domestic Journal* (April 1882 – September 1884), which had serialised Janet Carroll's novel *Magna: An Australian Girl* in 1882 – the first novel, in fact, to bear the title of this character type. The Australian girl is a projection, an ideal. But the *Australian Woman's Magazine* also reminds us that she emerges out of real conditions, which means thinking about the sorts of opportunities local colonial life can offer women in terms of education and employment. In 'Woman's Work', 'Vaga' cautions colonial women against frivolity but keeps her counsel rather vague; here, 'work' has more to do with nurture and duty, especially towards the husband. As in so much commentary on the Australian girl, matrimony is her taken-for-granted destination.

By the 1890s, the Australian girl had a great deal of currency. In this section we have included two Australian girl stories from around this time, which show the ways in which narratives about this character type explored various models and trajectories: opening up some possibilities, but also setting limits. The Victorian teacher and naturalist William Gillies' story 'The New Governess', from Blackwell's *Centennial Magazine*, was published in the same year as Catherine Martin's *An Australian Girl*. In Martin's novel, a local girl chooses between two suitors, an Englishman and an Australian squatter. But in Gillies's story, a young lawyer who takes a teaching position at a ladies' college finds himself caught between two Australian girls: the governess Margaret Forbes, and a student from a remote bush station who seems 'wild': 'no governess had been able to govern her...' The story asks us to think about which kind of Australian girlhood offers the best promise for a happy and prosperous (matrimonial) future. The independence of the Australian girl could be either an advantage or a disadvantage, depending on the case.

In the story by 'The J Nib' from *Cosmos*, Stella Eldridge acts courageously in the bush, winning the admiration of her English suitor – and bearing out Woollacott's point about the way in which the Australian girl was valued over her English counterpart. A girl's independence and her prospects as a wife-to-be jostle with each other through the narratives this character type inhabits. Ethel Turner's complaint – also in *Cosmos* – is that, for the new heroine of literary fiction, even marriage isn't satisfying. The short piece on 'The Australian Girl' from George Taylor's satirical magazine, *Ha! Ha: A Merry Newspaper Magazine for Australians*, is also searching for an ideal literary heroine that would provide Australian girls with something they could aspire to. *Cosmos* – one of the few colonial journals at the time to be edited by a woman, Annie Bright – was especially interested in debates about femininity and the ways in which Australia, as it edged closer to nationhood, could invest in its young women to realise their best potential. For the South Australian school teacher Jane Steele Millan in her article, 'The Women of the Future', education is therefore the key. Drawing on an earlier account of the radical American feminist, Victoria Woodhull Martin, Millan advocates the proper training of Australian girls, partly to enable them to make the right matrimonial decisions later on. Her article develops a poetic vision of the future of the Australian girl, drawing on Walt Whitman and the English literary critic and political radical Frederic Harrison's essay on John Stuart Mill. It is interesting to note that, in the pages of a popular colonial journal, she also advises young Australian girls to keep away from 'worthless and ephemeral light literature'.

Those colonial journals specifically aimed at women readerships were invested in the education of women as a way of shaping both their employment prospects and the successful management of domestic life. Louisa Lawson's *Dawn: The Journal for Australian Women* wrote about work and labour, but also advised on household economy and even fashion and feminine entertainments. T. Shaw Fitchett's *New Idea*, which claimed a circulation of 100,000 readers, was less radical and tied more to popular literary forms, making ample space for 'light literature': ghost stories, detective fiction, romances, and so on. But it also published important colonial women writers like Miles Franklin, Mary Gilmore and (as we have noted) Katharine Susannah Prichard, and it could treat feminist issues seriously. Rose Scott was a leading advocate for women's suffrage in New South Wales. In *New Idea*'s interview with her, Scott shows off her home, talks about her life and hobbies, speaks up for women's education at school, and reminisces about the early days of colonial suffrage campaigns. She describes what was originally a literary network of progressive women and men, which included Caroline L. Montefiore, who wrote stories and articles for *Cosmos*; Margaret Windeyer, a member of Louisa Lawson's Dawn Club and the Women's Literary Society; the journalist, novelist and poet Emily Manning, who published under the name 'Australie' and wrote for the *Australian Town and Country Journal* and the *Sydney Mail*; and the Sydney artist Julian Ashton and his wife Eliza Ashton.

New Idea was also interested in women's experiences at work: Mary Gilmore wrote about her experiences as a teacher in the bush, Prichard wrote about her life as a governess, and in 1903 the social journalist Helen Davis went undercover to write exposés of women's work conditions in a variety of institutions (factories, boarding houses, and so on). In 1907, the journalist and writer Beatrix Tracy wrote another fascinating series of articles about Australian women in the workplace—for the *Lone Hand*—under the general title 'Explorations in Industry'. One of these, 'The Girl in Waiting', looks at the tea-room girl or waitress, and weighs up the benefits and drawbacks of the role. Tea-room girls, she says, are 'well-connected young women', or at least 'pretend to be'. Their rates of pay are low, but the girls form a 'fraternity' and are generally well looked after. Tracy had been involved in colonial theatre and married Howard E. Carr, the musical director for J. C. Williamson's Comic Opera Company; she talked about her theatrical background in an article about the 'the chorus girl' in her *Lone Hand* series. Florence Young was one of J. C. Williamson's star performers who was greatly admired by colonial audiences. She also wrote about the chorus-girl for the *Lone Hand*, recuperating for serious discussion what might have once been dismissed as a frivolous profession. The chorus girl is trained to perform a demanding role; because of this, the question of women's labour (and rates of remuneration etc.) is just as important in the colonial entertainment industries as it is anywhere else. Young's article is a valorisation of the Australian girl at work: 'any girl blessed with an object in life', she writes, 'becomes a better woman than the pampered and useless dolls of society'.

In spite of these investments, the Australian girl was also available as an emblem of middle class recreation – which meant she ran the risk of being reduced to an image defined entirely by her good looks and fashionability. George Taylor had already spoken about the Australian girl as a national ideal or 'model' in his journal *Ha! Ha: A Merry Magazine for Australians*. In 1907 – the same year as Beatrix Tracy's 'Explorations in Industry' series – he wrote 'The Quest of the Australian Girl' for *A.A.A.: All About Australians*, a lively review of visual representations of this character type by a number of prominent colonial artists, such as Mabelle Edmonds, Norman Lindsay, Percy Spence and Fred Leist. For William George Moore in *The Story of*

COLONIAL TYPES: THE AUSTRALIAN GIRL

Australian Art, 'Fred Leist […] was the first Australian artist to draw the Australian girl as a type'.[3] Taylor describes the 'Leist Girl' as a 'wild, frolicsome, happy hearted damsel', although the sketch we reproduce here seems instead to suggest a more metropolitan, sophisticated aesthetic. Florence Young had mentioned the 'Gibson girl' as a representative American type, referring to the illustrations of the American artist Charles Dana Gibson, which celebrated a confident, aristocratic kind of feminine beauty. For Taylor, the Gibson girl is a source of inspiration for Australian artists, but the local scene has different imperatives – and his discussion of 'racial purity' reminds us that the Australian girl was also instrumental in the valorisation of whiteness in the newly-formed nation. It is not surprising, then, that a journal like the *Lone Hand* – which had invested so heavily in a white Australia – exhibited the Australian girl at every opportunity. In D. H. Souter's 1912 article 'The Australian Girl', this character type is lifted out of the workplace altogether and celebrated instead for her erotic appeal, her whimsy, her frivolousness. A fickle creature of fashion, she is now almost entirely emptied of content; even so, she still has enough representative power to make even those who leave Australia want to return.

1   de Serville, *Rolf Boldrewood: A Life*, p. 173.
2   Woollacott, *To Try Her Fortune in London*, p. 158.
3   Moore, *The Story of Australian Art*, p. 110.

'VAGA', 'WOMAN'S WORK'
Australian Woman's Magazine and Domestic Journal
1 July 1882

Woman's mission and woman's work is a topic that has engaged much attention and has almost been torn to tatters in debate. In writing upon this subject we do not mean to argue in favor of any particular form of work or destiny, more than this, that love and gentleness ought to run like a golden thread through all a woman's life and duties.

Woman's mission is one of sympathetic love and fostering care. A woman devoid of a feeling heart, sympathy, and gentleness, is like a flower lacking fragrance. The perfume of a flower attracts you, and controls your finer senses, so also do the feminine attributes of a woman. She is essentially the earthly guardian spirit of humanity. Hundreds of authors have in their writings testified to the power, purpose, and influence of women.

The earthly work and mission of woman is immeasurably harder than that of man. She has to bear her own share and yet be the consoler and comforter of man. She has to "suffer and be strong." We do not assume that woman is meant to be man's superior; she was made "a companion." Man is her king—her lord; one whom she can reverence and love, and in whose love and praise she finds her reward; but he is not her *master*. That is where the mistake comes in. If the women of our age would only realize their power of doing good there would be less crime, sin, and discontent in the world. Many women of the present day flit through life like butterflies of summer, and almost as purposely, the principal object of living apparently being the love of dress and admiration. Thus the nobler qualities are crushed and only the frivolities of her nature are seen. This is a grievous pity. Strength and determination can accomplish a great deal, but gentleness and sympathy can do more. Then, sisters, banish all foolish thoughts and wrong desires. Stand up noble women, fulfilling the grand destiny of woman.

WILLIAM GILLIES, 'THE NEW GOVERNESS'
Centennial Magazine
June 1890

I was returning to town from a holiday in the bush. It was hot, drowsy weather. I was the sole occupant of my compartment, and was lazily reviewing the past year of my life, and wondering what the next year held in store for me. I was a student of law and expected to be called to the bar in three months' time. I had paid my way by teaching in a school for young ladies and by occasional journalism. I was glad to think that I would soon be free from the Oskaloosa Ladies' College; for, though I was no hater of Woman, I was not fond of Girl.

COLONIAL TYPES: THE AUSTRALIAN GIRL

I had almost dropped off to sleep, when the train stopped at one of those wayside stations which are equally distant from everywhere. A young lady, neatly dressed in a grey travelling costume, was standing guard over a pile of luggage. The guard opened the door of my compartment, thrust in the luggage and said: "Here you are, Miss;" and, as she hesitated, "Jump in please, we're late." She looked at me timidly through pretty, brown eyes, and then obeyed the guard.

The train started with a jerk, and one of her bags, a large one hastily placed in the rack overhead, was thrown out, and would have fallen on her had I not caught it just in time. The action brought our faces close together, and a sudden conviction that this was the one face in the world for me flashed through my mind. "Stung by the splendor of this sudden thought," I hardly noticed her words of thanks, or how she blushed as she spoke.

She moved to the window and looked out and backwards, as if taking farewell of the place. A bullock-team was crawling along the white, dusty road that ran beside the line, and she waved her hand to the driver. He was the only human being within sight, and he did not see her.

Presently, through a break in the nearer bush, a range of hills in the background became visible, and, dimly through the smoke-haze, one could see the white walls of a cottage. Tears filled the girl's eyes, and she kept her head out of the window long after the cottage was lost to view. It was a grave face, but, sure, no sweeter soul ever looked through human eyes.

When she drew in her head our eyes met, and I said,

"It's hard to leave the old place, is it not?"

"Yes," she replied, and the voice was soft and musical, "it is hard!"

Her eyes began to fill again, and she turned aside and busied herself with her baggage.

After a little she took out a book which I recognized at once as a Latin grammar—A workman knows the tools of his trade. She put down the book open as we stopped at a station, and my eye caught the heading, "*Qui* with the Subjunctive." There is a book called "Latin Without Tears." I do not think my old friend "*Qui* with the Subjunctive" can have been allowed within the boards of that book.

I stole an occasional glance as the study proceeded, and saw the lines of struggle come into her brow. I thought I knew just what it was that puzzled her. Had I not guided—how painfully let teachers say, a hundred pupils through this maze? But what joy to help this girl!

Presently we stopped at a station where ten minutes were allowed for refreshment. Here was a chance to break through her reserve. I brought her a cup of tea. It was a little thing, but the fervor and tenderness in my heart made it a great thing; and she blushed slightly as she thanked me. The ice was broken and we talked freely.

Her father, she told me, had been a clergyman in the bush. She was an only child, and her father, who was a man of quiet scholarly tastes, had taught her all she knew. On his death she found it necessary to work for a living, and she was going to act as governess at the Oskaloosa Ladies' College.

"Oskaloosa!" I exclaimed, "good, we shall be fellow-workers," and I joyfully handed her my card.

"Oh!" she exclaimed, "I am glad. One face, at least, won't be quite strange. I am anxious, Mr. Webb, about it all; for it's all new to me."

I made light of her difficulties: not quite honestly, perhaps: but what would you, with those grave, sweet eyes looking timorously into the future? Her face lit up with smiles, her reserve was gone, and in a few minutes we were talking and laughing like old friends.

The slow train became a fast train, and the suburbs of the city came all too soon. As I put her into a cab I read the name on her baggage—Margaret Forbes. I wondered that people could call their girls any name but Margaret: it seemed the one name for a woman. And Forbes! Yes, the name was worthy of her.

PART II

School work had begun. I had helped the lady-principal to receive parents and to classify pupils, for, like many of her class, she could do everything but teach. I had also helped to allocate the classes among the staff, and had contrived so that Margaret Forbes would not be over-taxed, and also that she would be teaching close to me for part of the time of my visit to the school.

That fixed, I drew out and sent to her a list of probable pupils she would have, adding comments like the following:—

Emily Quick: A lazy girl; needs the spur.

Annie Upright: A mean girl; a tale-bearer; can lie without winking.

Jessie Smith: True as steel, but shy and slow.

Laura Primrose: Forward, vain, officious; needs occasional snub.

Jane Cheerful: Sullen and vindictive if you cross her.

Eve Silence: Full of tricks, but not a bad girl at heart.

I also added a few hints on the errors young teachers generally fall into, and I had the great satisfaction of seeing that by the end of the first week Margaret Forbes was mistress of the situation.

On the following Monday there was a new pupil, a girl from a remote station whose education was backward. No governess had been able to govern her, and she had run wild. At times, when the fit seized her, she would learn, and then she would learn rapidly. She was eighteen, and looked her age. She was fair and had a clear, fresh complexion: and she was tall and graceful in movement. Something in her features, the eyes and the nose, suggested a trace in her veins of Jewish blood. This, probably, was a wrong inference, since the only interest any Jews I know have in pastoral pursuits lies through mortgages on the land and liens on the wool-clip. Her name was Edna Howson.

Miss Howson gave me a good deal of trouble to bring her into line with the others. I found her, indeed, docile enough, though she moved about with the air of one who was not subject to the rules of the school. She was very attentive, but I soon found that her interest was not in the thing explained, but in him who explained it. As a teacher with some experience among senior girls I knew how to deal with cases of this kind. Do not think me vain, dear reader, because I say this. The experience is a professional commonplace.

When Miss Howson's eye was not the eye of the student I refused to catch it, and I treated her, in all respects, like the other girls. At first I bent over her desk frequently to give her the extra help she required; but when I found that she colored and became confused, I ceased to do this and made her come to my desk in front of the class.

Meantime, Margaret Forbes and I were becoming good friends. I watched her class as well as my own. At the close of school I gave her hints and warnings, and her mischievous pupils soon found that they were under two pair of eyes instead of one pair.

It did not strike me that my own class were watching this little game. Judge therefore, of my surprise when, one day, after a written examination, I found on a torn page which had unintentionally been handed in with other papers, the following extra question appended to the questions set:—"II Mention of the number of times per hour that Mr. Webb looks at Miss Forbes. Explain shortly his reasons, and give historical parallels." The writing was that of Miss Howson.

About this time, Miss Howson, who had stood aloof from the other girls, began to show a friendly spirit, and as she could be genial and charming in manner, and had plenty of pocket-money, she soon became popular.

Soon after, Margaret Forbes complained to me that Miss Howson, who had sullenly opposed her from the first, was becoming unbearably insolent, and, what was more serious, was trying to draw the other girls into revolt. Now I understood her friendly advances to the other girls. I saw that there was but one remedy: to have Miss Howson removed from Margaret's classes; and this, with some difficulty, I persuaded the Principal to do.

That Edna Howson understood all this I am certain, and, now and again, I fancied there was a wicked gleam in her eye as she looked towards Margaret.

Margaret, on her part, showed no sign; and, indeed, it was against her wish that Miss Howson was removed from her class. She would not own that she was beaten, and she made no difference in her conduct towards Miss Howson when she met her about the house. In taking this line she was guided partly by her own good sense and partly by my advice, that she should never allow a pupil to see that she had the power to annoy her. It was a hard role to keep up;

for, in all social functions—dances, charades, tennis-parties, and so on—Miss Howson played a leading part, and was able to put many a slight on Margaret.

One hot afternoon Margaret was in charge of a party of boarders at the sea baths. As a country girl she had not learned to swim, but Edna Howson, who was one of the party, had become quite at home in the sea during the annual visits of her folks to St. Kilda.

Here was a chance to humiliate Margaret. All the girls of the party could swim, and Miss Howson led them to steps where the water was too deep for any but swimmers. "Here you are, girls," she cried, "here are the steps for all but the muffs."

Margaret, ill at ease and uncertain, felt that she, and not Miss Howson, ought to say where the girls were to enter the water; but while she hesitated they dived, one after the other, all except a timid girl who had only just learned to swim. Margaret ran forward to stop her. "Come on, Lucy!" cried Miss Howson. "Don't Lucy!" cried Margaret, as she rushed down the steps. It was too late. The girl was braced for the dive, and Margaret, reaching forward to catch her, stumbled and fell into the water. No one was near her except Lucy, who had enough to do to swim into shallow water. Edna Howson saw what had happened and swam to the rescue at once. Margaret had risen to the surface the second time, when she caught her and pushed her to the steps. An ambulance class was included in the College curriculum, and Miss Howson had been an apt pupil. She knew the drill for restoring the half drowned, and in two minutes Margaret recovered consciousness.

Next day, after school, I was sitting alone in my room making up returns, when Miss Howson came back for a book she had forgotten. I beckoned her to me, and said: "You did nobly yesterday, I hope you'll follow it up. You have saved Miss Forbes' life; try to make that life happy."

"Ah!" she exclaimed, with rising color and a quick frown, "always Miss Forbes; you think of no one but Miss Forbes." And she lifted her books and swept out of the room.

Next morning I received a note, which ran thus:—"Dear Mr. Webb, you are right. Forgive me. I have written to Miss Forbes. Good bye. Edna Howson."

When Margaret was well enough she was allowed to read the following:—"Dear Miss Forbes, I have behaved badly to you, but you have a woman's heart and can understand. Forgive me."

I never saw her again. She went to the house of an uncle in another suburb, and then to a school near Sydney. Two years after she was carried off to England by an officer of the Navy.

A load seemed to have been lifted from Margaret's life, and a new buoyancy gave charm to her grave manner. My afternoons at Oskaloosa College were all too short. No duty was irksome, no pupil tiresome when Margaret Forbes was in the room. I was told that a glad light was in my eye, and I know that goodwill to every pupil was in my heart.

And if I was changed so also was my class. They worked for me with a will, and a word of rebuke was as effective as formerly a long "imposition." When, at the end of the session, I gave up school work, each girl gave me her photograph; and there are marks on some of the cards which I firmly believe are tears.

When, a year after, I came back to take away Margaret Forbes to her new home, there was much crying over her, and clinging and kissing. Oskaloosa College lost the best governess it had ever had, and I won the sweetest wife that ever made a man happy.

ETHEL TURNER, 'WOMEN'S DEPARTMENT'
Cosmos
20 October 1894

An exchange says the heroine of fiction is generally a type of the day. If that is so, then this year she is a clever, beautiful, bloodless creature who at twenty-two is bored to death with everything except mountain storms, scientific studies and suicides. She has ceased to be a chatterer: she speaks only in epigrams. She is not given to tears; about once in seven hundred pages her body is shaken with great, tearless sobs. She is not a flirt; she is cold, indifferent—very often absolutely rude. She beats the record for eccentricity; she drives tandem, smokes over billiards, goes out at night unattended, and refuses to be bored by matrimony. In spite of everything, however, she gets along all right; and when she commits suicide, it is not because she is not having a good time, but because she is not going to accept her good time with the complacency that any ordinary woman would. She objects to be happy like ordinary cabbage-rose women; so she takes laudanum out of pure "cussedness." What will the next type be like? Our novels used to end with marriage; now they begin with it. Our heroines of the past year have been all married women; maidens are out of it. Why not take up the middle-aged woman next and invest her with some romance? She would be a change.

'THE J NIB', 'AN AUSTRALIAN GIRL'
Cosmos
19 November 1896

Neligen, the homestead of Thomas Eldridge, looks calm and beautiful in the warm, white moonlight of the summer evening. From the French windows, thrown wide open, great shafts of light stream across the broad verandah; and now the hum of conversation and ripple of laughter from within die away, and the magnificent chords of the "Marche Hongroise" peal forth, causing the little birds nestling in the shrubbery around the house to bring their heads from beneath their wings, and, half-awakened, sleepily twitter in response. Then the music ceases, the hum of voices is resumed, and the birds are at rest again.

Inside, where a party of friends are met at the invitation of their host, a girl of eighteen sits at the piano, looking up, with bright eyes and smiling lips, into the face of the young fellow who leans over her. No need for a second glance to tell that they are in that happy state, which usually, after a brief *tête-a-tête,* culminates in the term "engaged."

Stella Eldridge is the sister of the young proprietor of Neligen, already betrothed to Hazel Royce, and it is the brother of the latter young lady who leans so tenderly over Stella. It is probable that the second engagement would have been announced ere this were it not for one little peculiarity in the character of the gentleman, one, too, unfortunately shared by many of his countrymen, for be it known that Francis Royce is English—with a capital E,—and with the conservative prejudice born of inexperience, deems it the correct thing to speak in disparaging terms of things Australian. Stella is Australian—with a capital A,—and meets his earnest protestations with a laughing quotation of his nearest approach to commendation—"Pity I'm not English."

That very day he had made an attempt to bring matters to a crisis, without success. A party of the guests had been shooting in the wild gullies that bounded one side of the estate, and returning earlier than usual, amused themselves firing at pinecones thrown up on the lawn before the house. Hazel had witnessed the sport with the equanimity of a man, and had even fired off her *fiancée*'s gun without flinching; but Stella had put her hands to her ears with a little scream at every report, and when at last, after much persuasion, she fired Royce's gun, had shut her eyes, turned away her head, and almost dropped the weapon when it went off. Presuming on the fact that *he* had been the only one who could induce her to discharge a gun, Royce took the opportunity as they walked towards the house to press his suit, only to be put out of court by the jesting reply, "Pity I'm not English, isn't it?"

This evening, however, he meant to settle the matter. Another lady took Stella's place at the piano, and in the most inconsequent manner in the world the pair strolled out into the garden. Then the little birds perched in a certain tree awoke once more, and listened to a conversation carried on in low tones beneath them. The male voice seemed pleading in his cause with success, to judge by the tone of the female voice in the rare intervals of its reply, and the little birds hitched up against one another and nodded as they listened. But suddenly there came a change; Royce had the misfortune to decry Australians even at the supreme moment; "If she accepted him, they would leave this country and live in England, where they could associate with people who," &c. Then the birds saw her take him by the arm and point to the knot of stalwart young men standing in the glare of light in the drawing-room. They heard her demand in indignant tones whether they were not as good—aye, fifty times better than any of his countrymen. They heard her ask how it was if Englishmen were so superior to her own people he had the bad taste to choose an Australian for his wife. They saw her release his arm, and without waiting for his reply, walk, with her head erect, straight back to the house, leaving him to follow at his leisure. Then the little birds hitched back to their places, winked their little eyes, and went to sleep again.

Two days after the scene in the garden there is bustle and excitement in the household, though not of a pleasurable nature. Taking advantage of the bright moonlight of the previous evening, Eldridge and his guest went 'possum-shooting, and though it is now early forenoon neither has returned. At the solicitation of their young mistress, the men employed about the station set off in small parties and scoured the bush in all directions in search of the missing men, only to straggle back at midday to report their unsuccess, and after providing themselves with food for a prolonged absence, at once started out again to renew their search.

As hour after hour drags slowly on, every minute adding to the torturing suspense felt by the two girls who have hitherto borne bravely up under their anxiety, the dormant characteristic of their respective natures manifests itself. Little by little the quiet self-possession of the English girl—which contrasts so strongly with the excitement of her future sister-in-law—gives way, and she betakes herself to her room, there to weep helplessly until Stella comes in and finds her. "Hazel, Hazel, *don't* cry!" she implores, while her own pale face and moist lashes tell how near she is to following her friend's example; "come outside and *do* something." "Oh, I shall go mad if they don't come soon!" Then, as Hazel only answers by a sob to her exhortation, takes her hand and tries to raise her to her feet. "Come," she says desperately, "let us go and look for them ourselves;" and, again, receiving no reply but renewed tears, darts out, picking up her hat as she passes through the house, and hurries away across the paddocks to the bush, with the hot, slanting rays of the setting sun throwing a long purple shadow before her.

Where to look for the lost men, or what on earth she was going to do should she find them, never cost her a thought, and it was only when after going straight in the direction of the gullies for a mile or so that the downright madness of her action struck her. Climbing down the side of a creek, she suddenly drew back with a half-suppressed scream as a big brown snake went gliding down before her, its wicked head sideways and forked tongue flickering in and out as it travelled. That was the first check. She decided to climb up and follow the crown of the gully—and did so until she was met by another creek, running into the one she was following. Then she felt bewildered, and decided to go home, but couldn't find her way, and nightfall saw her wandering aimlessly about in the bed of a dry creek, half mad with fear, now and then calling in a tremulous shriek for help upon those she had started out to rescue. At length she sat down exhausted in the bottom of a dark gully, and gazed appealingly at the trees crowning the range, that caught the light from the tardy moon. Suddenly she started, as a hideous, long-drawn howl echoed through the ravine, and sent her stumbling and staggering afresh in wild-eyed terror. Reaching a point where yet another gully rounded into the creek, she paused to listen for a repetition of the dingo's howl, and regaining courage from the continued silence, again cried for help.

Could she be mistaken? Was that an answer to her cry? Once more she sent forth a shriek—"Coo-oo-ee!" Pressing her hand to her heart, she listened intently. There was no mistake. "Co-oo-ee!" came faintly back from close at hand. Like a mad thing, she rushed forward over rocks and brushes, her white dress fluttering and tearing as it caught the branches, till with a cry of "Oh, Frank!" "Oh, Tom!" she sank on her knees beside two figures that lay huddled up on the ground.

She had found the missing ones, but in evil case. Her brother, who had answered to her coo-ee, half-reclined on the ground, his right leg fractured below the knee; while Frank Royce, with some ribs broken and a bad scalp wound, alternately sat up and rolled about in delirium.

Tom, after enquiring for Hazel, in a few sentences punctuated with groans, told her what had happened. "We were coming back along the edge of the gully," he said, "and Frank leaned out to get a shot at a 'possum. He slipped. I tried to save him, and we both went over and rolled down here. I've crawled down there to the creek twice for water, but my strength gave out, and we must have died shortly had you not found us. Get some water, for Heaven's sake!"

Forgetting all her fears, Stella took her brother's hat—she had lost her own—and made her way through the black bush towards the waterhole indicated. Twice she made the journey, bringing sufficient water to quench their burning thirst and bathe Royce's wounded head; and having under her brother's directions built a fire, and made them as comfortable as possible, found a piece of ribbon somewhere about her dress and tied back the hair which had tumbled over her face and shoulders, then, seating herself between the two men, asked Tom what next was to be done.

"You can do nothing, Stella," he answered. "If the men are still out they will probably camp till morning. At daylight you must fire signal shots for awhile, and if there's no answer, I'll give you your course, and you must try to get back and bring assistance."

Slowly the moon crawled up the sky, till at last her beams came through the trees in the gully, and fell in ragged patches upon the three figures grouped close to the fire. Eldridge had fallen into a fitful sleep, broken by the pain of his injured limb; and Royce, who was still semi-conscious, tossed about muttering and moaning incoherently. Poor Stella sat, cold and miserable, listening in the intervals of quietude of the men to the hundred weird noises of the bush—the snore of the morepork, the unaccountable splashing in the water-hole, the scamper of the bandicoot and opossum over the dead leaves, or the startling crash of a falling bough. As the night advanced, the ravings of her lover became more pronounced, and taking Tom's hat, she once more filled it at the creek, and drawing Royce's head on her lap, bathed his temples with the cool water. After a time he became calmer, and finally dozed off; then, overcome by excitement and utter weariness, she too was on the point of falling asleep, when a stealthy rustle in the undergrowth caused her to look sharply round. At first she saw nothing, but presently noticed two clear, green points of light shining out from the shadow of a bush. She closed her eyes, and looked again. The points of light were gone. Reassured, she turned her gaze elsewhere, and saw in the open a similar pair of spots, surrounded by a dull grey shape that told her they were eyes. With a thrill of fear she now looked about her, and saw in other directions the counter-part of those sinister green eyes.

Alone with two disabled men, who were powerless to protect her, the presence of those awful eyes brought to her mind the many stories she had heard of attacks made by packs of dingoes upon men left helpless and unarmed in the bush. She knew that they were encompassed by the cowardly brutes, but, instead of increasing her fears, the thought that danger menaced the two men she loved gave her strength. Gently removing Royce's head from her lap, she rose to her feet and replenished the fire, and as the bright flames leapt up, her glance rested on one of the guns lying a few yards from where she stood. Picking it up, she saw it was uninjured, and opening the breech found it to be loaded; then, as though accustomed from her infancy to the use of firearms, swung round in search of the eyes that had so startled her. They were gone as if by magic. Instead of returning to her seat, she stood in the shadow of a tree near the two men, and waited. Gradually, as the fire died down, she saw the long, grey forms come stealing out of the darkness, ever drawing closer and closer as the circle of light narrowed towards the dying fire, until she distinctly saw the outlines of several dingoes within a few paces of her, their eyes fixed on the two restless figures on the ground. Presently one huge brute, bolder than the rest, crouched forward until his broadside was in full view, and, quietly raising the weapon without a trace of the nervousness that she had displayed on the afternoon of the dance, took deliberate aim and fired.

As the thunder of the report rolled down the valley, there was a rush and scamper of feet as the dingoes took flight, leaving their leader kicking and struggling in the agony of death. But a more cheering sound followed. Scarcely had the echoes died away when from far down the creek came an answering shot, followed by a faint coo-ee. Instantly discharging the other barrel, Stella sent forth a wild cry, in which her whole heart seemed embodied. Later, from a nearer point came another shot and another shout, and in a few minutes a party of the station hands clambered down the rocks and clustered about them.

It was a long while before Eldridge and Royce fully recovered from the effects of their injuries and exposure; but some months later there was a double weeding at Neligen, and now, when Mr. and Mrs. Eldridge visit Mr. and Mrs. Royce, Tom looks at the big dingo skin that ornaments Stella's dining-room, and while thankful that Hazel was spared the sufferings of

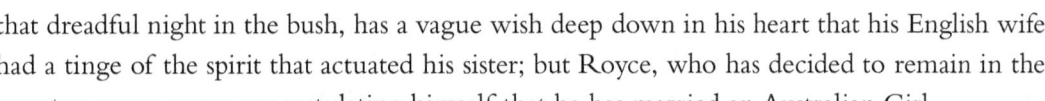

that dreadful night in the bush, has a vague wish deep down in his heart that his English wife had a tinge of the spirit that actuated his sister; but Royce, who has decided to remain in the country, never ceases congratulating himself that he has married an Australian Girl.

J. STEELE MILLAN, 'THE WOMEN OF THE FUTURE'
Cosmos
19 February 1897

The article of Mrs. Hirst Alexander, in the November number of *Cosmos*, entitled "Mrs. Victoria W. Martin,—A Woman of the Times," evoked my sympathy, and is responsible for the following suggestions made to such as are interested in the education and mental culture of the women of the very near future,—the girlhood of Australia.

The fact that I have been engaged in educational work in Australia for the last fifteen years, and for as many more, previous to that, in England and South Africa, may perhaps excuse and explain my doing so. I am thus in a position in which I can compare the capabilities of the girls of three English-speaking countries, and I can truthfully say that I have found the mental capacity and ability of the girlhood of Australia in no whit inferior to those of girls of a similar age in the other lands mentioned. To the true teacher—and the teacher, like the poet, is born, not made—the work of education is a delightful one. It is certainly one, however, of great responsibility. The ideal teacher should feel that teaching is her special vocation—that the privilege is hers of leading ever onward and upward, young, enthusiastic, ardent, impressionable minds. She should train and encourage her girls to think for themselves, and by no means to allow others to do all their thinking for them. She should direct their attention to the writings of those authors whose teachings are in accord with mental and spiritual freedom, and away from the worthless and ephemeral light literature, too often productive of nothing but the growth of foolish and chimerical expectations. I believe in training girls to form correct judgments as to the comparative merits of the works of the various authors with whom it is desirable they should become acquainted—in helping them to distinguish between the mere sweet and euphemistic in poetry and in prose and the lofty, powerful and original. Some have said that there is danger in making a girl too imaginative and idealistic. I think not, if one only gives her high ideals, and tempers her imaginative faculty by the cultivation and encouragement of good sound sense.

Just think how narrow and meager the education of the sex has, *as a rule,* hitherto been! A few accomplishments and perhaps a foreign language or two, in addition to a, too often, superficial and limited acquaintance with their own,—that has been all. Mental training, in its proper sense, has been entirely wanting. But suppose all that changed! Suppose this all-important work, the training and education of the future mothers of the race; in fit and proper hands,—there are women who might make it a labour of love—what then? Do you think that girls, educated on such lines as these, could ever be contented with the wretched, superficial lives of the mere pleasure-seeker?—with the infinite littleness of fashionable frivolity?—with an empty-headed *masher* for a husband? No, I trow not! They could not possibly be so.

We women need not dwell reproachfully, for ever, upon the one-sided justice that has so long been meted out to the sexes. Even in twin children who have come into the world of different sexes, the *feminine* one it is true has been handicapped throughout life by being debarred from the privileges accorded to the masculine twin, as if he were undoubtedly the superior animal! However, it is sad to reflect that this injustice extended even to the cultivation of their brains. How much may have been lost to the world by the assumption that the feminine brain could not grasp anything abstruse, or that involved deep research, study and thought! Not only in modern times but all through past history that theory has been disproved by facts. And do we not find now-a-days, that when girls are given the *chance*, their attainments and success are equal to those of their masculine compeers? Not that I think it desirable to educate the sexes on exactly similar lines. But there surely need to be no rivalry of a mean or jealous kind between them. The one sex is the complement of the other. Mr. Frederic Harrison says:—"The truth lies not in the equality, but in the inter-dependence of the sexes; not in their identities or similarities but in their hetero-geneities and correlations."

I can quite understand and follow the conviction of Mrs. Woodhull Martin that the "process of evolution will eventually produce a perfect woman possessing every virtue and worthy attribute of her sex, from whose progeny will spring a perfect race," only I would speak in the *plural*, and say that, eventually, there may be produced such *women* whose progeny will naturally inherit nobility of nature! Walt Whitman says:

> "Roaming in thought over the universe, I saw the little that is Good steadily hastening towards immortality,
> And the vast all that is called Evil I saw hastening to merge itself and become lost and dead."

To this prophecy may all the people say amen!

One last thought: Can none of our Australian women do what Mrs. Woodhull Martin has done, namely, imitate receptions of the "*salon*" type?—receptions, the passport to which, the "Open Sesame," will, or should be, genius, brilliancy, worth, goodness—the aristocracy of talent, and distinction of whatever kind, so that it be admirable and loveable,—for in its literal sense of "*the best*" one can reverence an aristocracy—tho' certainly not the plutocracy. How delightful such receptions might become! No pleasure can approach that of intercourse with congenial spirits, nor can any be purer or more elevating. In spite of what dear, brave, old Walt Whitman calls his "barbaric yawp" his lines are often soul-inspiring. I shall close it by citing a few—

> "Ages, precedents, have long been accumulating undirected materials.
> America brings builders and brings its own styles (*so does Australasia.*)
> The immortal poets of Asia and Europe have done their work and passed to other spheres.
> A work remains – the work of surpassing all they have done.
>
> ★   ★   ★   ★
>
> For the great Idea, the idea of perfect and free individuals,
> For that, the bard walks in advance, the leader of leaders.
> For the great Idea,
> That, O my brethren, *that* is the mission of poets!"

GEORGE TAYLOR, 'THE AUSTRALIAN GIRL'
Ha! Ha: A Merry Magazine for Australians
9 April 1898

No we cannot laugh just here. We are thinking of the Australian girl in colonial literature. When will any of our writers make a start and give us a girl character that will stand as a model for all colonial girls to copy—a girl that we can look on as a true Australian type?—she is wanted badly. The writers who are filling us up week after week give us but one type, and, alas! she happens to be a girl who is untrue to all sense of womanly virtue. Are there no pure and noble-minded Australian girls whose self-denying lives are worthy of molding into print? Thousands! And now we wait with happy hopes the immortalizing of a type that will be a copy for all our girls, and in a great way develop the purest and noblest in Australian women.

COLONIAL TYPES: THE AUSTRALIAN GIRL

'SYDNEY'S LEADING POLITICAL LADY'
New Idea
1 January 1903

"If all women suffragists were like Miss Rose Scott," once observed a crusty old bachelor—who simply hated women who speak in public with a perfect hatred—after hearing that lady on the platform, "I would vote for the women's franchise tomorrow."

One can readily understand the exception thus made in Miss Scott's favor. Of all the women who clapped their hands in an ecstasy of delight a few weeks back, when the New South Wales State Parliament followed the example of the Federal Parliament, and passed the Women's Franchise Bill, there is none more charming in the truest sense of the word than Miss Rose Scott. She is so delightfully and delicately unconventional, and withal so entertaining, that interviewing becomes a positive pleasure.

She welcomed us on the front verandah of her pretty little cottage home, "Lynton," Woollahra, and inside of five minutes every vestige of nervousness had left us, and we were at home.

ASPIRATIONS

"As a child I longed to be a sort of Joan of Arc, and do something for my country," our host confided, as she began to tell in miniature the story of her life. "Then I began to hear of the wrongs of women, and it appealed to me. Then I was led to read all I could on the women's suffrage movement. The book that finally settled me was John Stuart Mill's 'Subjection of Women.'

"When our league was first formed in Sydney, I was asked to become the secretary. Oh, it was dreadful, the very idea of it, and I shrank from the bare suggestion. In the end, however, I was persuaded.

"Do you know?" Miss Scott threw in by way of parenthesis, "I have always found that whatever one seeks for in life is not satisfactory; while that which you do not seek for succeeds. It certainly has seemed that way to me.

"Then, again, when once I had turned my attention to the women's suffrage question, it seemed as if everything tended in that direction. I was independent, and unmarried, moreover, and could do just as I liked; while I suppose, naturally, I had a way of thinking and acting for myself.

"I often used to think I might die without seeing the suffrage accomplished. People used to seek to discourage me by telling me so. I have sometimes said that I should be content to die when we got the suffrage, but I am not dead yet!

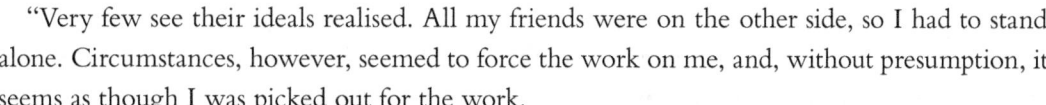

"Very few see their ideals realised. All my friends were on the other side, so I had to stand alone. Circumstances, however, seemed to force the work on me, and, without presumption, it seems as though I was picked out for the work.

FROM THE BUSH

"For ten years I was a little bush girl, and I always thank Heaven for that. Life is less conventional in the bush, and there one learns to think for one's self. I never saw a shop until I was ten years of age. My father was a very rich man before I was born. He came to this country in the 'twenties,' and my mother in the 'thirties.' My mother's father (Mr. Rusden) was the first clergyman in Maitland. My father was a squatter at Glendon, on the Hunter River. He, however, lost his money in the bank smash, and later was appointed a police magistrate, first at Carcoar, then at Louisa Creek, and Wollombi, and finally, for twenty years, at Newcastle.

"The first event in my life, after passing my tenth year, was to pay a visit to my uncle, the late Dean Selwyn, on the Clarence. He was a very fine man, and interested me greatly. I remember hearing the question asked at the store, 'Have you any fresh butter?' and the answer, 'No, but we are expecting some by the next boat,' and lo! a keg of butter from Cork.

"That, however, was a long time ago, for I was born in 1847. We arrived in Sydney on Easter morning. That was my very first experience of Sydney—hearing the bells ring on Easter morning.

A NOTED ANCESTRY

"Really, you know, my people's history is more interesting than my own. My uncle, Capt. Scott, of the Bengal Light Cavalry, was a police magistrate in Sydney for many years. My father's father was president of the Medical Board in Bombay. When the great Duke of Wellington was Sir Arthur Wellesley, he attended him in an illness sustained in India. He subsequently wrote of him in a letter to my grandmother, 'I am very interested in that young man. I shouldn't be surprised if he came to be somebody.' Grandfather wrote a book on the arts of India, a subject in which he was greatly interested. My uncle George wrote a history of New Zealand and Australia, and got into a fearful libel action with a Mr. Bryce.

WOMEN SUFFRAGE IN N.S.W.

"The history of our movement? Oh, yes! The women's suffrage campaign commenced ten years ago. It was Mrs. Montefiore (now in England) who asked us to start it. Eight people went to her house. Besides Mrs. Montefiore there were Miss Margaret Windeyer, Miss Manning (who went to England recently), Mr. William Suttor, and Mr. and Mrs. Julian Ashton; but these had left the suffrage, and I was the only one of the party remaining.

COLONIAL TYPES: THE AUSTRALIAN GIRL

"Previously we had a little Women's Literary Society, and it was there I read my first paper. It was on the subject of Education and 'Stuffing.' The first time I appeared in print was in a letter written to the 'Sydney Morning Herald' against home lessons.

"Yes, the women's franchise question has been part of my religion. It is of far more importance than people think, because it is really a phase of liberty—and to free a whole continent of women is the most wonderful thing that has happened for women. I used to hope that my country would become the freest country in the world, and set an example in legislation; but I broke my heart over federation—and then, the labour [sic] people, and the way they act. I like them, but I feel disgusted with the selfishness of their legislation, for selfishness never pays in the end.

"'In the woman and the workers,' said Ibsen, 'lies the hope of the future.' That being so, the women will have to wake up."

"Has the realization of your wishes in securing the franchise brought you much additional work?" we queried.

"Yes, indeed," replied Miss Scott. "I thought we should get a rest after securing the franchise, but there has been more work since than there was before—such numbers of letters from women all over the country, wanting to know what is the best thing to do, how to form an association, asking advice on points of law, and requesting me to speak.

"I have just come back from a little tour. It was intensely interesting to see the earnest desire of women to do right, to feel their responsibility—and their humility. 'What can we do?' 'What can we learn?'

"You will have noticed how all the political parties are wanting to get hold of the women. But we want to keep free from parties, and free from sectarianism.

"On my tour I visited Maitland, Wallsend, Newcastle, Glen Innes. At Wallsend my host came home all black. He was a miner, and I hadn't met him before. 'I can't shake hands with you yet,' he pleaded. It was such a nice little evening that I had at Wallsend. One saw the earnestness of the women everywhere. At Glen Innes they collected my expenses, and insisted on paying for my sleeping berth. In other places they offered my expenses. I really cannot go to all the places I have been asked to visit.

A NEW INTEREST FOR WOMEN

"The fact is this franchise gives the women a new interest in life—something else to think of. Some of the men agree to say that the earnestness of the women in this matter has done them good; but the responsibility, and the grandeur, and the duty of the vote has not struck all men. Personally I see magnificent possibilities. The thing now is for men and women to work together, and if they trust each other there is nothing they could not do.

"Any hobbies? Quite a number—autographs, book plates, and my garden—oh, I love my garden. I am very much interested in photographs, and have made a collection of all the persons of any note who have come to Australia. Many of the autograph letters I have will become historical. There is all the correspondence in connection with the women's suffrage and the National Council of Women.

"I am on the committee of the Free Kindergarten, and a vice-president of the Women's Club. I was a vice-president of the old Early Closing Association.

"I really take a great interest in housekeeping. I think you would be surprised at the interest I take in cooking and housework. Arranging the meals for the day is my first duty in the morning. Then I attend to my house and garden. My biggest hobbies are flowers and human beings. There is something interesting in everybody if you can get at them—the Chinaman, the butcher, the baker, they are all interesting. And life itself is so interesting that one can't help being jolly, though there is the sad, pathetic side. But the little things of the home life keep you from feeling sad and despondent.

"I have been surrounded with books ever since I had to climb up on to the bookcase as a girl, to reach the books I wanted. My own very precious books about women and social questions are kept packed away in my private room.

"Joan of Arc, Florence Nightingale, Grace Darling, Lady Godiva, Charlotte Corday are my human inspirations. Next to John Stuart Mill, or I might say equal to him, comes Mazzini. They have both been splendidly on the side of women.

"Yes, I am very fond of poetry and art—more so than of music. My mother used to read Shakespeare to us when little things, before I could read. She always left some part unfinished till the next day, and it made us think a lot in the interval. Andersen's 'Fairy Tales' were given to me when ten years old, and I love them still."

GEORGE TAYLOR, 'THE QUEST OF THE AUSTRALIAN GIRL'
A.A.A.: All About Australians
1 February 1907

Some one once remarked that he did not care who made the laws of his country so long as he made its songs.

Similarly C. Dana Gibson the Great American Artist and the limner of the world famous Gibson-Girl may have remarked that he cared not what cartoonist molded the politics of his country so long as he drew its women.

The influence of an artist is unquestionably immense. A great statesman remarked that "treaties between nations may be made by Cabinet Ministers, but it rested with those who had the ear and, still better, the eye of the public, to make them effective;" hence the artist holds a power which may be as wide spread as the limits of postal communication and as long-lived as the perishability of the medium upon which the picture in painted.

It is erroneous to say that the artist creates. He simply takes what appears to the outsider as "the matter of fact" and he clothes it with his own personality. He revivifies the idea and re-echoes it with all the glory his soul is capable of expressing.

The beautiful, homely and lovable English girl, immortalized by Du Maurier in "Punch" didn't materially exist. He took the type nearest to his ideal, and clothed it with some of the beauty of his own spirit and the resultant figure reflects the ego of its adapter. Therefore in considering the artists whose typical "girls" are famous, we can discern therein that after all, they are but a reflex of their own natures.

When one considers that artists can thus build up entities that are embraced as national ideals, can one say the power of the artist is in any way over estimated?

Though Dana Gibson's tall, athletic, graceful conception appealed to his fellow Americans as the ideal American girl, yet Gibson simply took a type of woman, in his case the woman he loved and wedded. He draped her in all the beauty of his ideality and as he was one of the few mortals who could realize for others the heights to which his soul reached, his nation saw the result and admired. The men applauded and the women, ever imitative, began to copy her dress, her carriage, grace, and, I am sure, the beauty of soul underlying the loveliness; so we find to-day the Gibson Girl in society, in the theatre, and round the world generally as a distinct type; and without a doubt the coming American generation will benefit from this imitation of the artist's ideal in the growth of the strong, virile, and out-door loving girl and boy that Gibson loved to depict.

Dana Gibson was fortunate in being an American. He had a country in the final stages of development, a country of variegated types, a country where the units had only just settled into solidity; and a type to imitate, to show the way to better, was being looked for as the wise men of old watched for the Star; hence its immediate popularity. If Gibson had been a German, a Russian, or had developed his ideal in an old-world nation, his girl would not be world known.

Just as America ten years ago was ripe for the creation of the American girl, so Australia to-day awaits the realization of the Australian girl. We have conditions similar to America, but of a more acute type. A young country in which the elements of population are not so variegated as the American, we are not so hybrid, the general racial tone of the Australian nation being purer and more civilized, not only from the fact that it is newer in history, but so far, we have held to racial purity; and the foreign element so manifest in America is not so apparent here.

The Australian girl type then should rise higher in ideality than any other, and as the units of our population have ceased to simmer, and we have grown into nationality, it is about time Australia got its "girl."

Like Jason in his quest of the golden fleece, I will sally forth and enquire of the artists if she has yet arrived. Of the Australian artists whose clever pencils depict girl types, may be mentioned Messrs. Fred Leist, D.H. Souter, Alex. Sass, Norman Lindsay, Minns, Spence, Cotton, Shelden, Miss Ethel Wood, and Miss Mabelle Edmonds.

I will endeavor to introduce their "girls" to you, and you can judge how far they reach the standard of your ideality.

Mr. Fred Leist is by nature fond of open-air life, free and merry in all his methods and optimistic to a degree, hence his "best" girl is a wild, frolicsome, happy hearted damsel, never at her happiest unless she is out of doors, happier still if she has left her hat at home, and in the seventh heaven of delight if a sharp breeze is tossing her tresses about. If she is in love, she is of that clinging, trustful nature that we so often see—"on the stage." She is ubiquitous, can bare her arms and milk the cows, and later on parade before you dressed in a neat, but quiet style; but the same jovial, happy-go-lucky face smiles at you ever.

A rustle of skirts—a shiver of silk—and the Souter girl bounces in. She doesn't want an introduction. Bold, dashing and devil-may-care, she juggles with hearts as easy as kissing her hand. But as they are only cynical old fossils and fashionable prize-fighters, who fall under her spell, it doesn't matter so much. She dresses weeks ahead of the fashions, and has remarkably good taste in clothes, evidently selecting the most original and expensive things in the shop—and—she puts them on with a pitchfork. The Souter girl is not wicked at heart—it being my private belief that she was seriously in love long years ago—and no doubt being disappointed, henceforth treated hearts simply as pawns in the game. But she doesn't care while her hair is black, her maxim being "Eat, drink and be merry, for to-morrow we 'dye.'" I'm afraid the Souter girl will end badly unless she meets her first lover, and satisfactory explanations follow.

Mr. Souter personally is a phlegmatic, hard-headed man of the world—cynical, ever optimistic and independent of criticism. He puts his own value on friendship and other things, and is ever generous and delightfully versatile.

A timid, apologetic cough at the door, and Mr. Norman Lindsay peeps in.

Personally he is a loveable young genius, with a heart bubbling over with optimism. He lives at express speed to enjoy every atom of his existence. Nerves working overtime, he fires his words at you like a "maxim"; good-natured to a degree, and with eyes sparkling with very joy that it is real good and jolly to be alive, he introduces his "girl."

She is young, fullblooded, ever ready for him. She dances and trips through her life, careless and merry. She is the type of girl the men call a "jolly" sort, and the woman "a forward young minx," and doesn't she enjoy life! She is something of a tomboy, too, and romps with the other sex in a general, sisterly fashion. She is a frolicsome, happy-go-lucky Trilby, and should marry early. I sometimes think that Lindsay's "girl" was once the Souter "girl," but that was long ago,

COLONIAL TYPES: THE AUSTRALIAN GIRL

before she was disappointed in love, and long before she grew cynical and cruel, and flirted with baldheaded reprobates and aforesaid society pugilists.

The type of girl Alex. Sass presents is a buxom, full-busted young lady, with eyes like a startled deer. She always appears as if she was surprised to see things as they are, but that is only make-believe. I often fancy she is employed in her business hours as a barmaid at some high class hotel. She is too dainty and regal for the threepenny bars, and will only be found where queenly dignity is necessary to make the sixpenny drink twice the value of the same liquor served by a less lady-like individual.

She eventually marries a squatter and lives happily ever after.

Mr. Sass personally is of a free and easy-going nature, optimistic, never worrying, and always looking on the bright side of things.

The girl B.E. Minns delights to depict is a simple young person, who always appears to be a young mother in the early years of married life—before "the marriage lines" show in wrinkles on her fair brow. She, however, is lately becoming very English, a sort of sister to Lewis Baumer's "English girl." Minns, who is at present in England, would no doubt, if he returned, evolve a distinct Australian type, as he has all the gracefulness and experience.

Mr. Percy Spence, prior to leaving for England some years ago, was first favorite for finding and drawing the Australian girl. But his stay in fashionable English circles, coupled with his sensitive nature, has evolved a damsel of the "wilo-waly" type.

The "Spence" girl is pretty, but delicate and anaemic. Too sickly to fall in love with anything alive, her chief joy is to sit about and look nice.

The "Spence" girl will eventually die an old maid, as live men do not care to mate with a piece of female confectionery.

Mr. Spence personally is a dainty, well-groomed gentleman. His daintiness permeates all his work, so that little of it betokens any vigor. If he depicts a jackaroo dashing through the scrub the horse will always canter gracefully, and the jackaroo will undoubtedly have hair parted in the centre, his moustache nicely curled with just the requisite amount of brilliantine thereon.

In a wild, erratic dream I once imagined Spence's jackaroo married to the "Spence" girl, but the combination was too humorous.

A new type of girl has been peering at us during the last few years. Her adaptor, H. Cotton, being a matter-of-fact young man, whose style, though rather wiry just at present, presents a distinct original. His "girl" is a cheeky party always, well dressed in a starched linen, but soulless. I wager she is a desperate flirt, but flirts simply for the same reason the small boy pulls the wings off the fly before casting it back into the world.

I came across a clever girl sketch by a promising young artist—Selden—a merry, optimistic young man, whose type of girl seems to reflect his merry Bohemian temperament.

And now we come to a peculiar anomaly in art. In older worlds the girl-artists in black and white are rare. In England, with its teeming millions, only two have risen any height above the ruck, Hilda Cowham and Florence Upton. In America the same scarcity exists, but in Australia we find the lady artists in the arena, shoulder to shoulder with their brother artists. Of the girl artists of note who black and white in Australia are Miss Alice Muskett, Ruby Lindsay, Mabelle Edmonds, Ethel Wood, Miss Nichols, Beryl Reid, and Ida Rentoul.

Of the above, Misses Muskett, Nichols and Rentoul do not evolve "girl types." Miss Lindsay has not yet struck a distinct type, but Misses Wood and Edmonds have original types out of which the desired ideal may develop.

Miss Edmonds' "girl" is a cheeky, flirty maiden, ever making love and meaning it. She is the opposite to the "Souter" girl, being as sweet and true as the latter is cynical and cold-hearted. Miss Edmonds' "girl" will die happy. In her dashing flight through the days she will attract a host of moths, and will have the sense to lift one out of the pack who will keep her nicely dressed, and will let her wear gowns that will make that stuck-up "Spence girl" green with envy.

The girl type that carries Ethel Wood's name is the work of a young, happy little lady, whose entry into art though recent, is most promising. The "E. Woods' girl," or, I should say, "woman," has a heart; you can see it in her face; but, unlike all other types, she doesn't flirt. She is sensible, and likes a joke occasionally, but please don't make her laugh too much; she looks more soulful if her lips are locked. With the rapid progress Miss Wood is making in her art, I can safely predict that with the freedom of drawing experience will give her, this young lady will without doubt make a distinct hit with her girl type, and it would not be surprising if the ideal type developed under her pen.

Of the other Australian artists who draw girls Lionel Lindsay's type is not yet distinct, and the McCrae "girl" is not yet an entity.

I am anxious to see the McCrae "girl." He has the requisite temperament, originality and the poetic instinct to evolve a distinct type, and some fine day, when his clever condensed cartoonlets have grown to full pages, he may find a corner from which the McCrae "girl" will make her first peep.

The Selden "girl" is of somewhat recent creation. A characteristic sample is reproduced herewith, but as the girl is of the pink-and-white variety much of the effect is lost when the impression is conveyed in cold black. Selden is a young artist who wears an everlasting smile, and the smile shines through his work.

Such are the girls our artists are developing, and as to any evolving into a national type, the future only can reveal.

When the Australian "girl" does arrive—when she steps on the threshold of our nationality, and holds aloft the wreath for her conqueror, from what I know of the Australian "boy" she will find no lack of enthusiastic champions.

COLONIAL TYPES: THE AUSTRALIAN GIRL

The Leist Girl.

BEATRIX TRACY, 'THE GIRL IN WAITING'
Lone Hand
1 June 1908

Said the Editor: "Now, the Waitress and the Barmaid! Those ladies require attention!"

"They'd prefer it from a masculine source, Mr. Editor!"

"Perhaps, yes. But—to your exploring work!"

And I fared again into the wilderness—this time as a seeker for a situation as a waiting-maid. Under the general term "waitress" are grouped several types of worker—from the fashionable barmaid down to the slattern who carries dishes in the fried-fish shop of some greasy Levantine. At her lowest, the lot of the waitress is far beneath that of the poorest domestic servant; at her highest, she shares the meretricious glories of the chorus-girl. I cannot pretend to have enjoyed personal experience of all the several degrees. For one thing, it would have taken too long to acquire it. Then one avenue of industry was blocked by the fact that I lacked the qualifications of a successful bar-tender; for yet another, I knew there would be cockroaches in the Levantine kitchen (and before a floppety cockroach I am weak like a swaddled baby, and defenseless, and could never have rescued the fish from its possession). To be definite, my experience was limited to a tea-room, and a couple of days in a quiet city hotel of a fair average type. What I learned of other branches of this industry was the result of inquiry.

In searching for employment on the basis of being an inexperienced and poverty-stricken girl, I found that I had no hope of getting an enviable situation, either as a bar or café maid. The better restaurants and hotels are inundated with applications from women who have good references, and who are circumstanced so that they can wait for a congenial engagement. The girl who must either earn a living wage or starve, has to take deplorable chances of being sweated or demoralized in the waitress positions that are available at short notice. Short of testimonials as to efficiency, marked comeliness is the strongest recommendation one can offer an enterprising employer of waitresses.

But, somehow, great beauty and want seldom go together, so few women can avail themselves of that adventitious aid to industrial employment.

I went the rounds of Sydney tea-rooms and had my name noted by two or three with a view to future consideration. At length I was engaged by the proprietor of a large catering business, and placed in one of his most popular shops. It struck me that at least one thing promised well for the tea-room girl. Her male employer was courteous to her femininity, which is not the case in many braches of female industry. With further knowledge of her lot, I retained my first favorable impressions, and personally found "waitressing" a tolerable way of earning two-thirds of a livelihood.

It goes without saying that the women who adopt café work reflect their employers. In a large establishment run by a company, or by a business man, the workers will be the normal congregation of "middle-class" girls—some, ambitious for diversions beyond their purses and their resources, who are inclined to be indiscreet; some who are not desirable in any intimate regard; and a big majority who are hard-working, matter-of-fact creatures, taking the world and its trials in courageous spirit, and going their respective ways without ostentation. In a feeding-shop run by some coarse, old woman, one will find girls picked out of adjoining alleys. In tea-rooms presided over by a superacilious dame, who has a grudge against the universe because she has had to reconcile her "good-breeding" with hard work, one will encounter well-connected young women, or, at least, those who pretend to be so. Therefore, a woman wishing to be a waitress should pick her wage-payer with care—if her capital will permit of self-consideration—for her employer will strike the keynote for her associates.

The experience and wages gained by workers in restaurants which are uncompromisingly business-like are preferable to any other. The treatment of the girls is framed upon a set of moderately equitable rules; though, of course, some unfair advantages always remain with the employer. Their hours are settled quantities; and the supervision of the employee's character, while close and protective in most cases, has none of the insult of espionage. This latter is a point which liked me. In the tea-room where I worked, there were regulations—some of them quite subtle—which saved the girls from their own follies, and from misconceptions on the part of male customers. A waitress was not allowed to enter into conversation with patrons, nor stand in close attendance upon any one person. She was forbidden to wear jewellery, which prevented one or two girls at least from flaunting signs of inconsistent luxury. All were uniformly dressed—which was an incentive to each one to make the best of her appearance, to cultivate an amiable manner, and develop a personality. And they were under the direct control of a manageress—to my knowledge a kindly woman who found food for pride in the respectability and contentment of her corps.

My own engagement was as an afternoon waitress; my hours from 3 o'clock till 7; my wages 12S. weekly and my evening meal each day. I was quite innocent of any previous practice in such work, so I considered this a just payment for the hours. I learned that a woman working 54 hours a week could earn close up to a sovereign, sometimes more. In some rooms they pay a minimum salary of 9S., and give 6d. in the £ commission on the orders taken. If a woman is popular, and has three or four tables in her charge, this arrangement may bring her in anything up to 10S. or 15S. a week in addition to her wages. The premium system is good both for employer and employee. It ensures energetic service on the one hand, and imposes a sense of self-responsibility on the other, which things tend to make their common relations satisfactory. A woman who is engaged to wait only during luncheon time—about two-and-a-half hours—will get from 5S. to 7S. a week. This payment is insufficient, I think; although the hours leave her an opportunity to supplement it.

These rates are usual only in the largest and best-conducted food-shops. In the small tea-rooms one finds most reprehensible sweating the rule, and censurable conduct the result very often. The eating den where the cockroach dwells, to dispute his hash with the hungry stevedore, is the place where one finds the nadir of the waitress type. She is a drab, undistinguished by any deftness or other merit as an attendant, and is much worse situated than she would be as a servant in a private house. She has all the hardships, without the comforts, of domestic service, and may consider herself lucky if she is paid 8S. a week. The one recompense for the squalor and dirtiness of such employment is the nightly liberty it allows, and the intercourse with a passing crowd in the day time.

Since capable waitresses are paid an average of from 15S. to 18S., and may be "tipped" to the extent of several further shillings per week, the wage-scale of the upper grades of the industry cannot be condemned very fiercely. But the minimum wage should be raised, and the number of daily working hours limited to not more than eight. (Of this I shall speak later. But is an important objection to nearly all branches of waiting-work.)

As to my own career as a waitress, I'm rather proud of it. After a few hours I learned to slide a trayful of crockery on to a table without making a deafening noise. During the whole period I never broke a plate, and I called for "one strong tea, one bread-and-butter" in the tones of a patriot evoking salvation for her country. My first day I was given into the charge of a senior girl. I just took orders, and served them. She made out the dockets, and I was not bothered with that part of my business until I was thoroughly at ease in the remainder.

The girls had a dressing-room to themselves, where they changed into their uniforms from street clothes. There it was one got in touch with them. In the tea-rooms they were too preoccupied with their work. On the whole, they were very nice to each other—helpful in practical ways, sympathetic and cheerful. As a class, I think they were more fraternal, "chummy" girls than any others I have come in contact with during my explorations. Their attitude to one another was in contradistinction to that they adopted towards women customers. To work beside a woman breeds tolerance in her neighbor; to work for one breeds resentment, it would appear.

The general sentiment amongst waitresses is a preference for doing service to men. One girl voiced it rather exaggeratedly, saying: "I'd rather be 'slushy' in a man's house than companion to a woman—men treat you better." I fancy this idea is nourished by knowledge to some extent. Men are less apt to make trouble and labor [sic] for waitresses and domestics than are the majority of women. But on that point something later.

Café work is bright. It is not exciting. Beyond the conditions of the workers and the peculiarities of a few customers, there is little to be said concerning it. Perhaps my place was exceptionally placid. During my tenure of it, everyone and everything was refreshingly commonplace, yet all was interesting.

COLONIAL TYPES: THE AUSTRALIAN GIRL

The odds and ends of conversation that assailed one's ears were entertaining. Going from one table to another, a phrase of amorous cooing might be drowned in an argument about a grocer's bill between some plump pair of housewives close by. Men came in and sat over pots of untouched tea for long whiles, urgently discussing subjects that they treated as secrets.

Deep schemes are hatched in the shallow stream of a tea-room, I imagine. Youths of the "young man about town" kind lounged in after hours. They were the people who gave me most bother. Sometimes it was necessary to be very positive in discouragement of proffered familiarity to secure anything like polite conduct. They seemed to think that the sixpences which paid for their tea and scones bought also the waitress's submission to their pitiable efforts in badinage, and their burlesque sentimentality.

Occasionally one saw an appealing evidence of devotion shown by a customer to a girl-in-waiting. A wan man, with a straggling yellow beard, used to come in two or three times a day, always to sit at the same table. So infatuated was he with the damsel who served him that once he ate the paper serviette which accompanied his meat-pie. He poured Worcestershire sauce over both, and munched the horrid combination while he devoured her with his blinded eyes.

While most of the trials come from the customer, so do the rewards. It is very gratifying to see the satisfaction of unprejudiced persons with one's labors [sic]. The half-friendly smiles of a pleased diner, and his or her return to one's table, are trifles which go towards making work a pastime. After all, a love of approbation is the leading characteristic of women. (That women seldom yield praise freely to their sisters may be one reason for the common objection to serving them. Men are prodigal of it.)

The waitress is not an ill-used young woman, I should say. She is fed well; and if she gets three meals a day, and earns about 15S. a week, she can be described as self-supporting. If her work does keep her indoors all day, it does not deprive her of exercise, and it does not impose any malignant strain upon her strength, if she is ordinarily strong.

If it is necessary that there should be occupations for young women outside their homes, waiting, next to domestic help, seems one of the most desirable. There is no particular temptation. (Certainly a waitress meets many men, has many chances to make irregular friendships; but nowadays she has almost as good—or bad—opportunities without going into any employment. And a sensible girl should find it easy to arrive at a fair standard of valuation of herself in the study of the mixed stream which flows through a big restaurant.)

A pleasant feature in the waitress's life is the good diet she can enjoy. Good meals mitigate the dangers of constant work, and maintain self-respect and cheeriness to an extent that can only be appreciated by those who have gone hungry. With some reforms, the waitress can be allowed to stand as a tolerable woman industrial. Her calling is not unsuited to her femininity; it gives her some degree of independence, and it does not interfere seriously with her chances of matrimony, which is the most vital consideration of all.

FLORENCE YOUNG, 'THE AUSTRALIAN CHORUS-GIRL'
Lone Hand
1 June 1908

If I had to select an Australian type of girl who is as representative of the country as the Gibson girl is of America, I think I should point to the chorus-girl. And why not? She is bright, *chic*, vivacious, pretty, and lady-like. What more do you want?

Thank goodness the time has gone by when to be a chorus-girl was to be—oh, well, condemned. Nowadays, the chorus-girls—or the ladies of the chorus, if you please—are a much better class all round then [sic] they used to be a few years ago. If they are not, what has become of the stage-door Johnny? That beautiful specimen of humanity has beaten the Australian aborigines by about three generations in the race for extinction. What has become of dear old Cholly or Bertie, who would spend half of his week's allowance to take a ballerina to supper, who carried a bouquet of flowers to the stage door without fear of being accused of aesthetic tendencies, and whose home was a hansom cab? He has gone—not because mankind has changed, but because stage girls have been growing more self-respecting, and they have learned the consequences of being seen in the society of men of that type.

There is another reason. A great deal more is demanded of the chorus-girl today than mere physical attractiveness. She must study singing, acting, dancing, and stage deportment. That keeps her busy, and to be busy is to be out of mischief. Nearly every chorus-girl has some principal to understudy, or—if she really means to succeed in the profession—she is studying privately. That gives her a definite existence, and any girl blessed with an object in life becomes a better woman than the pampered and useless dolls of society. Nearly every mail brings me letters from girls who want to go on stage. Most of them excuse themselves for writing, by saying that their friends all think they ought to be on the stage, and have advised them to write to me. It reminds me of an American humorism.

"Is she a pretty girl?"

"Is she? Why, even her own mother thinks she is pretty."

And so in the case of many of these young ladies; even their own mothers think they can act, which is, of course, the last word of recommendation. There is also another class, who confide to me the dark and dreadful secret that they were born for the stage, but their cruel parents want them to stay at home and cook. Shall they stay at home and cook? Never! So they would like to meet me, and would I hear their voice, and advise them what to do? Fortunately, I have an easy reply, since nearly every Tuesday, at 1 o'clock, a trial of stage aspirants takes place at Her Majesty's Theatre, and all I can do, except in special cases, is to notify them to be there. But who—oh! ye national testimonialists—is going to reimburse me for all those postage stamps?

These voice trials are both interesting and amusing. Mr. J.C. Williamson has made it a rule never to refuse anyone a hearing, and to treat everyone alike. So at the fatal hour of 1 o'clock the stage director takes his seat near the footlights, attended by a clerk with a notebook, in which the names of the aspirants are enrolled. A piano is on the stage, and an accompanist in attendance. One by one the aspirants are admitted. There is no ceremony, no trouble, no embarrassment. The caller walks up to the piano, hands her music to the accompanist, and sings. Sometimes the sound might be better described as a shriek, a howl, a yell, or a sob of despair. And at others, it might be the crude and untutored expression of a soul filled with beautiful music. Sometimes, though rarely, it is a "discovery." The stage director is brief and decisive with those in the former category. A polite intimation that the lady will not suit, a hurried "good-day" and she disappears—to go home, let us hope, and lend some practical aid to the solution of the domestic service problem.

But she of the Voice, crude and undeveloped though it be, gets other treatment. Her name and address is taken and she is given the best possible advice. If she is sufficiently trained a vacancy will be found for her at the earliest opportunity. The rest is with herself. But no real talent ever passes by unnoticed or unaided. Mr. Williamson attends many of these trials and takes the greatest interest in them. He has the reputation of being the keenest judge of a voice in Australia. Our girls should appreciate this opportunity, for I am sure there is no better medium for exploiting talent in the world. Of course many girls go away dissatisfied with the test. They blame the accompanist, or complain of distracting influences. But the born artist takes no heed of these things. You could turn on the stage thunder, but what would the true nightingale care if she was determined to be heard?

Not only must the voice be passable, but a girl cannot be engaged for the chorus if she lacks appearance, or if her carriage is impossible. These things are noted the moment she enters the door, and an experienced eye can tell at once whether she is suitable or adaptable in those respects.

It goes without saying that a chorus-girl must work hard and study if she wishes to succeed, but she has many compensations. In the first place, she can travel and see her native land from end to end, which is an experience worth much to any woman. In her interludes she should be able to find some agreeable leisure. Again, there is no occupation which offers young girls such high rewards. The average chorus-girl gets a considerably larger salary than the best paid lady-stenographer, and about twice as much as the ordinary shop-assistant. Then she has a chance to earn more money than the most successful women in any other professions, even allowing for the exaggeration of artists' salaries. For instance, a present favorite, who was a chorus-girl six years ago, is earning £10 per week to-day, and there are many other examples, in my own knowledge, of ambitious girls who have, in the course of a brief period, risen from the ranks to make contracts on terms which the average civil servant, country bank manager, head law clerk or other men in responsible positions would consider the realization of all their hopes.

How do our chorus-girls compare with the English? Well, I reckon they could easily win four out of five test matches. A better comparison would be with the Americans, who are treated like goods in the shop-window of an Italian fruit-vendor—the rosiest peaches in the front row.

The much-vaunted American girl might have been a new species of humanity found in the North Pole if we didn't know her origin. In other words, she looks as though a sculptor had been working on an iceberg. Superciliousness and self-consciousness are kept working overtime with a certain type of American show girl. But many of them certainly are beautiful, and if they seem as they do, it is only because they are placed on too high a pedestal. The successful New York chorus-girl, for instance, has figured prominently in some notorious way in the daily press, and has her pictures continually published in leading papers and magazines. Her doings are chronicled as much, almost, as those of people who earn their livings by their cleverness, and she is sometimes paid out of all proportion to her capabilities. I knew of one girl in a leading burlesque house who received £15 a week to walk on in tights, because it was considered she had an exceptional figure. Many of these girls lead lives as high as their native skyscrapers, and never strive for artistic success.

How much sweeter, then, are our Australian girls, with their bright, ingenuous dispositions! The atmosphere of the stage in this country is so much purer than it is in the older world that no mothers need fear for the welfare of their daughters—at least, so far as theatre influences are concerned. Indeed, I know of no manner of life in which a girl of natural exuberance of spirits, and gifted with the magnetic power to please, can live so well as upon the Australian stage to-day.

D.H. SOUTER, 'THE AUSTRALIAN GIRL'
Lone Hand
February 1912

Over nineteen hundred years ago Julius Cæsar remarked that "the crowd in the Appian Way never grew any older." If the late eminent potentate were in a position to review our Australian streets to-day, he would say the same thing about the Australian Girl.

The Australian Girl is a delightful subject, and one worthy of something more than mere serious study. A philosophic poet named Pope asserted that "the noblest study of mankind is man"; but as he predeceased the discovery of the Australian continent by something like forty

COLONIAL TYPES: THE AUSTRALIAN GIRL

years, we will acquit him of the slight which at first glance he seems to cast upon the majority of our Australian womanhood.

Speaking as one who, in the face of almost insuperable obstacles, has yet been able to devote considerable attention to this entrancing subject, I can affirm it to be a most absorbing one, and it is a matter of life-long regret to me that I have never had the means nor the opportunity to grasp more than its chief details.

The age of the Australian Girl is somewhere between eighteen and eight and twenty. Sometimes she stresses this limit, but she never looks a day older or a day younger than the particular age which she deems to go best with her bust measurement or the cast of her complexion. That she occasionally assists Nature to preserve those charms with which she was originally dowered is but one more virtue to be laid to her credit; and that she now and then paints the lily is but another indication of her desire to please. And where is the man who does not feel flattered by the delicate attention?

Compared with her sisters of other parts of the globe, the Australian Girl has a particular claim on our affections because of her immediate and unfailing proximity. To use a vulgar colloquialism, she is "on the spot." One has only to step outside his own door to find her slamming the gate of the adjacent cottage; she sits next to you in the tram, opposite you at the lunch table, rubs shoulders with you in the street, swims with you in the same breaker, and when—but that's another story.

She walks with a freer step, talks with a wider intelligence, and meets you on a more level plane of equality than the girl born and bred under conditions less kindly than those obtaining in Australia. At election time she records her vote for the nicest candidate, irrespective of his political or other convictions; and holds that oblique feet, or a preposterous taste in neckties, should shut the door of public life on a man for ever. If you offer her your seat in the tram she will accept it as her right without a murmur, or refuse it with a delightful smile and an explanation that she is only going as far as the next corner, and prefers to stand, anyhow. She is perfectly oblivious of the fact that her dressmaker has made it impossible for her to catch on to the roof straps, and that, in consequence of the absence of sufficient means of physical support, she is stepping all over your feet, and her curves are swaying up and down the compartment in a way that makes it impossible for you to read your newspaper. She plays tennis; before she was a girl she played hockey. When she plays golf she ceases to be a girl, and therefore does not come within the scope of the present enquiry. She is not ashamed of her bifidate construction, and since tight skirts have been in vogue not one serious note of censure has been passed on the Tramway Commissioners.

In many respects she is a menace to public safety. The soft light in her eyes, the ruddy lusciousness of her lips, the audacious contour of her chin, and the appealing whiteness of the nape of her neck speak volumes for the firm hold which the majority of men keep on their emotions. Even in her last stage of girlhood she abates no jot of her attractiveness. Her charms merely mature. She no longer pursues nor invites pursuit, but, confident in the fullness of her powers, she lifts a languid eyelid and marks you for her own.

This year she is much slimmer than last; also more attractive. The female form divine being long accorded Nature's masterpiece, whatever extraneous drapery was hung on it served only to conceal its beauty. Surely it was some jealous Turk who invented the hoop skirt, or an envious harridan who designed the poke bonnet and the impervious veil. Sweet woman, ever amenable to flattery, accepted these monstrosities as necessary adjuncts to her safety until her inherent artistry taught her the half-concealment that was more enticing than the open allurement, and, playing on our vanity, piquing our curiosity, she discovered the fatal effect of the fleeting glimpse, the desirability of the seemingly unattainable, and the impossibility of man to do without what he believes he cannot have.

I have read with interest the press interviews of many returned Australians. They all finish like this:—

"And now—how do you find Australia?"

"The best on earth. I am glad I went away, because I am so glad to be back to it again."

For "it" read "her"; for "her" understand some Australian Girl, and you won't be far from the true genesis of the sentiment.

PART 9

Race and the Frontier
KEN GELDER & RACHAEL WEAVER

'On the Civilisation of the Aborigines', *South Australian Magazine*, February 1843
353

'The Chinese Puzzle', *Melbourne Monthly Magazine*, May 1855
354

Thomas McCombie, 'The History of Victoria' (extract), *Illustrated Journal of Australasia*, February 1858
357

'Yarns by the Camp Fire II', *Colonial Monthly*, November 1869
360

Ernest Favenc, 'The Attack on Barrow Creek', *Sydney Mail*, 14 May 1881
362

John Mackie, 'In the Far North', *Sydney Quarterly Magazine*, February 1885
363

W.L. Lumley, 'The Crimson Thread of Brotherhood', *Pacific Quarterly*, August 1890
369

'Black Detectives', *Yabba*, 17 January 1900
373

'Ganesha' (Louis Esson), 'Round the Corner', *Lone Hand*, 1 December 1908
374

Unsigned, 'Velly Good Lettucee', *Centennial Magazine*, January 1889
379

9

Race and the Frontier
KEN GELDER & RACHAEL WEAVER

THE COLONIAL JOURNALS OFTEN REFLECTED carefully on questions of race; at the same time, they casually reproduced the virulent kinds of racism that were pervasive right across the settler colonies. A whole range of questions and dispositions come into play here: to do with the impact of colonial settlement on Aboriginal people, the role of government policy and the law, the 'civilising' agendas of Christian missions, the intellectualisation of racial categories (under the growing influence of evolutionary anthropology), the prevailing opinions about importing labour from elsewhere, and the way settler colonies might manage or respond to increasingly diverse immigrant populations. Some colonial journals were more progressive and humanitarian than others as far as these questions are concerned, but there is never any consistency here. Coming in the wake of the global abolition of slavery, settlement in Australia nevertheless utterly relied on the legitimation of forced labour: convict gangs, indentured workers from the Pacific Islands, and so on. And the imperative to 'civilise' Aboriginal people only helped to consolidate the discourses that characterised them as 'savage' and destined for extinction. Indeed, as Ian J. McNiven and Lynette Russell note, 'the nineteenth century heralded a new era for discourses of savagery as Aboriginal Australians superseded Native Americans as exemplars of primordial man'.[1] Patrick Brantlinger has neatly expressed the way that even progressive views on race were always enmeshed in the assumptions and biases of their times: 'humanitarians', he writes, 'could be both abolitionists and racists'.[2] The full range of these contradictions is played out right across the colonial journals and across the various genres of writing they invest in, from chronicles of frontier violence and adventure to panoramic surveys of racial diversity in the colonial metropolis.

James Allen and Thomas Young Cotter's *South Australian Magazine* (July 1841 – November 1843) was an early attempt to produce a journal that would speak to the conditions of the new colony and influence its future development. The anonymously authored article, 'On the Civilisation of the Aborigines', is especially interesting here because it is a direct response to what it perceives as the colonial government's failure to protect its citizens against Aboriginal attacks. The focus here is Port Lincoln, on the western frontier, where the recent death of a white settler had led to escalating violence – quickly transforming the settlement into 'a shattered community'.³ For this article, the 'civilisation' of Aboriginal people is therefore a matter of urgency. It looks as if its author has a Christian, humanitarian stake in all this, but his arguments are entirely guided by colonial self-interest, a stark recognition that Aboriginals must adopt settler lifestyles ('to resign the right of private vengeance – to respect the laws – to learn to depend on their own industry for their maintenance') in order for settlement itself to proceed unencumbered. We have also reproduced an extract from Thomas McCombie's 'The History of Victoria' in this part, first published in the *Illustrated Journal of Australasia* in February 1858. McCombie was a squatter, journalist and novelist who was intensely interested in the processes of colonisation and the treatment of Aboriginal people. The extract here is another response to violent contact between Aboriginals and settlers, in northern Victoria: where the spearing of a young pastoralist, Andrew Beveridge, leads to the arrest of two Aboriginal men and their trial and execution in Melbourne. McCombie brings a similar kind of Christian, humanitarian understanding to these events, deliriously imagining the religious conversion of the two men taking place as they move out of incarceration and towards their deaths. But he also reproduces the narrative tropes of colonial adventure fiction as he describes settlers in the bush under siege from 'the most daring and blood-thirsty tribe in the colony'.

The colonial journals published a lot of short narrative sketches of colonial frontier experience, all of which worked to consolidate a set of generic conventions that enabled extreme forms of racism to flow freely. 'Yarns by the Camp Fire II' is one of a series of reminiscences of bush life published in Marcus Clarke's *Colonial Monthly* in late 1869. By this time, violent encounters with Aboriginal people are already subsumed into tales of adventure that brutally express settler triumphalism. The most famous (or notorious) author of this kind of Australian story is Ernest Favenc, an explorer, bush worker and journalist who wrote for a number of colonial journals, including the *Bulletin*, the *Australian Town and Country Journal*, the *Queenslander*, and *Cosmos*. His short article 'The Attack on Barrow Creek', published in the *Sydney Mail* in May 1881, turns back to an Aboriginal raid on an isolated telegraph station seven years earlier, which led to violent reprisals. Amanda Nettlebeck and Robert Foster describe these events in their book, *In the Name of the Law: William Willshire and the Policing of the Australian Frontier* (2007), reading the attack as a violent preamble to a fledgling colonial modernity: 'Central Australia was, in that historical moment, a space on the threshold of a radical change that had not quite arrived. The drama of the Barrow Creek story lies in the contradictions of a belated frontier which was still in the making'.⁴ Favenc, however, has none of McCombie's faith in Christianity's 'civilising' mission; in keeping with the masculine logic of colonial adventure fiction, he invests instead in a future that is punitive and disciplinary. Significantly, both 'Yarns by the Camp

Fire II' and Favenc's 'The Attack on Barrow Creek' also draw attention to the precarious role of those young Aboriginal men who were co-opted to protect settler life and property. Colonial authorities had used Aboriginal trackers since the 1830s, and native police corps were established in the colonies in the 1840s and 1850s. By the time we get to the turn of the century, the derisively named journal *Yabba* could talk about 'Black Detectives'. This short article from 1900 places its Aboriginal trackers entirely in the service of the colony, as they search for the murderers of a stockrider carrying a large amount of his station owner's money. The narrative ends with a kind of late colonial inversion of McCombie's account, its Aboriginal trackers assimilated into the policing and protection of settler interests – but still subject to a belated racist system of classification in terms of speech, natural instinct, etc.

The short-lived *Melbourne Monthly Magazine* (May–November 1855) wrote enthusiastically about the commercial prosperity of the city in the wake of the Victorian gold rush, its interest in the economic life of the colony unfolding alongside an investment in local literary production (serialised stories about emigration, the bush, and so on) and the development of key cultural institutions (such as the public library). The unsigned article 'The Chinese Puzzle' is a lively, satirical reaction to colonial panic over the rapid growth in Chinese immigration in the early 1850s. It lampoons a series of sensationalised newspaper reports about Chinese immorality, but it also responds to debates about the need for legislation and taxes to limit the number of new arrivals. 'They have not a weapon amongst them', the article dryly observes; 'nevertheless they have terrified us'. Written not long after the Eureka Stockade, the question of what makes a good colonial citizen – who is able to assimilate into the colonial economy, who can contribute, who can improve the fortunes of the colony – is something this article wonders about in the framework of deep racial and religious divisions. Much later on, in 1890, the bookseller E. W. Cole published the *Pacific Quarterly* (August 1890), a journal that only lasted for one issue, with contributions by Alexander Sutherland and W. N. Pratt, among others. W. M. Lumley's wonderfully titled 'The Crimson Thread of Brotherhood' reminded colonial readers that 'civilisation' wasn't exclusive to the West and argued that Australians need to develop a more enlightened, educated outlook towards the Chinese and other Asian nations in the region. This is a spirited call for a colonial cosmopolitanism, infused with a poetic idealism that sees Lumley quoting enthusiastically from his own work ('Australia's Springtime' was later published in *The Coo-ee Reciter* in 1904). Interestingly, Cole himself went on to publish a pamphlet called *Better Side of the Chinese Character* (1905), a passionate defence of the Chinese against the hostilities and prejudices of the White Australia policies that were instituted just after Federation.

John Mackie was a boys' adventure novelist whose stories were syndicated across Australia through the regional newspapers. His article 'In the Far North', from the *Sydney Quarterly Magazine* in 1885, takes us to the edges of the colonial frontier to chronicle a place where – as he puts it – 'civilization was just in the chrysalis stage'. Here, Chinese fossickers are cast as untrustworthy, and Aboriginal people are 'villainous-looking' and threatening. Mackie returns us to the conventions of colonial adventure fiction here, also touching the Gothic as he discovers a 'white man's grave'. A group of arrivals recall 'the spectre crew in the "Ancient Mariner"' and a 'weird and ghastly' landscape evokes the work of the American artist, Elihu Vedder. This is a literary response to the frontier that looks forward, almost evangelically, to a prosperous future that will somehow mark the end of 'savagery'.

Lurid expressions of racism were often to be found in the *Lone Hand*, too, and we reproduce a particularly lively example from 'Ganesha', a pseudonym used by the prolific poet and dramatist, Louis Esson. 'Round the Corner' turns to the slums of Melbourne, another kind of frontier that seems to exist on the fringes of civilisation. For Esson, 'the call of the slums is as that of the sea and the bush'; this is a thrilling, colourful place that throws together an assortment of different ethnic types and pursuits, all of which suggest a kind of 'anarchic freedom' in which illicit activity is constantly evading the gaze of the police ('rossers'). This is a landscape that once again inspires a literary imagination, tied in this case to a long tradition of bohemian encounters with the seamier side of city life that ends up, finally, in Australia: 'Villon, Burns, Walt Whitman, Maxim Gorki, Henry Lawson', Esson writes, 'the alleys have had no want of bards'. As we will see in the next part, this view of the underbelly of metropolitan experience continually troubles those colonial commentators who invest in the progress and prosperity of the nation.

1   McNiven and Russel, *Appropriated Pasts: Indigenous People and the Colonial Culture of Archaeology*, p. 32.
2   Brantlinger, *Taming Cannibals: Race and the Victorians*, p. 54.
3   Foster and Nettlebeck, *Out of the Silence: The History and Memory of South Australia's Frontier Wars*, p. 50.
4   Foster and Nettlebeck, *In the Name of the Law: William Willshire and the Policing of the Australian Frontier*, p. 8.

'ON THE CIVILISATION OF THE ABORIGINES'
South Australian Magazine
February 1843

Until the British standard was planted on these shores, the native roamed at will through forest land and over prairie; from these he is now shut out—they are the property of the white man. Each individual had then his separate portion of territory, his exclusive title to all upon which was undisputed. Where are now his possessions?—they are usurped by the white man. Where are now the kangaroo, the emu, and the multitude of other game upon which he formerly subsisted?—they have been either killed or driven away by the white man. If, therefore, we have deprived the native of the means of procuring his subsistence after his own fashion, are we not bound to instruct him in the art of procuring it after ours? If we punish him for committing a breach of our laws, are we not bound to instruct him in the great moral principles upon which they are founded? If we curtail the enjoyments of his savage state, are we not bound to teach him the superior blessings of civilisation? There can be but one answer to these questions: we have usurped the territory of the native, and we are bound to make him the only compensation it is in our power to bestow, by imparting to him the blessings of Christian civilization. We know that there are some who think, with Mr. Baron [sic] Field, that the natives are incapable of civilization; and hence they have justified to themselves all the horrors which have been committed in the elder settlements—horrors which have exceeded even those of the slave trade. It has likewise been said, by the same authority, and upon equally just grounds, that the North American Indians are incapable of civilization; but we now know that the Choctaws have devoted a large portion of the annuity to which they are entitled from the United States, in return for some territory which was purchased from them, to the establishment of schools; and that, at one of the general councils, one thousand dollars in money and eighty cows and calves, were subscribed for the use of these schools—making the total amount of subscriptions for this object 70,000 dollars. We know, too, that the Cherokee Indians possess a substantial court-house, four circuit judges, and a printing establishment; that they have adopted the English language for all official purposes, and are said to be rapidly conforming to the laws and customs of their brethren. The question of civilization is, therefore, no longer one of mere speculation, and, as far as the poor natives of this province are concerned, we are bound at least to make the attempt; and the more so, because our better feelings are daily outraged by the exhibition of vices and diseases which the natives have acquired by the example or instruction of the Europeans, and because our flocks and herds, nay, the safety of our homesteads, and the individual members of our families, depend on the good understanding which may exist between us and them—for which there can be no security until they are taught to give up their wandering habits—to resign the right of private vengeance—to respect the laws—to learn to depend on their own industry for their maintenance—and, above all, until they acquire a knowledge of the principles of the Christian religion. A lamentable proof of this fact has been exhibited in the settlement of Port Lincoln. None could have behaved with greater general kindness and forbearance than the individuals, both masters and servants, who formed that settlement; they were ever ready to give them food or shelter when they were required, and nothing could exceed the good understanding which seemed to prevail between the two races; but to uncivilised man the present moment is of all importance—the gratification of his appetite can alone afford him pleasure—and the refusal of a favour, although from one who may have heaped daily or hourly acts of kindness upon him, and for whom he would have been willing to have sacrificed his life to have shown his gratitude, excites a deadly hatred which often nothing but the destruction of the individual giving offence can overcome—hence the destruction of so many valuable lives at Port Lincoln; and the history of that place will become that of each of our out-stations in turn, unless some steps are taken to enforce upon the aborigines the adoption of the habits and customs of civilized life.

This is a subject which has engrossed a large portion of the attention of philanthropists and Christian philosophers. The fact that, wherever modern colonization has extended, the aboriginal inhabitant has been swept from the face of the earth, has induced the governments of every British settlement to place the natives under the protection of the laws, and to enforce kindness and forbearance on the part of the whites in all their intercourse with them; and for this purpose officers, called protectors, have been appointed;—but this alone has been found totally insufficient for the purpose. At some out-station, far from the eye of the protector, food and clothing is demanded and refused, a quarrel ensues, which terminates in bloodshed, the whole tribe take it up as a family quarrel, and a war is the result, which becomes one of extermination to the weaker party.

'THE CHINESE PUZZLE'
Melbourne Monthly Magazine
May 1855

The Vandemonian alarm having died away, and the State Trials being now absolutely a bore, a new excitement has opportunely sprung up—a trial to Mayoral jurisprudence, an exercise for Young Collingwood oratory—the Chinese puzzle.

It has, of course, been our lot to witness the commencement of that terrible irruption of Pagans (as they are now invariably called) which threatens the Christianity (and the diggings) of Victoria. With horror we have heard of the barbarian hordes about to be poured into this happy land, and of their obvious intention of exterminating the British—and indeed, (in spite of Colonel Vern) the whole European population. With horror we have read those foul and wicked prints which, when exposed in the police-court, brought the blush of shame and indignation into the cheek of His Worship, and sent a highly respectable lady of the name of Bridget (we believe from Sligo) into fits.

These things are, at first sight, horrible, we must admit; but let us look at them again, to be quite sure whether they are as monstrous as they appear.

No doubt, to get over the preliminary objection which has brought up *Paterfamilies* in his wrath, certain pictures, said—by undoubted judges—to be of an immoral tendency, have been sold by certain Pagans to certain Christians; and no doubt more—we are not told how many—have been fished up by our vigilant and intelligent police. Very well: the Collector of Customs should have stopped these in the Bay; but the offenders, either by way of sale or publication, may be punished when they get on shore. They have adopted this country, and they must, with it, take its laws. We believe they do, most submissively. Some individuals, out of an immigration said to amount to very many thousands, have then been detected in an offence and punished for it. Is their sin to be visited on their country-men? And shall we, in common justice, hang simultaneously a few of our leading booksellers in consideration of the vice of Holywell Street? "Down they shall be put," said Sir Charles Hotham, rather too aristocratically, of foreigners in general, the other day. "Down they shall be put," say many wise people, of the Chinese now. But why, and how?

For our part, we doubt the policy as well as the legality of any such proceedings as our intensely European fellow-citizens are calling for, against the Pagans from the land of tea. We think it would be at least wise to reflect a little before setting out on so eminently unchristian a crusade, as Peter—beg pardon, John Thomas—the hermit is getting up at this crisis.

Look at John Chinaman as you see him in Collins Street, with his happy and intelligent—and, we ought to add, clean—face, and compare him with a few of our fellow-countrymen as they first appear in the colony. If he is not a Christian, this is your opportunity to make him one; if he is, so much the better. But, as a citizen, how is he objectionable? Nobody seems willing to answer that.

We submit then, in the first place, that we want colonists, and that till there is a clear case against John Chinaman, we want *him*. We see him marching through the street in European dress, and we are much obliged to him for his custom; we see him consuming European food, and we admire his appetite. (We only hope he has imported his taste for little dogs, and will consume the few thousand useless curs which the government *won't* tax.) We see him refusing European drink, and we respect his sobriety! There he is, a Victorian from Asia—a Pagan, certainly, but ready to be converted, reverend and dear sir, whenever you like to begin! There he is, we say, a Victorian, who has brought his speciality of industry, whatever it may be, and his producing power, to add to the real wealth of the colony. A Victorian, obedient to our laws, and likely to be more useful to us in many ways than many of our importations from home, however meritorious and well-meaning they may be. If he be an inferior animal, as we are informed the intellectual Brown believes, let him do inferior animals' work, of which there is plenty required; if this be an error on the part of Brown, why then let the Chinaman improve us; let him be Lieutenant-Governor, if the post will fit him; let us do anything, in fact, except declare war upon a friend—against a visitor, at any rate—in whom we see a good servant to begin with, and possibly a good customer into the bargain.

As to any danger to our laws from Chinamen, we confess our fears lie in a different direction. We look with some alarm at the habits of despotism likely to be engendered amongst our small authorities, by the too ready submission of the thousands of Celestials whom they will now have the opportunity of bullying to the top of their bent. "The Chinaman," says an undisputed authority, "is bred up to civil obedience *tenero ab ungui*, with every chance of proving a quiet subject at least. Such institutions certainly do not denote the existence of much liberty; but, if peaceful obedience and universal order be the sole objects in view, they argue, on the part of the governors, some knowledge of human nature, and an adaptation of the means to the end." So John Chinaman would be peaceful—even at Ballaarat [sic]. One question: Was Peter Lalor, late Commander-in-Chief of the Insurgents, a Chinaman?

To our minds there is something contemptible in the rush from panic to panic for which Melbourne is so sadly distinguished. The Russians have not invaded us; the *Great Britain*, spite of her cannonading, has left of us safe; special constables have been sworn in to save us from Ballaarat: Ballaarat stands where it did, and so does Melbourne—not a constable being required. And now, at length, there being nothing left of our Rifle Brigades and our Sepoys to talk valorously about, we have a chattering of Tartar domination and anti-Celestial morals; we are to exclude industry and energy from the colony, on the plea that it is not European; and with a shout of "China for the Chinese," we are to shut ourselves within such lands as our own wise system allows us, to despise foreigners, and to be the laughing-stock of all sensible mankind, in all quarters of the world.

If anybody could tell us what we were afraid of; if we were not mere children, seeing ghosts in the dark, and only in the dark, our terrors would be respectable; but, really, our present condition is absurd. Take any British citizen aside and ask him what he is afraid of—why he wishes to exclude the Chinese—and whether he is sure that he wishes to exclude them at all. His answer is terribly confused. "Morals, sir, morals, must be attended to. Pagans, you know Pagans. No Mrs. Chisholm at the Chinese ports—no distressed needlewomen—no wives for Pagans, sir. Prints, sir, improper prints. Very proper observation of Mayor. Pagans' wives—prints—pictures—mayor—inferior race—Asiatic Tartar.—Must be put a stop to!"

This is all we can learn against the Chinese, an intelligent, educated, and industrious class of immigrants who, we think, may be made immensely serviceable to us (the English) in the development of the industrial resources of this colony. A prejudice has been got up against them, and that prejudice has sought every possible pretext for doing them wrong. It has sought to make our little Legislature exclude the Chinese, assuming an imperial right, and pretending that we are an independent state with a voice in the matter. It has sometimes called itself by sacred names, and sometimes announced itself in a mere political character; but it is a prejudice, and worse, it is a panic. We are afraid of the Chinese, and we have not the moral courage to say so. They have not a weapon amongst them; nevertheless they have terrified us. And the Attorney-General is preparing a bill to relieve our minds—a bill for the exclusion of skilled artisans and admirable agriculturists, a bill to cause a further delay in the cultivation of our lands. That is Mr. Stawell's present amusement and occupation, since, without the assistance of Mr. Molesworth, he acquitted all the state prisoners. But let us wait a little. Let us do nothing in haste. Let us give Chinese colonists a chance, and not commence legislating against them till we know the reason why. And even then let us consider whether we wish to exclude them from the colony or only from the diggings, and whether, by cutting them off from the gold-fields and opening the land, we could not make their industry of vast value to ourselves. In short, let us look at this question as selfishly as possible. Let us assure the Chinese that they are Pagans and our inferiors, and let us bastinado them from time to time, if that oriental mode of punishment be thought desirable; but if we can get anything out of them let us do so, and unless we are a perfectly irrational people, let us stay Mr. Stawell's hand till we see whether he is about to slay an Asiatic goose come here to lay golden eggs.

Meanwhile, Mrs. Chisholm is requested to smuggle us a few China women, and, by all means, to let those she brings be young. It is, we believe, a melancholy truism, applicable to the whole people, "that with the progress of age, the old men come very ugly, and the old women, if possible, more so." (*Vide Penny Cyclopædia,* article China.)

Such being the case, perhaps some of the Pagans will unite themselves to more durable British spinsters, and, attaching themselves to the soil of Victoria, found a new family upon the face of the earth.

We say nothing of the expediency of such marriages, except that in no case, we trust, will the lady find that by any accident she has "caught a Tartar!"

THOMAS MCCOMBIE, 'THE HISTORY OF VICTORIA' (EXTRACT)
Illustrated Journal of Australasia
February 1858

A murder was perpetrated by the aborigines on the 23rd of August, 1846, under circumstances of unwonted barbarity. The victim was a young settler, of considerable promise, named Andrew Beveridge, who, with his brother, occupied a tract of country on the bank of the Lower Murray.

From the evidence of two men named Kelly and Ryan, who were present, it appeared that six of the natives had remained on the station during the night of the 22nd, and that, on the morning of the 23rd while at breakfast, some of them "cooied," and Mr. Beveridge went out. Two black men, named Bobby and Ptolemy, had their spears in their hands, which they threw at Mr. Beveridge, who immediately retreated towards the hut; one of the spears had entered his body about six inches, and the unfortunate young man almost instantly expired. The two men, Kelly and Ryan, got on their horses in the confusion and rode away. The murderers were afterwards captured by three of the Western Port Border police, assisted by Messrs. Kirby, French, and Mr. Beveridge, the brother of the murdered gentleman. The police, disguised as bushmen, proceeded to Mr. Coghill's station, and concealed their arms from observation in a hut. The blacks were camped on the opposite side of the Murray, but were very shy and afraid of policemen. The troopers represented themselves as white men looking for a run, and offered to pay the blacks if they would cut bark for building purposes. The hut had a yard with a palisade in front; a large fire was made within it, and an enormous pot placed on it; the blacks were invited to dine on a pudding made of flour, sugar, and water, which was being made ready. The police got six plates out, and informed the tribe that only six black fellows could enter the yard at one time; they took care that the three murderers of Mr. Beveridge should dine in one party, and, after great difficulty, they managed to rush upon the party suddenly and to throw strong cords round the necks of Bobby, Bullet-eye, and Ptolemy, and in this manner pinned them to the ground. The rest of the blacks dashed across the river, yelling fearfully; and such were the frantic efforts of the prisoners to get clear, that they dragged their captors over the palisade, and it was only by force of arms that they were at length finally secured, and carried into the hut. The police, aware of the hazard as they ran from the general attack which would inevitably be made on the hut, despatched mounted messengers to the two adjoining stations for aid. The reinforcements received before night-fall only amounted to three men, who came in from Mr. Beveridge's station; so that there were only eight individuals to man the little fortress which had to withstand the onset of the most daring and blood-thirsty tribe in the colony, or, perhaps, in the whole Australian continent. The garrison were on the alert all night, but the attack did not commence until just before daybreak. The blacks mustered on the bank of the river, and took up a strong position in the scrub; an advanced body of about seventy picked men came on immediately to attack the hut; just as the first faint streaks of daylight began to glimmer in the horizon they marched forward with silent tread, until they perceived that they were observed, when they gave forth the most savage and hideous yells, and sprang like tigers on the hut, clearing the palisade at a bound, and sending their spears against it with such force that they went halfway through the slabs, and penetrated the doors and shutters, wounding Johnston, the sergeant of police, who had the command. The defenders were momentarily paralysed by the sudden energy of attack, but soon recovered their coolness, and fired a volley from various apertures in the walls of their little fortress; and the leader of the attack, "Dick the Needle," as he was called, a chief of the Murumbidgee tribe, fell dead with a convulsive spring. Still the attack continued, the blacks endeavouring to unroof the hut, and force an entrance by that means, and the besieged defending this part as the most vulnerable point. The cool resolution of the Europeans checked the violence of the onset, and the party of aborigines retreated to their friends on the bank of the river. It was now broad daylight, and the garrison were calmly awaiting a second attack; they had heavy anticipations, it may be well supposed, for they would have to meet a fresh column of enemies while they were exhausted with the previous struggle. Assistance, however, was at hand, and, before any farther injury could be inflicted, a party of armed horsemen, who had galloped seventy-five miles to aid them, reached the scene and changed the aspect of affairs very quickly. The aborigines had to retreat, and the police, assisted by a strong body of civilians, set forth with the prisoners for Melbourne. It is but right to state that one of the party who defended the hut was severely wounded in the hand by his own pistol, which accidently went off in the affray, and he lost the use of the injured limb. The Government were petitioned to assist this unfortunate gentleman, and gave him the very inadequate sum of fifty pounds as compensation.

The prisoners were brought to trial at Melbourne, and the usual defence was attempted to be made on their behalf—that they were not sufficiently acquainted with the proceedings. After some delay, however, parties were obtained who could interpret to all the three, and, the evidence being conclusive against Bobby and Ptolemy, they were convicted and sentenced to death. There was no evidence to implicate Bullet-eye, and he was discharged.

The huge, dreary mass of dark stone which looms on the rising ground in the rear of the Hospital and Courthouse has, during the brief period that it has been in use as the receptacle of criminals, witnessed many sad and shocking spectacles; but it is questionable if ever a more afflicting drama has been enacted within its gloomy portals than that of the 30th April, 1847. The unfortunate murderers of Mr. Beveridge, Bobby and Ptolemy, were led forth, neatly clad in duck frocks and trowsers, attended by the Rev. A.C. Thompson, rector of St. James's Church, Mr. Protector Thomas, Mr. French, and various other persons interested in them. They were sensible of their awful position, and the powerful working of their feelings was fully exhibited by the twitching of the muscles of their faces during the time that the prayers usual upon such occasions were read. When they were pinioned their feelings overpowered them, and they cried and sobbed in a manner most painful to behold. As the two sable denizens of the far-off forests emerged from the gloomy corridor of the gaol into the open air the sun shone forth on their upturned countenances with uncontrollable splendour. In a scene, strange, new, and terrible,—haunted by the fear of a terrible death, and shut up, as they had been, for many months from the blessed light of heaven, they looked on the glorious orb for a moment, and their faces lightened up as if they had met a dear friend. No doubt their thoughts wandered to their hunting ground and mia-mias on the Murray, to their relations and companions, and, for that instant, they heeded not the terrible engine which was now in full view. It seemed a happy, but, alas! a brief moment. The terrible reality of the actual scene again presented itself; they gave a dread shudder, and, with a quiet, subdued air, awaited their terrible doom. Ptolemy died almost instantaneously, but Bobby struggled for a considerable time, having broken his fall by standing with one foot off the platform.

Britain established the Protectorate with the excellent intention of preventing the white race from oppressing or injuring the aboriginal natives. She spent something like sixty thousand pounds in the experiment, which proved a failure. This spasmodic effort to civilize and protect the black man was attended with no result. It was a grave error. The Government appointed men invested with civil power to protect the natives, and they, in many cases, came into contact with the Europeans who were colonizing and settling in the country. Disputes arose, and the protectors, in not a few instances, became spys on the actions of the settlers. The protectorate did not join cordially and in a generous spirit with the people to ameliorate the condition of the aborigines; it assumed an antagonistic position, and, becoming intolerable to all classes, was abandoned as an acknowledged failure. The Government ought to have liberally supplied the wants of the aborigines by giving them food when hungry and unable to procure it; it ought farther to have employed Christian missionaries to labour in the bush, endeavouring to convert the blacks and to maintain a brotherly feeling between them and the legitimate colonists.

'YARNS BY THE CAMP FIRE II'
Colonial Monthly
November 1869

In 1864 I was in charge of a new station between the Lachlan and the Bogan. I started one fine morning to look for springs, and was accompanied by a darkie, called Jacky, who had come with me from another part of the country. After riding nearly all day, we found a beautiful spring, and giving our horses a drink we turned them up a gully in the hopes they would not come near the spring, as we could see wild horses watered at it in the night. We made our fire a few yards from the spring, and, while the quarts were boiling, Jacky began looking for wood for the night. Directly afterwards I heard him give a "*wagh*" and look very white, or rather a pale green. I asked him what was the matter, and he told me strange blacks were about, he had just got their fresh tracks. I went over to him, and sure enough there were four fresh tracks not more than an hour old. Though I felt no fear of the blacks myself, yet I knew they

would murder Jacky if they got the chance; so, putting out our fire, we had our tea, and taking our blankets, and planting our saddles in some rocks, we walked about a quarter of a mile to windward of the spring, and laid down in some long, dry grass. I was soon asleep, for we had ridden a long way. Just before daybreak, Jacky woke me, and whispered that the "warrigals" were after us. I sat up, and I could see four shadowy forms moving about, evidently looking for our trail. At last they got within a hundred yards of us, and though they had not been able, on account of the faint light, to make sure where we were, yet I knew, as soon as day broke fairly, they could follow our trail at a run. Jacky begged me to shoot, but I hardly felt justified in killing one of them until they commenced the attack. However, I thought I would give them a start; so taking aim over their heads with my pea-rifle, I fired. They disappeared like lightening, and for some time we saw nothing of them, and we were just thinking of going to the spring, and making our pot of tea, when we found ourselves in a nice fix. The black devils had crawled to windward of us, and fired the long grass, and it came down towards us like lightening. They had got upon some big rocks to the right and left of us, so we had nothing for it but to scud for the spring. We ran for life, and you may be sure we did our best. The blacks began to yell as soon as we started, and to throw spears; one came so close to my cheek that it riled me, and, turning round short, I let one chap have a pill from the old rifle that doubled him up, and brought him off his perch, and we had the pleasure of hearing the brute yell as the fire caught him. When we got within fifty yards of the spring, the fire caught us. Straining every nerve, we flew rather than ran, and next moment, half smothered with smoke, and minus some of our hair, we were standing safe in the spring. The fire swept past, and we felt quite safe for the sun was just rising, and I knew the rifle and my revolver were a match for the three remaining blacks. After a short spell we came out of our bath, and were thinking of going for our horses, when I got a jack spear right through my leg; I turned in the direction it came from, and there were the three blacks on the top of a large rock. Though generally of an excellent temper, I really was vexed now, and taking aim at one chap, who had his arm raised in the act of throwing another spear, I let him have it hot. He came down an awful cropper about sixteen feet of the rock, and I concluded he was safe, as I heard no complaint from him. I then drew my revolver and let go a couple of charges at the two remaining ones; but they could not see the fun of being made targets of, and they soon disappeared. Jacky cut the spear close to my leg, and drew it out the other side, and made some poultice of herbs and put on it; he then went and got the two horses—who were only about a hundred yards away, coming down for a drink—and lifting me on mine, we pushed for home, quite satisfied with our morning's sport.

RACE AND THE FRONTIER

ERNEST FAVENC, 'THE ATTACK ON BARROW CREEK'
Sydney Mail
14 May 1881

That it is possible to tell *old* tales of *new* country seems at first blush to be a paradox, but now, as Hamlet says, "the time gives it proof."

Central Mount Stuart, the centre of our Continent, as laid down by Macdougall Stuart in 21° 23° South latitude and 134° 25° longitude East is but a comparatively small hill—not the lofty mountain that such a continent as Australia should (if we consider what is termed the eternal fitness of things) boast as a central point. Nature, however, despising conventional rules, has given us Mount Stuart as the point Stuart failed to reach, and the hill that occupies the position he hoped his central sea did.

In point of fact, however, it is not with Central Mount Stuart itself we have to do, but the nearest inhabited point to it, and that is some forty miles to the north-east—namely, Barrow Creek telegraph station. Truly there is a nearer inhabited point—a solitary grave on the telegraph line only a few miles to the eastward, but the occupant of that grave is not one of the actors in our story. Barrow Creek, the most central settlement of white men in Australia, is situated in the line of broken ridges that Stuart so carefully followed in his expeditions.

The station, like most of those on the line in the interior, is substantially built of rough stone, and forms in itself three sides of a square, a thick wall pierced by a large gate forming the fourth side. In the neighbourhood are the usual sandstone peaks and table-topped hills of Central Australia.

Up to the time of our story friendly intercourse existed between the whites and the natives, and the attack made on the evening of February, 1874, was undreamt of and unexpected. At that time of the day all the inmates of the station were outside its walls, congregated on the side furthest removed from the gateway, talking and smoking. Not one of the whites was armed—a black boy from another district, who was in the employ of the S.A. Government, had a revolver on his belt. Suddenly about eighty or a hundred natives appeared on the ridge at the back of the station, almost succeeding in cutting the party off from their only means of escape. Fortunately they were not well enough up in strategy to think of taking possession of the yard, which they might easily have done, and then the married men outside would have all been sacrificed. As it was the assailed being without weapons to make any defence had the benefit of having to run round one side of the building and through the gateway under a shower of spears and boomerangs. The unfortunate station-master, H.J. Stapleton, was mortally wounded by one of the first spears thrown at the commencement of the attack. In the one-sided fight that followed, J. Frank, a linesman, was speared through the heart as he was running through the gate, and another man was badly wounded in the thigh. Meantime, the black boy had behaved like a hero, firing deliberately at the blacks with his revolver, and thereby greatly assisting his companions to reach cover; in fact his own escape was almost cut off, and after receiving two spear wounds he was dragged in through one of the windows of the building. Once inside the station in possession of their fire-arms the blacks were easily beaten off and the attack was over, but it was only by accident of misfortune that any survivors were left to tell the tale. To show how much gratitude or anything akin to that feeling is to be found in savage nature it was only that morning that the station-master had been dressing a sore place on one of the blacks who led the attack. The two murdered men were buried a short distance from the station, and their graves formerly marked by a rough fence are now enclosed by an iron railing. The station itself has also undergone some slight alteration since that day, and the Government have always had a mounted trooper stationed at Barrow Creek since then. Whether the sight of his uniform (if he wears one), or some sharp reprisals inflicted upon the blacks have had the desired effect I cannot say, but of late years the natives have given little trouble.

JOHN MACKIE, 'IN THE FAR NORTH'
Sydney Quarterly Magazine
February 1885

After leaving Thursday Island and navigating Torres' Straits, we find ourselves in the Gulf of Carpentaria. Here we meet with the bronzed pioneer squatter, with his easy self-reliant style, who has just returned from a well won spell "down South". There is that air of vitality and contentment about him that characterises his native Cloncurry. Here, also, we come in contact with a motley crew belonging to the rolling stone species of stockmen and bushmen, who have come round with the "first in charge" to muster large mobs of cattle somewhere about Normanton, and then to travel with them westward into the far Northern Territory to stock up fresh country.

When we get a glimpse of the coast at all we find it flat, low and densely wooded with great mangrove forests down to the very water's edge. The cannibal black and the alligator have a long lease of the shores of this Gulf, the waters of which are rather puzzling to the strange navigator, for there being only one tide in the day, and the waters being remarkably shallow, when any of the shifting winds freshen a nasty chopping sea springs up. In a short time we reach the mouth of the Norman River, and after bumping over the awkward bars, enter. The little signalling and telegraph station called Kimberley, on the left bank, telegraphs some 70 miles up to Normanton that we are in the River.

RACE AND THE FRONTIER

It was in the month of November last when we first sailed up it and I confess that for the first few hours we admired the dense mangrove-fringed banks, swarming with thousands of white cockatoos, as much as ever we did the Rhine or the Kyles of Bute; but then after admiring nothing save a chopping sea for some days back, one is almost liable to wax poetical over an ant-hill. There can be no doubt that it was slightly warm, the thermometer standing at 112° in the shade. It is wonderful how things physical influence the peculiar channel in which our reasoning faculties run, for when the spot or selection on which the new Boiling-Down Works would probably be erected, was pointed out to me, I absently remarked—as I wrung the perspiration from my shirt like water—"That it would suit admirably, the saving of fuel being a great consideration." Again, in the evening when the vast armies of mosquitoes and sandflies came, our thoughts dwelt upon Job, and we came to a speedy conclusion that the loss of flocks and herds were as nothing compared to the loss of a mosquito-net, and when about morning we fell into a fitful slumber we cherished the sweet delusion that the winged curses had gone, and we were only enjoying the comparative luxury of a plague of evils.

The Norman River twists and winds about much after the manner of an eel when it is suddenly landed on a sandbank. It may not be quite as undecided in its course as a Cabinet Minister, but to compare it to a corkscrew would be a gross injustice—to the corkscrew. Normanton is the commercial *entrepot* and centre, which supplies an area of country much larger than Great Britain, comprising the distant regions of Georgetown and Cloncurry, abounding in incalculable mineral wealth, with which last-named locality it will most likely soon be connected by rail. Within the last few years it has progressed rapidly and has generally a population of about six hundred souls. They are about to provide themselves with a church and a hospital. Of the former they have as much need as of the latter, though Normanton is often described as "that fever-haunted town." The Chinese have a monopoly in the religious line. In fact, the Chinese are the most pious people we know, for they have praying wheels, which, with a little expenditure of elbow grease, get through an extraordinary amount of piety. We knew a Chinaman, named Ah Sin, who lived on the banks of a creek; he was a most notorious horse-thief and opium-smoker, but was somehow always reckoned among the righteous. We could never understand this, until one day we discovered his praying wheel fixed in the running stream working out most industriously the absolution of Ah Sin.

Your first impression of Normanton, on ascending the slightly rising ground on which it is built, is a rather mixed affair. You see an irregular association of galvanized iron, canvas, drays, wagons and telegraph poles. A singular phenomena also came under our observation here, which made us surmise that something was surely wrong with the earth's centre of gravity in this quarter of the globe—the burnt and bearded bushmen and bullock-drivers moving about seemed to have the utmost difficulty in preserving their perpendicular; indeed, at certain times, the oscillation became so violent that they were forced to assume the horizontal. One of the most peculiar sights in Normanton is a complete wall of glass which nearly encircles the town; it is about twelve feet in breadth and four or five feet high and is composed of empty bottles. Whatever geological era the last was in the earth's history this is essentially the bottle period. It also clearly indicates that if the Celestials worship at the shrine of Fusiyama, the Christian population are not less zealous in its [sic] devotion to Bacchus. The hostels here, which are mere shanties, do a roaring trade despite all drinks being a shilling. Under the verandah of one of them we observed an appreciative crowd watching a skipper of the bottle-nosed species called Smith, receiving well-merited interest in Chancery from a gentleman of colour whom he had challenged.

After a few days we left Normanton by steamer, passed the mouth of the Leichhardt and entered the Albert River, which is not unlike the Norman, and shortly after reached Burketown, the *ultima thule* of civilization in this part of Australia. When we arrived here the town was just on the eve of resurrection after a most remarkable sleep of about thirteen years. Then it was that the Gulf country was opened up, and Robert Towns established boiling-down works upon the great plain, giving employment to about two or three hundred people. A plague, believed to be of Asiatic importation, soon, however, took possession of the little settlement and mowed down the people as grass before the reaper's scythe. The disease spread all round the district, and a severe drought following, all the settlers were driven out of the place. Thus in less than a year from date of establishment the Gulf settlement was completely abandoned. Strange and wild are the tales told of these dreadful days when the very grog-shanties were called by such names as "The House of Blazes," "The Dead Finish" and others I care not to mention, More than one grave-digger dug his own grave. Most of the buildings were hurriedly pulled down and carried a distance of one hundred and eighty miles overland to Normanton, and the dying were left to bury the dead.

Not a soul trod in its silent street for years. The wild dog howled in its ruins and the cannibal black made it his corroborree ground.

When we arrived two shanties were on the eve of completion, a butcher and a baker of colour had come, a Police Barrack was being constructed, and an able and respected Magistrate named McArthur was already on the ground. A large store was also being built for the go-a-head shipping firm of Burns, Philip and Co., nevertheless civilization was just in the chrysalis stage. Nobody wore a coat, save the Police Magistrate, who was looked up to as a swell in consequence. Few, indeed, there were without a revolver, cartridges and knife stuck in their belt, for as evil a looking mob of blacks hung round the township as one could wish to see. A few days before we came a black boy belonging to the butcher had been decoyed scarcely a mile from the township by some of the blacks, and murdered—part of his body chopped up was found in the river. Every now and again these niggers go-a-hunting, spearing the cattle in the neighbourhood, and, strange to say, always have the sense to come back into the township immediately afterwards, for there they know they cannot be dispersed. "Crocodile," a crafty, huge and villainous-looking savage, is the ringleader and principal actor in every murder and raid, but still he always manages to keep a whole skin. One day I went down by the river to have a shot at the alligators, with which the river swarms, and met "Crocodile." I think I only once before saw such a horrible diabolical head on human shoulders, and that was only on canvas in the Wirtz Gallery at Brussels. However, I won his heart by giving him a piece of tobacco, then I let fall a few remarks expressing my profound contempt for the police. So we became confidential and I am afraid I led him to believe I was something in the horse-stealing line. We then sat down on a log—my Colt handy to stop his little games forever, should I consider it advisable—and enjoyed each other's company immensely. We descanted on the merits of cannibalism, for which, I made him infer, I had a great partiality. How his gentle heart warmed to me. I got a standing invitation to the camp and a significant hint that a little tobacco and rum might purchase a little banquet *a la* —, if my appetite were good. When I am weary of the burden of this life and want someone to release me of it I'll go to that camp, but not till then. Burketown is the farthest-out bush town in the north-western portion of Queensland, Port Darwin being some nine hundred miles from here. (Point Parker about fifty miles from Burketown is certainly the most suitable and central place in this rapidly developing Gulf country for a port; deep water sufficient to float the very largest vessels coming close up to the very shore the site for a town is undeniable, and it is quite useless for any, otherwise interested, persons who have never been there, to gainsay it.)

After a little stay here we set out for the Queensland border which is about one hundred and sixty miles to the westward in Longitude 148°. Having crossed the Gregory we reached a lightly timbered and fairly well-watered country which stretches on for hundreds of miles almost without a rise into the Northern Territory. Here were the Eucalypti, the Bloodwood and the Woolybutt in a park-like *demesne*, and now the track crawled along the banks of a lagoon on which the drooping Pandanus grew and where the Native Companion stalked. We passed on through a thicket of Silver Wattle and a sombre Tea-tree scrub. Then over the dry sandy bed of the Nicholson; here the men had a little piece of excitement—"double-banking"—to get the wagons over. Every other day some travel-stained horseman would come in and tell us how ahead the blacks were playing up and spearing cattle and horses under the very noses of those who were with the travelling mobs and how they could not get at them. Then no one dare to go down to the creek without his revolver, and at night you were not safe unless your revolver or rifle lay alongside you, for one or two men had been obliged to hand in their checks through the wily savage. The black in this part of Australia is a giant compared to the specimen you see further south.

We passed Corinda, still pursuing our track across the weary plain. One day, riding on in advance, I came to a little rising ground and a few yards off the track saw one of those solitary sacred spots not unfrequently met with in the Australian bush—a white man's grave. Within a rough slab enclosure were some loose bleaching bones, they were those of this poor fellow's dog. The story of his fate resembles that of many another. He was returning to the Gulf from Port Darwin overland, and had reached the Macarthur when the blacks speared three of his horses, and left him with one only on which he put his swag. Leading it, he set out to walk a distance of four hundred miles. His rations had run out, and he lived on iguanas, berries and currajong roots; then his boots gave way, but still he trudged heavily on with bruised and bleeding feet. His strength began to fail him and strange fancies to flit across his brain; somehow his mind had lately been always running upon his past life, trivial incidents and scenes that had taken place when he was a boy were always before him and colouring his dreams. His step grew feebler and feebler and his face careworn and thin as that of an old man. At last the dreaded day came when he staggered to this ridge and gazed anxiously ahead and around. But he could see nothing affront but the unbroken forest of tree tops, which stretched on and on until they merged into the faint blue line of the horizon. His limbs shook under him, and, staggering, he sank to the ground, and his pack-horse wandered away into the bush. The fever had taken a firm hold of him now. The fierce sun had gone down and the moon was full up, and his poor dog was licking his face and hands. He managed to crawl to a waterhole and quenched his thirst. There was a mor-poke somewhere near him that kept up its strange chant. Then a curlew passed over him with its weird eerie cry. And in the dark and silent hour that precedes the dawn he fell asleep.

In his sleep it appeared to him that he was a boy again and back in the old country: that he was roaming about in the shadow-flecked fields and the Spring woods all day looking for the early primrose, and that the light-hearted laughter of his brothers and sisters had never ceased; that he had gone to his bed looking out upon the cherry orchard weary, and he had lived in his dreams all the sunshine of childhood's happy days over again. Daylight was coming on through the half open casement, which was wreathed with the wisteria and honeysuckle, and the fragrance of the hawthorn was sweet upon the air. And his eyes wandered away over the tree tops and climbed the distant hill on which the old church stood and which he knew so well. Then a little bird awoke and called sleepily to its mate among the boughs. Then another awoke, then another and another until there was a glorious burst of song. Then the sun peeped o'er the dew and the spirit of May stirred in that glorious dawn. Surely he heard a well-known footstep in the garden beneath his window. Suddenly a voice he knew had long been silent called on him by name.

But ere he could cry out in his joy he awoke, and the glaring tropical summer's sun that scorched him, the Go-go-burra that shrieked its mocking "Ha-ha-ha!" above him, and the vultures and ravens that whirred in circles over him was a strange awakening from such a pleasant dream. And as the awful present crushed down with all its horror upon him the great Hereafter stared him in the face. That blood-red after-glow he had seen two nights before in the sky was not of this earth; could he not accept it as a symbol of that divine redemption he had read of when a child? Then the end came, but he did not live in this hard and forlorn present, but was lying in his cot again on the other side of the world looking out upon that glorious Spring dawn.

And, suddenly, a voice called him, and starting up exclaiming, "I am coming, I am coming!" he went out to meet Him in the mysterious Hereafter.

His body lay there in the glaring sun, and his dog faithful still to death drove away the birds and beasts of prey. But in two days a great mob of cattle came crawling over the plain, and in advance was a travel-stained rider, who came up and stared with an awestruck recognition of the corpse. Then another came, "Good Heavens! lad," he said, "it's our brother Bill. Go back to the wagon and get the tools, and send the cattle round by the right." And these rough time-worn men buried their long lost brother under a shady Bohemia tree and left him to his rest.

This is but one of the many bush graves that mark the last camping grounds of the explorer and the pioneer in this great lone land of ours.

About sixty miles from Burketown we left the Nicholson River which we crossed and skirted keeping to the right. Travelling mobs *en route* for Western Australia strike off here to the left. At Turn-off Lagoon we came upon a party of three, who had a strange tale to tell. They had been camped on the edge of a waterhole, and one of them had gone out for two days looking for horses, and had left his swag rolled up a little apart from the others. Late in the evening he came back and rolling himself in his blanket lay down in the exact spot where it had lain. Towards morning he was rudely disturbed, for suddenly he felt himself lifted up in a pair of strong arms. On shrieking out he was flung violently to the ground, and was just in time to see a huge black scuttle over a ridge where he had joined some more of his companions. These blacks had watched the swag for two days and made up their mind to steal it, but the worthy savage who had been deployed off to do it probably went back to say, as one of the black boys, who immensely relished the joke, remarked, "All a same, whitefellow devil-devil jump up along a swag."

Our track now approached the ranges, winding along by the foot of them, and after a journey of about one hundred and thirty miles from Burketown we arrived at the last place in Queensland; in fact, the only place where you could get a pound of flour to save yourself from starving on this side of Port Darwin. It is called West-morland or Lagoon Creek where the Mackintosh is always ready to welcome the traveller with true Highland hospitality.

It is a squatting station. In the run there is about 1,200 square miles of splendidly-grassed and abundantly-watered country, the range converting it into a convenient natural paddock. The house, store and other buildings have only been up a few months for the station has not long since been formed.

Here our wagons and drays were unloaded, and, truly, the necessities of life out here are worth their weight in gold. It is a pretty spot in front of the house. A lawn-like vista of large trees, a flourishing garden, and at the foot of it a long strip of clear water, on which the water lilies grow; while on the banks the Native Companion stalks, and the waterfowl move fearlessly about knowing that no harm can come to them there.

While we were here a party arrived with pack-horses for provisions, who had been out forming a station on the Macarthur River some two hundred and twenty miles westward, which was to consist of a run of 15,000 square miles. They looked for all the world like the spectre crew in the "Ancient Mariner," for the vessel which was to have brought them round supplies, by some unavoidable cause not having shown up, they had been living on a bill of fare comprising iguanas and snakes, currajong roots and berries. Truly, a *menu a la Nature*. At about twenty-five miles westward, the boundary line—the 148° of longitude is supposed to be, but a party with camels are at present travelling overland from Adelaide to fix it definitely. A Border Township will spring up here, most likely at no distant day.

One day crossing the range of huge boulders, about thirty miles to the S.W. of this place and ascending a mount on which, I believe, no white man had ever set foot before, my eye wandered over the far-stretching panorama of hill and dale and misty mountain top. It was a scene as weird and ghastly in its solitude and sense of desolation as a landscape by Vedder. My mind speculated on the past of this great conglomerate country and if it would reveal a land of Ophir in the future. But mine was the first footstep there, save that of the dusky savage, and the present was wrapped in the mystery that seemed to brood over it.

But the day is close at hand when these rocks must give their testimony, and the mist of ages shall break up and roll away from this Never Never Country.

W.L. LUMLEY, 'THE CRIMSON THREAD OF BROTHERHOOD'
Pacific Quarterly
August 1890

One of the remarkable things in this progressive age of ours is the way in which the brotherhood of man is being preached, and is practically influencing human thought. This is seen in the strong aversion everywhere shown to slavery, and in many other ways. Although there are not many men, perhaps, who can say with the same broad and universal philanthropy as John Wesley, "The world is my country," and, although humanity must greatly advance in its ideas before it overtakes that grand old man, still it *is* advancing in that direction. Those prejudices which separate one nation or one class from another are being assailed, and are showing signs of growing weakness. The spread of Democratic ideas is an evidence and a cause of this. There was a time, for instance, when people of aristocratic pretensions were regarded, or regarded themselves as being composed of finer clay than ordinary mortals, but that time has passed. Now other ideas are being attacked, and must in time give way. The right of certain individuals to huge monopolies of land and wealth, bringing about immense riches side by side with terrible poverty—the right of others to the power of throwing nations into war—such rights are being questioned in a way that argues strongly against their long continuance. The idea that all men are brothers, and, as such, have equal rights, is the moving principle in these reforms, and it is interesting to see how it is manifesting itself in our world today, and to enquire what we have to do with it.

Some time ago an international congress of working men was held in Paris. Even Australia was represented by a delegate, and questions affecting working men everywhere were discussed. Straws showing which way the wind blows are seen in the Australian and other contributions to the Dock Labourers' Strike Fund, and the proposal to establish a universal labour federation. They show that the feeling is growing that nations ought to regard each other not as enemies, but as brothers, and it is a hopeful sign of our world's progress towards the standard set before us in the gospel, "Whatsoever ye would that men should do to you, do ye even so to them." Men are not striving after union because they have learned to love one another better, but rather because the union which self interest creates will lead to greater love for their fellows. In countries where travelling is accomplished by means of sleighs drawn by dogs, it is said that if two dogs become unfriendly, the best cure is to put them side by side in the traces, when they soon become fast friends. This principle applies to men as well as to dogs.

Statesmen now-a-days are ruled by public opinion, and public opinion is made up of what *we* think. So it is important that Australians should think rightly, and further, that our minds should not contract into the little circle of our own local affairs, but should take as broad a flight over the outside world as our opportunities permit. Above all, we should cultivate a brotherly sympathy for all men, for God has made of one blood all the nations of the earth.

People should love their own country best, but, at the same time, have a good word for other countries. We may truly think that there is no place like Australia. We are proud to call ourselves by her name. We rejoice in her prosperity, the comfort and happiness of her working classes, the freedom and enlightenment of her laws, her broad and free democracy, and the wonderful future before her. The foundations of her greatness have been laid broad and deep, and the great building is slowly rising in majestic proportions.

> "'Tis the Springtime of Australia, and the dazzled eye may see
> Wondrous dreams of future greatness, of the glories yet to be;
> Visions, not of martial conquest, not of carnage, blood and fire,
> But of lands, by noble actions, growing greater, grander, higher!
> Of the wond'ring nations turning, gazing with admiring eyes,
> While oppress'd and toiling millions feel new hopes and thoughts arise,
> In the march of human progress as Australia leads the van
> To the world's great federation and the Parliament of Man."

So far so good. But most young Australians think too much of themselves and their country, and too little of others. We hear Australia held up as the height of perfection—right or wrong. Let a comparison be made by anyone between Australia and any other place, and usually, some enthusiastic colonial will be found to maintain that his country can "lick creation," as an American would say. A good sample of young Australia was a youth heard the other day to declare that for statuary no place could equal Ballarat. Such specimens may be rare, but, nevertheless, there are numbers who think it their duty to maintain that Australia excels every other place in every respect, whether they have truth on their side or not.

Instead of such ideas we should cultivate a more friendly feeling towards other countries, and get rid of our foolish jealousies. If by any means thought can be given to any other subject than unending football, we should look out to find the good points of others, and see what good things can be said of them.

And then there is the grand old land we are all proud to belong to. After all, there is no place like Old England, no country so guided by principles of righteousness, no country so true at heart. Mighty in war, she yet loves peace, and her might has often been used to defend the right and to help the weak. A royal nation—for centuries she has led the van of the world's progress, and still leads. And, even now, though under her flag are still done deeds of abominable wrong, though she is far from perfect, and needs, perhaps, as much as even the application of purifying influences—even now she is a centre of righteousness and moral power. She is growing better and purer and grander; long-existing wrongs are being dragged to the light of day, remedies for which are being applied, and we all say, "England, with all thy faults we love thee still."

> "Hugged by the clinging billow's clasp,
> From sea-weed fringe to mountain heather,
> The British oak, with rooted grasp,
> Her slender handful holds together
> With cliffs of white and bowers of green
> And ocean narrowing to caress her,
> And hills with threaded streams between
> Our little Mother Isle—God bless her!"

But something more is wanted. Our friendly feelings should go out to France, Germany and Russia, and to all the world. We have all read histories of England *by Englishmen*. Should we be so proud of ourselves if we were to read our history by a Frenchman? Should we have fancied Waterloo "so glorious a victory" if we had ready only the French account of it? The fact is that all, or nearly all, the histories or the descriptions that we read of ourselves or other people are exaggerated and one-sided, and if we knew the truth sometimes about ourselves and our neighbours it would take much of the conceit out of us, and we would be more ready to acknowledge that we are not the only people possessed of all the virtues. We have a great dislike to the Chinese, for instance. The real reason of this is that they enter into competition with us, and so touch us in that tender part—the pocket. Of course, we are justified in protecting ourselves against their unfair competition by every lawful means; but when we talk about their dirt, their immorality, their opium and so forth, in the way some of us do, we commit a moral wrong against them; and when we treat the subjects of a friendly power, as we did some time ago—refusing to permit them to land on our shores, and robbing them of the passage money they had paid in good faith and on the understanding that we were a civilised community—when we do a thing like this we are guilty of a gross act of injustice.

The average Chinaman is not more dirty nor more immoral than the average Englishman. If he smokes opium we must not forget that Britain's power is at this moment forcing China against her will to admit the drug from India, and it ill becomes us to cast that failing in her teeth. And the Chinaman is much in advance of the Englishman as regards intoxicating drink. The Chinese amongst us are their lower classes. Did you ever speak civilly to one and get an uncivil answer? Did you ever see one of them loafing about bar doors or street corners, and giving abuse and bad language to passing ladies? Did you ever see one able to work, going about begging? Did you ever treat one kindly and find him ungrateful? Never; but you have seen all these things from the lower classes of colonials. The Chinese are a wonderful race. They have a civilisation dating back long before the time when our forefathers wandered about in wolf skins. When Isaiah was writing his poetry, when Solomon was building his temple, when Moses was minding his sheep, when Abraham was leading his flocks away from his native place, the Chinese were there—a civilised and enlightened people—and he who despises them displays both ignorance and folly. "Is your father a Christian?" a boy was once asked. "Yes; but he don't work at it now!" was the reply. We are a professedly Christian nation; but we do not always show our faith by our works. Our principles ought to shine out in our dealings with, and our feelings towards, other nations, as well as towards other individuals; and while we think that we are better than most others we are not quite perfect.

> "If each before his own door swept
> The sidewalk would be clean,"

and if everyone did his duty our land would be a Paradise, true brotherhood would reign and the Millennium would be *here*.

'BLACK DETECTIVES'
Yabba
17 January 1900

None of the marvellous unravellings of mystery by the impossible detectives of fiction can surpass in ingenuity the work done by our own black trackers of Australia. The following story of a stockrider who, travelling with large sum of money, disappeared will give some idea of the cleverness of the blacks in tracking. The stockrider's horse had returned riderless to the station, and without saddle or bridle. A search was at once instituted, but proved fruitless. The horse's hoofmarks were followed to the very boundary of the run, near which stood a hut occupied by two shepherds. These men when questioned declared that neither man or horse had passed that way. Then a native who worked on the station was pressed into service, and starting from the house, walking with downcast eyes, and occasionally putting his nose to the ground, he easily followed the horse's tracks to the shepherd's hut, where he at once offered some information. "Two white man walk here," he said, pointing to indications he alone could discover on the ground. A few yards further he cried—"Here fight; here large fight!" and it was seen that the grass had been trampled down. Again, close at hand, he shouted, in great excitement—"Here kill, kill!" A minute examination of the spot showed that the earth had been moved recently, and on turning it over a quantity of clotted blood was found below .... The black now discovered the tracks of men by the banks of a stream hard by .... The stream was shrunk to a tiny thread after the long drought, and here and there was swallowed up by sand. But it gathered occasionally into deep, stagnant pools, which marked its course. Each of these the native examined, still finding footmarks on the margin. At last they reached a pond larger than any, wide, and seemingly very deep. The tracker, after circling round and round the bank, said the trail had ceased, and bent all his attention on the surface of the water, where a quantity of dark scum was floating. Some of this he skimmed off, tasted, and smelt, and decided positively—"White man here."

The pond was dragged, and the mangled remains of the stockrider were found in a sack weighted with stone. Suspicion fell upon the shepherds, who were arrested and sent to Melbourne. The saddle-bags were still to be found. The black followed the tracks of the two men's feet, and after some time came upon a dry watercourse, in the middle of which was a high pile of stones.

The tracks ended at a stone on the side, when the native said he smelt leather. When several stones had been taken down the saddle-bags, saddle and bridle were found hidden in a inner receptacle.

The money, no less than £2000, was still in the bags. The shepherds were both hanged at Melbourne.

RACE AND THE FRONTIER

'GANESHA' (LOUIS ESSON), 'ROUND THE CORNER'
Lone Hand
1 December 1908

Round the corner there, from Russell to Exhibition streets, runs Little Lon., the main artery of the slums, the Mecca of all outcasts of society. Herein gather, drawn as by some magnet, the strange denizens of Slumtown. At a corner hotel, a gramaphone [sic] blaring popular airs attracts a motley crowd; thieves and spielers come in from the suburbs to their favourite pub with religious regularity. It is a summer's night, and people laze around. The moon makes pictures out of squalid materials—tumble-down hovels, narrow lanes, windows, lamp-posts, chimneys. Bedraggled women squat on doorsteps, blowing cigarettes; shadows sneak up and down dim-lighted lanes; a turbaned Hindu passes; then a swaggie, who seems "bushed"; a Dutch seaman. Through the crowd shuffles a smug Celestial; "bucks" muster at the corners.

There is no point duty on this beat. Fully armed, the "rossers," working in pairs, have a roving commission. The night squad begins operations at a quarter to nine, and continues till five next morning.

"How are we?" inquires the constable, as if addressing an old friend.

"Glad to see you—but there's nothing doing."

The speaker is an elderly, grey haired man, clean-shaven, sturdily-built, and dressed in sober black. On his honoured grey hairs rests the record of 17 convictions, totalling over 47 years' imprisonment. A quiet, soft-spoken man, modest as befits a hero, this is the daddy of them all—the prince, the plum.

At the next corner, listening to the gramaphone, lounges a blue-eyed young man in a grey suit. This is "Smithy the Liar." (A big percentage of thieves have blue eyes, states an expert.) Smithy seems a pleasant chap, full of anecdotes of his personal prowess, most of them unfounded on fact. Smithy explains that he can't afford to miss a chance, and is planning a big job now. When not "in smoke" (*i.e.*, in hiding), the cheerful Smithy sometimes "fights in the 'alls," but is usually knocked out about the third round.

A good-looking young woman, with bobbing feathers in her hat, accosts the policeman.

"Hullo, 'Renie; back again?"

'Renie's husband is a lumper at Port Melbourne—a giant famous for his Achillean wrath and battles with the police. A hard grafter, he married this girl from Little Lon., and though usually steady, whenever she drifts back—and drift back she must, the call of the slums is as that of the sea and the bush—Bill goes on a jamboree, and tries to push over the post office.

'Renie takes Fishy Kate and Rhinoceros Liz to the pub.

"'Ow's Bill?" they ask.

Her troubles!

The "talent" pours in—thieves, pick-pockets, vagrants, flash spielers, sailors who have gone down to the pub from ships, gaudily dressed women, Asiatics—they all add spice and colour to the narrow streets.

◉

Down a foetid lane there is an "opium joint," kept by an impassive Chinaman. There is nothing attractive about this form of vice. The smokers lie on platforms, covered with cocoanut-matting [sic], their heads resting on bags. The only light in the place comes from the opium lamps, which are nothing but wicks stuck in fat and surrounded by glass. A tray contains the paraphernalia—the pipe, a thick wooden apparatus, with a large solid bulb, through which a tiny hole has been pierced; the opium, a black, sticky, tar-like mixture, contained in a little pot, odourless when raw, but giving out when "cooked" a smell like unto that of coffee beans; the long needle, with which the stuff is held over the lamp and cooked; and a little dish of "enchee," the ash, worth several shillings an ounce, that serves when eaten as a substitute for a smoke when the pipe is unprocurable.

It is a fallacy to think opium-smoking creates beautiful dreams. It is a sedative, occasionally a pick-me-up. Cigarettes are smoked between pipes, for opium has no taste.

Huddled together lie Chinese merchants, clerks, street musicians, professional men, market gardeners, bound by the democracy of human weakness. Everything is hushed in the tainted room. Calm as a joss the proprietor sits behind the counter. Opium-smokers cause no disturbance; they hurt only themselves.

There is a number of Asiatics on this beat, making a little Asia in Australia.

The Syrians, who have no relationship with the old Assyrians who built the walls of Babylon, are subtle folk, born traders. They will deal in anything, and are among the plutocracy of Slumtown. Rarely do they come into collision with the law. The women, who are kept strictly secluded, bend day and night over their machines, expert in sewing skirts and fancy blouses. In a Syrian shop one is regaled with curious drinks, and still more curious music on stringed instruments. Most Melbourne Syrians belong to the Greek Church. Arabic is their language. Though many merchants return to Beyrout and the Levant, the younger generation tends to become Australian, too easily one thinks.

The Hindus, mainly hawkers, collect in many unsavoury portions of the city. The Mahommedan, who follows the teachings of the Koran, despises the Hindu, whose creed, however quaintly symbolised by images of incomprehensible gods and goddesses, is based on the Vedic hymns and the elaborate metaphysic of the Brahmins. The few Hindus in Melbourne are usually of low caste. A third body represented in the alleys are the warlike Sikhs, who neither smoke nor cut hair. Though the ramifications of creed and caste are followed less minutely in Australia than in India, holy wars are not infrequent among the conflicting sects.

In McCormack Place the Mussulmans have built themselves a little mosque. In the same quarter lodge a Dago harpist, a maker of ice-cream, another Dago, a Cockney seller of red and blue toy balloons, Australian outcasts, and other nondescripts familiar in the city streets. Near by, in Cumberland Place, there is a church wherein Syrian children are taught by the Sisters of Mercy. By the beard of the Prophet, a strange assemblage!

In many a dark lane and alley China predominates. Little Bourke Street, however, which suffers more than formerly from official interference, has lost something of its color, and smell, and picturesqueness. But gambling, from roulette-like games down to simple ticket-marking, still proceeds darkly, and the bank, with which the lottery shops are all connected, is rarely raided.

One finds a variety of all-night cook-shops and coffee-stalls. One is kept by an Australian aboriginal; another by a Jap, whose explanation of slackness of trade—"don't serve thief"—must gall his rivals; a famed and gorgeous oyster saloon, managed by a Levantine Greek, and other establishments at odd corners, run by a Syrian, a negro, and a half-caste "Pat."

This last caboose is in Little Lon.; it is a centre of light and learning, one of the most popular haunts of the neighborhood. The cuisine is plain Australian; but Celestial delicacies are served to connoisseurs—short and long soup, duck-fowl, smoked pork sausages, Chinee mushrooms, eggs fried in peanut oil, sodden fancy cakes, etc. A Chinaman can digest anything.

It is a great night. At the tables sit two young Jap clerks, "advanced" Japs, full of half-baked information and inordinate conceit; letters are piled by their plates to show their importance in the commercial world. In comparison, a sedate Chinese storekeeper looks quite dignified. A weedy little fellow, another Jap, his hat thrust back, a cane by his chair, is described, in whispers, as a phenomenal jui-jitsu wrestler. Two or three "fancy" men drop in; a sharp-shooter from a Wild West show, a couple of sailors, spielers, and other night-hawks.

The waiter is an astounding person, half Chinese, half larrikin. Talkative, confident, a "boshter bloke," he professes great faith in China, and, like most half-castes, his sentiments are all Celestial.

Putting down a plate of sausages, he informs the company that he comes from a clan that literally "eats gunpowder and drinks blood"; "the greatest soldiers in the world," he says, "some of them 8ft. high."

"'Ow do you know, Waka?" asks a gruff voice.

"Didn't they arst me over ter Chiner at £10 a week? The Guvermint wanted 25 of us ter gow over and educite them. They carn't git too many like us. We speak English and Chinese fluently. Yet pan—fish and chips."

Waka begins in Chinese, but usually finishes in Australian.

"Are yer goin', Wak?"

"Dickin'. They carn't buy my brains."

Waka presumes to speak only five Chinese dialects. His pals say he has never seen China and can't speak 40 words of the language. But Waka supports everything Chinese. "Dogs? You must go to China for dogs. Nerve specialists? There are no nerve specialists here; they are all in China. Flying machines? *We* invented *them* 600 years ago." Chinese carving, Chinese cookery, Chinese sailors, Chinese vegetables—these are all, in his opinion, the finest in the world.

"Er bloke cum in 'ere t'other night an' started ter dror—er long, skinny slab—an' got some of us blokes ter sit for ther piper. But 'e cudn't dror. Y'orter gow ter Chiner"—

This is an all-night restaurant, and at one time or another one meets there all the distinguished personalities of the cosmopolitan alleys.

A sly grog shop is worth seeing. One enters a hovel, and goes down to a cellar that suggests a Hogarthian interior. In this den many plots are hatched, many "jobs" planned. Thieves and their doxies are found here, visitors from Sydney, deserters from foreign ships. Social evenings are sometimes held, for the criminals form a distinctive community with their own habits and amusements. Though less highly organised than a Chinese secret society, they band together to take up subscriptions for fines, bail out a pal; hold, when desirable, a wake; defray funeral expenses, or indulge in a "hop" or "ballum rancum."

"Slimy Jonah," the proprietor, has never yet been trapped. Beneath the first cellar he has a lower cellar wherein the poisonous liquor is kept. It is reached by an ingenious trap-door. At any suspicion of raid, the glasses are placed on the table, which sinks through the trap-door to the lower cellar, and the company is discovered innocently playing cards.

Thieves rarely "drop their bundle," that is, give information to the police; such information must be sought among the women. A woman must talk, even to a policeman, if a man swing for it.

Round and round the beat tramp the "rossers," though now the streets are almost deserted. Only the vagrant is in evidence, lying out in some dilapidated shed or deserted hovel, under trees in the parks, in secluded doorways, or in that reserve near the Exhibition Gardens that has been called the "plantation" or "Spion Kop." Occasionally they raise the price of a bed in some low doss house; but more often they are found in the streets and charitably "run in." These are the outcasts, the derelicts, creatures that once were men—and women—drifting aimlessly between the gaol and the hospital. Their last refuge is Koolgardie Square, the most dismal place in Melbourne. Under a gloomy archway one comes on this square, conspicuous by its tumbledown fences, lamps hanging from blackened beams, a litter of orange-peel, old hats, kerosene tins, stones, papers, all manner of debris. Through a narrow slit in an iron gate, built like a monkey-cage, a glimpse is obtained of a Chinese den; on a wooden bench behind the bars there is a bowl of rice, some vegetables, and pork in an enamelled basin. A woman is lying out at the gate. This is the lane that has no turning; for when the vagrant reaches Koolgardie Square the next step is the river and the morgue.

A cock crows shrilly, heralding the dawn. In Little Bourke Street the "Pats" are loading carts with bananas and vegetables for the market. The "rosser's" round is almost done.

During the night they may have "run in" garrotters, pickpockets, or merely inoffensive drunks. They have noted whether some "old hand," just "out," is back to his old haunts; and kept an eye on any suspicious strangers knocking round the beat. They have explored every nook and cranny; inspected low pubs, fish shops, thieves' kitchens, doss houses, Asiatic dens; and, as watchmen, examined and bolted tempting-looking doors and windows. They have listened to many tales of trouble—the doxy's lament about her "bloke" who beat her, complaints of mugs who have been taken-down, and maunderings of drunks who have lost their way and have forgotten where they live.

Villon, Burns, Walt Whitman, Maxim Gorki, Henry Lawson—the alleys have had no want of bards. And though bounded by the pub, the gambling den, the "jug," and the morgue, there is such spice of adventure in the life, such hazardous contrasts, such anarchic freedom that few hardened habitués would exchange it for the humdrum paths of respectability.

"VELLY GOOD LETTUCEE."

PART 10

Colonial Modernity
KEN GELDER & RACHAEL WEAVER

'Sydney and its Suburbs No. II: Bondi',
Month: A Literary and Critical Journal,
September 1857
385

Grosvenor Bunster, 'By Way of a Prologue.
No. 1—Concerning Sydney',
Australian Journal, 2 March 1867
388

'Waif Wander' (Mary Fortune),
'Down Bourke Street', *Australian Journal*,
16 January 1869
391

'Banking Up-country',
Colonial Monthly, July 1869
405

'The Duties of a Leisure Class in Colonial
Society', *Australian Magazine of Contemporary
Colonial Opinion*, August 1886
410

Alexander Sutherland, 'The Yarra',
Centennial Magazine, August 1888
419

W.B.S. (Walter Baldwin Spencer),
'The Destruction of Eucalypts',
Australasian Critic, 1 May 1891
424

'Notes on Cycling', *Block*, 15 August 1896
426

J.D. Fitzgerald, 'Sydney: The Cinderella
of Cities', *Lone Hand*,
1 May 1907
428

New South Wales tourism advertisement,
Lone Hand, 1 June 1907
433

10

Colonial Modernity
KEN GELDER & RACHAEL WEAVER

So much of the writing we see in colonial Australia registers the changing features of the physical landscape: the evolution of the colonial cities, the radical transformation of bush and country. The journals were especially committed to giving definition to the ways in which urban and regional spaces alike were utterly reshaped through the processes of financial speculation and colonial expansion. New social and material structures superimpose themselves on existing ones, which they displace or marginalise – but those older forms also return over and over to give the new its self-definition. Richard Dennis makes this point in his book *Cities in Modernity* (2008): modernity ushers in 'the realisation that now is not the same as then', but it also throws these two radically different temporal moments together, recreating 'the past as "other" as a continuing proof of the superiority of the new'.[1] The idea of a *colonial* modernity folds this point into a further realisation that, as colonisation progresses, an otherwise remote place like Australia is at the same time embedded in global frameworks for the flow of capital and commodities. For Robert Dixon, 'the term colonial modernity [...] refers to a series of developments in the late nineteenth and early twentieth centuries that linked apparently provincial cultures like those of the Australian colonies into a busy traffic in personnel, cultural practices, texts and intellectual property around the English-speaking world'.[2] This section of our book shows the many ways in which the early Australian journals registered the 'busy traffic' of colonial modernity, as writers navigated their way through increasingly crowded urban streets and the demands of capital impacted on every aspect of daily life: from the rapid growth of business centres across the country to the systematic degradation of the forests and waterways.

The anonymously written 'Sydney and its Suburbs No. II: Bondi' is part of a series of descriptions of walking tours through colonial Sydney, published in the *Month: A Literary and Critical Journal* (July 1857 – December 1858). Frank Fowler, the editor, was an English immigrant who spent three years in Australia working as a journalist, publishing a lively, caustic account of Australian life, *Southern Lights and Shadows* (1859), not long after he had left the colonies. He was also a member of the Stenhouse circle in Sydney, a literary coterie that included Charles Harpur, Henry Kendall and John Sheridan Moore, who edited the last few issues of the *Month* after Fowler's departure. This good-natured journal was modelled on Edinburgh's *Blackwood's Magazine*, mixing Australian material with appreciations of British and European literary culture. The article about tramping from Bondi to the Heads and travelling back to Woolloomooloo begins with a wonderfully delirious description of the wild Sydney coastline and the sheer nightmare of the ocean voyage. Walking to Bondi – in this early stage of Sydney's development – is then cast as a mock-heroic expedition into the wilderness, something unexpectedly dangerous and disorienting. Grosvenor Bunster was a Hobart-born novelist, journalist and dramatist who contributed stories and sketches to the *Australian Journal* for over thirty years. In 'Concerning Sydney', the city itself is cast as a kind of wilderness, a global destination for displaced populations: 'a depot', as he puts it, 'of the nations of the earth'. Written in 1867, this article already sees Sydney as a city entirely driven by capital. But its rapidly expanding modernity also means that its newness is consistently compromised, the past and the present now impossible to distinguish: 'a strange hugger-mugger of buildings', Bunster writes, 'old and new, mean and princely'.

A second article from the *Australian Journal* that we have included in this section, Mary Fortune's 'Down Bourke Street,' offers a similarly panoramic account of the modern metropolis, representing the myriad sights and activities of bustling, downtown Melbourne as a series of spectacles or attractions for the reader to consume. When the article was published in 1869, Fortune was still a relative newcomer to Melbourne. Lucy Sussex has talked about Mary Fortune's pseudonym, 'Waif Wander', noting that its 'connotation of homelessness' was unusual 'in an era when femininity was identified with domesticity'.[3] Fortune's narrative is touristic, but her relationship to the colonial commodities on offer is tentative: immersed in some ways, disengaged in others. To a degree, her role is that of the *flaneuse* or female *flaneur*, someone who taps into the nervous energy of modernity by registering 'the fleeting, ephemeral, impersonal nature of encounters in the urban environment'.[4]

Wealth accumulation is often treated ambivalently in the colonial journals. On the one hand, it is a visible marker of progress and success; on the other, it can seem to override more important questions to do with cultural attainment and national self-definition. 'Banking Up-country', from the *Colonial Monthly* – while Marcus Clarke was its editor – thinks carefully about the social role of banks as they branch out into the provinces. The 1860s goldrushes in Victoria, as Jim Bain puts it, 'confirmed Melbourne's commercial destiny',[5] and opened the way for financial and trading institutions to establish themselves in the outlying regional centres. In this article, the narrator takes charge of a country bank and tells us what happens when modern finance meets small-town communities. But he also wonders about the future of banks in the city, with a new generation of narcissistic colonial employees ('such terrible young "swells"') challenging the financial sector's ability to operate as efficiently as it used to. James McDougall's short-lived *Australian Magazine of Contemporary Colonial Opinion* often thought carefully about colonial prosperity. 'The Duties of a Leisure Class in Colonial Society' is a different kind of response to wealth accumulation. A privileged colonial class has emerged that no longer needs to work: so what do they do? For this article, these people turn out to be crucial to the development of the nation since they have the resources necessary to nurture its cultural life. 'Art and Literature are tender plants', the author tells us; 'the cold breath of commercial calculation will blight their growth. It is here that we require a leisure class to exercise its beneficent and appreciative influence'.

The flow of colonial modernity out of the cities and into the country was counteracted by various investments in a kind of pastoral poetics that wanted to see the natural world as something permanent in the midst of change. Alexander Sutherland was a literary critic and university lecturer who co-authored *The Development of Australian Literature* in 1898, contributing biographical essays on Adam Lindsay Gordon and Henry Kendall. He also wrote a series of essays on the Yarra for *Centennial Magazine,* the first of which we include here. Sutherland's tribute to this 'enchanted' river is a kind of exaggerated pastoral that sees the source of the Yarra as an impenetrable wilderness (even though it isn't very far away). But as it reaches into the city, Sutherland recognises that modernity has already transformed the river into something ruined and polluted. Walter Baldwin Spencer's 'The Destruction of Eucalypts' – from the *Australasian Critic* – comes in the wake of what Tim Bonyhady in *The Colonial Earth* (2008) describes as the aesthetic and environmental recuperation of the eucalypt towards the end of the nineteenth century. In fact, Baldwin's remarks about 'the mania for ringbarking' during this time are echoed in Bonyhady's discussion of an emergent colonial environmentalism – involving other, like-minded scientists such as William Woolls and Alfred William Howitt – that had already begun to worry about the effects of native deforestation.[6] Baldwin's essay is remarkably prescient in the way it ties land clearance to climate change: 'it is surely evident', he writes, 'that the complete changing of the nature of the surface of the country must, in the long run, produce some definite climactic result'.

Modernity brings with it a promise of rationality and order: a transparent metropolitan structure, wide boulevards, organised (and orderly) civic spaces, and so on. In the colonial cities, however, this is a promise that is not always completely fulfilled. For a progressive metropolitan journal like the *Block*, the bicycle is a symbol of everything modernity is supposed to deliver, especially for women. Arriving in colonial cities in the late 1870s, it enabled freedom of movement, encouraged sensible attire ('rational dress'), and lent women the opportunity to consolidate family relationships and develop new forms of social recreation. For other commentators, however, the colonial cities seemed to *refuse* to modernise. John Daniel

COLONIAL MODERNITY

Fitzgerald, a prominent barrister involved in local government, wrote a series of controversial articles about Sydney for the *Lone Hand*. The journal spoke up for Fitzgerald's 'passionate civic enthusiasm', but his articles in fact give a devastating critique of the city's predicament. Sydney is polluting its bays and destroying the surrounding forests; it seems more provincial than global; it has failed to live up to the aesthetic standards of other cities; and, as its slums proliferate, it seems that 'civic anarchy' prevails. Typically for the *Lone Hand*, these criticisms also fuel anxieties to do with racial degeneration, as if the fate of a colonial city – and the nation itself by this time – rests entirely on its ability to put its streets and buildings in good order.

1. Dennis, *Cities of Modernity: Representations and Productions of Metropolitan Space, 1830–1940*, p. 1.
2. Dixon, *Photography, Early Cinema and Colonial Modernity: Frank Hurley's Synchronized Lecture Entertainment*, p. xxix.
3. Sussex, *Women Writers and Detectives in Nineteenth-Century Crime Fiction: The Mothers of the Mystery Genre*, p. 131.
4. Wolff, *Feminine Sentences: Essays on Women and Culture*, p. 35.
5. Bain, *A Financial Tale of Two Cities: Sydney & Melbourne's Remarkable Contest for Commercial Supremacy*, p. 7.
6. See Bonyhady, *The Colonial Earth*, pp. 178–82.

'SYDNEY AND ITS SUBURBS NO. II: BONDI'
Month: A Literary and Critical Journal
September 1857

With cruel and insatiate hunger—feeding her "white flames" on the souls of men—has flowed the everlasting Sea of late. A little blood plashed on the channelled face of the antique rock—a fragment or two of splintered wreck—a few blanched limbs, cut and mangled by the merciless green spume—a human body, gnawed by the white teeth of the surge, cast here and there upon the beach, have vindicated, with sullen power—with a deathly emphasis, as solemn and mournful, perhaps, as the world has ever heard—the slumbering might and majesty of the imperishable Deep! Some of our noblest and best—young hopeful hearts—faces keenly bright with thoughts of home and hearty greeting—children buoyant with the knowledge of having given and taken their last "Good Night" upon the waters—old sea veterans, fresh with the brine on which they had made their home since boyhood—brave but tender lads on their first voyage, kneeling at their sea-chests writing promised letters of safe-arrival to old England friends—all these to be drawn down by the pitiless salt waves, with scarcely time for one brief prayer to Him, who holds the sea as it were within "the hollow of His hand,"—a big ship and her brave company to vanish in an instant from the deep, as a shadow from a glass,—is a thought from which the strongest mind shrinks and cowers as from the great blank horror of a dream!

Shaking her white mane over her devoured prey, all night long roars the Sea out there at Bondi. Licking the sharp angle of the Northern-most Rock that—like some fossil, old-world Tantalus—stretches and stretches for ever to the wave, the white tongues of foam dart at the dipping wings of the screeching gulls, or break in showers of feathery spray upon the giant crags laid prone along the shore.

And when the stars and moon are out! When the little scant vegetation on the rocks casts its shadow in the wave, and the long dark hills towards the Beacon show out in a cold, defined blackness; when the broken crags look dimly grey, and the phosphorescent water gleams and glows like one vast burning lake; when the waves shoot up like flame, and seethe and smoke in the wild vortex of the Inferno; when the pebbles "raked" over and over with the retreating wave, shriek demonically, or seem to be borne down with a low despairing wail; when you look into the boiling maelstrom as into the crater of a volcano, or watch the reflection of the moon broken in the thousand pieces by the bursting wave, as though it were a bark of pearl dashed upon a rock, or a casque of a steel shattered by a strong blade and arm into a rain of dazzling splinters!

From Bondi to the Heads—tramping through the entangled scrub; leaping over gaps in the rocks, down which the eye sees the old sea creeping hundreds of feet below; climbing over crags with faces eaten by the waves into monster honeycombs, or carven into uncouth arabesques; stumbling through narrow rocky passes, with overhanging top-stones, meeting so close nearly half a furlong over head, that only narrow rifts of sky show through to bring out, as it were, the ugliness of the broken stones covered with green lymphic fungus over which the timid foot goes sliding towards the ocean, thundering and roaring below, and angrily dashing its sharp stress of foam far up the narrow gap in the face of the adventurer,—from Bondi to the Heads, we say, is a walk so fraught with fears and dangers, that no one but a Borrow or a Livingstone would care to take it more than once in a lifetime.

We performed the expedition under the most harassing difficulties. Trying, to body and nerve, must be at all times the walk along those five or six miles of coast. But when the excursionist is a novice, and the scrub is one mass of palpitating bog,—when the mind is veiled with the conviction that beneath the shadow of the rocks a ship went down at midnight, and broke to pieces amid the savage breakers howling there below,—beneath such facts and thoughts as these, the walk is robbed of every element that might otherwise redeem it and render it agreeable.

At nine o'clock at night, with just a few pale stars overhead, we found ourselves still fighting our way through the dense scrub about a mile from the Light-house. We were up to our hips in water; our precious face and fingers were most gloriously lacerated with the burrs and brambles; our nether integuments were thickly perforated with the rigid barbs of the grass-tree, on which we had more than once alighted from the recoil of the bushes through which we had tried to force a path; and our shoes were fast filling with the rain water, which the leaves of the shrubs persisted in emptying into them, and we trudged along.

We had reached Bondi at noon—had stood on the southernmost head at one—and immediately afterwards commenced our walk towards the Light-house. From two o'clock till nine we had been toiling through scrub, jumping over gaps, and climbing up rocks, and still another long and dreary mile lay before us. Shall we ever cease to remember that delicious drink—the first we had had since sun-rise—from the little pool of rain-water lying in the bosom of a great brown rock like a sea-nymph in the arms of a satyr? How cool it gleamed, beneath the stars, in its rough basin! How fresh and sweet it came to the parched palate; and how, after a refreshing draught, taken as we lay full length upon the earth, we made up our mind to join the standard of the Temperance Crusade if ever we were fortunate enough to reach Sydney. Presently, and just as we had begun to despair, the curve of red road, leading to the rear of the hotel near the Light-house, came in sight. It was now ten o'clock, and the lights in the windows of the hostelrie shone very pleasantly. A thin wreath of smoke rose from one of the square white chimneys, like incense from the altar of the jolly god, Hospitality. There were a few shaggy well-conditioned goats munching some carrot-tops in front of the house, while an old asthmatical Cochin-China was "making night hideous" with his unearthly crowings. With all kinds of joyful feelings we entered the house; and—O Man! O Weakness! O Frail Human Nature!—laughed at our temperance resolves and called for—shall we confess it?—a "thumping glass of brandy-and-water." The taste of that same cogniac [sic] remains with us as we write. It was pale and hot as gold just ladelled from the furnace—light and beautiful, with a curl of lemon peel winding through it, as a block of straw-ribbed amber—exhilarating to the heart and provoking to the taste as a goblet of ambrosia! In the wild excitement of our dissipation we invoked blessings on Silenus, snapped our fingers at the Band of Hope, and—positively called for a second jorum!

But how were we to return to Sydney? "How far is it to Wolloomooloo?" said we to the fair waitress as she brought us word that no conveyance was going into town that night. "Ten miles and we've good beds," she replied in a breath. Now certainly the "good beds" halved the distance, but even five or six miles was too far to walk. In fact as we tried to rise from our seats to take a peep at the night, we felt a most unpleasant sensation about the upper part of the legs, as if some one had screwed us to the chair. We managed at length to hobble to the door, when, to our inexpressible delight, a cab drove into the yard. "Going back?" we asked of jarvey, as jumping off the seat he began wildly flapping his arms—as is the manner of the tribe—like the sails of a wind-mill. "I'm engaged to this 'ere gent," said cabbie, touching his hat. The stranger looked at us—took pity on our woe-begone aspect—our scratched face and tattered drapery—generously consented to stay at the hotel all night, and left his cab at our disposal. That man, we wish it to be distinctly understood, was what Sir Robert Peel would call a Brick. Phaeton himself was glad of an extra fee, remounted the box with surprising nimbleness, and with a pleasant smack of his whip set off at full trot towards Sydney. We let down the window, lighted our cigar, and throwing our legs along the seat blessed our stars that the preliminaries of sketch No. 2 of "Sydney and its Suburbs" were completed. In a few moments our cigar fell from our mouth (we believe, in our excessive fatigue, our very teeth slumbered), and we dropped, after one or two dislocating jerks, into a profound slumber. Strange visions haunted us. We had not had two beckers [sic] of pale brandy for nothing. We dreamt we were Emperor of Rome—one of the Twelve Cæsars, as well as we can remember—that the plebs had risen in revolt, and that we were deposed and condemned to be hurled from the Tarpeian Rock. Yoked to a bullock-dray we were ignominiously driven through Paddington to Waverley, and from thence to Coogee. Shall we ever forget being led by two common-councilmen, dressed in lappets of ermine with white ferules in their hands, to the highest rock near Bondi? Shall we never forget, too, inspector S—— driving us, as a Public Nuisance, to the brow of the crag, and shouting as he hurled us over, ——

"Here you are, sir,—what part of Woolloomooloo do you want to go to?"

COLONIAL MODERNITY

GROSVENOR BUNSTER, 'BY WAY OF A PROLOGUE. NO. 1—CONCERNING SYDNEY'
Australian Journal
2 March 1867

The author calls them Vagabond sketches, not, let him most impressively remark, because they are the production of a vagabond, but because they bear about them—as will be seen by those who may have the patience to read them—a certain free and easy, devil-may-care indifference to the rules of ordinary composition, identical with the careless and haphazard characteristics of vagabondage; because, too, as the tramp sets forth in the morning upon a journey, whither he knows not and cares not, so the writer will treat of no particular subject, jotting down his ideas in a slouching, idle manner, as they may come to him. In short, like the tramp, he sets forth upon his journey by the first road that presents itself, trusting to good fortune for inspiration as he goes along. He purposes to gossip, ladies and gentlemen. If—as mayhap he will, and often—he may maunder somewhat, and be unutterably dull and prosy, why, skip his folly and forgive it. Let us see if the wheat shall not outcrop the tares in the matter he presents to you; whether, in short, his vagabond sense may not outweigh the vagabond nonsense of which he will doubtless be guilty occasionally. And even here, he bethinks him, fooling, if it be wisely placed, is not always unacceptable. The best of us can laugh—aye, and heartily and honestly—at the antics of Mr. Merryman, and we think none the worse of that gentleman that we know he is a very sensible fellow and a very respectable citizen. What if the writer dress himself in motley, and, hiring a tub, harangue you in *his* way? Honestly, you will have seen many a greater fool make a good thing of it. Take him as he comes forth, disguised in professional paint and bravery; he may weary occasionally—then set him aside, and smoke a pipe. He may be commonplace—indeed, he claims no originality—and, treating of every-day affairs and scenes, must needs, to a certain degree, appear an echo. But what more dear to us than familiar topics spoken of in familiar language? He speaks not of the moon, nor the stars, nor the firmament above us, but gossips of commonplace matters in a homely style. But there!—Bother apology.

NO. I.—CONCERNING SYDNEY

One of the queerest cities I ever set foot in. A strange hugger-mugger of buildings, old and new, mean and princely; narrow streets, too, ill-paved and badly-drained—noble roads and broad avenues, tree lined, shady, and cool. A city of many wharfs and warehouses, of rocks and sandhills, of grand parks and water-views, of gardens and pleasure grounds. A city, likewise, of numerous shaky rookeries, abodes of thieves and rats, vice and wickedness; of foul lanes and by-ways, where the brave sun never shines—where filth and drunkenness, and debauchery and utter misery reign triumphant—and this, too, alongside grand buildings where dwell the rich and fair and luxurious. Astonishing contrasts! The beggar's rags and broadcloth divided by but a wall—Lazarus and Dives within stone's throw of each other. This you see in Sydney.

A city, too, is Sydney, of great bustle and activity; a grand mart for selling, and buying, and—cheating; where, all the livelong day, the streets are crowded with passengers, and omnibuses and cabs rattle up and down incessantly. Many shops also has Sydney, rich in silks, and cloth, and jewels and all the frippery of civilization; and in front of these you behold the carriages of the "big-wigs" and the powerful of the land. During the afternoons, ladies—some fair and comely, many the reverse, adorned and bejeweled—fill these chariots, and pass their leisure (eternal leisure theirs, fortunate females!) in running up bills for their husbands' delectation. In a small way, just such a picture and satire as you'll look upon in any great city of the world.

George-street, which is the main artery of Sydney, from which all the lesser ones spring, is the representative street. Here you will behold every type of the inhabitants, and there are many, curious and interesting. Yonder, behold the business man, common everywhere; there, the loafer, also, no rarity. See, likewise, the squatter, who walks listlessly down the street, having, possibly—if his account with his agents be on the right side of the ledger—no other business to transact than that which concerns his pleasure. Leaning languidly against a lamp-post, behold a lanky, long-haired, dried-up looking youth, yellow complexioned, with an indescribable air of *ennui* about him, a London exquisite might envy—the native youth, ladies and gentlemen, in whom, as enthusiastic M.P.'s will tell you, you may regard the future glory of the country. Well, I dare say. These youngsters sometimes show pluck and energy (though very often in a bad cause), which will go a long way towards the "glory" result. There is much of the Yankee in our cornstalk; and, apart from his personal habits, I respect Jonathan prodigiously. And there is much in common with these two representatives of youthful nations.

Israel is largely settled in this city, and the hook nose and swarthy visage of the ancient people abound. Energetic, indomitable, never-tiring, they are worthy and useful citizens; a little over fond of "the monish, my tear," but never backward in giving to a good cause. You can see them in droves in George-street during business hours, and at night behold them in the balconies of the finest houses of the town, smoking the best cigars that money can purchase. I would I were a Hebrew, for faith, Dame Fortune seems to have marked them for her own. Shuffling along in their slippers and pigtails, comes a string of Chinamen; another race of money makers, having the leaven of the money lender and hoarder strongly developed. Some of these carry ducks in their hands, others, joints of pork, which, after much haggling and diplomacy on either side, they have purchased from some dealer in the market for their dinners, for tomorrow is a festival among them. John has a passion for poultry and pork. Indeed, judging from our Celestial friends' fondness for pig, I see no reason to doubt dear old Elia.

Then you may see Germans, and Italians, and Spaniards, plentiful as blackberries, in George-street—a commercial city. It is a depot of the nations of the earth, whose children wander hither in the grand pursuit in which we are all engaged—the pursuit of gold. Burly and bearded diggers, slouching teamsters, jolly sailors, spic-and-span exquisites, jostle cheek by jowl as the surging crowd passes up and down the narrow pavements of the street. Ah! those pavements. What boots have I worn out, what corns outraged, what curses deep have I muttered as, stumbling over these abortive sideways, I have experienced the benefits of municipal legislation. Old as the oldest among us are these pavements, and in their youth and freshness have been trodden by bucks in floured wigs and extravagant neckties. Governors Bligh and Hunter, Colonel Johnston and Anthony Van Kemp, and a host of bygones, I'll swear, have stepped upon them, and they still exist, effete remnants of a past age. And, save by spasmodic efforts, our aldermen and councilors make no remedy; for which, methinks, the only corn-cutter of the town must daily remember them in his prayers.

While speaking of nuisances, my mind turns to omnibuses—great lumbering, rattling, shivering conveniences—the noise of which sets my teeth on edge. We have no light, easy cars, as in Melbourne. No, sir, being Tory, we retain what did our forefathers. Have we not uprooted the tramway, which, in a mad moment of absurd improvement, we laid down in Pitt-street? and we'll have nothing better (there is nothing better) than those dear old rattling arks on wheels, with their dirty straw carpets, and nations of fleas, their greasy drivers, and impertinent youthful conductors, which have served us so long and well.

I have said youthful conductors, and literally, as referring to their ages, the expression is proper; but it is impossible, while regarding the imps perched on the step of the vehicle, to avoid the impression that they are so many resuscitated old men; for their wizen faces, having none of the freshness and bloom of boyhood, contracted, shriveled up, and screwed into the faces rather of satyrs, unnatural, unwholesome, and revolting, carry in their expression the undeniable evidence of outrageous precocity. Youngsters in years, in cunning, and sharp practice; in blaspheming and low habits, in slang and pipe smoking, they are veterans. *Jehu* and these, too, are the future glory of the country. I'll take my hat, and casting into it a dozen pieces of paper, draw ten forth again, and wager with you that, as I tear these up and scatter the atoms to the wild, so will ten out of twelve of these weird boys live a bad life, pass much time in gaol, and mayhap, terminate their career on the scaffold! Ugh—a bad lot! But, there, my anger is appeased by this little outburst. After all, I may be severe, but I have suffered much indignity at the hands of these men children; have been cheated of pence, bullied and sworn at, thrust violently into the vehicle, and my earnest importunities to be allowed to get out, entirely disregarded; I have been borne onwards past my destination. Is it wonderful my satire is as the west wind, and cutteth deep?

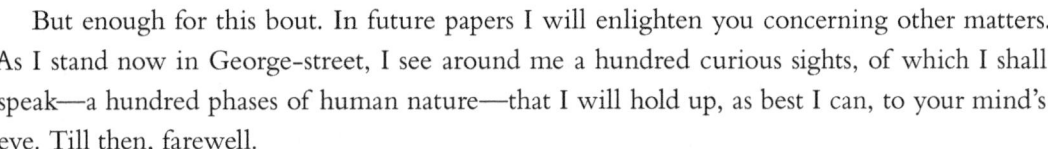

But enough for this bout. In future papers I will enlighten you concerning other matters. As I stand now in George-street, I see around me a hundred curious sights, of which I shall speak—a hundred phases of human nature—that I will hold up, as best I can, to your mind's eye. Till then, farewell.

'WAIF WANDER' (MARY FORTUNE), 'DOWN BOURKE STREET'
Australian Journal
16 January 1869

"Well, are you going down Bourke-street tonight!"

"Down Bourke-street? What for?"

"What for!" with a wide, open stare, and the most plainly expressed disgust at my verdancy, "for a walk, to be sure, and to see 'Paddy's' Market. Why, *everybody* goes down Bourke-street on a Saturday night."

And one might almost believe the broad assertion. If you want to get a fair idea of the crowds that do go down Bourke-street on a Saturday night, just go up to the back of the Parliamentary reserve and take a look at the streams that are pouring down the flagged channels that cross it from one suburb to swell the tide of people who go down Bourke street. It puzzled me to keep in the channel, that is to say, *on* the flags, among the moving crowd of rustling, clattering, chattering, laughing people, of all sizes and shapes, who hurried along the path; and it is very fortunate for all concerned that nobody was silly enough to fence in that flagway, or to even provide it with a kerbstone.

"You might a' knocked me over with a feather—when I got that new belt and the—bottle of gin that she never paid for.—Oh! I never!—past the Haymarket with such a thunderin'—lie! I said so!—ma'am, I'll trouble you to stand off my gownd!" were some of the scraps of conversation that rewarded part of my passage through the Parliamentary reserve; for as to give the whole of them, I might as well try to write Chinese.

If it were for nothing else that you had been pushed and dragged in the greatest of Bourke street crowds for two consecutive hours, save to get five good minutes' look at that identical street, from its head in Spring-street, you would be amply rewarded. I cannot at this moment recall to recollection a more noble and beautiful street among the many noble-looking and beautiful streets it has been my wandering fate to see.

Of course we must all rejoice that the early closing movement has placed so much valuable time at the disposal of those hardly-wrought young men whose unenviable lot it is to stand behind counters on bright sunny days and dull wintry ones, and to humour the trying whims of women who very often do not really know what they require; but we nevertheless, that is, we who walk down Bourke-street in the evening, miss the brilliantly-lighted windows and doors, the broad sheets of decorated plate glass, and, more than all, the magnificent *coup d'œil* that used to await us when we emerged from the Parliamentary reserve, and paused to let the streams of people diverge to right and left of the gleaming thoroughfare.

And a brilliant spectacle it still is, though only now on Saturday night. On that last night of the week floods of light are pouring from door and from window. Did the lamps not stand out independently, and the pavement width away from those blazing gasaliers, their lights would fade into an insignificance unworthy of that broad street. But, stretching away down in brilliant star-like rows, and sweeping up the distant acclivity where Bourke-street West leaves the noble Post Office behind, and creeps away into the far distance, those brilliant lamps stand like dusky soldiers with radiant helmets guarding the wide thoroughfare, and the wealth full emporiums that line its sides.

Light in broad glares from broad, colour-lined windows—light streaming out from narrow doorways, and up from barred areas—light, glowing strangely in great, round, red, and green, and blue, and golden balls through chemists' windows—and light, sending vividly illuminated letters out into the gleaming darkness. Light, battling with night's darkness in a hundred different forms, and gaining the victory down Bourke street! Light, in squares—light, in balls—light, in circles—light, in stars! Light, streaming, glaring, glowing, flickering, blazing, for a long mile of a vista almost worth coming to the antipodes to see.

Choose your own side of Bourke street on Saturday night, but if you follow me you will turn to the right. At that side you will find the most vivid gasaliers, the most tempting windows. It will be impossible for you to go down that side without stopping to admire and to sigh—that is, if you are one of the sex, naturally weak in mind as well as in body; and, indeed, though you should proudly wear a "bell-topper," *could* you pass those attractive gentlemen's emporiums without wishing to try "a suit off this piece, newest style, at three guineas?"

First, you will pass that well known letter receiver. Will you wonder, as I often do, how many sighs and broken hearts in words lie at the bottom of it? If there are sharp, bold, business letters, or ill-pelled, vulgar, scrawls, or scratchy, angular words, meaning nothing but folly, waiting, in the dark recess of that dumb receptacle, for that smart, scarlet-coated official to gather them all up in the early morning?

But you won't have either time or patience to think anything at all about it; for, on Saturday night, at all events, you *must* "push on."

Certainly you must, and whether you like it or not; for you are getting into the stream now, and such a stream of forms, and colours and noises, as was never seen flowing between the banks of any stream in the known world. Little girls—growing girls—full grown girls and women—old and young. Pups of boys and fops of men—tall and short—young and old. Fat and lean; rich and poor. Flaunting in all the colours of a lighted prism, or hanging in dirty tatters of no colour; all bodies moving and talking, and all going down Bourke-street.

Before you get very far down Bourke-street, there is some possibility of your being able to pause and indulge your curiosity at the attractive windows, without the imminent danger of being pitched head foremost into what brilliant sea of plate glass, and its island of "loves of bonnets" spread out before you. As for myself, being naturally an arrant coward (where my pocket is concerned); I never can enjoy, as I otherwise should, a full, delightful examination of those ravishing concoctions of tuille and ribbon and lace and flower and feather. Horrid visions of being precipitated into that maze of colour by some vindictive enemy, and of finding myself borne by fierce drapers' assistants into the clutches of some vicious policeman, while the real criminal has hurried away in the hiding crowd, rises up between me and the distracting view, and hastens me onward in affright.

Here, however, can you pause, you will see two dowdy, middle-aged matrons, carrying market baskets, or, perchance, the more genteel bag, on their arms, lost in a serious consultation about the form, colour, external and internal arrangement, of a bonnet that is to adorn the sandy head of one of the ladies, and has already created virulent symptoms of the green-eyed monster's presence in the bosom of the other.

"I think as I'll have it blue, Martha; with a few small roses and a coople of feathers. And if the ties were blue, I'd have 'em fastened behind, and that 'ud show my new earrings, you know."

"Ay, so it would. Mrs. Perkins; but I'm afraid that the blue and the roses wouldn't become your complexion, ma'am. You see, you're rather sandy, ma'am, an' for my peart I thinks that when a femiale comes to the likes of your age, Mrs. Perkins, the less she 'sposes her wrinkles the better."

"To hear *you* talk, Marthy! 'pon my word, one would think you were about twenty yourself, and a born beauty into the bargain, umph." And Mrs. Perkins tosses her head with that indescribable snuff of disdain so full of expression and meaning.

I wish I could write down some resemblance to that so frequently heard snuff of disdain which *cannot* be written. I should take out a patent for it. But alas! I have tried it in all ways in vain. How can one write down a sound which is simply an expulsion of air through the nostrils, and not a sound formed by the combination of any letters? No, I give up, and class it with that other unwritable click of the tongue against that palate, and which means almost anything.

But this is not going down Bourke-street; and we are still at that absorbing draper's window. Do you see that trio of giggling and conceited girls, who are, in appearance, any age from twelve to twenty? Perhaps I am not quite correct at the present time in calling them a giggling trio, as they are too deeply engaged in a consequential discussion of millinery matters to giggle just at present. Look at the aping chignon and the frizzled ringlets; mark the dangling, valueless eardrops, and the flaring brooches; notice the disgusting fast airs of these poor children and wonder with me what on earth the mothers of Australia are about!

"Now, which would you like best, Maria, if you had your choice? Oh! isn't that a beauty; that one with the sweet feather and the coronet? Look. Ellen! there's one, I declare, just like Fanny Glen's; a nasty thing, I call it."

"Well. I'd rather have the green one, Clara, it would be more becoming."

"Oh! I say (this latter in a loud whisper)—there's William Ray and George Hopwood behind! I hope they'll see us!"

Again, if I could write that sound, expressing disgust, of which I spoke a little ago, I should put it at the end of that last paragraph; not as "sic." you know, but as a private expression of my own private feelings.

"Move on." It is dangerous to linger here, and the crowd thickens. We are getting on famously. Passing, oh, such appetising confectioners' shops, with their tempting buns, and seed cakes, and iced plum cakes, and tarts. And those lolly shops, where the little ones dare not stop else would their little hearts break. "Lemon drops, one penny per ounce;" cocoa-nut tablet, one penny ditto; and the tantalizing Everton lolly, as ditto ditto! This latter is the stuff for the boys, who, boy-like, will invariably patronize the dirtiest of all dirty sweetness.

Go on! Why, we shall never get down Bourke-street if we stop this way. But here is a jeweller's; is it within the power of woman to pass that array? Does even male moral courage resist this fresh temptation?

I think not. I have often noticed the gentlemen more frequent examiners of jewellery than ladies, and invariably, I think, with a more practicable object in view. You will see the *youngish* ones examining the array of signet-rings, or wrist-links, or scarf-pins. These gentlemen are bent upon the decoration of self, you may perceive, while older and quieter-looking men are examining the jewelled rings of small circumference—the sets of broaches and earrings and bracelets—or the pretty miniature watches, intended to decorate the belt of some fair lady. It is no difficult matter to guess that, when you see one of these gentlemen entering the enchanted premises of the jeweller, he is about to purchase a present for some fair, and perhaps, beloved, friend.

Apropos of the simplicity of being able to put two and two together and make four. I saw, on Sunday last, and in Fitzroy Gardens, a serious and sensible-looking gentleman lying under a shady tree in a quiet spot engaged in the intent perusal of a letter. I quite sympathized with him in his search for quietness to enjoy an evidently absorbing communication, but, as I passed onward it was impossible for one of my observing character *not* to observe that the letter contained a photograph, at which he gazed frequently. On the following day I happened to visit a jeweller's shop, and there I saw that same gentleman purchasing a handsome gold locket, a gentleman's. Do you think the guess that it was intended to enclose that portrait was very far wide of the fact?

And if I may confess a personal weakness in peace, it is for the windows of those aggravating jewellers' shops. Bonnets or dresses have no temptation for me. Lollies are an abomination, and pastry beneath my notice; but a jeweller's window is my weakness.

And the weakness of many wiser than I, we may judge. What frequent hushed pauses are made at these windows by the passers by! And is it not strange that they are hushed pauses? You will hear a great deal of talk going on in the glaring front of a draper's, but those very same talkers cease to speak when they pause in front of a jeweller's window; or, at most, they speak in subdued tones, as if there was something awe inspiring in the wealth that lies in such small compass, and in such beautiful forms, in those unostentatious rosewood cases.

Jewellers do not indulge in much *glare* either; their wares are sufficiently valuable in themselves to prevent any adventitious aids to show being necessary. There are no tickets in these windows with the shillings in large, black letters to attract your eye, and the pence (nearly always eleven) in small penciled ones, to deceive it. There is no necessity here for huge placards to insult one's own judgment by the assertion that some trumpery article is the "latest style," or the "most recherché," or the "choicest mode," for diamonds, and emeralds, and rubies, and onyx, are always in fashion, and always "most recherché," and always valuable; and so, were I not Cæsar, you know, I would be a jeweller.

But, for mercy sake, go on, or we'll be crushed flat! Do you see that man standing there by the pavement, with his eyes fast closed and placard on his breast? The placard asks you to "Please assist the stone blind," and I should like to assist the stone blind, and be sorry for him, but the world is so full—so very full of humbug, that I dare not. It would be a different thing, you see, if the coin he asks for would be unmissed by me or mine, for I could then afford to be charitable, and risk the humbug; but, as it is, the innocent must often be punished for the sins of the guilty.

Two or three yards further on you will see a fruit stall at a corner of an intersecting street, and on *it* a placard, declaring it also to be "for the benefit of the blind." Now, that looks like *mean* humbug, for certainly the women attending it are keen-eyed enough, and also quite strong enough to work for the blind. I wouldn't buy an apple or an orange from that stall on any consideration; far better would it be to deposit the value in the placarded man's box, as he at least begs for himself openly.

We are getting almost bewildered now, for as many seem to be coming up as going down Bourke-street. There seems to be a general, but by no means invariable, tendency to take the right, and many are the collisions between the ups and the downs. Oh, bless us! do you see those chignons—those *frizzes*—those trains? Heaven help us with brains! Do you observe the eardrops, and the ribbons, and the glittering jet ornaments hanging in and on every conceivable, or at least perceivable, article of attire?

Are you not overpowered by the bewildering charms of these bedizened women, and oppressed by the loud, vulgar laugh, and—the smell of stale, inferior *eau de cologne?* I am; let us move on quickly.

Stale *eau de cologne* indeed! Why, this is infinitely worse. We are passing the "Royal" now, at least we are being bodily hustled past it, and there is only one word—which I dare not write, you know—that can at all describe the odour with which you are so nearly poisoned. Heaven knows who these loafers around the door of the Royal are; I don't; but I know that they smoke vicious tobacco and drink poisonous spirits, and that you must endure it until you are wriggled past the creatures, or not attempt to go down Bourke-street at all.

Turn back? Yes, I think we have had quite enough of it. That tall man who goes onward as straight as he can, without looking to right or left, eh? "Oh! thank you infinitely, my friend; *my* pocket is on the other side, and there is no purse in it." *That* is your tall, gentlemanly looking man, who takes not the slightest notice of anything as he passes onward. I should like to pick *his* pocket some day.

We will cross over here. Although at night we have still some little danger of being run over by cab or carriage, but nothing in comparison with what we should meet with during the day. Now, don't you find this side quieter? But just wait until we get in the vicinity of "Paddy's Market."

A good deal devoted to feeding the public is this side. Lots, heaps of oysters here, and big, knobby cray fish. Pie shops occasionally, and everywhere the inevitable "public." "Drinks at threepence" very frequently, and (astonishing to relate) a flower shop. Bouquets are here, looking wonderfully fresh, considering all things, and suggestive of stalls.

Ah! I thought so. Here is the old Haymarket Theatre, you see, and what do you hear? Bedlam—or all the bedlams of the universe amalgamated, or Glasgow Green on a Fair night. Well, Paddy's Market does bear a faint and small resemblance to that wild festival, Glasgow Fair by lamp light.

"Daily *Age!*" "Daily *Argus!*" "Daily *Argus!*" "Daily *Age!* *Evenin' Star!* Only one penny! All the latest news by the Panama mail." "Just arrived! All the latest news from Panama and New Zealand; latest news of the week—*Leader! Australasia!*"

That is what you hear, in all tones, as you pass the Haymarket, and just here you turn the corner into Paddy's Market. In all tones, from the most "profondo basso" to the very shrillest of altos; from little, cute-looking, town boys, and from tall, grown men; from each and every one of these you may purchase the very latest news.

Here we are, amid crowds of people, and in an atmosphere redolent of fish. (Faugh!) let us get out of this as quick as the crowd will let us, for I was never a fish eater, and most determinedly detest the stench of it in any shape. "Fish alive O! fish alive! All alive here, *and* kicking! Come, try and buy, and buy and try—anything under a bushel for fourpence! Alive O—alive O! Fish alive! Fish alive!"

"Cherry ripe—cherry ripe! fresh as daises and sweet as sugar! Cherries at twopence a pound! Twopence a pound, ripe cherries! Here, ma'am, give a fellow a turn! There's not finer cherries in the market. Come, taste 'em, I say. Cherry ripe—cherry ripe! Two pence a pound! Cherries at only twopence a pound!"

"Strawberries!—fine ripe strawberries! Turn in and try the strawberries! Roll up, and buy the strawberries! That's it, missus; they're fit for anything—pies and puddin's, and jams, and all sorts! Fine ripe strawberries—fine ripe strawberries!"

"I'll trouble you to keep your elbows out o' my ribs, mister! Drat the man! Look at my gown torn to shivers."

"Cherry ripe—cherry ripe! All alive and kicking—fish O! Fish O! All alive at twopence a pound! Roll up here—roll up!"

Oh no! You must not get bewildered, or disgusted, or stunned, and feel like flying for bare life into some dark street leading away from the noisy spot; nor must your head ache "like to split," or your limbs give way and want to deposit you on that heap of green, limp vegetables. By no means; you must "do" Paddy's Market from one end to the other; you must go up one row of stalls and down another, until every inch of it is covered, and until you are "ready to drop," and until, in short, you are as sick of it as I am.

Look at that tempting array of glittering trash. There are at least eight square yards covered with it. "The choice of any article for one shilling," or "the choice of any article at sixpence." Could you ever conceive such a brilliant collection of shining, glittering, glass and tinsel ornaments? Yes, nearly all ornaments, and ornaments for the female person. God help the mechanic who has a wife fond of worthless finery, if she should happen to drop on this stall at Paddy's Market! Why, there are gold and jet chains (fine long ones, that will rattle and loop, you know) to be had for one shilling, and what's the matter of a Sunday's dinner in comparison with *that*?

Stalls of rich, ruddy fruit, mountains of cherries, piles of oranges, and mole hills of strawberries; stalls of cabbages and new potatoes, and of onions dry and green; stalls of boots and shoes, not by any means tempting these, but strong and serviceable-seeming; stalls of villanous, rancid bacon, and shocking cheese; and stalls of "old cloes! Old cloes!"

A veritable bundle of the articles themselves attends to this latter stall—a bundle well filled out, and not particularly graceful in form, or lady-like in deportment. As she dives between a half dozen of suspended "gowns," of no particular hue or material, and in distressing condition, and leaves nothing visible but a pair of huge ankles and slipshod feet, not intended for exhibition, she looks—well, funny.

A magnificent array of crockery ware and general ironmongery, spread out broadly and attractively on the ground, will be sure to attract your eye as you are crowd-driven past. Here examine and bargain, sensible and generally sturdy-looking women, who value an extra chimney ornament, or new pudding dish, more than a long "jet" chain "at one shilling." There is much haggling about the prices, and many assurances that "the last one as I bought from you wor cracked, missus," etc., etc.; but if you wait long enough you will see the bargain concluded, and doubtless with perfect satisfaction to both parties.

There, you have reached the pleasantest spot in the whole market. Surely you will never complain of headache here, where there is nothing unpleasant in either sight or smell, to remind you of disagreeables. Here are baskets of all shapes and sizes, and articles of all shapes and sizes in basket work. If I were rich I would spend money on this spot—such a lot of money as would astonish you; and I should go home rich in basket-work of multitudinous uses.

I should have jolly market baskets, and pretty little knitting or crochet baskets, and baskets of plain willow, as well as baskets coloured and varnished. I should have baby baskets, and waste paper baskets (and help to fill the latter, eh, Mr. Editor?) and clothes baskets. I should have baskets with lids and baskets without lids, and square baskets and round baskets, and oval baskets; and I should have baskets neither square or round or oval, but of shapes only imaginable and not describable.

And I should have chairs of basket-work fit to ornament any drawing-room, and little suggestive chairs for the baby. And I should have high chairs for the pretty little boys and girls to sit on when they were admitted to the honour of dining with big people; and I should have half a dozen glorious cradles for the baby. Bless your heart, if I had plenty of money, I should take a wagon load of basket-work away from Paddy's Market.

Just look at the crowds of people pushing, and driving, and elbowing one another; and do you observe that cherries are an institution of the market tonight? Every man, woman, and child appears to be supplied with a paper bag containing cherries, and such munching goes on as you would hardly credit. It is beginning to be dangerous for slightly shod ladies to walk on the pavement, so numerous are the cherry stones scattered about. But what business have slightly shod ladies in Paddy's Market?

There is a steady-looking mechanic in front of that stall, you see, and by his side is a comfortable-looking woman, carrying a fat baby, who is making insane attempts to push a whole tangled bunch of cherries into its gaping mouth. The father is supplying two little ones, who stand around him with upstretched hands, from the paper bag of cherries he holds in his hand. The eager delight pictured in the little, anxious faces is worth waiting to see; but will they cry for more when those are done, like big children, or will the fruit make them sick, poor little toddlers, and very cross and troublesome, as they go home from Paddy's Market?

Here are three schoolboys gathered around another paper bag full of cherries. There they stand, a triangular group, keeping their ground in the middle of the moving crowd, and in spite of it. Indeed, they are oblivious of the crowd, so far as their privacy is concerned, and as thoroughly comfortable as if they were in the quietest right-of-way in Melbourne.

"I'd rather have lollies—blowed if I wouldn't! By golly, ain't they sour!"

"You be jiggered; they're fine! Now, you, Jim, you're patchin' away the stones; half's mine, you know!"

"Rat the stones! Why, there's bushels of 'em lying about. I don't care; I've got seven hundred and twenty in my nut bag. I'm tired of that game. I wish 'cherry nuts' was out; don't you, Jack?"

"Blowed if I know. I wonder what'll be in next. Marbles, I guess."

So you see that the "cherry nut" game is "in" now among the town boys, and marbles "is" for the present "out."

"Cherries ripe! All hot—cherries all hot!" What a facetious chap, to be sure. "Cherries going—going—and nearly all gone! That's it, my boy—twopence a pound—as cheap as dirt. There you are! Sold again, and got the money!"

Next pleasantest thing to the baskets in Paddy's Market is, in my humble opinion, a dainty little stall where white muslin ready for embroidering is sold. It is simply a table, or some such contrivance, surrounded by a tolerable high rail, which is covered, as well as the table, with specimens of clean, white muslin, covered with cut-out patterns. There you may have your choice of chemisettes and collars, and strips for trimming anything. Of all widths and of all patterns, white "slip bodies," white vandyking, and white frilling—everything pure looking and attractive, even amid the noises and stenches of Paddy's Market.

It is pleasant to see a woman stop here, although I am sorry to say that as far as my personal experience goes, not many *do* stop. Better the odd pennies spent in a strip of English embroidery, to be worked pleasantly by the home fireside, and to afterwards decorate the little one's petticoats, than three yards of the most conspicuous chain to hang with rattling elegance from the most stylish of chignons. Good luck attend the vendor of muslin whose wares are disposed of without noise.

"The celebrated soap which will remove stains from all sorts of linen and cloth! An invaluable boon to the public! Removes kerosene and oil of all sorts from all clothes!"

This crier is elevated a little higher than his wares; but from his manner of enunciation I should judge that *he* is not the immortal inventor. Because why? He doesn't seem to care much whether he sells his celebrated soap or not; and drawls out his words heavily, as if they were lies (!) and choked him. Over and over again he repeats his parrot-like lesson, pausing between each word to permit of its due effect upon the audience, of whom he takes no more notice than if they were in China.

It's a pity that man has to open his mouth, for it is most evidently a great trouble to him to do so. It would doubtless be more satisfactory to himself if he could sit up in a little box and masticate cherries, like poor Jacko there.

What is it? Why, don't you see it's a monkey, and a monkey for whose appearance and characteristics I have the most unbounded respect? He presides over some sort of a lottery arrangement, by which small quantities of lollies find their way into the stomachs of young Australia, and large quantities of copper coin into the pockets of the proprietors. No, I don't think poor Jacko benefits much by the profits; his imitation of a jacket, and the short petticoats that pretend to cover his miserable bits of legs, are very raggy and tawdry.

Bits of pink and white calico they were originally, and of the same material is the flat pretence of a cap that is tied on his head, doubtless to his great discomfort. Poor Jacko! how wretched an object he looks, and yet look at the cool content of his expressive face! He's not the size of a small cat, you see; and his box, turned on its side to form a frontless house, is barely large enough to hold him sitting on his haunches; but Jacko little cares; he is resigned to his hard fate.

Yes, that is the expression I admire in poor Jacko's face—its perfect resignation. He looks as if he had been so hardly used that fate had nothing worse in store for him. See how he munches his cherries, and manipulates them actively with his long fingers, as the soft pulp is greedily abstracted from the stone. His cap has slipped down—a round, puckered frill of pink, glazed calico—and it now hangs on his right shoulder an objectless article.

And his keen, restless, observant eyes, they range over the moving crowd, in front of his dwelling, as sharp and quick as if there was reason and speculation in them—now here, now there; sometimes resting for a second on a lad who offers him some more cherries, only, however, to pass him without a sign; and always manipulating his nut, and munch-munching with his funny jaws. Poor Jacko, I should like to see you up on the highest cocoa-nut palm-tree in your native land.

One last look at that glowing stall overspread with heaps of lollies of aggravating appearance. How attractive is this corner to the boys! How lovingly they linger around it! Watch the eager delight of these two lads, happy in the possession of threepence between them. If the fate of empires depended on it, could they be more anxious in their selection of favourable investment? What is it to be? Cocoa-nut ice, pink and slushy, or almond tablet, firm and durable? Shall the purchase consist of lozenges or drops, bulls' eyes or peppermints? Little lads—will it matter fifteen minutes hence when the lollies are devoured?

Here we come again in contact with the most piteous objects we have seen in Paddy's Market; and they are neither blind, halt, or lame, hungry or thirsty, cold or ill-clad—they are simply young and silly. Two girls they are, who have been wandering purposelessly up and down and in and out of every alley in the market; for surely we cannot call a plain anxiety to be seen a lawful purpose for two poor girls, of thirteen or fourteen. Look at the taller one's hair, frizzled so absurdly as to resemble a very ill-used mop; and the other's dark ringlets tossed about her shoulders with each affected toss of the wearer's head. Mark the silly giggle and the conscious swagger as they fancy the observation of every male eye in the vicinity to be upon them. Have these girls no little brothers or sisters at home to wash, and tuck snugly into bed on Saturday night, so that the little ones may waken, clean and rosy, in the morning, and lighten the Sabbath morning's work. Or have they no brothers to accompany them to Paddy's Market, or no mothers, to order their stay at home? If this latter question can be answered in the affirmative, what then, ask we again, are the mothers of Melbourne about?

In comparison with these precocious girls who sweep past him with elevated chins, that boy is a useful and respectable member of society. His object is a lawful and laudable one, at least, if it is not in reality what it seems to be, viz, the explosion of himself. His wares consist of cabbages. You see only cabbages; and yet if they were jewels of price, he could not be more anxious to trumpet their virtues. With an extended palm at either side of his mouth, he is shouting, as if in a storm, until his cheeks are at the point of cracking, and each as red as a peony.

"Cabbages! Cabbages!! Cabbages!!!" There is no variety, you perceive, and the boy is evidently not afflicted with a powerful imagination. He has but one idea, and he is determined to carry it. That idea is to make a louder noise in his legitimate profession than that gruff-voiced opponent of his; and he is doing it—more power to the lad! Shout on, my boy! *You'll* never stick in the world for want of perseverance, and thrive none the less for the want of the originality which prevents your framing a more taking puff about your wares than your neighbour. I wish to heaven, that in every trade lying advertisements of all sorts—including tickets labeled "latest style," and "most recherché," etc—were put down by our wise government, and that every vendor was restricted to the simple declaration of the article in which he dealt. Wouldn't it be quite refreshing to read and hear, as you went down Bourke-street, every window and every tradesman reiterating one simple word—"Tea!" or "Bonnets!" or even "Cabbages!" like my boy of the market?

Are we nearly out of the din at last? Well, just let us have a look at the butchers' stalls before we cross that dim Stephen-street. Now, that is a pleasant sight, if you like—a very pleasant sight indeed, and a cleanly. There is no noise here. People will buy meat without much coaxing, and they soon find out the best shops, and stick to them. One could not imagine much room for artistic arrangement in a butcher's shop until they had seen a town one, and then they will believe that even with so unlikely a material as dead bullocks, or dead sheep, or dead pigs even, so beautiful an effect could be created. But there is room for taste in every walk of life, you know.

How wild it looks here in the shadow of the market, with those glaring and unshaded gas lights driven about by the night wind. There is a regular dust-storm sweeping down Bourke-street just now; and clouds of white rolling dust are rising up into the darkness far above the lights of the street and the din of Paddy's Market. They look like volumes of white smoke, or of wreathing steam bellowing out progressively against the background of dark sky above the house tops. Higher up and higher, until lost in the darkness; even dust, then, has a tendency to mount skywards, has it?

COLONIAL MODERNITY

Whew! how cold it is sweeping round this corner, blowing the flaring lights under the dim stalls out one by one, and leaving them still dimmer in Stephen street. Let us get over the way and home, for surely we've had enough of Paddy's Market.

But what is this strange object coming noiselessly around the corner? Is it a phantom? It shows no horses, and yet it moves—a black, huge thing, with imps behind it. Bless us all, what is it?

Dare you go nearer to see? There is one bigger demon than the rest tossing black bags out of it now, for it has stopped; and there is another performing some strange mysteries behind—quietly though, and with a matter-of-fact air. I don't see his eyes blazing in the dark, nor do any flames belch out of the mouth of this attendant spirit; I think we might venture a little nearer.

A long cylindrical object, not black on nearer inspection, but green; an object on four wheels, with an aspiring chimney standing sturdily in front. On its side, in proud letters, may be traced as it opens its huge eyes, "Young England." Why this is, as sure as you live, the wonderful "Hot potatoes and saveloy engine," that has commenced a new era of street cookery in Melbourne.

Its huge eyes? To be sure; it has three, I think—a red and a green one down by its sides, and a furious white one up behind its chimney. Well, of course, they're lamps—can't I see that for myself? and can't you understand a poetical way of talking when you're favoured with polite company?

Well, let us watch "Young England" a little, although if that is not a strange misnomer, I don't know one when I see it. You perceive that those jumping imps behind are simply a few little boys looking out for fun and hot potatoes—anxious and impatient for the latter, if one may guess from the eager watch they keep on the dispenser's movements.

And a great many movements there are. First, those big lamps have to be hooked into their places, and the silent monster fed with one of those black bags full of something—coke, I should be inclined to guess from the sound it made as it was tossed on the ground. "Young England" is just getting up you see, after having reposed all day in some unknown region, and they are giving him his breakfast as soon as he opens his eyes.

Nay, he must have had an early French breakfast in bed I think, and this is a second. Lo! there is heat and cookery in his back premises. And now that dark man opens and shuts two or three little doors behind in a manner that leads one to suppose he has been accustomed to practice the shuffling art of legerdemain; and now he flings an observation to the audience, which is highly interesting to the main portion of it, viz., the boys:

"All hot, gentlemen, all hot! Potatoes and saveloys, all hot!" And, in reply to unheard (by me) orders, click goes the little iron door, and in and out pops the speaker's hand, dispensing supplies of some eatable to the little lads behind him.

What is he dispensing? I am sadly disappointed. In the first place, I am very doubtful if this much-talked of steam engine does anything but cook potatoes and saveloys; and in the second, I am afraid it doesn't cook them according to my preconceived ideas of the management, which is, you must acknowledge, a very unfair proceeding on the part of the proprietors toward— myself. From newspaper descriptions, I had fancied a smart engine, puffing, and screaming, and revolving its own wheel through the streets of happy and benefitted Melbourne, whereas I am sadly afraid that someone shoves it behind.

And I had fancied steam-cooked potatoes, snowy and floury, and melting in one's mouth; such potatoes as I have seen in the days of old cooked in our own kitchen-range. Alas! what, then, are these black shriveled things that this man fingers out of his iron door that clicks, and has no one any objection to their *being* fingered? And what, in the name of curiosity, *are* saveloys?

Well, I'll be blessed if I can tell you. Suppose we invest? Come now, you need not be particular in the dark you know, and as you *are* the cheekiest of the two (hem!) I'll find the cash if you'll go and purchase. Is it a bargain? Well, there.

"Ho! ho! sixpence worth of potatoes and a saveloy! All hot, gentlemen, all hot! Potatoes and saveloys all hot!" The potatoes in your cap, eh? and the saveloy in a bit of very dirty play-bill? Well, never mind, the one is, I dare say, not much dirtier than the dispenser's fingers; and as for the play-bill, well, it's good enough for the looks of the saveloy anyway.

For it looks a dried up, shriveled bit of pork sausage, that's what it looks like, my friend, and its cost is twopence; there you are quite welcome to it, I assure you, and "may good digestion," etc., etc.

One, two, three, four, and four. Eight hot baked potatoes—black, soapy, sticky potatoes, that you would be expatriated for selling in fair Ireland twenty years ago. "One halfpenny each for hot baked potatoes, to be sold here a bargain at three a penny!" No, "Young England," I may be prejudiced I know, but I cannot conscientiously recommend you to the patronage of Young Australia.

And so we really go home at last, enjoying with delight the comparative cool and quiet of the streets. Across the Parliamentary reserve there still flows a thin stream of people, mostly homewards though, and more silent than they were a couple of hours ago. The most delightful enjoyment tires people at times you know.

What is that building to the left there, shadowy and ghost-like in the darkness? There is a long tunnel-like vista through it, illuminated with a solitary dim lamp, hung far up; is it among the rafters? Ghosts of vehicles are there in the obscurity, defying one to define their forms or ages, and far in—away through the tunnel—things are moving obscurely. I should judge the whole affair to be a livery-stable of some sort, and the moving objects to be far-away feeding horses, were it not for a strange object that performs strange motions in the middle distance of this strange picture.

COLONIAL MODERNITY

Under that dim and solitary lamp it is; a dark, distant figure, or rather shadow of a figure, for so it seemed in that dim space, surrounded by ghosts of carriages. Mopping and mowing it was, twirling and twisting, and performing the strangest antics that was ever performed by humanity—if the thing was human—in the dim light of that tunnelled lamp. Was it really only in reality some stable boy performing a *pas seul* for his own delectation and amusement, or as an exercise conducive to the warmth of his toes?

But hush! we are coming near holy ground; not from the vicinity of St. Peter's at all, but from the thrilling warnings that are thundered there in the darkness every Saturday night. Now, if you want to hear eloquence, and see a performance such as would do credit to a professional gymnast, go by all means, and stand within sight and hearing for five minutes. If you exceed that space of time, then I've done with you, and set you down as a decidedly irreligious person, although you have been listening to a sermon.

And for this reason, that any reverent person must be thoroughly disgusted with the man's roaring, blustering, sing-song desecration of the subject on which he pretends to discourse. The advisability of street preaching at all I do not attempt to deal with; it is, I suppose, a matter of opinion. But if we must be waylaid in park and street, let it in mercy be by people of education, who will neither destroy the Queen's ordinary English or shock our preconceived ideas of reverence as connected with religion. Of course, he gathers an audience. If I myself were to go into that self-same spot and shout "Cabbages!" like that lad in the market, I should in fifteen minutes have a larger audience than ever listened to his psalms and hymns!

Just look at the man's antics! Could Lola Montez—were she in the body—rival that pirouette, or equal that bound? It is to take in the circle with a regular sweep, you see, that he pirouettes out that fearful warning; and to fix upon the minds of his hearers the immutability of their sentence that he brings his heels down upon the pavement with such a crash.

"O O O! my friends, look at the lake of fire and brimstone! Think on your fate be-*fore* it be too late. O O O! repent! O O O! my friends, repent before it is *too o o* late! A-And cry out in the be-ewtiful words of the poet—'none but' (shall we say David?) 'none but—!'"

Please move aside, my absorbed and, doubtless, repentant friend, I wish to pass on. Being a person of hardened disposition and most unimpressible temperament, I infinitely prefer the performance of my friend in the livery-stable over the way, and have some intention of returning to witness it again, to take "the taste of this" objectionable "one out of my mouth."

Here we are at Victoria-parade, and here comes a swirl of dust along it, that momentarily obliterates lamps and illuminated shop windows.

But here is another orator doing *his* performance of religion! I can hear the stentorian bellow from where I stand. Hope to mercy the dust *won't* fill his mouth up so "chock" full that he won't be able to open it for a month, eh?

'BANKING UP-COUNTRY'
Colonial Monthly
July 1869

I believe there is no country in the world where banks have made such rapid progress as in Victoria. What town of the age of Melbourne could support so many of those institutions? I think none. There are now in Melbourne ten banks of issue, four of which are local. To these may be added the Land Mortgage, the Melbourne Banking Corporation, and the Maritime Company, all of which may be classed as banks, although not issuing their own notes. These institutions are apparently doing well. We have first rate half-yearly reports from nearly all, and the shareholders enjoy capital dividends. It has been said that the profits in many instances are not quite legitimately obtained, but about this I am not going to speak, nor is it my intention to write an essay on banking morality. My idea is to give a few of the experiences of a country bank manager, more or less amusing.

Every country town with any pretensions to importance has its bank—a branch of one or other of the ten establishments in the city. It was my duty, some five years ago, to proceed to one of these country branches of the institution to which I belonged, to relieve the manager, Mr. Carker (no relation to Carker of Dombey and Son), who was ill, and had obtained sick leave. This little branch (let us call it Burkeville) could only boast of one officer, who was therefore manager, accountant, teller, ledger-keeper, and everything else beside. I must here explain that I was anything but a fit and proper person to take charge of a branch, being utterly ignorant of everything connected with the working, etc. One year's experience in the head office had taught me nothing. In fact, in a large office, a clerk learns how to keep certain ponderous ledgers or cash books, but little or nothing of how to manage a bank. Carker being ill, very naturally wished to be off at once; but this I could not agree to, as I had to be initiated into the mysteries, and eventually persuaded him to stay a day with me. The evening of my arrival I took over the cash, and a pretty time it took me to count those notes. I was not surprised at Carker's disgust at my slowness, for it was nearly midnight when I had finished. He said it was a positive cruelty to send a hand of my inexperience to take charge of a branch—a way of thinking to which I came after he left me.

Burkeville was a small town, not unpleasantly situated, entirely supported by mining—some half dozen alluvial companies, and a host of Chinese fossickers. Gold buying, therefore, formed part of the manager's duties, and, for those unaccustomed to it, a disagreeable enough job it is. The gold (all fine) is placed in a copper "blower," and a magnet passed over it to extract any iron. Then, holding the tray in both hands, keeping it moving, you blow it till your ears tingle and your head feels a sensation like cracking. When the dust is blown out the gold is weighed. An incident occurred on the day Carker remained with me which was rather amusing. He was buying some 3 dwts. of gold from a half-dozen dirty Chinese—this, by the way, being the joint week's find of the party—and had got it in the scale. Several of the Celestials were leaning over the counter, eagerly watching the process. Suddenly, and to my no slight surprise, Carker doubled his fist, and sent one particularly attentive John spinning to the other side of the bank with a blow between the eyes. Whilst pretending to see justice done him in the matter of weight, he had been quietly *blowing down* the scale containing the gold.

"That's the only way to deal with those fellows. That scoundrel won't try that on again," said Carker, after they had gone.

And he proceeded to explain that Chinamen in general required to be sharply looked after. They were all swindlers and rogues, according to his idea.

"Don't trust any of them; test their gold."

And he explained the use of a piece of charcoal, a blow-pipe, and a spirit lamp. How the beggars used to grin, I remember, when I pulled out the apparatus.

"Oh, welly good gold—welly good gold," John would expostulate, as if he felt hurt at the insinuation.

I learnt by after experience that a Chinaman who offers spurious gold for sale invariably bolts at the sight of the "tester."

Carker and family left next morning, and I was alone in charge, and I wished myself well out of it. Being naturally nervous, everything worried me. Gold buying bothered me; paying cheques bothered me; customers requiring "further accommodation" bothered me; and I was conscious of a want of firmness—recommended by Gilbart as essential to a banker—towards the latter, which I could not conquer; they saw it, and took advantage accordingly. I was in a fever of trouble and bother all day. I gave one man ten fives instead of ones, which he was honest enough to bring back. By closing time, my books, notes, vouchers, etc., were in such a fog, that it was past eleven at night before I had balanced, and could go over to the public house to dinner! I could see that the people in the hotel looked upon me as a greenhorn. The landlady (I could have kissed her) said, "she supposed Mr. Carker had left things in a muddle over at the bank, from my being so late." But her spouse (I could have brained him) thought "that couldn't be so, as Mr. Carker was a first-rate man of business, and rather expected I was new to it." As the room was full of gossipers, I endeavored to disabuse mine host, and talked "big" about "when I was in charge at so and so on, and so and so," etc., etc. But I saw them winking at each other, so went over to the bank to bed. Tired, and with a villanous [sic] headache, I turned in; feeling, however, I know not why, a little nervous about housebreakers. There was a pistol certainly in the bank, but I had little faith in its utility in case of need, as Carker informed me it had not been fired off for eighteen months. He, no doubt, felt safe enough, having his family in the house; but I was alone, and, to say the least of it, felt lonely.

And now I come to the thrilling part of my story. But, before I proceed to it, I must explain that the bank building was of wood, in fact, a mere bandbox, with calico walls and ditto ceiling. Any noise outside was distinctly audible within. The road was three chains wide, and the bank almost isolated in position. Well, I soon fell asleep—a sort of dog's sleep. At the faintest noise outside I awoke with a start. At about two a.m., I was startled by a grinding noise close to the bank door. What could this mean? I listened. It sounded as though some one were trying to force in the boards, or bore through them.

"Here's a pretty go, and this pistol's no more good that a ruler," thought I, as I stealthily, and I own, tremblingly, crept out of bed, and walked on tiptoe into the bank. Pistol in hand, I crouched behind the counter, prepared to receive whoever might enter.

The pushing and grating grew fiercer, and I had now no doubt that the bank was to be stuck-up. It would not have so much mattered had I been sure the pistol would go off. There was the rub, however; should it snap, I should be shot or brained on the spot. For a moment, I thought of deserting the place to its fate, and bolting by the back door; but the dread of a newspaper account of the affair, and (probably, a more potent reason) that, no doubt, some one would be posted there to prevent escape, put an end to that. These ideas flashed through my mind like lightning as I stood, quaking with fear, behind that memorable counter, on that bitter cold morning.

Just as I expected, from the last vigorous effort, which made the whole building tremble and my hair to stand on end, that an entrance would be effected in another minute, the noise ceased. Hark! retreating footsteps. I summoned up courage to go to the window and peep out.

What?—Eh?—No! Yes, it was though. An old white cow was to be seen in the moonlight, leisurely walking across the road, and had evidently been, cow like, rubbing her huge sides against the bank for the last ten minutes, and was now walking off in the most unconcerned manner, as if she had not nearly frightened the life out of a harmless human being—*que le diable l'importe!* From that hour I hate cows. Though relieved in mind, I was shivering in body, and turned into bed again, invoking a malediction on cattle in general, and that white cow in particular.

I am inclined to think that most men in my predicament, viz., in a bank by myself, and a safe on the premises containing over £5000, would have felt uneasy, if not terrified, under the circumstances.

Nothing of any importance took place on the following day, beyond my dishonouring the cheque of our best customer for five pounds, who might have been allowed to overdraw to almost any amount. I mistook his signature for that of a customer of the same name, who "was not to have a penny." Every little error I made flurried me, and, of course, led to others; and, in fact, by the end of the day, everything had got itself into a delicious fog.

However, as day by day passed on, the fog gradually dispersed, and the work had clearer weather of it. By the end of a month (the period of my stay at Burkeville), I felt capable of managing the head office itself.

I think I hear some one say, "It's all twaddle to suppose that a bank would send such a raw hand to take so important a post." All I can say is, Friend Sceptic, that I have myself been relieved by just as great "muffs" as I was when sent to Burkeville. I am far, however, from advocating such a practice. It is no kindness to the individual. In fact, it is a positive cruelty, and might lead to great loss to the bank, both in cash and reputation. One certainly gains experience rapidly by being placed in such a position, but the anxiety and worry are enormous, and, to my mind, are scarcely compensated for.

A country business has peculiarities of its own, of which general managers in town know nothing. In a small community you are so thrown amongst your clients, and are so intimately connected with everyone's monetary affairs, to what you would be in a large town. You say to yourself, "How can Jones afford that new silk dress his wife had on in church? Only yesterday I had to dishonour his cheque for £1." Or, "Too bad of Johnston to play unlimited loo every night when he knows his account is overdrawn," etc., etc. Then you are the financial father confessor of the whole town, and many a tale of woe is poured into your ear. How a starving family, for instance, may be saved from destruction by a temporary advance of £20, which is "sure to be paid back in a month." You know the unfortunate man, perhaps, to be honest and industrious, but he finds it a difficult matter to earn a livelihood at his particular craft, and I can tell you, Mr. General Manager, the heart sometimes requires a deal of steeling to arrive at the required state of hardness to refuse some of these poor fellows. Were it not for the appalling question to be asked by the inspector next time he calls, "What security do you hold for this advance?" the "poor unfortunates" would far oftener get the advantage of us. Your country customer is a queer customer indeed. Whilst one man will take it as the greatest condescension on your part to receive the money he pays in, another can scarcely be persuaded that he is not trusting you too much in leaving his paltry £10 or £20 in your hands. Some will enter the bank with a proper notion as to the importance of the institution, and those employed in it; others again, will come in, scowling at you as though you were their natural enemy, and only awaited the faintest opportunity to swindle them. The most difficult thing is to persuade some persons that you have given them the correct amount of interest on their deposit. I sincerely believe that many go away with the idea that you have kept some of it for your private pocket. Only the other day I was informed by a female depositor that the interest on her deposit of £30 for three months, at three per cent., ought to be £3; and when handed the four-and-sixpence, she threw it on the counter and declared in elegant terms that "she'd have the law on us," etc., etc.

An instance of the genus borrower may be afforded by the following account of an interview between myself and a specimen of that class:

Intending Borrower. "I want to borrow some money." Tone of voice conveys that he is doing you a favour.

Myself. "Yes. How much do you want?"

I.B. "A hundred pound."

Myself. "Very well. What security can you offer?"

I.B. (indignantly). "What do you mean by security?"

Myself. "Why, have you no deeds to leave with us as a collateral security?"

I.B. (emphatically). "I don't understand anything about collateral security. I want a hundred pound."

Myself. "No doubt. But we must be secured in some way."

I.B. "All right, then. Take my team of bullocks that's outside, and the dray, too, if you think I'm going to bolt with your money."

Myself. "No, my good man; your bullocks are no use to me. I am afraid I shall not be able to accommodate you."

I.B. "What's a bank for, I should like to know, but to lend money. But I suppose you think I'm a rogue, and want to rob you," etc., etc.; and exit *I.B.*, very wroth. That man is your personal enemy for life, and would do anything to thwart you.

The bank service is a good one; much better than that of the Government, in being safer, and not subject to periodical reduction. Another reason, certainly there is, why it is better, viz., the regularity with which the employés get their "screw." But, no doubt, stoppages of salary are no longer an inconvenience to Government officials, as they must, ere this, have become accustomed to them. *On s'accoutume á tout.* A good service it is, but nevertheless, it is deteriorating. The boy element is now being introduced into banks at an alarming extent; and the vacancies left by men, are in far too many instances filled up with youngsters.

I do not wish the boys any harm, but they are an unmistakable nuisance, especially where there are many of them together. Go into any one of the Melbourne banks, and count the number of boys at work; are they not daily increasing? And such terrible young "swells," too. What confiding tailors they must have! As, in most instances, two boys are required to do the work of one man, the number of hands has necessarily increased without a like result in the efficiency of the staff. Whether this new state of things is brought about by a system of patronage, or a consideration of cheapness on the part of the management, I do not pretend to say; but I am fully convinced that, if cheapness is the object, it is, in the long run, far from being attained. Sift most of the cases where forgeries have been paid, or where petty embezzlements have taken place, in nearly every instance a boy's carelessness will be found to have caused the former, or his want of honesty—probably through pressure of his principal creditors, his tailor or jeweller—the latter. Yet, on the other hand, the old question crops up: "What are we to do with our boys?" Well, I positively cannot say. (I have one of my own, fortunately very young though.) A bank offers a first-rate opening for a youngster; but a better system of discipline will have to be instituted. Boys are apt to be "cheeky" and obstructive, and customers do not relish that.

'THE DUTIES OF A LEISURE CLASS IN COLONIAL SOCIETY'
Australian Magazine of Contemporary Colonial Opinion
August 1886

New communities and young countries are usually intolerant of what is called a Leisure Class. It is supposed that everyone, without exception, who lives ought to work for his living. In the very early stages of "starting a colony," of course, a leisure class cannot exist. At such a time the precept, "If you want a thing done, do it yourself," is enforced on everyone in a practical and even rough way. But after a while good work pays, and some men cannot, and many will not, go on working all their lives. Sooner or later, in all countries, we find a considerable number of citizens who, without further exertion, can live on property they have either laboriously amassed for themselves, or acquired by taking the trouble of being born—a leisure class in fact. But, notwithstanding this, if an "intelligent traveller," with all the voracious inquisitiveness of his species, asks the average Colonial citizen whether the Colonies have a class of wealthy leisure people, the answer is almost sure to be "No, we have no idle people here; everyone is a real working man with us." The idea is rather widely spread in the Colonies that it is a fine boast not to have any leisure people. But if, at the present high state of advancement of most of the Australian Colonies, the existence of a leisure order is not regarded with hearty satisfaction, we may be sure of finding one of two faults in Colonial Societies: either the mass of the people have, unfortunately, as yet not become thoughtful enough to appreciate the advantages of such a class, or else that class has been blameably remiss in convincing the other people of the highest warrant for its existence. If this pride in having no idle people in Colonial Society arose from a true belief in the nobility of work for work's sake, we should have nothing to say against it. But it does not, it is to be feared, spring from anything implying such an exalted ideal. It rather comes from the conviction that the man who is not actively employed in earning his bread—in money-making and that alone—is a foolish drone or a useless dreamer.

But, whatever may be thought of them, there is no doubt that we have in Colonial Society a considerable number of leisure people. From a reason pointed out further on, this number is rather under-estimated. We have many people of whom it may be said that all they have to do is to do nothing, and that they do it nobly. A certain degree of civilisation will certainly always create a leisure class. The average extent to which that class recognises its public and social duties, and the general degree of its culture and education, is a good index of the worth of this civilisation to those who are enabled to take the fullest advantage of it. People with a sense of their public and private duties, who are above the necessity of earning their daily bread, are among the most useful of all possible citizens. Though the reason may not lie on the surface, they are more than ordinarily useful in a democracy. A democracy consists of good and bad people, all of whom have an equal voice in the government of the State. Those who properly employ their leisure are those who, having every facility for cultivating their better tastes and higher qualities, do so. The more they improve these capabilities, the more useful they are as good citizens. They, of course, thus increase the number of good citizens, and shine conspicuously out from the crowd. In a level and homogeneous democracy their social example is more patent and powerful than in other forms of political government. In a hard-working democratic Colonial community, the leisure class are in the happy position of being removed from those more or less sordid and hardening cares of money-making, and making a living, which blunt all human faculties except those of cunning and acquisitiveness. Their employment of their leisure is (to repeat) at once an index of their own mental resources and tastes, and of the higher products of our civilisation, which are laid under contribution to satisfy these resources and tastes. The class which, rather than any other, should give a distinction to our Society, and form an aristocracy in the best sense, is a leisure, as distinguished from a merely wealthy, active class. The man of leisure is, in spite of himself, raised up on a higher level than the rest of the community. While the workers are pressing forward in the closely-packed ranks of the battle for life, unable to stop and look round to see how far they have progressed for fear of a competitor jostling in front of them, the man of leisure can observe the struggle without taking part in it, like a general watching the movements of an army from a height. Such a man can, perhaps, influence the direction of the moving mass. He can certainly see whither the great confused body is drifting more clearly than those who are themselves engaged in the thick of the struggle. The judgments which come from those who themselves are outside or above those whom they judge are usually more correct than the opinions of observers who are part and parcel of those they judge, and are really trying to criticize themselves and their own tendencies. Hence the opinions of well-qualified travellers, because they are usually unprejudiced and fearless, are generally of more use to a people than the most weighty words of critical advice addressed to them by their own leaders, who, from the very fact of being chosen their leaders, must possess most of their peculiarities of character and consequent imperfection of judgment. Now, the ideal leisure man (and it is only of him we here speak) is somewhat in the position of such a traveller. He should be a more safe pilot in many public or social matters than those who have no time to think of anything but their own immediate and limited sphere of work. He can, at his ease, take a survey of all public or social forces at work around him. Others have their judgment warped by considerations of inevitable expediency, and have to bend their will to circumstances. He is independent, and should be able to look at matters dispassionately. He can nearly always do what he thinks best; the others have often to put up with the second-best course of action. Hence, there is no body of men more desirable for undertaking political duties in a country than an intelligent leisure class. It is among them indeed that many of the best patriots, who have at different times served their countries in Politics, War, or Letters, have been found. They need not ingratiate themselves with any man to assure their livelihood, and their freedom from petty worrying cares enables them to devote their unreserved energies to carrying out their views. Such men have a most aptly fitting sphere of exercise in the Colonies.

But there is another, and even more important, direction in which the influence of our leisure class should be noticeable in Colonial Society. The great danger to Colonial Society, as has been so often pointed out to unhearing ears, is an ardent devotion to merely material interests, to the exclusion of anything which is not convertible into current coin of the realm. Money, of course, is useful in any nation to every person, and the English bishop who preached a diatribe against it, and continued to draw his income of £7,000 a-year, exhibited much saintly inconsistency. But we fear that, in the Australian Colonies more than anywhere else, money itself is the god, and making it is the goal, of nearly every member of the community—ambition for this, we mean, *and for nothing else.* No one says that the practical nature of colonists, their commercial enterprise and love of pecuniary success, are bad qualities; but their indifference to anything beyond this is a most alarming symptom. Mere economic prosperity, and a sole regard for and striving after that, will never make great men nor a great nation. Great nations have always shown their greatness in other ways beyond the amount of money they can make, and the importance they attach to making it. Their greatness has forced itself out in devotion to or death for an ideal, in unshrinking national sacrifices, and, above all, in their Literature, Science, and Art. But any honest man will admit that the general criterion of excellence of any pursuit or achievement in the Colonies is simply this pocket-searching question—Will it pay? But all nations find, sooner or later (to their cost sometimes), that it is just those very qualities that do not pay that form their protection in hours of national calamity or social danger. A great historian has well said, that a nation without sentiment may as well cease to be a nation at all. But where is sentiment to appear among a people solely devoted to buying or selling, only intent on over-reaching each other in ways more or less legitimate, and looking on life as merely a prolonged opportunity for making safe investments? Now, nothing is so effectual an antidote to this national money-grubbing as a widespread interest among the people in those higher intellectual developments of which man is capable, as expressed in Art, Literature, or Science. Students of European nations will immediately recognize in the wonderfully rapid advance of Germany a most cogent instance of the union of the practical and the sentimental feelings as a means of real national progress. Who more extravagantly romantic, even lachrymose, than Germans singing heart-felt songs about the "Vaterland"? Who shrewder or keener commercial travellers and agents all over the world? Both from the inherent nature of the case, and from the result of comparative observation, it is found that these higher products of the intellect, so useful in their influence on national character, can only be called forth and fostered to any considerable extent by a leisure class. Art and Literature are tender plants; the cold breath of commercial calculation will blight their growth. It is here that we require a leisure class to exercise its beneficent and appreciative influence. To think out and encourage every scheme for the intellectual and æsthetic (if this word will be forgiven us) amelioration of the people, as distinguished from their material improvement, is the very work which a leisure class, and they only, can perform in the Colonies. The business and professional men are, as we have said, running in the race of life, and have not sufficient time to assist much in the important work. It is our leisure class which should come forward as patrons of all that is beautiful and elevating beyond being merely useful. They should, by an intelligent and well-educated money-spending, counteract the prevailing mania of money-making. If they do this, they will do their country service by forwarding the growth of intellectual interests, by driving home the idea that worldly success is not the be-all and end-all of citizenship; and they will thereby infuse into the clay of our popular body the inspiring breath of an exalted ideal, and a national, as opposed to a ledger-balancing, sentiment.

A glance elsewhere will show that this is not an impossible and wildly-imagined ideal. If we look attentively at the rather degenerate England of the present crisis, we shall see the immense influence exerted by the men of leisure in different branches of life. In politics, the men of leisure, though decreasing in numbers, are still numerous. Many consider, too, that it is owing to their gradual exclusion from this field of action that much of the narrow-sighted, small, and unimaginative, legislation of recent times is due. Socially, the influence of the leisure class in England is supreme, and it is noticeable that from it have come most of the reforms in the way of simplifying and lessening the pompous formalities of every-day life: in this it is notorious that it has opposed the more actively commercial and "city" classes. Even the very "fads" and follies which have been taken up in London and Paris, for instance, have not been altogether unhealthy in their results. The effect of the absurd æsthetic craze, for instance, has been to distinctly increase the susceptibility of people to beauty in their immediate surroundings, and to promote the cultivation of individual taste. Many would be thankful that such manifestations of so-called eccentricity are not possible in the Australian Colonies. Though it may be unpopular—and hence very likely true—to say so, we are not sure that they are right. To ride an idea to death is bad; but it is better than the dull well-fed indifference which cannot grasp one. To abstain and stand aloof from all intellectual movements may show the reposeful contemplation of a well-balanced mind; but what if this mental inaction is the result of a comatose intellect?

COLONIAL MODERNITY

Now, what are our leisure classes doing in the Colonies? The answer is a sad one. They are, for the most part, lurking in a wealthy obscurity. As far as any tangible public action is concerned, they seem to be burying their individual personalities under the tumulus of their gold. Many of those who are worth so much in money are themselves worthless to the community. The idea of their responsibilities, or the capacity for influence they possess, has never flashed upon them. We know that there are, of course, exceptions; but, on the whole, these remarks, if strong, we believe to be true; in their truth only is their strength. The older pioneers of the Australian Colonies deserve nothing but praise for their undaunted courage and ingenious resource in successfully conquering almost insurmountable obstacles to material success, and for building up their princely fortunes. They deserved their rich reward. But the progress of most of their descendants, the inheritors of their wealth, is almost a retrograde one. The greater number of our wealthy younger generation, despite of great advantages, have not advanced. They travel, they are educated, they come under all the influence of European culture, and they return to us—to shake their culture and education off. They relapse into all their fathers' roughness and "Philistinism," which their chances of improvement should have made distasteful to them, and yet they have lost much of their fathers' sturdy energy. It is sad to think that, from present appearances, it would seem that the distinguishing characteristic of most of our future landowners, for instance, is to be a more or less amiable bucolicism. The conversation of most of them is bovine or ovine, their reading is the stock report, their public spirit is undiscernible to the keenest scrutiny. We assert that, unless they are galvanized into some sort of intellectual activity, many of our landed gentry will become, in all but name, a wealthy peasantry.

When the great object of everyone is to make money, those who possess most will be considered the most successful men. It is, however, by using their money liberally and thoughtfully that our leisure class could properly differentiate themselves from the rest of the commonwealth. Unless they do so we shall become, in everything but money, more and more mediocre every year. Those who would be able to recognise or reward talent or genius in any shape are too dull to discern it, and too mean-spirited to substantially help it. Unless our leisure classes try and brighten with some spark of higher life the dull mass of our colonial democracies, we shall every year attain more and more nearly to the perfection of the worst style of a Plutocracy. If people who have money to spend cannot spend it at all, or cannot spend it wisely and well, then we find them becoming proud of money itself, instead of the many excellent and improving results and objects money can bring. The idea poisons the well-springs of all large-hearted and generous public action. We shall then have no emulation in anything save the making and keeping of money. We shall have matured more fully what is patent enough already—a certain vulgar disdain of those who "have not" by those who have; and, as usual, those who "have not" will retaliate by trying to "take" from those who have.

What are our leisure class doing in active politics? Holding aloof. No wonder we have the cry that respectable men will not go into Parliament. Surely if in England, with a constitution almost as democratic as ours, peers of the realm, weighted down with what is to an increasingly large number of voters the opprobrium of nobility, can get returned to Parliament by the sheer force of ability, earnest work, and active oratory, then in our land, where no such class distinctions exist, many of our wealthy leisure men should succeed in winning the suffrages of those among whom they ought daily to move. Turn from politics to learning, and still it is the same refrain. Those who have leisure to do so much are doing nothing. Australians have gone through our Australian universities by the score; many of them have received degrees at the great English universities. Of these an undoubtedly large number are men of wealth and of leisure. Yet no one has had a sufficiently high ideal of "learned leisure" (as was pointed out in a lecture at a colonial university not long ago) to investigate thoroughly (and we take only one branch of knowledge) the languages of our own aborigines, to say nothing of those of important adjacent islands. How many of our leisure classes take interest in promoting our public libraries or lectures, in the improvement of our popular literature, or any other process of that sort? How few, comparatively, are taking any work in our military schemes? No; it is our business men, our active men, who have to take the burden of all such important matters. Our leisure class do not even look on; they are hardly aware that any public work of this sort is being done for them to look at. Their apathetic ignorance is not ashamed at its own apathy.

This defection of our leisure class from the party of those who are doing the best work in our communities is noticeable in many of the directions we have suggested. Even in the smaller, but important, sphere of amusements they are not to the fore. Public amusements are a pretty safe test of public taste. Examples of neglect of our leisure class to assist or elevate public taste in this way are almost ludicrous in their conclusiveness. A leisure class should form a school of taste. They should enjoy the luxury of supporting the Drama, Music, Art, Letters. They should at least relish the higher and more cultivated forms of amusement, and be willing to pay for them according to their value. But how have great artists, actors, or musicians been received in the Colonies? Some years ago, when Madame Ristori, the greatest actress of the last three or four decades, was in Melbourne, it was found that the wealthy classes objected to pay seven shillings and sixpence to hear her and a splendid company. Italian Opera failed for a similar reason. Theatrical and concert managers have found that, with all our classes and leisure people, they dare not charge a sum of above five shillings for admission to performances by world-renowned artists. For this extra half-crown reason, one of the greatest *virtuosi* in the world, Willhelmj, who creates a *furore* wherever he appears in Europe, played in Melbourne to empty benches. In Sydney, want of appreciation of talent has been even more notoriously ridiculous. In England or in Paris, when great travellers, men of letters, artists, musicians, and actors appear, they are made the lions of drawing-rooms and the cynosure of *salons*; Society tries to surpass itself in doing them honour. What tribute do the leisure classes of social Australia pay to such gifted visitors? The tribute of sluggish indifference and careless neglect. Our *nouveaux riches* are not quick enough to see that they might in these cases shine a little by reflected light.

A great deal of this want of appreciation of culture arises from the grossly mistaken way in which many of our so-called higher classes, male and female, mis-spend their leisure time. Our sons devote their spare hours almost entirely to sport. Love of sport is an evidence of manly spirit, and is somewhat of a safeguard against dissipation or self-indulgent habits. But sport should not fill the whole of the mental horizon of our younger generation. There is no doubt that a successful oarsman or cricketer will receive a more enthusiastic and general welcome in the Colonies than a poet laureate or a famous general. When our daughters are not playing tennis, or dancing, they are frittering away their time in cristoleum painting, or we know not what other illicit process of accomplishment and back-door entrance to art, or in tolerating novels of impossible and impassable silliness. After learning foreign languages for some years at school, too many of them are usually unable to cope with the linguistic task of asking for a pair of gloves in a continental shop without making almost as many mistakes as there are words in a sentence. Our wealthy parents have estimated the value of music and French lessons, we shall say, according to the sum they have paid for them. Their children show the amount of instruction which has been pressed into them—just taking these two studies as examples—by complete ignorance of Racine and Moliere, and by a stolid preference for waltzes and opera bouffes to Wagner or Beethoven. Few of our leisure people, young or old, can earn the doubtful praise of being even dilettanti. It is from our middle and poorer classes that our thorough students, our hard-working, well-educated leaders of future thought, are coming. As we have said, "hobbies" are not altogether delightful social objects, but we would sooner see our younger wealthy people taking them up than wasting their lives in low-souled slothful luxury, or in vapid frivolity very seldom tempered by wit. There ought to be a distinct advance in the amount of personal influence exercised on the community by our new generation beyond that exercised by the old. But we fear they have not made their individuality so prominent as their rougher forefathers. Our leisure class must surely possess some faculties; if they let these rust, they will decay for want of use. Heredity will make their children less highly endowed than even their parents, and we shall sink lower in the intellectual scale than ever. Those who have wealth and time at their disposal should not consider the mere possession of these as forming a sufficient and distinguishing mark of superiority. Let them do something and be something; at present they do nothing, and are nothing in particular, except idle and wealthy.

There is one type of our leisure classes which we only glance at to pass by. We mean those whose ideas of the responsibilities of wealth consist in spending it as brutishly as possible—the prodigals and spend-thrifts. They have the reward for their conduct in the uncomfortable truth that, unfortunately, one case of faculties misused and resources abused will do more harm, and stir up more popular prejudice against their class, than ten cases of negatively correct lives will do good to it. The best thing that the Colonies can wish for such blighting existences (luckily not very numerous among us) is, that a regular course of drinking bad liquor, and of vicious dissipation, will soon remove them to another sphere, and prevent their spreading harm around with every penny they spend. One cannot help applying to these blind and low cumberers of our social ground the wonderfully apt and tremendous words of Dante:—

> "E la lor cieca vita è tanto bassa
> Fama di loro il mondo esser non lassa
> Non ragioniam di lor, ma guarda e passa."

It may be thought that these strictures are too sweeping and too vague. As to their sweepingness, we admit that throughout our Colonies there are brilliant and honourable exceptions to the shortcomings of the class we deal with. As to vagueness, such a charge cannot be honestly made by any of those to whom our remarks are directed, if they will take the trouble of a moment's thought. The opportunities for our leisure class doing the duty to the country which only they can do, are so numerous that it would take another article to point some of them out. What we insist earnestly on is this: Let our leisure class have the spirit of responsibility infused into them: Let them firmly grasp the idea that they are really answerable to the community for some beneficial uses of their fortunate and comfortable position. As the amount of taxation for material purposes of the State should be proportionately larger in the case of the wealthy than of the poor, so should our wealthy leisure classes contribute more to the stock of the intellectual and spiritualising treasury of the popular mind. As soon as this spirit of responsibility animates them, it will prompt numberless occasions of opportune exercise.

Our wealthy men might, for instance, very well play a little more the part of the *grand seigneur* in its better aspects. At present, the chief use they make of their wealth—one of the few extravagances they seem capable of devising—is keeping racehorses or greyhounds. The stable and the kennels are well filled, but the library is unused, and the picture gallery is non-existent. Perfecting the breed of sheep and cattle entails much anxious care, but the means of in any way improving the mass of our great Australian nation are never thought of. Let us have the good sheep and cattle by all means, but we expect more than this from their wealthy owners. We do not wish such men to spend too much money in any objects of social amelioration. In a country where the moralist is almost inclined to think there is too much wealth that is not necessary, a little money more often and judiciously expended is what is wanted. Even in more modest ways much may be done. Cannot our leisure people use any such talents as they have to philanthropically amuse or instruct the poor, the sick and needy. In London, men and women of the highest rank in the land have given concerts, lectures, and other amusements to thousands of the poorer classes with a success almost unparalleled, opening to them fields of pure enjoyment never dreamt of in their cheerless lives. Relief of deserving poverty has also become there, in some measure, a fashionable pastime, and, to a great extent, a really serious sustained movement on the part of the higher classes. It is this sort of spirit which must be looked to for preventing what is called the spread of Socialism, and for welding the different classes of a people into one vast humanized and mutually dependent whole. In these Colonies we may not have any considerable class so poor as to need free amusement to brighten or sweeten their hard lives; but our asylums are filled with poor, feeble, or bed-ridden people, to whom life is one perpetual round of days of dreary pain or uneventful dullness. Could not our rich young ladies of leisure, our great and increasing army of amateurs, exercise their pleasure-giving talent, and their leisure time, as happily here as before fashionable audiences? Something is done already in this way, and all honour to those who do it; but what remains undone calls for a large reinforcement of workers. Again, among our crowded cities, there are very many of those saddest "cases" of well-educated persons—governesses, professional men in failing health—who have fallen into blameless distress. Here are the very cases which can only be dealt with adequately by a sympathetic and interested leisured patron. Let our leisure classes take a keener interest in literature, native and otherwise. A poet like Gordon or Kendall, a novelist like Marcus Clarke, will do more to force on the attention of all the rest of the world the fact that there is an Australian nation than numberless victories in the cricket field. Let those who have picture galleries throw them open to the general public, and "compel them to come in." Let those who have time and money assist, nay, even search out after, any young and struggling talent among us. Let them encourage high-class popular concerts by subscribing to them. Let them buy good colonial pictures. Our leisure man should have a thoughtful care in watching all public movements, and doing his full share in helping them on, and guiding them aright. He should remove from himself the stigma of being ill-instructed and listless, of being *ignavus ignarusque,* as the old Latin epigrammatically puts it. We expect our leisure people to cultivate diligently whatever higher talents they have, rather than to vegetate in easy-going sloth. Such cultivation is one of the cases where self-indulgence of a man's own tastes not only gratifies him but indirectly elevates his surroundings and the community. Our leisure classes must wake up to show us there is intellectual as well as animal and commercial life in them. It is their duty to remove the possibility of a reproach that they, who can enjoy to the greatest degree all the benefits of our civilisation, do nothing to diffuse these benefits through the mass of the people. It will be said that it is too soon for all this, that we are not ripe for it. But surely it is better to arrest, if possible, a downward tendency in any social class at once than to let it grow into an ineradicable habit of life and thought. Our leisure classes it is who must lift our communities out of an undue regard to commercial and material prosperity, and that alone, up to a higher ideal of national spirit, and to the possibility of a more elevated conception of national success. Let these wealthy classes transmute their leisure into a watchful activity in furthering, to their full power, all the possible higher developments of public opinion and public effort. Those who choose to lead a leisure life in our Colonies should look on it, not as an excuse for inactivity, not as apology for public incompetency, but as a powerful means of raising the social well-being and intellectual standard of the community. Thus, and thus only, will our great nation develop in its aggregate nature an appreciable number of great qualities. It will gain the whole world much easier if, meantime, it does *not* lose its soul.

ALEXANDER SUTHERLAND, 'THE YARRA'
Centennial Magazine
August 1888

If there lived in truth, some of those kindly fairies whom our earliest years adored, who, with the waft of their wings could bear the objects of their care afar from prosy days into the very heart of the realms of enchantment, then, if my prayers could touch them, I would entreat them, when the weariness of the city fell upon me, when I was filled by that vague but futile yearning to be mingled in the vastness of Nature, I would beseech them to let my waking be, after our airy flight, in no other enchanted world than the beechen forest whence the infant Yarra gathers its confluent rills. For the glories of that forest, unknown, untrodden, and remote, are indeed a world of enchanted beauty. Those beeches, that there in that solitary forest form league on league of dimly solemn aisles; with pillar on pillar, span on span, and vaults of fretted boughs and leaves are nowhere else to be found in Australia, nor anywhere else in the world save in a few lonely mountains of Tasmania. There is a patch of forest of the allied species on a lofty ridge of Queensland, for in Australia this majestic tree, that carries its exquisite foliage two hundred feet into upper air, will grow on no ordinary soil. Three thousand feet must its roots be above the level of the sea; moist and mossy must the earth be where it spreads its gloomy grandeur, and nowhere but on that ridge that runs from Mount Juliet, and bends at an angle into the lofty crests of the Baw Baw Range, only in that one district is the *fagus Cunninghami* to be seen.

And yet not very easily, it is to be seen, at least where the infant Yarra tinkles in limpid threads. Robert Hoddle, the first surveyor-general of Victoria, was a well-trained bushman, inured to the roughest travelling. In 1844 he declared that he would pierce to the source of the Yarra. With him he took a party of men and pack horses, well provisioned, and well equipped, with axes and saws for a laborious journey. He was gone from Melbourne seven months, and in that time he travelled only eighty miles and back. He reached that beechen glory four thousand feet high, though perhaps his lips did not taste the icy coolness of the remotest spring, but what a sacrifice of labor had it cost him? For in that gorge between Mount Juliet and the Baw Baws what an astounding profusion of vegetation has Nature thrown in dense entanglement. Valley and slope and mountain crest are alike the home of the tallest trees that the bosom of our earth lifts upwards to the heavens; giants of gum trees whose tapering stems of smooth and glistening white end at heights that make the brain grow dizzy when we strain our necks to look up at them, four hundred feet above the enormous masses that form their feet, of girth not to be circled by ten men in a ring. These tapering spires wave their thin leaves in stately forests, but as many more lie prostrate. This way and that, they interweave their mighty lines; no horse can cross them, and the man who has surmounted a hundred in half-a-mile has done his day's work and may rest his aching limbs. For all between these prostrate giants the undergrowth is strong, and rank, and luxuriant. Musk trees, and dog-bush, and blanket-bush form a scarcely penetrable jungle; while the scented sassafras joins to make still wilder the vast wildernesses, and the rotting stems of fallen fern trees league on league, make the footing rough beyond conception. For this is the chosen home of the tree-fern. Nowhere, not even in the steaming forests of Borneo is that graceful form seen in such limitless profusion. Its stems rise high with ponderous masses of fronds, the growth of a dozen seasons gracefully bent in every variety of curve, from the pendent brown to the nearly vertical shoot of tender green. Thirty feet is a common height, forty and fifty not altogether uncommon, and Baron von Mueller has measured them seventy feet. And all Nature can show no lovelier sight than a hollow in the hills where from out the tangle these charming orphans of a bygone creation, lift their emerald stars, each after each in thousands and in tens of thousands, down the slope and over all the hollow and up the opposite bank, till they make one perfect sea, of a gracefulness that refreshes not merely the eye, but the very soul of the beholder.

Even now, when the railway will carry the traveller thirty miles of the way from Melbourne and a coach that bowls upon a good road among delightful scenery will take him another twenty, even now the remaining thirty are but little penetrated, and not a dozen men have ever trod the upper regions of these wilds where the Yarra tinkles in its first and gentlest little tones a purling music that fills the else too silent forest.

Let us dream then dear reader, that our fairy spirit has gently carried us thither in soothing trance, and has laid us within that beechen forest more than three thousand feet high. There is no tangle here, it is an open glade, we can see a quarter of a mile on every hand, but we can see no blue of heaven, for though the leaves of this species of beech trees are excessively small, no longer than a house-fly, yet they hang in rich sheets like those of the laburnum, and with twigs and branches interlaced form fretwork above fretwork till the blue is lost and all the wide expanse of the woodlands is a sombre twilight. Yet from time to time there are breaks, and then how exquisitely beautiful are the places where the sunlight falls in a shower of golden rays. For all the earth beneath our feet is carpeted with moss and tender ferns, and the light that plays upon them in a fleckered circle, wakes them into the most delicate of earthly beauty.

Now let us tread onwards, with tree-ferns like solitary sentinels at intervals on either hand. Here they do not grow close together as in the valleys; but they wave their mighty fronds in stately solitude. Hark, how the earth cracks and crunches beneath our feet. For this is no common earth; it is a layer of twigs and boughs all damp, and rotting, and green, with soft cushions of moss; and underneath them lie the relics of forests that grew before the white man ever trod the shores of Australia. All these in moist decay give sustenance to a world of delicate ferns, a hundred species that carpet the floors of this magnificent temple, remote and silent among the dreamy hills.

But hush! a long deep note; a rich contralto! It came from yonder hollow, where a little grove of wattles nestle beneath the all embracing forest. That was the note of a lyrebird. And there comes a plaintive response. Let us step cautiously onwards, while from time to time we hear the mellow phrases roll softly through the forest. If we are very careful we may see these shy and timid creatures at play in their own, their unmolested haunt. Now we see them. They hop in gamesome mood from one black branch to another. We can count a dozen and more; see how that nimble one is exciting himself to amuse his female companions! What courtly bows he makes; how artfully he turns his head with quick, and yet tender glances! And each in turn, all unwitting of our presence, they coo and gabble in notes of melting lusciousness those garrulous vows of love, those vocal sweets and endearments, that belong to their honeymoon season.

And this is where the infant Yarra springs? Yes, if you peer beyond the birds and through the twilight gloom of the wattle trees, you will see the hollow glistening with a few inches of water, a silver surface but broken with the floating leaves of a bright green marsh-plant and with the tiny stars of white that are its flowers. This we shall choose as the central one of many such slender little shallow pools that sleep in the beechen forest and we shall make it our starting point. We are to follow the streamlet hence, from its babyhood in purity, in solitude, in loveliness, with only sweet and innocent things to be its companions—follow it away through all its devious courses, till foul and dirty, and be-draggled with stench and slime and the infernal plash of brick-built sewers, it ends its polluted career among crafts, whose crews are too often but obscene and drunken comrades for the once pure and joyous beauty that trilled its little life beneath the beeches.

But that is far in the future, and now as we follow it down its gently sloping hollow, though we scarce can detect the little rill, yet its waters are bright with the sparkle of perfect purity. At times we lose it altogether, it dodges in among a tangle of moss-grown fern trunks, that compels us to leave it and keep a little higher than the trickling current at the bottom of the hollow. But in that way we chanced to see a curious little sight. It is a little patch of bareness, rising into a tiny mound like an ant-hill, but with no ants. It is formed of twigs and gravel, and is an almost perfect circle of brown in the illimitable green of moss and fern that carpets all the forest. This is a dancing place of the lyre bird. If we traversed the woodlands far enough, we should from time to time stumble across these little places, which when the season comes will be lively sights for those who might then behold them. For when the male birds are adorned in all the glory of their lyre-like tails, those graceful feathers, white, and brown, with their tip of coquettish black, they will hither resort to show their splendour. Here, when these ornaments are erect, to show their elegant curves the gallant suitors will strut, and posture, and dance, while the more sober suited females will circle round and admire the amorous rivalry. Then will each aspirant strain his every muscle in the dance, for a notable prize awaits the victor, the love of not one but many of the circling females, who will need but small caressment ere with heavy whirring wings they flit along with him to be his brides, far in the scented recesses of some wattle brake.

But the sight of these courtly tournaments will not be granted to us, they are the rare pastimes of sunset hours in spring. We have the little stream to follow down the course of its dreamy hollow. That shallow valley becomes more and more pronounced until it is a little glen with sides that would be rocky but for the all-embracing mosses that stand in round cushions of delicious greens, or in lines of gleaming emerald along the twigs and branches of upright sassafras or prostrate wattle.

The glen becomes a gorge, on whose side the tree-ferns rise innumerable. The beechen forest is ended, and we are in the realm of giant white-gums. From out of the gorge and its steep sides, the great pillars rise from roots like buttresses and mingle at stupendous heights their branches and their quivering leaves.

And the stream is now a mountain burn. From many another source its rills have gathered and its waters are now a yard in width. How wild the little thing appears, with all the wayward yet lovable whims of infancy.

> Its murmuring waters now concealed,
> Now peeping out till half revealed,
> Now bounding forth with foam and spray,
> To tumble down their rocky way.
> And still, the current as it passes,
> Just flouts the twigs and waves the grasses;
> And in and out at every turn
> Bedews the moss and beads the fern.

So onward it flows, down and downward ever, very still in an occasional brown pool wherein the white cloudlets float upon the azure of far inverted skies, but very noisy in its tiny leaps over moss-grown boulders; and very passionate, growing white with childish temper where the fallen tree-ferns, with fronds and trunks, have blocked its path. How deep and silent the great valley now becomes, the crests of its sloping sides far, far above us while we are in a reign whose stillness is broken only by the occasional sweetness of the bell-bird's cadence, or after twilight by the chuckle with which the native bear derides the moon, when first he puts forth his furry little head to creep outward for his meal on dew-bathed gumleaves.

Another deep gorge joins this wild chasm of ours, a long furrow descending from another part of the Baw Baw Ranges. It seems of equal loveliness, and at least of equal wildness. It contains a similar little brawling rivulet which with a sudden rush delivers its gliding waters into those of the rill whose laughter has made glad our way for a mile or two down the gully. And so the river, increased to nearly two yards in width, and with its silvery tinkle converted to a muffled roar, rushes, and glides, and foams, and tumbles; at every mile its valley grows more and more choked with vegetation. Long sassafras trunks, whose bark has a refreshing scent, lie like bridges spanning the waters, and resting on these are masses of tree-ferns, borne down by bygone floods; and out of their rotting substance grow perfect little ferneries, where amid broad-leafed species and fronds of darker tint the dainty elegance of the star fern or the delicate tracery of the coral fern tremble to the wind that is caused by the rushing and leaping waters.

Thus, gathering volume as it goes, the little river prepares itself for its great descent, which Professor Kernot estimates as in all about eight hundred feet. Its first leap is about seventy feet in a splendid double cascade, the water bursting into foam upon a rocky ledge about half-way down. Then, enclosed within narrow walls of glistening rock, it drops by steps of twenty, thirty, or sometimes fifty feet in height, scarcely resting from one cascade ere it is hurried to cast itself headlong over another. The whole valley is filled for ever with the roar of waters, which returns in softened echoes from the all-enclosing ranges. And the river which thus in a mile has made its great descent, has left its mountain heights, its beeches and its tree-ferns, to flow in calmer measure on a more level ground. Away below, where forests of giant gum trees wave in sunny expanses mile after mile till they rise in bluer tints upon the hill sides, there flows the river in gloomier forests, bordered by pathless wilderness, and shaded by over-arching evergreens.

Its wilding life of early childhood is over. It must conform a little to regular ways. It is grown a peaceable, steady, and well-conducted little river. It has still its beauty and its poetry; but never again can it dance with the wild exuberant joy, with the rippling laughter, with the graceful waywardness of its course among these heaven-kissing hills.

COLONIAL MODERNITY

W.B.S. (WALTER BALDWIN SPENCER), 'THE DESTRUCTION OF EUCALYPTS'
Australasian Critic
1 May 1891

To those who are at all accustomed to the apparently endless gum-forests of Australia, any idea of their destruction, to more than a most limited extent, will doubtless appear very strange. And yet there is probably some danger of this being carried on in a much greater and more wide-spread way than we imagine. In a paper recently read before the Field Naturalists' Club of Victoria, the author, Dr. Woolls, of Sydney has brought together some interesting data with regard to this subject. His facts naturally deal more with New South Wales than with the other colonies, but what is true of one portion of Australia is in all likelihood true of the rest. It was, of course, absolutely necessary that clearings should be made as settlements gradually spread inland from the sea coast, but everywhere it has seemed to be the policy of the settlers to completely clear off the gum-forest, irrespective of the industrial value of the trees or any subsequent need of them for such purposes as fencing or firewood. This absolute clearance of the land has been carried on, and is still being carried on, to far too great an extent.

Opinions are very much divided as to the influence on climate produced by the destruction of trees. Some say that the rainfall is thereby much diminished; others are equally certain that no result of this kind follows. Though the data at our command are not sufficient as yet to allow of the formation of a very definite conclusion, it is surely evident that the complete changing of the nature of the surface of the country must, in the long run, produce some definite climatic result, and it is much to be hoped that some stop may be put to the indiscriminate clearing of the forest. In many parts, for example, of Gippsland the hillsides are completely denuded of the woods which once clothed them to their summits. It would be thought that at least large clumps of forest might be left without much loss to the settlers, and the axe has been freely applied in the most wanton manner. That the destruction has been excessive is borne evidence to by the very existence of our State nurseries, which are now engaged in the task of rearing and distributing young forest trees to districts which have suffered in this way.

Everyone who has travelled in the country parts, far beyond the towns and settlements, has been struck at times by the strange and weird appearance of larger or smaller tracts of dead gum forests. Sometimes the dead forest forms a large patch, at others a long belt, extending, it may be, for miles, sharply marked out from the surrounding living forest. In these cases some other agency than man has been at work. These natural agencies may be roughly classified as floods, droughts, and parasites.

Even the so-called river-gum which lives by water-courses and in damp low-lying districts is unable to endure a prolonged flood. Of all countries Australia seems the most liable to prolonged periods of excessive drought and flood. So much is this the case that trees may grow during a long series of years, and even attain to nearly full size, in the beds of what are potential lakes. This has been noticed apparently in the cases of Lakes Regent George and Bathurst, whose dimensions vary according to the season. For years gum saplings may flourish on parts which in wet years form the bed of the shallow lake, and when once the flood comes and lasts for any length of time they die. Mr. Russell, in particular, has shown that this has been true of Lake George.

Droughts, with their intense heat and accompanying bush fires, do much damage but apparently not so much as floods for the gum-tree shows a remarkable recuperative power after being scorched and fired.

Dr. Woolls in his paper referred to the damage done to the trees by the opossums. We should, however, doubt much whether any serious harm arises from what must, at all events, be the very limited ravages of this animal when it feeds upon the young gum leaves. There seems to be but very little evidence, if any, to connect the opossums directly with the destruction of the gum-forest nor do they probably exist anywhere in such vast numbers as to form a great source of danger from their leaf-eating propensities.

On the other hand, there is no doubt whatever that parasites, certainly animals, and perhaps also plants, form an important source of danger. The Baron v. Mueller has stated that the common forest-gum, *Eucalyptus tereticornis,* and the river-gum, *Eucalyptus rostrata,* become occasionally destroyed over extensive areas by a phasmatideous insect which devours their foliage. Mr. Howitt found that in Gippsland the same trees were destroyed by a moth, which Sir W. Macleay stated to be allied to the form *Orgyria*. Another gum-tree, *Eucalyptus odorata,* suffers apparently from the ravages of a nocturnal cockchafer, which devours the leaves, and may finally destroy the whole tree. So far back as 1863-4 Mr. Howitt, one of our best observers, noted that a belt of red-gums extending across the Gippsland plains between Sale, Maffra, and Stratford was beginning to die. All gradually perished. Still later, in 1878, he observed the red-gum forests of the Mitchell River to be dying, and, on investigating the subject, found that the trees were infested with myriads of the larvæ of a nocturnal Lepidoptera which devoured the upper and under epidermis of the leaves. Some of these larvæ were hatched out and have proved to be those of *Urubra lugens*. A very curious fact in connection with this is that the insect only attacks, to any extent, the red-gums whilst it leaves unharmed the white and swamp gums growing in the same neighborhood.

The same naturalist has drawn attention to the fact that the long-continued use of the country for pasturage has greatly hardened the soil, so that rain which once soaked into the soil now runs off, with the result that the gum-trees at once suffer from lack of moisture, and being thereby weakened, are rendered more susceptible to attacks of parasites. In fact, one apparently slight change in the environment of the gum-tree becomes at once the centre of an ever-increasing circle of changes, the far-reaching effects of which cannot possibly be foreseen.

At the same time, it is interesting to note that so acute an observer as Mr. Howitt is of opinion, as the result of long observations, that settlement on the land has in certain respects favoured the growth of gum-trees. He has himself watched the increase of forests of young saplings in parts such as the valley of the Snowy River, which, since the advent of the white man, have so increased that now "it is difficult to ride over parts which one can see by the few scattered old giants were at one time open, grassy country." The growth of these forests Mr. Howitt attributes to the care taken, as far as possible, to prevent bush fires and the consequent opportunity of growth given to young saplings. Along with this, however, goes the multiplication of insect life unchecked by fire and the consequent devastation of grass and crops. We are, in fact, at present only in the experimental stage and it is earnestly to be desired that the governments of the various colonies will, meanwhile, spare no efforts both to form forest reserves, to maintain the present forests and in some way to check the prevalent mania of often useless ring-barking. Both New South Wales and Victoria have able and active conservators of forests and we may hope that under their fostering care there will always exist forests capable of providing a good supply of timber requisite for the various needs of the colony.

'NOTES ON CYCLING'
Block
15 August 1896

It has always been a dream of the poets for women to stand on an equality with men. Shelley wrote:

> "Never can peace and human nature meet,
> Till free and equal men and women greet
> Domestic peace."

Whitman is for ever urging that the proper development of the physical frame of woman will be the inauguration of a new race of human beings upon earth. It seems as though the bicycle is destined to be one of the most potent factors in this social revolution. As regards health, a leading physician said lately that "not within 200 years had there been any one thing which had so benefitted mankind as the invention of the bicycle," mainly from the fact that it has put all the world out of doors. "You may be sure," he says, "these people are not going to be put indoors again having tasted the pleasures of air and sunshine. Wheels will be cheap in a short time, their present high price is because demand is so great that enormous profits can be secured by manufacturers, middlemen, and retailers." But signs are abundant that prices will soon be lowered by dint of competition, and bicycles will be deemed as necessary a part of the household as a stock of umbrellas.

W.T. Stead thinks the bicycle will play an important part in rationalising the dress of women. In one of his sprightly "notes" in the *Review of Reviews,* Mr. Stead says:—"Among all the agencies which have been influential in humanising women,—that is to say, giving them a share of the common life with its common humanities, with its weariness, thirst, hunger and adventures and general commingling with the common life of our common world, the cycle stands easily first. It is also possible, although not probable, that it will leave a permanent trace upon the dress of one half of the race. When women cycle, whatever dress they wear, whether it be rational or skirted, they break once and for all with the tradition that it is indelicate for any one to show a stockinged calf, and when once that ancient tradition is broken down the scope for variation in female costume will be indefinitely increased."

But perhaps the most important function will be the strengthening of ties between husband and wife when they find there is an outdoor recreation that both can share and enjoy. This influence of the wheel as a factor in domestic felicity has not been prominently brought forward. Wives and husbands, notably those who have reached the early forties and beyond, have found a bond of companionship in the bicycle that is as strong as it is oftentimes unconscious. The advent of children and the encroachments of business cares are two elements of life that slowly force a man and wife apart to a greater or less extent, till, after twenty years of matrimony, it not unfrequently happens that without any jar or conscious estrangement the two are spending most of their time in separate pursuits. Into this breach the wheel has slipped with a magnetic power. A common enthusiasm for the steel steed brings them together in interest; their daily spins in company make them amusement sharers, and the silver wedding anniversary is likely to stretch on to the golden one, if they are spared to see it, with their lives largely welded.

To the closely united couples, too, the wheel has to come. Said a wife recently: "I am going to learn to ride a wheel this Summer while I am out of town. My husband, the most conservative of men, has resisted the craze till now, but he is about to take it up, and I foresee dire results if I do not also. In all our married life, despite various cares and anxieties, it has been our habit to take little outings together—sometimes only a day, sometimes a week, or a month, as it happened, but always together, walking, driving, or sailing. Now, if he rides a bicycle and I do not, it will mean separation on these expeditions. From now on we need each other more than ever, for our sons and daughters are nearly ready to go out into the world. So, though the children smile at the idea of 'mamma on a wheel,' that is where she is going to be."

COLONIAL MODERNITY

J.D. FITZGERALD, 'SYDNEY: THE CINDERELLA OF CITIES'
Lone Hand
1 May 1907

The parallel suggested in the title will not, on consideration, be found far-fetched. Sydney is in the position of the Cinderella of the fairy tale—in the kitchen, covered with soot and grime, slovenly and out-at-heels, bedraggled and neglected; yet with the beauty of face, and all the natural charms of form and color, obscured, but not eclipsed. The fairy god-mother will come, sooner or later, and the Cinderella city will show the beauty that is hers, and the world will look towards her from afar, and marvel at the charms and perfections which are now hidden. Travelers will come from the uttermost horizons to pay homage to her; poets will sing of her; and she shall sit, in the time to come, like a beautiful princess enthroned by her sparkling waters.

Let us consider this problem: Here is this city of Sydney, with the finest natural position on the globe's surface. All "the glory that was Greece and the grandeur that was Rome" in beauty of site is hers. What have her citizens done with it? The citizens of Athens turned their mountain tops to glorious account; they crowned them with exquisite marble temples and shrines. The old ædiles of Rome capped their seven hills with noble structures. Paris has been torn to pieces and beautified. Hamburg and Vienna, and even Manila (in the dreamy regions of the Asiatic), have cast down their mediæval walls, and filled up their moats to make gardens, and ring streets and park girdles. Slow, flat, ponderous, self-satisfied London has grooved out its crowded central places, and constructed noble streets on the sites of slum and alley.

But Sydney! Suppose the fate of fabled Winetha—swallowed for its sins by the waves of the Baltic, but visible to the eye of the mariner on calm days, with its silver ramparts, its marble columns, its noble palaces, towers and walls beneath the water, rising from the ocean "to sun itself in daylight" on Good Friday, only to be submerged on Easter Monday—suppose that Winetha's fate overtook Sydney, and the blue Pacific rolled over her merchants' and bankers' and traders' palaces—over the domes and cupolas, the spires and towers of her civic, her State, her religious halls and ministers, her cathedrals and pavilions, what could Sydney show in her record of civic existence to justify the title to occupy so noble a site? What answer could she make to the accusation which History would hurl at her—she, the city of the beautiful bay which she had polluted with her sewerage; of the noble cliffs and headlands which she had disfigured with architectural monstrosities; of the splendid natural forests which she had wasted to replace with alien vegetation, not a hundredth part as beautiful; of the fairy islands which she had delivered over to other than picturesque uses?

By her own exertions what has she done but "uglify" the primeval beauty of her site? Nature poured all natural advantages into her lap, and she has despised and mutilated them. As a seaport and commercial entrepôt she can vie with Tyre and Sidon and Carthage, with the Hanse towns in the North, and the glories of Venice, Pisa, and Genoa in the South of Europe in their golden days of pomp and power. But her "merchant princes" have no civic patriotism. In ancient Rome the great men were builders of palaces and aqueducts and cloacas; they were citizens first, and rulers of the world afterwards. Rome was a city Republic. The civic spirit manifested itself in noble improvement schemes—in baths, and palaces, and temples, theatres, and colosseums. Her ruined monuments to-day show the greatness of her civic conceptions. If the city were ill-governed the Roman populace strangled or crucified an ædile or two, and by this means the civic Furies were appeased, and things went better. (In Sydney the citizens would have to dispose of nearly 500 ædiles before any good result would follow.) In the Hanse towns and the Italian seaports the civic spirit made the citizens co-mates and peers of emperors and kings, makers of treaties, and rulers of provinces.

Now, let us glance for a moment at the situation of this Cinderella city, and measure the advantages which Nature has lavished upon her. The first thing to remark, in view of future expansion, is that she lies in the very centre of a network of salt-water lakes—the waters of the blue Pacific surging and pulsing in and out through high, bluff entrances; between shelving shores, with milk-white and saffron-hued beaches, over-looked and commanded by high promontories and miniature capes. The southern most of these lakes, Port Hacking, stretches into the forests of the Illawarra region—a region to which the twining vine and the cabbage palm give the appearance of a coral patch which has drifted from the North Pacific and anchored itself to the great island-continent. A flat plain holds the waters of Botany Bay, and, north of that, bold cliffs barrier back the sea, until they crack asunder to make an entrance to Port Jackson. To the north again, past silver and saffron beaches, the waters of Narrabeen Lake; and further again, the varied beauties of Broken Bay, broad and restless at the mouth, converging into the lake and island scenery of the Hawkesbury River, which excels the Rhine in all the characteristics of bold headland, picturesque island, smiling cultivation, and forest-covered crag and peak, olive-green under the bluest of skies. All this lake and harbor region is the site of the Sydney of the future—not occupied yet, but to be occupied in the not distant days to come.

In the very centre of this system of salt water basins, the ocean runs through a narrow throat between cliffs of sandstone—a fissure in the walls of rock—into a noble bay. On this bay, Port Jackson, is built a city, favored *in excelsis* by reason of its natural conformation, its perfect scenery, its protected berthage, its depth of water, its salubrity of climate, its commercial position, its hygienic advantages. In this bay the primeval forest yet runs down to the white sandy beaches; the masts of the world's ships contend with the foliage of giant red, blue and spotted gum, turpentine, iron and stringy bark; the spars and yards and cordage of the one blending, in a picturesque etcher's dream, with the lofty limbs and fantastic tracery of the other. The watery reaches of this Bay spread abroad to the long arms of the Middle Harbour, the quiet nooks of Lane Cove River and Villa Maria, and the Parramatta River with its clumps of mangrove and swampy shores.

Amid all this panorama of lake and stream, harbor and shore—the city, huge, amorphous, spreads itself year by year with increasing haste, in ever-widening circles. Through the central gateway of the Pacific—through the massive portals of the North and South Head—the ships of the world are proclaiming, with their hundred flags, the commercial greatness of the present, and heralding the greater future of this city—a city flung down in a crazy mass, formless, inorganic, a maze of slums, of ruelles, defilés, cul-de-sacs; a tangle of competing and incompetent civic, governmental, and private authorities; its commercial centre crowded and embarrassed and choked by the narrowness of its planless thorough-fares; its outer suburbs reproducing the defects and the mistakes of the inner core of the city. In the beginning of its history, when the skilful engineer, the architect, the artist, and the landscape gardener should have conspired together to mould the cradle of the great city that was to be, the wandering cattle, the bullock wagon, the vagrant bush track set the plan for the future. In every respect, from the first, civic anarchy has had its own way with Sydney.

To-day the planlessness of the city is as apparent as it was when the convict woodcutter, or the pig-tailed soldier, carved out George-street or Pitt-street with the casual axe, or traced them with the pioneer's cart wheel. The criminal negligence of the past is matched by a criminal content and neglect as to the possibilities of present improvement and of future growth. The government of the great civic whole is split up into small, helpless fragments. Legions of authorities—municipal, statutory, governmental, private enterprise—war and clash on the area of Greater Sydney. Forty-three municipal authorities—buried to the knees and walled within their own small areas, incapable of combining for the organization of Sydney's future greatness—retard its progress by jealous incompetence.

We look abroad, and see Glasgow and Birmingham re-built, and beautified, and rendered healthy and wealthy in the re-building. We see the model city—the garden of Paris—with its avenues and its boulevards, tree-lined, and miles long. We see the citizens of Boston or of Philadelphia pointing to his hundred mile avenues, broad and straight, and piercing the horizon. We see Melbourne with its spacious plan. We look from one hill in Bourke-street up a noble boulevard to the hill topped by the Federal Houses, or from the Market buildings in Collins-street to the Treasury hill; we see the gardens multiplied and the flower-beds planted in the very centre of the business parts, and we sigh with envy. Adelaide draws our admiration for its broad plan and splendid possibilities. Is it not possible for Sydney to emulate the achievements of other races of city dwellers; to carve out the city and re-build it on a new plan; to restore and increase its natural beauty without diminishing its commercial advantages? Can we not also demolish the slum—"the slum, which disgraces our civilisation," said King Edward VII.—and beautify the area, and create new commercial centres? Can we not cover the city with parks and gardens and flower-plots, and erect triumphal arches and glistening fountains, and open out the spaces before our public buildings, and plant lines of trees in our streets?

And there are other considerations, not less important. There is the future of the race. In every progressive community the tendency is for people to crowd into cities and towns. Australia no longer regards its territory as a gigantic sheep run. It is beginning to put its mind to manufacturing. It is beginning to grow rich, and to have a higher appreciation of the value of its men—of how they shall live, and how they shall be clothed and fed and paid. It looks out at possible foes, and the dangers to our wealth from the cupidity of Northern nations. To hold its own it must guard the stamina of the race. If the destiny of a progressive race is fixed as that of town-dwellers in the future, then country conditions must, so far as possible, be combined with city conveniences. "You cannot rear an Imperial race in the slums," said Rosebery. "Look!" said John Burns, one day, pointing out a group of stunted London *gamins* to the writer, "There are the dwarfs of Savage London. The Country Council is going to make men of the next generation."

Sydney, so full of contrasts—contrasts of wealth and poverty, of palace and slum, of commercial concentration and efficiency, with civic ineptitude and dismemberment—will repay study. The student of the civic problems, that are well on the way to solution in Great Britain and America, has here virgin soil in which to plant his ideas. It is worth while. Sydney has a strange power of attraction for those who have once sojourned within her walls. Brady, the poet who has sung of ships and wharves and quays; who has, with his poet's intuition, fathomed the mind of the nomads of the deep, has told us their thoughts of the City of the Harbor:—

> *She has subjects to her homage, has the Siren of*
> *the South—*
> *With a crown upon her forehead, and a love-song*
> *in her mouth;*
> *With her gold and purple raiment, and her eyes of*
> *witchery.*
> *Will you come and walk on Sunday with the*
> *Lady by the Sea?*
>
> *She recalls you with a perfume, she compels you*
> *with her eyes—*

COLONIAL MODERNITY

*Oh! the pleasant pleasure places, and her Harbor
    and her skies!*
*She is Athens, she is Delhi, she is Mecca, she is
    Rome,*
*When you count your collars over, and you mark
    your kit for home.*
*In the steerage, in the cabin, lie the stripling and
    the sire,*
*In the "sleeper" or the "second," who are brothers
    in desire.*
*She is Venice, she is Florence, she is Athens, she
    is Rome,*
*When the Little Mother calls them, and her
    wanderers come home.*

A study of Sydney in its physical plan, in the spirit of its civic institutions, in the possibilities of its future development and improvement, in the evolution of the race of city dwellers inhabiting it, has not yet been attempted. The effort will be made by articles from time to time in THE LONE HAND to preach civic reform for all Australia, with Sydney usually as "the shocking example." The proposition will be laid down, and the advancement of commercial activity and of physical adornment and beautification may be pursued simultaneously, and the greatness and the beauty of a city advanced with equal foot.

BIBLIOGRAPHY

Bain, Jim, *A financial tale of two cities: Sydney & Melbourne's remarkable contest for commercial supremacy*, University of New South Wales Press, Sydney, 2007.

Barton, G. B., *Literature in New South Wales*, Thomas Richards, Sydney, 1866.

Baudelaire, Charles, *The painter of modern life*, trans. P. E. Charvet, Penguin, London, 2010.

Bellanta, Melissa, *Larrikins: a history*, University of Queensland Press, St Lucia, Qld, 2012.

Bode, Katherine, *Reading by numbers: recalibrating the literary field*, Anthem Press, London and New York, 2012.

Bonyhady, Tim, *The colonial earth*, Melbourne University Press, Carlton, 2000.

Brantlinger, Patrick, *Taming cannibals: race and the Victorians*, Cornell University Press, Ithaca, NY, 2011.

Cannon, Michael, *The land boomers: the complete illustrated history*, Melbourne University Press, Carlton, 1995.

Cantrell, Leon, ed., 'A. G. Stephens's *Bulletin* Diary' in Bruce Bennett, ed., *Cross-currents: magazines and newspapers in Australian literature*, Longman Cheshire, Melbourne, 1981.

Cohen, Stanley, *Folk devils and moral panics*, MacGibbon and Kee, London, 1972.

Dennis, Richard, *Cities of modernity: representations and productions of metropolitan space, 1830–1940*, Cambridge University Press, Cambridge, 2008.

de Serville, Paul, *Rolf Boldrewood: a life*, Melbourne University Press, Melbourne, 2000.

Dixon, Robert, *Photography, early cinema and colonial modernity: Frank Hurley's synchronized lecture entertainment*, Anthem Press, London, 2011.

Docker, John, *The nervous nineties: Australian cultural life in the 1890s*, Oxford University Press, Melbourne, 1991.

Green, H. M., *A history of Australian literature, volume 1, 1789–1923*, Sydney, Angus & Robertson, 1961.

Greenop, Frank S., *History of magazine publishing in Australia*, K.G. Murray Publishing Company, Sydney, 1947.

Grove Day, A., *Louis Becke*, Hill of Content, Melbourne, 1967.

Johnson-Woods, Toni, *Index to serials in Australian periodicals and newspapers. Nineteenth century*, Mulini Press, Canberra, 2001.

Jose, Arthur W., *The romantic nineties*, Angus and Robertson, Sydney, 1933.

Lawson, Sylvia, *The Archibald paradox: a strange case of authorship*, Penguin, Melbourne, 1983.

MacKaness, George and Walter W. Stone, *The books of the Bulletin 1880–1952: an annotated bibliography*, Angus and Robertson, Sydney, 1955.

McNiven, Ian J. and Lynette Russell, *Appropriated pasts: indigenous people and the colonial culture of archaeology*, AltaMira Press, Oxford, 2005.

Mirmohamadi, Kylie and Susan K. Martin, *Colonial Dickens: what Australians made of the world's favourite writer*, Australian Scholarly Press, Melbourne, 2012.

Moore, William George, *The story of Australian art* (vol. 2), Angus and Robertson, Sydney, 1934.

Morrison, Elizabeth, 'Serial fiction in Australian colonial newspapers', in John O. Jordan and Robert L. Patten, eds., *Literature in the marketplace: nineteenth-century British publishing & reading practices*, Cambridge University Press, Cambridge, 1995.

Nettlebeck, Amanda and Robert Foster, *Out of the silence: the history and memory of South Australia's frontier wars*, Wakefield Press, Kent Town, SA, 2012.

——, *In the name of the law: William Willshire and the policing of the Australian frontier*, Wakefield Press, Kent Town, SA, 2007.

Potter, Simon J., *News and the British world: the emergence of an imperial press system*, Oxford University Press, Oxford, 2003.

Sadrin, Anny, 'Foreign English-language editions', in Paul Schlicke, ed., *Oxford reader's companion to Dickens*, Oxford University Press, Oxford, 2000.

Stuart Sayers, *The company of books: a short history of the Lothian Book Companies 1888–1988*, Lothian Publishing Company, Melbourne, 1988.

Sheridan, Susan, 'Temper, romantic; bias, offensively feminine: Australian women writers and literary nationalism', *Kunapipi*, vol. VII, nos 2 and 3, 1985.

Stuart, Lurline, *Australian periodicals with literary content, 1821–1925: an annotated bibliography*, Australian Scholarly Publishing, Melbourne, 2003.

——, *James Smith: the making of a colonial culture*, Allen & Unwin, Sydney, 1989.

Sussex, Lucy, *Women writers and detectives in nineteenth-century crime fiction: the mothers of the mystery genre*, Palgrave Macmillan, London, 2010.

Sussex, Lucy and Elizabeth Gibson, eds, *Mary Helena Fortune (Waif Wander/W.W.), c.1833–1910: a bibliography*, Victorian Fiction Research Unit 27, University of Queensland, St Lucia, 1998.

Waters, Catherine, *Commodity culture in Dickens's Household Words: the social life of goods*, Ashgate, London, 2008.

Webby, Elizabeth, 'Before the *Bulletin*: nineteenth century literary journalism', in Bruce Bennett, ed., *Cross-currents: magazines and newspapers in Australian literature*, Longman Cheshire, Melbourne, 1981.

Wolff, Janet, *Feminine sentences: essays on women and culture*, University of California Press, Berkeley, 1990.

Woollacott, Angela, *To try her fortune in London: Australian women, colonialism, and modernity*, Oxford University Press, Oxford, 2001.

ACKNOWLEDGMENTS

A NUMBER OF PEOPLE HAVE assisted greatly in the development and production of this book. Susan Millard and the librarians in the Special Collections Room at the Baillieu Library, University of Melbourne, have been especially welcoming, allowing us unlimited access to their valuable materials. The librarians at the State Library of Victoria and the Mitchell Library in Sydney have also been extremely helpful.

We want to thank Jane Brown, manager of the Visual Cultures Resource Centre in the School of Culture and Communication at the University of Melbourne, for generously lending us her expertise and time in preparing the images we've used in this book for publication. Thanks also to Christian Gelder for his assistance with transcribing a number of the original documents.

Terri-ann White's enthusiasm for this project from the beginning has been very much appreciated, and both Terri-ann and Anne Ryden at UWA Publishing have been a pleasure to work with. We also want to thank Anna Maley-Fadgyas and Deb Fitzpatrick.

The publication subsidy committee in the Faculty of Arts at the University of Melbourne has significantly contributed to the production of this book; thanks also to the School of Culture and Communication. We are very grateful to the Australian Research Council for funding a Discovery Project (2011–2013) that enabled us to undertake the research needed to bring this book to completion.

Note: where possible, we have retained the original formatting, punctuation and spelling of the transcribed documents, preserving the distinctiveness of their styles. The titles of some colonial journals vary over time and this is reflected in our book: for example, the 1902 *New Idea: A Women's Home Journal for Australasia* becomes *New Idea for Australasian Women* in 1906.

About the Authors

KEN GELDER is Professor of English at the University of Melbourne. His books include the co-authored *Uncanny Australia: Sacredness and Identity in a Postcolonial Nation* (MUP 1998) and *After the Celebration: Australian Fiction 1989–2007* (MUP 2009). His most recent book is *New Vampire Cinema* (BFI/Palgrave 2012).

RACHAEL WEAVER is an Australian Research Council Research Fellow in English at the University of Melbourne. She is author of *The Criminal of the Century* (Arcadia/ASP 2006), and co-editor with Ken Gelder of four anthologies of colonial Australian popular fiction published by Melbourne University Publishing.